Annual Editions: Anthropology, 40/e

Elvio Angeloni

http://create.mheducation.com

ISBN-10: 1259666417   ISBN-13: 9781259666414

Contents

Detailed Table of Contents

Unit 1: Anthropological Perspectives

The September 11 Effect on Anthropology, Lara Deeb and Jessica Winegar, *Middle East Report*, 2011
The September 11, 2001 attacks have had a considerable effect on anthropological research in the Middle East and beyond. Along with the fact that job opportunities have increased in some areas and diminished in others, anthropologists have become increasingly concerned about the politics of funding and the ethics of particular kinds of projects offered. In general, pressures are mounting with respect to scholars' ability to maintain academic freedom and, perhaps, even tenure itself.

Eating Christmas in the Kalahari, Richard Borshay Lee, *Natural History*, 1969
Anthropologist Richard Borshay Lee gives an account of the misunderstanding and confusion that often accompany cross-cultural experience. In this case, he violated a basic principle of the Kung Bushmen's social relations—food sharing.

Tricking and Tripping: Fieldwork on Prostitution in the Era of AIDS, Claire E. Sterk, Social Change Press, 2000
As unique as Claire E. Sterk's report on prostitution may be, she discusses issues common to anthropologists wherever they conduct fieldwork: How does one build trusting relationships with informants and what are the ethical obligations of an anthropologist toward them?

The Trials of Alice Goffman, Gideon Lewis-Kraus, *The New York Times*, 2016
As a fieldworker, Alice Goffman's foray into the mixed-income neighborhood of West Philadelphia was from its beginning a dicey enterprise. In her efforts to maintain the trust of her subjects, she had to strike a balance between what she owed to her professional community—an objective, well-documented, fact-based ethnography—with what she owed to her subjects—a personal and impressionistic account of their day-to-day experiences that only she, and they, could know was true or not. Either way, she was bound to be criticized.

Why Manners Matter, Valerie Curtis, *New Scientist Magazine*, 2013
A crucial factor in human evolution has to do with the problem of getting close to others without sharing pathogens. Disgustologist Valerie Curtis shows that the solution to this problem has to do with good manners.

On the Origin of Faith, Joseph Henrich, Princeton University Press, 2015
The key to the success of the human species has been not to simply rely on one's wits alone, but upon our genetically endowed ability to selectively focus on the cultural know-how from prior generations.

Unit 2: Culture and Communication

Baby Talk, Patricia K. Kuhl, *Scientific American*, 2017
While it is true that human infants are natural-born linguists, it takes "parentese" with its exaggerated inflections, immersive social interaction, and even computational skills to effectively learn all the nuances and complexity of a language. And when it comes to learning a second language, the earlier the better.

War of Words, Mark Pagel, *New Scientist Magazine*, 2012
In taking on the task of explaining why humans communicate with thousands of mutually unintelligible languages, in direct contradiction with the principle that language is supposed to help us exchange information, the author finds that languages have diverged from each other because of migration, geographical isolation, and a deeply rooted need for tribal identity.

Armor against Prejudice, Ed Yong, *Scientific American*, 2013
Even subtle reminders of prejudice against one's sex, race, or religion can hinder performance in school, work, and athletics. Researchers have found new ways to reverse and prevent this effect.

Preface

This edition of *Annual Editions: Anthropology* contains a variety of articles on contemporary issues in social and cultural anthropology. In contrast to the broad range of topics with minimum depth that is typical of standard textbooks, this anthology provides an opportunity to read first-hand accounts by anthropologists of their own research. In allowing scholars to speak for themselves about the issues in which they are experts, we are better able to understand the kinds of questions anthropologists ask, the ways in which they ask them, and how they go about searching for answers. Indeed, where there is disagreement among anthropologists, this format allows the readers to draw their own conclusions. Given the very broad scope of anthropology—in time, space, and subject matter—the present collection of highly readable articles has been selected according to a certain criteria. The articles have been chosen from both professional and nonprofessional publications for the purpose of supplementing standard textbooks that are used in introductory courses. Some of the articles are considered classics in the field, while others have been selected for their timely relevance.

Finally, it should be pointed out that an *Author's Note* is available for some of the classic articles that have been in this book since they were originally published. These updates consist of fresh perspectives on important issues, written by the authors themselves exclusively for this book.

Included in this volume are a number of features that are designed to make it useful for students, researchers, and professionals in the field of anthropology. Each unit is preceded by an overview, which provides a background for informed reading of the articles and emphasizes critical issues. *Learning Outcomes* accompany each article and outline the key concepts that students should focus on as they are reading the material. *Critical Thinking* questions, found at the end of each article, allow students to test their understanding of the key points of the article. The *Internet References* section can be used to further explore the topics online.

Those involved in producing this volume wish to make the next one as useful and effective as possible. Your criticism and advice are always welcome. Any anthology can be improved. This continues to be—annually.

Editor

Elvio Angeloni received his BA from UCLA in 1963, MA in anthropology from UCLA in 1965, and MA in communication arts from Loyola Marymount University in 1976. He has produced several films, including *Little Warrior,* winner of the Cinemedia VI Best Bicentennial Theme, and *Broken Bottles,* shown on PBS. He served as an academic adviser on the instructional television series *Faces of Culture.* He received the Pasadena City College Outstanding Teacher Award in 2006 and has since retired from teaching. He is also the academic editor of *Annual Editions: Physical Anthropology* and co-editor of *Annual Editions: Archaeology.* His primary area of interest has been indigenous peoples of the American Southwest. evangeloni@gmail.com

Academic Advisory Board

Members of the Academic Advisory Board are instrumental in the final selection of articles for the *Annual Editions* series. Their review of the articles for content, level, and appropriateness provides critical direction to the editor(s) and staff. We think that you will find their careful consideration reflected in this book.

Lauren Arenson
Pasadena City College

Deborah Augsburger
University of Wisconsin—Superior

Victoria Bernal
University of California—Irvine

Mary Jill Brody
Louisiana State University

Daniel Cring
University of Louisiana—Lafayette

Christina Dames
Lindenwood University

Ronald Enders
Ashland Community Technical College

Beverly Fogelson
Oakland University

Josephine Fritts
Ozarks Technical Community College

Jeremy L. Goldstein
St. George's School

Angela Guy-Lee
Ferris State University

Carol Hayman
Austin Community College

Elias S. Kary
Monterey Peninsula College

Melissa Kirkendall
University of Hawai'i Maui College

Roberta Lenkeit
Modesto Junior College

Diane A. Lichtenstein
Baldwin-Wallace College and Cleveland Institute of Art

Heather Smith Mode
Gaston College

Sabina Trumble
University of Phoenix

Tim Vermande
Art Institute of Indianapolis

Mary Vermilion
Saint Louis University

John D. Wilkins
Grand Canyon University

Unit 1

UNIT

Prepared by: Elvio Angeloni, *Pasadena City College*

Anthropological Perspectives

For at least a century, the goals of anthropology have been to describe societies and cultures throughout the world and to compare and contrast the differences and similarities among them. Anthropologists study in a variety of settings and situations, ranging from small hamlets and villages to neighborhoods and corporate offices of major urban centers throughout the world. They study hunters and gatherers, peasants, farmers, labor leaders, politicians, and bureaucrats. They examine religious life in Latin America as well as revolutionary movements.

Wherever practicable, anthropologists take on the role of "participant observer." Through active involvement in the life ways of people, they hope to gain an insider's perspective without sacrificing the objectivity of the trained scientist. Sometimes the conditions for achieving such a goal seem to form an almost insurmountable barrier, but anthropologists call on persistence, adaptability, and imagination to overcome the odds against them.

The diversity of focus in anthropology means that it is earmarked less by its particular subject matter than by its perspective. Although the discipline relates to both the biological and social sciences, anthropologists know that the boundaries drawn between disciplines are highly artificial. For example, while in theory it is possible to examine only the social organization of a family unit or the organization of political power in a nation-state, in reality it is impossible to separate the biological from the social, from the economic, from the political. The importance of the cultural aspects of our being can be stated very simply in the anthropology axiom: Biology is not destiny.

One might get the impression while reading about some of the anthropological field experience that the field has had primarily to do with the exotic and the unusual and, therefore, is not particularly relevant to the larger world in which most of us live. On the contrary, much is at stake in our attempts to achieve a more objective understanding of the diversity of peoples' ways. The more we understand why others do as they do, the more we come to appreciate why we are as we are and vice versa. After all, the purpose of anthropology is not only to describe and explain, but also to develop a special vision of the world in which cultural alternatives (past, present, and future) can be measured against one another and used as guides for human action.

Article   Prepared by: Elvio Angeloni, *Pasadena City College*

The September 11 Effect on Anthropology

LARA DEEB AND JESSICA WINEGAR

Learning Outcomes

After reading this article, you will be able to:

- Understand the effects of September 11 on the field of anthropology.

Conventional wisdom among scholars of the Middle East is that the September 11, 2001 attacks left behind a threatening professional environment. Graduate students and faculty alike speak of hostile infiltrators in their classrooms, inevitably bitter tenure battles and the self-censorship that both can produce. At the same time, in the aftermath of September 11 Middle East scholars anticipated that the perennially spotty job market might improve.

Our research for *Anthropology's Politics,* a book project under contract with Stanford University Press, thus far confirms that scholars have in fact gained new "opportunities" during the past decade, but with government agencies or NGOs rather than in academe, where tenure-track jobs (as in most fields) have become scarcer. Our data also shows that scholars employed at universities, particularly those without tenure, labor under greater surveillance and suspicion. While trepidation about this climate is general to Middle East anthropologists regardless of specialty, the vast majority of actual incidents have been related to scholars' analysis of the conflict in Israel-Palestine.

Time and time again, in our interviews with anthropologists of the Middle East, they describe their jobs as "a minefield." They may have problems explaining research on politically sensitive topics to their universities' institutional review boards; they may see their grant funding denied or withdrawn; they may encounter prejudice among colleagues on hiring and tenure committees; and they may experience conflict with students when presenting critical perspectives on the US-led "war on terror." Whether or not their difficulties were expressly tied to politics, faculty frequently linked their personal stories to the political climate. One person described the resulting fear as "knowing that people who fall on the wrong side can suffer in their careers."

Scholars are increasingly worried about losing access to field sites and control over the use of their work. The new "security"

orientation of the study of the Middle East and Islam has led to more frequent invitations from government agencies, Washington think tanks and military subcontractors. These invitations often make anthropologists nervous, as they do not want to be identified with US Middle East policy or have their insights employed in its formulation.

But when it comes to tangibly negative effects on careers and academic freedom, Palestine—not the "war on terror"—is the enduring issue. "The word on the street" in graduate school, many anthropologists say, is that "if you work on Palestine you will never get a job," at least not in the United States. Indeed, Palestine frequently rose as a specter in anthropologists' job interviews in the 2000s. In the words of one Palestine scholar, "It's not what I said, it's the subject I work on. . . . People don't want to open themselves up to controversy—once the word Palestine is there, people say, 'Why do we want to make everyone upset?'" Even scholars who research other countries were often questioned about their politics on Palestine during campus visits, sometimes point blank.

Quantitatively, we have found that Palestine is the number-one cause of persecution of faculty in the classroom, despite anthropologists' assumption that everyone is at risk in the post-September 11 political climate. Many whose research does not focus on Palestine avoid it in their teaching, in part because they feel "on less sure ground," but also due to worries about classroom consequences. Well-publicized right-wing attacks—from inside and outside the discipline—foment this atmosphere of apprehension. On Campus Watch, the most robust of the conservative websites that collects reports on scholars of the Middle East, the vast majority of the articles about Middle East anthropology or anthropologists concern Israel-Palestine. The question of Palestine also dominates the websites Discover the Network and Students for Academic Freedom, both sponsored by right-wing activist David Horowitz. This focus is not a post-September 11 phenomenon, but a continuation of decades of concerted agitation against those speaking out about Palestinian rights. There does, however, seem to be a difference in the scale and organization of the attacks, which are facilitated by the Internet and other new media, and have been strengthened by the deeper Islamophobia of the post-September 11 era.

Nevertheless, there were in fact more job opportunities for Middle East anthropologists in the 2000s than in the preceding decade. Our quantitative analysis shows, however, that the increase paled in comparison to increases in fields such as history, political science and religious studies—presumably because those disciplines are thought to provide birds-eye views of the region or explanations for the September 11 events. At the same time, the US government has presumed that anthropology is able to provide on-the-ground information useful for counter-terrorism, and thus anthropologists are heavily recruited to staff "Human Terrain Systems" or other military projects that depend on local knowledge. The recruitment efforts have met with little success, as they run up against the anthropological Code of Ethics and anthropologists' political sensibilities, both of which prohibit such collaboration. The 2009 version of the Code of Ethics, currently under revision, clearly states that it is a set of guidelines for anthropologists rather than a binding document that adjudicates violations for its members. It states that "anthropological researchers must ensure that they do not harm the safety, dignity or privacy of the people with whom they work, conduct research or perform other professional activities, or who might reasonably be thought to be affected by their research." The vast majority of anthropologists understand providing information to the US military to contradict this tenet of the code.

September 11 affected scholarly life by pushing many scholars to speak publicly about the Middle East and Islam. In this regard, the "war on terror" is viewed as both opportunity and danger-filled obligation, an ambivalence perfectly captured in one anthropologist's phrase, "poisoned chalice." While a few resisted sipping from this cup, explaining that their scholarly work was not so conventionally political, most felt that they faced an ethical imperative to correct stereotypes and dispel misunderstandings—even if they became subject to slander and libel.

September 11 also shaped scholars' choices of field site and topic. Many anthropologists continue to shy away from Israel-Palestine. Some have begun to work on US military engagement in the region. Others have moved toward studies of Islam, although many anthropologists express concern that religion has come to stand in for the Middle East in the academy as it has in public discourse. It remains to be seen what impact the "Arab spring" might have on this trend.

In general, Middle East anthropologists share other Middle East scholars' sense that American institutions of higher education have become battlegrounds pitting defenders of academic freedom against defenders of various state policies, particularly those of Israel. The explosion of media outlets and the corporatization of universities in the 2000s have created a feeling that off-campus forces have more power today than in the past to shape scholarly discourse. Even scholars with tenure often find civic engagement unpleasant, not because they do not want to speak to the public, but because uninformed political opinion often trumps fact-based discussion in these forums. Those without tenure, especially those whose specialties or views generate controversy, have to fear for their job security as well. Those who call for eliminating tenure would do well to recognize that such a move might diminish the supply of in-depth knowledge of the Middle East to the American public.

Critical Thinking

1. What has been the conventional wisdom among scholars of the Middle East as a result of the September 11, 2001 attacks?
2. What did the authors' discover as a result of their research?
3. Why do anthropologists of the Middle East describe their jobs as "a minefield"? Why they are increasingly worried?
4. What is the "enduring issue" and why? Why is there a difference in the scale and organization of the attacks on anthropologists since September 11 even though this has been a decades-long issue?
5. How do the authors assess the job opportunities for Middle East anthropologists compared to other fields?
6. Why have recruitment efforts met with little success?
7. Why has the "war on terror" been viewed as both an opportunity and a danger-filled obligation?
8. How has September 11 shaped scholars' choices of field site and topic?
9. In what respects have American institutions of higher education become battlegrounds? What might be the result of eliminating tenure?

Create Central

www.mhhe.com/createcentral

Internet References

Anthropology Links
http://anthropology.gmu.edu
Archaeology and Anthropology Computing and Study Skills
www.isca.ox.ac.uk/index.html
Introduction to Fieldwork and Ethnography
http://web.mit.edu/dumit/www/syl-anth.html
The Institute for Intercultural Studies
www.interculturalstudies.org/main.html

LARA DEEB, an editor of this magazine, teaches anthropology at Scripps College. **JESSICA WINEGAR** teaches anthropology at Northwestern University.

Deeb, Lara; Winegar, Jessica. From *Middle East Report*, Winter 2011, pp. 42–43. Copyright © 2011 by Middle East Research & Information Project. Reprinted by permission.

Article

Prepared by: Elvio Angeloni, *Pasadena City College*

Eating Christmas in the Kalahari

RICHARD BORSHAY LEE

Learning Outcomes

After reading this article, you will be able to:

- Describe some of the unique research strategies of anthropological fieldwork.

- Explain how anthropologists who become personally involved with a community through participant observation maintain their objectivity as scientists.

- Explain the ways in which the results of fieldwork depend on the kinds of questions asked.

The !Kung Bushmen's knowledge of Christmas is third-hand. The London Missionary Society brought the holiday to the southern Tswana tribes in the early nineteenth century. Later, native catechists spread the idea far and wide among the Bantu-speaking pastoralists, even in the remotest corners of the Kalahari Desert. The Bushmen's idea of the Christmas story, stripped to its essentials, is "praise the birth of white man's god-chief"; what keeps their interest in the holiday high is the Tswana-Herero custom of slaughtering an ox for his Bushmen neighbors as an annual goodwill gesture. Since the 1930s, part of the Bushmen's annual round of activities has included a December congregation at the cattle posts for trading, marriage brokering, and several days of trance-dance feasting at which the local Tswana headman is host.

As a social anthropologist working with !Kung Bushmen, I found that the Christmas ox custom suited my purposes. I had come to the Kalahari to study the hunting and gathering subsistence economy of the !Kung, and to accomplish this it was essential not to provide them with food, share my own food, or interfere in any way with their food-gathering activities. While liberal handouts of tobacco and medical supplies were appreciated, they were scarcely adequate to erase the glaring disparity in wealth between the anthropologist, who maintained a two-month inventory of canned goods, and the Bushmen, who rarely had a day's supply of food on hand. My approach, while paying off in terms of data, left me open to frequent accusations of stinginess and hard-heartedness. By their lights, I was a miser.

The Christmas ox was to be my way of saying thank you for the cooperation of the past year; and since it was to be our last Christmas in the field, I determined to slaughter the largest, meatiest ox that money could buy, insuring that the feast and trance-dance would be a success.

Through December I kept my eyes open at the wells as the cattle were brought down for watering. Several animals were offered, but none had quite the grossness that I had in mind. Then, ten days before the holiday, a Herero friend led an ox of astonishing size and mass up to our camp. It was solid black, stood five feet high at the shoulder, had a five-foot span of horns, and must have weighed 1,200 pounds on the hoof. Food consumption calculations are my specialty, and I quickly figured that bones and viscera aside, there was enough meat—at least four pounds—for every man, woman, and child of the 150 Bushmen in the vicinity of /ai/ai who were expected at the feast.

Having found the right animal at last, I paid the Herero £20 ($56) and asked him to keep the beast with his herd until Christmas day. The next morning word spread among the people that the big solid black one was the ox chosen by /ontah (my Bushman name; it means, roughly, "whitey") for the Christmas feast. That afternoon I received the first delegation. Ben!a, an outspoken sixty-year-old mother of five, came to the point slowly.

"Where were you planning to eat Christmas?"

"Right here at /ai/ai," I replied.

"Alone or with others?"

"I expect to invite all the people to eat Christmas with me."

"Eat what?"

"I have purchased Yehave's black ox, and I am going to slaughter and cook it."

"That's what we were told at the well but refused to believe it until we heard it from yourself."

"Well, it's the black one," I replied expansively, although wondering what she was driving at.

"Oh, no!" Ben!a groaned, turning to her group. "They were right." Turning back to me she asked, "Do you expect us to eat that bag of bones?"

"Bag of bones! It's the biggest ox at /ai/ai."

"Big, yes, but old. And thin. Everybody knows there's no meat on that old ox. What did you expect us to eat off it, the horns?"

Everybody chuckled at Ben!a's one-liner as they walked away, but all I could manage was a weak grin.

That evening it was the turn of the young men. They came to sit at our evening fire. /gaugo, about my age, spoke to me man-to-man.

"/ontah, you have always been square with us," he lied. "What has happened to change your heart? That sack of guts and bones of Yehave's will hardly feed one camp, let alone all the Bushmen around ai/ai." And he proceeded to enumerate the seven camps in the /ai/ai vicinity, family by family. "Perhaps you have forgotten that we are not few, but many. Or are you too blind to tell the difference between a proper cow and an old wreck? That ox is thin to the point of death."

"Look, you guys," I retorted, "that is a beautiful animal, and I'm sure you will eat it with pleasure at Christmas."

"Of course we will eat it; it's food. But it won't fill us up to the point where we will have enough strength to dance. We will eat and go home to bed with stomachs rumbling."

That night as we turned in, I asked my wife, Nancy: "What did you think of the black ox?"

"It looked enormous to me. Why?"

"Well, about eight different people have told me I got gypped; that the ox is nothing but bones."

"What's the angle?" Nancy asked. "Did they have a better one to sell?"

"No, they just said that it was going to be a grim Christmas because there won't be enough meat to go around. Maybe I'll get an independent judge to look at the beast in the morning."

Bright and early, Halingisi, a Tswana cattle owner, appeared at our camp. But before I could ask him to give me his opinion on Yehave's black ox, he gave me the eye signal that indicated a confidential chat. We left the camp and sat down.

"/ontah, I'm surprised at you: you've lived here for three years and still haven't learned anything about cattle."

"But what else can a person do but choose the biggest, strongest animal one can find?" I retorted.

"Look, just because an animal is big doesn't mean that it has plenty of meat on it. The black one was a beauty when it was younger, but now it is thin to the point of death."

"Well I've already bought it. What can I do at this stage?"

"Bought it already? I thought you were just considering it. Well, you'll have to kill it and serve it, I suppose. But don't expect much of a dance to follow."

My spirits dropped rapidly. I could believe that Ben!a and /gaugo just might be putting me on about the black ox, but Halingisi seemed to be an impartial critic. I went around that day feeling as though I had bought a lemon of a used car.

In the afternoon it was Tomazo's turn. Tomazo is a fine hunter, a top trance performer . . . and one of my most reliable informants. He approached the subject of the Christmas cow as part of my continuing Bushman education.

"My friend, the way it is with us Bushmen," he began, "is that we love meat. And even more than that, we love fat. When we hunt we always search for the fat ones, the ones dripping with layers of white fat: fat that turns into a clear, thick oil in the cooking pot, fat that slides down your gullet, fills your stomach and gives you a roaring diarrhea," he rhapsodized.

"So, feeling as we do," he continued, "it gives us pain to be served such a scrawny thing as Yehave's black ox. It is big, yes, and no doubt its giant bones are good for soup, but fat is what we really crave and so we will eat Christmas this year with a heavy heart."

The prospect of a gloomy Christmas now had me worried, so I asked Tomazo what I could do about it.

"Look for a fat one, a young one . . . smaller, but fat. Fat enough to make us //gom ('evacuate the bowels'), then we will be happy."

My suspicions were aroused when Tomazo said that he happened to know of a young, fat, barren cow that the owner was willing to part with. Was Tomazo working on commission, I wondered? But I dispelled this unworthy thought when we approached the Herero owner of the cow in question and found that he had decided not to sell.

The scrawny wreck of a Christmas ox now became the talk of the /ai/ai water hole and was the first news told to the outlying groups as they began to come in from the bush for the feast. What finally convinced me that real trouble might be brewing was the visit from u!au, an old conservative with a reputation for fierceness. His nickname meant spear and referred to an incident thirty years ago in which he had speared a man to death. He had an intense manner; fixing me with his eyes, he said in clipped tones:

"I have only just heard about the black ox today, or else I would have come here earlier. /ontah, do you honestly think you can serve meat like that to people and avoid a fight?" He paused, letting the implications sink in. "I don't mean fight you, /ontah; you are a white man. I mean a fight between Bushmen. There are many fierce ones here, and with such a small quantity of meat to distribute, how can you give everybody a fair share? Someone is sure to accuse another of taking too much or hogging all the choice pieces. Then you will see what happens when some go hungry while others eat."

The possibility of at least a serious argument struck me as all too real. I had witnessed the tension that surrounds the distribution of meat from a kudu or gemsbok kill, and had documented many arguments that sprang up from a real or imagined slight in meat distribution. The owners of a kill may spend up to two hours arranging and rearranging the piles of meat under the gaze of a circle of recipients before handing them out. And I also knew that the Christmas feast at /ai/ai would be bringing together groups that had feuded in the past.

Convinced now of the gravity of the situation, I went in earnest to search for a second cow; but all my inquiries failed to turn one up.

The Christmas feast was evidently going to be a disaster, and the incessant complaints about the meagerness of the ox had already taken the fun out of it for me. Moreover, I was getting bored with the wisecracks, and after losing my temper a few times, I resolved to serve the beast anyway. If the meat fell short, the hell with it. In the Bushmen idiom, I announced to all who would listen:

"I am a poor man and blind. If I have chosen one that is too old and too thin, we will eat it anyway and see if there is enough meat there to quiet the rumbling of our stomachs."

On hearing this speech, Ben!a offered me a rare word of comfort. "It's thin," she said philosophically, "but the bones will make a good soup."

At dawn Christmas morning, instinct told me to turn over the butchering and cooking to a friend and take off with Nancy to spend Christmas alone in the bush. But curiosity kept me from retreating. I wanted to see what such a scrawny ox looked like on butchering and if there *was* going to be a fight, I wanted to catch every word of it. Anthropologists are incurable that way.

The great beast was driven up to our dancing ground, and a shot in the forehead dropped it in its tracks. Then, freshly cut branches were heaped around the fallen carcass to receive the meat. Ten men volunteered to help with the cutting. I asked /gaugo to make the breast bone cut. This cut, which begins the butchering process for most large game, offers easy access for removal of the viscera. But it also allows the hunter to spot-check the amount of fat on the animal. A fat game animal carries a white layer up to an inch thick on the chest, while in a thin one, the knife will quickly cut to bone. All eyes fixed on his hand as /gaugo, dwarfed by the great carcass, knelt to the breast. The first cut opened a pool of solid white in the black skin. The second and third cut widened and deepened the creamy white. Still no bone. It was pure fat; it must have been two inches thick.

"Hey /gau," I burst out, "that ox is loaded with fat. What's this about the ox being too thin to bother eating? Are you out of your mind?"

"Fat?" /gau shot back, "You call that fat? This wreck is thin, sick, dead!" And he broke out laughing. So did everyone else. They rolled on the ground, paralyzed with laughter. Everybody laughed except me; I was thinking.

I ran back to the tent and burst in just as Nancy was getting up. "Hey, the black ox. It's fat as hell! They were kidding about it being too thin to eat. It was a joke or something. A put-on. Everyone is really delighted with it!"

"Some joke," my wife replied. "It was so funny that you were ready to pack up and leave /ai/ai."

If it had indeed been a joke, it had been an extraordinarily convincing one, and tinged, I thought, with more than a touch of malice as many jokes are. Nevertheless, that it was a joke lifted my spirits considerably, and I returned to the butchering site where the shape of the ox was rapidly disappearing under the axes and knives of the butchers. The atmosphere had become festive. Grinning broadly, their arms covered with blood well past the elbow, men packed chunks of meat into the big cast-iron cooking pots, fifty pounds to the load, and muttered and chuckled all the while about the thinness and worthlessness of the animal and /ontah's poor judgment.

We danced and ate that ox two days and two nights; we cooked and distributed fourteen potfuls of meat and no one went home hungry and no fights broke out.

But the "joke" stayed in my mind. I had a growing feeling that something important had happened in my relationship with the Bushmen and that the clue lay in the meaning of the joke. Several days later, when most of the people had dispersed back to the bush camps, I raised the question with Hakekgose, a Tswana man who had grown up among the !Kung, married a !Kung girl, and who probably knew their culture better than any other non-Bushman.

"With us whites," I began, "Christmas is supposed to be the day of friendship and brotherly love. What I can't figure out is why the Bushmen went to such lengths to criticize and belittle the ox I had bought for the feast. The animal was perfectly good and their jokes and wisecracks practically ruined the holiday for me."

"So it really did bother you," said Hakekgose. "Well, that's the way they always talk. When I take my rifle and go hunting with them, if I miss, they laugh at me for the rest of the day. But even if I hit and bring one down, it's no better. To them, the kill is always too small or too old or too thin; and as we sit down on the kill site to cook and eat the liver, they keep grumbling, even with their mouths full of meat. They say things like, 'Oh this is awful! What a worthless animal! Whatever made me think that this Tswana rascal could hunt!' "

"Is this the way outsiders are treated?" I asked.

"No, it is their custom; they talk that way to each other too. Go and ask them."

/gaugo had been one of the most enthusiastic in making me feel bad about the merit of the Christmas ox. I sought him out first.

"Why did you tell me the black ox was worthless, when you could see that it was loaded with fat and meat?"

"It is our way," he said smiling. "We always like to fool people about that. Say there is a Bushman who has been hunting. He must not come home and announce like a braggard, 'I have killed a big one in the bush!' He must first sit down in silence until I or someone else comes up to his fire and asks, 'What did you see today?' He replies quietly, 'Ah, I'm no good for hunting. I saw nothing at all [pause] just a little tiny one.' Then I smile to myself," /gaugo continued, "because I know he has killed something big."

"In the morning we make up a party of four or five people to cut up and carry the meat back to the camp. When we arrive at the kill we examine it and cry out, 'You mean to say you have dragged us all the way out here in order to make us cart home your pile of bones? Oh, if I had known it was this thin I wouldn't have come.' Another one pipes up, 'People, to think I gave up a nice day in the shade for this. At home we may be hungry but at least we have nice cool water to drink.' If the horns are big, someone says, 'Did you think that somehow you were going to boil down the horns for soup?'

"To all this you must respond in kind. 'I agree,' you say, 'this one is not worth the effort; let's just cook the liver for strength and leave the rest for the hyenas. It is not too late to hunt today and even a duiker or a steenbok would be better than this mess.'

"Then you set to work nevertheless; butcher the animal, carry the meat back to the camp and everyone eats," /gaugo concluded.

Things were beginning to make sense. Next, I went to Tomazo. He corroborated /gaugo's story of the obligatory insults over a kill and added a few details of his own.

"But," I asked, "why insult a man after he has gone to all that trouble to track and kill an animal and when he is going to share the meat with you so that your children will have something to eat?"

"Arrogance," was his cryptic answer.

"Arrogance?"

"Yes, when a young man kills much meat he comes to think of himself as a chief or a big man, and he thinks of the rest of us as his servants or inferiors. We can't accept this. We refuse one who boasts, for someday his pride will make him kill somebody. So we always speak of his meat as worthless. This way we cool his heart and make him gentle."

"But why didn't you tell me this before?" I asked Tomazo with some heat.

"Because you never asked me," said Tomazo, echoing the refrain that has come to haunt every field ethnographer.

The pieces now fell into place. I had known for a long time that in situations of social conflict with Bushmen I held all the cards. I was the only source of tobacco in a thousand square miles, and I was not incapable of cutting an individual off for non-cooperation. Though my boycott never lasted longer than a few days, it was an indication of my strength. People resented my presence at the water hole, yet simultaneously dreaded my leaving. In short I was a perfect target for the charge of arrogance and for the Bushmen tactic of enforcing humility.

I had been taught an object lesson by the Bushmen; it had come from an unexpected corner and had hurt me in a vulnerable area. For the big black ox was to be the one totally generous, unstinting act of my year at /ai/ai, and I was quite unprepared for the reaction I received.

As I read it, their message was this: There are no totally generous acts. All "acts" have an element of calculation. One black ox slaughtered at Christmas does not wipe out a year of careful manipulation of gifts given to serve your own ends. After all, to kill an animal and share the meat with people is really no more than Bushmen do for each other every day and with far less fanfare.

In the end, I had to admire how the Bushmen had played out the farce—collectively straight-faced to the end. Curiously, the episode reminded me of the *Good Soldier Schweik* and his marvelous encounters with authority. Like Schweik, the Bushmen had retained a thorough-going skepticism of good intentions. Was it this independence of spirit, I wondered, that had kept them culturally viable in the face of generations of contact with more powerful societies, both black and white? The thought that the Bushmen were alive and well in the Kalahari was strangely comforting. Perhaps, armed with that independence and with their superb knowledge of their environment, they might yet survive the future.

Critical Thinking

1. To what extent do the Bushmen typically celebrate Christmas?
2. Why did Lee wish to slaughter an ox for the Bushmen?
3. What was it about the Bushman ways of life and Lee's role as an anthropologist that led to their reactions to his generosity?
4. Why was the Bushman reaction "strangely comforting" to Lee in the final analysis?

Create Central

www.mhhe.com/createcentral

Internet References

Anthropology Links
   http://anthropology.gmu.edu
Archaeology and Anthropology Computing and Study Skills
   www.isca.ox.ac.uk/index.html
Introduction to Fieldwork and Ethnography
   http://web.mit.edu/dumit/www/syl-anth.html
The Institute for Intercultural Studies
   www.interculturalstudies.org/main.html

RICHARD BORSHAY LEE is a full professor of anthropology at the University of Toronto. He has done extensive fieldwork in southern Africa, is coeditor of *Man the Hunter* (1968) and *Kalahari Hunter-Gatherers* (1976), and author of *The !Kung San: Men, Women, and Work in a Foraging Society*.

Lee, Richard Borshay. From *Natural History*, December 1969, pp. 14–22, 60–64. Copyright © 1969 by Natural History Magazine. Reprinted by permission.

Article   Prepared by: Elvio Angeloni, *Pasadena City College*

Tricking and Tripping
Fieldwork on Prostitution in the Era of AIDS

CLAIRE E. STERK

Learning Outcomes

After reading this article, you will be able to:

- Explain how anthropologists who become personally involved with a community through participant observation maintain their objectivity as scientists.

- Give examples of the kind of ethical obligations fieldworkers have toward their informants.

The way to do that, the cultural anthropologist would say, is to ask and to listen.

As you read this selection, ask yourself the following questions:

- What happens when Sterk says, "I'm sorry for you" to one of her informants? Why?
- Why do you think fieldwork might be a difficult job?
- Do you think that the fact that Sterk grew up in Amsterdam, where prostitution is legal, affected her research?
- Which of the six themes of this work, described at the end of the article, do you think is most important?

Students often think of anthropological fieldwork as requiring travel to exotic tropical locations, but that is not necessarily the case. This reading is based on fieldwork in the United States—on the streets in New York City as well as Atlanta. Claire Sterk is an anthropologist who works in a school of public health and is primarily interested in issues of women's health, particularly as it relates to sexual behavior. In this selection, an introduction to a recent book by the same title, she describes the basic fieldwork methods she used to study these women and their communities. Like most cultural anthropologists, Sterk's primary goal was to describe "the life" of prostitution from the women's own point of view. To do this, she had to be patient, brave, sympathetic, trustworthy, curious, and nonjudgmental. You will notice these characteristics in this selection; for example, Sterk begins her book with a poem written by one of her informants. Fieldwork is a slow process, because it takes time to win people's confidence and to learn their language and way of seeing the world. In this regard, there are probably few differences between the work of a qualitative sociologist and that of a cultural anthropologist (although anthropologists would not use the term "deviant" to describe another society or a segment of their own society).

Throughout the world, HIV/AIDS is fast becoming a disease found particularly in poor women. Sex workers or prostitutes have often been blamed for AIDS, and they have been further stigmatized because of their profession. In reality, however, entry into prostitution is not a career choice; rather, these women and girls are themselves most often victims of circumstances such as violence and poverty. Public health officials want to know why sex workers do not always protect their health by making men wear condoms. To answer such questions, we must know more about the daily life of these women.

One night in March of 1987 business was slow. I was hanging out on a stroll with a group of street prostitutes. After a few hours in a nearby diner/coffee shop, we were kicked out. The waitress felt bad, but she needed our table for some new customers. Four of us decided to sit in my car until the rain stopped. While three of us chatted about life, Piper wrote this poem. As soon as she read it to us, the conversation shifted to more serious topics—pimps, customers, cops, the many hassles of being a prostitute, to name a few. We decided that if I ever finished a book about prostitution, the book would start with her poem.

This book is about the women who work in the lower echelons of the prostitution world. They worked in the streets and other public settings as well as crack houses. Some of these women viewed themselves primarily as prostitutes, and a number of them used drugs to cope with the pressures of the life. Others identified themselves more as drug users, and their main reason for having sex for money or other goods was to support their own drug use and often the habit of their male partner. A small group of women interviewed for this book had left prostitution, and most of them were still struggling to integrate their past experiences as prostitutes in their current lives.

The stories told by the women who participated in this project revealed how pimps, customers, and others such as police officers and social and health service providers treated them as "fallen" women. However, their accounts also showed their strengths and the many strategies they developed to challenge these others. Circumstances, including their drug use, often forced them to sell sex, but they all resisted the notion that they might be selling themselves. Because they engaged in an illegal profession, these women had little status: their working conditions were poor, and their work was physically and mentally exhausting. Nevertheless, many women described the ways in which they gained a sense of control over their lives. For instance, they learned how to manipulate pimps, how to control the types of services and length of time bought by their customers, and how to select customers. While none of these schemes explicitly enhanced their working conditions, they did make the women feel stronger and better about themselves.

In this book, I present prostitution from the point of view of the women themselves. To understand their current lives, it was necessary to learn how they got started in the life, the various processes involved in their continued prostitution careers, the link between prostitution and drug use, the women's interactions with their pimps and customers, and the impact of the AIDS epidemic and increasing violence on their experiences. I also examined the implications for women. Although my goal was to present the women's thoughts, feelings, and actions in their own words, the final text is a sociological monograph compiled by me as the researcher. Some women are quoted more than others because I developed a closer relationship with them, because they were more able to verbalize and capture their circumstances, or simply because they were more outspoken.

The Sample

The data for this book are qualitative. The research was conducted during the last ten years in the New York City and Atlanta metropolitan areas. One main data source was participant observation on streets, in hotels and other settings known for prostitution activity, and in drug-use settings, especially those that allowed sex-for-drug exchanges. Another data source was in-depth, life-history interviews with 180 women ranging in age from 18 to 59 years, with an average age of 34. One in two women was African-American and one in three white; the remaining women were Latina. Three in four had completed high school, and among them almost two-thirds had one or more years of additional educational training. Thirty women had graduated from college.

Forty women worked as street prostitutes and did not use drugs. On average, they had been prostitutes for 11 years. Forty women began using drugs an average of three years after they began working as prostitutes, and the average time they had worked as prostitutes was nine years. Forty women used drugs an average of five years before they became prostitutes, and on the average they had worked as prostitutes for eight years. Another forty women began smoking crack and exchanging sex for crack almost simultaneously, with an average of four years in the life. Twenty women who were interviewed were ex-prostitutes.

Comments on Methodology

When I tell people about my research, the most frequent question I am asked is how I gained access to the women rather than what I learned from the research. For many, prostitution is an unusual topic of conversation, and many people have expressed surprise that I, as a woman, conducted the research. During my research some customers indeed thought I was a working woman, a fact that almost always amuses those who hear about my work. However, few people want to hear stories about the women's struggles and sadness. Sometimes they ask questions about the reasons why women become prostitutes. Most of the time, they are surprised when I tell them that the prostitutes as well as their customers represent all layers of society. Before presenting the findings, it seems important to discuss the research process, including gaining access to the women, developing relationships, interviewing, and then leaving the field.[1]

Locating Prostitutes and Gaining Entree

One of the first challenges I faced was to identify locations where street prostitution took place. Many of these women worked on strolls, streets where prostitution activity is concentrated, or in hotels known for prostitution activity. Others, such as the crack prostitutes, worked in less public settings such as a crack house that might be someone's apartment.

I often learned of well-known public places from professional experts, such as law enforcement officials and health care providers at emergency rooms and sexually transmitted disease clinics. I gained other insights from lay experts, including taxi drivers, bartenders, and community representatives such as members of neighborhood associations. The contacts universally mentioned some strolls as the places where many women worked, where the local police focused attention, or where residents had organized protests against prostitution in their neighborhoods.

As I began visiting various locales, I continued to learn about new settings. In one sense, I was developing ethnographic maps of street prostitution. After several visits to a specific area, I also was able to expand these maps by adding information about the general atmosphere on the stroll, general characteristics of the various people present, the ways in which the women and customers connected, and the overall flow of action. In addition, my visits allowed the regular actors to notice me.

I soon learned that being an unknown woman in an area known for prostitution may cause many people to notice you, even stare at you, but it fails to yield many verbal interactions. Most of the time when I tried to make eye contact with one of the women, she quickly averted her eyes. Pimps, on the other hand, would stare at me straight on and I ended up being the one to look away. Customers would stop, blow their horn, or wave me over, frequently yelling obscenities when I ignored them. I realized that gaining entree into the prostitution world was not going to be as easy as I imagined it. Although I lacked such training in any of my qualitative methods classes, I decided to move slowly and not force any interaction. The most I said during the initial weeks in a new area was limited to "how are you" or "hi." This strategy paid off during my first visits to one of the strolls in Brooklyn, New York. After several appearances, one of the women walked up to me and sarcastically asked if I was looking for something. She caught me off guard, and all the answers I had practiced did not seem to make sense. I mumbled something about just wanting to walk around. She did not like my answer, but she did like my accent. We ended up talking about the latter and she was especially excited when I told her I came from Amsterdam. One of her friends had gone to Europe with her boyfriend, who was in the military. She understood from her that prostitution and drugs were legal in the Netherlands. While explaining to her that some of her friend's impressions were incorrect, I was able to show off some of my knowledge about prostitution. I mentioned that I was interested in prostitution and wanted to write a book about it.

Despite the fascination with my background and intentions, the prostitute immediately put me through a Streetwalker 101 test, and apparently I passed. She told me to make sure to come back. By the time I left, I not only had my first conversation but also my first connection to the scene. Variations of this entry process occurred on the other strolls. The main lesson I learned in these early efforts was the importance of having some knowledge of the lives of the people I wanted to study, while at the same time refraining from presenting myself as an expert.

Qualitative researchers often refer to their initial connections as gatekeepers and key respondents. Throughout my fieldwork I learned that some key respondents are important in providing initial access, but they become less central as the research evolves. For example, one of the women who introduced me to her lover, who was also her pimp, was arrested and disappeared for months. Another entered drug treatment soon after she facilitated my access. Other key respondents provided access to only a segment of the players on a scene. For example, if a woman worked for a pimp, [she] was unlikely . . . to introduce me to women working for another pimp. On one stroll my initial contact was with a pimp whom nobody liked. By associating with him, I almost lost the opportunity to meet other pimps. Some key respondents were less connected than promised—for example, some of the women who worked the street to support their drug habit. Often their connections were more frequently with drug users and less so with prostitutes.

Key respondents tend to be individuals central to the local scene, such as, in this case, pimps and the more senior prostitutes. Their function as gatekeepers often is to protect the scene and to screen outsiders. Many times I had to prove that I was not an undercover police officer or a woman with ambitions to become a streetwalker. While I thought I had gained entree, I quickly learned that many insiders subsequently wondered about my motives and approached me with suspicion and distrust.

Another lesson involved the need to proceed cautiously with self-nominated key respondents. For example, one of the women presented herself as knowing everyone on the stroll. While she did know everyone, she was not a central figure. On the contrary, the other prostitutes viewed her as a failed streetwalker whose drug use caused her to act unprofessionally. By associating with me, she hoped to regain some of her status. For me, however, it meant limited access to the other women because I affiliated myself with a woman who was marginal to

the scene. On another occasion, my main key respondent was a man who claimed to own three crack houses in the neighborhood. However, he had a negative reputation, and people accused him of cheating on others. My initial alliance with him delayed, and almost blocked, my access to others in the neighborhood. He intentionally tried to keep me from others on the scene, not because he would gain something from that transaction but because it made him feel powerful. When I told him I was going to hang out with some of the other people, he threatened me until one of the other dealers stepped in and told him to stay away. The two of them argued back and forth, and finally I was free to go. Fortunately, the dealer who had spoken up for me was much more central and positively associated with the local scene. Finally, I am unsure if I would have had success in gaining entrance to the scene had I not been a woman.

Developing Relationships and Trust

The processes involved in developing relationships in research situations amplify those involved in developing relationships in general. Both parties need to get to know each other, become aware and accepting of each other's roles, and engage in a reciprocal relationship. Being supportive and providing practical assistance were the most visible and direct ways for me as the researcher to develop a relationship. Throughout the years, I have given countless rides, provided child care on numerous occasions, bought groceries, and listened for hours to stories that were unrelated to my initial research questions. Gradually, my role allowed me to become part of these women's lives and to build rapport with many of them.

Over time, many women also realized that I was uninterested in being a prostitute and that I genuinely was interested in learning as much as possible about their lives. Many felt flattered that someone wanted to learn from them and that they had knowledge to offer. Allowing women to tell their stories and engaging in a dialogue with them probably were the single most important techniques that allowed me to develop relationships with them. Had I only wanted to focus on the questions I had in mind, developing such relationships might have been more difficult.

At times, I was able to get to know a woman only after her pimp endorsed our contact. One of my scariest experiences occurred before I knew to work through the pimps, and one such man had some of his friends follow me on my way home one night. I will never know what plans they had in mind for me because I fortunately was able to escape with only a few bruises. Over a year later, the woman acknowledged that her pimp had gotten upset and told her he was going to teach me a lesson.

On other occasions, I first needed to be screened by owners and managers of crack houses before the research could continue. Interestingly, screenings always were done by a man even if the person who vouched for me was a man himself. While the women also were cautious, the ways in which they checked me out tended to be much more subtle. For example, one of them would tell me a story, indicating that it was a secret about another person on the stroll. Although I failed to realize this at the time, my field notes revealed that frequently after such a conversation, others would ask me questions about related topics. One woman later acknowledged that putting out such stories was a test to see if I would keep information confidential.

Learning more about the women and gaining a better understanding of their lives also raised many ethical questions. No textbook told me how to handle situations in which a pimp abused a woman, a customer forced a woman to engage in unwanted sex acts, a customer requested unprotected sex from a woman who knew she was HIV infected, or a boyfriend had realistic expectations regarding a woman's earnings to support his drug habit. I failed to know the proper response when asked to engage in illegal activities such as holding drugs or money a woman had stolen from a customer. In general, my response was to explain that I was there as a researcher. During those occasions when pressures became too severe, I decided to leave a scene. For example, I never returned to certain crack houses because pimps there continued to ask me to consider working for them.

Over time, I was fortunate to develop relationships with people who "watched my back." One pimp in particular intervened if he perceived other pimps, customers, or passersby harassing me. He also was the one who gave me my street name: Whitie (indicating my racial background) or Ms. Whitie for those who disrespected me. While this was my first street name, I subsequently had others. Being given a street name was a symbolic gesture of acceptance. Gradually, I developed an identity that allowed me to be both an insider and an outsider. While hanging out on the strolls and other gathering places, including crack houses, I had to deal with some of the same uncomfortable conditions as the prostitutes, such as cold or warm weather, lack of access to a rest room, refusals from owners for me to patronize a restaurant, and of course, harassment by customers and the police.

I participated in many informal conversations. Unless pushed to do so, I seldom divulged my opinions. I was more open with my feelings about situations and showed empathy. I learned quickly that providing an opinion can backfire. I agreed that one of the women was struggling a lot and stated that I felt sorry for her. While I meant to indicate my "genuine concern for her," she heard that I felt sorry for her because she was a failure. When she finally, after several weeks, talked with me again, I was able to explain to her that I was not judging her, but rather felt concerned for her. She remained cynical and many times asked me for favors to make up for my mistake. It took me months before I felt comfortable telling her that I felt I had done enough and that it was time to let go. However, if she was not ready, she needed to know that I would no longer go along. This was one of many occasions when I learned that although I wanted to facilitate my work as a researcher, that I wanted people to like and trust me, I also needed to set boundaries.

Rainy and slow nights often provided good opportunities for me to participate in conversations with groups of women. Popular topics included how to work safely, what to do about condom use, how to make more money. I often served as a health educator and a supplier of condoms, gels, vaginal douches, and other feminine products. Many women were very worried about the

AIDS epidemic. However, they also were worried about how to use a condom when a customer refused to do so. They worried particularly about condom use when they needed money badly and, consequently, did not want to propose that the customer use one for fear of rejection. While some women became experts at "making" their customers use a condom—for example, "by hiding it in their mouth prior to beginning oral sex—others would carry condoms to please me but never pull one out. If a woman was HIV positive and I knew she failed to use a condom, I faced the ethical dilemma of challenging her or staying out of it.

Developing trusting relationships with crack prostitutes was more difficult. Crack houses were not the right environment for informal conversations. Typically, the atmosphere was tense and everyone was suspicious of each other. The best times to talk with these women were when we bought groceries together, when I helped them clean their homes, or when we shared a meal. Often the women were very different when they were not high than they were when they were high or craving crack. In my conversations with them, I learned that while I might have observed their actions the night before, they themselves might not remember them. Once I realized this, I would be very careful to omit any detail unless I knew that the woman herself did remember the event.

In-Depth Interviews

All interviews were conducted in a private setting, including women's residences, my car or my office, a restaurant of the women's choice, or any other setting the women selected. I did not begin conducting official interviews until I developed relationships with the women. Acquiring written informed consent prior to the interview was problematic. It made me feel awkward. Here I was asking the women to sign a form after they had begun to trust me. However, often I felt more upset about this technicality than the women themselves. As soon as they realized that the form was something the university required, they seemed to understand. Often they laughed about the official statements, and some asked if I was sure the form was to protect them and not the school.[2] None of the women refused to sign the consent form, although some refused to sign it right away and asked to be interviewed later.

In some instances the consent procedures caused the women to expect a formal interview. Some of them were disappointed when they saw I only had a few structured questions about demographic characteristics, followed by a long list of open-ended questions. When this disappointment occurred, I reminded the women that I wanted to learn from them and that the best way to do so was by engaging in a dialogue rather than interrogating them. Only by letting the women identify their salient issues and the topics they wanted to address was I able to gain an insider's perspective. By being a careful listener and probing for additional information and explanation, I as the interviewer, together with the women, was able to uncover the complexities of their lives. In addition, the nature of the interview allowed me to ask questions about contradictions in a woman's story. For example, sometimes a woman would say that she always used a condom. However, later on in the conversation she would indicate that if she needed drugs she would never use one. By asking her to elaborate on this, I was able to begin developing insights into condom use by type of partner, type of sex acts, and social context.

The interviewer becomes much more a part of the interview when the conversations are in-depth than when a structured questionnaire is used. Because I was so integral to the process, the way the women viewed me may have biased their answers. On the one hand, this bias might be reduced because of the extent to which both parties already knew each other; on the other, a woman might fail to give her true opinion and reveal her actions if she knew that these went against the interviewer's opinion. I suspected that some women played down the ways in which their pimps manipulated them once they knew that I was not too fond of these men. However, some might have taken more time to explain the relationship with their pimp in order to "correct" my image.

My background, so different from that of these women, most likely affected the nature of the interviews. I occupied a higher socioeconomic status. I had a place to live and a job. In contrast to the nonwhite women, I came from a different racial background. While I don't know to what extent these differences played a role, I acknowledge that they must have had some effect on this research.

Leaving the Field

Leaving the field was not something that occurred after completion of the fieldwork, but an event that took place daily. Although I sometimes stayed on the strolls all night or hung out for several days, I always had a home to return to. I had a house with electricity, a warm shower, a comfortable bed, and a kitchen. My house sat on a street where I had no fear of being shot on my way there and where I did not find condoms or syringes on my doorstep.

During several stages of the study, I had access to a car, which I used to give the women rides or to run errands together. However, I will never forget the cold night when everyone on the street was freezing, and I left to go home. I turned up the heat in my car, and tears streamed down my cheeks. I appreciated the heat, but I felt more guilty about that luxury than ever before. I truly felt like an outsider, or maybe even more appropriate, a betrayer.

Throughout the years of fieldwork, there were a number of times when I left the scene temporarily. For example, when so many people were dying from AIDS, I was unable to ignore the devastating impact of this disease. I needed an emotional break.

Physically removing myself from the scene was common when I experienced difficulty remaining objective. Once I became too involved in a woman's life and almost adopted her and her family. Another time I felt a true hatred for a crack house owner and was unable to adhere to the rules of courteous interactions. Still another time, I got angry with a woman whose steady partner was HIV positive when she failed to ask him to use a condom when they had sex.

I also took temporary breaks from a particular scene by shifting settings and neighborhoods. For example, I would invest most of my time in women from a particular crack house for several weeks. Then I would shift to spending more time on one of the strolls, while making shorter and less frequent visits to the crack house. By shifting scenes, I was able to tell people why I was leaving and to remind all of us of my researcher role.

While I focused on leaving the field, I became interested in women who had left the life. It seemed important to have an understanding of their past and current circumstances. I knew some of them from the days when they were working, but identifying others was a challenge. There was no gathering place for ex-prostitutes. Informal networking, advertisements in local newspapers, and local clinics and community settings allowed me to reach twenty of these women. Conducting interviews with them later in the data collection process prepared me to ask specific questions. I realized that I had learned enough about the life to know what to ask. Interviewing ex-prostitutes also prepared me for moving from the fieldwork to writing.

It is hard to determine exactly when I left the field. It seems like a process that never ends. Although I was more physically removed from the scene, I continued to be involved while analyzing the data and writing this book. I also created opportunities to go back, for example, by asking women to give me feedback on parts of the manuscript or at times when I experienced writer's block and my car seemed to automatically steer itself to one of the strolls. I also have developed other research projects in some of the same communities. For example, both a project on intergenerational drug use and a gender-specific intervention project to help women remain HIV negative have brought me back to the same population. Some of the women have become key respondents in these new projects, while others now are members of a research team. For example, Beth, one of the women who has left prostitution, works as an outreach worker on another project.

Six Themes in the Ethnography of Prostitution

The main intention of my work is to provide the reader with a perspective on street prostitution from the point of view of the women themselves. There are six fundamental aspects of the women's lives as prostitutes that must be considered. The first concerns the women's own explanations for their involvement in prostitution and their descriptions of the various circumstances that led them to become prostitutes. Their stories include justifications such as traumatic past experiences, especially sexual abuse, the lack of love they experienced as children, pressures by friends and pimps, the need for drugs, and most prominently, the economic forces that pushed them into the life. A number of women describe these justifications as excuses, as reflective explanations they have developed after becoming a prostitute.

The women describe the nature of their initial experiences, which often involved alienation from those outside the life. They also show the differences in the processes between women who work as prostitutes and use drugs and women who do not use drugs.

Although all these women work either on the street or in drug-use settings, their lives do differ. My second theme is a typology that captures these differences, looking at the women's prostitution versus drug-use identities. The typology distinguishes among (a) streetwalkers, women who work strolls and who do not use drugs; (b) hooked prostitutes, women who identify themselves mainly as prostitutes but who upon their entrance into the life also began using drugs; (c) prostituting addicts, women who view themselves mainly as drug users and who became prostitutes to support their drug habit; and (d) crack prostitutes, women who trade sex for crack.

This typology explains the differences in the women's strategies for soliciting customers, their screening of customers, pricing of sex acts, and bargaining for services. For example, the streetwalkers have the most bargaining power, while such power appears to be lacking among the crack prostitutes.

Few prostitutes work in a vacuum. The third theme is the role of pimps, a label that most women dislike and for which they prefer to substitute "old man" or "boyfriend." Among the pimps, one finds entrepreneur lovers, men who mainly employ streetwalkers and hooked prostitutes and sometimes prostituting addicts. Entrepreneur lovers engage in the life for business reasons. They treat the women as their employees or their property and view them primarily as an economic commodity. The more successful a woman is in earning them money, the more difficult it is for that woman to leave her entrepreneur pimp.

Most prostituting addicts and some hooked prostitutes work for a lover pimp, a man who is their steady partner but who also lives off their earnings. Typically, such pimps employ only one woman. The dynamics in the relationship between a prostitute and her lover pimp become more complex when both partners use drugs. Drugs often become the glue of the relationship.

For many crack prostitutes, their crack addiction serves as a pimp. Few plan to exchange sex for crack when they first begin using; often several weeks or months pass before a woman who barters sex for crack realizes that she is a prostitute.

Historically, society has blamed prostitutes for introducing sexually transmitted diseases into the general population. Similarly, it makes them scapegoats for the spread of HIV/AIDS. Yet their pimps and customers are not held accountable. The fourth theme in the anthropological study of prostitution is the impact of the AIDS epidemic on the women's lives. Although most are knowledgeable about HIV risk behaviors and the ways to reduce their risk, many misconceptions exist. The women describe the complexities of condom use, especially with steady partners but also with paying customers. Many women have mixed feelings about HIV testing, wondering how to cope with a positive test result while no cure is available. A few of the women already knew their HIV-infected status, and the discussion touches on their dilemmas as well.

The fifth theme is the violence and abuse that make common appearances in the women's lives. An ethnography of prostitution must allow the women to describe violence in their neighborhoods as well as violence in prostitution and drug-use settings. The most common violence they encounter is from customers. These men often assume that because they pay for sex they buy a woman. Apparently, casual customers pose more

of a danger than those who are regulars. The types of abuse the women encounter are emotional, physical, and sexual. In addition to customers, pimps and boyfriends abuse the women. Finally, the women discuss harassment by law enforcement officers.

When I talked with the women, it often seemed that there were no opportunities to escape from the life. Yet the sixth and final theme must be the escape from prostitution. Women who have left prostitution can describe the process of their exit from prostitution. As ex-prostitutes they struggle with the stigma of their past, the challenges of developing a new identity, and the impact of their past on current intimate relationships. Those who were also drug users often view themselves as ex-prostitutes and recovering addicts, a perspective that seems to create a role conflict. Overall, most ex-prostitutes find that their past follows them like a bad hangover.

Notes

1. For more information about qualitative research methods, see, for example, Patricia Adler and Peter Adler, *Membership Roles in Field Research* (Newbury Park: Sage, 1987); Michael Agar, *The Professional Stranger* (New York: Academic Press, 1980) and *Speaking of Ethnography* (Beverly Hills: Sage, 1986); Howard Becker and Blanche Geer, "Participant Observation and Interviewing: A Comparison," *Human Organization* 16 (1957): 28–32; Norman Denzin, *Sociological Methods: A Sourcebook* (Chicago: Aldine, 1970); Barney Glaser and Anselm Strauss, *The Discovery of Grounded Theory: Strategies for Qualitative Research* (Chicago: Aldine, 1967); Y. Lincoln and E. Guba, *Naturalistic Inquiry* (Beverly Hills: Sage, 1985); John Lofland, "Analytic Ethnography: Features, Failings, and Futures," *Journal of Contemporary Ethnography* 24 (1996): 30–67; and James Spradley, *The Ethnographic Interview* (New York: Holt, Rinehart and Winston, 1979) and *Participant Observation* (New York: Holt, Rinehart and Winston, 1980).

2. For a more extensive discussion of informed consent procedures and related ethical issues, see Bruce L. Berg, *Qualitative Research Methods for the Social Sciences,* 3rd edition, Chapter 3: "Ethical Issues" (Boston: Allyn and Bacon, 1998).

Critical Thinking

1. How do prostitutes gain a sense of control over their lives?

2. How does the author describe the women in her study?

3. How does the author describe people's reactions when she tells them what her research is about?

4. How and where did she find places of prostitution?

5. What was the main lesson she learned in her early efforts?

6. How does she describe "key respondents"?

7. How did she manage to develop relationships with prostitutes? What was the single most important technique?

8. How did the author handle situations involving ethical questions?

9. Describe the author's interview techniques and the rationale behind them.

10. How did the author feel about being able to "leave the field" daily?

11. Under what circumstances would she leave a scene temporarily?

12. What explanations do the women themselves give for their involvement in prostitution?

13. What is the author's typology regarding prostitutes? What kinds of strategies are thereby explained? Which has the most bargaining power? Which has the least?

14. How does the author describe the different kinds of pimps?

15. Who is historically held responsible for the spread of HIV/AIDS? Who is not held responsible?

16. How does the author describe the violence and abuse suffered by prostitutes and who is likely to inflict it?

17. With what do ex-prostitutes come to struggle?

Create Central

www.mhhe.com/createcentral

Internet References

Anthropology Links
http://anthropology.gmu.edu

Archaeology and Anthropology Computing and Study Skills
www.isca.ox.ac.uk/index.html

Introduction to Anthropological Fieldwork and Ethnography
http://web.mit.edu/dumit/www/syl-anth.html

Women Watch
www.un.org/womenwatch/about

Article

Prepared by: Elvio Angeloni

The Trials of Alice Goffman

GIDEON LEWIS-KRAUS

Her first book, *On the Run*—about the lives of young black men in West Philadelphia—has fueled a fight within sociology over who gets to speak for whom.

Learning Outcomes

After reading this article, you will be able to:

- Discuss Alice Goffman's approach to doing ethnography and why it has been criticized.

- Describe the potential conflict between what an ethnographer owes to the professional community versus that which is owed to informants.

- Discuss the need of some social scientists for "figures, charts, and graphs."

- Discuss the problem of bridging the gap between ethnography as science and maintaining one's membership in the community being studied.

Before the morning last September when I joined her at Newark Airport, I had met Alice Goffman only twice. But in the previous months, amid a widening controversy both inside and outside the academy over her research, she and I had developed a regular email correspondence, and she greeted me at the gate as if I were an old friend. A 34-year-old untenured professor of sociology at the University of Wisconsin, Madison, Goffman had just begun a year of leave at the Institute for Advanced Study in Princeton, which she hoped she might use to escape her critics and get back to work. Now, though, she was returning to Madison for a four-day visit, to deliver a lecture and catch up with her graduate students.

The object of dispute was Goffman's debut book, *On the Run*, which chronicles the social world of a group of young black men in a mixed-income neighborhood in West Philadelphia, some of them low-level drug dealers who live under constant threat of arrest and cycle in and out of prison. She began the project as a 20-year-old undergraduate at the University of Pennsylvania; eventually she moved to be closer to the neighborhood, which in the book she calls "Sixth Street," and even took in two of her subjects as roommates. While most ethnographic projects are completed over a year and a half, Goffman spent more than six years working in the neighborhood, which evolved from a field site into what she still basically considers her home. Her field notes, which she kept with obsessive fidelity—often transcribing hourslong conversations as they happened in real time—ran to thousands of pages. She had to spend more than a year chopping up and organizing these notes by theme for her book: the rituals of court dates and bail hearings; relationships with women and children; experiences of betrayal and abandonment. All those records had now been burned: Even before the controversy began, Goffman felt as though their ritual incineration was the only way she could protect her friend-informers from police scrutiny after her book was published.

At the gate in Newark, Goffman unshouldered a bulky zippered tote bag. "I'm so happy," she said with visible and somewhat exaggerated relief, "that I didn't give you this to take through security yourself." Over the course of our correspondence, I had asked her from time to time if she had any book artifacts that escaped destruction. In this tote was some material she had forgotten about: unpaid bills, bail receipts, letters from prison and a few extant fragments of hastily scrawled *in situ* field notes. But it wasn't until the security line that she remembered what the tote probably once held, memorabilia from her time on Sixth Street: bullets, spent casings, containers for drugs. She passed safely through the scanner in a state of agitation, not about the risk she took but by how blithely she was treated by T.S.A. agents.

'How much do we sacrifice to become public intellectuals? At the end of the day, we have to be careful about how much pandering we do to the masses.'

"And who did they stop?" she said. "Not me and my bag of contrabandy stuff, but a young man with brown skin. I tried to exchange a look of solidarity with him, but he wouldn't look at me. Compare that to the interactions I've had at this airport—people smiling at me, holding the door for me. You don't think, as a white person, about how your whole day is boosted by people affirming your dignity all day long. This isn't news. But it is stuff that, for me, at the beginning . . ." She didn't finish the sentence.

When the University of Chicago Press published *On the Run* in 2014, it was met with a level of mainstream attention—profiles, reviews, interviews—that many sociologists told me they had never witnessed for a first book in their field. Malcolm Gladwell called the work "extraordinary," and in *The New York Review of Books*, Christopher Jencks hailed it as an "ethnographic classic." Despite the many years it took Goffman to finish the book, its timing turned out to be propitious: The work of scholars like Michelle Alexander had turned America's staggering incarceration rates, especially for black men, into one of the very few territories of shared bipartisan concern. In the year after publication, Goffman did 32 public speaking appearances, including a TED talk. But by the time that TED talk received its millionth view, a rancorous backlash to the book had begun.

Within her discipline, attitudes toward Goffman's work were conflicted from the beginning. The American Sociological Association gave *On the Run* its Dissertation Award, and many of Goffman's peers came to feel as though she had been specially anointed by the discipline's power elite—that she had been allowed, as the future public face of sociology, to operate by her own set of rules. As a qualitative researcher, Goffman paid relatively scant attention to the dominant mode of her data-preoccupied field, instead opting to work in a hybrid fashion, as something between a reporter and an academic. She has also mostly refused to play the kinds of political games that can constitute a large part of academic life, eschewing disciplinary jargon and citing the work of other scholars only when she felt like it.

Worse, perhaps, was Goffman's fondness in her writing for what could seem like lurid detail. Some of the flourishes in *On the Run* were harmless or even felicitous—one character's "morning routine of clothes ironing, hair care, body lotion and sneaker buffing"—but others seemed to play up her own peril or pander to audience expectations. In one scene, two white officers in SWAT gear break down a house door, "with guns strapped to the sides of their legs." She continues, "The first officer in pointed a gun at me and asked who was in the house; he continued to point the gun toward me as he went up the stairs." In another, Goffman writes that the house of a family "smelled of piss and vomit and stale cigarettes, and cockroaches roamed freely across the countertops and soiled living-room furniture."

Above all, what frustrated her critics was the fact that she was a well-off, expensively educated white woman who wrote about the lives of poor black men without expending a lot of time or energy on what the field refers to as "positionality"—in this case, on an accounting of her own privilege. Goffman identifies strongly and explicitly with the confident social scientists of previous generations, and if none of those figures felt as though they had to apologize for doing straightforward, readable work on marginalized or discredited populations, she didn't see why she should have to. As another young professor told me, with the air of reverent exasperation that people use to talk about her, "Alice used a writing style that today you can't really use in the social sciences." He sighed and began to trail off. "In the past," he said with some astonishment, "they really did write that way." The book smacked, some sociologists argued, of a kind of swaggering adventurism that the discipline had long gotten over. Goffman became a proxy for old and unsettled arguments about ethnography that extended far beyond her own particular case. What is the continuing role of the qualitative in an era devoted to data? When the politics of representation have become so fraught, who gets to write about whom?

These criticisms, though heated, had been carried out in the public, respectable, self-correcting way of any social-scientific debate. Last spring, however, the discussion lost its academic gentility. In May, an unsigned, 60-page, single-spaced document was emailed from a throwaway address to hundreds of sociologists, detailing a series of claims casting doubt on the veracity of events as Goffman described them. The book, according to the anonymous accuser, has her attending a juvenile criminal proceeding that must have been closed to outsiders; it misrepresents the amount of time she spent living in the neighborhood; it describes scenes containing characters that by Goffman's own account were by then dead. In one place, the document notes, Goffman says she went to nine funerals, while in another place she says 19. She claims that her close friend "Chuck"—she uses pseudonyms for all her subjects—was shot in the head but also describes him in his hospital bed as covered in casts. The allegations, some of them trivial in isolation, seemed in their profusion hard to write off.

At the recommendation of her trade publisher, Goffman prepared, but did not distribute, an almost equally lengthy point-by-point response to the charges, and her department investigated the accusations and declared them without merit. But journalists and legal scholars had seized on the anonymous critique, and over the course of last spring and summer, critical pieces appeared in *The Chronicle of Higher Education* and *The New Republic*. Her critics compared her to fabricators like

Stephen Glass and Jonah Lehrer, who invented quotations or characters out of whole cloth. Some went so far as to accuse her of a felony, based on a brief but vivid account in the book's appendix. Chuck, her friend and sometime roommate, has been murdered by neighborhood rivals, and Goffman describes driving her other roommate, Mike, on his manhunt for the killer—a de facto and prosecutable confession, her critics said, of conspiracy to commit homicide. Goffman generally refused to respond to the allegations against her, but she did come forward to recharacterize this episode, despite the stark blood lust she originally described, as something akin to a mere mourning ritual. This made for a considerably attenuated version of the story, and her critics responded that she was thus either a felon or a liar.

I reached out to Goffman last summer, at the height of the controversy over her work. She responded to me in part, I think, because despite the sleeplessness, depression, and anxiety the scandal provoked, she was unable to quiet her curiosity about the norms and social structure of a discipline—i.e., journalism—that is so similar to and yet so different from what she herself does. We struck up a correspondence based on the comparison, about how we each balance what we owe to our professional communities and what we owe to our subjects, and about how to seduce subjects to cooperate in the first place. She saw the ethical predicament of her tribe as arguably worse than that of mine. "People aren't letting you in because they want to be seen," she wrote, "because you're an academic and nobody's gonna read what you write. They're letting you in because you're friends by now, and they forget that you're writing a book at all, even when you keep bringing it up. So it's more like the betrayal of telling secrets about your own family members, of selling out the people you care about most."

The discipline as a whole does not seem to know quite how to react to Goffman's case. Sociologists are proud that the work that comes out of their departments is so heterodox and wide-ranging—and, especially when it comes to issues like mass incarceration, so influential in policy debates—but it is a fractured field, and many sociologists worry that over the last few decades they have ceded their great midcentury prestige and explanatory power to economists on one side and social psychologists on the other. There has been a lot of hand-wringing about Goffman, and even her sympathizers mostly declined to speak to me on the record for fear of contamination. "I've done nothing for months but talk to my colleagues about Alice," one sociologist told me, in the context of how much he admires her and her work. "But we're in uncharted waters here. There have been a hundred years of debates about the reliability of ethnography, but this is the first time the debate is being carried out in the Twitter age."

It does not help that Goffman, when challenged about her book—or about the privilege, defiance, and sloppiness to which

critics attribute its weaknesses—tends to respond with willful naïveté or near-grandiose self-possession. Once, when I asked her what she made of a sustained series of attacks by one critic, a respected quantitative sociologist, she said it was hard to pay proper attention to him when other people were accusing her of felonies. Besides, she said, in a world in which a majority of black men without high-school degrees have been in prison, she had little patience for internecine quarrels. "I can't even muster that much interest," she wrote by way of conclusion. "Because there's a big, mysterious world out there, and I want to understand a little more of it before I die. That and tear down the prisons."

A kind of benign self-neglect, along with a comprehensive absent-mindedness, extends outward to everything in Goffman's life that isn't fieldwork or her students. People who spend a lot of time with her often arrange themselves to take care of her, lest she get lost. I knew her for only two days before I found myself making sure, for example, that her phone was plugged in. In our four days in Madison, she could not remember that her room was a right turn out of the elevator. Goffman is short, with big, round chestnut eyes, dirty-blond hair that she rarely knows what to do with, a slightly reedy quaver in her voice and a performatively childlike manner that softens a relentlessly inquisitive and analytic intelligence. If she ever stopped asking questions, you might notice her only as someone's tagalong little sister.

This mien helps her enlist everyone she meets as a cooperating informer. In Madison, we were picked up between appointments by an Uber driver in blue scrubs; he told us he was studying radiology at a local community college but had taken the year off to earn money as a transport coordinator in a hospital. He was from Jackson, Miss., and had arrived in Madison via Milwaukee.

Goffman turned to the driver, who was black, to ask—in the offhand way you might ask an Uber driver about his experiences with the company—"What have your local experiences with racism been like?"

He thought for a moment. "It's like, people smile at me, smile at me, smile at me, and then BAM!" He paused.

"Something happens, and you feel put in your place?" Goffman said.

The driver nodded emphatically and asked Goffman what she did for a living. When she answered, he told her he saw the social forces that organized human behavior as if they were a school of fish guiding each member.

"Go on," she said, taking notes on her phone.

"You just can't go from A to Z," he continued. "You go from A to B and then maybe to C, but then you're back to B again, then to C and back to B, and you never know why."

"That's so good," Goffman said. She gave him her email address and asked him if she could persuade him to switch over to sociology, and he laughed. By the time we got out of the car, he seemed a little dazed, unsure how he came to talk about this stuff over the course of a five-minute ride.

Goffman was raised to be a sociologist, though she tends to prefer the homelier designation of "fieldworker." Her father, Erving, who died at 60 of stomach cancer when she was an infant, was perhaps the most important sociologist of the last 50 years—and easily the most consequential sociologist in the public discourse. Though Erving's work was varied and deliberately unsystematic, he is best known for his elaboration of the self as a series of performances. His daughter has taken over his idea that static character is less interesting or relevant than the dynamics of exchange. "I don't think," she once told me—after calling herself "chameleonlike"—"that I have real preferences, just desires that emerge in social interactions."

Her mother, Gillian Sankoff, and her adoptive father, William Labov, are eminent sociolinguists themselves, and when Goffman was a child, she was sent on the full-time, perpetual errand of collecting noteworthy linguistic misunderstandings for her parents' collection. Goffman was partly raised by an Italian family in South Philadelphia whom her mother found through a want ad for child care; they were so different from her "professor parents" that she got in the habit of taking field notes on family conversations. Goffman spent a gap year between high school and college volunteering for U.S.A.I.D. in the Philippines, and her parents remember that she sent home pages and pages of letters that said little about her own life and quite a bit about, for example, the local varieties of queue formation.

In her first semester as an undergraduate at the University of Pennsylvania, she took a graduate-level class on urban sociology, and within a few weeks it was clear to her professor, David Grazian, that she was the most talented and committed person in the class. "I sent her out on a fieldwork assignment to sit at a diner and record what she saw, and she came back after an hour with 14 single-spaced pages." Through a project for that class, on the lives of the mostly black cafeteria employees at Penn, she came to tutor a teenager named Aïsha, the granddaughter of a cafeteria supervisor. Goffman grew close to Aïsha and her family, and it was through them that she met the men whose lives she describes in *On the Run*: an intermittent drug dealer she calls Mike, as well as a family: three brothers, Chuck, Reggie and Tim, and their mother, Miss Linda.

Even while Goffman was still an undergraduate, word of her intensive fieldwork circulated among senior ethnographers, and one recruited her to study under him in a PhD program at Princeton; she commuted to New Jersey from Philadelphia, and the project she began at 20 ultimately became her dissertation. The general impression was that, as a member of the Princeton department told me, her work was brilliant but not all that dissimilar from other contemporary works of ethnography,

except in the depth of her fieldwork. Recent years have seen comparable projects on drug dealers in an unidentified city, by Waverly Duck of the University of Pittsburgh; on drug robbers in the South Bronx, by Randol Contreras of the University of Toronto; on reform-school students in Pennsylvania, by Jamie Fader of Temple University; and others. One member of that cohort described Goffman to me as "very humble, very down to earth," and Goffman herself has always categorized what she did as only an incremental contribution to the cumulative work in the field.

But from the beginning, critics worried that her book, which refused to contextualize itself with "positional" humility or some powerful theory, would serve only to reinforce popular stereotypes. The most glaring such stereotype was that young black men are invariably involved in crime, and critics felt that she drastically overstated the extent to which her characters were representative, rather than anomalous, in their criminal activity.

Sociologists who distrust her strain of richly descriptive ethnography saw this as an unfortunate consequence of the ethnographer's tendency to become "too close" to her subjects, to forgo rigor and skepticism in favor of taking at face value the accounts that subjects give of themselves. In Goffman's case, this extended both to discussions of criminality (her subjects, some critics suggested, played up their exploits to impress her) and to the various exigencies that shaped their lives. When her subjects told her that they were afraid to go to the hospital to witness the birth of their children because it was standard practice among police officers to check visitors for arrest warrants, she was deemed too quick to accept their beliefs and superstitions as accurate representations of police practice. Too often she presented events or descriptions without qualifying comment—a perfectly valid approach for a journalist, who often tells a particular story and leaves the reader to do the generalizing, but a more problematic one for a sociologist, who is expected to do the generalizing herself.

It was the media's celebration of *On the Run*—and particularly of its more sensational elements—that turned the response within the discipline from contentious to personal. This ill will was made explicit at the 2014 annual meeting of the American Sociological Association in San Francisco, where it seemed as if Goffman had become a celebrity: Some attendees remember seeing a poster-size photo of her, hands in her jeans pockets, outside a prison. Goffman had been chosen for an "Author Meets Critics" panel, an honor rarely visited upon a book so soon after publication. The event was, extraordinarily, standing room only; people in neighboring panels reported that they could barely pay attention to what was going on in front of them because of the fanfare down the hall. Two people told me they tried to get in, were turned away and went to their hotel rooms to watch the drama unfold on Twitter.

By all accounts, the session felt unusually hostile. As Victor Rios, one of the panelists and a sociologist at the University of California, Santa Barbara, who studies similar communities, framed the problem, she had engaged in the "Jungle Book trope": She visits the jungle, sees the wild animals in their natural habitat, loses her way and, thanks to the kindness of beasts, lives to tell the story.

Rios, a former gang member, told me later that he understood the pressures on Goffman and that he was urged to write his story in a way that would command broad attention—"My best friend was killed in front of me; I ended up in juvie." But he resisted it, out of worry about his tenure prospects and also on principle. "How much do we sacrifice to become public intellectuals?" he said. "At the end of the day, we have to be careful about how much pandering we do to the masses."

Sociology as a discipline emerged, in the late 19th century, from the idea that things called "social facts" might be studied the way a chemist studies compounds or a biologist studies organisms. While political economists and psychologists studied the individual actor, with his or her particular preferences and utility-maximizing behavior, sociologists believed that the group was primary to its members—that we are evolving products of contingent social norms. What this insight has subsequently produced in practice is a discipline that now encompasses everything from statistical analyses of census data to accessible monographs about why people shoplift or the social processes of divorce. Over the past few decades, the field has gone through cycles of tribalism, rived by arguments among quantitative analysts; theory-heavy scholars working in the tradition of the French sociologist Pierre Bourdieu; critical race scholars, who have brought up important but tricky points about who gets to study whom; and the urban "symbolic interactionists" with whom Goffman identifies.

People in Goffman's camp trace their work to Robert E. Park and the so-called First Chicago School, which set itself to the project of understanding the new vigor and clash of the American city, then driven by the dynamism of industrialization and immigration. Park had spent 10 years as a journalist and was working for Booker T. Washington at the Tuskegee Institute when he was asked, in 1914, to join the young sociology department at the University of Chicago. This was a Chicago that would produce new sorts of Americans, characters like Saul Bellow's Augie March, and Park's team went on to put together canonical, sympathetic studies of the city's black, Jewish, Chinese, and Polish neighborhoods. As Richard Wright put it in his introduction to *Black Metropolis*, St. Clair Drake and Horace Cayton's classic study of Chicago's "black belt," the ethnographers of the First Chicago School "were not afraid to urge their students to trust their feelings for a situation or an event, were not afraid to stress the role of insight, and to warn against a slavish devotion to figures, charts, graphs and sterile scientific techniques."

Their painstaking empirical efforts, modeled on the anthropology of Franz Boas, were carried out in the hope that they might refute the reigning theoretical paradigm of the day, which looked to eugenics and social Darwinism to explain racial inferiority and the "social problems" introduced by immigration. The project was explicitly liberal and meliorative, of a piece with the work of journalists like Jacob Riis and early social workers like Jane Addams. The first step toward sensible policy-driven solutions, the First Chicago School believed, was work that would convince the broader public that these immigrant enclaves, which seemed so foreign and inscrutable, actually represented ordered social worlds structured by familiar norms.

This sort of detail required deep, sustained, participatory attention. Some monographs produced by Park's team were written by "native informants"—Louis Wirth on the Jewish ghetto, Paul Siu on the Chinese laundryman, Drake and Cayton on the black belt—and others by outsiders. These practitioners, especially when they sought to examine and explain criminal behavior, faced many of the same problems Goffman did as a participant-observer: William Foote Whyte, in his 1943 study of Boston's North End, admitted in his methodological appendix that he had been an accessory to election fraud. But it was understood that part of the ethnographer's project was a suspension of belief in conventional assumptions about deviant behavior, and that if you wanted to understand more fully how and why people broke the law, you had to see their world from the inside.

Part of the problem for both native informants and outside observers, Wright saw at the time, was that this sort of detail-heavy, participatory intensity was always in danger of being taken the wrong way. As Wright put it in his introduction to *Black Metropolis*: "This is no easy book. . . . There is no attempt in *Black Metropolis* to understate, to gloss over, to doll up or to make harsh facts pleasant for the tender-minded." The work represented important racial progress insofar as it treated black lives as worthy of full, lavish, unblinkered description.

After World War II, immigration slowed and the university was expanding, and what became known, under the leadership of Everett Hughes, as the Second Chicago School was less interested in ethnic minorities than it was in the processes of professionalization—how some people come to self-identify as "doctors" or "lawyers"—as well as the mechanics by which some subcultures were labeled "deviant." Though Erving Goffman did only two stints as a fieldworker—once in the Shetland Islands, the work that ultimately became his 1959 classic *The Presentation of Self in Everyday Life*, and again for a year in a mental institution, the experience that was the basis for his 1961 book *Asylums*—he had a strong affinity with this school, especially with the work of Howard S. Becker, who wrote widely read essays about the socialization of marijuana users. These books, lucid and elegant in their style and argumentation, were acclaimed far outside sociology departments and often led their writers to positions of influence on policy. (Goffman ended up on an important committee to review the mental-health system.)

But by the 1970s, this style of qualitative work was threatened on all sides. It became easier, in the context of the Cold War expansion of the American university, to secure funding if you could point to exactly the figures, charts and graphs that Wright considered sterile. Universities were turning out a newly diverse array of graduates, and the critical race studies movement arose to question the methods and prejudices of "intrepid" white scholars in pith helmets. As these young scholars pointed out, especially in Joyce Ladner's landmark 1973 anthology, *The Death of White Sociology*, a number of the books produced by the First Chicago School did, despite their best intentions, traffic in sensationalism and stereotypes. At the same time, sociologists—keen to keep up with their colleagues in economics departments—strove to put themselves on the secure path of a science. The view was that statistics were facts and everything else mere impressionism.

And, worse than impressionistic, ethnography had also come to seem exploitative. The most glaring case was that of the Washington University scholar Laud Humphreys, who wrote in 1970 about anonymous sex between men in public restrooms. As part of his research, he took down the license plates of the "tearoom" visitors, and many months later went to interview them, under false pretexts, at home and often in front of their families. The press attacked the work as unethical, often in the same language with which Goffman was criticized. The scandal destroyed Humphreys's entire department, and the moral was clear: Ethnography was shady work.

On our flight back from Madison, Goffman came to find me in the rear of the plane and silently handed me two black notebooks, both marked 2003. She used them during her sophomore and junior years of college, when she and Mike and Chuck were first getting close. She had hesitated to show them to me because they were one of the few sentimental things she had left from that time, and now, she figured, she would have to destroy them just as she had destroyed her field notes.

The notebooks are extraordinary records of a young scholar's intellectual and personal development. They present two parallel processes of socialization. In the fall of 2003, she is about to turn 22; she is in her junior year at Penn, but she is already applying to graduate school. Her life on Sixth Street has become much more real to her than her life on campus, but still she remained committed to sociology. The notebooks show her makeshift attempts to reconcile what she is learning in class

with what she is seeing on the street. She is taking a course, with the eminent sociologist Randall Collins, on the history of sociological theory; another class on the history of the South; a third on African-American literature; and a fourth, which she will drop, on statistics. The only time either notebook mentions Erving Goffman is on the first page, where she takes down what seems to be a quote from a posthumously published talk on fieldwork: "The most difficult thing about doing fieldwork is remembering who you are."

In class, Goffman is learning about the history of racial discrimination, and on Sixth Street, she is witnessing Mike's inability to secure a job. "After months of limited involvement in the drug trade," she writes, "his man [Chuck] is home and he is ready to stop being broke and get back in more seriously." She moves easily in and out of an academic register, writing in one sentence about her attempts to "chart Mike's socioecon wave" and elsewhere on the same page about the minor transactions of their growing friendship: "I tell him to call PO [parole officer]—it's the 15th—and ask if he'll help me move my couch tomorrow and he says I got you."

Mike and Chuck come to her house—they're not living with her yet—to do their laundry. They tease her, often for what she's wearing, and she teases them back. It's clear in her mischievous play, her ability to generate urgent affection and her speed on the uptake that this is the same Goffman I have gotten to know. At a certain point, the group returns to a waiting black Lincoln Navigator, and her friend Steve has taken her seat: "I say Get the [expletive] out of my seat [Steve]! And he and [Mike] think this is the funniest thing they ever heard and [Mike] says proudly: Yo she be gangster sometimes." There are moments where she pauses to reflect on the changes she has undergone since she started her fieldwork—"I'm a vegetarian and used to be a gymnast"—but for the most part she does nothing to indicate that she feels as though she is being transformed or remade by the experience.

Threaded through her descriptions of these young-adult encounters—in between her course notes on Richard Wright, W.E.B. Du Bois, Ned Polsky, and Emile Durkheim—is the sort of sociological work that David Riesman described as a "conversation between the classes." Over the course of the final few weeks of that notebook, jottings on the theories of Georg Simmel or an outline of the history of the Scottsboro boys alternates with a comprehensive lexicon she begins to assemble: "fall back: to cool it. fall back! said to a boy trying to holla. 'I'm falling back from hustlin'." There are entries for "cake/cakin'" and "to smash," followed by pages with definitions of Weber's concepts of "*erklären*" and "*verstehen*."

Critics have been quick to point out, implicitly and otherwise, that the similar code-switching in *On the Run* looks a lot like what Erving warned about: forgetting who you are. As one detractor told me, it seemed to many people as if

"Alice thought she was turning black," and *Philadelphia* magazine has compared her to Rachel Dolezal, the N.A.A.C.P. president in Spokane, Wash., who was revealed to have been passing as black. On occasion, this discomfort has been crudely sexualized; when Goffman was an undergraduate, professors in her department asked her advisers if she was sleeping with her informers, and that insinuation makes regular appearances in anonymous posts about her on sociology message boards. The conversation between the classes had grown so obviously intimate that a lot of people could understand it only in terms of lust and fetish.

It's true that ethnography has come somewhat back into fashion since the 1970s and that no contemporary sociologist would agree with the call, tweeted by a Buzzfeed writer and echoed elsewhere, to "ban outsider ethnographies." As one sociologist put it to me, "If Alice Goffman isn't allowed to write about poor black people, then sociologists who come from poor communities of color, like Victor Rios, aren't allowed to write about elite institutions like banks or hedge funds, and that, in the end, hurts Victor Rios much more than it hurts Alice Goffman."

But even within sociology departments, there isn't a lot of agreement about how to go about the process of bridging social distance in a way that is both respectful and rigorous—a researcher is always in danger of being accused of having stayed too far away or gotten too close. Ethnographers have always dealt with questions about where their allegiances lie, and more than one ethnographer has been accused of being too close to her subjects to evaluate their self-reports. I asked Goffman's undergraduate adviser, Elijah Anderson, an august ethnographer—mostly of urban black communities—now at Yale, about the criticism of Goffman as an adventurer or tourist, or as a wide-eyed, credulous observer. He said she had carried out her work just as any ethnographer should. He elliptically handed me a copy of *Stigma*—one of Erving Goffman's most famous books, from 1963—and invited me to look up the part on "courtesy stigma." Erving anticipates exactly the sort of criticism brought to bear five decades later on the work of his daughter:

> The person with a courtesy stigma can in fact make both the stigmatized and the normal uncomfortable: By always being ready to carry a burden that is not "really" theirs, they can confront everyone else with too much morality; by treating the stigma as a neutral matter to be looked at in a direct, offhand way, they open themselves and the stigmatized to misunderstanding by normals who may read offensiveness into this behavior.

Most of the problems *On the Run* has encountered, especially outside the field, have to do with the fact that it falls between the stools of journalism and ethnography. If the book was too journalistic—too descriptive, too irresponsible, too sensationalistic, too taken with its own first-person involvement—to

count as properly rigorous sociology, it was too sociological to count, for many journalists, as proper reporting. Most journalists believe that true stories are necessarily personal, about the ways particular people choose to act in the world; the language of journalism, like the language of law, is almost always the language of individual moral responsibility. For a sociologist, whose profession since the turn of the century has taken it as axiomatic that society is primary to the individual, the language of individual moral responsibility is often a way of avoiding talk about structural conditions that favor the powerful.

Many of the things for which journalists and legal scholars have berated Goffman are considered standard practice for sociologists, and most sociologists have found the mainstream criticisms of the book to be baseless. Procedurally, journalists object to the pseudonymity of sources and the destruction of her field notes; sociologists point out that institutional review boards mandate that identities be obscured and that they often require the destruction of field notes that could be subject to subpoena in a criminal investigation. Regarding most of the book's internal inconsistencies, virtually every single ethnographer I talked to described the enormously difficult logistical problem of how to keep track of pseudonymous notes over years and admitted that if you subjected almost any work in the field to that kind of punitive audit, you would almost certainly come up with similar trivial confusions. This is true of even the most organizationally composed people, [one] of which Goffman is not. She cannot, off the top of her head, remember which year she finished high school, which year she finished college or which year she spent three months in the hospital after almost being killed on her bike by a bus.

Goffman has declined to make public the long, point-by-point rebuttal of her anonymous attacker, but after we got to know each other well, she shared it with me. It is blunt and forceful and, in comparison with the placidity of her public deportment, almost impatient and aggrieved in tone, and it is difficult to put the document down without wondering why she has remained unwilling to publicize some of its explanations. She acknowledges a variety of errors and inconsistencies, mostly the results of a belabored anonymization process, but otherwise persuasively explains many of the lingering issues. There is, for example, a convincing defense of her presence in the supposedly closed juvenile court and a quite reasonable clarification of the mild confusion over what she witnessed firsthand and what she reconstructed from interviews—along with explanations for even the most peculiar and deranged claims of her anonymous attacker, including why Mike does his laundry at home in one scene and at a laundromat in another.

Many claims against her are also easy to rebut independently. Some critics called far-fetched, for example, her claim that an F.B.I. agent in Philadelphia drew up a new computer surveillance system after watching a TV broadcast about the

East German Stasi. If you search the Internet for "Philadelphia cop Stasi documentary," a substantiating item from *The Philadelphia Inquirer* from 2007 is the second hit. When it comes to Goffman's assertion that officers run IDs in maternity wards to arrest wanted fathers, another short Internet search produces corroborating examples in Dallas, New Orleans, and Brockton, Mass., and a Philadelphia public defender and a deputy mayor told me that the practice does not at all seem beyond plausibility. The most interesting question might not be whether Goffman was telling the truth but why she has continued to let people believe that she might not be.

The hardest elements of her story to confirm are the ones that feel like cinematic exaggerations, especially with respect to police practices; several officers challenged as outlandish her claim that she was personally interrogated with guns on the table. To Goffman, however, the fact that a journalist or a legal scholar would turn to the police to confirm accusations against them is representative of the broader failure of American society to take seriously the complaints of disempowered minority communities. It's the definition of institutional racism. When I reminded her that it was my job to try to find independent confirmation of some of her claims, she understood my own disciplinary needs and was forthcoming, if slightly begrudging, in helping me out. But at one point, when I pressed her on one of these issues, she wrote back that I seemed to be saying, "The way to validate the claims in the book is by getting officials who are white men in power to corroborate them." She went on: "The point of the book is for people who are written off and delegitimated to describe their own lives and to speak for themselves about the reality they face, and this is a reality that goes absolutely against the narratives of officials or middle-class people. So finding 'legitimate' people to validate the claims—it feels wrong to me on just about every level."

In this her discipline stands behind her, over and against journalistic or legal practice. As Randall Collins, whose course she was taking when she was writing in the black notebooks, put it: "She got in deep enough so that not only does she understand things from their point of view, she doesn't give priority to laws, official morals, all the things that conventional people take for granted. I not only am not going to play the shock game, but I don't have much respect for people who can't see that their being shocked is part of the way their social world is constructed around them."

What has united her critics, academic and otherwise, is the accusation that in going "deep enough" to disregard laws, she did in fact lose herself in the process and confuse her own ethnographic standing with actual membership in the community she studied. This comes to the fore in the book's final scene, the nighttime drive to find Chuck's killer. The legal and journalistic position would stipulate that either the last scene occurred as it was initially written, as a manhunt, or it occurred as she later described it—as a mourning ritual and face-saving ceremony.

But what her critics can't imagine is that perhaps both of the accounts she has given are true at the same time—that this represents exactly the bridging of the social gap that so many observers find unbridgeable. From the immediate view of a participant, this was a manhunt; from the detached view of an observer, this was a ritual. The account in the book was that of Goffman the participant, who had become so enmeshed in this community that she felt the need for vengeance "in my bones." The account Goffman provided in response to the felony accusation (which read as if dictated by a lawyer, which it might well have been) was written by Goffman the observer, the stranger to the community who can see that the reason these actors give for their behavior—revenge—is given by the powerless as an attempt to save face; that though this talk was important, it was talk all the same.

The problem of either-or is one that is made perhaps inevitable by the metaphor of "immersion." The anthropologist Caitlin Zaloom, who studies economic relationships, explained to me that it's a metaphor her own field has long given up on. The metaphor asks us to imagine a researcher underwater—that is, imperiled, unreachable from above—who then returns to the sun and air, newly qualified to report on the darkness below because the experience has put a chill in her bones. This narrative of transformation is what strikes critics like Rios as so patronizing and self-congratulatory. But Goffman herself never understood her work to be "immersive" in that way. The almost impossible challenge Goffman thus set before herself is the representation of both these views—of drive as manhunt and drive as ritual—in all their simultaneity.

Goffman could have covered herself by adding another paragraph of analysis, one that would have contextualized but also undercut the scene as the participants experienced it. Almost all of her early readers thought she should do that. It would have made her life easier. But she didn't. This was a book about men whose entire lives—whose whole network of relationships—had been criminalized, and she did not hesitate to criminalize her own. She threw in her lot.

For the last five years, Goffman hadn't had the opportunity to spend much time in Philadelphia: after finishing her dissertation in 2010, she spent two years on a postdoctoral fellowship in Michigan (she threw away the two years of field notes she took there, fearing an even worse version of the criticisms she got for *On the Run*) and then moved to Madison for her new job there. But now that she was in Princeton for the year, she had told her Sixth Street friends that she would be back on the block again.

It had been at least a year since she visited Miss Linda, and when we went to see her in October, she engulfed Goffman until her tiny person almost disappeared into the embrace. Reggie, himself a man of considerable bulk, stood there on the sidewalk, his phone ringing unanswered, for two minutes until Goffman was put down and it was his turn. Goffman had come down in part to catch up with the family and in part to distribute the royalty checks she shares evenly with the book's central characters. (She did the math last year without setting aside money to cover taxes, so she had to pay them out of pocket.) She chose that Friday because it was Reggie's birthday and because Mike had called to tell her that he might be getting out of prison that day, though he had been thinking that for a few weeks.

The Sixth Street neighborhood, four or five square blocks in all, is bounded by some geographical features that make it feel mostly self-contained; it's not an area one would be likely to pass through en route to anywhere else, so it was, Goffman explained, not a place for strangers. She wasn't sure how they would receive another outsider, but it was clear from our arrival that Goffman was family, so anyone she brought along was family, too. Reggie wore a black T-shirt over the contours of a black tank top and fitted gray sweatpants; he had a short fauxhawk and a wide, pointy beard, which gave his large head the shape of a big, dark diamond. He removed his headphones from his ears and put his sunglasses—large and round and stylishly effeminate in an early-1980s way, like the sunglasses Mia Farrow wears in "Broadway Danny Rose"—atop his mohawk, then smiled broadly and extended his hand to introduce himself.

"You write books, too? Like Alice?"

"I do, yeah."

"I write books, too." He explained that he had done a lot of writing in prison, but that being back at home was too distracting to get much done. Alice fished in her wallet and handed him a check. "This for our book?" She nodded. He asked me if I had read their book. I said that I had and that I really liked it. He was pleased. He said "our book" a few more times. Goffman was clearly happy that he was so proud of it.

After a while, Goffman, who eats an astonishing amount of junk food, was hungry and wanted to go to a Jamaican place nearby. She asked Reggie and Miss Linda if they wanted to come, but Miss Linda was happy sitting in the sun, and she told us that as long as Reggie's phone was ringing off the hook, he wasn't going anywhere. We went to get food and bring it back, and Reggie came over to the car to make sure we would be joining him for his birthday party that night. Goffman got out and gave him a hug and said she would be in touch. As she got back into the car, she called out, "I love you."

I had spent a lot of time with her, and I had never seen her in such high spirits as she seemed in the car that day, crisscrossing

Philadelphia to see everyone she was close to. We were off to meet some of her other friends from the book, one group in what she described as a poorer neighborhood nearby, then a quick visit to a friend of hers in the hospital, and finally to a more middle-class, mixed-ethnicity neighborhood in another part of the city. Before we arrived at each stop, Goffman gave me a demographic and historical rundown of the block and the community it hosted, with the sort of fine-grained understanding of the class differences in the community that she was accused of lacking in the book. She seemed entirely herself: an observer upon whom nothing is lost, an irremediable sociologist and the prodigal baby sister of Sixth Street home at last.

Many of the people we met knew that Goffman hadn't had the easiest year, and they greeted her like an infantryman on leave from a traumatic campaign—though each seemed to have a slightly different idea of what it was Goffman actually did. Most of them knew she wrote books, and some thought she was a teacher. She told some of her friends that she was thinking about quitting her job, and she asked them what they thought she could do if she moved back to town. They said that she would be a great schoolteacher, but that unfortunately she was a little too small to be a home health aide. By the end of the night, Goffman was beginning to drag, and she told Mike's mom, with whom she is particularly close, that she didn't know what to do.

Mike's mom smoothed Goffman's knotty hair, then gave her a stern lecture about persistence. "You just got to pull your pants up," she said, "and keep going."

Critical Thinking

1. How should an ethnographer strike a balance between what is owed to the discipline versus what is owed to the community being studied?
2. How should an ethnographer report findings with respect to figures, charts, and graphs versus a more descriptive personal account?
3. What should an ethnographer do if conducting fieldwork might involve breaking the law?

Internet References

Anthropology Links
 http://anthropology.gmu.edu
Human Relations Area Files
 http://hraf.yale.edu
Introduction to Anthropological Fieldwork and Ethnography
 http://web.mit.edu/dumit/www.syl-anth.html

GIDEON LEWIS-KRAUS is a contributing writer for the magazine.

Article

Prepared by: Elvio Angeloni, *Pasadena City College*

Why Manners Matter

VALERIE CURTIS

Learning Outcomes

After reading this article, you will be able to:

- Discuss the importance of manners as an evolutionary adaptation.
- Describe and explain the "disgust system" as a psychological adaptation.
- Explain why manners have become particularly important in recent human history.

You wake up in the morning. Your partner burps and drags on a smelly dressing gown. You can't find your toothbrush so you use his and then wipe some muck off the floor with it. Leaving the house, you step over a turd deposited by a neighbour, then drive into a traffic jam caused by everyone ignoring the lights. In your office, everyone interrupts each other until a spitting match breaks out. Leaving work, ill-groomed strangers press up against you in the lift and one sneezes in your face.

What a grim picture. A world without manners hardly seems worth living in. Yet manners are so ingrained in our lives that we hardly notice them.

I believe that they are too important to ignore. We need to better understand manners for two reasons: first, because they are a principal weapon in the war on disease, and second, because manners underpin our ability to function as a cooperative species. In my new book on the evolution of disgust, *Don't Look, Don't Touch*, I argue that, far from being an old-fashioned set of rules about which fork to use, manners are so important that they should be up there with fire and the invention of language as a prime candidate for what makes us human.

The first, and most ancient, function of manners is to solve the problem of how to be social without getting sick. Imagine that you and I encounter each other. Although I'd like to hang

around in case you have information or goods to exchange, it might be more sensible if I ran away because, to me, you are a walking bag of microbes. With every exhalation you might emit millions of influenza viruses, and your handshake might transfer salmonella bacteria or scabies mites. More intimate contact could give me hepatitis, syphilis, or worse. Your proximity to me is potentially deadly. You too, of course, make the same subconscious calculation. So how can we get close enough to share benefits but avoid sharing our microbes? This is the job of manners.

Manners dictate that if I want to interact with you I should stay at a safe distance; far enough away not to spray you with microbe-laden saliva. They tell me that I should clean and cover my body, especially the smelly bits where microbes might lurk, and to share my food with you, but not any leftovers that I have already bitten into. And manners tell me to invite you to my dwelling, but only once I've cleaned it of my bodily wastes. I do all of this because I cannot afford to disgust you. If I fail in my manners, you may reject and ostracise me and refuse further collaboration. Worse, you may gossip about my lapses in hygiene and tarnish my reputation, denying me access to the benefits of life as a member of an intensely social species.

This ability to be mannerly is supported by two psychological adaptations. One is the disgust system, which motivates us to recognize and avoid potential pathogen hot zones. The other is the ability to feel shame, which, I hypothesise, evolved to help us learn to avoid becoming disgusting to others. A study by Roger Giner-Sorolla at the University of Kent, UK, confirmed that we feel shame if someone looks at us with a disgusted expression. And research from Richard Stevenson's lab at Macquarie University in Sydney, Australia, suggests that parents use disgust expressions to teach hygiene behaviour to their children. Indeed, I suspect that one of the reasons we evolved the ability to communicate disgust via its characteristic facial and vocal expression is to teach others good manners. By pulling a face and exclaiming "Eeeugh!" we demonstrate disgust for another person's poor hygiene. This elicits shame in the target, and as a result, they modify their manners, which protects us.

But manners have acquired another function besides disease avoidance. As group sizes grew from related individuals, to clans, tribes and beyond, the problem of how to cooperate with unrelated others became more serious. Individuals who tried to get the benefits of social life without paying their share of the costs could derail the whole cooperative enterprise. Humans became adept at looking for clues as to who was likely to cooperate and who was not. Manners provided an indicator. Those who were careful with hygiene were good candidates, as were those who demonstrated that they put the interests of others before themselves. The child who passes a plate of food before serving herself is showing that she can control her selfish tendencies. In effect, she is saying: "Look how well my mother taught me. If I can show such self-control now, how useful a member of this society I will be in the future. In the meantime, you can safely do business with my family." The child taught restraint with cake now by her mother would be likely to receive a greater total of cooperative cake in her lifetime.

Those who master manners are set to reap the many benefits that come from living in a highly cooperative ultra-society. Manners are therefore a sort of proto-morality, a set of behaviors that we make "second nature" early in life so that we can avoid disgusting others with our parasites and antisocial behavior.

There are, of course, exceptions to these rules. A study on manners that my team at the London School of Hygiene and Tropical Medicine has just completed in Nepal showed that rules of hygiene are often suspended for close family members. This is probably because sharing saliva-contaminated food with someone who is already an intimate is unlikely to have disease consequences. We also saw that courtesy manners are suspended as guests become more familiar, probably because in an established cooperative relationship there is less need to signal cooperative intent. Of course, in intimate relationships, hygiene manners can be suspended entirely. Perhaps we find kissing attractive because it signifies that one's partner is serious, so much so that they will contemplate sharing our pathogens.

We play out a mannerly dance every day, getting close, but not too close, offering tokens of goodwill, but not giving away too much, in every social interaction. Yet we do the dance largely unaware of why we do it. We don't rationally calculate how to avoid inflicting our pathogens on others, nor do we consciously calculate that a small courtesy now might lead us to a big trading opportunity later. Instead, we have vague intuitions that it would be better not to disgust a guest by appearing unkempt or by offering them a dirty towel, and we follow the rules of politeness that were drummed into us as children. When we fail in these civilities, the disgust shown by our interlocutor provokes shame and teaches us not to repeat the offence.

My team is now investigating whether we can use manners to encourage better hygienic behavior, for example, in campaigns to prevent disease by improving hand washing and food hygiene in Nepal and Zambia. But it may be that understanding manners can bring us an even bigger prize.

The acquisition of manners was one of the first baby steps humans took on the road to large-scale cooperation, and cooperation, underpinned by our moral sense, was the great leap forward that allowed humans to become a hyper-social species. We have since worked together to achieve technical dominance of the planet. If we can better understand how microbes gave us manners and manners then shaped our morality, it might hold clues for our future as a species.

Critical Thinking

1. Discuss the role of manners for human beings and what they specifically dictate.
2. Describe and explain the psychological adaptations related to the "disgust system."
3. Why have manners become particularly important as group sizes have increased in human history?
4. Discuss the circumstances in which the rules of hygiene are suspended.

Create Central

www.mhhe.com/createcentral

Internet References

Everyday Health
www.everydayhealth.com/
Good Health
www.goodhealth.com.au

VALERIE CURTIS is a disgustologist and director of the Hygiene Centre at the London School of Hygiene and Tropical Medicine. This essay is based on her new book, *Don't Look, Don't Touch: The science behind revulsion* (Oxford University Press/University of Chicago Press).

Article   Prepared by: Elvio Angeloni

On The Origin Of Faith

JOSEPH HENRICH

Learning Outcomes

After reading this article, you will be able to:

- Discuss the importance of the accumulated wisdom implicit in the practices and beliefs of a people rather than their own intuitions and personal experiences.

- Discuss the success of humanity as a consequence of both our genetic endowment and our cultural adaptiveness.

- Discuss the importance of taboos in human adaptiveness.

- Discuss divination as a way to overcome the "Gambler's Fallacy."

- Explain the good taste of spices such as the chili pepper.

- Using housebuilding among weaverbirds and Inuit as an example, explain why natural selection is insufficient to explain the success of the human species.

As one of the world's staple crops, manioc (or cassava) is a highly productive, starch-rich tuber that has permitted relatively dense populations to inhabit drought-prone tropical environments. I've lived on it, both in Amazonia and in the South Pacific. It's tasty and filling. However, depending on the variety of manioc and the local ecological conditions, the tubers can contain high levels of cyanogenic glucosides, which release toxic hydrogen cyanide when the plant is eaten. If eaten unprocessed, manioc can cause both acute and chronic cyanide poisoning. Chronic poisoning, because it emerges only gradually after years of consuming manioc that tastes fine, is particularly insidious and has been linked to neurological problems, developmental disorders, paralysis in the legs, thyroid problems (e.g., goiters), and immune suppression. These so-called "bitter" manioc varieties remain highly productive even in infertile soils and ecologically marginal environments, in part due to their cyanogenic defenses against insects and other pests.[1]

In the Americas, where manioc was first domesticated, societies who have relied on bitter varieties for thousands of years show no evidence of chronic cyanide poisoning. In the Colombian Amazon, for example, indigenous Tukanoans use a multistep, multiday processing technique that involves scraping, grating, and finally washing the roots in order to separate the fiber, starch, and liquid. Once separated, the liquid is boiled into a beverage, but the fiber and starch must then sit for two more days, when they can then be baked and eaten.

Such processing techniques are crucial for living in many parts of Amazonia, where other crops are difficult to cultivate and often unproductive. However, despite their utility, one person would have a difficult time figuring out the detoxification technique. Consider the situation from the point of view of the children and adolescents who are learning the techniques. They would have rarely, if ever, seen anyone get cyanide poisoning, because the techniques work. And even if the processing was ineffective, such that cases of goiter (swollen necks) or neurological problems were common, it would still be hard to recognize the link between these chronic health issues and eating manioc. Most people would have eaten manioc for years with no apparent effects. Low-cyanogenic varieties are typically boiled, but boiling alone is insufficient to prevent the chronic conditions for bitter varieties. Boiling does, however, remove or reduce the bitter taste and prevent the acute symptoms (e.g., diarrhea, stomach troubles, and vomiting). So, if one did the common-sense thing and just boiled the high-cyanogenic manioc, everything would seem fine. Since the multistep task of processing manioc is long, arduous, and boring, sticking with it is certainly nonintuitive. Tukanoan women spend about a quarter of their day detoxifying manioc, so this is a costly technique in the short term.[2]

Now consider what might result if a self-reliant Tukanoan mother decided to drop any seemingly unnecessary steps from the processing of her bitter manioc. She might critically examine the procedure handed down to her from earlier generations and conclude that the goal of the procedure is to remove the bitter taste. She might then experiment with alternative procedures by dropping some of the more labor-intensive or time-consuming steps. She'd find that with a shorter and much less labor-intensive process, she could remove the bitter taste. Adopting this easier protocol, she would have more time for other activities, like caring for her children. Of course, years or decades later her family would begin to develop the symptoms of chronic cyanide poisoning.[3]

Thus, the unwillingness of this mother to take on faith the practices handed down to her from earlier generations would result in sickness and early death for members of her family. Individual learning does not pay here, and intuitions are misleading. The problem is that the steps in this procedure are causally opaque—an individual cannot readily infer their functions, interrelationships, or importance. The causal opacity of many cultural adaptations had a big impact on our psychology.

Wait. Maybe I'm wrong about manioc processing. Perhaps it's actually rather easy to individually figure out the detoxification steps for manioc? Fortunately, history has provided a test case.

At the beginning of the seventeenth century, the Portuguese transported manioc from South America to West Africa for the first time. They did not, however, transport the age-old indigenous processing protocols or the underlying commitment to using those techniques. Because it is easy to plant and provides high yields in infertile or drought-prone areas, manioc spread rapidly across Africa and became a staple food for many populations. The processing techniques, however, were not readily or consistently regenerated. Even after hundreds of years, chronic cyanide poisoning remains a serious health problem in Africa. Detailed studies of local preparation techniques show that high levels of cyanide often remain and that many individuals carry low levels of cyanide in their blood or urine, which haven't yet manifested in symptoms. In some places, there's no processing at all, or sometimes the processing actually increases the cyanogenic content. On the positive side, some African groups have in fact culturally evolved effective processing techniques, but these techniques are spreading only slowly.[4]

The point here is that cultural evolution is often much smarter than we are. Operating over generations as individuals unconsciously attend to and learn from more successful, prestigious, and healthier members of their communities, this evolutionary process generates cultural adaptations. Though these complex repertoires appear well designed to meet local challenges, they are not primarily the products of individuals applying causal models, rational thinking, or cost-benefit analyses. Often, most or all of the people skilled in deploying such adaptive practices do not understand how or why they work, or even that they "do" anything at all. Such complex adaptations can emerge precisely because natural selection has favored individuals who

often place their faith in cultural inheritance—in the accumulated wisdom implicit in the practices and beliefs derived from their forbearers—over their own intuitions and personal experiences. In many crucial situations, intuitions and personal experiences can lead one astray. To see this more clearly, let's look at some more cultural adaptations.

Taboos during Breast-Feeding and Pregnancy?

We were eating a large, tasty moray eel when I noticed that Mere was not eating any of the eel, only the manioc. I asked her why she was not eating the eel. I recall Mere saying something like "A tabu; qi sa bukete," which translates as, "It's taboo; I'm pregnant." "Interesting," I thought; this suggested to me that there may be some taboos against consuming certain foods during pregnancy. I had noticed Mere not eating because I'd been worried about eating the moray eel myself, since I'd read that this species is known to carry high levels of ciguatera toxin. Of course, following the ethnographers' axiom, I pressed on eating the eel since no one else seemed at all worried. Many folks were even enthusiastic about the eel, since it has a richer flavor than the typical white fish. This incident, early in my fieldwork in Fiji, sparked my interest and led me to investigate pregnancy practices and food taboos more deeply over the next several years.[5]

To tap her experience with public health research, pregnancy, and breastfeeding, I teamed with my wife, Natalie, on this project. Here's what we found: during both pregnancy and breast-feeding, women on Yasawa Island (Fiji) adhere to a series of food taboos that selectively excise the most toxic marine species from their diet. These large marine species, which include moray eels, barracuda, sharks, rock cod, and several large species of grouper, contribute substantially to the diet in these communities; but all are also known in the medical literature to be associated with ciguatera poisoning. Ciguatera toxin is produced by a marine microorganism that thrives on dead coral reefs. The toxin accumulates up the food chain to achieve dangerous levels in some large and long-living members of these species. The acute symptoms of poisoning, which last about a week, involve diarrhea, vomiting, headache, itchiness, and a distinctive hot-cold reversal on the skin. My village friends say they know they've been poisoned when they bathe. Bathing is always done with cool water, and when poisoned, the water provokes a burning sensation on their skin. These symptoms sometimes return periodically, weeks or even months later. Little is known about the effects of ciguatera toxin on fetuses, though we know that pregnant women have reduced resistance to toxins, and I found cases in the medical literature showing that fetuses can be highly disturbed by ciguatera poisoning. Like other toxins, it seems likely that ciguatera can accumulate in mother's milk and endanger nursing infants. For adults, ciguatera poisoning results in death in a small percentage of cases. While you have probably never heard of ciguatera toxin, it's the most common form of fish poisoning and creates a health problem for any population that routinely consumes tropical reef species.[6]

This set of taboos represents a cultural adaptation that selectively targets the most toxic species in women's usual diets, just when mothers and their offspring are most susceptible. To explore how this cultural adaptation emerged, we studied both how women acquire these taboos and what kind of causal understandings they possess. As adolescents and young women, these taboos are first learned from mothers, mothers-in-law, and grandmothers. However, this initial repertoire is then updated by a substantial portion of women who learn more taboos from village elders and prestigious local yalewa vuku (wise women), who are known for being knowledgeable about birthing and medicinal plants. Here we see Fijian women using cues of age, success or knowledge, and prestige to figure out from whom to learn their taboos. As explained in earlier chapters, such selectivity alone is capable of generating an adaptive repertoire over generations, without anyone understanding anything.

We also looked for a shared underlying mental model of why one would not eat these marine species during pregnancy or breastfeeding—a causal model or set of reasoned principles. Unlike the highly consistent answers on what not to eat and when, women's responses to our why questions were all over the map. Many women simply said they did not know and clearly thought it was an odd question. Others said it was "custom." Some did suggest that the consumption of at least some of the species might result in harmful effects to the fetus, but what precisely would happen to the fetus varied greatly, though a nontrivial segment of the women explained that babies would be born with rough skin if sharks were eaten and smelly joints if morays were eaten.

Unlike most of our interview questions on this topic, the answers here had the flavor of post-hoc rationalization: "Since I'm being asked for a reason, there must be a reason, so I'll think one up now." This is extremely common in ethnographic fieldwork, and I've personally experienced it in the Peruvian Amazon with the Matsigenka and with the Mapuche in southern Chile.[7] Of course, it's not particularly difficult to get similar responses from educated Westerners, but there remains a striking difference: educated Westerners are trained their entire lives to think that behaviors must be underpinned by explicable and declarable reasons, so we are more likely to have them at the ready and feel more obligated to supply "good" reasons upon request. Saying "it's our custom" is not considered a good

reason. The pressure for an acceptable, clear, and explicit reason for doing things is merely a social norm common in Western populations, which creates the illusion (among Westerners) that humans generally do things based on explicit causal models and clear reasons.[8] They often do not.

Finally, our evidence from Yasawa suggests that these taboos, while causally opaque, do actually work. We compared women's chances of getting fish poisoning during pregnancy and breast-feeding with the rest of their adult lives. Our analyses show that rates of fish poisoning are cut by a third during pregnancy and breast-feeding. Thus, the taboos are cultural prescriptions that reduce fish poisoning.

Why Put Ash in the Corn Mix?

One morning in 1998, when I was living in rural southern Chile and working with the indigenous Mapuche, I arrived at my friend Fonso's farmhouse to find him preparing what he called mote, a traditional Mapuche corn dish. He showed me how you have to scoop fresh ash out of the wood stove and put it into the corn mix for soaking, before heating it. I thought that was curious, so I asked him why he mixed the wood ash in with the corn. His answer was, "It's our custom." And a wise custom it is.

In the Americas before 1500 CE, corn was the [staple] crop for many farming societies. However, relying heavily on corn presents some tricky nutritional issues. A diet based on corn can leave one short on niacin (vitamin B). Failure to get enough niacin results in a disease called pellagra, a horrible condition characterized by diarrhea, lesions, hair loss, tongue inflammation, insomnia, dementia, and then death. There is actually niacin in corn, but it's chemically bound and cannot be freed by normal cooking. To release this niacin, populations throughout the New World culturally evolved practices that introduced an alkali (a base) into their corn preparations. In some places, the alkali came from burning seashells (generating calcium hydroxide) or the ash of certain kinds of wood. Elsewhere, there were natural sources of lye (providing potassium hydroxide). Mixing the alkali into the recipe in the right way chemically releases the otherwise unavailable niacin in the corn, which stops pellagra in its tracks, and allowed corn-based agricultural populations to grow and spread.[9]

Perhaps mixing nonfood substances, like wood ash or burned seashells, with foods during cooking is easy for a big-brained ape like us to figure out?

History, again, provides us with a natural experiment, because corn was brought from the New World to Europe after 1500. By 1735, some populations in Italy and Spain had already become reliant on cornmeal as a staple, and pellagra had emerged. The condition was theorized to be a form of leprosy or somehow caused by spoiled corn. Pellagra spread across Europe with this new staple crop into Romania and Russia but remained confined mostly to poor populations, who relied on it almost exclusively through the winter—making pellagra the "springtime disease." Experiments were done, and laws were passed to address the problem, by prohibiting the sale of spoiled or moldy corn. This did little to reduce pellagra, since spoilage is not the issue—the Europeans developed the wrong causal model.[10]

Later, pellagra also emerged in the southern United States during the late nineteenth and early twentieth century and spread in epidemic fashion until the 1940s. Millions died, because poor people and institutions, including prisons, sanitariums, and orphanages, had come to rely heavily on diets of cornmeal and molasses. Despite alarms raised by the Surgeon General, special commissions, medical conferences, and private donations to find a cure, the plague raged on for 30 years.

One man, Dr. Joseph Goldberger, investigated orphanages, performed controlled experiments on prisoners, and had begun to construct the right causal model by 1915. However, at the time, the medical community was convinced that pellagra must be an infectious disease, so Goldberger was ineffective and his ideas thought "absurd." Goldberger even injected his wife and friends with blood from people suffering from pellagra to demonstrate the noninfectious nature of the condition. These studies were dismissed by asserting that Goldberger's staff must have been "constitutionally resistant" to the disease.[11]

Thus, not only did people—Europeans and Americans in this case—not figure out the right causal model, but they actively resisted it when it was presented to them by Goldberger. Instead, they preferred to hold firmly to the wrong causal model, probably because the right model was rather less intuitive. Spoiled food and contamination were, and are, relatively "easy to think" about with regard to food compared to the concept of chemical reactions initiated by the introduction of nonfoods, like burnt seashells, into culinary recipes. Cultural evolution had produced a rather nonintuitive fix for the pellagra challenge.

Note, if you are educated and Western, you might be thinking that my numerous examples of toxic plants and animals are merely special cases, because you might be under the impression that few plants need detoxification and that nature's bounty is pure and safe. For many Westerners, "it's natural" seems to mean "it's good." This view is wrong and comes from shopping in supermarkets and living in landscaped environments. Plants evolved toxins to deter animals, fungi, and bacteria from eating them. The list of "natural" foods that need processing to detoxify them goes on and on. Early potatoes were toxic, and the Andean peoples ate clay to neutralize the toxin. Even beans can be toxic without processing. In California, many hunter-gatherer populations relied on acorns, which, similar to manioc, require a labor intensive, multiday leaching process. Many small-scale societies have similarly exploited hardy, tropical plants called cycads for food. But cycads contain a nerve toxin. If not properly processed, they can cause neurological symptoms, paralysis, and death. Numerous societies, including hunter-gatherers, have culturally evolved an immense range of detoxification techniques for cycads.[12] By contrast with our species, other animals have far superior abilities to detoxify plants. Humans, however, lost these genetic adaptations and evolved a dependence on cultural know-how, just to eat.

Divination and Game Theory

. . . [M]uch work in psychology shows that people (well, at least educated Westerners) are subject to the Gambler's Fallacy, in which we perceive streaks in the world where none exist or we believe that we are "due" after an extended losing streak. In fact, we struggle to recognize a sequence of hits and misses as random—instead, we find phony patterns in the randomness. One famous version of this is the hot-hand fallacy in basketball, in which people perceive a player as suddenly better than his long-term scoring average would suggest (it's an illusion). This is a problem for us, since the best strategies in life sometimes require randomizing. We are just not good at shutting down our mental pattern recognizers.[13]

When hunting caribou, Naskapi foragers in Labrador, Canada, had to decide where to go. Common sense might lead one to go where one had success before or to where friends or neighbors recently spotted caribou . . . The caribou are mismatchers and the hunters are matchers. That is, hunters want to match the locations of caribou while caribou want to mismatch the hunters, to avoid being shot and eaten. If a hunter shows any bias to return to previous spots, where he or others have seen caribou, then the caribou can benefit (survive better) by avoiding those locations (where they have previously seen humans). Thus, the best hunting strategy requires randomizing. Can cultural evolution compensate for our cognitive inadequacies?

Traditionally, Naskapi hunters decided where to go to hunt using divination and believed that the shoulder bones of caribou could point the way to success.[14] To start the ritual, the shoulder blade was heated over hot coals in a way that caused patterns of cracks and burnt spots to form. This patterning was then read as a kind of map, which was held in a prespecified orientation. The cracking patterns were (probably) essentially random from the point of view of hunting locations, since the outcomes depended on myriad details about the bone, fire, ambient temperature, and heating process. Thus, these divination rituals may have provided a crude randomizing device that helped hunters avoid their own decision-making biases . . .

This is not some obscure, isolated practice, and other cases of divination provide more evidence. In Indonesia, the Kantus of Kalimantan use bird augury to select locations for their agricultural plots. The anthropologist Michael Dove argues that two factors will cause farmers to make plot placements that are too risky. First, Kantu ecological models contain the Gambler's Fallacy and lead them to expect that floods will be less likely to occur in a specific location after a big flood in that location (which is not true).[15] Second . . . Kantus pay attention to others' success and copy the choices of successful households, meaning that if one of their neighbors has a good yield in an area one year, many other people will want to plant there in the next year.

Reducing the risks posed by these cognitive and decision-making biases, the Kantu rely on a system of bird augury that effectively randomizes their choices for locating garden plots, which helps them avoid catastrophic crop failures. The results of divination depend not only on seeing a particular bird species in a particular location, but also on what type of call the bird makes (one type of call may be favorable, and another unfavorable).[16]

The patterning of bird augury supports the view that this is a cultural adaptation. The system seems to have evolved and spread throughout this region since the seventeenth century when rice cultivation was introduced. This makes sense, since it is rice cultivation that is most positively influenced by randomizing garden locations. It's possible that, with the introduction of rice, a few farmers began to use bird sightings as an indication of favorable garden sites. On average, over a lifetime, these farmers would do better—be more successful—than farmers who relied on the Gambler's Fallacy or on copying others' immediate behavior. Whatever the process, within 400 years, the bird augury system had spread throughout the agricultural populations of this Borneo region. Yet it remains conspicuously missing or underdeveloped among local foraging groups and recent adopters of rice agriculture, as well as among populations in northern Borneo who rely on irrigation. So, bird augury has been systematically spreading in those regions where it is most adaptive.

This example makes a key point: not only do people often not understand what their cultural practices are doing, but sometimes it may even be important that they don't understand what their practices are doing or how they work. If people came to understand that bird augury or bone divination didn't actually predict the future, the practice would probably be dropped or people would increasingly ignore ritual findings in favor of their own intuitions.

Manufacturing complex technologies is also causally opaque. Consider just one element of the archery package found among hunter-gatherers, the arrow. Let's also pick a society known to possess one of the least complex toolkits known, the hunter-gatherers of Tierra del Fuego, who entered the historical record when they encountered Ferdinand Magellan and, later, Charles Darwin. Among the Fuegians, making an arrow requires a fourteen-step procedure that involves using seven different tools to work six different materials. Here are some of the steps:

- The process begins by selecting the wood for the shaft, which preferably comes from chaura, a bushy, evergreen shrub. Though strong and light, this wood is a nonintuitive choice since the gnarled branches require extensive straightening. (Why not start with straighter branches?)
- The wood is heated, straightened with the craftsman's teeth, and eventually finished with a scraper. Then, using a preheated and grooved stone, the craftsman presses the shaft into the grooves and rubs it back and forth, pressing it down with a piece of fox skin. The fox skin becomes impregnated with the dust, which prepares it for the polishing stage. (Does it have to be fox skin?)
- Bits of pitch, gathered from the beach, are chewed and mixed with ash. (What if you don't include the ash?)
- The mixture is then applied to both ends of a heated shaft, which must then be coated with white clay. (What about red clay? Do you have to heat it?) This prepares the ends for the fletching and arrowhead.
- Two feathers are used for the fletching, preferably from upland geese. (Why not chicken feathers?)
- Right-handed bowman must use feathers from the left wing of the bird, and vice versa for lefties. (Does this really matter?)
- The feathers are lashed to the shaft with sinews from the back of the guanaco, after they are smoothed and thinned with water and saliva. (Why not sinews from the fox that I had to kill for the aforementioned skin?)

Next is the arrowhead, which must be crafted and then attached to the shaft, and of course, there is also the bow, quiver, and archery skills. But I'll leave it there, since I think you get the idea.[17] It's an extensively causally opaque process.

"Overimitation" in the Laboratory

Crucial to making cultural adaptations like manioc, corn, or nardoo processing work is not only faithfully copying all the steps, but also sometimes actually avoiding putting much emphasis on causal understandings that one might build on the fly, on one's own. As shown above, dropping seemingly unnecessary steps from one's cultural repertoire can result in neurological disorders, paralysis, pellagra, reduced hunting success, pregnancy problems, and death. In a species with cumulative cultural evolution, but only in such a species, faith in one's cultural inheritance often favors greater survival and reproduction.

Dovetailing with the above field observations, experimental work with children and adults on the fidelity of cultural learning allows us to put a microscope on the cultural transmission process. Recently, psychologists have studied the when and why of people's willingness to copy the seemingly irrelevant steps used by another to get to a reward. In a typical experiment, a participant sees a model engage in a multistep procedure that involves using simple tools to push, pull, lift, poke, and tap an "artificial fruit" (often a large box with doors and holes). The procedure usually results in obtaining some desirable outcome, such as a toy or snack. Some of the steps in the procedure are not apparently required to achieve the goal of getting the reward. Sometimes people even copy steps with no evident material-physical connection to the outcome. Notorious for inappropriately naming behavioral patterns, psychologists have labelled this not-particularly-shocking phenomenon overimitation.

Let's examine a specific experiment that has been tested and replicated with children, adults, and chimpanzees. In the experiment, participants first observe a model engage in a series of steps using a slender rod to access a reward in an "artificial fruit." The fruit is a large opaque box with two entry points. The first entry point is sealed by bolts, which can be (a) pushed or (b) dragged out of the away—using the rod—to provide access to the tube. This tube, however, merely dead ends—it's a decoy and is irrelevant to obtaining the reward. The second entry point is concealed by a doorway, which can be (a) slid or (b) lifted. The rod, which has a Velcro tip, can then be maneuvered down the tube to obtain the reward, a sticker for the kids or food for the chimps.[18]

The robust results from these kinds of experiments are that children and adults are rather inclined to copy whatever the model does to obtain the reward. People even copy the irrelevant actions when they are alone, after they think the experiment is over, and when they've been told explicitly not to copy any irrelevant actions.[19] However . . . people are more likely to copy irrelevant actions when the model is older and higher in prestige. This is also not merely some tendency of little children: assuming the problem is sufficiently opaque, the magnitude of "overimitation" increases with age.[20] This also isn't just educated Western peoples. Research in the Kalahari Desert in southern Africa, whose populations lived as foragers until recent decades, show them to be at least as inclined to high-fidelity cultural transmission as Western undergraduates.[21]

As you may anticipate, the chimpanzees outperformed their big-headed cousins . . . In this work, the comparative psychologists Vicki Horner and Andy Whiten used the same opaque "artificial fruit" used above and also a clear version of the fruit in which one could readily see that the top slot was not connected to the area with the reward. When the causality was more transparent, with the clear box, the chimpanzees immediately dropped all irrelevant actions, whereas the three-to four-year-old Scottish kids copied the irrelevant actions as much as with the opaque fruit. Chimpanzees did learn some stuff by watching the model work on the fruit: it helped them assess the affordances of the apparatus. They learned how different parts of the fruit could move. But once they had visual evidence that these actions would not do anything, they dropped them.[22] Though chimps clearly have some culture, they aren't a cultural species.[23]

. . .[H]umans have also evolved to use mimicry to build social relationships and to cue status differences. So we also mimic others to say, "Hey, I wanna relate to you; you're swell." . . . Culture-gene coevolution generates many reasons why our species is inclined to copy all the steps or closely follow the local protocols.[24]

Our reliance on cultural transmission, however, goes much deeper. In addition to acquiring practices and beliefs, which may violate our intuitive understandings, we can also acquire tastes, preferences, and motivations. These too can be acquired in the face of our instinctual or innate inclinations. Such acquisitions do not mean we lack instincts or innate inclinations, but merely that natural selection has endowed our cultural learning systems with the ability to, under the right conditions, overwrite or work around them.

Overcoming Instinct: Why Chili Peppers Taste Good

Why do we use spices in our foods? In thinking about this question keep in mind that (1) other animals don't spice their foods, (2) most spices contribute little or no nutrition to our diets, and (3) the active ingredients in many spices are actually aversive chemicals that evolved to keep insects, fungi, bacteria, mammals, and other unwanted critters away from the plants that produce them.

Several lines of evidence indicate that spicing may represent a class of cultural adaptations to the problem of food-borne pathogens. Many spices are antimicrobials that can kill pathogens in foods. Globally, the common spices are onions, pepper, garlic, cilantro, chili peppers (capsicum), and bay leaves. Here's the idea: the use of many spices represents a cultural adaptation to the problem of pathogens in food, especially in meat. This challenge would have been most important before refrigerators came on the scene. To examine this, two biologists, Jennifer Billing and Paul Sherman, collected 4578 recipes from traditional cookbooks from populations around the world. They found three distinct patterns.[25]

1. Spices are, in fact, antimicrobial. The most common spices in the world are also the most effective against

bacteria. Some spices are also fungicides. Combinations of spices have synergistic effects, which may explain why ingredients like chili powder (a mix of red pepper, onion, paprika, garlic, cumin and oregano) are so important. And ingredients like lemon and lime, which are not on their own potent antimicrobials, appear to catalyze the bacteria-killing effects of other spices.

2. People in hotter climates use more spices, and more of the most effective bacteria killers. In India and Indonesia, for example, most recipes used many antimicrobial spices, including onions, garlic, capsicum, and coriander. Meanwhile, in Norway, recipes use some black pepper and occasionally a bit of parsley or lemon, but that's about it.

3. Recipes appear to use spices in ways that increase their effectiveness. Some spices, like onions and garlic, whose killing power is resistant to heating, are deployed in the cooking process. Other spices, like cilantro, whose antimicrobial properties might be damaged by heating are added fresh in recipes.[26]

Thus, many recipes and preferences appear to be cultural adaptations that are suited to local environments and that operate in subtle and nuanced ways not understood by those of us who love spicy foods. Billing and Sherman speculated that these evolved culturally, as healthier, more fertile, and more successful families were preferentially imitated by less successful ones. This is quite plausible given what we know about our species' evolved psychology for cultural learning, including specifically cultural learning about foods and plants.

Among spices, chili peppers are an ideal case. Chili peppers were the primary spice of New World cuisines prior to the arrival of Europeans and are now routinely consumed by about a quarter of all adults globally. Chili peppers have evolved chemical defenses, based on capsaicin, that make them aversive to mammals and rodents but desirable to birds. In mammals, capsicum directly activates a pain channel (TrpV1), which creates a burning sensation in response to various specific stimuli, including acid, high temperatures, and allyl isothiocyanate (which is found in mustard and wasabi). These chemical weapons aid chili pepper plants in their survival and reproduction, because birds provide a better dispersal system for the plants' seeds than other options (like mammals). Consequently, chilies are innately aversive to nonhuman primates, babies, and many human adults. Capsaicin is so innately repellent that nursing mothers are advised to avoid chili peppers lest their infants reject their breast milk, and in some societies, capsicum is even put on a mother's breasts to initiate weaning. Yet adults who live in hot climates regularly incorporate chilies into their recipes. And those who grow up among people who enjoy eating chili peppers not only eat chilies but love eating them. How do we come to like the experience of burning and sweating—the activation of pain channel TrpV1?[27]

Research by the psychologist Paul Rozin shows that people come to enjoy the experience of eating chili peppers mostly by reinterpreting the pain signals caused by capsicum as pleasure or excitement. Based on work in the highlands of Mexico, children acquire this preference gradually, without being pressured or compelled.[28] They want to learn to like chili peppers, to be like those they admire. This fits with what we've already seen: children readily acquire food preferences from older peers. In chapter 14, I will further examine how cultural learning can alter our bodies' physiological response to pain, and specifically to electric shocks. The bottom line is that culture can overpower our innate mammalian aversions when necessary and without us knowing it.

As a product of this long-running duet between cumulative cultural evolution and genes, our brains have genetically adapted to a world in which information crucial to our survival was embedded implicitly in a vast body of knowledge that we inherit culturally from previous generations. This information comes buried in daily cooking routines (manioc), taboos, divination rituals, local tastes (chili peppers), mental models, and tool-manufacturing scripts (arrow shafts). These practices and beliefs are often (implicitly) MUCH smarter than we are, as neither individuals nor groups could figure them out in one lifetime. As you'll see in later chapters, this is also true of some institutions, religious beliefs, rituals, and medical practices. For these evolutionary reasons, learners first decide if they will "turn on" their causal-model builders at all, and if so, they have to carefully assess how much mental effort to put into them. And if cultural transmission supplies a prebuilt mental model for how things work, learners readily acquire and adhere to those.

Of course, people can, and do, attempt to break down complex procedures and protocols in order to understand the causal links between them and to engineer better versions. They also alter practices through experimentation, errors in learning, and idiosyncratic actions. Nevertheless, as a cultural species, we have an instinct to faithfully copy complex procedures, practices, beliefs, and motivations, including steps that may appear causally irrelevant, because cultural evolution has proved itself capable of constructing intricate and subtle cultural packages that are far better than we could individually construct in one lifetime. Often, people don't even know what their practices are actually doing, or that they are "doing" anything. Spicy-food lovers in hot climates don't know that using recipes involving garlic and chili peppers protect their families from meat-borne pathogens. They just culturally inherited the tastes and the recipes, and implicitly had faith in the wisdom accumulated by earlier generations.

Finally, we humans do, of course, construct causal models of how the world works. However, what's often missed is that the construction of these models has long been sparked and fostered by the existence of complex culturally evolved products. When people have accurately speculated on why they do something, this realization often occurs after the fact: "Why do we always do it this way? There must be a reason . . . . Maybe it's because . . . " However, just because some people have speculated accurately as [to] why they themselves, or their groups, do something in a particular way does not mean that this is the reason why they do it. An enormous amount of scientific causal understanding, for example, has developed in trying to explain existing technologies, like the steam engine, hot air balloon, or airplane. A device or technology often preexisted the development of any causal understanding, but by existing, such cultural products opened a window on the world that facilitated the development of an improved causal understanding. That is, for much of human history until recently, cumulative cultural evolution drove the emergence of deeper causal understandings much more than causal understanding drove cultural evolution.[29]

. . .

Move Over, Natural Selection

Famous evolutionary psychologists, from Steve Pinker to David Buss, are fond of claiming that natural selection is the only process capable of creating complex adaptations that are functionally well designed to meet environmental challenges or the demands of organisms' lives.[30] They are impressed by the fact that products of natural selection—like eyes, wings, hearts, spider webs, nests, and polar bear snow caves—seem well suited or fit to the problems they solve. Save for certain telltale imperfections, these adaptations look well designed, even engineered. Eyes seem crafted for seeing and wings for flying; yet, there's no engineer or designer, and no agents had intentions to create them or a mental model of how they work. I largely agree with this view and certainly share their sense of awe at the stunning power of natural selection. However, I part ways with them on the word "only." At least since the rise of cumulative cultural evolution, natural selection has lost its status as the only "dumb" process capable of creating complex adaptations well fit to local circumstances. . . . [C]ultural evolution . . . is fully cable of generating these complex adaptive products, which no one designed or had a causal mental model of before they emerged.

To see this, let's compare two types of houses—two artifacts—one built by natural selection and one built by cumulative cultural evolution. In Africa, male village weaverbirds construct strong, kidney-shaped nests with downward-facing tubular entrances that effectively protect two to three eggs from larger predators. Each species of weaver uses a stereotyped set of techniques to build the house in the same step-by-step pattern. Weavers first create an attachment and then construct a ring, roof, egg chamber, antechamber, and entryway. Weaving, in different parts of the house, involves one of three knots (overhand, half hitch, and slipknot) and three different weave patterns. To build the house, weavers must locate and harvest particularly stout strips from tall grasses or palm fronds. The shape of the interior combined with the downward-facing entry tunnel means that predators will have a hard time getting at the eggs. The thickness and layered construction of the woven floor means that the eggs can even survive a fall, should the nest be knocked off its branch. None of these techniques or layouts are learned from other birds. Weavers either just know them innately or are geared to reliably figure them out on the fly, on their own. Natural selection has constructed many such complex artifacts, and invertebrates such as termites, wasps, and spiders make many such beautiful structures without any mental model of their final form.[31]

Inuit snow houses are also a complex adaptation for living in many parts of the Arctic . . . Architecturally, these snow houses are unique in that they are constructed from snow blocks cut from drifts created during a single snowfall to form an aerodynamic dome-shape that can stand against strong Arctic winds. Properly constructed, with blocks cut to fit, this dome is strong enough for a person to stand on without danger of collapse. Heated by small soapstone lamps that are fueled with rendered fat from marine mammals, the insulating properties of snow mean that inside temperatures are 10°C (50°F). This internal warmth slightly melts the snow, thereby allowing the walls and ceiling to freeze together even more solidly. Properly oriented, the long tunnel entrance not only blocks the wind, but also uses pressure differences to create a heat trap. Windows, created from translucent membranes cut from seal guts or sheets of ice, provide light inside, and small holes maintain air circulation.[32]

Like village weaver nests, Inuit snow houses look designed and are clearly functionally well fit to life in the Arctic. In fact, they appear to call for a team of engineers with knowledge of aerodynamics, thermodynamics, material science, and structural mechanics . . . It's a product of cumulative cultural evolution and contains features that many or most Inuit builders just learn as "that's the way you do it" without any big causal model. Of course, there's little doubt that bits and pieces of causal models were culturally transmitted along with the procedures, rules, and protocols, since partial or minimodels help builders make sure the parts are working and to adapt to changing or unusual circumstances. However, most of these causal mini-models are themselves transmitted culturally as part of the overall package, not built on the fly by individuals.

Recognizing the power of cultural evolution to produce such adaptive complexity has serious implications for studying humans. It means that when we observe something functionally well suited to address an adaptive challenge outside of conscious awareness, whether it be a snow house or complex cognitive ability (like subtracting 16 from 17), we can't assume that the complexity comes from either natural selection acting on genes or intentional construction. It might be a product of cumulative cultural evolution.

Overall, cultural evolution is smarter than we are, and our species evolved genetically in a world full of cultural stuff—ranging from sophisticated technologies like snow houses to nuanced protocols like using ash to chemically release key nutrients from corn—that people had to just put their faith in. Relatively early in our species' lineage, surviving by one's wits alone without leaning on any cultural know-how from prior generations meant getting outcompeted by better cultural learners, who put their efforts into focusing selectively on what and from whom to learn. However, even if you can figure out what to learn and from whom, it doesn't mean that those who possess the most valuable cultural know-how will be motivated to permit you to hang around them and freely tap their accumulated wisdom. It's this evolutionary challenge that gave us prestige.

Notes

1. For a review of the health effects, see Nhassico et al. 2008.
2. See Dufour 1984, 1985.
3. This appears to have happened in the Democratic Republic of Congo (Tylleskar et al. 1991, 1992).
4. The emergence of specific negative health impacts is complex and depends on other factors such as the presence of sulfur in the diet (Jackson and Jackson 1990, Tylleskar et al. 1992, 1993 Peterson, Legue, et al. 1995, Peterson, Rosling, et al. 1995). Jackson and Jackson discuss a processing technique that actually increases cyanogenic content. See Padmaja 1995 for a review of processing techniques.
5. I replaced all personal names from my ethnographic work with pseudonyms.
6. See Henrich and Henrich 2010. Also see Henrich and Broesch 2011.
7. See Henrich 2002.
8. We also elicited descriptions of any actual cases of fish poisoning that women might have heard. Almost everyone relayed the same few cases. This means that the repertoire of taboos cannot be composed of "case knowledge," with individual women assembling their taboos from stories—most of the tabooed species appear in zero of the reported cases.
9. See Katz, Hediger, and Valleroy 1974 and Mcdonough et al. 1987.
10. See Bollet 1992 and Roe 1973.
11. This is from Bollet 1992. The quotations "constitutionally resistant" and "absurd" are on p. 217. See Jobling and Petersen 1916.
12. See Whiting 1963, Beck 1992, and Mann 2012.
13. On the Gambler's Fallacy and our problems with randomness, see Kahneman 2011 and Gilovich, Griffin, and Kahneman 2002.
14. Beaver hips were used for hunting beavers and fish jaws for locating fish.
15. Statistical data shows that rainfall patterns and floods are random, without distinguishable cycles or streaks.
16. See Dove 1993 and Henrich 2002. For a similar case, see Lawless 1975.
17. On arrow making, see Lothrop 1928. For an extended discussion and more examples, see Henrich 2008.
18. McGuigan 2012, McGuigan, Makinson, and Whiten 2011, McGuigan et al. 2007, Horner and Whiten 2005.
19. See Lyons, Young, and Keil 2007.
20. This assumes that the relative competence, age, and skill of the model is appropriately adjusted. Adults won't overimitate three year olds . . . much.
21. See Nielsen and Tomaselli 2010, McGuigan, Gladstone, and Cook 2012, McGuigan 2012, 2013, and McGuigan, Makinson, and Whiten 2011.
22. See Horner and Whiten 2005.
23. For a detailed discussion of chimpanzee culture see Henrich and Tennie, forthcoming.
24. For important lines on work on all these angles, see Herrmann et al. 2013, Over and Carpenter 2012, 2013, and Kenward 2012.
25. See Billing and Sherman 1998, Sherman and Billing 1999, Sherman and Flaxman 2001, and Sherman and Hash 2001.
26. The evidence for this is only suggestive at this point (Billing and Sherman 1998, Sherman and Billing 1999, Sherman and Flaxman 2001, Sherman and Hash 2001).
27. It's worth noting that cultural learning has overcome other aversions that are probably innate. For example, we likely have innate aversions to eating feces, but Inuit foragers will eat deer poop like berries (apparently, they are good in soup: Wrangham 2009), and Hadza hunter-gatherers enjoy picking the partially digested nuts from baboon poop (Marlowe 2010).
28. See Rozin, Gruss, and Berk 1979, Rozin and Schiller 1980, Rozin, Mark, and Schiller 1981, Rozin, Ebert, and Schull 1982, and Rozin and Kennel 1983. There is some evidence of a weak desensitization to the pain-inducing effects of capsicum after high levels of capsicum consumption (Rozin and Schiller

1980, Rozin, Mark, and Schiller 1981). However, this doesn't account for the clear enjoyment of the burning sensation and for preferences for chili peppers. Efforts to train rats to like capsicum have failed (Rozin, Gruss, and Berk 1979), though they can be trained to selectively eat capsicum-containing food if the unpleasant burning sensation is correlated with future desirable states (less pain). In Mexico, dogs and pigs, who can only survive by eating chili-laden-food garbage, come to be indifferent to capsicum (which is a big step, since otherwise it's aversive). The only nonhuman evidence for acquiring a taste for capsicum is from two juvenile, human-reared chimpanzees and three pet dogs. Rozin and Kennel (1983) argue that it's the experience of human environments during ontogeny that sets the stage for such taste acquisitions.

29. See Williams 1987 and Basalla 1988.

30. See Buss et al. 1998 and Pinker and Bloom 1990.

31. See Boyd, Richerson, and Henrich 2013.

32. See Boyd, Richerson, and Henrich 2011a.

Critical Thinking

1. How has the success of the human species been dependent upon both natural selection and accumulated wisdom?
2. In what sense have human taboos been adaptive?
3. How has divination helped humans to overcome such subjective strategies as intuition?
4. Why have spices become an important part of human adaptiveness?
5. How can a functionally adaptive Inuit snow house come about without the purposeful design or mental model of a single individual?

Internet References

American Academy of Religion
  https://www.aarweb.org/publications/journal-american-academy-religion

Apologetics Index
  www.apologeticsindex.org/site/index-c

Henrich, Joseph. "On the Origin of Faith", *The Secret of Our Success: How Culture Is Driving Human Evolution, Domesticating Our Species, and Making Us Smarter,* October 2015. Copyright © 2015 by Princeton University Press. Used with permission.

Unit 2

UNIT

Prepared by: Elvio Angeloni, *Pasadena City College*

Culture and Communication

Anthropologists are interested in all aspects of human behavior and how they interrelate. Language is a form of such behavior (albeit, primarily verbal behavior) and, therefore, worthy of study. Although it changes over time, language is culturally patterned and passed down from one generation to the next through learning, not instinct. In keeping with the idea that language is integral to human social interactions, it has long been recognized that human communication through language is, by its nature, different from the communication found among other animals. Central to this difference is the fact that humans communicate abstractly, with symbols that have meaning independent of the immediate sensory experiences of either the sender or the receiver of the message. Thus, for instance, humans are able to refer to the future and the past and not just the present.

Recent experiments have shown that anthropoid apes can be taught a small portion of Ameslan or American Sign Language. It must be remembered, however, that their very rudimentary ability has to be tapped by painstaking human effort and that the degree of difference between apes and humans serves only to emphasize the peculiar need of humans for, and development of, language.

Just as the abstract quality of symbols lifts our thoughts beyond our immediate sense perceptions, so also it inhibits our ability to think about and convey the full meaning of our personal experience. No categorical term can do justice to its referents—the variety of forms to which the term refers. The degree to which this is an obstacle to clarity of thought and communication relates to the degree of abstraction involved in the symbols. The word "chair," for instance, would not present much difficulty, as it has objective referents. However, consider the trouble we have in thinking and communicating with words whose referents are not tied to immediate sense perception—words such as "freedom," "democracy," and "justice." At best, the likely result is *symbolic confusion:* an inability to think or communicate in objectively definable symbols. At worst, language may be used to purposefully obfuscate.

A related issue has to do with the fact that languages differ as to what is relatively easy to express within the restrictions of their particular vocabularies and grammatical structure. Thus, although a given language may not have enough words to cope with a new situation or a new field of activity, the typical solution is to invent words or to borrow them. In this way, it has been claimed that any language can be used to say anything.

While we often become frustrated with the ways in which symbolic confusion cause misunderstandings between individuals or groups, we should also pause to admire the beauty and wonder inherent in this uniquely human form of communication—in all of its linguistic diversity—and the tremendous potential of recent research to enhance effective communication among all of us.

Article   Prepared by: Elvio Angeloni

Baby Talk

Every infant is a natural-born linguist capable of mastering any of the world's 7,000 languages like a native.

PATRICIA K. KUHL

Learning Outcomes

After reading this article, you will be able to:

- Discuss the important of "parentese" in babies' language acquisition.
- Discuss ways in which babies learn languages in general.
- Discuss the optimal circumstances for learning a second language.

An infant child possesses an amazing, and fleeting, Gift: the ability to master a language quickly. At six months, the child can learn the sounds that make up English words and, if also exposed to Quechua and Tagalog, he or she can pick up the unique acoustic properties of those languages, too. By age three, a toddler can converse with a parent, a playmate, or a stranger.

I still marvel, after four decades of studying child development, how a child can go from random babbling to speaking fully articulated words and sentences just a few years later—a mastery that occurs more quickly than any complex skill acquired during the course of a lifetime. Only in the past few years have neuroscientists begun to get a picture of what is happening in a baby's brain during this learning process that takes the child from gurgling newborn to a wonderfully engaging youngster.

At birth, the infant brain can perceive the full set of 800 or so sounds, called phonemes, that can be strung together to form all the words in every language of the world. During the second half of the first year, our research shows, a mysterious door opens in the child's brain. He or she enters a "sensitive period," as neuroscientists call it, during which the infant brain is ready to receive the first basic lessons in the magic of language.

The time when a youngster's brain is most open to learning the sounds of a native tongue begins at six months for vowels and at nine months for consonants. It appears that the sensitive period lasts for only a few months but is extended for children exposed to sounds of a second language. A child can still pick up a second language with a fair degree of fluency until age seven.

The built-in capacity for language is not by itself enough to get a baby past the first utterances of "Mama" and "Dada." Gaining mastery of the most important of all social skills is helped along by countless hours listening to parents speak the silly vernacular of "parentese." Its exaggerated inflections—"You're a preettee babbee"—serve the unfrivolous purpose of furnishing daily lessons in the intonations and cadences of the baby's native tongue. Our work puts to rest the age-old debates about whether genes or the environment prevails during early language development. They both play starring roles.

Knowledge of early language development has now reached a level of sophistication that is enabling psychologists and physicians to fashion new tools to help children with learning difficulties. Studies have begun to lay the groundwork for using recordings of brain waves to determine whether a child's language abilities are developing normally or whether an infant may be at risk for autism, attention deficit or other disorders. One day a routine visit to the pediatrician may involve a baby brain examination, along with vaccinations for measles, mumps and rubella.

The Statistics of Baby Talk

The reason we can contemplate a test for language development is that we have begun to understand how babies absorb language with seeming ease. My laboratory and others have shown that infants use two distinct learning mechanisms at the earliest stages of language acquisition: one that recognizes sound through mental computation and another that requires intense social immersion.

To learn to speak, infants have to know which phonemes make up the words they hear all around them. They need to discriminate which 40 or so, out of all 800, phonemes they need to learn to speak words in their own language. This task requires detecting subtle differences in spoken sound. A change in a single consonant can alter the meaning of a word—"bat" to "pat," for instance. And a simple vowel like "ah" varies widely when spoken by different people at different speaking rates and in different contexts—"Bach" versus "rock." Extreme variation in phonemes is why Apple's Siri still does not work flawlessly.

My work and that of Jessica Maye, then at Northwestern University, and her colleagues have shown that statistical patterns— the frequency with which sounds occur—play a critical role in helping infants learn which phonemes are most important. Children between eight and 10 months of age still do not understand spoken words. Yet they are highly sensitive to how often phonemes occur—what statisticians call distributional frequencies. The most important phonemes in a given language are the ones spoken most. In English, for example, the "r" and "l" sounds are quite frequent. They appear in words such as "rake" and "read" and "lake" and "lead." In Japan, the English-like "r" and "l" also occur but not as often. Instead the Japanese "r" sound is common but is rarely found in English. (The Japanese word "raamen" sounds like "laamen" to American ears because the Japanese "r" is midway between the American "r" and "l.")

The statistical frequency of particular sounds affects the infant brain. In one study of infants in Seattle and Stockholm, we monitored their perception of vowel sounds at six months and demonstrated that each group had already begun to focus in on the vowels spoken in their native language. The culture of the spoken word had already pervaded and affected how the baby's brain perceived sounds.

What exactly was going on here? Maye has shown that the brain at this age has the requisite plasticity to change how infants perceive sounds. A Japanese baby who hears sounds from English learns to distinguish the "r" and the "l" in the way they are used in the U.S. And a baby being raised among native English speakers could likewise pick up the characteristic sounds of Japanese. It appears that learning sounds in the second half of the first year establishes connections in the brain for one's native tongue but not for other languages, unless a child is exposed to multiple languages during that period. Later in childhood, and particularly as an adult, listening to a new language does not produce such dramatic results—a traveler to France or Japan can hear the statistical distributions of sounds from another language, but the brain is not altered by the experience. That is why it is so difficult to pick up a second language later on.

A second form of statistical learning lets infants recognize whole words. As adults, we can distinguish where one word ends and the next begins. But the ability to isolate words from the stream of speech requires complex mental processing. Spoken speech arrives at the ear as a continuous stream of sound that lacks the separations found between written words. Jenny Saffran, now at the University of Wisconsin-Madison, and her colleagues—Richard Aslin of the University of Rochester and Elissa Newport, now at Georgetown University—were the first to discover that a baby uses statistical learning to grasp the sounds of whole words. In the mid-1990s Saffran's group published evidence that eight-month-old infants can learn word-like units based on the probability that one syllable follows another. Take the phrase "pretty baby." The syllable "pre" is more likely to be heard with "ty" than to accompany another syllable like "ba."

In the experiment, Saffran had babies listen to streams of computer-synthesized nonsense words that contained syllables, some of which occurred together more often than others. The babies' ability to focus on syllables that coincide in the made-up language let them identify likely words.

The discovery of babies' statistical-learning abilities in the 1990s generated a great deal of excitement because it offered a theory of language learning beyond the prevailing idea that a child learns only because of parental conditioning and affirmations of whether a word is right or wrong. Infant learning occurs before parents realize that it is taking place. Further tests in my lab, however, produced a significant new finding that lends an important caveat to this story: the statistical-learning process does not require passive listening alone.

Baby Meet and Greet

In our work, we discovered that infants need to be more than just computational geniuses processing clever neural algorithms. In 2003 we published the results of experiments in which nine-month-old infants from Seattle were exposed to Mandarin Chinese. We wanted to know whether infants' statistical-learning abilities would allow them to learn Mandarin phonemes.

In groups of two or three, the nine-month-olds listened to Mandarin native speakers while their teachers played on the floor with them, using books and toys. Two additional groups were also exposed to Mandarin. But one watched a video of Mandarin being spoken. Another listened to an audio recording. A fourth group, run as a control, heard no Mandarin at all but instead listened to U.S. graduate students speaking English while playing with the children with the same books and toys. All of this happened during 12 sessions that took place over the course of a month.

Infants from all four groups returned to the lab for psychological tests and brain monitoring to gauge their ability to single out Mandarin phonemes. Only the group exposed to Chinese from live speakers learned to pick up the foreign phonemes. Their performance, in fact, was equivalent to infants in Taipei who had been listening to their parents for their first 11 months.

Infants who were exposed to Mandarin by television or audio did not learn at all. Their ability to discriminate phonemes matched infants in the control group, who, as expected, performed no better than before the experiment.

The study provided evidence that learning for the infant brain is not a passive process. It requires human interaction—a necessity that I call "social gating." This hypothesis can even be extended to explain the way many species learn to communicate. The experience of a young child learning to talk, in fact, resembles the way birds learn song.

I worked earlier with the late Allison Doupe of the University of California, San Francisco, to compare baby and bird learning. We found that for both children and zebra finches, social experience in the early months of life was essential. Both human and bird babies immerse themselves in listening to their elders, and they store memories of the sounds they hear. These recollections condition the brain's motor areas to produce sounds that match those heard frequently in the larger social community in which they were being raised.

Exactly how social context contributes to the learning of a language in humans is still an open question. I have suggested, though, that parents and other adults provide both motivation and necessary information to help babies learn. The motivational component is driven by the brain's reward systems—and, in particular, brain areas that use the neurotransmitter dopamine during social interaction. Work in my lab has already shown that babies learn better in the presence of other babies—we are currently engaged in studies that explain why this is the case.

Babies who gaze into their parents' eyes also receive key social cues that help to speed the next stage of language learning—the understanding of the meaning of actual words. Andrew Meltzoff of the University of Washington has shown that young children who follow the direction of an adult's gaze pick up more vocabulary in the first two years of life than children who do not track these eye movements. The connection between looking and talking makes perfect sense and provides some explanation of why simply watching an instructional video is not good enough.

In the group that received live lessons, infants could see when the Mandarin teacher glanced at an object while naming it, a subtle action that tied together the word with the object named. In a paper published in July, we also showed that as a Spanish tutor holds up new toys and talks about them, infants who look back and forth between the tutor and the toy, instead of just focusing on one or the other, learn the phonemes as well as words used during the study session. This example is an illustration of my theory that infants' social skills enable—or "gate"—language learning.

These ideas about the social component of early language learning may also explain some of the difficulties encountered by infants who go on to develop disorders such as autism. Children with autism lack basic interest in speaking. Instead they fixate on inanimate objects and fail to pay attention to social cues so essential in language learning.

Say, "Hiiiii!"

An infant's ability to learn to speak depends not only on being able to listen to adults but also on the manner in which grown-ups talk to the child. Whether in Dhaka, Paris, Riga or the Tulalip Indian Reservation near Seattle, researchers who listen to people talk to a child have learned one simple truth: an adult speaks to a child differently than to other adults. Cultural ethnographers and linguists have dubbed it "baby talk," and it turns up in most cultures. At first, it was unknown whether baby talk might hinder language learning. Numerous studies, however, have shown that motherese or parentese, the revisionist name for baby talk, actually helps an infant learn. Parentese, in fact, is not a modern invention: Varro (116 to 27 BC), an ancient Roman expert on syntax, noted that certain shortened words were used only when talking to babies and young children.

My lab—and those of Anne Fernald at Stanford University and Lila Gleitman at the University of Pennsylvania—has looked at the specific sounds of parentese that intrigue infants: the higher pitch, slower tempo, and exaggerated intonation. When given a choice, infants will choose to listen to short audio clips of parentese instead of recordings of the same mothers speaking to other adults. The high-pitched tone seems to act as an acoustic hook for infants that captures and holds their attention.

Parentese exaggerates differences between sounds—one phoneme can be easily discriminated from another. Our studies show that exaggerated speech most likely helps infants as they commit these sounds to memory. In a recent study by my group, Nairan Ramirez-Esparza, now at the University of Connecticut, had infants wear high-fidelity miniature tape recorders fitted into lightweight vests worn at home throughout the day. The recordings let us enter the children's auditory world and showed that if their parents spoke to them in parentese at that age, then one year later these infants had learned more than twice the number of words as those whose parents did not use the baby vernacular as frequently.

Signatures of Learning

Brain scientists who study child development are becoming excited about the possibility of using our growing knowledge of early development to identify signatures of brain activity, known as biomarkers, that provide clues that a child may be running into difficulty in learning language. In a recent study in my lab, two-year-old children with autism spectrum disorder listened to both known and unfamiliar words while we monitored their brain's electrical activity when they heard these words.

We found the degree to which a particular pattern of brain waves was present in response to known words predicted the child's future language and cognitive abilities, at ages four and six. These measurements assessed the child's success at learning from other people. They show that if a youngster has the ability to learn words socially, it bodes well for learning in general.

The prospect for being able to measure an infant or toddler's cognitive development is improving because of the availability of new tools to judge their ability to detect sounds. My research group has begun to use magnetoencephalography (MEG), a safe and noninvasive imaging technology, to demonstrate how the brain responds to speech. The machine contains 306 SQUID (superconducting quantum interference device) sensors placed within an apparatus that looks like a hair dryer. When the infant sits in it, the sensors measure tiny magnetic fields that indicate specific neurons firing in the baby's brain as the child listens to speech. We have already demonstrated with MEG that there is a critical time window in which babies seem to be going through mental rehearsals to prepare to speak their native language.

MEG is too expensive and difficult to use in a neighborhood medical clinic. But these studies pave the way by identifying biomarkers that will eventually be measured with portable and inexpensive sensors that can be used outside a university lab. If reliable biomarkers for language learning can be identified, they should help determine whether children are developing normally or at risk for early-life, language-related disabilities, including autism spectrum disorder, dyslexia, fragile X syndrome, and other disorders. By understanding the brain's uniquely human capacity for language—and when exactly it is possible to shape it—we may be able to administer therapies early enough to change the future course of a child's life.

Critical Thinking

1. How and why does "parentese" help babies learn to talk?
2. In what respects is language acquisition dependent upon both mental computation and intense social immersion?
3. What are the optimal circumstances for learning a second language and why?

Internet References

How Your Newborn Grows: Infant Development
   http://www.webmd.com/parenting/baby/infant-development-9/baby-talk

The linguistic genius of babies
   https://www.ted.com/talks/patricia_kuhl_the_linguistic_genius_of_babies?language=en

Pathways
   https://pathways.org/

Article   Prepared by: Elvio Angeloni, *Pasadena City College*

War of Words

Mark Pagel

Learning Outcomes

After reading this article, you will be able to:

- Discuss the origins and functions of linguistic diversity in human societies.

- Discuss the future of linguistic diversity in terms of its direction and causes.

For anyone interested in languages, the north-eastern coastal region of Papua New Guinea is like a well-stocked sweet shop. Korak speakers live right next to Brem speakers, who are just up the coast from Wanambre speakers, and so on. I once met a man from that area and asked him whether it is true that a different language is spoken every few kilometres. "Oh no," he replied, "they are far closer together than that."

Around the world today, some 7,000 distinct languages are spoken. That's 7,000 different ways of saying "good morning" or "it looks like rain"—more languages in one species of mammal than there are mammalian species. What's more, these 7,000 languages probably make up just a fraction of those ever spoken in our history. To put human linguistic diversity into perspective, you could take a gorilla or chimpanzee from its troop and plop it down anywhere these species are found, and it would know how to communicate. You could repeat this with donkeys, crickets or goldfish and get the same outcome.

This highlights an intriguing paradox at the heart of human communication. If language evolved to allow us to exchange information, how come most people cannot understand what most other people are saying? This perennial question was famously addressed in the Old Testament story of the Tower of Babel, which tells of how humans developed the conceit that they could use their shared language to cooperate in the building of a tower that would take them to heaven. God, angered at this attempt to usurp his power, destroyed the tower and to ensure it would not be rebuilt he scattered the people and confused them by giving them different languages. The myth leads to the amusing irony that our separate languages exist to prevent us from communicating. The surprise is that this might not be far from the truth.

The origins of language are difficult to pin down. Anatomical evidence from fossils suggests that the ability to speak arose in

our ancestors sometime between 1.6 million and 600,000 years ago (*New Scientist,* 24 March, p. 34). However, indisputable evidence that this speech was conveying complex ideas comes only with the cultural sophistication and symbolism associated with modern humans. They emerged in Africa perhaps 200,000 to 160,000 years ago, and by 60,000 years ago had migrated out of the continent—eventually to occupy nearly every region of the world. We should expect new languages to arise as people spread out and occupy new lands because as soon as groups become isolated from one another their languages begin to drift apart and adapt to local needs (*New Scientist,* 10 December 2011, p. 34). But the real puzzle is that the greatest diversity of human societies and languages arises not where people are most spread out, but where they are most closely packed together.

Papua New Guinea is a classic case. That relatively small land mass—only slightly larger than California—is home to between 800 and 1,000 distinct languages, or around 15 per cent of all languages spoken on the planet. This linguistic diversity is not the result of migration and physical isolation of different populations. Instead, people living in close quarters seem to have chosen to separate into many distinct societies, leading lives so separate that they have become incapable of talking to one another. Why?

Thinking about this, I was struck by an uncanny parallel between linguistic and biological diversity. A well-known phenomenon in ecology called Rapoport's rule states that the greatest diversity of biological species is found near to the equator, with numbers tailing off as you approach the poles. Could this be true for languages too? To test the idea, anthropologist Ruth Mace from University College London and I looked at the distribution of around 500 Native American tribes before the arrival of Europeans and used this to plot the number of different language groups per unit area at each degree of latitude (*Nature,* vol 428, p. 275). It turned out that the distribution matched Rapoport's rule remarkably well.

The congruity of biological species and cultures with distinct languages is probably not an accident. To survive the harsh polar landscape, species must range far and wide, leaving little opportunity for new ones to arise. The same is true of human groups in the far northern regions. They too must cover wide geographical areas to find sufficient food, and this tends to blend languages and cultures. At the other end of the spectrum, just as the bountiful, sun-drenched tropics are a cradle of biological speciation, so this rich environment has allowed humans to thrive and splinter into a profusion of societies.

Of course that still leaves the question of why people would want to form into so many distinct groups. For the myriad biological species in the tropics, there are advantages to being different because it allows each to adapt to its own ecological niche. But humans all occupy the same niche, and splitting into distinct cultural and linguistic groups actually brings disadvantages, such as slowing the movement of ideas, technologies and people. It also makes societies more vulnerable to risks and plain bad luck. So why not have one large group with a shared language?

An answer to this question is emerging with the realisation that human history has been characterised by continual battles. Ever since our ancestors walked out of Africa, beginning around 60,000 years ago, people have been in conflict over territory and resources. In my book *Wired for Culture* (Norton/Penguin, 2012) I describe how, as a consequence, we have acquired a suite of traits that help our own particular group to outcompete the others. Two traits that stand out are "groupishness"—affiliating with people with whom you share a distinct identity—and xenophobia, demonising those outside your group and holding parochial views towards them. In this context, languages act as powerful social anchors of our tribal identity. How we speak is a continual auditory reminder of who we are and, equally as important, who we are not. Anyone who can speak your particular dialect is a walking, talking advertisement for the values and cultural history you share. What's more, where different groups live in close proximity, distinct languages are an effective way to prevent eavesdropping or the loss of important information to a competitor.

In support of this idea, I have found anthropological accounts of tribes deciding to change their language, with immediate effect, for no other reason than to distinguish themselves from neighbouring groups. For example, a group of Selepet speakers in Papua New Guinea changed its word for "no" from *bia* to *bune* to be distinct from other Selepet speakers in a nearby village. Another group reversed all its masculine and feminine nouns—the word for he became she, man became woman, mother became father, and so on. One can only sympathise with anyone who had been away hunting for a few days when the changes occurred.

The use of language as identity is not confined to Papua New Guinea. People everywhere use language to monitor who is a member of their "tribe." We have an acute, and sometimes obsessive, awareness of how those around us speak, and we continually adapt language to mark out our particular group from others. In a striking parallel to the Selepet examples, many of the peculiar spellings that differentiate American English from British—such as the tendency to drop the "u" in words like colour—arose almost overnight when Noah Webster produced the first American Dictionary of the English Language at the start of the 19th century. He insisted that: "As an independent nation, our honor [sic] requires us to have a system of our own, in language as well as government."

Use of language to define group identity is not a new phenomenon. To examine how languages have diversified over the course of human history, my colleagues and I drew up family trees for three large language groups—Indo-European languages, the Bantu languages of Africa, and Polynesian languages from Oceania (*Science*, vol 319, p. 588). These "phylogenies," which trace the history of each group back to a common ancestor, reveal the number of times a contemporary language has split or "divorced" from related languages. We found that some languages have a history of many divorces, others far fewer.

When languages split, they often experience short episodes during which they change rapidly. The same thing happens during biological evolution, where it is known as punctuational evolution (*Science*, vol 314, p. 119). So the more divorces a language has had, the more its vocabulary differs from its ancestral language. Our analysis does not say why one language splits into two. Migration and isolation of groups is one explanation, but it also seems clear that bursts of linguistic change have occurred at least in part to allow speakers to assert their own identities. There really has been a war of words going on.

So what of the future? The world we live in today is very different from the one our ancestors inhabited. For most of our history, people would have encountered only their own cultural group and immediate neighbours. Globalisation and electronic communication mean we have become far more connected and culturally homogenised, making the benefits of being understood more apparent. The result is a mass extinction of languages to rival the great biological extinctions in Earth's past.

Although contemporary languages continue to evolve and diverge from one another, the rate of loss of minority languages now greatly exceeds the emergence of new languages. Between 30 and 50 languages are disappearing every year as the young people of small tribal societies adopt majority languages. As a percentage of the total, this rate of loss equals or exceeds the decline in biological species diversity through loss of habitat and climate change. Already a mere 15 of the Earth's 7,000 languages account for about 40 per cent of the world's speakers, and most languages have very few speakers.

Still, this homogenisation of languages and cultures is happening at a far slower pace than it could, and that is because of the powerful psychological role language plays in marking out our cultural territories and identities. One consequence of this is that languages resist "contamination" from other languages, with speakers often treating the arrival of foreign words with a degree of suspicion—witness the British and French grumblings about so-called Americanisms. Another factor is the role played by nationalistic agendas in efforts to save dying languages, which can result in policies such as compulsory Welsh lessons for schoolchildren up to the age of 16 in Wales.

Linguistic Creativity

This resistance to change leaves plenty of time for linguistic diversity to pop up. Various street and hip-hop dialects, for example, are central to the identity of specific groups, while mass communication allows them easily to reach their natural constituencies. Another interesting example is Globish, a pared-down form of English that uses just 1,000 or so words and simplified language structures. It has spontaneously evolved among people who travel extensively, such as diplomats and international business people. Amusingly, native English speakers can be disadvantaged around Globish because they use words and grammar that others cannot understand.

In the long run, though, it seems virtually inevitable that a single language will replace all others. In evolutionary terms, when otherwise equally good solutions to a problem compete, one of them tends to win out. We see this in the near worldwide standardisation of ways of telling time, measuring weights and distance, CD and DVD formats, railway gauges, and the voltages and frequencies of electricity supplies. It may take a very long time, but languages seem destined to go the same way—all are equally good vehicles of communication, so one will eventually replace the others. Which one will it be?

Today, around 1.2 billion people—about 1 in 6 of us—speak Mandarin. Next come Spanish and English with about 400 million speakers each, and Bengali and Hindi follow close behind. On these counts Mandarin might look like the favourite in the race to be the world's language. However, vastly more people learn English as a second language than any other. Years ago, in a remote part of Tanzania, I was stopped while attempting to speak Swahili to a local person who held up his hand and said: "My English is better than your Swahili." English is already the worldwide lingua franca, so if I had to put money on one language eventually to replace all others, this would be it.

In the ongoing war of words, casualties are inevitable. As languages become extinct we are not simply losing different ways of saying "good morning," but the cultural diversity that has arisen around our thousands of distinct tribal societies. Each language plays a powerful role in establishing a cultural identity—it is the internal voice that carries the memories, thoughts, hopes and fears of a particular group of people. Lose the language and you lose that too.

Nevertheless, I suspect a monolinguistic future may not be as bad as doomsayers have suggested. There is a widely held belief that the language you speak determines the way you think, so that a loss of linguistic diversity is also a loss of unique styles of thought. I don't believe that. Our languages determine the words we use but they do not limit the concepts we can understand and perceive. Besides, we might draw another, more positive, moral from the story of Babel: With everyone speaking the same language, humanity can more easily cooperate to achieve something monumental. Indeed, in today's world it is the countries with the least linguistic diversity that have achieved the most prosperity.

Critical Thinking

1. Discuss the linguistic diversity among humans in comparison to animal communication.
2. What is the "intriguing paradox" at the heart of human communication?
3. How does the author explain the original diversity of human languages?
4. Where on earth is the greatest diversity of human languages and why?
5. How do *groupishness* and *xenophobia* both play a role in linguistic diversity? Be familiar with the evidence cited by the author in support of this idea.
6. What are the factors involved in why a language splits into two?
7. What is the future for linguistic diversity and why? Why is the pace of "homogenization" slower than it could be?
8. In what contexts does linguistic diversity continue to pop up?
9. What does the author see as the future for linguistic diversity? Why might a "monolinguistic future" not be as bad as doomsayers have suggested?

Create Central

www.mhhe.com/createcentral

Internet References

Exploratorium Magazine: "The Evolution of Languages"
www.exploratorium.edu/exploring/language

Language and Culture
http://anthro.palomar.edu/language/default.htm

Language Extinction
www.colorado.edu/iec

Showcase Anthropology
www.anthropology.wisc.edu

Article   Prepared by: Elvio Angeloni, *Pasadena City College*

Armor against Prejudice

ED YONG

Learning Outcomes

After reading this article, you will be able to:

- Discuss the impact of negative stereotypes on many minorities.

- Discuss the effect of "stereotype threat" on individual performance.

- Explain the interventionist approach to stereotype threat and its possible positive outcome.

Neil deGrasse Tyson, the renowned science communicator, earned his PhD in astrophysics from Columbia University in 1991. About 4,000 astrophysicists resided in the country at the time. Tyson brought the total number of African-Americans among them to a paltry seven. In a convocation address, he spoke openly about the challenges he faced: "In the perception of society, my academic failures are expected and my academic successes are attributed to others." Tyson said. "To spend most of my life fighting these attitudes levies an emotional tax that is a form of intellectual emasculation. It is a tax that I would not wish upon my enemies."

Tyson's words speak to a broad truth: negative stereotypes impose an intellectual burden on many minorities and on others who think that the people around them perceive them as inferior in some way. In many different situations—at school, at work or in sports stadiums—these individuals worry that they will fail in a way that affirms derogatory stereotypes. Young white athletes fear that they will not perform as well as their black peers, for example, and women in advanced math classes worry that they will earn lower grades than the men. This anxiety—Tyson's "emotional tax"—is known as stereotype threat. Hundreds of studies have confirmed that stereotype threat undermines performance, producing the very failure they dread. Sometimes, people become trapped in a vicious cycle in which poor performance leads to more worry, which further impedes performance.

In recent years, psychologists have greatly improved their understanding of how stereotype threat affects individuals, why it happens and, most important, how to prevent it. Although the threat is real, some researchers question how well some of the relevant laboratory studies mirror anxiety in real-world settings; they also note that it is just one of many factors that contribute to social and academic inequality. Yet it is also one of the factors that can be easily changed. In studies conducted in actual schools, relatively simple interventions—such as self-esteem-boosting writing exercises completed in less than an hour—have produced dramatic and long-lasting effects, shrinking achievement gaps, and expelling stereotype threat from the classroom and students' minds. Some educators are working on ways to scale up these interventions to statewide education programs.

Identifying the Threat

Two psychologists, Claude Steele of Stanford University and Joshua Aronson, then also at Stanford, coined the term "stereotype threat" in 1995. Then, as now, black students across the U.S. earned worse grades on average than their peers and were more likely to drop out early at all levels of education. The various explanations for this gap included the pernicious idea that black students were innately less intelligent. Steele and Aronson were not convinced. Instead, they reasoned, the very existence of this negative stereotype might impair a student's performance.

In a now classic experiment, they presented more than 100 college students with a frustrating test. When they told the students that the exam would not measure their abilities, black and white students with comparable SAT scores did equally well. When Steele and Aronson told the students that the test would assess their intellectual ability, however, the black students' scores fell, but those of their white peers did not. Simply asking the students to record their race beforehand had the same effect.

The study was groundbreaking. Steele and Aronson showed that standardized tests are far from standardized. When presented in a way that invokes stereotype threat, even subtly, they put some students at an automatic disadvantage. "There was a lot of skepticism at first, but it's reducing with time," Aronson says. "In the beginning, even I didn't believe how strong the effects were. I thought, 'Somebody else has to replicate this.'"

Many researchers have. To date, hundreds of studies have found evidence of stereotype threat in all manner of groups. It afflicts students from poorer backgrounds in academic tests and men in tasks of social sensitivity. White students suffer from it when pitted against Asian peers in math tests or against black peers in sports. In many of these studies, the strongest students suffer the greatest setbacks. The ones who are most invested in succeeding are most likely to be bothered by a negative stereotype and most likely to underperform as a result. Stereotype threat is nothing if not painfully ironic.

Exactly how pervasive stereotype threat is in real-world settings remains somewhat unclear, however, largely because the relevant studies face the same problems that plague much of social psychology. Most were conducted with small numbers of college students—which increases the chances of statistical flukes—and not all studies found a strong effect. Some critics also note that laboratory experiments are often a poor substitute for the real world. Paul Sackett of the University of Minnesota has argued that outside the lab, stereotype threat could be less common and more easily overcome. Last year Gijsbert Stoet, then at the University of Leeds in England, and David C. Geary of the University of Missouri—Columbia examined every study that looked for stereotype threat among women taking math tests—a phenomenon that Steele and his colleagues first identified in 1999. Out of 20 that repeated the 1999 experiment, only 11 concluded that women performed worse than men. Geary is not ready to discount stereotype threat, but he thinks it may not be as strong as it is sometimes portrayed.

Ann Marie Ryan of Michigan State University has identified some plausible reasons for such inconsistent conclusions. In 2008 she and Hanna-Hanh Nguyen, then at California State University, Long Beach, compared the results of 76 different studies on stereotype threat in high schoolers and undergraduates. They found that in the lab, scientists are able to detect the threat only under certain conditions, such as when they give volunteers an especially difficult test or when they work with people who strongly identify with their social group.

In the past decade, psychologists have shifted from showing that stereotype threat exists to understanding how it works. Researchers have demonstrated that the threat operates in the same way across different groups of people. Anxiety arrives; motivation falls; expectations lower. Building on these findings, Toni Schmader of the University of British Columbia surmised that the threat preys on something fundamental. The most obvious culprit was working memory—the collection of cognitive skills that allows us to temporarily hold and manipulate information in our mind. This suite of skills is a finite resource, and stereotype threat can drain it. Individuals might psychologically exhaust themselves by worrying about other people's prejudices and thinking about how to prove them wrong. To test this idea, Schmader gave 75 volunteers a difficult working memory test, during which they had to memorize a list of words while solving mathematical equations. She told some volunteers that the test would assess their memory skills and that men and women may have inborn differences in their abilities. Sure enough, women who were told of this supposed discrepancy kept fewer words in mind, whereas their male colleagues had no such problems.

This depletion of working memory creates various stumbling blocks to success. People tend to overthink actions that would otherwise be automatic and become more sensitive to cues that might indicate discrimination. An ambiguous expression can be misread as a sneer, and even one's own anxiety can become a sign of imminent failure. Minds also wander, and self-control weakens. When Schmader stopped women in the middle of a math test and asked them what they were thinking of, those under stereotype threat were more likely to be daydreaming.

Expelling Stereotypes

Most recently, researchers have moved the study of stereotype threat out of the lab and into schools and lecture halls, where they try to dispel or prevent the threat altogether. "I see three waves of research," Schmader says. "The first was identifying the phenomenon and how far it travels. The second was looking at who experiences the effect and its mechanisms. The third wave is now to translate these results into interventions."

Geoffrey Cohen, also at Stanford, has achieved particularly impressive results. His method is disarmingly simple: he asks people to consider what is important to them, be it popularity or musical ability, and write about why it matters. The 15-minute exercise acts like a mental vaccine that boosts students' self-confidence, helping them combat any future stereotype threat.

In 2003 Cohen visited racially diverse middle schools in California and put his exercise through a randomized controlled trial—the gold-standard test in medicine that checks if an intervention works by pitting it against a placebo. Cohen administered his exercise to seventh graders: half wrote about their own values, and the rest wrote about things that were unimportant to them. The trial was double-blinded, meaning that neither Cohen nor the students knew who was in which group.

At the end of the term, black students who completed the exercise had closed a 40 percent academic gap between them and their white peers. Best of all, the students at the bottom of the class benefited most. Over the next two years, the same students took two or three booster versions of the original exercise. Only 5 percent of the poorest students who wrote about their values ended up in remedial classes or repeated a grade, compared with 18 percent of those in the control group. Ultimately, the black students' grade point averages rose by a quarter of a point and by 0.4 point among the worst performers.

A few fractions of a point here and there might not seem like a huge improvement, but even small changes in confidence—whether positive or negative—have a cumulative effect. Children who do poorly at first can quickly lose self-confidence or a teacher's attention; conversely, signs of modest progress can motivate far greater success. By intervening early on, Cohen asserts, educators can turn vicious cycles into virtuous ones.

Cohen's task is so simple that Ryan and others are not entirely convinced by his results. "It was hard for us to believe, but we've replicated it since," Cohen says. In the past five years, he has used his exercise to swing the fortunes of black students in three different middle schools and to largely close the gender gap in a college-level physics class. Skeptics, though, still hope that independent researchers will try to replicate these studies.

Meanwhile Cohen is seeking new ways to help students. He has collaborated with Greg Walton, also at Stanford, to counter a kind of isolation that stereotype threat often induces. Many minorities worry that their academic peers will not fully accept them. Walton combated these worries with survey statistics and quotes from older students showing that such feelings are common to everyone regardless of race and that they disappear with time. "It makes them reframe their own experiences through the lens of this message, rather than of race," Walton explains.

Walton and Cohen tested their hour-long exercise with college students in their first spring term. Three years later, when the students graduated, the achievement gap between blacks and whites had been halved. The black students were also happier and healthier than their peers who did not take part in Walton's exercise. In the past three years, they had made fewer visits to the doctor. Walton acknowledges that such a simple exercise may look trivial to an outsider. But, he says, for students who are "actively worried about whether they fit in, the knowledge that those concerns are shared and temporary is actually very powerful."

Cohen and Walton are now scaling up their simple and inexpensive interventions from individual schools to entire states. The pair—as well as Carol Dweck and Dave Paunesku—both also at Stanford, created PERTS (the Project for Education Research That Scales), which allows them to rapidly administer their interventions online. They can also combine the programs or pit them against one another to see which have the greatest effects.

Even if the programs work as planned, researchers who study stereotype threat admit that undoing it is not a panacea against inequality. Cohen, for example, tested his initial writing exercise only in schools with mixed ethnicities, and he is unsure if it would work in predominantly minority schools. "There are many reasons why we have achievement gaps—inequality of resources, bad schools, less well-trained teachers," Walton adds. "There doesn't seem to be much hope of addressing these structural barriers. What's exciting about stereotype threat is that we can make headway in the face of those things."

Recent work on the phenomenon not only offers realistic hope for alleviating some truly tenacious problems—it also upends pervasive beliefs. By thwarting stereotype threat, researchers have shown that the stereotypes themselves are unfounded. Performance gaps between black and white students or between male and female scientists do not indicate differences in ability; rather they reflect prejudices that we can change. "The things we thought were so intractable 15 years ago aren't," Aronson says, "and that's a hugely positive message."

Critical Thinking

1. In what ways do negative stereotypes impose an intellectual burden on many minorities?
2. Discuss the effect of "stereotype threat" on performance and how it can be changed.
3. How did the experiment by Steele and Aronson illustrate the effects of stereotype threat?
4. Discuss the findings of the various studies on stereotype threat.
5. Why has it been difficult to assess the effects of stereotype threat outside the lab settings?
6. How does Ann Marie Ryan explain the inconsistent conclusions?
7. Discuss the ways in which stereotype threat actually works.
8. Discuss the interventionist methods of Geoffrey Cohen and Greg Walton and why they seem to reduce the effects of stereotype threat.
9. Explain why undoing stereotype threat is not a panacea and yet offers a realistic hope.

Create Central

www.mhhe.com/createcentral

Internet References

Language and Culture

http://anthro.palomar.edu/language/default.htm

Linguistic Society of America

www.linguisticsociety.org/resource/sociolinguistics

Understanding Prejudice

http://www.understandingprejudice.org/apa/

ED YONG is a science writer based in England. He has written for *Nature, Wired, National Geographic* and *New Scientist,* among other publications.

Article   Prepared by: Elvio Angeloni, *Pasadena City College*

Strong Language Lost in Translation: You Talkin' to Me?

CAROLINE WILLIAMS

Learning Outcomes

After reading this article, you will be able to:

- Discuss body language in terms of what it can actually tell us about a person.

- Discuss the relationship between body language and sexual attraction.

- Discuss the ways in which body language can be used to increase success and influence how we feel.

When Tom Cruise and Katie Holmes announced their divorce last year, tabloid journalists fell over themselves to point out that they had seen it coming. "Just look at their body language!" the headlines screamed, above shots of Holmes frowning while holding Cruise at arm's length. "Awkward!" And when Barack Obama lost last year's first US presidential debate to Republican nominee Mitt Romney, some commentators blamed it on his "low-energy" body language and tendency to look down and purse his lips, which made him come across as "lethargic and unprepared."

Popular culture is full of such insights. After all, it is fun to speculate on the inner lives of the great and the good. But anyone with a sceptical or logical disposition cannot fail to notice the thumping great elephant in the room—the assumption that we can read a person's thoughts and emotions by watching how they move their body. With so many myths surrounding the subject, it is easy to think we understand the coded messages that others convey, but what does science have to say about body language? Is there anything more in it than entertainment value? If so, which movements and gestures speak volumes and which are red herrings? And, knowing this, can we actually alter our own body language to manipulate how others perceive us?

A good place to start looking for answers is the oft-quoted statistic that 93 percent of our communication is non-verbal, with only 7 percent based on what we are actually saying. This figure came from research in the late 1960s by Albert Mehrabian, a social psychologist at the University of California, Los Angeles. He found that when the emotional message conveyed by tone of voice and facial expression differed from the word being spoken (for example, saying the word "brute" in a positive tone and with a smile), people tended to believe the non-verbal cues over the word itself. From these experiments. Mehrabian calculated that perhaps only 7 percent of the emotional message comes from the words we use, with 38 percent coming from tone and the other 55 percent from non-verbal cues.

Mehrabian has spent much of the past four-and-a-bit decades pointing out that he never meant this formula to be taken as some kind of gospel and that it only applies to very specific circumstances—when someone is talking about their likes and dislikes. He now says that "unless a communicator is talking about their feelings or attitudes, these equations are not applicable" and that he cringes every times he hears his theory applied to communication in general.

So the oldest stat in the body language book isn't quite what it seems, and the man who came up with the formula would like everyone to please stop going on about it. After all, if we really could understand 93 percent of what people are saying without recourse to words, we wouldn't need to learn foreign languages and no one would ever get away with a lie.

Clearly, people can lie successfully. And, generally, though it is useful to lie occasionally, we would rather that others could not. Which is why a lot of the interest in body language concerns detecting lies. Legend has it that liars give themselves away with physical "tells", such as looking to the right, fidgeting, holding their own hands or scratching their nose. How much of this stacks up?

The first item is easy to dispatch. A study published last year, the first to scientifically test the "liars look right" assertion, found no evidence to back it up. A team led by psychologist Richard Wiseman from the University of Hertfordshire in Hatfield, UK, observed the eye movements of volunteers telling lies in lab-based experiments. They also studied footage of people at police press conferences for missing persons, where some of the emotional pleas for information came from individuals who turned out to be involved in the disappearance. In neither case did the liars look to the right any more than in other directions (*PLoS One,* vol. 7, p. e40259).

As for other tells, a meta-analysis of more than 100 studies found that the only bodily signs found in liars significantly more often than in truth-tellers were dilated pupils and certain kinds of fidgeting—fiddling with objects and scratching, but not rubbing their face or playing with their hair. The best way to spot a liar, the study found, was not to watch a person's body language but to listen to what they were saying. Liars tended to talk with a higher-pitched voice, gave fewer details in their accounts of events, were more negative and tended to repeat words.

Overall, the researchers concluded, subjective measures—or a gut feeling—might be more effective for lie detection than any available scientific measure. The problem with relying on body language is that while liars may be slightly more likely to exhibit a few behaviors, people who are telling the truth do the same things. In fact, the signals you might think of as red flags for lying, like fidgeting and avoiding eye contact, tend to be signs of emotional discomfort in general, and a non-liar is more likely to express them under the pressure of questioning. This is perhaps why, despite having a vested interest in spotting liars, we are generally pretty bad at it. In fact, US psychologist Paul Ekman has found that most people perform no better than would be expected by chance. And the success rate of judges, police, forensic psychiatrists, and FBI agents is only marginally higher.

So it might be best not to go around accusing people of lying based on their body language. And there are lots of other examples in which our preconceptions of non-verbal communication are off-beam or even totally misleading. Take crossed arms. Most people believe that when someone folds their arms they are being defensive or trying to fend off another individual or their opinions. This may be true. "But the same arm-cross can mean the opposite if the torso is super-erect, bent back somewhat—then it conveys invulnerability," says David McNeill, who studies gestures at the University of Chicago. Besides, an arm crosser might simply be cold, trying to get comfortable, or just lacking pockets.

McNeill is also not convinced by claims trotted out by public-speaking consultants about the importance of hand gestures. It is often said, for example, that "steepling" your fingers, makes you look authoritative and an open hand signals honesty. He says that these are examples of metaphorical gestures that have the meanings that people in management perceive, but they are not limited to these meanings. In other words, these well-known "rules" of body language are arbitrary. An open hand, for example might be a metaphor for trustworthiness, but it could just as easily signal holding the weight of something. The gesture is ambiguous without context and cues from spoken language.

So far, our scientific approach has provided little support for those who claim to speak fluent body-ese, but it turns out there are some gestures everyone understands. At the 2008 Olympic and Paralympic Games, athletes from all cultures made the same postures when they won: arms up in a high V, with the chin raised. The same was true for athletes who had been blind from birth, suggesting that the victory pose is innate, not learned by observation. Defeat postures seemed to be universal too. Almost everyone hunches over with slumped shoulders when they lose.

In fact, if you are hunting for signs of victory or defeat, the body may be a better place to look than the face. Hillel Aviezer at Princeton University and colleagues revealed last year that the facial expressions of professional tennis players when they won or lost an important point were so similar that people struggled to tell them apart. However, the body language was easy to read even when the face was blanked out (*Science,* vol. 338, p. 1225).

Other recent studies indicate that we can glean important clues about people from the way they move. Men judge a woman's walk and dance as significantly sexier when she is in the most fertile part of her menstrual cycle, suggesting that a woman's body language sends out the message that she is ready to mate, whether or not she—or the men around her—realise it. Meanwhile, women and heterosexual men rate the dances of stronger men more highly than those of weaker men, which might be an adaptation for women to spot good mates and men to assess potential opponents.

Using body language to assess sexual attraction can be risky, though. Karl Grammer at the University of Vienna in Austria found support for the popular notion that women signal interest in a man by flipping their hair, tidying their clothes, nodding, and making eye contact. But he also discovered that they make the same number of encouraging signals in the first minute of meeting a man whether they fancy him or not. Such flirting is only a sign of real interest if it keeps going after the first four minutes or so. Grammer interprets this as women using body language to keep a man talking until they can work out whether he is worth getting to know.

Even when there is general agreement about how to interpret body language, we can be wrong, as has been revealed in new research on gait. Psychologist John Thoresen at the University of Durham, UK, filmed people walking and then converted the images to point-light displays to highlight the moving limbs while removing distracting information about body shape. He found that almost everyone judged a swaggering walk to signal an adventurous, extroverted, warm, and trustworthy person. A slow, loose and relaxed walk, on the other hand, was associated with a calm, unflappable personality. However, when the researchers compared the actual personalities of the walkers to the assumptions other people made about them, they found no correlation (*Cognition,* vol. 124, p. 2621).

Arguably, it doesn't really matter what your body language actually reveals about you. What matters is what other people think it is telling them. So can it be faked?

Fake It to Make It

Thoresen says that it should certainly be possible to fake a confident walk. "I have no data to back this up," he says, "but I do believe people can be trained to change perceived personality." There are other corporeal tricks that may help in impression management, too. For example, people in job interviews who sit still, hold eye contact, smile, and nod along with the conversation are more likely to be offered a job. Those whose gaze wanders or who avoid eye contact, keep their head still and don't change their expression much are more likely to be rejected. If it doesn't come naturally, consciously adopting a confident strut, a smile and nod and some extra eye contact probably won't hurt—unless you overdo it and come across as a bit scary.

Faking calmness and confidence may change the way others perceive us, but psychologist Dana Carney at the University of California, Berkeley, believes that it can do far more than that. She says we can use our body language to change ourselves. Carney and her colleagues asked volunteers to hold either a "high-power" or "low-power" pose for two minutes. The former were expansive, including sitting with legs on a desk and hands behind the head and standing with legs apart and hands on hips, while the latter involved hunching and taking up little space. Afterward, they played a gambling game where the odds of winning were 50:50, and the researchers took saliva samples to test the levels of testosterone and cortisol—the "power" and stress hormones, respectively—in their bodies. Those who had held high-power poses were significantly more likely to gamble than those who held low-power poses (86 percent compared with 60 percent). Not only that, willingness to gamble was linked to physiological changes. High-power posers had a 20 percent increase in testosterone and a 25 percent decrease in cortisol, while low-power posers showed a 10 percent decrease in testosterone and a 15 percent increase in cortisol (*Psychological Science,* vol. 21, p. 1463).

"We showed that you can actually change your physiology," says Carney. "This goes beyond just emotion—there is something deeper happening here." The feeling of power is not just psychological: increased testosterone has been linked with increased pain tolerance, so power posing really can make us more powerful.

And this is not the only way body language can influence how you feel. Carney points to studies showing that sitting up straight leads to positive emotions, while sitting with hunched shoulders leads to feeling down. There is also plenty of evidence that faking a smile makes you feel happier, while frowning has the opposite effect. In fact, there is evidence that people who have Botox injections that prevent them from frowning feel generally happier.

Despite these interesting results, if science has shown us anything it is that we should always question our preconceptions about body language. Even when people from diverse cultures are in agreement about the meaning of a particular movement or gesture, we may all be wrong. As the evidence accumulates, there could come a time when we can tailor our body language to skillfully manipulate the messages we send out about ourselves. For now, at least our popular conceptions can be modified with a little evidence-based insight. Or as Madonna almost put it: "Don't just stand there, let's get to it, strike a pose. There's something to it."

Critical Thinking

1. Discuss the source of the notion that 93 percent of our communications is non-verbal, with only 7 percent based on what we are actually saying. What is the truth of the matter?
2. Discuss the evidence regarding the various methods proposed for detecting lies.
3. Discuss the meaning of such body language as arm-crossing, arms up in a high V, defeat postures, and facial expression when losing or winning.
4. What is the evidence regarding body language and sexual attraction?
5. Is there any relationship between the way a person walks and one's personality?
6. How can one increase the likelihood of a successful job interview?
7. Discuss the evidence for the idea that body language can influence how you feel.

Create Central

www.mhhe.com/createcentral

Internet References

Center for Nonverbal Studies
    www.library.kent.edu/resource.php?id = 2800
Nonverbal Behavior
    www.usal.es/~nonverbal/researchcenters.htm

CAROLINE WILLIAMS is a writer based in Surrey, UK.

Article   Prepared by: Elvio Angeloni, *Pasadena City College*

Vanishing Languages

RUSS RYMER

Learning Outcomes

After reading this article, you will be able to:

- Explain the importance of the variety of human languages in today's world.

- Discuss the different ways in which languages highlight the varieties of human experience.

Tuvan
The Compassion of Khoj Özeeri

One morning in early fall Andrei Mongush and his parents began preparations for supper, selecting a black-faced, fat-tailed sheep from their flock and rolling it onto its back on a tarp outside their livestock paddock. The Mongush family's home is on the Siberian taiga, at the edge of the endless steppes, just over the horizon from Kyzyl, the capital of the Republic of Tuva, in the Russian Federation. They live near the geographic center of Asia, but linguistically and personally, the family inhabits a borderland, the frontier between progress and tradition. Tuvans are historically nomadic herders, moving their *aal*—an encampment of yurts—and their sheep and cows and reindeer from pasture to pasture as the seasons progress. The elder Mongushes, who have returned to their rural aal after working in the city, speak both Tuvan and Russian. Andrei and his wife also speak English, which they are teaching themselves with pieces of paper labeled in English pasted onto seemingly every object in their modern kitchen in Kyzyl. They work as musicians in the Tuvan National Orchestra, an ensemble that uses traditional Tuvan instruments and melodies in symphonic arrangements. Andrei is a master of the most characteristic Tuvan music form: throat singing, or *khöömei*.

When I ask university students in Kyzyl what Tuvan words are untranslatable into English or Russian, they suggest khöömei, because the singing is so connected with the Tuvan environment that only a native can understand it, and also *khoj özeeri*, the Tuvan method of killing a sheep. If slaughtering livestock can be seen as part of humans' closeness to animals, khoj özeeri represents an unusually intimate version. Reaching through an incision in the sheep's hide, the slaughterer severs a vital artery with his fingers, allowing the animal to quickly slip away without alarm, so peacefully that one must check its eyes to see if it is dead. In the language of the Tuvan people, khoj özeeri means not only slaughter but also kindness, humaneness, a ceremony by which a family can kill, skin, and butcher a sheep, salting its hide and preparing its meat and making sausage with the saved blood and cleansed entrails so neatly that the whole thing can be accomplished in two hours (as the Mongushes did this morning) in one's good clothes without spilling a drop of blood. Khoj özeeri implies a relationship to animals that is also a measure of a people's character. As one of the students explained, "If a Tuvan killed an animal the way they do in other places"—by means of a gun or knife—"they'd be arrested for brutality."

Tuvan is one of the many small languages of the world. The Earth's population of seven billion people speaks roughly 7,000 languages, a statistic that would seem to offer each living language a healthy one million speakers, if things were equitable. In language, as in life, things aren't. Seventy-eight percent of the world's population speaks the 85 largest languages, while the 3,500 smallest languages share a mere 8.25 million speakers. Thus, while English has 328 million first-language speakers, and Mandarin 845 million, Tuvan speakers in Russia number just 235,000. Within the next century, linguists think, nearly half of the world's current stock of languages may disappear. More than a thousand are listed as critically or severely endangered—teetering on the edge of oblivion.

In an increasingly globalized, connected, homogenized age, languages spoken in remote places are no longer protected by national borders or natural boundaries from the languages that dominate world communication and commerce. The reach of Mandarin and English and Russian and Hindi and Spanish and Arabic extends seemingly to every hamlet, where they compete with Tuvan and Yanomami and Altaic in a house-to-house battle. Parents in tribal villages often encourage their children to move away from the insular language of their forebears and toward languages that will permit greater education and success.

Who can blame them? The arrival of television, with its glamorized global materialism, its luxury-consumption pros-elytizing, is even more irresistible. Prosperity, it seems, speaks English. One linguist, attempting to define what a language is, famously (and humorously) said that a language is a dialect with an army. He failed to note that some armies are better equipped than others. Today any language with a television station and a currency is in a position to obliterate those without, and so residents of Tuva must speak Russian and Chinese if they hope to engage with the surrounding world. The incursion of dominant Russian into Tuva is evident in the speaking competencies of the generation of Tuvans who grew up in the mid-20th century, when it was the fashion to speak, read, and write in Russian and not their native tongue.

Yet Tuvan is robust relative to its frailest counterparts, some of which are down to a thousand speakers, or a mere handful, or even one individual. Languages like Wintu, a native tongue in California, or Siletz Dee-ni, in Oregon, or Amurdak, an Aboriginal tongue in Australia's Northern Territory, retain only one or two fluent or semifluent speakers. A last speaker with no one to talk to exists in unspeakable solitude.

Increasingly, as linguists recognize the magnitude of the modern language die-off and rush to catalog and decipher the most vulnerable tongues, they are confronting underlying questions about languages' worth and utility. Does each language have boxed up within it some irreplaceable beneficial knowledge? Are there aspects of cultures that won't survive if they are translated into a dominant language? What unexpected insights are being lost to the world with the collapse of its linguistic variety?

Fortunately, Tuvan is not among the world's endangered languages, but it could have been. Since the breakup of the Soviet Union, the language has stabilized. It now has a well-equipped army—not a television station, yet, or a currency, but a newspaper and a respectable 264,000 total speakers (including some in Mongolia and China). Yet Tofa, a neighboring Siberian language, is down to some 30 speakers. Tuvan's importance to our understanding of disappearing languages lies in another question linguists are struggling to answer: What makes one language succeed while another dwindles or dies?

Aka
The Respect of Mucrow

I witnessed the heartrending cost of broken languages among the Aka people in Palizi, a tiny, rustic hamlet perched on a mountainside in Arunachal Pradesh, India's rugged northeastern most state. It is reachable by a five-hour drive through palm and hardwood jungles on single-track mountain roads. Its one main street is lined with unpainted board-faced houses set on stilts and roofed with thatch or metal. Villagers grow their own rice, yams, spinach, oranges, and ginger; slaughter their own hogs and goats; and build their own houses. The tribe's isolation has bred a radical self-sufficiency, evidenced in an apparent lack of an Aka word for job, in the sense of salaried labor.

The Aka measure personal wealth in mithan, a breed of Himalayan cattle. A respectable bride price in Palizi, for instance, is expressed as eight mithan. The most cherished Aka possession is the precious *tradzy* necklace—worth two mithan—made from yellow stones from the nearby river, which is passed down to their children. The yellow stones for the tradzy necklaces can no longer be found in the river, and so the only way to have a precious necklace is to inherit one.

Speaking Aka—or any language—means immersing oneself in its character and concepts. "I'm seeing the world through the looking glass of this language," said Father Vijay D'Souza, who was running the Jesuit school in Palizi at the time of my visit. The Society of Jesus established the school in part because it was concerned about the fragility of the Aka language and culture and wanted to support them (though classes are taught in English). D'Souza is from southern India, and his native language is Konkani. When he came to Palizi in 1999 and began speaking Aka, the language transformed him.

"It alters your thinking, your worldview," he told me one day in his headmaster's office, as children raced to classes through the corridor outside. One small example: *mucrow*. A similar word in D'Souza's native language would be an insult, meaning "old man." In Aka "mucrow" means something more. It is a term of respect, deference, endearment. The Aka might address a woman as mucrow to indicate her wisdom in civic affairs, and, says D'Souza, "an Aka wife will call her husband mucrow, even when he's young," and do so affectionately.

American linguists David Harrison and Greg Anderson have been coming to Arunachal Pradesh to study its languages since 2008. They are among the scores of linguists worldwide engaged in the study of vanishing languages. Some have academic and institutional affiliations (Harrison and Anderson are both connected with National Geographic's Enduring Voices Project), while others may work for Bible societies that translate Scripture into new tongues. The authoritative index of world languages is *Ethnologue,* maintained by SIL International, a faith-based organization. The researchers' intent may be hands-off, to record a grammar and lexicon before a language is lost or contaminated, or it may be interventionist, to develop a written accompaniment for the oral language, compile a dictionary, and teach native speakers to write.

Linguists have identified a host of language hotspots (analogous to biodiversity hotspots) that have both a high level of linguistic diversity and a high number of threatened languages. Many of these are in the world's least reachable, and often least hospitable, places—like Arunachal Pradesh. Aka and its neighboring languages have been protected because Arunachal Pradesh has long been sealed off to outsiders as a restricted border region. Even other Indians are not allowed to cross into the region without federal permission, and so its fragile microcultures have been spared the intrusion of immigrant labor, modernization—and linguists. It has been described as a black hole of linguistics because its incredible language variety remains so little explored.

Much of public life in Palizi is regulated through the repetition of mythological stories used as forceful fables to prescribe behavior. Thus a money dispute can draw a recitation about a spirit whose daughters are eaten by a crocodile, one by one, as they cross the river to bring him dinner in the field. He kills the crocodile, and a priest promises to bring the last daughter back to life but overcharges so egregiously that the spirit seeks revenge by becoming a piece of ginger that gets stuck in the greedy priest's throat.

Such stories were traditionally told by the elders in a highly formal version of Aka that the young did not yet understand and according to certain rules, among them this: Once an elder begins telling a story, he cannot stop until the story is finished. As with linguistic literacy, disruption is disaster. Yet Aka's young people no longer follow their elders in learning the formal version of the language and the stories that have governed daily life. Even in this remote region, young people are seduced away from their mother tongue by Hindi on the television and

English in the schools. Today Aka's speakers number fewer than 2,000, few enough to put it on the endangered list.

One night in Palizi, Harrison, Anderson, an Indian linguist named Ganesh Murmu, and I sat cross-legged around the cooking fire at the home of Pario Nimasow, a 25-year-old teacher at the Jesuit school. A Palizi native, Nimasow loved his Aka culture even as he longed to join the outside world. In his sleeping room in an adjacent hut was a television waiting for the return of electricity, which had been out for many months thanks to a series of landslides and transformer malfunctions. After dinner Nimasow disappeared for a moment and came back with a soiled white cotton cloth, which he unfolded by the flickering light of the cooking fire. Inside was a small collection of ritual items: a tiger's jaw, a python's jaw, the sharp-toothed mandible of a river fish, a quartz crystal, and other objects of a shaman's sachet. This sachet had belonged to Nimasow's father until his death in 1991.

"My father was a priest," Nimasow said, "and his father was a priest." And now? I asked. Was he next in line? Nimasow stared at the talismans and shook his head. He had the kit, but he didn't know the chants; his father had died before passing them on. Without the words, there was no way to bring the artifacts' power to life.

Linguistics has undergone two great revolutions in the past 60 years, on seemingly opposite ends of the discipline. In the late 1950s Noam Chomsky theorized that all languages were built on an underlying universal grammar embedded in human genes. A second shift in linguistics—an explosion of interest in small and threatened languages—has focused on the variety of linguistic experience. Field linguists like David Harrison are more interested in the idiosyncrasies that make each language unique and the ways that culture can influence a language's form. As Harrison points out, some 85 percent of languages have yet to be documented. Understanding them can only enrich our comprehension of what is universal to all languages.

Different languages highlight the varieties of human experience, revealing as mutable aspects of life that we tend to think of as settled and universal, such as our experience of time, number, or color. In Tuva, for example, the past is always spoken of as ahead of one, and the future is behind one's back. "We could never say, I'm looking forward to doing something," a Tuvan told me. Indeed, he might say, "I'm looking forward to the day before yesterday." It makes total sense if you think of it in a Tuvan sort of way: If the future were ahead of you, wouldn't it be in plain view?

Smaller languages often retain remnants of number systems that may predate the adoption of the modern world's base-ten counting system. The Pirahã, an Amazonian tribe, appear to have no words for any specific numbers at all but instead get by with relative words such as "few" and "many." The Pirahã's lack of numerical terms suggests that assigning numbers may be an invention of culture rather than an innate part of human cognition. The interpretation of color is similarly varied from language to language. What we think of as the natural spectrum of the rainbow is actually divided up differently in different

tongues, with many languages having more or fewer color categories than their neighbors.

Language shapes human experience—our very cognition—as it goes about classifying the world to make sense of the circumstances at hand. Those classifications may be broad—Aka divides the animal kingdom into animals that are eaten and those that are not—or exceedingly fine-tuned. The Todzhu reindeer herders of southern Siberia have an elaborate vocabulary for reindeer; an *iyi düktüg myiys,* for example, is a castrated former stud in its fourth year.

If Aka, or any language, is supplanted by a new one that's bigger and more universally useful, its death shakes the foundations of the tribe. "Aka is our identity," a villager told me one day as we walked from Palizi down the path that wound past the rice fields to the forests by the river. "Without it, we are the general public." But should the rest of the world mourn too? The question would not be an easy one to frame in Aka, which seems to lack a single term for world. Aka might suggest an answer, though, one embodied in the concept of mucrow—a regard for tradition, for long-standing knowledge, for what has come before, a conviction that the venerable and frail have something to teach the callow and the strong that they would be lost without.

Critical Thinking

1. In what respects does the Mongush family "inhabit a borderland"?

2. Why are some Tuvan words untranslatable?

3. How many languages are there in the world? Why are so many of them disappearing?

4. What are some of the underlying questions about languages' worth and utility? How is the language of Tuvan important to our understanding of disappearing languages?

5. In what ways does the Aka language reflect Aka culture?

6. What is the difference between a linguist's "hands-off" approach versus an "interventionist approach"?

7. In what respects is the Aka language located in a "language hotspot"? How have they been protected?

8. Why are Aka youth no longer learning the stories that have governed daily life?

9. How does the author illustrate the fact that different languages highlight the varieties of human experience?

Create Central

www.mhhe.com/createcentral

Internet References

Intute: Anthropology
www.intute.ac.uk/anthropology

RUSS RYMER is the author of *Genie: A Scientific Tragedy,* the story of an abused child whose case helped scientists study the acquisition of language.

Article   Prepared by: Elvio Angeloni, *Pasadena City College*

My Two Minds

CATHERINE DE LANGE

Learning Outcomes

After reading this article, you will be able to:

• Discuss the origins of human linguistic diversity.

• Discuss the advantages of being bilingual.

When I was just a newborn baby, my mother gazed down at me in her hospital bed and did something that was to permanently change the way my brain developed. Something that would make me better at learning, multitasking and solving problems. Eventually, it might even protect my brain against the ravages of old age. Her trick? She started speaking to me in French.

At the time, my mother had no idea that her actions would give me a cognitive boost. She is French and my father English, so they simply felt it made sense to raise me and my brothers as bilingual. Yet as I've grown up, a mass of research has emerged to suggest that speaking two languages may have profoundly affected the way I think.

Cognitive enhancement is just the start. According to some studies, my memories, values, even my personality, may change depending on which language I happen to be speaking. It is almost as if the bilingual brain houses two separate minds. All of which highlights the fundamental role of language in human thought. "Bilingualism is quite an extraordinary microscope into the human brain," says neuroscientist Laura Ann Petitto of Gallaudet University in Washington DC.

The view of bilingualism has not always been this rosy. For many parents like mine, the decision to raise children speaking two languages was controversial. Since at least the 19th century, educators warned that it would confuse the child, making them [sic] unable to learn either language properly. At best, they thought the child would become a jack-of-all-trades and master of none. At worst, they suspected it might hinder other aspects of development, resulting in a lower IQ.

These days, such fears seem unjustified. True, bilingual people tend to have slightly smaller vocabularies in each language than their monolingual peers, and they are sometimes slower to reach for the right word when naming objects. But a key study in the 1960s by Elizabeth Peal and Wallace Lambert at McGill University in Montreal, Canada, found that the ability to speak two languages does not stunt overall development. On the contrary, when controlling for other factors which might also affect performance, such as socioeconomic status and education, they found that bilinguals outperformed monolinguals in 15 verbal and non-verbal tests (*Psychological Monographs*, vol 76, no 27, p. 1).

Unfortunately, their findings were largely overlooked. Although a trickle of research into the benefits of bilingualism followed their study, most researchers and educators continued to cling to the old ideas. It is only within the last few years that bilingualism has received the attention it deserves. "For 30 years I've been sitting in my little dark room doing my thing and suddenly in the last five years it's like the doors have swung open," says Ellen Bialystok, a psychologist at York University in Toronto, Canada.

In part, the renewed interest comes from recent technological developments in neuroscience, such as functional near-infrared spectroscopy (fNIRS)—a form of brain imaging that acts as a silent and portable monitor, peering inside the brains of babies as they sit on their parents' laps. For the first time, researchers can watch young babies' brains in their initial encounters with language.

Using this technique, Petitto and her colleagues discovered a profound difference between babies brought up speaking either one or two languages. According to popular theory, babies are born "citizens of the world," capable of discriminating between the sounds of any language. By the time they are a year old, however, they are thought to have lost this ability, homing in exclusively on the sounds of their mother tongue. That seemed to be the case with monolinguals, but Petitto's study found that bilingual children still showed increased neural activity in response to completely unfamiliar languages at the end of their first year (*Brain and Language*, vol 121, p. 130).

She reckons the bilingual experience "wedges open" the window for learning language. Importantly, the children still reached the same linguistic milestones, such as their first word, at roughly the same time as monolingual babies, supporting the idea that bilingualism can invigorate rather than hinder a child's development. This seems to help people like me acquire new languages throughout our lives. "It's almost like the monolingual brain is on a diet, but the bilingual brain shows us the full, plump borders of the language tissue that are available," says Petitto.

Indeed, the closer the researchers looked, the more benefits they discovered, some of which span a broad range of skills.

Bialystok first stumbled upon one of these advantages while asking children to spot whether various sentences were grammatically correct. Both monolinguals and bilinguals could see the mistake in phrases such as "apples growed on trees," but differences arose when they considered nonsensical sentences such as "apples grow on noses." The monolinguals, flummoxed by the silliness of the phrase, incorrectly reported an error, whereas the bilinguals gave the right answer (*Developmental Psychology*, vol 24, p. 560).

Bialystok suspected that rather than reflecting expertise in grammar, their performance demonstrated improvement in what is called the brain's "executive system," a broad suite of mental skills that centre on the ability to block out irrelevant information and concentrate on a task at hand. In this case, they were better able to focus on the grammar while ignoring the meaning of words. Sure enough, bilingual kids in subsequent studies aced a range of problems that directly tested the trait. Another executive skill involves the ability to switch between different tasks without becoming confused, and bilinguals are better at these kinds of challenges too. When categorising objects, for instance, they can jump from considering the shape to the colour without making errors (*Bilingualism: Language and Cognition*, vol 13, p. 253).

A Second Viewpoint

These traits are critical to almost everything we do, from reading and mathematics to driving. Improvements therefore result in greater mental flexibility, which may explain why the bilingual people performed so well in Peal and Lambert's tests, says Bialystok.

Its virtues may even extend to our social skills. Paula Rubio-Fernández and Sam Glucksberg, both psychologists at Princeton University, have found that bilinguals are better at putting themselves in other people's shoes to understand their side of a situation. This is because they can more easily block out what they already know and focus on the other viewpoint (*Journal of Experimental Psychology: Learning, Memory and Cognition*, vol 38, p. 211).

So what is it about speaking two languages that makes the bilingual brain so flexible and focused? An answer comes from the work of Viorica Marian at Northwestern University in Evanston, Illinois, and colleagues, who used eye-tracking devices to follow the gaze of volunteers engaged in various activities. In one set-up, Marian placed an array of objects in front of Russian-English bilinguals and asked them to "pick up the marker," for example.

The twist is that the names of some of the objects in the two languages sound the same but have different meanings. The Russian word for stamp sounds like "marker," for instance, which in English can mean *pen*. Although the volunteers never misunderstood the question, the eye-tracker showed that they would quickly glance at the alternative object before choosing the correct one (*Bilingualism: Language and Cognition*, vol 6, p. 97).

This almost-imperceptible gesture gives away an important detail about the workings of the bilingual brain, revealing that the two languages are constantly competing for attention in the back of our minds. As a result, whenever we bilinguals speak, write, or listen to the radio, our brain is busy choosing the right word while inhibiting the same term from the other language. It is a considerable test of executive control—just the kind of cognitive workout, in fact, that is common in many commercial "brain-training" programs, which often require you to ignore distracting information while tackling a task.

It did not take long for scientists to wonder whether these mental gymnastics might help the brain resist the ravages of ageing. After all, there is plenty of evidence to suggest that other forms of brain exercise can create "cognitive reserve," a kind of mental padding that cushions the mind against age-related decline. To find out, Bialystok and her colleagues collected data from 184 people diagnosed with dementia, half of whom were bilingual. The results, published in 2007, were startling—symptoms started to appear in the bilingual people four years later than in their monolingual peers (*Neuropsychologia*, vol 45, p. 459). Three years later, they repeated the study with a further 200 people showing signs of Alzheimer's disease. Again, there was around a five-year delay in the onset of symptoms in bilingual patients (*Neurology*, vol 75, p. 1726). The results held true even after factors such as occupation and education were taken into account. "I was as surprised as anyone that we found such large effects," Bialystok says.

Besides giving us bilinguals a brain boost, speaking a second language may have a profound effect on behaviour.

Neuroscientists and psychologists are coming to accept that language is deeply entwined with thought and reasoning, leading some to wonder whether bilingual people act differently depending on which language they are speaking. That would certainly tally with my experience. People often tell me that I seem different when I speak English compared with when I speak French.

Such effects are hard to characterise, of course, since it is not easy to pull apart the different strands of yourself. Susan Ervin-Tripp, now at the University of California, Berkeley, found an objective way to study the question in the 1960s, when she asked Japanese-English bilinguals to complete a set of unfinished sentences in two separate sessions—first in one language, then the other. She found that her volunteers consistently used very different endings depending on the language. For example, given the sentence "Real friends should" a person using Japanese replied "help each other out," yet in English opted for "be very frank." Overall, the responses seemed to reflect how monolinguals of either language tended to complete the task. The findings led Ervin-Tripp to suggest that bilinguals use two mental channels, one for each language, like two different minds.

Her theory would seem to find support in a number of recent studies. David Luna from Baruch College in New York City and colleagues, for example, recently asked bilingual English-Spanish volunteers to watch TV adverts featuring women—first in one language and then six months later in the other—and then rate the personalities of the characters involved. When the volunteers viewed the ads in Spanish, they tended to rate the women as independent and extrovert, but when they saw the advert in English they described the same characters as hopeless and dependent (*Journal of Consumer Research,* vol 35, p. 279). Another study found that Greek-English bilinguals reported very different emotional reactions to the same story depending on the language—finding themselves "indifferent" to the character in one version, but feeling "concerned" for his progress in the other, for example (*Journal of Multilingual and Multicultural Development,* vol 25, p. 124).

One explanation is that each language brings to mind the values of the culture we experienced while learning it, says Nairán Ramírez-Esparza, a psychologist at the University of Washington in Seattle. She recently asked bilingual Mexicans to rate their personality in English and Spanish questionnaires. Modesty is valued more highly in Mexico than it is in the US, where assertiveness gains respect, and the language of the questions seemed to trigger these differences. When questioned in Spanish, each volunteer was more humble than when the survey was presented in English.

Some of the behavioural switches may be intimately linked to the role of language as a kind of scaffold that supports and structures our memories. Many studies have found that we are more likely to remember an object if we know its name, which may explain why we have so few memories of early childhood. There is even some evidence that the grammar of a language can shape your memory. Lera Boroditsky at Stanford University in California recently found that Spanish speakers are worse at remembering who caused an accident than English speakers, perhaps because they tend to use impersonal phrases like "Se rompió el florero" ("the vase broke itself") that do not state the person behind the event (*Psychonomic Bulletin Review,* vol 18, p. 150).

The result seems to be that a bilingual person's recollections will change depending on the language they are [sic] speaking. In a clever but simple experiment, Marian and Margarita Kaushanskaya, then at Northwestern University, asked Mandarin-English bilinguals a general knowledge question, first in one language then the other. For instance, they were asked to "name a statue of someone standing with a raised arm while looking into the distance." They found people were more likely to recall the Statue of Liberty when asked in English, and a statue of Mao when asked in Mandarin (*Psychonomic Bulletin & Review,* p. 14, vol 925). The same seems to occur when bilinguals recall personal, autobiographical memories. "So childhood memories will come up faster and more often when you are reinstating that language," Marian says.

Despite the recent progress, the researchers may just be seeing the tip of the iceberg when it comes to the impact of bilingualism, and many questions remain. Chief among them will be the question of whether any monolingual person could

cash in on the benefits. If so, what better incentive to bolster language education in schools, which is flagging in both the UK and US.

Much has been made of the difficulties of learning a new language later in life, but the evidence so far suggests the effort should pay off. "You can learn another language at any age, you can learn it fluently, and you can see benefits to your cognitive system," says Marian. Bialystok agrees that late language-learners gain an advantage, even if the performance boost is usually less pronounced than in bilingual speakers. "Learn a language at any age, not to become bilingual, but just to remain mentally stimulated," she says. "That's the source of cognitive reserve."

As it is, I'm grateful that particular challenge is behind me. My mother could never have guessed the extent to which her words would change my brain and the way I see my world, but I'm certain it was worth the effort. And for all that I just have to say: Merci!

Critical Thinking

1. What was the view of educators regarding bilingualism from the 19th century until recently?
2. What has recent evidence shown regarding bilinguals?
3. How has new technology sparked renewed interest in this subject?
4. What has been the popular theory regarding babies learning language? How do bilingual babies compare with monolingual babies with respect to acquiring new languages? With respect to spotting grammatical correctness in sentences?
5. What skill differences have been showing up in further tests?
6. In what ways do these skills extend beyond the linguistic?
7. What do such studies reveal about "executive control" in bilinguals?
8. What appears to be the relationship between "gymnastic abilities" and resistance to the ravages of aging?
9. What is the evidence that bilinguals are affected by the language they speak in terms of their values, how they perceive others, and what they remember?
10. Why should people be encouraged to learn a language at any age?

Create Central

www.mhhe.com/createcentral

Internet References

Exploratorium Magazine: "The Evolution of Languages"
www.exploratorium.edu/exploring/language
Linguistic Inquiry and Word Count
www.liwc.net

Unit 3

UNIT

Prepared by: Elvio Angeloni, *Pasadena City College*

The Organization of Society and Culture

Human beings do not interact with one another or think about their world in random fashion. They engage in structured and recurrent physical and mental activities. Such patterns of behavior and thought—referred to here as the organization of society and culture—may be seen in a number of different contexts, from the mating preferences of hunter-gatherer bands to whether a mother breastfeeds her child to the decisions made by neighboring tribes as to whether they shall go to war or establish peaceful relations with each other.

Of special importance are the ways in which people make a living—in other words, the production, distribution, and consumption of goods and services. It is only by knowing the basic subsistence systems that we can hope to gain insight into other levels of social and cultural phenomena, for they are all inextricably bound together. Noting the various aspects of a sociocultural system in harmonious balance, however, does not imply an anthropological seal of approval. To understand infanticide

(killing of the newborn) in the manner that it is practiced among some peoples is neither to condone nor condemn it. The adaptive patterns that have been in existence for a great length of time, such as many of the patterns of hunters and gatherers, probably owe their existence to their contributions to long-term human survival.

Anthropologists, however, are not content with the data derived from their individual experiences with others. On the contrary, personal descriptions must become the basis for sound anthropological theory. Otherwise, they remain meaningless, isolated relics of culture in the manner of museum pieces. In other words, while anthropological accounts of field are to some extent descriptive, they should also serve to challenge both the academic and "commonsense" notions about why people behave and think the way they do. They remind us that assumptions are never really safe and if anthropologists are kept on their toes, it is the field as a whole that benefits.

Article   Prepared by: Elvio Angeloni

How We Hounded Out the *Neanderthals*

Soon after humans arrived in Europe, *Neanderthals* died out. Was this because we had "living weapons", asks Pat Shipman.

PAT SHIPMAN

Learning Outcomes

After reading this article, you will be able to:

- Discuss the advantages our ancestors had that allowed them to replace the *Neanderthals* in Europe.
- Discuss the factors that made our ancestors better hunters.
- Discuss the reintroduction of wolves into Yellowstone National Park as a model for understanding *Neanderthal* replacement in Europe.
- Discuss the evidence for the domestication of dogs and how it happened.
- Discuss the advantages of the human domestication of dogs.

Humans are natural invaders, the mammalian equivalent of Burmese pythons, cane toads, and Asian carp. Our species came from Africa and invaded Europe about 50,000 years ago. Perhaps surprisingly, this invasiveness may explain why we have outlasted our last close relatives, *Neanderthals*, by tens of thousands of years. I believe that the key to our success as invaders lies in our partnership with a weapon with a wagging tail: the domestic dog.

When early modern humans first entered Europe, *Neanderthals* had been living there for roughly 250,000 years. They knew the terrain and ecosystem intimately. They shared many of our physical and behavioural traits, such as large brains, specialised abilities for making tools and fire, and methods for hunting the same large game. Genetically, *Neanderthals* were so much like us that we interbred, albeit rarely. Yet the evidence is very clear that we thrived during the period of overlap, while *Neanderthals* went extinct. Why?

Climate instability has been a favourite candidate. Severe fluctuations from warmer and wetter to colder and drier, and back again, started about 45,000 years ago. Until recently, *Neanderthal* sites appeared to show a pattern of progressive retreat to more southerly, milder locations, ending with their extinction about 27,000 years ago. However, improvements in radiocarbon dating have dramatically undercut this interpretation.

All well-dated Neanderthal sites have been found to be at least 39,000 years old and no southerly shift through time is evident. Besides, we faced the vacillating climate at the same time as the *Neanderthals* and they had survived similar cold periods before our arrival. Some new factors were at work.

Our presence was one element. Did we force *Neanderthals* into extinction? Yes, but not through violence or killing—once a preferred hypothesis. We were simply better at hunting than they were. A model for understanding how one invasive predator might outcompete a similar rival comes from the reintroduction of wolves to Yellowstone National Park in the US. Though wolves were integral to that ecosystem for millennia, they were wiped out there by settlers by about 1920. The effects of removing the wolf were striking. Coyotes formed larger, more wolf-like packs, while elk populations soared, changing the vegetation close to rivers by eating young trees and shrubs. Pronghorn antelope populations dropped as more coyotes preyed on their offspring; beavers disappeared from the park and songbirds declined in number.

Reintroducing just 31 wolves in the mid-1950s transformed the ecosystem again. Wolves targeted their closest competitor, killing coyotes in confrontations over carcasses and consuming enough prey to hinder their survival. Coyotes avoided areas favoured by wolves and shifted to smaller prey. Coyote packs fragmented and their overall population declined sharply. More pronghorns survived; elk herds diminished; and riverine vegetation came back, encouraging the return of beavers and songbirds.

In a similar way, *Neanderthals* bore the brunt of our invasive impact. They might have abandoned areas where their rivals were numerous, as coyotes did, but unlike them did not shift to different prey. Wolves dominate coyotes by sheer size and power. We humans dominated through our diverse hunting skills. One advantage is that we had projectile weapons, while *Neanderthals* had only handheld or muscle-powered weapons. Distance killing exposed us to far fewer risks and expended less energy. More food for less work meant more energy for reproduction. The second advantage is that, at about the time of the demise of the *Neanderthals*, we "invented" dogs.

We did not set out to create dogs. There were no other domesticated animals at the time and, until recently, no one thought domestic dogs appeared until about 15,000 years ago. In 2009, a team led by my Belgian colleague Mietje Germonpré began investigating ways to tell dogs apart from wolves using statistical methods. These two canids are so similar that they can and do interbreed; no simple genetic or physical trait distinguishes them. However, a complex analysis of skull shape reliably separates wolves from both modern dogs and from the accepted prehistoric wild dogs. Analysing additional fossil canid skulls, the team recognised a group of ancient dog-like animals intermediate in shape between wolves and prehistoric dogs. I call them wolf-dogs, not because I believe they were hybrids, but because deciding which group they belonged to is not easy.

Whatever wolf-dogs were, they were different from contemporary wolves. Chemical analysis of their bones shows their diets differed from those of humans or wolves at the same sites. Wolf-dog mitochondrial DNA differs from that of any other canid and is very primitive compared with that of other modern and fossil dogs and wolves.

The oldest wolf-dog yet identified (there are now more than 40) is an astonishing 36,000 years old, much older than expected for a domesticated animal. How long would domestication take when no one could possibly know how to do it? The oft-cited silver fox farm experiment, conducted in Siberia, produced a domesticated fox in 40 generations. However, the original foxes were not wild—their ancestors had been in captivity for 50 years—and they were caged, so only those chosen by experimenters bred. These conditions were not like those in the first domestication, which probably took thousands of years of trial and error. If it did, then wolf-dog domestication started before *Neanderthals* went extinct. The telltale evidence of early domestication should lie in behaviour. Dogs travel with us, bond with us, cooperate with us, and change our lives. They are our best friends. Wolves are not.

The prediction that the presence of wolf-dogs would coincide with a behavioural shift in humans is borne out by the archaeological record. All known wolf-dogs occur in sites created by humans, not *Neanderthals*. The sites themselves are extraordinary and contain the bones of dozens, even hundreds, of woolly mammoths, though mammoths were previously rare in archaeological sites. Some were clearly hunted, their bones butchered, skinned, and charred. The sites include hearths, tools and huts built from mammoth bones. Though top predators are always rare in ecosystems, wolf remains at these sites are so abundant that they must have been targeted. Their luxuriant fur would be useful in near-Arctic conditions, and territorial wolf-dogs—like wolves and dogs today—would probably not tolerate the presence of any other canid.

Even if wolf-dogs were poorly domesticated, cooperating with them would have offered huge advantages. We gave them food, shelter, and protection. They provided faster pursuit of prey and the ability to track by smell. They could surround and harass large prey until they tired, making our long-distance weapons more successful and saving wolf-dogs from risk. Territorial wolf-dogs defended the carcasses, the camp, and us, enabling us to have longer-term settlements close to the kill site. Wolf-dogs enlarged our ecological niche, enabling us to out-compete *Neanderthals*.

This hypothesis still requires elaboration and testing. Not everyone accepts the evidence that wolf-dogs were domesticated so very early, or that they were instrumental in pushing *Neanderthals* into extinction. But I think that the combination of humans and dogs was unstoppable. Since then, we and our best friends have invaded other continents and initiated the sixth global extinction. Working with humans, dogs are deadly weapons.

Pat Shipman is a palaeoanthropologist and former adjunct professor of biological anthropology at Pennsylvania State University. Her book *The Invaders: How humans and their dogs drove Neanderthals to extinction* is out this month.

Critical Thinking

1. Why does the author think that climate change cannot explain the replacement of the *Neanderthals* by our ancestors?
2. What factors made our ancestors better hunters than the *Neanderthals*?
3. How does the reintroduction of wolves into Yellowstone National Park serve as a model for understanding *Neanderthal* replacement in Europe by our ancestors?
4. How and why did the domestication of dogs occur?

Internet References

Max Planck Institute for Evolutionary Biology
   http://wwwstaff.eva.mpg.de/~paabo/
Origin of the domestic dog
   https://en.wikipedia.org/wiki/Origin_of_the_domestic_dog

Article   Prepared by: Elvio Angeloni

From Wolf to Dog

Scientists are racing to solve the enduring mystery of how a large, dangerous carnivore evolved into our best friend.

VIRGINIA MORELL

Learning Outcomes

After reading this article, you will be able to:

- Discuss the differences between dogs and wolves that seem to be the result of dog domestication.
- Discuss the difficulty in identifying the time and place of dog domestication.
- Discuss the evidence for dog domestication during the hunter-gatherer era.
- Identify the physical characteristics that distinguish domesticated dogs from wolves.

When you have cared for dogs and wild wolves from the time they are little more than a week old and have bottle-fed and nurtured them day and night, you are wise to their differences. Since 2008 Zsófia Virányi, an ethologist at the Wolf Science Center in Austria, and her colleagues have been raising the two species to figure out what makes a dog a dog—and a wolf a wolf. At the center, the researchers oversee and study four packs of wolves and four packs of dogs, containing anywhere from two to six animals each. They have trained the wolves and dogs to follow basic commands, to walk on leashes and to use their nose to tap the screen of a computer monitor so that they can take cognition tests. Yet despite having lived and worked with the scientists for seven years, the wolves retain an independence of mind and behavior that is most undoglike.

"You can leave a piece of meat on a table and tell one of our dogs, 'No!' and he will not take it," Virányi says. "But the wolves ignore you. They'll look you in the eye and grab the meat"—a disconcerting assertiveness that she has experienced on more than one occasion. And when this happens, she wonders yet again how the wolf ever became the domesticated dog.

"You can't have an animal—a large carnivore—living with you and behaving like that," she says. "You want an animal that's like a dog; one that accepts 'No!'"

Dogs' understanding of the absolute no may be connected to the structure of their packs, which are not egalitarian like those of the wolves but dictatorial, the center's researchers have discovered. Wolves can eat together, Virányi notes. Even if a dominant wolf flashes its teeth and growls at a subordinate, the lower-ranked member does not move away. The same is not true in dog packs, however. "Subordinate dogs will rarely eat at the same time as the dominant one," she observes. "They don't even try." Their studies also suggest that rather than expecting to cooperate on tasks with humans, dogs simply want to be told what to do.

How the independent-minded, egalitarian wolf changed into the obedient, waiting-for-orders dog and what role ancient humans played in achieving this feat baffle Virányi: "I try to imagine how they did it, and I really can't."

Virányi is not alone in her bafflement. Although researchers have successfully determined the time, location and ancestry of nearly every other domesticated species, from sheep to cattle to chickens to guinea pigs, they continue to debate these questions for our best friend, *Canis familiaris*. Scientists also know why humans developed these other domesticated animals—to have food close at hand—but they do not know what inspired us to allow a large, wild carnivore into the family homestead. Yet dogs were the first domesticated species, a status that makes the mystery of their origin that much more perplexing.

As inscrutable as the mystery is, scientists are piecing it together. In the past few years they have made several break-throughs. They can now say with confidence that contrary to received wisdom, dogs are not descended from the gray wolf species that persists today across much of the Northern Hemisphere, from Alaska to Siberia to Saudi Arabia, but from an unknown and extinct wolf. They are also certain that this domestication event took place while humans were still hunter-gatherers and not after they became agriculturalists, as some investigators had proposed.

At what time and in what location wolves became dogs and whether it was only a one-time event are questions that a large research team, composed of once competing scientists, has just started to tackle. The researchers are visiting museums, universities and other institutions around the world to study collections of canine fossils and bones, and they are readying genetic samples from ancient and modern dogs and wolves for the most comprehensive comparison to date. When they are finished, they will be very close to knowing when and where—if not exactly how—wolves first began down the path toward becoming our trusted companions. Answers to these questions will complement the growing body of evidence for how humans and dogs influenced one another after that relationship was first forged.

Mixed Signals

When modern humans arrived in Europe perhaps 45,000 years ago, they encountered the gray wolf and other types of wolves, including the megafaunal wolf, which pursued large game such as mammoths. By that time wolves had already proved themselves among the most successful and adaptable species in the canid family, having spread across Eurasia to Japan and into the Middle East and North America. They were not confined to a single habitat type but flourished in tundra, steppelands, deserts, forests, coastal regions, and the high altitude of the Tibetan Plateau. And they competed with the newly arrived humans for the same prey—mammoths, deer, aurochs, woolly rhinoceroses, antelopes, and horses. In spite of this competition, one type of wolf, perhaps a descendant of a megafaunal wolf, apparently began living close to people. For many years scientists concurred on the basis of small portions of the genome that this species was the modern gray wolf (*Canis lupus*) and that this canid alone gave rise to dogs.

But last January geneticists discovered that this long-held "fact" was wrong. Repeated interbreeding between gray wolves and dogs, which share 99.9 percent of their DNA, had produced misleading signals in the earlier studies. Such consorting between the two species continues today: wolves with black coats received the gene for that color from a dog; shepherd dogs in Georgia's Caucasus Mountains mate so often with the local wolves that hybrid ancestors are found in both species' populations, and between 2 and 3 percent of the sampled animals are first-generation hybrids. (Building on the admixture theme, in June researchers writing in *Current Biology* reported on the sequencing of DNA from a 35,000-year-old wolf fossil from Siberia. This species appears to have contributed DNA to high-latitude dogs such as huskies through ancient interbreeding.)

Analyzing whole genomes of living dogs and wolves, last January's study revealed that today's Fidos are not the descendants of modern gray wolves. Instead the two species are sister taxa, descended from an unknown ancestor that has since gone extinct. "It was such a long-standing view that the gray wolf we know today was around for hundreds of thousands of years and that dogs derived from them," says Robert Wayne, an evolutionary geneticist at the University of California, Los Angeles. "We're very surprised that they're not." Wayne led the first genetic studies proposing the ancestor–descendant relationship between the two species and more recently was one of the 30 co-authors of the latest study, published in *PLOS Genetics*, that debunked that notion.

More surprises may come from renewed efforts to nail down the timing and location of dog domestication. Previous studies left a confusing trail. The first analysis, carried out in 1997, focused on the genetic differences between dogs and gray wolves and concluded that dogs may have been domesticated some 135,000 years ago. A later study by some members of the same group indicated that dogs originated in the Middle East.

But another analysis, which examined the DNA of 1,500 modern dogs that was published in 2009, argued that dogs were first domesticated in southern China less than 16,300 years ago. Then, in 2013, a team of scientists compared the mitochondrial genomes of ancient European and American dogs and wolves with their modern counterparts. It concluded that dogs originated in Europe between 32,000 and 19,000 years ago.

Evolutionary biologist Greger Larson of the University of Oxford, who is co-leading the recently launched multidisciplinary dog-domestication project, says the previous studies, while important, have shortcomings. He faults the 1997 and 2009 studies for relying solely on DNA from modern dogs and the last one for its geographically limited samples. "You can't solve this problem by using modern animals alone as windows to the past," Larson says. The studies of modern dog DNA are not sufficiently informative, he explains, because people have moved and interbred dogs around the world numerous times, blurring their genetic heritage. Any regional signatures that might have helped identify where they were domesticated has long since been lost.

To further muddy the picture, "wolves have a ridiculously broad distribution across the world," Larson explains. In contrast, he points out, the ancestors of most other domesticated species, such as sheep and chickens, had much smaller geographical ranges, making it far easier to trace their origins.

Larson suspects that several geographically disparate populations of the ancestral wolf species may have contributed to the making of today's dog. It would not be the first time such a thing happened: Larson has shown that pigs were domesticated twice—once in the Near East and once in Europe. Intriguingly, enigmatic fossils from Belgium, the Czech Republic and southwestern Siberia that date to between 36,000 and 33,000 years ago and exhibit a mix of wolf and dog features hint at the possibility of at least three independent instances of domestication attempts from an ancestral wolf. But the anatomical characteristics of these fossils alone cannot answer the question of where dogs came from.

To solve the dog-domestication puzzle, Larson and his collaborators are using two key techniques employed in the pig study: they are undertaking a more thorough analysis of thousands of modern and ancient samples of dog and wolf DNA from individuals across the globe and are using a fairly new technique for measuring bones. Called geometric morphometrics, this method enables scientists to quantify certain traits, such as the curves of a skull, and so better compare the bones of individuals. Previously researchers relied primarily on the length of a canid's snout and the size of the canine teeth to distinguish dogs from wolves. Dogs' snouts are generally shorter, their canines are smaller, and their teeth are on the whole more crowded than those of wolves. The new method should identify other, perhaps more telling differences. Together these techniques should yield a far more detailed picture of dog domestication than any other approach has to date.

Close Encounters

Although the when and where of dog domestication remain open questions, scientists now have a general idea of which kind of human society was the first to establish a close relationship with dogs. Perhaps not surprisingly, this question, too, has generated debate over the years. Some investigators have argued that settled agriculturalists had that distinction. After all, the other domesticated animal species all entered the human realm after people started farming and putting down roots. But other researchers credited earlier hunter-gatherers with being the first to have dogs. Wayne says that his team's latest DNA study has at last ended this part of the debate. "The domestication of the dog occurred prior to the agricultural revolution," he asserts. "It happened when people were still hunter-gatherers," sometime between 32,00 and 18,800 years ago. (Agriculture is thought to have begun in a big way roughly 12,000 years ago in the Middle East.)

And that finding leads back to the questions Virányi and most everyone who owns and loves a dog has: How did these hunter-gatherers do it? Or did they? What if the first dogs—which, it is important to remember, would have at first been more wolf than dog—showed up on their own?

The genus *Canis* goes back about 7 million years, and although some members of that group, such as jackals and the Ethiopian wolf, lived in Africa, the birthplace of humanity, there is no evidence that the earliest humans tried to domesticate any of these species. Only after modern humans spread out from Africa and into Europe 45,000 years ago did the wolf-dog-human triad begin to form.

Hints about the evolving relationship between canids and early modern humans have come from the paleontological and archaeological records. Take the canid remains unearthed between 1894 and 1930 at Předmostí, a roughly 27,000-year-old settlement in the Bečva Valley in what is now the Czech Republic. The ancient people who lived and died there are known to us as the Gravettians, after a site with similar cultural artifacts in La Gravette, France. The Czech Gravettians were mammoth hunters, killing more than 1,000 of the great creatures at this one site alone. They ate the behemoths' meat, used their shoulder blades to cover human remains and decorated their tusks with engravings. They also killed wolves. Canids are the most abundant type of mammal at the site after mammoths, and their remains include seven complete skulls. But some of the canid skulls do not look exactly like those of wolves. Three in particular stand out, says Mietje Germonpré, a paleontologist at the Royal Belgian Institute of Natural Sciences in Brussels. Compared with the wolf skulls found at Předmostí, the three unusual ones "have shorter snouts, broader braincases and crowded teeth," she notes.

These kinds of anatomical changes are the first signs of domestication, Germonpré and others say. Similar changes are found in the skulls of the silver foxes that are the focus of a famous, long-running experiment at Novosibirsk State University in Russia. Since 1959, researchers there have selected the foxes for tameness and bred them. Over the generations their coats have become spotted, their ears floppy, their tails curly, their snouts shorter and wider—even though the scientists have been selecting only for behavior. Similar changes are seen in other domesticated species, including rats and mink. Investigators have yet to explain why docile animals are consistently altered in these ways. They do know that the tame silver foxes have smaller adrenal glands and much lower levels of adrenaline than their wild counterparts.

Last year other scientists came up with a testable hypothesis: tame animals may have fewer or defective neural crest cells. These embryonic cells play a key role in the development of the teeth, jaws, ears and pigment-producing cells—as well as the nervous system, including the fight-or-flight response. If they are right, then all those cute domestic traits—spotted coats, curly tails, floppy ears—are a side effect of domestication.

Germonpré suspects that the apparent domestication at Předmostí was a dead-end event; she doubts that these animals are related to today's dogs. Nevertheless, to Germonpré, "they are dogs—Paleolithic dogs." She says these early dogs probably looked very much like today's huskies, although they would have been larger, about the size of a German shepherd. Germonpré calls the Předmostí specimens "dogs" because of what she interprets as some type of relationship between the canids and the Gravettians. For instance, a dog's lower jaw was found near a child's skeleton, according to the diary of the original excavator.

The dogs were also included in rituals in ways that other species were not. In one case, a Gravettian tucked what is most likely a piece of mammoth bone between the front teeth of one of the dog skulls after the animal died and arranged its jaws so that they clamped together on the bone. Germonpré suspects that an ancient mammoth hunter placed the bone there as part of a ritual related to hunting, or to help sustain in death an animal the hunter revered, or to enable the dog to assist a human in the afterlife. "You see this kind of thing in the ethnographic record," she says, citing, as one example, a Chukchi ceremony in Siberia for a deceased woman in the early twentieth century. A reindeer was sacrificed and its stomach placed in the mouth of a dead dog's head, which was then positioned to protect the woman on her death journey.

Many researchers imagine that these early people set about making the wolf into the dog to help us hunt big game. In her book *The Invaders*, published by Harvard University Press earlier this year, anthropologist Pat Shipman argues that the first dogs (or wolf-dogs, as she calls them) were like a new and superior technology and helped the mammoth-hunting modern humans outcompete the *Neanderthals*. But she, Wayne, Larson and others think that wolves joined forces with humans on their own; that the canny, adaptable canids identified us as a new ecological niche they could exploit. The alternative scenario—people brazenly raiding wolf dens to steal pups young enough for taming—would have been a dangerous undertaking. And raising wolves in camps with young children would have presented another serious risk.

"We didn't do [domestication] deliberately; not at first," Larson surmises. Instead wolves most likely started following people for the same reason that ants trail into our kitchens—"to take advantage of a nutritional resource, our trash." Over time, some of these camp-following wolves increasingly lost their fear of people—and vice versa—and a mutually beneficial relationship developed. Wolf-dogs would sniff out prey for us, and we would share the resulting meat with them. (Circumstantial evidence for this scenario comes from the silver fox experiment. By selecting foxes that were less fearful of humans, the researchers at Novosibirsk eventually developed a silver fox

that runs to greet people. Most silver foxes in captivity hide in the back of their cage.)

There is just one problem with this imagined event, at least at Předmostí: Germonpré's early dogs were not eating mammoth meat even though that is what the humans were dining on; isotopic analysis of the Paleolithic dogs' bones indicates that they were eating reindeer, which was not a favored food of the people who inhabited the site. The Předmostí dogs also had broken teeth and severe facial injuries, many of which had healed. "Those could be signs of fighting with other dogs," Germonpré says, "or of being hit with sticks." She pictures the human-dog bond developing via the mammoth hunters' canid rituals. In this scenario, the hunter-gatherers brought pups to their camps, perhaps after killing the adult wolves, just as many modern nomadic peoples bring baby or young animals to their settlements. The mammoth bones at Předmostí show no signs of being gnawed by canids, which suggests they were not free to roam and scavenge people's scraps. Rather humans probably tied the canids up, fed them what appears to have been second-rate food, given that the humans were not eating it, and even bred them—all to ensure a ready supply of victims for their ritualistic sacrifices.

Breeding wolves in captivity would lead to the anatomical changes that Germonpré has documented in the Předmostí dogs and could even produce a less fearful and independent animal as seen in the Novosibirsk silver foxes.

Confined, beaten, fed a restricted diet, the dogs at Předmostí would likely have understood the meaning of "No!" There is no evidence at Předmostí or other comparably old sites where dog remains have been uncovered that the ancient hunter-gatherers there regarded the canines as their friends, companions or hunting pals, Germonpré observes. "That relationship came later."

Shifting Fortunes

If Germonpré is right, then dog domestication may have begun quite early and under circumstances that were not favorable for the dogs. Not every scientist agrees that Germonpré's dogs are dogs, however. Some prefer the wolf-dog designation or simply "wolf" because their taxonomic status is not clear either from their morphology or genetics. (Larson expects to resolve this question over the course of his mega project.)

The earliest undisputed dog on record, a 14,000-year-old specimen from a site called Bonn-Oberkassel in Germany, tells a very different story of dog domestication, evincing a much more affectionate bond between humans and canines. In the early 1900s archaeologists excavating the site found the dog's skeleton interred in a grave with the remains of a man about 50 years old and a woman about 20 to 25. When researchers see such associations, they know they are looking at a fully domesticated animal—one that is treasured and regarded so highly that it is given a burial as if it, too, were a member of its human family.

The Bonn-Oberkassel dog is not the only ancient hound to have received such honors. In Israel, at Ain Mallaha, a hunter-gatherer site dating to 12,000 years ago in the upper Jordan Valley, archaeologists discovered what is perhaps the most famous dog-human burial. The skeleton of an elderly person lies curled on its right side, its left arm stretched out under the head, with the hand resting gently on a puppy. The dog was about four to five months old and was placed there, archaeologists think, to be a companion to the deceased. Unlike the Předmostí dogs, this puppy was not battered; its remains were arranged lovingly with someone who may have cared for it.

Although such touching dog-human scenes are rare during this period, dog burials are not. And after about 10,000 years ago, the practice of entombing dogs increased. No other animal species is so consistently included in human mortuary rituals. People had come to see dogs in a different light, and this shift in attitude had a profound effect on dogs' evolution. Perhaps during this period dogs acquired their human social skills, such as abilities to read our facial expressions, understand our pointing gestures and gaze into our eyes (which increases oxytocin—the love hormone—in both dog and owner). "Dog burials happen after hunting moves away from the open plains and into dense forests," says Angela Perri, a zooarchaeologist at the Max Planck Institute for Evolutionary Anthropology in Leipzig, Germany, and a specialist on these burials. "Dogs in open environments might be good for helping you transport meat from killed mammoths but wouldn't necessarily help you hunt them," she says, noting that elephant hunters do not use dogs. "But dogs are excellent for hunting smaller game, such as deer and boar," that live in forests.

Beginning at least 15,000 years ago and probably somewhat earlier, Perri says, hunter-gatherers in Europe, Asia and the Americas began depending on their dogs' hunting skills for survival. Researchers cannot trace a direct genetic line from those animals to our pet pooches; nevertheless, they say, these animals were unquestionably dogs. "Good hunting dogs can find fresh tracks, and guide the hunters to the prey, and hold them at bay," says Perri, who has joined traditional hunters and their dogs in Japan and the U.S. "When people start using dogs for hunting, you see a switch in how people view them, and you start finding dog burials across the world." Such burials are not rituals or sacrifices, she emphasizes. "These are burials of admiration, where the dogs are interred with ocher, stone points and blades—male tools of hunting."

One of the most elaborate dog burials comes from Skateholm, Sweden, and is dated to about 7,000 years ago. Several dogs were found interred in the same area with dozens of humans. One was particularly celebrated and given the finest treatment

there of anyone, human or dog. "The dog was laid on its side, flint chips were scattered at its waist, and red deer antlers and a carved stone hammer were placed with it, and it was sprinkled with red ocher," Perri says. There is no indication of why this dog was so revered, but she suspects it must have been an excellent hunter and that its human owner mourned its death. "You see this relationship among hunters and their dogs today and in the ethnographic record," Perri observes, noting that Tasmanian hunter-gatherers in the late 19th century were quoted as saying, "Our dogs are more important than our children. Without them, we couldn't hunt; we wouldn't survive."

Early dogs provided other important services, too. The first known attempt at the kind of intentional selection that has shaped the evolution of *C. familiaris* comes from a site in Denmark dating to 8,000 years ago. The ancient hunter-gatherers there had three sizes of dogs, possibly bred for certain tasks. "I didn't expect to see something like dog breeds," Perri says, "but they had small, medium and large dogs." It is not clear what they used the small dogs for, but the medium-sized animals had the build of hunting dogs, and the larger ones, which were the size of Greenland sled dogs (about 70 pounds), most likely transported and hauled goods. With their warning barks, all the dogs would have served as camp sentinels, too.

The dog's status plunged when people developed farming. In early agricultural settlements, dog burials are rare. "The difference is so strong," Perri says. "When people are living as hunter-gatherers, there are tons of dog burials." But as agriculture spreads, the burials end. "Dogs are no longer as useful." That fall from grace, though, did not doom them to extinction—far from it. In many places, they began to turn up on the dinner table, providing a new reason to keep dogs around.

Not all agricultural cultures consigned Fido to the menu, however. Among those groups that tended livestock, dogs were sometimes bred for herding. Those that proved their worth could still end up pampered in the afterlife. In 2006 archaeologists discovered 80 mummified dogs buried in graves next to their human owners at a 1,000-year-old cemetery near Lima, Peru. The dogs had protected the Chiribaya people's llamas and, in return for their service, were well treated in life and death. Nearly 30 of the dogs were wrapped in finely woven llama-wool blankets, and llama and fish bones were set close to their mouth. The region's arid climate mummified the dogs' remains, preserving their fur and tissue. Unwrapped, the mummies resemble the small street dogs that roam Lima today, looking for a human to take them in and tell them what—and what not—to do. (That resemblance notwithstanding, the Chiribaya herding dogs are not related to Lima's modern-day mutts. Nor is there any evidence to support claims linking any of the breeds of antiquity anywhere to the modern, standard breeds of the American Kennel Club.)

Although the Chiribaya dogs and other dog burials in the Americas hail from the wrong place and time to represent the earliest stages of domestication, Larson and his colleagues are happily measuring their bones and sampling their DNA. That is because these early North American dogs descended from ancient European or Asian dogs; their bones and genes will help the scientists determine how many dog-domestication events occurred and where they took place. Thus far, in their attempt to study as many ancient canids as possible, the researchers have analyzed upward of 3,000 wolves, dogs, and other specimens that do not readily fall into either box. More than 50 scientists worldwide are helping with the effort. They expect to have a paper ready on their initial findings by this summer. Will we then finally know where and when the dog became domesticated? "I expect we'll be very close to an answer," Larson says. But we still won't know exactly how some long-lost type of wolf managed to become a creature that respects "No."

Critical Thinking

1. How do dogs differ from wolves anatomically and behaviorally?
2. When were dogs domesticated and why?
3. Discuss the "human social skills" of dogs.
4. How has the relationship between dogs and humans changed over time and why?

Internet References

Breeding Business
   https://breedingbusiness.com/origin-and-evolution-of-the-domestic-dog/
Duke Canine Cognition Center
   https://evolutionaryanthropology.duke.edu/research/dogs/research

VIRGINIA MORELL is a science writer based in Oregon. She covers evolution and animal behavior for *Science* and *National Geographic*, among other publications. Her latest book is *Animal Wise* (Crown, 2013).

Article   Prepared by: Elvio Angeloni, *Pasadena City College*

Breastfeeding and Culture

Katherine Dettwyler

Learning Outcomes

After reading this article, you will be able to:

- Discuss the benefit of breastfeeding for child, mother, and society.
- Discuss the factors that affect the practices of breastfeeding in various cultures.

In a perfect world—one where child health and cognitive development were optimal—all children would be breast-fed for as long as they wanted. As large-bodied, highly intelligent primates, that would be for a minimum of 2.5 years and as long as 6 or 7 years, or longer. In a perfect world, all mothers would know how to breastfeed and be supported in their efforts to do so by health care providers, spouses, friends, neighbors, co-workers, and the general beliefs of their culture.

Breastfeeding is, first and foremost, a way to provide protective immunities and health-promoting factors to children. Breast milk should be the primary source of nutrition for the first two years of life, complemented by appropriate solid foods around six months of age. Breast milk provides important immunities and nutrients, especially for growing brains, for as long as the child is breastfed. It is a source of physical and emotional comfort to a child, and for the mother it is the wellspring of the important mothering hormones, prolactin and oxytocin.

Ordinarily, childbirth is followed by breastfeeding, with its flood of prolactin, the "mothering hormone," and oxytocin, "the hormone of love." Both hormones elicit caretaking, affective, and protective behaviors by the mother towards her child. If the mother does not breastfeed, her body interprets this as "the baby died," and enters a state of hormonal grieving, preparing for a new attempt at reproduction. The mother, however, still has to cope with a newborn, and later a toddler, without the calming and nurturing influence of prolactin and oxytocin.

Like childbirth, however, breastfeeding is influenced by a variety of cultural beliefs, some directly related to breastfeeding itself, and others pertaining to a woman's role in society, to the proper relationship between mother and child, to the proper relationship between mother and father, and even to beliefs about breasts themselves.

One way of thinking about cultural influences on breastfeeding initiation and duration is based on the Demographic Transition, in which societies move from a pre-transition state of high birth and death rates, through a transitional stage of high birth but low death rates (resulting in rapid population growth), and eventually into a post-transition stage of low birth and death rates. Margaret Mead was the first to recognize an "Infant Feeding Transition." A culture begins in a pre-transition state of almost everyone breastfeeding for several years, then moves through a transitional stage of bottle-feeding. Three main forces conspire to move women away from breastfeeding: (1) the separation of their productive labor and their reproductive labor, as societies shift from subsistence-based economies to wage labor-based economies, and/or women are taken away from both productive and reproductive work to be their husband's social partners; (2) increasing confidence in the power of science to provide "better living through chemistry" coupled with decreasing confidence in the ability of women's bodies to function normally, and (3) the rise of commercial interests intent on making a profit by convincing women that breastfeeding is less healthy, difficult, primitive, and/or shameful. The transition is initiated by women with more education and higher incomes turning to shorter and shorter durations of breastfeeding, and eventually only wet-nursing (in previous centuries) or bottle-feeding (in the 20th and 21st centuries) from birth.

As time goes by, women with less education and lower income levels emulate their social superiors and adopt bottle-feeding as well. By the time the last of the lower classes have adopted bottle-feeding as being "modern and scientific," the well-educated upper-class women are returning to breastfeeding, first for short periods, and then for increasing durations. They have moved on to the post-transition stage. The return to breastfeeding by well-educated upper-class women is fueled by several factors, including research during the last few decades clearly documenting the superiority of breastfeeding over formula in terms of maternal and child health and child cognitive development, feminism's insistence that women's reproductive powers are of great value, and a general backlash against the infant formula companies for promoting their products in unethical ways. Primarily, in the United States it has been well-educated middle- and upper-class women who have fought for legislation to protect the rights of mothers to breastfeed in public, and for better maternity care and on-site child care facilities.

In the late 1950s, anthropologist Margaret Mead urged researchers to: "Find out how we can get from the working class mothers who breastfeed to the upper middle-class women who also breastfeed, without a generation of bottle feeders in between" (Raphael 1979). We still haven't figured out how to do this.

There are still a number of "pre-transition" cultures in the world, in which all women breastfeed each child for several years, but Western influence—particularly in the form of aggressive infant formula marketing strategies and the export of Western cultural beliefs about breasts as sex objects—is affecting even the remotest regions of the world. Korea, for example, is in the early stages of the transition from universal long-term breastfeeding to the adoption of bottles. Survey data reveal a decline in breastfeeding incidence and duration from the 1960s to the 1990s, led by upper-class, well-educated urban Korean women. China, likewise, has begun the transition to bottle-feeding, experiencing a rapid decline in the prevalence of breastfeeding in urban and periurban areas. Not surprisingly, China has been targeted by the infant formula companies as the next great market for their products.

Cuba is at the beginning of the infant feeding transition, with mothers of higher educational levels having the shortest duration of breastfeeding. Cuba seems to be well ahead of the United States in meeting established goals for maternal and child health through breastfeeding, with national strategies for supporting and promoting breastfeeding, including having all government hospitals participate in the World Health Organization's Baby-Friendly Hospital Initiative, and developing educational programs for day care centers and elementary and secondary schools to try to create a breastfeeding-friendly culture among both males and females from an early age. Cuba may be able to avoid a complete switch to bottle-feeding.

The Arabian Gulf countries (Bahrain, Kuwait, Oman, Qatar, Saudi Arabia, and the United Arab Emirates) are fully into the transitional phase, with middle- and upper-class women seldom breastfeeding, or only for a few weeks, and older women nursing longer than younger women. The influence of oil revenues on the lifestyles of these women, including the common employment of foreign housemaids and nannies, who bottle-feed the children, is fascinating and disturbing. The transition from full breastfeeding to almost full bottle-feeding has been particularly swift in this part of the world. "Westernized" hospital practices have been especially harmful, with hospital personnel and private clinics being used to promote the use of formula.

Australia, Canada, and the United States represent societies farthest along this "Infant Feeding Transition," with women of higher incomes and more education initiating breastfeeding in great numbers, and with increasing durations as well. This trend began in the 1970s, but was helped by the 1997 statement by the American Academy of Pediatrics that all children in the United States should be nursed for a minimum of one year (and thereafter as long as both mother and child wish), as well as by recent research showing that formula-fed children have lower IQs than their breastfed counterparts. In the United States, breastfeeding to the age of three years or beyond is becoming more and more common, as is breastfeeding siblings of different ages, known as "tandem nursing" (Dettwyler 2001). In the last decades, the

biggest leaps in initiating breastfeeding in the United States have been among WIC clients (women, infants, and children), who tend to be poor and less well-educated, indicating a trickle-down effect of breastfeeding from the upper classes, as well as the success of WIC Peer Counselor training programs.

Exactly how a particular region responds to influence from the Western industrialized nations and from the multinational infant formula companies depends on many different social, political, and economic factors. This makes it difficult to predict how the infant feeding transition will look in a specific region, or how long the bottle-feeding stage will last.

Cultural beliefs affect breastfeeding in other ways as well. Among the Bambara of Mali, people believe that because breast milk is made from a woman's blood, the process of breastfeeding creates a special relationship between a child and the woman who breastfeeds that child, whether or not she is the child's biological mother. In addition, breastfeeding creates a bond among all of the children who nurse from the same woman, whether or not they are biological siblings.

Having milk-siblings expands one's kinship network, providing more people one can call on for help in times of need. However, these kinship ties also prohibit marriage between the related children. In order to reduce the impact on potential marriage partners, women try to breastfeed other women's children only if they would already be excluded as marriage partners. Thus, a woman might wet-nurse the children of her co-wives, the children of her husband's brothers, or her grandchildren, while avoiding breastfeeding the children of her best friend, who she hopes will grow up to marry her own children. Similar beliefs about the "milk tie" are found among people in Haiti, Papua New Guinea, the Balkans, Burma, and among the Badawin of Kuwait and Saudi Arabia. In cultures where everyone is breastfed, or where everyone is bottle-fed, one's identity does not hinge on how one was fed. But in cultures entering or leaving the transition, feeding practices can be very important to one's identity. In a culture just entering the transition, to be bottle-fed is to have high status and be wealthy and modern. In a culture entering the final stage, to be breastfed is to have high status and be wealthy and modern.

In a wide variety of cultures, males are breastfed longer than females, sometimes much longer. These practices are supported by a variety of cultural beliefs, including the ideas that earlier weaning for girls insures a much-desired earlier menopause (Taiwan), that boys must be nursed longer so they will be willing to take care of their aged parents (Ireland), and that breast milk is the conduit for machismo, something boys need, but girls do not (Ecuador). Additionally, a number of societies have noted that males are physiologically weaker than females, more prone to illness and early death, so mothers nurse their sons longer to help ensure their survival.

Cultural beliefs about birth can have a profound influence on the success or failure of breastfeeding. Breastfeeding works best when the mother and baby are un-drugged at delivery, when they are kept together after birth, when the baby is not washed, when the baby is fed at the first cue (long before crying), when breastfeeding occurs early and often, when free formula samples and other gifts are not given to the mother, and when all those who surround the mother are knowledgeable and supportive of breastfeeding. Where the culture of birthing meets most or all of these criteria, we find higher rates of breastfeeding as well as longer durations. The World Health Organization's Baby-Friendly Hospital Initiative provides both a blueprint for optimal breastfeeding conditions and references to support their recommendations.

Cultural beliefs about how often children should breastfeed can help or hinder the process. The composition of human milk, as well as studies of human populations where children are allowed to breastfeed on demand, suggests that the natural frequency of breastfeeding is several times an hour for a few minutes each time, rather than according to a schedule, with longer feedings separated by several hours. Infrequent feeding in the early days and weeks of breastfeeding can permanently affect a mother's milk supply. As control of breast milk production gradually shifts from primarily endocrine (prolactin) to primarily autocrine (based on breast fullness) during the first few months postpartum, women who have been nursing on a three- to four-hour schedule may find that they no longer have sufficient milk to meet their babies' needs. A simple strategy of unrestricted breastfeeding from birth onwards would prevent this supply problem.

Perhaps the most pernicious cultural belief affecting breastfeeding is the one found in the United States and a small number of other (mostly Western) cultures—the belief that women's breasts are naturally erotic. American culture is obsessed with the sexual nature of women's breasts and their role in attracting and keeping male attention, as well as their role in providing sexual pleasure. This is reflected by the "normal" circumstances under which breasts are exposed in the United States (*Playboy* centerfolds, low-cut evening gowns, bikinis), by the phenomenon of breast augmentation surgery, by the association of breasts with sexual pleasure, and by the reactions of some people when they see women breastfeeding (embarrassment, horror, disgust, disapproval). In fact, the cultural belief that breasts are intrinsically erotic is just that, a cultural belief of limited distribution—one that has devastating consequences for women who want to breastfeed their children.

The mammary glands play no role in sexual behavior in any species other than humans. Among humans, the cross-cultural evidence clearly shows that most cultures do not define the breasts as sex objects. Extensive cross-cultural research in the 1940s and 1950s, published by Ford and Beach, found that, of 190 cultures surveyed, only 13 viewed women's breasts as sexually attractive. Likewise, 13 cultures out of 190 involved women's breasts in sexual activity. Of these latter 13, only three are also listed among the 13 where breasts are considered sexually attractive.

In most cultures, breasts are viewed solely as functional body parts, used to feed children—similar to how the typical American male views women's elbows, as devices to bend arms. Thus, in most cultures, it doesn't matter whether they are covered or not, or how big they are; husbands do not feel jealous of their nursing children, and women are never accused of breastfeeding for their own sexual pleasure. In the United States, and increasingly where Western ideas about breasts as sex objects are taking hold, women find that they must be

extremely discreet about where and how they breastfeed. They may get little support for breastfeeding, or even active resistance from jealous husbands; they may receive dirty looks or rude comments or be asked to go elsewhere (often the bathroom) to nurse. Still others are accused of sexually abusing their children for breastfeeding them longer than a year (Dettwyler 2001).

The evolution of cultural beliefs about breasts is difficult to pin down. Carolyn Latteier and Marilyn Yalom provide the most thorough research on the history of Western culture's obsession with breasts. The rise of both the infant formula industry and commercial pornography following World War II contributed to modern views of breasts as sex objects, rather than glands for producing milk for children.

Among health care providers themselves, a culture of denial about the health risks of formula contributes to the persistence of bottle-feeding. Many physicians view bottle-feeding as "almost as good" in spite of overwhelming research to the contrary. It is estimated that for every 1,000 deaths of infants in the United States, four of those deaths can be directly attributed to the use of infant formula. Additionally, children who are formula-fed have higher rates of many illnesses during childhood including diabetes, ear infections, gastrointestinal and upper respiratory infections, lymphoma, Sudden Infant Death Syndrome, and allergies. They continue to have higher rates of illnesses throughout life, including heart disease, some types of cancer, and multiple sclerosis. Children who are formula-fed likewise have lower average scores on intelligence tests and lower grades in school. Mothers who breastfeed their children, especially for longer durations, have lower rates of reproductive cancers (especially breast cancer), and lower rates of osteoporosis.

Unfortunately, obstetricians often view infant nutrition as the responsibility of the pediatrician, while the pediatrician claims that by the time the child is born, the mother has long since made up her mind about how she will feed her child. Many health care professionals say that they hesitate to discuss the dangers of formula for fear of "making women feel guilty." This is patronizing of parents and robs them of their chance to make an informed decision about this important area of child care.

In a perfect world, all cultural beliefs would support breastfeeding. The World Health Organization's Baby-Friendly Hospital Initiative and the Coalition for Improving Maternity Services' Mother-Friendly Childbirth Initiative are two attempts to clarify the best cultural practices for initiating breastfeeding. The Internet has also had a major impact on the culture of breastfeeding support. LactNet is an e-mail list for professionals who work in the lactation field. Kathleen Bruce and Kathleen Auerbach, both lactation consultants in the United States, began the list in March of 1995. It has grown to include more than 3,000 individuals from 38 countries who share ideas, beliefs, research studies, and clinical experience. Documents such as the Baby-Friendly Hospital Initiative and the Mother-Friendly Childbirth Initiative, and resources such as LactNet, are creating and sustaining a global culture of breastfeeding support.

Additional Resources

For Internet links related to this chapter, please visit our website at www.mhhe.com/dettwyler,

Ford, C. S., and F. A. Beach. *Patterns of Sexual Behavior.* New York: Harper & Row, 1951.

Giuliani, Rudolph W. (Introduction) and the editors of LIFE Magazine. *One Nation: America Remembers September 11, 2001.* New York: Little Brown & Company, 2001.

Kear, Adrian, and Deborah Lynn Steinberg, eds. *Mourning Diana: Nation, Culture and the Performance of Grief.* New York: Routledge, 1999.

Latteier, C. *Breasts: The Women's Perspective on an American Obsession.* Binghamton, NY: Haworth Press, 1998.

Podolefsky, Aaron, and Peter J. Brown, eds. *Applying Anthropology: An Introductory Reader.* 7th ed. New York: McGraw-Hill Higher Education, 2002.

Raphael, D. "Margaret Mead—A Tribute." *The Lactation Review* 4, no. 1 (1979), pp. 1–3.

Simopoulos, A. P., J. E. Dutra de Oliveira, and I. D. Desai, eds. *Behavioral and Metabolic Aspects of Breastfeeding: International Trends. World Review of Nutrition and Dietetics, Volume 78.* Basel, Switzerland: S. Karger, 1995.

Stuart-Macadam, Patricia, and Katherine A. Dettwyler, eds. *Breastfeeding: Biocultural Perspectives.* New York: Aldine de Gruyter Publishers, 1995.

Walker, M. "A Fresh Look at the Hazards of Artificial Infant Feeding, II." 1998. Available from the International Lactation Consultants Association.

Yalom, M. *A History of the Breast.* New York: Random House, Inc., 1997.

Critical Thinking

1. Discuss the importance of breastfeeding for both mother and child.
2. What kinds of cultural factors influence breastfeeding?
3. Discuss the main forces that move women away from breastfeeding.
4. What factors have fueled the return to breastfeeding?
5. How has Western influence brought about bottle-feeding in countries that are undergoing a transition? Why might Cuba be an exception in this regard?
6. Why are the Arabian Gulf countries "fully into the transitional phase"?
7. Describe the "Infant Feeding Transition" and why it is occurring.
8. How do cultural beliefs affect breastfeeding?
9. Why are males breastfed more often than females?
10. What are some of the detrimental effects of not breastfeeding?

Create Central

www.mhhe.com/createcentral

Internet References

Journal of Human Lactation
http://jhl.sagepub.com

American Anthropological Association Children and Childhood Interest Group
http://aaacig.usu.edu

Article   Prepared by: Elvio Angeloni, *Pasadena City College*

Meghalaya: Where Women Call the Shots

Many Indian women cry out for equality, but a matrilineal culture thrives with little parallel in the northeast.

SUBIR BHAUMIK

Learning Outcomes

After reading this article, you will be able to:

- Describe the matrilineal kinship system of the tribes of Meghalaya.

- Contrast marriage as a modern institution with traditional practices.

- Discuss the ways in which the political system contrasts with the economic system in Meghalaya.

In a far corner of India, a country where women usually cry out for equality, respect, and protection, there's a state where men are asking for more rights.

Meghalaya—"Home of Clouds"—is picturesque state with its capital Shillong a regional hub for education and the trend-setter for the Westernised culture that's accepted by most tribes in the country's northeast.

The two major tribes of Meghalaya, Khasis and Jaintias, are matrilineal with a vengeance. Children take the mother's surname, daughters inherit the family property with the youngest getting the lion's share, and most businesses are run by women.

Known as the "Khatduh", the youngest daughter anchors the family, looking after elderly parents, giving shelter and care to unmarried brothers and sisters, and watching over property.

The Khasi Social Custom of Lineage Act protects the matrilineal structure.

Some trace the origins of the system to Khasi and Jaintia kings, who preferred to entrust the household to their queens when they went to battle. This custom has continued to provide women the pride of place in the tribal society.

"Matriliny safeguards women from social ostracism when they remarry because their children, no matter who the father was, would be known by the mother's clan name. Even if a woman delivered a child out of wedlock, which is quite common, there is no social stigma attached to the woman in our society," says Patricia Mukhim, a national award-winning social activist who edits the *Shillong Times* newspaper.

Mukhim says her society will not succumb to the dominant patriarchial system in most of India.

"We have interfaced with several cultures and our women have married people from other Indian provinces and from outside India. But very few Khasi women have given up their culture," says Mukhim. "Most have transmitted the culture to their children born out of wedlock with non-Khasis."

Matrilineal Culture

Anirban Roy, a Bengali married to a Jaintia woman whom he met as a fellow student in a veterinary college, says he faced no problem adjusting to the matrilineal culture of his wife's family.

"Everyone in the wife's clan made it a point to come and introduce themselves and invite me to their houses either for lunch or for dinner to know each other better. Whenever we face a problem, the members of my wife's clan rushed to our help," said Roy. "As a groom, I enjoyed great respect and privilege."

But many Khasi and Jaintia men complain, and some formed the equivalent of a "men's liberation group" called Syngkhong Rympei Thymai (SRT) back in 1990.

"Our men now have no roles as fathers or uncles. Since ancient times, fathers have been the protector and bread-earner, but this notion is not so much of a reality in our society now," says Keith Pariat, SRT's founder.

"In our society, there is applause and celebration when a girl is born, but the birth of a boy is just taken in the stride," Pariat says.

Some tribal families have been switching over to patrilieany, where the father assumes leadership of the family, Pariat says. But he admits that such cases are rare.

SRT has only about 3,000 members, but most are silent members who are too nervous to publicly challenge matrilineal traditions of the Khasi-Jaintia society.

"We hope things will change and we will get a more meaningful role to play in our society. But we cannot force a change," says Anthony Kharkhongor, an SRT member.

C Joshua Thomas, regional director of the Indian Council of Social Science Research, says religious beliefs also help perpetuate the matrilineal system. Thomas is based in Shillong and has closely watched the tribal societies in Meghalaya in his long career as a social scientist.

"This system will survive because the people zealously guard this system. It has support from many quarters, including the indigenous religious systems Seng Khasi and also from the mainline Christian churches both from the Catholics and Protestant orders. The NGOs in Meghalaya also support this system," he says.

Khasi-Jaintia women, meanwhile, say the men have enough of a role to play in society—if they want to.

"Even in our matrilineal society, we treat the fathers as the head of the family, and they take important family decisions. Men are given due recognition even in major family decisions," says Iwbih Nylla Tariang, a female employee with Meghalaya's animal husbandry department.

But Tariang is keen that the present matrilineal system stays as is.

"Unlike elsewhere in India, we have followed a unique matrilineal society for centuries. Our society in Meghalaya always gave respect to women. The children taking mother's family name is the biggest respect," she says.

"Disgruntled Individuals"

The social activist Mukhim calls the SRT a "bunch of disgruntled individuals."

"Khasis, as a whole, do not find any problem with matriliny. It is a small group of urban males who seem dissatisfied having to live with the wife's family," Mukhim says.

"Khasi men were known to be polygamous and marriages are brittle. Marriage as an institution came about only after Christianity and is practised only among Christians. Those who follow the indigenous faith, or who are outside the purview of any religion, still practise cohabitation or living together. So our system works."

In India, where women often become victims of "honour killings" if seen with a male from another caste, Khasi-Jaintia

women enjoy remarkable social mobility and can accompany any men without taboo.

Unlike elsewhere in India where the bride's family is generally required to pay a dowry to the groom's family, the women of Khasi-Jaintia society do not.

Nor are there any arranged marriages.

Khasi women are enterprising and run small businesses well. In Shillong's oldest market, the Lewduh, women operate almost all businesses.

Many Khasi political leaders are apprehensive about outsiders coming to settle in Meghalaya and marrying local women.

In 2007, the Khasi Hills Autonomous District Council (KHADC), which gives the tribes self-governance, declared a policy of encouraging Khasi women to have more children.

Some Khasi mothers who had given birth to 15 or more offspring were handed out cash rewards.

"We have a lot of land but migrants from other parts of India and neighbouring Bangladesh are coming into Meghalaya in some numbers," says KHADC chief HS Shylla, justifying cash rewards in a country where the federal government advocates strict family planning.

"We may be swamped by them, like neighbouring Tripura or Assam, if we don't grow in numbers."

One crucial area exists, however, where women are not the dominant figures. The Dorbar Shnong—or the grassroots political institution of the tribes—debars women from holding office and remains a male-centric institution.

"Women would be represented at the Dorbar by male members of the family such as their husbands, brothers, or uncles. These days women attend the Dorbar but cannot hold office as executive members, and certainly not as the headman," says Thomas.

The 60-member Meghalaya state assembly also has only four women lawmakers—an unusual situation in a society where social and economic powers rest with females.

"This is one reason why women in Meghalaya have been uncertain about entering electoral politics. There is an inherent feeling that politics is a male domain," says Mukhim.

Critical Thinking

1. Describe the matrilineal social system of the tribes of Meghalaya.

2. Discuss the claims and counterclaims with respect to the discontent expressed by some men.

3. How does marriage as a modern institution contrast with the traditional practice?

4. How does the experience of women in Meghalaya contrast with that of women in the rest of India?

5. Discuss the concerns of Khasi political leaders regarding the influx of outsiders.

6. How does the political system contrast with the economic system in Meghalaya?

Create Central

www.mhhe.com/createcentral

Internet References

Kinship and Social Organization
www.umanitoba.ca/anthropology

Sex and Marriage
http://anthro.palomar.edu/marriage/default.htm

Article Prepared by: Elvio Angeloni, *Pasadena City College*

The Inuit Paradox

How can people who gorge on fat and rarely see a vegetable be healthier than we are?

Patricia Gadsby

Learning Outcomes

After reading this article, you will be able to:

- Identify the traditional Inuit (Eskimo) practices that are important for their survival in the circumstances they live in and contrast them with the values professed by the society you live in.

- Discuss what contemporary hunter-collector societies teach us about the quality of life in the prehistoric past.

- Define the "Inuit paradox" and explain what we can learn from it with regard to modern-day eating practices.

Patricia Cochran, an Inupiat from Northwestern Alaska, is talking about the native foods of her childhood: "We pretty much had a subsistence way of life. Our food supply was right outside our front door. We did our hunting and foraging on the Seward Peninsula and along the Bering Sea."

"Our meat was seal and walrus, marine mammals that live in cold water and have lots of fat. We used seal oil for our cooking and as a dipping sauce for food. We had moose, caribou, and reindeer. We hunted ducks, geese, and little land birds like quail, called ptarmigan. We caught crab and lots of fish—salmon, whitefish, tomcod, pike, and char. Our fish were cooked, dried, smoked, or frozen. We ate frozen raw whitefish, sliced thin. The elders liked stinkfish, fish buried in seal bags or cans in the tundra and left to ferment. And fermented seal flipper, they liked that too."

Cochran's family also received shipments of whale meat from kin living farther north, near Barrow. Beluga was one she liked; raw muktuk, which is whale skin with its underlying blubber, she definitely did not. "To me it has a chew-on-a-tire consistency," she says, "but to many people it's a mainstay." In the short subarctic summers, the family searched for roots and greens and, best of all from a child's point of view, wild blueberries, crowberries, or salmonberries, which her aunts would mix with whipped fat to make a special treat called *akutuq*—in colloquial English, Eskimo ice cream.

Now Cochran directs the Alaska Native Science Commission, which promotes research on native cultures and the health and environmental issues that affect them. She sits at her keyboard in Anchorage, a bustling city offering fare from Taco Bell to French cuisine. But at home Cochran keeps a freezer filled with fish, seal, walrus, reindeer, and whale meat, sent by her family up north, and she and her husband fish and go berry picking—"sometimes a challenge in Anchorage," she adds, laughing. "I eat fifty-fifty," she explains, half traditional, half regular American.

No one, not even residents of the northernmost villages on Earth, eats an entirely traditional northern diet anymore. Even the groups we came to know as Eskimo—which include the Inupiat and the Yupiks of Alaska, the Canadian Inuit and Inuvialuit, Inuit Greenlanders, and the Siberian Yupiks—have probably seen more changes in their diet in a lifetime than their ancestors did over thousands of years. The closer people live to towns and the more access they have to stores and cash-paying jobs, the more likely they are to have westernized their eating. And with westernization, at least on the North American continent, comes processed foods and cheap carbohydrates—Crisco, Tang, soda, cookies, chips, pizza, fries. "The young and urbanized," says Harriet Kuhnlein, director of the Centre for Indigenous Peoples' Nutrition and Environment at McGill University in Montreal, "are increasingly into fast food." So much so that type 2 diabetes, obesity, and other diseases of Western civilization are becoming causes for concern there too.

Today, when diet books top the best-seller list and nobody seems sure of what to eat to stay healthy, it's surprising to learn how well the Eskimo did on a high-protein, high-fat diet. Shaped by glacial temperatures, stark landscapes, and protracted winters, the traditional Eskimo diet had little in the way of plant food, no agricultural or dairy products, and was unusually low in carbohydrates. Mostly people subsisted on what they hunted and fished. Inland dwellers took advantage of caribou feeding on tundra mosses, lichens, and plants too tough for humans to stomach (though predigested vegetation in the animals' paunches became dinner as well). Coastal people exploited the sea. The main nutritional challenge was avoiding starvation in late winter if primary meat sources became too scarce or lean.

These foods hardly make up the "balanced" diet most of us grew up with, and they look nothing like the mix of grains, fruits, vegetables, meat, eggs, and dairy we're accustomed to seeing in conventional food pyramid diagrams. How could such a diet possibly be adequate? How did people get along on little else but fat and animal protein?

The diet of the Far North shows that there are no essential foods—only essential nutrients.

What the diet of the Far North illustrates, says Harold Draper, a biochemist and expert in Eskimo nutrition, is that there are no essential foods—only essential nutrients. And humans can get those nutrients from diverse and eye-opening sources.

One might, for instance, imagine gross vitamin deficiencies arising from a diet with scarcely any fruits and vegetables. What furnishes vitamin A, vital for eyes and bones? We derive much of ours from colorful plant foods, constructing it from pigmented plant precursors called carotenoids (as in carrots). But vitamin A, which is oil soluble, is also plentiful in the oils of cold-water fishes and sea mammals, as well as in the animals' livers, where fat is processed. These dietary staples also provide vitamin D, another oil-soluble vitamin needed for bones. Those of us living in temperate and tropical climates, on the other hand, usually make vitamin D indirectly by exposing skin to strong sun—hardly an option in the Arctic winter—and by consuming fortified cow's milk, to which the indigenous northern groups had little access until recent decades and often don't tolerate all that well.

As for vitamin C, the source in the Eskimo diet was long a mystery. Most animals can synthesize their own vitamin C, or ascorbic acid, in their livers, but humans are among the exceptions, along with other primates and oddballs like guinea pigs and bats. If we don't ingest enough of it, we fall apart from scurvy, a gruesome connective-tissue disease. In the United States today we can get ample supplies from orange juice, citrus fruits, and fresh vegetables. But vitamin C oxidizes with time; getting enough from a ship's provisions was tricky for early 18th- and 19th-century voyagers to the polar regions. Scurvy—joint pain, rotting gums, leaky blood vessels, physical and mental degeneration—plagued European and U.S. expeditions even in the 20th century. However, Arctic peoples living on fresh fish and meat were free of the disease.

Impressed, the explorer Vilhjalmur Stefansson adopted an Eskimo-style diet for five years during the two Arctic expeditions he led between 1908 and 1918. "The thing to do is to find your antiscorbutics where you are," he wrote. "Pick them up as you go." In 1928, to convince skeptics, he and a young colleague spent a year on an Americanized version of the diet under medical supervision at Bellevue Hospital in New York City. The pair ate steaks, chops, organ meats like brain and liver, poultry, fish, and fat with gusto. "If you have some fresh meat in your diet every day and don't overcook it," Stefansson

declared triumphantly, "there will be enough C from that source alone to prevent scurvy."

In fact, all it takes to ward off scurvy is a daily dose of 10 milligrams, says Karen Fediuk, a consulting dietitian and former graduate student of Harriet Kuhnlein's who did her master's thesis on vitamin C. (That's far less than the U.S. recommended daily allowance of 75 to 90 milligrams—75 for women, 90 for men.) Native foods easily supply those 10 milligrams of scurvy prevention, especially when organ meats—preferably raw—are on the menu. For a study published with Kuhnlein in 2002, Fediuk compared the vitamin C content of 100-gram (3.55-ounce) samples of foods eaten by Inuit women living in the Canadian Arctic: Raw caribou liver supplied almost 24 milligrams, seal brain close to 15 milligrams, and raw kelp more than 28 milligrams. Still higher levels were found in whale skin and muktuk.

As you might guess from its antiscorbutic role, vitamin C is crucial for the synthesis of connective tissue, including the matrix of skin. "Wherever collagen's made, you can expect vitamin C," says Kuhnlein. Thick skinned, chewy, and collagen rich, raw muktuk can serve up an impressive 36 milligrams in a 100-gram piece, according to Fediuk's analyses. "Weight for weight, it's as good as orange juice," she says. Traditional Inuit practices like freezing meat and fish and frequently eating them raw, she notes, conserve vitamin C, which is easily cooked off and lost in food processing.

Hunter-gatherer diets like those eaten by these northern groups and other traditional diets based on nomadic herding or subsistence farming are among the older approaches to human eating. Some of these eating plans might seem strange to us—diets centered around milk, meat, and blood among the East African pastoralists, enthusiastic tuber eating by the Quechua living in the High Andes, the staple use of the mongongo nut in the southern African !Kung—but all proved resourceful adaptations to particular eco-niches. No people, though, may have been forced to push the nutritional envelope further than those living at Earth's frozen extremes. The unusual makeup of the far-northern diet led Loren Cordain, a professor of evolutionary nutrition at Colorado State University at Fort Collins, to make an intriguing observation.

Four years ago, Cordain reviewed the macronutrient content (protein, carbohydrates, fat) in the diets of 229 hunter-gatherer groups listed in a series of journal articles collectively known as the Ethnographic Atlas. These are some of the oldest surviving human diets. In general, hunter-gatherers tend to eat more animal protein than we do in our standard Western diet, with its reliance on agriculture and carbohydrates derived from grains and starchy plants. Lowest of all in carbohydrate, and highest in combined fat and protein, are the diets of peoples living in the Far North, where they make up for fewer plant foods with extra fish. What's equally striking, though, says Cordain, is that these meat-and-fish diets also exhibit a natural "protein ceiling." Protein accounts for no more than 35 to 40 percent of their total calories, which suggests to him that's all the protein humans can comfortably handle.

Wild-animal fats are different from other fats. Farm animals typically have lots of highly saturated fat.

This ceiling, Cordain thinks, could be imposed by the way we process protein for energy. The simplest, fastest way to make energy is to convert carbohydrates into glucose, our body's primary fuel. But if the body is out of carbs, it can burn fat, or if necessary, break down protein. The name given to the convoluted business of making glucose from protein is gluconeogenesis. It takes place in the liver, uses a dizzying slew of enzymes, and creates nitrogen waste that has to be converted into urea and disposed of through the kidneys. On a truly traditional diet, says Draper, recalling his studies in the 1970s, Arctic people had plenty of protein but little carbohydrate, so they often relied on gluconeogenesis. Not only did they have bigger livers to handle the additional work but their urine volumes were also typically larger to get rid of the extra urea. Nonetheless, there appears to be a limit on how much protein the human liver can safely cope with: Too much overwhelms the liver's waste-disposal system, leading to protein poisoning—nausea, diarrhea, wasting, and death.

Whatever the metabolic reason for this syndrome, says John Speth, an archaeologist at the University of Michigan's Museum of Anthropology, plenty of evidence shows that hunters through the ages avoided protein excesses, discarding fat-depleted animals even when food was scarce. Early pioneers and trappers in North America encountered what looks like a similar affliction, sometimes referred to as rabbit starvation because rabbit meat is notoriously lean. Forced to subsist on fat-deficient meat, the men would gorge themselves, yet wither away. Protein can't be the sole source of energy for humans, concludes Cordain. Anyone eating a meaty diet that is low in carbohydrates must have fat as well.

Stefansson had arrived at this conclusion, too, while living among the Copper Eskimo. He recalled how he and his Eskimo companions had become quite ill after weeks of eating "caribou so skinny that there was no appreciable fat behind the eyes or in the marrow." Later he agreed to repeat the miserable experience at Bellevue Hospital, for science's sake, and for a while ate nothing but defatted meat. "The symptoms brought on at Bellevue by an incomplete meat diet [lean without fat] were exactly the same as in the Arctic . . . diarrhea and a feeling of general baffling discomfort," he wrote. He was restored with a fat fix but "had lost considerable weight." For the remainder of his year on meat, Stefansson tucked into his rations of chops and steaks with fat intact. "A normal meat diet is not a high-protein diet," he pronounced. "We were really getting three-quarters of our calories from fat." (Fat is more than twice as calorie dense as protein or carbohydrate, but even so, that's a lot of lard. A typical U.S diet provides about 35 percent of its calories from fat.)

Stefansson dropped 10 pounds on his meat-and-fat regimen and remarked on its "slenderizing" aspect, so perhaps it's no surprise he's been co-opted as a posthumous poster boy for Atkins-type diets. No discussion about diet these days can avoid Atkins. Even some researchers interviewed for this article couldn't resist referring to the Inuit way of eating as the "original Atkins." "Superficially, at a macronutrient level, the two diets certainly look similar," allows Samuel Klein, a nutrition researcher at Washington University in St. Louis, who's attempting to study how Atkins stacks up against conventional weight-loss diets. Like the Inuit diet, Atkins is low in carbohydrates and very high in fat. But numerous researchers, including Klein, point out that there are profound differences between the two diets, beginning with the type of meat and fat eaten.

Fats have been demonized in the United States, says Eric Dewailly, a professor of preventive medicine at Laval University in Quebec. But all fats are not created equal. This lies at the heart of a paradox—the Inuit paradox, if you will. In the Nunavik villages in northern Quebec, adults over 40 get almost half their calories from native foods, says Dewailly, and they don't die of heart attacks at nearly the same rates as other Canadians or Americans. Their cardiac death rate is about half of ours, he says. As someone who looks for links between diet and cardiovascular health, he's intrigued by that reduced risk. Because the traditional Inuit diet is "so restricted," he says, it's easier to study than the famously heart-healthy Mediterranean diet, with its cornucopia of vegetables, fruits, grains, herbs, spices, olive oil, and red wine.

A key difference in the typical Nunavik Inuit's diet is that more than 50 percent of the calories in Inuit native foods come from fats. Much more important, the fats come from wild animals.

Wild-animal fats are different from both farm-animal fats and processed fats, says Dewailly. Farm animals, cooped up and stuffed with agricultural grains (carbohydrates) typically have lots of solid, highly saturated fat. Much of our processed food is also riddled with solid fats, or so-called trans fats, such as the reengineered vegetable oils and shortenings cached in baked goods and snacks. "A lot of the packaged food on supermarket shelves contains them. So do commercial french fries," Dewailly adds.

Trans fats are polyunsaturated vegetable oils tricked up to make them more solid at room temperature. Manufacturers do this by hydrogenating the oils—adding extra hydrogen atoms to their molecular structures—which "twists" their shapes. Dewailly makes twisting sound less like a chemical transformation than a perversion, an act of public-health sabotage: "These man-made fats are dangerous, even worse for the heart than saturated fats." They not only lower high-density lipoprotein cholesterol (HDL, the "good" cholesterol) but they also raise low-density lipoprotein cholesterol (LDL, the "bad" cholesterol) and triglycerides, he says. In the process, trans fats set the stage for heart attacks because they lead to the increase of fatty buildup in artery walls.

Wild animals that range freely and eat what nature intended, says Dewailly, have fat that is far more healthful. Less of their fat is saturated, and more of it is in the monounsaturated form (like olive oil). What's more, cold-water fishes and sea mammals are particularly rich in polyunsaturated fats called n-3 fatty acids or omega-3 fatty acids. These fats appear to benefit the heart and vascular system. But the polyunsaturated fats in most Americans' diets are the omega-6 fatty acids supplied by vegetable oils. By contrast, whale blubber consists of 70 percent monounsaturated fat and close to 30 percent omega-3s, says Dewailly.

Dieting is the price we pay for too little exercise and too much mass-produced food.

Omega-3s evidently help raise HDL cholesterol, lower triglycerides, and are known for anticlotting effects. (Ethnographers have remarked on an Eskimo propensity for nosebleeds.) These fatty acids are believed to protect the heart from life-threatening arrhythmias that can lead to sudden cardiac death. And like a "natural aspirin," adds Dewailly, omega-3 polyunsaturated fats help put a damper on runaway inflammatory processes, which play a part in atherosclerosis, arthritis, diabetes, and other so-called diseases of civilization.

You can be sure, however, that Atkins devotees aren't routinely eating seal and whale blubber. Besides the acquired taste problem, their commerce is extremely restricted in the United States by the Marine Mammal Protection Act, says Bruce Holub, a nutritional biochemist in the department of human biology and nutritional sciences at the University of Guelph in Ontario.

"In heartland America it's probable they're not eating in an Eskimo-like way," says Gary Foster, clinical director of the Weight and Eating Disorders Program at the Pennsylvania School of Medicine. Foster, who describes himself as open-minded about Atkins, says he'd nonetheless worry if people saw the diet as a green light to eat all the butter and bacon—saturated fats—they want. Just before rumors surfaced that Robert Atkins had heart and weight problems when he died, Atkins officials themselves were stressing saturated fat should account for no more than 20 percent of dieters' calories. This seems to be a clear retreat from the diet's original don't-count-the-calories approach to bacon and butter and its happy exhortations to "plow into those prime ribs." Furthermore, 20 percent of calories from saturated fats is *double* what most nutritionists advise. Before plowing into those prime ribs, readers of a recent edition of the *Dr. Atkins' New Diet Revolution* are urged to take omega-3 pills to help protect their hearts. "If you watch carefully," says Holub wryly, "you'll see many popular U.S. diets have quietly added omega-3 pills, in the form of fish oil or flaxseed capsules, as supplements."

Needless to say, the subsistence diets of the Far North are not "dieting." Dieting is the price we pay for too little exercise and too much mass-produced food. Northern diets were a way of life in places too cold for agriculture, where food, whether hunted, fished, or foraged, could not be taken for granted. They were about keeping weight on.

This is not to say that people in the Far North were fat: Subsistence living requires exercise—hard physical work. Indeed,

among the good reasons for native people to maintain their old way of eating, as far as it's possible today, is that it provides a hedge against obesity, type 2 diabetes, and heart disease. Unfortunately, no place on Earth is immune to the spreading taint of growth and development. The very well-being of the northern food chain is coming under threat from global warming, land development, and industrial pollutants in the marine environment. "I'm a pragmatist," says Cochran, whose organization is involved in pollution monitoring and disseminating food-safety information to native villages. "Global warming we don't have control over. But we can, for example, do clean-ups of military sites in Alaska or of communication cables leaching lead into fish-spawning areas. We can help communities make informed food choices. A young woman of child-bearing age may choose not to eat certain organ meats that concentrate contaminants. As individuals, we do have options. And eating our salmon and our seal is still a heck of a better option than pulling something processed that's full of additives off a store shelf."

Not often in our industrial society do we hear someone speak so familiarly about "our" food animals. We don't talk of "our pig" and "our beef." We've lost that creature feeling, that sense of kinship with food sources. "You're taught to think in boxes," says Cochran. "In our culture the connectivity between humans, animals, plants, the land they live on, and the air they share is ingrained in us from birth.

"You truthfully can't separate the way we get our food from the way we live," she says. "How we get our food is intrinsic to our culture. It's how we pass on our values and knowledge to the young. When you go out with your aunts and uncles to hunt or to gather, you learn to smell the air, watch the wind, understand the way the ice moves, know the land. You get to know where to pick which plant and what animal to take."

"It's part, too, of your development as a person. You share food with your community. You show respect to your elders by offering them the first catch. You give thanks to the animal that gave up its life for your sustenance. So you get all the physical activity of harvesting your own food, all the social activity of sharing and preparing it, and all the spiritual aspects as well," says Cochran. "You certainly don't get all that, do you, when you buy prepackaged food from a store."

"That's why some of us here in Anchorage are working to protect what's ours, so that others can continue to live back home in the villages," she adds. "Because if we don't take care of our food, it won't be there for us in the future. And if we lose our foods, we lose who we are." The word Inupiat means "the real people." "That's who we are," says Cochran.

Critical Thinking

1. What kinds of diseases are on the increase among the Inuit and why?

2. How does their traditional high-protein, high-fat diet compare with the "balanced diet" most of us grew up with? What does this mean, according to Harold Draper?

3. What are the contrasting sources of vitamins A, D, and C between our diet and the diet of the Inuit? What is the advantage of eating meat and fish raw?

4. What is a "protein ceiling"? How did hunter-gatherers cope with this problem?

5. Where do the more healthful fats (monounsaturated and omega-3 fatty acids) come from? What are their benefits?

6. Why is it that Atkins-dieters are not really eating in an "Eskimo-like way"?

7. What are the differences between the subsistence diets of the Far North and "dieting"?

8. Were people of the Far North fat? Why not? In what ways did the old way of eating protect them?

9. How is the northern food chain threatened?

10. In what sense is there a kinship with food sources in the Far North that our industrial societies do not have? Why is it also a part of one's development as a person?

Create Central

www.mhhe.com/createcentral

Internet References

The Paleolithic Diet Page
    www.paleodiet.com

The Institute for Intercultural Studies
    www.interculturalstudies.org/main.html

Sociology Guy's Anthropology Links
    www.trinity.edu/~mkearl/anthro.html

Article

Prepared by: Elvio Angeloni, *Pasadena City College*

Cell Phones, Sharing, and Social Status in an African Society

Daniel Jordan Smith

Learning Outcomes

After reading this article, you will be able to:

- Discuss the economics, the politics, and the sociality of cell phone use in Nigeria.
- Discuss the ways in which cell phones are perceived as status symbols in Nigeria.

Contemporary processes of globalization have stimulated many anthropologists to begin asking new research questions. One important area of innovative research pertains to the global spread of technology and its influence on local people, practices, values, and behaviors. Globalization involves the worldwide transfer of technology, capital, industry, people, and cultural ideas. It has made the world a smaller place, but it has also increased social inequalities across the "digital divide."

In the twentieth century, radio and television played powerful roles in creating linkages between previously disconnected areas of the world. Without a doubt, new mass media brought the signs, symbols, images, and cultural values of the industrialized "First World" to people and communities in poorer "Third World" regions. The globalization of technology is not a top-down, unidirectional process. New technologies create new ways in which small groups of people can shape the ideas, values, political opinions, and even the actions of large groups of people within a particular town, district, country, or world region.

Recent technological developments are influencing people and communities in new ways, raising new research questions for anthropologists. One such development is the Internet, although on a global scale fewer people have access to that technology than the topic of this selection: cell phones. Like radio and television before them, cell phones create new and unprecedented opportunities for communication across distances. As this selection vividly demonstrates, the ways in which people use cell phones are powerfully influenced by local ideas, values, customs, and practices. In other words, global processes always take place within local contexts. Both the symbolic

meaning and the social rules for using cell phones change in different cultural contexts.

Introduction

On July 19, 2004, the popular BBC Africa Service morning news program, *Network Africa,* carried a curious story from its Nigeria correspondent. He described a recent epidemic of rumors circulating in the country, purporting that anyone who answered calls on their cellular telephones originating from several specific numbers risked madness, and even death. I had heard a similar story in the previous few days from dozens of friends and acquaintances in and around the towns of Owerri and Umuahia in southeastern Nigeria, where I was conducting research. Ironically, cell phone usage around the country surged in the wake of the rumors, as people phoned and sent text messages to friends and relatives, warning them of the "killer numbers."

Once the popular rumors circulated widely, Nigerian newspapers carried stories printing some of the suspected numbers and incorporating quotations from citizens who allegedly witnessed the effects of these sinister calls (Akinsuyi 2004). But the newspapers also published statements from spokespersons for the country's major mobile telephone service providers, denying that such killer numbers existed (Ikhemuemhe 2004). Further, they published interviews with government authorities and university scientists disputing the technological feasibility of transmitting witchcraft through cell phones. Radio call-in programs and television talk shows buzzed with debate about the story, mesmerizing the nation for the better part of two weeks. Eventually, popular attention faded, as it had with regard to a previous rumor suggesting that men who carried cell phones in their pockets or strapped them to their belts risked becoming infertile.

The rumors that mobile phones might be implicated in infertility, madness, and murder are a testament to how dramatically this new technology has affected Nigeria. A few elite Nigerians had access to older cellular telephone technologies beginning in the 1990s, but the number of such phones was minuscule. The introduction of the Global System for Mobile Communications (GSM) technology to Nigeria in 2001 and the liberalization of Nigeria's previously government-controlled telecommunications industry transformed cell phones from an extreme rarity into an everyday technology to which literally millions of ordinary citizens have access. When GSM technology was first introduced in Nigeria, the country had only approximately 500,000 landlines for over 100 million people (Obadare 2004), a number which had not increased significantly in many years. By the end of 2004, less than four years after the first GSM cellular phones and services went on sale to the Nigerian public, the country had over 7 million subscribers (Mobile Africa 2005), with some recent estimates putting the number of mobile phones users in Nigeria at over 11 million (PANA 2005).

In addition, millions more people without their own phones were provided easy access to cell phone service, as individual cell phone owners became small-scale entrepreneurs, converting their personal phones into informal businesses. By the time the BBC story was broadcast, thousands of call centers, most with just one or two phones and a single attendant, dotted Nigeria's landscape. Every major city and many small towns are now connected, and countless rural and urban communities that have no running water and little or no electricity service are integrated into the country's vast and expanding mobile telephone network.

Cell phones have produced dramatic changes in communication in Nigeria, with many positive effects. Mobile phones have been integrated into long-standing patterns of social relationship, enabling Nigerians separated by great distances to continue to interact based on expectations of sharing and reciprocity. But just as important, they have become symbols of social status. Nigerians assert and express modern identities by purchasing, using, and publicly displaying the latest consumer commodities. Mastery of the new phone technology is a marker of being middle class, educated, and urban. Yet the reality is that cell phones represent a level of economic achievement that is out of reach to most Nigerians. The majority of new cell phone consumers experience the costs of usage as exorbitant, reinforcing the sense that middle-class status remains elusive. Thus, while the burgeoning popularity of cell phones in Nigeria, and throughout sub-Saharan Africa, represents the aspirations of ordinary people for better lives, this new technology exposes the pronounced and enduring nature of social inequality.

Cell Phone Economics

Owning and using a cell phone in Nigeria requires three primary investments: (1) buying a phone; (2) accessing service from one of the country's four major providers through the purchase of a SIM (Subscriber Identity Module) card that is installed in the back of the phone to connect it to the service network; and (3) procuring "recharge cards," through which call time is paid for by loading a unique pin number each time one wants to add credit to an individual account. While the phone and the SIM card are one-time acquisitions, access to service depends on the regular purchase of the recharge cards to load call time as previously purchased amounts are exhausted.

In 2005, new phones are available in Nigeria for as little as 6,000 naira (approximately 45 U.S. dollars), and as much as 60,000 naira (over U.S. $450), depending on the brand, the model, and the complexity of features offered on the phone.

The price of SIM cards declined dramatically in the past several years, to about five to ten dollars, with companies sometimes offering free SIM cards as part of periodic marketing campaigns. The vast majority of customers use the "pay as you go" recharge card system.

Most crucial from the perspective of ordinary Nigerians is the cost of calls themselves. As with every other feature of cell phone service, the cost of calls has declined significantly over the four years since GSM service was introduced. But the price of calls per minute and per second (a choice between these rates is now available to most consumers) is still expensive, relative to both Nigerians' purchasing power and the cost of cell phone service in other countries (Obadare 2004). Importantly, although incoming calls are free, every outgoing call is charged—there are no free minutes per month or at night and on weekends, though lower rates apply in off-peak hours. Further, recharge cards expire. Credit not utilized within a specified period of time is forever lost. For example, ten dollars of credit would typically need to be used within about two weeks.

Initially, when GSM cell phone service was first introduced, domestic calls cost approximately 50 naira (37 U.S. cents) per minute. Recently, the cost has declined to about 25 naira (19 cents) per minute, with the precise amount depending upon the volume of calls per month, whether the call is in or out of network, the time of day, and so on. Each of the country's four main service providers (Glomobile, Mtel, MTN, and Vmobile) offers a diverse range of service packages and special deals, but most consumers cannot afford to make enough calls to qualify for the plans that offer the cheapest calling rates. Indeed, an entire discourse of complaint about the high cost of cell phone calls has emerged in Nigeria (Obadare 2004). Popular reaction to the economics of personal cell phone use has generated a new lexicon and a growing repertoire of behaviors designed to mitigate the financial burdens of cell phone ownership.

"The Fire That Consumes Money"

In southeastern Nigeria, where I work, and where the predominant language is Igbo, the vernacular name for a cell phone is *oku na iri ego,* which translates literally as "the fire that consumes money." This popular local name reflects ordinary citizens' frustrations with the perceived exorbitant costs of cell phone calls. New linguistic turns of phrase and innovative social practices that have evolved with the proliferation of cell phone technology build on people's aggravation over the strain of cell phone ownership, but they also indicate the degree to which cell phone culture has taken root in everyday life.

Nigerians have adapted their cell phone usage to suit their economic circumstances, and some aspects of the service plans offered by the country's main providers are clearly designed to attract and keep customers who cannot afford to make a high volume of phone calls. For example, the Short Messaging Systems (SMS), through which customers can send "text messages," is extremely popular in Nigeria and typically costs only 15 naira (about 10 U.S. cents) per message. Text messages must be limited in size, usually no more than 160 characters. Text messaging is particularly popular with younger customers and it has generated its own lexicon of abbreviations, an economy of language that has also become part of Nigeria's youth culture, as it has in other settings (for literature on text messaging generally see Fox 2001; Dooring 2002; and Sylvia and Hady 2004).

Text messaging has become a common way for Nigerians who cannot afford regular phone calls to communicate using the new technology. But for older people, and even among young folks, using text messages too frequently without also calling can be interpreted as sign of unwillingness to spend money on a particular relationship—reflecting either stinginess or a lack of deep concern about the relationship or both. As a consequence, although text messaging is extremely popular, people are careful not to rely on it too exclusively, lest they become objects of criticism. In times of economic hardship, the willingness to spend money on a phone call is evidence of interest or commitment to a relationship, whether it is a friendship, a family tie, a business partnership, or a romance. The consequences of the microeconomics of cell phone use reflect the importance and the complexity of how issues of wealth, inequality, and status are negotiated in human relationships.

"Flash Me, I Flash You"

Other common practices besides text messaging illustrate the economics and micropolitics of cell phone behavior, and the importance of these behaviors in navigating issues of inequality in social relationships. For example, a major consequence of the fact that many cell phone owners cannot afford to maintain credit on a regular basis is the innovation of what Nigerians call "flashing." To "flash" someone means to call the recipient's line and allow the phone to ring just once, so that the incoming number is displayed to the recipient, but the caller hangs up before the recipient answers. This way, the recipient knows the number of the person trying to reach him or her, and hopefully has enough credit to call back. Flashing is possible because one can make a call without paying for it as long as no one picks up. Under the prevailing plans in Nigeria, it is possible to receive incoming calls even when one does not have any credit.

From my experience observing scores of friends and acquaintances receiving flashes, whether or not the recipient of the flash could identify the caller from the incoming number was not necessarily a good predictor of a callback. Sometimes knowledge of the identity of the incoming caller created the incentive to call back immediately, perhaps out of obligation, affection, or some prior awareness about the reason for the call. Conversely, on other occasions, knowledge of the identity of the caller had the opposite effect, the attitude being that anyone who had something important to communicate would find a way to pay for a call, even if only for a minute or two. People often refused to call back after a flash out of suspicion that the caller wanted the recipient to bear the cost of the conversation. Nevertheless, unidentified flashes often sparked curiosity, and people frequently responded to them.

Given that countless Nigerians who own cell phones are often in a position where credit is exhausted or very low, and therefore very precious, flashing can sometimes become a comical exchange in which no one wants to bear the costs of a call. In the Pidgin English that is often the lingua franca in Nigeria,

people expressed the phenomenon of reciprocal flashing, in which no one was willing to pay for a call, with the phrase "flash me, I flash you." Mostly in good humor, friends frequently suspected each other of trying to transfer and defray the costs of communication through flashing. As a consequence, people sometimes tried to answer their phones before the end of the first ring, engaging the call before the flasher could hang up. This practice was particularly common when someone flashed more than once, giving the recipient time to prepare for a quick answer. Over the past couple of years I witnessed numerous comic scenes where people plotted to "catch" flashers before they could hang up, making them pay for the connection.

Sharing Credit: Inequality and Sociality

Of course most people who communicate by telephone eventually see each other in person, and past episodes of flashing are often topics of discussion. A typical face-to-face conversation about flashing might include a query by the flasher as to why the recipient did not call back, followed by an admission (or assertion) by the recipient that he or she did not have any credit. The recipient, in turn, may accuse the flasher of having credit and being unwilling to use it. These mostly good-natured conversations reproduce some of the complexity of how people in Nigeria navigate the social representation of wealth more generally. On the one hand, using and sharing one's cell phone liberally are clear signals of wealth, and, like many kinds of conspicuous consumption in Nigeria, seemingly carefree cell phone usage can be rewarded with recognition and prestige. On the other hand, in Nigeria's current economic climate, in which most people are struggling to make ends meet, a strong ethos prevails in which even the relatively affluent portray themselves as just getting by, particularly among people who are otherwise their peers.

These contradictory dimensions of people's public representations of wealth play out constantly in the arena of cell phone socioeconomics. For those who really are struggling, claiming one has no credit can be a strategy for protecting a precious and dwindling resource. Conversely, using one's cell phone generously even when one cannot actually afford it can be a way of portraying or maintaining social status that is threatened by economic hardship. For those who are better off, claiming not to have credit can be a form of humility, representing oneself as just as much of a victim of Nigeria's unjust political economy as one's peers. But the balance can be precarious. Humility can easily be interpreted as stinginess if a wealthy person persists too long in feigning hardship. However, acting too carefree can be seen as ostentatious or arrogant. Ultimately, affluent people are meant to demonstrate and share their prosperity, but in ways that do not humiliate their peers. The proliferation of cell phones has created a very prominent sphere in which the micropolitics of social inequality in Nigeria are enacted (for other examples see Barber 1995; Cornwall 2002; and Smith 2004).

Although Nigerians' cell phone-related social behaviors illustrate the importance of economics in how people manage their phone usage, including strategizing about the social representation of one's wealth, it would be a mistake to emphasize only the economic dimensions of Nigeria's emerging cell phone culture and its associated behavior. A good deal of cell phone-related behavior requires a social rather than an economic interpretation.

Perhaps the most striking example is the way that Nigerians conceptualize cell phone credit. Clearly, everyone who uses cell phones knows how much phone calls cost, and people are aware of the exact amounts in which recharge cards are sold. Further, as the discussion above regarding the phenomenon of flashing suggests, there is a considerable degree of conscious jockeying with regard to sharing and spending one's credit. However, to a remarkable extent, Nigerians seem to think of cell phone credit in much different terms than they think of money. Once money is transformed into cell phone credit through the purchase and loading of recharge cards, cell phone credit becomes much more like food or drink than money, in the sense that people feel more entitled to share in it without the strict incursion of a debt that would be the case if one asked to borrow money. As with food or drink, there is a strong social expectation that cell phone credit should be shared if one has it.

My awareness of the difference between Nigerian and Western (or at least American) sensibilities in this matter was driven home to me by the experience of an American student who worked as my summer research assistant. She lived with a Nigerian family and found them amazingly hospitable and generous, to the point where they refused to allow her to pay rent or contribute to the household budget for food. She felt guilty about this, knowing the family's limited means, and we devised ways that she could contribute without offending her hosts. But when it came to the student's cell phone, the situation was quite the opposite. She had acquired a cell phone mainly so that her parents could call her at any time from the United States. Over the course of the summer, she found that people in the household had no compunctions about asking if she had credit, and, if she did, they had no hesitation in asking to use her phone to make calls. One young woman in the household asked to use her phone so often that the student finally became exasperated and reported it to me. She could not understand how the same family that was so generous and so unwilling to accept her money could expect to use her cell phone in ways that, from her perspective, seemed so insensitive.

Conceived of as a consumable commodity, cell phone credit was easily incorporated into long-standing traditions of sharing, gift giving, and reciprocity, in which people are expected and often genuinely desire to share without incurring the equivalent of a monetary debt. Of course money too is highly implicated in social relationships, and it can be gifted and shared as well as borrowed, lent, or spent, but it was clear from my student's experience, and from numerous similar interactions that I have since participated in and observed, that cell phone credit is transformed into a medium of social exchange that is much different from money once it is loaded into a phone. Nigerians routinely ask their friends and family, and even acquaintances of less intimacy, whether or not they have credit, in ways they would rarely, if ever, ask so openly about money.

The politics of sharing cell phone credit is nonetheless complicated, both because forms of nonmonetary sharing and reciprocity have their own moral economy, with numerous unspoken rules and expectations, and because cell phone credit is, in fact, in some ways more like money than are consumable commodities like food or drink. Even in the sharing of food and drink, in which Nigerians, like people in many societies, are extremely generous and social, there are expectations of generalized reciprocity (Bearman 1997). Although one does not incur a quantifiable debt by sharing someone's food, if, over time, one only takes and never gives, this will be recognized and admonished in some way. Similarly, with the sharing of cell phone credit, someone asking to make calls on another's phone cannot expect indefinite cooperation if favors are not eventually reciprocated.

However, cell phone credit is still more like money than is a beer or a plate of cooked meat. Although ordinary Nigerians have obviously participated in the conversion of cell phone credit from money into a commodity that carries a more social definition, this transformation is not complete. People routinely lied to their friends about their credit, and I observed countless instances in which people were "caught" misrepresenting their credit. At a club in Nigeria where I play tennis, men would commonly pick up a person's phone while he was on the court to check how much credit was available. Someone caught underreporting his credit would almost certainly have to relent and share his phone. Through such actions people contribute to the demonetization of cell phone credit. But this demonetization did not occur without ambivalence. Indeed, the social expectation that one must share phone credit contributed further to the notion that cell phones are a "fire that consumes money."

As these anecdotes suggest, sociality is at least as important a dynamic in Nigerian social life as inequality, and not just in terms of sharing, but also with regard to the importance of regularly greeting and communicating with people in one's social network. The preeminent value of sociality has greatly influenced cell phone usage, in ways that have significant economic implications, even if economic calculations are not always foremost in the minds of cell phone users. Although much of what I have described above demonstrates that Nigerians are highly conscious of the economics of cell phone use and deeply aware of the social implications of cell phone behavior, it is also true that people's penchant for regular communication for purely social purposes means that people make many calls just to say hello and to be in touch. To have a phone and not use it to reach out to family and friends is similar to the idea of living alone or preferring solitude and privacy to social interaction. For most Nigerians it is not only unconscionable, it is unthinkable (Uchendu 1965). As a consequence, although many Nigerians rightly extol the virtues of the country's new cell phone services for promoting business and facilitating a more effective and productive commercial sector, my observations suggest that the vast majority of ordinary customers use a good deal of their credit making calls that are the cellular telephone version of a friendly visit. All this suggests that while cell phone technology has sparked some changes in social life, in many ways the new technology has also adapted to and been incorporated into longer-standing behavioral customs.

"Glo with Pride:" Cell Phones as Status Symbols

As I sat down in the parlor of my friend's house in the south-eastern town of Owerri, her twenty-three-year-old son, Uzoma, inquired whether I owned a cell phone. I said I did, and he asked to see it. After a quick inspection of my very simple and obviously low-end Motorola phone, Uzoma declared dismissively: "This phone doesn't fit you." He meant that a person of my status should have a fancier and more expensive phone, preferably the type currently most popular in Nigeria, where the face flips open, the phone has numerous elaborate technical features, and the screen looks like a computer LCD. I defended my simple phone, but I was not surprised at Uzoma's evaluation. I had encountered this reaction to my phone many times before in a society where cell phones have become important markers of social status.[1]

The relatively educated, mostly urban, and at least marginally economically successful Nigerians who own the majority of the country's more than ten million cell phones are acutely aware of the status distinctions conferred by different models. People are constantly noting the quality of their peers' phones, openly conveying approval or disapproval in ways that consciously connect cell phones to social status. Even where people cannot afford to upgrade their phones, the quality of one's cell phone cover and the type and number of accessories owned can be the subject of more fine-grained attempts to assert both status and fashion. Indeed, as status symbols, the cell phones operate at the cusp between economics and fashion, marking both financial position and sense of style. Uzoma assumed I could afford a more expensive phone, so he concluded that I was either too cheap to own a phone fit for a man of my means or too fashion-challenged to know that my phone was a disgrace.

In a huge country like Nigeria, where many people migrate from their villages of origin to cities and towns in search of education, employment, and economic advancement (Geschiere and Gugler 1998; Gugler 2002), the advent of cell phones in a context where landlines served less than 1 percent of the population has revolutionized communication between family and friends separated by long distances. It is little wonder that so many people want cell phones, or that people who can barely afford some of the basic necessities of everyday life make extraordinary efforts to acquire one. But aside from the practical advantages of cell phone ownership, there is no doubt that cell phones have become an important form of symbolic capital, and that the social status conferred by owning a cell phone is a major motivation for many people (Bourdieu 1984). The cell phone companies cultivate and exploit the symbolic dimensions of cell phone ownership in their advertising, and the pressure of seeing peers enjoy the benefits and social recognition of cell phone ownership induces ever larger numbers of consumers to take the leap.

Whereas just ten years ago, before the advent of GSM technology in Nigeria, cell phones were the exclusive province of the superelite, by 2004 many Nigerians who were not wealthy enough to own their own houses and could not afford to buy a used car were able to acquire the latest marker of modernity.

The transition from an elite exoticism to an almost essential accessory for an aspiring middle class happened remarkably fast. Just two years ago, Umuahia, a small city of less than 200,000 that is the capital of Abia State, had not yet been linked to the network of any of the four main service providers. However, for those who really wanted cell phone service, a regional company called Baudex provided a mostly effective but very expensive service.

At the social club where I frequently played tennis, a playground for the town's elite, approximately fifteen to twenty men owned these Baudex phones in the summer of 2003. To call further attention to the status they displayed by owning and sporting these expensive phones, the owners formed a club within the club. They called themselves "*Ofo* United." "*Ofo*" refers to a mystical staff that is the emblem of traditional authority in Igbo society, a symbol that implies supernatural backing. "United" presumably refers to the name of famous football teams, most notably the world-famous Manchester United, but also to teams in Nigeria that use "United" in their names. The members of *Ofo* United sometimes further separated themselves from other members of the larger club, sharing a roasted goat and several cartons of beer, greeting each other saying "*Ofo* United," and brandishing their phones like some sort of secret society symbol. Just a year later, all this changed dramatically, as both MTN and Glomobile had established full service in Umuahia. By the time I left Nigeria in December of 2004, literally every member of the tennis club had a phone, as did the club's receptionists, one of the bar girls, and some of the kitchen staff. *Ofo* United was no more.

As cell phones have come within the reach of more ordinary citizens, their availability has only intensified the status competition associated with the new technology. Just as the poorest Nigerians have for many years worn watches that do not keep time in order to appear better off than they are, one now sees many young people carrying cell phones that are just shells—though being exposed in such a deception is worse than having no phone at all. Because so many people can aspire to having a cell phone, the distinctions noticed with regard to brands, models, and accessories have become even more fine-grained. Many wealthier people now own multiple phones, with one line for each provider, and they carry them wherever they go. Having a cell phone is no longer so distinctive, but having two or three is still notable. Similarly, making calls to friends or relatives in London or New York, seemingly without a care about the higher cost, can still impress one's peers. In late 2004, camera phones were just hitting the Nigerian market, and I have no doubt they will be all the rage in a very short time.

Conclusion

Although it is impossible to pinpoint the origin of the "killer numbers" rumors described at the start of this article, I suggest that their currency and appeal were related to popular discontents about the role of cell phones in highlighting and sometimes aggravating social inequality. Some speculated that the rumors were the work of one provider trying to undermine the business of another (the killer numbers were first associated with the phone numbers of one company, though, in time, it spread to them all). Others argued that the rumors were a form of consumer revenge, with the allegations meant to damage the reputation and profits of companies toward which customers felt increasing anger. Still others suggested that the rumors were started by some among the vast majority of Nigerians who still cannot afford to own cell phones, in order to strike fear into those who were intimidating their economic inferiors with their ostentatious use of this flashy new technology. More important than these theories about origin is the speed with which the rumors spread and the extent to which they captured popular imagination. The fascination they generated reflects the fact that, as happy as most Nigerians are for their newfound access to a modern communications technology, ordinary citizens remain extremely discontented over the extent of inequality in their society. The new technology is being interpreted, to a large extent, in relation to these discontents.

Note

1. In 2000, *The New York Times* published an article suggesting the importance of cell phones not only for displaying social status generally, but for the attraction of mates. The newspaper account drew on an article in the journal *Human Nature*, entitled "Mobile Phones as Lekking Devices among Human Males" (Lycett and Dunbar 2000). Regardless of whether one finds a sociobiological argument convincing, the association of cell phones with social status seems to strike a chord across many societies.

References

Akinsuyi, Yemi. 2004. Anxiety Over 'Satanic' GSM Phone Numbers. *This Day* (Nigeria), July 23.

Barber, Karin. 1995. Money, Self-Realization, and the Person Yoruba Texts. In *Money Matters: Instability, Values and Social Payments in the Modern History of West African Communities,* ed. J. Guyer, 205–224. Portsmouth, NH: Heinemann.

Bearman, Peter. 1997. Generalized Exchange. *American Journal of Sociology* 102(5): 1383–1415.

Bourdieu, Pierre. 1984. *Distinction: A Social Critique of the Judgement of Taste.* Translated by Richard Nice. Cambridge: Harvard University Press.

Cornwall, Andrea. 2002. Spending Power: Love, Money, and the Reconfiguration of Gender Relations in Ado-Odo, Southwestern Nigeria. *American Ethnologist* 29(4): 963–980.

Dooring, Nicolas. 2002. 'Kurzm-wird-gesendet'—Abbreviations and Acronyms in SMS Communication (Short-Message-Service). *Muttersparche.*

Fox, Barry. 2001. No 2MORO for Text Messaging Lingo. *New Scientist* 171(2298): 24.

Geschiere, Peter, and Josef Gugler. 1998. The Urban-Rural Connection: Changing Issues of Belonging and Identification. *Africa* 68(3): 309–319.

Gugler, Josef. 2002. The Son of a Hawk Does Not Remain Abroad: The Urban-Rural Connection in Africa. *African Studies Review* 45(1): 21–41.

Ikhemuemhe, Godfrey. 2004. The Killer Phone Rumour—Operators Cry Foul. *Vanguard* (Nigeria), July 26, 2004.

Lycett, John, and Robin Dunbar. 2000. Mobile Phones as Lekking Devices among Human Males. *Human Nature* 11(1): 93–104.

Mobile Africa. 2005. Cellular/Mobile Phone Networks in Africa, www.mobileafrica.net/mobile-phone-networks-in-africa.php. (Accessed June 7, 2005).

Obadare, Ebenezer. 2004. "The Great GSM (cell phone) Boycott: Civil Society, Big Business and the State in Nigeria." Dark Roast Occasional Paper Series, No. 18. Cape Town: South Africa: Isandla Institute.

PANA (Pan African News Agency). 2005. Nigeria's Phone Subscriber Base Hits 12 Million. *PanAfrican News Agency Daily Newswire,* May 4.

Smith, Daniel Jordan. 2004. Burials and Belonging in Nigeria: Rural-Urban Relations and Social Inequality in a Contemporary African Ritual. *American Anthropologist* 106(3): 569–579.

Sylvia, K. N., and S. W. Hady. 2004. Communication Pattern with SMS: Short Message Service and MMS: Multimedia Message Service as a Trend of Conduct of Modern Teenagers. *International Journal of Psychology* 39(5–6): 289.

Uchendu, Victor. 1965. *The Igbo of Southeast Nigeria.* Fort Worth, TX: Holt, Reinhart, Winston.

Critical Thinking

1. How and why does cell phone use touch upon wealth, inequality, and status in Nigeria? How are these issues reflected in the vernacular name, "the fire that eats money" and in the use of text messaging? In "flashing"?

2. Describe the economic dimensions of cell phone use and sharing.

3. How do Nigerians think about cell phone credit in different terms than they think of money?

4. In what sense is cell phone use a reflection of sociality?

5. In what respects can cell phones be seen as status symbols in Nigeria?

Create Central

www.mhhe.com/createcentral

Internet References

Smithsonian Institution
www.si.edu

The Royal Anthropological Institute of Great Britain and Ireland (RAI)
www.therai.org.uk

DANIEL JORDAN SMITH, "Cell Phones, Sharing, and Social Status in African Society." Reprinted with permission of the author.

Unit 4

UNIT

Prepared by: Elvio Angeloni, *Pasadena City College*

Other Families, Other Ways

Because most people in small-scale societies of the past spent their whole lives within a local area, it is understandable that their primary interactions—economic, religious, and otherwise—were with their relatives. It also makes sense that, through marriage customs, they strengthened those kinship relationships that clearly defined their mutual rights and obligations. More recently, the family structure has had to be surprisingly flexible and adaptive.

For these reasons, anthropologists have looked upon family and kinship as the key mechanisms for transmitting culture from one generation to the next. Social changes may have been slow to take place throughout the world, but as social horizons have widened, family relationships and community alliances are increasingly based upon new principles. Even when birth rates have increased, kinship networks have diminished in size and strength. As people have increasingly become involved with others as coworkers in a market economy, our associations depend more and more upon factors such as personal aptitudes, educational backgrounds, and job opportunities. Yet the family still exists. Except for some rather unusual exceptions, the family is small, but still functions in its age-old nurturing and protective role, even under conditions where there is little affection or under conditions of extreme poverty and a high infant mortality rate. Beyond the immediate family, the situation is in a state of flux. Certain ethnic groups, especially those in poverty, still have a need for the broader network and in some ways seem to be reformulating those ties.

We do not know where these changes will lead us and which ones will ultimately prevail. One thing is certain: Anthropologists will be there to document the trends, because the discipline of anthropology has had to change as well. Indeed, anthropologists exhibit a growing interest in the study of complex societies where old theoretical perspectives are inadequate. The current trends, however, do not necessarily depict the decline of the kinship unit. The large family network is still the best guarantee of individual survival and well-being in an urban setting.

Article   Prepared by: Elvio Angeloni, *Pasadena City College*

The Invention of Marriage

STEPHANIE COONTZ

Learning Outcomes

After reading this article, you will be able to:

- Explain why marriage was an early and vitally important human invention.
- Discuss the various social strategies people have used to create ties between groups and to defuse tensions among hunter-gatherers.

Marriage is a social invention, unique to humans. Of the hundreds of theories, stories, and fables explaining its origins, my favorite is a Blackfoot Indian tale recorded in 1911. I love this story not because I think it's any "truer" than the others but because it makes such a wonderful change from the equally fanciful theories most of us were taught in high school and college during the 1950s and 1960s. Before marriage was invented, according to the Piegan, or Blackfoot Indians:

> The men and women of the ancient Piegans did not live about together in the beginning. The women . . . made buffalo corrals. Their lodges were fine. . . . They tanned the buffalo-hides, those were their robes. They would cut the meat in slices. In summer they picked berries. They used those in winter. Their lodges all were fine inside. And their things were just as fine. . . . Now, the men were . . . very poor. . . . They had no lodges. They wore raw-hides. . . . They did not know, how they should make lodges. They did not know, how they should tan the buffalo-hides. They did not know, too, how they should cut dried meat, how they should sew their clothes.[1]

In the Blackfoot legend, it was the men, not the women, who needed marriage. Hungry and cold, the men followed the women and found out where they lived. Then they gathered on a nearby hill and waited patiently until the women decided to choose husbands and allow them into their lodges. The female chief selected her mate first, and the rest of the women followed suit.

This is only a folktale, of course, but it is no further off the mark than the story that some anthropologists and sociobiologists have told for years. Before marriage was invented, according to an Anglo-American anthropological theory,

The men hunted wild animals and feasted on their meat. Their brains became very large because they had to cooperate with each other in the hunt. They stood upright, made tools, built fires, and invented language. Their cave art was very fine. . . . But the women were very poor. They were tied down by childbearing, and they did not know how to get food for themselves or their babies. They did not know how to protect themselves from predators. They did not know, too, how to make tools, produce art, and build lodges or campfires to keep themselves warm.

In this story, as in the Blackfoot tale, the invention of marriage supplies the happy ending for the hapless sex. Here, however, women were the weaker gender. They initiated marriage by offering to trade sex for protection and food. Instead of the men waiting patiently on the hill for the women to pick their mates, the men got to pick the women, and the strongest, most powerful males got first choice. Then the men set their women up by the hearth to protect them from predators and from rival males.

The story that marriage was invented for the protection of women is still the most widespread myth about the origins of marriage. According to the protective or provider theory of marriage, women and infants in early human societies could not survive without men to bring them the meat of woolly mammoths and protect them from marauding saber-toothed tigers and from other men seeking to abduct them. But males were willing to protect and provide only for their "own" females and offspring they had good reason to believe were theirs, so a woman needed to find and hold on to a strong, aggressive mate.

One way a woman could hold a mate was to offer him exclusive and frequent sex in return for food and protection. According to the theory, that is why women lost the estrus cycle that is common to other mammals, in which females come into heat only at periodic intervals. Human females became sexually available year-round, so they were able to draw men into long-term relationships. In anthropologist Robin Fox's telling of this story, "The females could easily trade on the male's tendency to want to monopolize (or at least think he was monopolizing) the females for mating purposes, and say, in effect 'okay, you get the monopoly . . . and we get the meat.'"[2]

The male willingness to trade meat for sex (with the females throwing in whatever nuts and berries they'd gathered to sweeten the deal) was, according to Fox, "the root of truly human society." Proponents of this protective theory of marriage claim that the nuclear family, based on a sexual division of labor between the male hunter and the female hearth keeper, was the most important unit of survival and protection in the Stone Age.

People in the mid-twentieth century found this story persuasive because it closely resembled the male breadwinner/female homemaker family to which they were accustomed. The male breadwinner model of marriage, as we shall see later, was a late and relatively short-lived way of organizing gender roles and dividing work in human history. But in the 1950s, 1960s, and 1970s most people believed it was the natural and "traditional" family form.

In 1975, sociobiologist E. O. Wilson drew a direct line from the male hunter marriages that he imagined had prevailed on the African savanna at the dawn of human history to the marriages he observed in the jungle of Wall Street: "During the day the women and children remain in the residential area while the men forage for game or its symbolic equivalent in the form of money."[3] The protective theory is still periodically recycled to explain why women are supposedly attracted to powerful, dominant men, while men seek younger women who will be good breeders and hearth keepers.

But since the 1970s other researchers have poked holes in the protective theory of marriage. Some denied that male dominance and female dependence came to us from our primate ancestors. Among baboons, they pointed out, a female who pairs up with a male does not get more access to food than females outside such a relationship. Among chimpanzees, most food sharing occurs between mothers and their offspring, not between male and female sexual partners. Adult female chimps give food to other females (even unrelated ones) just as often as males give food to females, and female chimps are often more protective of other females than males are. A female chimp who wants food from a male may make sexual overtures, or a male chimp who has meat to spare may use it as a bargaining chip. But males cannot control the sexual behavior of the estrus females. And when members of the group, male or female, want food from a female, they hold or play with her infant, in effect offering babysitting for handouts.[4]

Studies of actual human hunting and gathering societies also threw doubt on the male provider theory. In such societies, women's foraging, not men's hunting, usually contributes the bulk of the group's food. The only exceptions to this rule are Eskimo and other herding or hunting peoples in areas where extremely hostile climates make foraging for plants difficult.[5]

Nor are women in foraging societies tied down by child rearing. One anthropologist, working with an African hunter-gatherer society during the 1960s, calculated that an adult woman typically walked about twelve miles a day gathering food, and brought home anywhere from fifteen to thirty-three pounds. A woman with a child under two covered the same amount of ground and brought back the same amount of food while she carried her child in a sling, allowing the child to nurse as the woman did her foraging. In many societies women also participate in hunting, whether as members of communal hunting parties, as individual hunters, or even in all-female hunting groups.

Today most paleontologists reject the notion that early human societies were organized around dominant male hunters providing for their nuclear families. For one thing, in the early phases of hominid and human evolution, hunting big game was less important for group survival than were gathering plants, bird eggs, edible insects, and shellfish, trapping the occasional small animal, and scavenging the meat of large animals that had died of natural causes.

When early humans began to hunt large animals, they did so by driving animals over cliffs or into swamps. These activities involved the whole group, women as well as men. That is what happens in the surrounds conducted by modern-day foragers, where the entire band encircles the game and gradually herds it into a trap.[6]

We cannot know for sure how the earliest hominids and humans organized their reproduction and family lives. But there are three general schools of thought on the subject. Some researchers believe that early humans lived in female-centered groups made up of mothers, sisters, and their young, accompanied by temporary male companions. Younger males, they suggest, left the group when they reached mating age. Other scholars argue that the needs of defense would have encouraged the formation of groups based on male kin, in which fathers, brothers, and sons, along with their female mates, stayed together. In this view, the female offspring rather than males left the group at puberty. A third group of researchers theorizes that hominid groups were organized around one male mating with several females and traveling with them and their offspring.[7]

But none of these three theories, not even the male with his harem, suggests that an individual male provided for "his" females and children or that the male–female pair was the fundamental unit of economic survival and cooperation. No one could have survived very long in the Paleolithic world if individual nuclear families had had to take primary responsibility for all food production, defense, child rearing, and elder care.[8]

A division of labor between males and females certainly developed fairly early and was reinforced when groups developed weapons effective enough to kill moving animals from a distance. Such weapons made it possible for small groups to hunt solitary, fast-moving animals. Hunting with projectile weapons became the domain of men, partly because it was hard for women to chase swift game while they were nursing. So wherever humans organized small hunting parties that left the main camp, they were likely to be all or mostly male. However, this did not make women dependent upon their individual mates.

Women, keeping their children near, were more likely to specialize in gathering and processing plants and shellfish, manufacturing clothing, trapping small animals, and making digging or cooking implements. This gender specialization led to greater interdependence between males and females. As these productive techniques became more complicated, people had to invest more time in teaching them to children, providing an incentive for couples to stay together for longer stretches.

Having a flexible, gender-based division of labor within a mated pair was an important tool for human survival. One partner, typically the female, could concentrate on the surer thing, finding food through foraging or digging. The other partner could try for a windfall, hunting for food that would be plentiful and filling if it could be caught. Yet this division of labor did not make nuclear families self-sufficient. Collective hunting and gathering remained vital to survival.[9]

Couples in the Paleolithic world would never have fantasized about running off by themselves to their own little retreats in the forest. No Stone Age lovers would have imagined in their wildest dreams that they could or should be "everything" to each other. That way lay death.

Until about twelve thousand years ago, say archaeologists Colin Renfrew and Paul Bahn, nearly all human societies were comprised of bands of mobile hunter-gatherers who moved seasonally between different sleeping camps and work sites, depending on the weather and food supply. Humans lived in these band-level societies and small, semipermanent hamlets far longer than the few millennia they have lived in more complex villages, cities, states, and empires.[10]

Reconstructions by archaeologists suggest that bands were made up of anywhere from a handful to as many as a hundred people, but commonly numbered around two dozen. Bands lived off the land, using simple tools to process a wide range of animals and plants for food, medicines, clothing, and fuel. They typically moved back and forth over a home territory until resources were depleted or other environmental changes spurred them to move on. Periodically they might travel longer distances to find valued raw materials and take advantage of seasonal game or fish runs.[11]

Sometimes the band would break down into individual family groups that foraged alone. But the archaeological record shows that families regularly came back to a main camp, or hooked up with a new one, for protection and to cooperate in communal hunts. Regional networks of camps routinely came together at water holes or to collectively exploit fish runs or seasonally abundant plants. During those times, dances, festivals, and other rituals took place, building connections between families and bands that were dispersed for much of the year. On such occasions, people might seek mates—or change them—from within the larger groups.

No one suggests that prehistoric bands existed in utopian harmony. But social interactions were governed by the overwhelming need to pool and share resources. The band's mobility made it impractical for people to accumulate significant surpluses, which would have to be lugged from place to place. In the absence of money and nonperishable wealth, the main currency in nomadic foraging societies would have been favors given and owed. Sharing beyond the immediate family or local group was a rudimentary form of banking. It allowed people to accumulate personal credit or goodwill that could be drawn on later.[12]

Using computer simulations and mathematical calculations to compare the outcome of different ways of organizing the production and consumption of food, economic anthropologist Bruce Winterhalder has established the decisive importance of prehistoric sharing. His calculations show that because the results of hunting and gathering varied on a daily basis, the surest way for individuals to minimize the risk of not having enough to eat on a bad day was not to save what they gathered or killed on good days for later use by their "own" nuclear family, but to pool and divide the whole harvest among the entire group every day.[13]

With few exceptions, hunting and gathering societies throughout history have emphasized sharing and reciprocity. Band-level societies put extraordinary time and energy into establishing norms of sharing. People who share gain status, while individuals who refuse to share are shunned and ostracized. Ethnographer Lorna Marshall reports that for the Dobe !Kung Bushmen of the Kalahari Desert in Africa, "the idea of eating alone and not sharing is shocking. . . . It makes them shriek with uneasy laughter." They think that "lions could do that, not men." In seventeenth-century America, William Penn marveled that the Indians always redistributed the gifts or trade goods that European settlers brought, rather than keep them for their own families. "Wealth circulateth like the Blood," he wrote. "All parts partake."[14]

Many simple hunting and gathering societies place so much emphasis on sharing that a person who kills an animal gets no more of its meat than do his companions. A review of twenty-five hunting and gathering societies found that in only three did the hunter get the largest share of his kill. In most, the hunter was obliged to share the meat equally with other camp members, and in a few he got less than he distributed to others. Anthropologist Polly Wiessner observes that these customs create total interdependence among families: "[T]he hunter spends his life hunting for others, and others spend their lives hunting for him."[15]

The idea that in prehistoric times a man would spend his life hunting only for the benefit of his own wife and children, who were dependent solely upon his hunting prowess for survival, is simply projection of 1950s marital norms onto the past. The male/female pair was a good way to organize sexual companionship, share child rearing, and divide daily work. A man who was a skilled hunter might have been an attractive mate, as would have been a woman who was skilled at foraging or making cooking implements, but marrying a good hunter was not the main way that a woman and her children got access to food and protection.

Marriage was certainly an early and a vitally important human invention. One of its crucial functions in the Paleolithic era was its ability to forge networks of cooperation beyond the immediate family group or local band. Bands needed to establish friendly relations with others so they could travel more freely and safely in pursuit of game, fish, plants, and water holes or move as the seasons changed. Archaeologist Brian Hayden argues that hunter-gatherers of the past used a combination of five strategies to create such ties with other groups and to defuse tensions: frequent informal visits, interband sharing, gift giving, periodic large gatherings for ritual occasions, and the establishment of marriage and kinship ties.[16]

All these customs built goodwill and established social networks beyond a single camp or a group of families. But using marriage to create new ties of kinship was an especially powerful way of binding groups together because it produced children who had relatives in both camps. The Maori of New Zealand say that "a gift connection may be severed, but not so a human link."[17]

However, a kin group that sent its daughters or sons to other groups as marriage partners also needed to make sure that it received spouses in return. Moreover, to create lasting links among groups, the exchange of spouses had to be renewed in later generations.

Sometimes such marriage exchanges would be very direct and immediate, a sister from one group being exchanged for a sister from the other. The exchange need not occur simultaneously, as long as the obligation to pay back one person with another was acknowledged. In other cases, spouses were not exchanged directly. Instead several lineages or clans would be linked in a pattern in which the sisters always married in one direction around the circle while the brothers always married in the opposite one. Lineage A would send its sisters and daughters as wives to lineage B, which sent wives to C, which sent them to A. As practiced among one present-day hunter-gatherer group, the Murngin of Australia, the circle of wife exchange takes seven generations to complete.[18]

Some people believe that from the very beginning, marriage alliances led to strict controls over a young person's choice of mates, especially a woman's. Among the Aborigines of Australia, one of the few places where hunter-gatherer societies lived completely untouched by contact with other societies for thousands of years, marriages were traditionally arranged when girls were still in their childhood and were strictly controlled by elders. Because of the scarcity of food and water in that harsh environment and the need to travel over long distances to ensure survival, Aboriginal elders had to ensure that their community's children were distributed in ways that gave the community family connections to the land and resources wherever they traveled. No rebellion against this system was tolerated.[19]

But the Indians of northeastern North America, who also lived for thousands of years in a "pristine" setting similar to the environment in which many of our Stone Age ancestors operated, traditionally took a very different approach toward marriage, divorce, and sexual activity from that of the Australian Aborigines. Among the Chippewyan people of Canada, the main function of marriage was also to build far-flung personal networks that gave people access to hunting, natural resources, or water holes in other regions. But in this more forgiving environment, individuals tended to make their own marital choices, and no one interfered if a couple decided to part.[20]

Nevertheless, many people argue that marriage originated as a way of exchanging women. Marriage alliances, the eminent anthropologist Claude Lévi-Strauss declared, were "not established between men and women, but between men by means of women." Women were merely the vehicle for establishing this relationship.[21]

In the 1970s several feminist researchers built on this idea to turn the protective theory of marriage on its head. They suggested that marriage originated not to protect women but to oppress them. These researchers argued that because women probably played a leading role in the invention of agriculture through their experimentation with plants and food preservation, and because women were certainly responsible for the physical reproduction of the group, the origins of marriage lay not in the efforts of women to attract protectors and providers but in the efforts of men to control the productive and reproductive powers of women for their own private benefit.[22]

According to this oppressive theory, men coerced women into marriage, often using abduction, gang rape, or wife beating to enforce their will. Brothers essentially traded their sisters for wives. Fathers gained power in the community by passing their daughters out to young men, who gave the fathers gifts and services in return. Rich men accumulated many wives, who worked for them and bore more daughters who could be exchanged to place other men in their debt.

Like the protective theory of marriage, the oppressive theory still has defenders. Philosopher Iris Marion Young maintains that the historical function of marriage was "to use women as a means of forging alliances among men and perpetuating their 'line.'" Even today, Young says, marriage is "the cornerstone of patriarchal power." Christine Delphy and Diana Leonard argue that marriage is one of the primary ways that "men benefit from, and exploit, the work of women."[23]

In today's political climate, in which men's power over their wives and daughters has greatly diminished, it is tempting to write off the oppressive theory of marriage as a product of 1970s feminist excesses. But there is strong historical evidence that in many societies marriage was indeed a way that men put women's labor to their private use. We can watch this process develop as recently as the eighteenth and nineteenth centuries among the Plains Indians.

In the Blackfoot legend about the origins of marriage, the men got dried meat and berries, warm robes, soft moccasins, and fine lodges only after the women chose to take them as husbands. In real life, men began to accumulate buffalo hides, large lodges, and other "fine" things, including, often, more than one wife, in a process that involved far less female choice.

Before the Europeans introduced the horse to the western United States, the Blackfoot and other Plains Indians hunted buffalo on foot, using surrounds. The entire group—men, women, and children—took part in driving the animals into traps or over cliffs. The men clubbed the buffalo to death, and the women dried the meat and tanned the hides. Although the men took on the more risky, up-close killing tasks, the work was evenly divided, and it was episodic; a good hunt could provide meat and clothes for a long time.[24]

But once Europeans introduced the horse, the gun, and the fur trade to North America, everything changed. Indian men were able to hunt buffalo individually. They had both the opportunity and incentive to kill more buffalo than they needed for their own subsistence because they could trade their surplus to whites for personal gain. This hugely increased the number of hides to be tanned and the amount of meat to be dried. The most successful hunters could now kill far more buffalo than one wife could process, and having more wives suddenly meant having more wealth. Richer men began to accumulate wives by offering horses to girls' fathers.

The expansion of the trade in buffalo hides brought a sharp increase in the number of wives per hunter. It also caused the age of marriage for women to drop to preadolescence, and it greatly multiplied social restrictions upon wives. According to nineteenth-century observers, the practice of keeping multiple wives was most common among groups that traded with the fur companies, and in these groups women's labor was much more intensive. These tribes too were more likely to practice forms of punishment such as cutting off a woman's nose for adultery.[25]

There are many other examples of societies in which men have exchanged women without consulting them and in which husbands have used the labor of their wives and children to produce surpluses that increased the men's prestige and power. It is also true that many more societies exchange women in marriage than exchange men, and there are some disadvantages to being the sex that moves after marriage. But in small-scale societies these disadvantages were not necessarily severe. Women could return home to their parents or call on their brothers for protection. Furthermore, in some societies men were the ones who moved at marriage. In these cases, one could just as easily argue that men were being exchanged by women.

In a current example, the Minangkabau of Indonesia, where marriage perpetuates the female line, refer to a husband as "the borrowed man." In traditional Hopi Indian marriages, a woman's kin made "a ceremonial presentation of cornmeal to the groom's household, conceptualized by the Hopi as 'paying for him.'" There is evidence that marriage systems in which men rather than women were circulated may have been more common in kinship societies of the distant past than in those observed over the past several hundred years.[26]

Even in cultures where women move at marriage, there has always been a huge variation in how much male dominance accompanies this arrangement. There are also enough exceptions to the practice of controlling women through marriage to call the oppressive theory into question. In the early eighteenth century a French baron, traveling among hunting and gathering peoples in what is now Canada, was scandalized to find that native parents believed "their Daughters have the command of their own Bodies and may dispose of their Persons as they think fit; they being at liberty to do what they please."[27]

In many hunting and gathering and simple horticultural societies, parents are likely to arrange a first marriage. They may even force a woman into a match. However, in most societies without extensive private property, marriages tend to be fragile, and women whose families have arranged their marriages frequently leave their husbands or run off with lovers without suffering any reprisals.[28]

I do not believe, then, that marriage was invented to oppress women any more than it was invented to protect them. In most cases, marriage probably originated as an informal way of organizing sexual companionship, child rearing, and the daily tasks of life. It became more formal and more permanent as groups began to exchange spouses over larger distances. There was nothing inherent in the institution of marriage that protected women and children from violence or produced the fair and loving relationships that many modern couples aspire to. But there was also nothing inherent in the institution of marriage, as there was, say, in slavery, that required one group to subordinate another. The effect of marriage on people's individual lives has always depended on its functions in economic and social life, functions that have changed immensely over time.

It is likely that our Stone Age ancestors varied in their behaviors just as do the hunting and gathering societies observed in more recent times. But in early human societies, marriage was primarily a way to extend cooperative relations and circulate people and resources beyond the local group. When people married into new groups, it turned strangers into relatives and enemies into allies.

That changed, however, as societies developed surpluses and became more sedentary, populous, and complex.[29] As kin groups began to assert permanent rights over territory and resources, some families amassed more goods and power than others. When that happened, the wealthier families lost interest in sharing resources, pooling labor, or developing alliances with poorer families. Gradually marriage exchanges became a way of consolidating resources rather than creating a circle of reciprocal obligations and connections.

With the growth of inequality in society, the definition of an acceptable marriage narrowed. Wealthy kin groups refused to marry with poorer ones and disavowed any children born to couples whose marriage they hadn't authorized. This shift constituted a revolution in marriage that was to shape people's lives for thousands of years. Whereas marriage had once been a way of expanding the number of cooperating groups, it now became a way for powerful kin groups to accumulate both people and property.

The Transformation of Marriage in Ancient Societies

Wherever this evolution from foraging bands to sedentary agriculturalists occurred, it was accompanied by a tendency to funnel cooperation and sharing exclusively through family ties and kinship obligations and to abandon more informal ways of pooling or sharing resources. In the American Southwest we can trace this transition through changes in architectural patterns. Originally surplus grains were stored in communal spaces in open, visible parts of the village. Later, storage rooms were enclosed within individual residences and could be entered only from the rooms where the family or household actually lived. Surpluses had become capital to be closely guarded, with access restricted to family members.[30]

As some kin groups became richer than others, they sought ways to enhance their own status and to differentiate themselves from "lesser" families. Excavations of ancient living sites throughout the world show growing disparities in the size and quality of dwellings, as well as in the richness of the objects buried with people.

Greater economic differentiation reshaped the rules of marriage. A kin group or lineage with greater social status and material resources could demand a higher "price" for handing over one of its children in marriage. Within the leading lineages, young men often had to borrow from their seniors in order to marry, increasing the control of elders over junior men as well as over women. A lineage that couldn't pay top prices for spouses had to drop out of the highest rungs of the marriage exchange system. Sometimes a poorer lineage would forgo the bridewealth a groom's family traditionally paid and give its daughters away as secondary wives or concubines to the leading lineages, in order to forge even a second-class connection with a leading family. But in other cases, lower-status kin groups were not allowed to intermarry with those of higher status under any circumstances.[31]

As dominant kin groups became more wealthy and powerful, they married in more restricted circles. Sometimes they even turned away from exogamy (the practice of marrying out of the group) and engaged in endogamy (marriage with close kin), in order to preserve and consolidate their property and kin members.[32] The more resources were at stake in marriage alliances, the more the relatives had an interest in whom their kin married, whether a marriage lasted, and whether a second marriage, which might produce new heirs to complicate the transmission of property, could be contracted if the first one ended.

In many ancient agricultural societies, if an heir was already in place and the birth of another child would complicate inheritance and succession, a woman might be forced to remain single and celibate after her husband's death. In a few cultures the ideal was for a widow to kill herself after her husband died.[33] More often, the surviving spouse was required to marry another member of the deceased's family in order to perpetuate the alliance between the two kin groups.

In India, early law codes provided that a widow with no son had to marry her husband's brother, in order to produce a male child to carry on his lineage. The Old Testament mentions several examples of the same custom. Indeed, it seems to have been preferred practice among the ancient Hebrews. A man who refused to marry his brother's widow had to go through a public ceremony of halizah, or "unshoeing." This passage from the Torah shows how intense the social pressure was against making such a choice: "Then shall his brother's wife come unto him in the presence of the elders, and loose his shoe from off his foot, and spit in his face, and shall answer and say, so shall it be done unto that man that will not build up his brother's house. And his name shall be called in Israel the house of him that hath his shoe loosed."[34]

As marriage became the primary vehicle for transmitting status and property, both men and women faced greater restrictions on their behavior. Men, like women, could be forced to marry women chosen by their parents. But because women could bear a child with an "impure" bloodline, introducing a "foreign interest" into a family, their sexual behavior tended to be more strictly supervised, and females were subject to severe penalties for adultery or premarital sex. The laws and moral codes of ancient states exhorted men to watch carefully over their wives "lest the seed of others be sown on your soil."[35]

Distinctions between legitimate and illegitimate children became sharper in all the early states. Children born into

unauthorized liaisons could not inherit land, titles, or citizenship rights and so in many cases were effectively condemned to slavery or starvation.

The subordination of wives in the ancient world was exacerbated by the invention of the plow. Use of the plow diminished the value of women's agricultural labor, because plowing requires greater strength than women were believed to have and is less compatible with child care than gardening with a hoe. Husbands began to demand dowries instead of giving bridewealth for wives, and daughters were devalued to the point that families sometimes resorted to female infanticide. The spread of warfare that accompanied the emergence of early states also pushed women farther down in the hierarchy.[36]

As societies became more complex and differentiated, upper classes sometimes displayed their wealth by adopting standards of beauty or behavior that effectively hobbled women. Restrictive clothing, heavy jewelry, or exceedingly long fingernails, for example, made a public statement that the family had slaves to do the work once done by wives and daughters. By the second millennium B.C. the practice of secluding women in special quarters had become widespread in the Middle East. This was done not just to guard their chastity but to signify that a family had so much wealth that its women did not even have to leave the home.

Much later, in China, binding the feet of young girls became a symbol of prestige. Upper-class girls had their feet bound so tightly that the small bones broke and the feet were permanently bowed over, making it excruciatingly painful to walk.[37]

In many societies, elaborate ideologies of purity grew up around the women of the highest-ranking classes. A man who courted a high-ranking woman outside regular channels faced harsh sanctions or even death, while women who stepped out of their assigned places in the marriage market were severely punished.

Assyrian laws from the twelfth and eleventh centuries B.C. guarded women's premarital virginity and condemned to death married women who committed adultery. Married women were required to wear veils, but concubines were forbidden to do so. A man who wanted to raise the status of his concubine and make her his wife could have her veiled. But a woman who veiled herself without the authority of a propertied husband was to be flogged fifty times, have tar poured over her head, and have her ears cut off.[38]

Women's bodies came to be regarded as the properties of their fathers and husbands. Assyrian law declared: "A man may flog his wife, pluck her hair, strike her and mutilate her ears. There is no guilt." The Old Testament suggests that a bride whose virginity was not intact could be stoned to death.[39]

Centuries later in China, Confucius defined a wife as "someone who submits to another." A wife, according to Confucian philosophy, had to follow "the rule of the three obediences: while at home she obeys her father, after marriage she obeys her husband, after he dies she obeys her son."[40]

But men too faced new controls over their personal behavior. If a woman could no longer choose her mate, this also meant that a man could not court a wife on his own initiative but needed to win her father's permission. And in many states, the confinement of wives to household activities "freed" their husbands to be drafted into the army or dragooned into back-breaking labor on huge public works projects.[41]

By the time we have written records of the civilizations that arose in the ancient world, marriage had become the way most wealth and land changed hands. Marriage was also the main vehicle by which leading families expanded their social networks and political influence. It even sealed military alliances and peace treaties.

With so much at stake, it is hardly surprising that marriage became a hotbed of political intrigue. Families and individuals developed elaborate strategies to create unions that furthered their interests and to block marriages that might benefit their rivals. Elites jockeyed to acquire powerful in-laws. If, after they had agreed to seal a match, a better one presented itself, they maneuvered (and sometimes murdered) to get out of the old one.

Commoners could no longer hope to exchange marriage partners with the elites. At best they might hope to have one of their children marry up. Even this became more difficult as intricate distinctions were created between the rights of primary wives, secondary wives, and concubines. Formal rules detailed what kinds of marriage could and could not produce legitimate heirs. In some places authorities prohibited lower-class groups from marrying at all or made it illegal for individuals from different social classes to wed each other.

The right to decide who could marry whom had become an extremely valuable political and economic weapon and remained so for thousands of years. From the Middle Eastern kingdoms that arose three thousand years before the birth of Christ to the European ones fifteen hundred years later, factions of the ruling circles fought over who had the right to legitimize marriages or authorize divorces. These battles often changed the course of history.

For millennia, the maneuvering of families, governing authorities, and social elites prevailed over the individual desires of young people when it came to selecting or rejecting marriage partners. It was only two hundred years ago that men and women began to wrest control over the right to marry from the hands of parents, church, and state. And only in the last hundred years have women had the independence to make their marital choices without having to bow to economic need and social pressure.

Have we come full circle during the past two centuries, as the power of kin, community, and state to arrange, prohibit, and interfere in marriages has waned? Legal scholar Harry Willekins argues that in most modern industrial societies, marriages are contracted and dissolved in ways that have more in common with the habits of some egalitarian band-level societies than the elaborate rules that governed marriage in more complex societies over the past 5,000 years.[42] In many contemporary societies, there is growing acceptance of premarital sex, divorce, and remarriage, along with an erosion of sharp distinctions between cohabitation and marriage and between "legitimate" and out-of-wedlock births.

Some people note this resemblance between modern family relations and the informal sexual and marital norms of many band-level societies and worry that we are throwing away the advantages of civilization. They hope to reinstitutionalize marriage as the main mechanism that regulates sexuality, legitimizes children, organizes the division of labor between men and women, and redistributes resources to dependents. But the last century of social change makes this highly unlikely. Yet if it is unrealistic to believe we can reimpose older social controls over marriage, it is also naive to think we can effortlessly revive the fluid interpersonal relationships that characterized simpler cultures. In hunting and gathering bands and egalitarian horticultural communities, unstable marriages did not lead to the impoverishment of women or children as they often do today. Unmarried women participated in the work of the group and were entitled to a fair share, while children and other dependents were protected by strong customs that mandated sharing beyond the nuclear family.

This is not the case today, especially in societies such as the United States, where welfare provisions are less extensive than in Western Europe. Today's winner-take-all global economy may have its strong points, but the practice of pooling resources and sharing with the weak is not one of them. The question of how we organize our personal rights and obligations now that our older constraints are gone is another aspect of the contemporary marriage crisis.

Critical Thinking

1. Explain why the story that marriage was invented for the protection of women was such a persuasive theory in the mid-twentieth century. In what ways have researchers poked holes in this theory?

2. What have been the three general schools of thought on how the earliest hominids and humans organized their reproduction and family lives?

3. How does the author characterize early hunter-gatherer societies and their gender-based division of labor and why?

4. What were such societies like, according to reconstructions by archaeologists?

5. Discuss the importance of prehistoric sharing. How is this contrary to the 1950s marital norms?

6. Why was marriage "an early and a vitally important human invention"?

7. According to archaeologist Brian Hayden, what were the five strategies used to create ties with groups and to defuse tensions?

8. Be familiar with some of the means by which marriage became an especially powerful way of binding groups together.

9. Discuss the "oppressive theory" as to the origin of marriage and the evidence provided by the author to contradict it.

10. How did the development of surpluses and a more sedentary life-style change the function of marriage?

11. How did greater economic differentiation reshape the rules of marriage, inheritance, and sexual behavior?

12. How was the subordination of wives in the ancient world exacerbated by the invention of the plow?

13. How is it that, as societies became more complex and differentiated, upper classes sometimes displayed their wealth by adopting standards of beauty or behavior that effectively hobbled women? What kinds of controls did men face?

14. In what ways did marriage become a "hotbed of political intrigue"?

15. Now that women have achieved some degree of economic independence and there is a degree of resemblance in family relations between ourselves and band-level societies, have we come full circle? Explain.

Create Central

www.mhhe.com/createcentral

Internet References

Kinship and Social Organization
www.umanitoba.ca/anthropology

Sex and Marriage
http://anthro.palomar.edu/marriage/default.htm

Wedding Traditions and Customs
http://worldweddingtraditions.com

Coontz, Stephanie. From *Marriage: A History*, Viking, 2005, pp. 1–13. Copyright © 2005 by Penguin Group (USA) Inc. Reprinted by permission.

Article   Prepared by: Elvio Angeloni, *Pasadena City College*

When Brothers Share a Wife
Among Tibetans, the Good Life Relegates Many Women to Spinsterhood

Melvyn C. Goldstein

Learning Outcomes

After reading this article, you will be able to:

- Discuss why "fraternal polyandry" is socially acceptable in Tibet but not in our society.

- Explain the disappearance and subsequent revival of fraternal polyandry in Tibet.

E ager to reach home, Dorje drives his yaks hard over the 17,000-foot mountain pass, stopping only once to rest. He and his two older brothers, Pema and Sonam, are jointly marrying a woman from the next village in a few weeks, and he has to help with the preparations.

Dorje, Pema, and Sonam are Tibetans living in Limi, a 200-square-mile area in the northwest corner of Nepal, across the border from Tibet. The form of marriage they are about to enter—fraternal polyandry in anthropological parlance—is one of the world's rarest forms of marriage but is not uncommon in Tibetan society, where it has been practiced from time immemorial. For many Tibetan social strata, it traditionally represented the ideal form of marriage and family.

The mechanics of fraternal polyandry are simple. Two, three, four, or more brothers jointly take a wife, who leaves her home to come and live with them. Traditionally, marriage was arranged by parents, with children, particularly females, having little or no say. This is changing somewhat nowadays, but it is still unusual for children to marry without their parents' consent. Marriage ceremonies vary by income and region and range from all the brothers sitting together as grooms to only the eldest one formally doing so. The age of the brothers plays an important role in determining this: very young brothers almost never participate in actual marriage ceremonies, although they typically join the marriage when they reach their mid-teens.

The eldest brother is normally dominant in terms of authority, that is, in managing the household, but all the brothers share the work and participate as sexual partners. Tibetan males and females do not find the sexual aspect of sharing a spouse the least bit unusual, repulsive, or scandalous, and the norm is for the wife to treat all the brothers the same.

Offspring are treated similarly. There is no attempt to link children biologically to particular brothers, and a brother shows no favoritism toward his child even if he knows he is the real father because, for example, his other brothers were away at the time the wife became pregnant. The children, in turn, consider all of the brothers as their fathers and treat them equally, even if they also know who is their real father. In some regions children use the term "father" for the eldest brother and "father's brother" for the others, while in other areas they call all the brothers by one term, modifying this by the use of "elder" and "younger."

Unlike our own society, where monogamy is the only form of marriage permitted, Tibetan society allows a variety of marriage types, including monogamy, fraternal polyandry, and polygyny. Fraternal polyandry and monogamy are the most common forms of marriage, while polygyny typically occurs in cases where the first wife is barren. The widespread practice of fraternal polyandry, therefore, is not the outcome of a law requiring brothers to marry jointly. There is choice, and in fact, divorce traditionally was relatively simple in Tibetan society. If a brother in a polyandrous marriage became dissatisfied and wanted to separate, he simply left the main house and set up his own household. In such cases, all the children stayed in the main household with the remaining brother(s), even if the departing brother was known to be the real father of one or more of the children.

The Tibetans' own explanation for choosing fraternal polyandry is materialistic. For example, when I asked Dorje why he decided to marry with his two brothers rather than take his own wife, he thought for a moment, then said it prevented the division of his family's farm (and animals) and thus facilitated all of them achieving a higher standard of living. And when I later asked Dorje's bride whether it wasn't difficult for her to cope with three brothers as husbands, she laughed and echoed the rationale of avoiding fragmentation of the family and land, adding that she expected to be better off economically, since she would have three husbands working for her and her children.

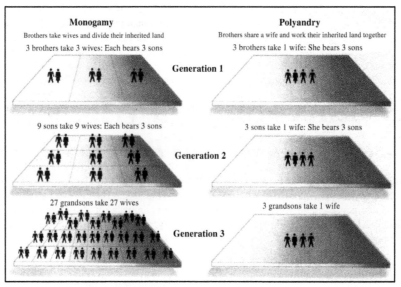

Joe LeMonnier

Family Planning in Tibet An economic rationale for fraternal polyandry is outlined in the diagram, which emphasizes only the male offspring in each generation. If every wife is assumed to bear three sons, a family splitting up into monogamous households would rapidly multiply and fragment the family land. In this case, a rule of inheritance, such as primogeniture, could retain the family land intact, but only at the cost of creating many landless male offspring. In contrast, the family practicing fraternal polyandry maintains a steady ratio of persons to land.

Exotic as it may seem to Westerners, Tibetan fraternal polyandry is thus in many ways analogous to the way primogeniture functioned in nineteenth-century England. Primogeniture dictated that the eldest son inherited the family estate, while younger sons had to leave home and seek their own employment—for example, in the military or the clergy. Primogeniture maintained family estates intact over generations by permitting only one heir per generation. Fraternal polyandry also accomplishes this but does so by keeping all the brothers together with just one wife so that there is only one *set* of heirs per generation.

While Tibetans believe that in this way fraternal polyandry reduces the risk of family fission, monogamous marriages among brothers need not necessarily precipitate the division of the family estate: brothers could continue to live together, and the family land could continue to be worked jointly. When I asked Tibetans about this, however, they invariably responded that such joint families are unstable because each wife is primarily oriented to her own children and interested in their success and well-being over that of the children of the other wives. For example, if the youngest brother's wife had three sons while the eldest brother's wife had only one daughter, the wife of the youngest brother might begin to demand more resources for her children since, as males, they represent the future of the family. Thus, the children from different wives in the same generation are competing sets of heirs, and this makes such families inherently unstable. Tibetans perceive that conflict will spread from the wives to their husbands and consider this likely to cause family fission. Consequently, it is almost never done.

Although Tibetans see an economic advantage to fraternal polyandry, they do not value the sharing of a wife as an end

in itself. On the contrary, they articulate a number of problems inherent in the practice. For example, because authority is customarily exercised by the eldest brother, his younger male siblings have to subordinate themselves with little hope of changing their status within the family. When these younger brothers are aggressive and individualistic, tensions and difficulties often occur despite there being only one set of heirs.

In addition, tension and conflict may arise in polyandrous families because of sexual favoritism. The bride normally sleeps with the eldest brother, and the two have the responsibility to see to it that the other males have opportunities for sexual access. Since the Tibetan subsistence economy requires males to travel a lot, the temporary absence of one or more brothers facilitates this, but there are also other rotation practices. The cultural ideal unambiguously calls for the wife to show equal affection and sexuality to each of the brothers (and vice versa), but deviations from this ideal occur, especially when there is a sizable difference in age between the partners in the marriage.

Dorje's family represents just such a potential situation. He is fifteen years old and his two older brothers are twenty-five and twenty-two years old. The new bride is twenty-three years old, eight years Dorje's senior. Sometimes such a bride finds the youngest husband immature and adolescent and does not treat him with equal affection; alternatively, she may find his youth attractive and lavish special attention on him. Apart from that consideration, when a younger male like Dorje grows up, he may consider his wife "ancient" and prefer the company of a woman his own age or younger. Consequently, although men and women do not find the idea of sharing a bride or bridegroom repulsive, individual likes and dislikes can cause familial discord.

Two reasons have commonly been offered for the perpetuation of fraternal polyandry in Tibet: that Tibetans practice female infanticide and therefore have to marry polyandrously, owing to a shortage of females; and that Tibet, lying at extremely high altitudes, is so barren and bleak that Tibetans would starve without resort to this mechanism. A Jesuit who lived in Tibet during the eighteenth century articulated this second view: "One reason for this most odious custom is the sterility of the soil, and the small amount of land that can be cultivated owing to the lack of water. The crops may suffice if the brothers all live together, but if they form separate families they would be reduced to beggary."

Both explanations are wrong, however. Not only has there never been institutionalized female infanticide in Tibet, but Tibetan society gives females considerable rights, including inheriting the family estate in the absence of brothers. In such cases, the woman takes a bridegroom who comes to live in her family and adopts her family's name and identity. Moreover, there is no demographic evidence of a shortage of females. In Limi, for example, there were (in 1974) sixty females and fifty-three males in the fifteen- to thirty-five-year age category, and many adult females were unmarried.

The second reason is also incorrect. The climate in Tibet is extremely harsh, and ecological factors do play a major role perpetuating polyandry, but polyandry is not a means of preventing starvation. It is characteristic, not of the poorest segments of the society, but rather of the peasant landowning families.

In the old society, the landless poor could not realistically aspire to prosperity, but they did not fear starvation. There was a persistent labor shortage throughout Tibet, and very poor families with little or no land and few animals could subsist through agricultural labor, tenant farming, craft occupations such as carpentry, or by working as servants. Although the per person family income could increase somewhat if brothers married polyandrously and pooled their wages, in the absence of inheritable land, the advantage of fraternal polyandry was not generally sufficient to prevent them from setting up their own households. A more skilled or energetic younger brother could do as well or better alone, since he would completely control his income and would not have to share it with his siblings. Consequently, while there was and is some polyandry among the poor, it is much less frequent and more prone to result in divorce and family fission.

An alternative reason for the persistence of fraternal polyandry is that it reduces population growth (and thereby reduces the pressure on resources) by relegating some females to lifetime spinsterhood. Fraternal polyandrous marriages in Limi (in 1974) averaged 2.35 men per woman, and not surprisingly, 31 percent of the females of child-bearing age (twenty to forty-nine) were unmarried. These spinsters either continued to live at home, set up their own households, or worked as servants for other families. They could also become Buddhist nuns. Being unmarried is not synonymous with exclusion from the reproductive pool. Discreet extramarital relationships are tolerated, and actually half of the adult unmarried women in Limi had one or more children. They raised these children as single mothers, working for wages or weaving cloth and blankets for

sale. As a group, however, the unmarried woman had far fewer offspring than the married women, averaging only 0.7 children per woman, compared with 3.3 for married women, whether polyandrous, monogamous, or polygynous. While polyandry helps regulate population, this function of polyandry is not consciously perceived by Tibetans and is not the reason they consistently choose it.

If neither a shortage of females nor the fear of starvation perpetuates fraternal polyandry, what motivates brothers, particularly younger brothers, to opt for this system of marriage? From the perspective of the younger brother in a land-holding family, the main incentive is the attainment or maintenance of the good life. With polyandry, he can expect a more secure and higher standard of living, with access not only to this family's land and animals but also to its inherited collection of clothes, jewelry, rugs, saddles, and horses. In addition, he will experience less work pressure and much greater security because all responsibility does not fall on one "father." For Tibetan brothers, the question is whether to trade off the greater personal freedom inherent in monogamy for the real or potential economic security, affluence, and social prestige associated with life in a larger, labor-rich polyandrous family.

A brother thinking of separating from his polyandrous marriage and taking his own wife would face various disadvantages. Although in the majority of Tibetan regions all brothers theoretically have rights to their family's estate, in reality Tibetans are reluctant to divide their land into small fragments. Generally, a younger brother who insists on leaving the family will receive only a small plot of land, if that. Because of its power and wealth, the rest of the family usually can block any attempt of the younger brother to increase his share of land through litigation. Moreover, a younger brother may not even get a house and cannot expect to receive much above the minimum in terms of movable possessions, such as furniture, pots, and pans. Thus, a brother contemplating going it on his own must plan on achieving economic security and the good life not through inheritance but through his own work.

The obvious solution for younger brothers—creating new fields from virgin land—is generally not a feasible option. Most Tibetan populations live at high altitudes (above 12,000 feet), where arable land is extremely scarce. For example, in Dorje's village, agriculture ranges only from about 12,900 feet, the lowest point in the area, to 13,300 feet. Above that altitude, early frost and snow destroy the staple barley crop. Furthermore, because of the low rainfall caused by the Himalayan rain shadow, many areas in Tibet and northern Nepal that are within the appropriate altitude range for agriculture have no reliable sources of irrigation. In the end, although there is plenty of unused land in such areas, most of it is either too high or too arid.

Even where unused land capable of being farmed exists, clearing the land and building the substantial terraces necessary for irrigation constitute a great undertaking. Each plot has to be completely dug out to a depth of two to two and half feet so that the large rocks and boulders can be removed. At best, a man might be able to bring a few new fields under cultivation in the first years after separating from his brothers, but he could not expect to acquire substantial amounts of arable land this way.

In addition, because of the limited farmland, the Tibetan subsistence economy characteristically includes a strong emphasis on animal husbandry. Tibetan farmers regularly maintain cattle, yaks, goats, and sheep, grazing them in the areas too high for agriculture. These herds produce wool, milk, cheese, butter, meat, and skins. To obtain these resources, however, shepherds must accompany the animals on a daily basis. When first setting up a monogamous household, a younger brother like Dorje would find it difficult to both farm and manage animals.

In traditional Tibetan society, there was an even more critical factor that operated to perpetuate fraternal polyandry—a form of hereditary servitude somewhat analogous to serfdom in Europe. Peasants were tied to large estates held by aristocrats, monasteries, and the Lhasa government. They were allowed the use of some farmland to produce their own subsistence but were required to provide taxes in kind and corvée (free labor) to their lords. The corvée was a substantial hardship, since a peasant household was in many cases required to furnish the lord with one laborer daily for most of the year and more on specific occasions such as the harvest. This enforced labor, along with the lack of new land and ecological pressure to pursue both agriculture and animal husbandry, made polyandrous families particularly beneficial. The polyandrous family allowed an internal division of adult labor, maximizing economic advantage. For example, while the wife worked the family fields, one brother could perform the lord's corvée, another could look after the animals, and a third could engage in trade.

Although social scientists often discount other people's explanations of why they do things, in the case of Tibetan fraternal polyandry, such explanations are very close to the truth. The custom, however, is very sensitive to changes in its political and economic milieu and, not surprisingly, is in decline in most Tibetan areas. Made less important by the elimination of the traditional serf-based economy, it is disparaged by the dominant non-Tibetan leaders of India, China, and Nepal. New opportunities for economic and social mobility in these countries, such as the tourist trade and government employment, are also eroding the rationale for polyandry, and so it may vanish within the next generation.

Author's Note

The Revival of Fraternal Polyandry in Tibet: Old Solutions for New Problems

In spite of my observation at the end of this article—that political and economic changes were eroding the rationality for fraternal polyandry—there has been a remarkable revival of polyandry in the Tibet Autonomous Region.

After the failed Tibetan Uprising in 1959, the Chinese government acted to end the traditional land-holding system and replace it with communes in which individual commune members worked under a set of managers. Fraternal polyandry ended, as families had no land to conserve and farm.

The rise to power of Deng Xiaoping in 1978 changed China radically. China now opened its doors to the West and adopted Western-style market economics complete with the

reintroduction of the profit motive and individual wealth seeking. In rural Tibet, this resulted in communes closing in 1980–81, with each commune member receiving an equal share of the commune's land regardless of age or sex. Thus, if each person received 1 acre, a family of 6 received 6 acres, on which it now managed to maximize production and income. However, families actually held this land as a long-term lease from the government so land could not be bought or sold. Consequently, as children were born and the size of families grew, land per capita began to decrease. At the same time, as sons reached the age of marriage, it was obvious that if families with several sons allowed each to marry and set up nuclear families, the land the family received from the commune would decline dramatically, and with no way to buy more land, each of the family units would have difficulty growing enough grain for subsistence. Families, therefore, as in the old society, began to utilize traditional fraternal polyandry to keep their sons together at marriage to conserve the family's land intact across generations.

A second factor underlying the widespread revival of fraternal polyandry concerned its concentration of male labor in the family. However, in the new socioeconomic environment, this has not been used to fulfill corvée labor obligations to one's lord (as mentioned in the article), but rather to increase family income by sending surplus labor (one or more of the set of siblings) to "go for income," i.e., to go outside the village as migrant laborers to earn cash income working for part of the year in cities or on rural construction projects. By the time of my last stint of fieldwork in rural Tibet in 2009, this had become the largest source of rural family income.

Fraternal polyandry has therefore undergone an unexpected revival in Tibet because its traditional functions of conserving land intact across generations and concentrating male labor in the family has offered families in the new economic system old solutions to new problems. Rapidly changing socioeconomic conditions, therefore, do not necessarily erode traditional cultural practices. They can, as in this case, revive and sustain them as well.

Critical Thinking

1. What is "fraternal polyandry"? How is it arranged?
2. How do marriage ceremonies vary? When do younger brothers typically join the marriage?
3. How are authority, work, and sex dealt with?
4. Describe the relationship between fathers and children. How is family structure reflected in kinship terminology?
5. What types of marriage are allowed in Tibetan society? Which are the most common? When does polygyny typically occur? Is fraternal polyandry a matter of law or choice? What happens if a brother is dissatisfied? What about his children?
6. How do the Tibetans explain fraternal polyandry? How is this analogous to primogeniture in 19th-century England?
7. Why does it seem that monogamous marriages among brothers in the same household would not work?

8. What kinds of problems occur with fraternal polyandry that make it less than ideal?

9. What two reasons have been commonly offered for the perpetuation of fraternal polyandry in Tibet and how does the author refute these?

10. What percentage of women remain unmarried in Tibetan society? What happens to them? To what extent does polyandry thereby limit population growth? Are the Tibetans aware of this effect?

11. Why would a younger brother accept such a marriage form?

12. How is the polyandrous family more adaptive to the system of hereditary servitude in traditional Tibet?

13. Why is the custom of fraternal polyandry in decline?

14. Explain the disappearence and subsequent revival of fraternal polyandry in Tibet.

Create Central

www.mhhe.com/createcentral

Internet References

Sex and Marriage
   http://anthro.palomar.edu/marriage/default.htm
Wedding Traditions and Customs
   http://worldweddingtraditions.com

MELVYN C. GOLDSTEIN, now a professor of anthropology at Case Western Reserve University in Cleveland, has been interested in the Tibetan practice of fraternal polyandry (several brothers marrying one wife) since he was a graduate student in the 1960s.

Article   Prepared by: Elvio Angeloni, *Pasadena City College*

No More Angel Babies on the Alto do Cruzeiro

A dispatch from brazil's revolution in child survival.

NANCY SCHEPER-HUGHES

Learning Outcomes

After reading this article, you will be able to:

- Describe and explain the "normalization" of infant death as it once occurred on the Alto do Cruzeiro in Brazil.

- Discuss the economic and political changes in Brazil that led to the decline in "angel babies."

It was almost 50 years ago that I first walked to the top of the Alto do Cruzeiro (the Hill of the Crucifix) in Timbaúba, a sugar-belt town in the state of Pernambuco, in Northeast Brazil. I was looking for the small mud hut, nestled in a cliff, where I was to live. It was December 1964, nine months after the coup that toppled the left-leaning president, João Goulart. Church bells were ringing, and I asked the woman who was to host me as a Peace Corps volunteer why they seemed to ring at all hours of the day. "Oh, it's nothing," she told me. "Just another little angel gone to heaven."

That day marked the beginning of my life's work. Since then, I've experienced something between an obsession, a trauma, and a romance with the shantytown. Residents of the newly occupied hillside were refugees from the military junta's violent attacks on the peasant league movement that had tried to enforce existing laws protecting the local sugarcane cutters. The settlers had thrown together huts made of straw, mud, and sticks or, lacking that, lean-tos made of tin, cardboard, and scrap materials. They had thrown together families in the same makeshift fashion, taking whatever was at hand and making do. In the absence of husbands, weekend play fathers did nicely as

long as they brought home the current baby's powdered milk, if not the bacon. Households were temporary; in such poverty women were the only stable force, and babies and fathers were circulated among them. A man who could not provide support would be banished to take up residence with another, even more desperate woman; excess infants and babies were often rescued by older women, who took them in as informal foster children.

Premature death was an everyday occurrence in a shanty-town lacking water, electricity, and sanitation and beset with food scarcity, epidemics, and police violence. My assignment was to immunize children, educate midwives, attend births, treat infections, bind up festering wounds, and visit mothers and newborns at home to monitor their health and refer them as needed to the district health post or to the emergency room of the private hospital—owned by the mayor's brother—where charity cases were sometimes attended, depending on the state of local patron-client relations.

I spent several months making the rounds between the miserable huts on the Alto with a public-health medical kit strapped on my shoulder. Its contents were pathetic: a bar of soap, scissors, antiseptics, aspirin, bandages, a glass syringe, some ampules of vaccine, several needles, and a pumice stone to sharpen the needles, which were used over and over again for immunizations. Children ran away when they saw me coming, and well they might have.

But what haunted me then, in addition to my own incompetence, was something I did not have the skill or maturity to understand: Why didn't the women of the Alto grieve over the deaths of their babies? I tucked that question away. But as Winnicott, the British child psychoanalyst, liked to say, "Nothing is ever forgotten."

Sixteen years elapsed before I was able to return to the Alto do Cruzeiro, this time as a medical anthropologist. It was in 1982—during the period known as the abertura, or opening, the beginning of the end of the military dictatorship—that I made the first of the four trips that formed the basis for my 1992 book, *Death Without Weeping: The Violence of Everyday Life in Brazil.* My goal was to study women's lives, specifically mother love and child death under conditions so dire that the Uruguayan writer Eduardo Galeano once described the region as a concentration camp for 30 million people. It was not a gross exaggeration. Decades of nutritional studies of sugarcane cutters and their families in Pernambuco showed hard evidence of slow starvation and stunting. These nutritional dwarfs were surviving on a daily caloric intake similar to that of the inmates of the Buchenwald concentration camp. Life on the Alto resembled prison-camp culture, with a moral ethic based on triage and survival.

If mother love is the cultural expression of what many attachment theorists believe to be a bioevolutionary script, what could this script mean to women living in these conditions? In my sample of three generations of mothers in the sugar plantation zone of Pernambuco, the average woman had 9.5 pregnancies, 8 live births, and 3.5 infant deaths. Such high rates of births and deaths are typical of societies that have not undergone what population experts call the demographic transition, associated with economic development, in which first death rates and, later, birth rates drop as parents begin to trust that more of their infants will survive. On the contrary, the high expectation of loss and the normalization of infant death was a powerful conditioner of the degree of maternal attachments. Mothers and infants could also be rivals for scarce resources. Alto mothers renounced breastfeeding as impossible, as sapping far too much strength from their own "wrecked" bodies.

Scarcity made mother love a fragile emotion, postponed until the newborn displayed a will to live—a taste (gusto) and a knack (jeito) for life. A high expectancy of death prepared mothers to "let go" of and to hasten the death of babies that were failing to thrive, by reducing the already insufficient food, water, and care. The "angel babies" of the Alto were neither of this Earth nor yet fully spirits. In appearance they were ghostlike: pale and wispy-haired; their arms and legs stripped of flesh; their bellies grossly distended; their eyes blank and staring; and their faces wizened, a cross between startled primate and wise old sorcerer.

The experience of too much loss, too much death, led to a kind of patient resignation that some clinical psychologists might label "emotional numbing" or the symptoms of a "masked depression." But the mothers' resignation was neither pathological nor abnormal. Moreover, it was a moral code. Not only had a continual exposure to trauma obliterated rage and protest, it also minimized attachment so as to diminish sorrow.

Infant death was so commonplace that I recall a birthday party for a four-year-old in which the birthday cake, decorated with candles, was placed on the kitchen table next to the tiny blue cardboard coffin of the child's nine-month-old sibling, who had died during the night. Next to the coffin a single vigil candle was lit. Despite the tragedy, the child's mother wanted to go ahead with the party. "Parabens para pace," we sang, clapping our hands. "Congratulations to you!" the Brazilian birthday song goes. And on the Alto it had special resonance: "Congratulations, you survivor you—you lived to see another year!"

When Alto mothers cried, they cried for themselves, for those left behind to continue the struggle. But they cried the hardest for their children who had almost died, but who surprised everyone by surviving against the odds. Wiping a stray tear from her eye, an Alto mother would speak with deep emotion of the child who, given up for dead, suddenly beat death back, displaying a fierce desire for life. These tough and stubborn children were loved above all others.

Staying alive in the shantytown demanded a kind of egoism that often pits individuals against each other and rewards those who take advantage of those weaker than themselves. People admired toughness and strength; they took pride in babies or adults who were cunning and foxy. The toddler that was wild and fierce was preferred to the quiet and obedient child. Men and women with seductive charm, who could manipulate those around them, were better off than those who were kind. Poverty doesn't ennoble people, and I came to appreciate what it took to stay alive.

Theirs were moral choices that no person should be forced to make. But the result was that infants were viewed as limitless. There was a kind of magical replaceability about them, similar to what one might find on a battlefield. As one soldier falls, another takes his place. This kind of detached maternal thinking allowed the die-offs of shantytown babies—in some years, as many as 40 percent of all the infants born on the Alto died—to pass without shock or profound grief. A woman who had lost half her babies told me, "Who could bear it, Nanci, if we are mistaken in believing that God takes our infants to save us from pain? If that is not true, then God is a cannibal. And if our little angels are not in heaven flying around the throne of Our Lady, then where are they, and who is to blame for their deaths?"

If mothers allowed themselves to be attached to each newborn, how could they ever live through their babies' short lives and deaths and still have the stamina to get pregnant and give birth again and again? It wasn't that Alto mothers did not experience mother love at all. They did, and with great intensity. But mother love emerged as their children developed strength and vitality. The apex of mother love was not the image of Mary and her infant son, but a mature Mary, grieving the death of her young adult son. The Pieta, not the young mother at the crèche, was the symbol of motherhood and mother love on the Alto.

In *Death Without Weeping*, I first told of a clandestine extermination group that had begun to operate in Timbaúba in the 1980s. The rise of these vigilantes seemed paradoxical, insofar as it coincided with the end of the 20-year military dictatorship. What was the relationship between democracy and death squads? No one knew who was behind the extrajudicial limpeza ("street cleaning," as their supporters called it) that was targeting "dirty" street children and poor young Black men from the shantytowns. But by 2000 the public was well aware of the group and the identity of its leader, Abdoral Gonçalves Queiroz. Known as the "Guardian Angels," they were responsible for killing more than 100 victims. In 2001 I was invited, along with my husband, to return to Timbaúba to help a newly appointed and tough-minded judge and state prosecutor to identify those victims whose relatives had not come forward. In the interim, the death squad group had infiltrated the town council, the mayor's office, and the justice system. But 11 of them, including their semiliterate gangster-boss, Queiroz, had been arrested and were going on trial.

The death squad was a residue of the old military regime. For 20 years, the military police had kept the social classes segregated, with "dangerous" street youths and unemployed rural men confined to the hillside slums or in detention. When the old policing structures loosened following the democratic transition, the shantytowns ruptured and poor people, especially unemployed young men and street children, flooded downtown streets and public squares, once the preserve of gente fina (the cultivated people). Their new visibility betrayed the illusion of Brazilian modernity and evoked contradictory emotions of fear, aversion, pity, and anger.

Excluded and reviled, unemployed Black youths and loose street kids of Timbaúba were prime targets of Queiroz and his gang. Depending on one's social class and politics, the band could be seen as hired serial killers or as justiceiros (outlaw heroes) who were protecting the community. Prominent figures—well-known businessmen and local politicians—applauded the work of the death squad, whom they also called "Police 2," and some of these leading citizens were active in the extrajudicial "courts" that were deciding who in Timbaúba should be the next to die.

During the 2001 death-squad field research expedition, I played cat-and-mouse with Dona Amantina, the dour manager of the cartorio civil, the official registry office. I was trying to assemble a body count of suspicious homicides that could possibly be linked to the death squad, focusing on the violent deaths of street kids and young Black men. Since members of the death squad were still at large, I did not want to make public what I was doing. At first, I implied that I was back to count infant and child deaths, as I had so many years before. Finally,

I admitted that I was looking into youth homicides. The manager nodded her head. "Yes, it's sad. But," she asked with a shy smile, "haven't you noticed the changes in infant and child deaths?" Once I began to scan the record books, I was wearing a smile, too.

Brazil's national central statistics bureau, the Instituto Brasileiro de Geografia e Estatística (IBGE), began reporting data for the municipality of Timbaúba in the late 1970s. In 1977, for example, IBGE reported 761 live births in the municipality and 311 deaths of infants (up to one year of age) for that same year, yielding an infant mortality rate of 409 per 1,000. A year later, the IBGE data recorded 896 live births and 320 infant deaths, an infant mortality rate of 357 per 1,000. If reliable, those official data indicated that between 36 and 41 percent of all infants in Timbaúba died in the first 12 months of life.

During the 1980s, when I was doing the research for *Death Without Weeping*, the then mayor of Timbaúba, the late Jacques Ferreira Lima, disputed those figures. "Impossible!" he fumed "This municipio is growing, not declining." He sent me to the local private hospital built by, and named for, his father, Jofo Ferreira Lima, to compare the IBGE statistics with the hospital's records on births and deaths. There, the head nurse gave me access to her records, but the official death certificates only concerned stillbirths and perinatal deaths. In the end, I found that the best source of data was the ledger books of the cartorio civil, where births and infant and child deaths were recorded by hand. Many births were not recorded until after a child had died, in order to register a death and receive a free coffin from the mayor's office. The statistics were as grim as those of the IBGE.

In 2001, a single afternoon going over infant and toddler death certificates in the same office was enough to document that something radical had since taken place—a revolution in child survival that had begun in the 1990s. The records now showed a completed birth rate of 3.2 children per woman and a mortality rate of 35 per 1,000 births. Subsequent field trips in 2006 and 2007 showed even further reductions. The 2009 data from the IBGE recorded a rate of 25.2 child deaths per 1,000 births for Timbaúba.

Though working on other topics in my Brazilian field trips in 2001, 2006, and 2007, I took the time to interview several young women attending a pregnancy class at a newly constructed, government-run clinic. The women I spoke with—some first-time mothers, others expecting a second or third child—were confident in their ability to give birth to a healthy baby. No one I spoke to expected to have, except by accident, more than two children. A pair—that was the goal. Today, young women of the Alto can expect to give birth to three or fewer infants and to see all of them live at least into adolescence. The old stance of maternal watchful waiting accompanied by deselection of infants viewed as having no "talent" for life had been replaced by a maternal ethos of "holding on" to every infant, each seen as likely to survive. As I had noted in the past as well, there was a preference for girl babies. Boys, women feared, could disappoint their mothers—they could kill or be killed as adolescents and young men. The Alto was still a dangerous place, and gangs, drug dealers, and the death squads were still in operation. But women in the state-run clinic spoke of having control over their reproductive lives in ways that I could not have imagined.

By 2001 Timbaúba had experienced the demographic transition. Both infant deaths and births had declined so precipitously that it looked like a reproductive workers' strike. The numbers—though incomplete—were startling. Rather than the more than 200 annual infant and child mortalities of the early 1980s, by the late 1990s there were fewer than 50 childhood deaths recorded per year. And the causes of death were specific. In the past, the causes had been stated in vague terms: "undetermined," "heart stopped, respiration stopped," "malnutrition," or the mythopoetic diagnosis of "acute infantile suffering."

On my latest return, just this June, the reproductive revolution was complete. The little two-room huts jumbled together on the back roads of the Alto were still poor, but as I visited the homes of dozens of Alto residents, sometimes accompanied by a local community health agent, sometimes dropping in for a chat unannounced, or summoned by the adult child of a former key informant of mine, I saw infants and toddlers who were plump and jolly, and mothers who were relaxed and breastfeeding toddlers as old as three years. Their babies assumed a high status in the family hierarchy, as precious little beings whose beauty and health brought honor and substance—as well as subsistence—to the household.

Manufactured cribs with pristine sheets and fluffy blankets, disposal diapers, and plastic rattles were much in evidence. Powdered milk, the number one baby killer in the past, was almost a banned substance. In contrast, no one, literally, breastfed during my early years of research on the Alto. It was breast milk that was banned, banned by the owners of the sugar plantations and by the bourgeois patrons (mistresses of the house) for whom the women of the Alto washed clothes and cleaned and cooked and served meals. Today, those jobs no longer exist. The sugar mills and sugar estates have closed down, and the landowning class has long since moved, leaving behind a population of working-class poor, a thin middle class (with washing machines rather than maids), and a displaced rural labor force that is largely sustained by the largesse of New Deal–style federal assistance.

Direct cash transfers are made to poor and unemployed families, and grants (bolsas, or "purses") are given to women, mothers, babies, schoolchildren, and youth. The grants come with conditions. The balsa familiar (family grant), a small cash payment to each mother and up to five of her young children, requires the mother to immunize her babies, attend to their medical needs, follow medical directions, keep the children in school, monitor their homework, help them prepare for exams, and purchase school books, pens and pencils, and school clothes. Of the 30 Alto women between the ages of 17 and 40 my research associate, Jennifer S. Hughes, and I interviewed in June, the women averaged 3.3 pregnancies—higher than the national average, but the real comparison here is with their own mothers, who (based on the 13 of the 30 who could describe their mothers' reproductive histories) averaged 13.6 pregnancies and among them counted 61 infant deaths. Jennifer is my daughter and a professor of colonial and postcolonial Latin American history at the University of California, Riverside. I like to think that her awesome archival skills were honed more than 20 years ago when I enlisted her, then a teenager, to help me count the deaths of Alto babies in the civil registry office. She agreed to help me on this most recent field trip, and it was our first professional collaboration.

Jennifer, for example, looked up Luciene, the first-born daughter of Antonieta, one of my earliest key informants and my neighbor when I lived on the Alto do Cruzeiro. Now in her 40s, Luciene had only one pregnancy and one living child. Her mother had given birth to 15 babies, 10 of whom survived. Daughter and mother now live next door to each other, and they spoke openly and emotionally about the "old days," "the hungry times," "the violent years," in comparison to the present. "Today we are rich," Antonieta declared, "really rich," by which she meant her modernized home on the Alto Terezinha, their new color television set, washing machine, and all the food and delicacies they could want.

Four of the 30 women we interviewed had lost an infant, and one had lost a two year old who drowned playing with a large basin of water. Those deaths were seen as tragic and painful memories. The mothers did not describe the deaths in a monotone or dismiss them as inevitable or an act of mercy that relieved their suffering. Rather, they recalled with deep sadness the date, the time, and the cause of their babies' deaths, and remembered them by name, saying that Gloria would be 10 today or that Marcos would be eight years old today, had she or he lived.

What has happened in Timbaúba over the past decades is part of a national trend in Brazil. Over the past decade alone, Brazil's fertility rate has decreased from 2.36 to 1.9 children per family—a number that is below the replacement rate and lower than that of the United States. Unlike in China or India, this reproductive revolution occurred without state coercion. It was a voluntary transition and a rapid one.

A footnote in *Death Without Weeping* records the most common requests that people made of me in the 1960s and again in the 1980s: Could I possibly help them obtain false teeth?

[A] pair of eyeglasses? [A] better antibiotic for a sick older child? But most often I was asked—begged—by women to arrange a clandestine sterilization. In Northeast Brazil, sterilization was always preferable to oral contraceptives, IUDs, and condoms. Reproductive freedom meant having the children you wanted and then "closing down the factory." "A fábrica é fechada!" a woman would boastfully explain, patting her abdomen. Until recently, this was the privilege of the upper middle classes and the wealthy. Today, tubal ligations are openly discussed and arranged. One woman I interviewed, a devout Catholic, gushed that God was good, so good that he had given her a third son, her treasure trove, and at the same time had allowed her the liberty and freedom of a tubal ligation. "Praise to God!" she said. "Amen," I said.

In Brazil, the reproductive revolution is linked to democracy and the coming into political power of President Fernando Henrique Cardoso (1995–2002), aided by his formidable wife, the anthropologist and women's advocate Ruth Cardoso. It was continued by Luiz Inacio Lula da Silva, universally called "Lula," and, since 2011, by his successor, Dilma Rousseff. President Lula's Zero Hunger campaign, though much criticized in the popular media as a kind of political publicity stunt, in fact has supplied basic foodstuffs to the most vulnerable households.

Today food is abundant on the Alto. Schoolchildren are fed nutritious lunches, fortified with a protein mixture that is prepared as tasty milk shakes. There are food pantries and state and municipal milk distribution programs that are run by women with an extra room in their home. The monthly stipends to poor and single mothers to reward them for keeping their children in school has turned elementary school pupils into valuable household "workers," and literacy has increased for both the children and their mothers, who study at home alongside their children.

When I first went to the Alto in 1964 as a Peace Corps volunteer, it was in the role of a visitadora, a public-health community worker. The military dictatorship was suspicious of the program, which mixed health education and immunizations with advocating for water, street lights, and pit latrines as universal entitlements—owed even to those who had "occupied public land" (like the people of the Alto, who had been dispossessed by modernizing sugar plantations and mills). The visitadora program, Brazil's version of Chinese "barefoot doctors," was targeted by the military government as subversive, and the program ended by 1966 in Pernambuco. Many years later President Cardoso fortified the national health care system with a similar program of local "community health agents," who live and work in their micro-communities, visiting at-risk households, identifying crises, diagnosing common symptoms, and intervening to rescue vulnerable infants and toddlers from premature death. In Timbaúba, there are some 120 community health

agents, male and female, working in poor micro-communities throughout the municipality, including dispersed rural communities. On the Alto do Cruzeiro 12 health agents each live and work in a defined area, each responsible for the health and well-being of some 150 families comprising 500 to 600 individuals. The basic requirement for a health worker is to have completed ensino fundamental, the equivalent of primary and middle school. Then, he or she must prepare for a public concurso, a competition based on a rigorous exam.

The community health agent's wage is small, a little more than the Brazilian minimum wage, but still less than US $700 a month for a 40-hour work week, most of it on foot up and down the hillside "slum" responding to a plethora of medical needs, from diaper rash to an emergency home birth. The agent records all births, deaths, illnesses, and other health problems in the micro-community; refers the sick to health posts, emergency rooms, and hospitals; monitors pregnancies and the health of newborns, the disabled, and the elderly. He or she identifies and reports communicable diseases and acts as a public-health and environmental educator. The agent participates in public meetings to shape health policies. Above all, the community health agent is the primary intermediary between poor people and the national health care system.

I am convinced that the incredible decline in premature deaths and useless suffering that I witnessed on the Alto is primarily the result of these largely unheralded medical heroes, who rescue mothers and their children in a large town with few doctors and no resident surgeons, pediatricians, and worst of all, obstetricians. A pregnant woman of the Alto suffers today from one of the worst dilemmas and anxieties a person in her condition can face: no certain location to give birth. The only solution at present is to refer women in labor to distant obstetric and maternity wards in public hospitals in Recife, the state capital, a 67-mile drive away. The result can be fatal: at least one woman in the past year was prevented (by holding her legs together) from delivering her baby in an ambulance, and both mother and child died following their arrival at the designated hospital in Recife. For this reason, Alto women and their health agents often choose prearranged cesarian sections well in advance of due dates, even though they know that C-sections are generally not in the best interest of mothers or infants.

Then, beyond the human factor, environmental factors figure in the decline in infant mortality in the shantytowns of Timbaúba and other municipalities in Northeast Brazil. The most significant of these is the result of a simple, basic municipal public-health program: the installation of water pipes that today reach nearly all homes with sufficient clean water. It is amazing to observe the transformative potential of material conditions: water = life!

Finally, what about the role of the Catholic Church? The anomaly is that, in a nation where the Catholic Church predominates in the public sphere and abortion is still illegal except in the case of rape or to save a mother's life, family size has dropped so sharply over the last two decades. What is going on? For one thing, Brazilian Catholics are independent, much like Catholics in the United States, going their own way when it comes to women's health and reproductive culture. Others have simply left Catholicism and joined evangelical churches, some of which proclaim their openness to the reproductive rights of women and men. Today only 60 percent of Brazilians identify as Roman Catholic. In our small sample of 30 women of the Alto, religion—whether Catholic, Protestant, Spiritist, or Afro-Brazilian—did not figure large in their reproductive lives.

The Brazilian Catholic Church is deeply divided. In 2009, the Archbishop of Recife announced the Vatican's excommunication of the doctors and family of a nine-year-old girl who had an abortion. She had been raped by her stepfather (thus the abortion was legal), and she was carrying twins—her tiny stature and narrow hips putting her life in jeopardy. After comparing abortion to the Holocaust, Archbishop José Cardoso Sobrinho told the media that the Vatican rejects believers who pick and choose their moral issues. The result was an immediate decline in church attendance throughout the diocese.

While the Brazilian Catholic hierarchy is decidedly conservative, the rural populace, their local clerics, and liberation theologians such as the activist ex-priest Leonardo Boff are open in their interpretations of Catholic spirituality and corporeality. The Jesus that my Catholic friends on the Alto embrace is a sensitive and sentient Son of God, a man of sorrows, to be sure, and also a man of compassion, keenly attuned to simple human needs. The teachings of liberation theology, while condemned by Pope John Paul II, helped to dislodge a baroque folk Catholicism in rural Northeast Brazil that envisioned God and the saints as authorizing and blessing the deaths of angel babies.

Padre Orlando, a young priest when I first met him in 1987, distanced himself from the quaint custom of blessing the bodies of dead infants as they were carried to the municipal graveyard in processions led by children. He also invited me and my Brazilian research assistant to give an orientation on family planning to poor Catholic women in the parish hall. When I asked what form of contraception I could teach, he replied, "I'm a celibate priest, how should I know? Teach it all, everything you know." When I reminded him that only the very unpredictable rhythm method was approved by the Vatican, he replied, "Just teach it all, everything you know, and then say, but the Pope only approves the not-so-safe rhythm method."

The people of the Alto do Cruzeiro still face many problems. Drugs, gangs, and death squads have left their ugly mark. Homicides have returned with a vengeance, but they are diffuse and chaotic, the impulsive murders one comes to expect among poor young men—the unemployed, petty thieves, and small-time drug dealers—and between rival gangs. One sees adolescents and young men of the shantytowns, who survived that dangerous first year of life, cut down by bullets and knives at the age of 15 or 17 by local gangs, strongmen, bandidos, and local police in almost equal measure. The old diseases also raise their heads from time to time: schistosomiasis, Chagas disease, tuberculosis, and even cholera.

But the bottom line is that women on the Alto today do not lose their infants. Children go to school rather than to the cane fields, and social cooperatives have taken the place of shadow economies. When mothers are sick or pregnant or a child is ill, they can go to the well-appointed health clinic supported by both state and national funds. There is a safety net, and it is wide, deep, and strong.

Just as we were leaving in mid-June, angry, insurgent crowds were forming in Recife, fed up with political corruption, cronyism, and the extravagant public expenditures in preparation for the 2014 World Cup in Brazil—when the need was for public housing and hospitals. Those taking to the streets were mostly young, urban, working-class, and new middle-class Brazilians. The rural poor were generally not among them. The people of the Alto do Cruzeiro (and I imagine in many other communities like it) are strong supporters of the government led by the PT (Partido dos Trabalhadores, or Workers' Party). Under the PT, the government has ended hunger in Pernambuco and has opened family clinics and municipal schools that treat them and their children with respect for the first time in their lives.

The protesters in the streets are among the 40 million Brazilians who were added to the middle class between 2004 and 2010, under the government of President Lula, and whose rising expectations are combustible. When the healthy, literate children of the Alto do Cruzeiro grow up, they may yet join future protests demanding more accountability from their elected officials.

Critical Thinking

1. Discuss the conditions on the Alto do Cruzeiro that help to explain the "normalization" of infant death.
2. Describe the demographic transition and the effect it has on a mother's trust that her infant will survive.
3. When and why do Alto mothers cry?
4. Describe and explain the egoism that is admired and demanded in the shantytown.
5. Explain "magical replaceability" regarding children.

6. Discuss the "detached maternal thinking" and the emergence of mother love in the context of religious beliefs.

7. Explain the appearance of the death squads.

8. Describe the demographic transition in terms of what has brought it about and the resulting attitudes toward having children.

9. Describe the deep divisions within the Brazilian Catholic Church with respect to family planning.

Create Central

www.mhhe.com/createcentral

Internet References

American Anthropological Association Children and Childhood Interest Group
http://aaacig.usu.edu/

Journal of Medical Ethics
http://jme.bmj.com/

Latin American Studies
www.library.arizona.edu/search/subjects

NANCY SCHEPER-HUGHES'S renowned book *Death Without Weeping* was preceded by her *Natural History* article of the same title in October 1989. More recently, Scheper-Hughes contributed "Truth and Rumor on the Organ Trail" (October 1998). Scheper Hughes's most recent books are *Commodifying Bodies,* co-edited with Loic Waquant (Sage Publications Ltd, 2002), and *Violence in War and Peace: An Anthology,* co-edited with Philippe Bourgois (Basil Blackwell Ltd, 2003). An updated and abridged paperback edition of *Death Without Weeping* will be published by the University of California Press in the summer of 2014. Scheper-Hughes is Chancellor's Professor of Anthropology at the University of California, Berkeley, and the cofounder and director of Organs Watch, a medical human-rights project.

Article

Prepared by: Elvio Angeloni, *Pasadena City College*

Arranging a Marriage in India

Serena Nanda

Learning Outcomes

After reading this article, you will be able to:

- List the pros and cons of arranged marriages versus love marriages.
- Discuss the factors that must be taken into account in arranging a marriage in India.

> Sister and doctor brother-in-law invite correspondence from North Indian professionals only, for a beautiful, talented, sophisticated, intelligent sister, 5'3", slim, M.A. in textile design, father a senior civil officer. Would prefer immigrant doctors, between 26–29 years. Reply with full details and returnable photo.
>
> A well-settled uncle invites matrimonial correspondence from slim, fair, educated South Indian girl, for his nephew, 25 years, smart, M.B.A., green card holder, 5'6". Full particulars with returnable photo appreciated.
>
> —*Matrimonial Advertisements,*
> India Abroad

In India, almost all marriages are arranged. Even among the educated middle classes in modern, urban India, marriage is as much a concern of the families as it is of the individuals. So customary is the practice of arranged marriage that there is a special name for a marriage which is not arranged: It is called a "love match."

On my first field trip to India, I met many young men and women whose parents were in the process of "getting them married." In many cases, the bride and groom would not meet each other before the marriage. At most they might meet for a brief conversation, and this meeting would take place only after their parents had decided that the match was suitable. Parents do not compel their children to marry a person who either marriage partner finds objectionable. But only after one match is refused will another be sought.

As a young American woman in India for the first time, I found this custom of arranged marriage oppressive. How could any intelligent young person agree to such a marriage without great reluctance? It was contrary to everything I believed about the importance of romantic love as the only basis of a happy marriage. It also clashed with my strongly held notions that the choice of such an intimate and permanent relationship could be made only by the individuals involved. Had anyone tried to arrange my marriage, I would have been defiant and rebellious!

At the first opportunity, I began, with more curiosity than tact, to question the young people I met on how they felt about this practice. Sita, one of my young informants, was a college graduate with a degree in political science. She had been waiting for over a year while her parents were arranging a match for her. I found it difficult to accept the docile manner in which this well-educated young woman awaited the outcome of a process that would result in her spending the rest of her life with a man she hardly knew, a virtual stranger, picked out by her parents.

"How can you go along with this?" I asked her, in frustration and distress. "Don't you care who you marry?"

"Of course I care," she answered. "This is why I must let my parents choose a boy for me. My marriage is too important to be arranged by such an inexperienced person as myself. In such matters, it is better to have my parents' guidance."

I had learned that young men and women in India do not date and have very little social life involving members of the opposite sex. Although I could not disagree with Sita's reasoning, I continued to pursue the subject.

Young men and women do not date and have very little social life involving members of the opposite sex.

"But how can you marry the first man you have ever met? Not only have you missed the fun of meeting a lot of different people, but you have not given yourself the chance to know who is the right man for you."

"Meeting with a lot of different people doesn't sound like any fun at all," Sita answered. "One hears that in America the girls are spending all their time worrying about whether they will meet a man and get married. Here we have the chance to enjoy our life and let our parents do this work and worrying for us."

She had me there. The high anxiety of the competition to "be popular" with the opposite sex certainly was the most prominent feature of life as an American teenager in the late fifties. The endless worrying about the rules that governed our behavior and about our popularity ratings sapped both our self-esteem and our enjoyment of adolescence. I reflected that absence of this competition in India most certainly may have contributed to the self-confidence and natural charm of so many of the young women I met.

And yet, the idea of marrying a perfect stranger, whom one did not know and did not "love," so offended my American ideas of individualism and romanticism, that I persisted with my objections.

"I still can't imagine it," I said. "How can you agree to marry a man you hardly know?"

"But of course he will be known. My parents would never arrange a marriage for me without knowing all about the boy's family background. Naturally we will not rely only on what the family tells us. We will check the particulars out ourselves. No one will want their daughter to marry into a family that is not good. All these things we will know beforehand."

Impatiently, I responded, "Sita, I don't mean know the family, I mean, know the man. How can you marry someone you don't know personally and don't love? How can you think of spending your life with someone you may not even like?"

"If he is a good man, why should I not like him?" she said. "With you people, you know the boy so well before you marry, where will be the fun to get married? There will be no mystery and no romance. Here we have the whole of our married life to get to know and love our husband. This way is better, is it not?"

Her response made further sense, and I began to have second thoughts on the matter. Indeed, during months of meeting many intelligent young Indian people, both male and female, who had the same ideas as Sita, I saw arranged marriages in a different light. I also saw the importance of the family in Indian life and realized that a couple who took their marriage into their own hands was taking a big risk, particularly if their families were irreconcilably opposed to the match. In a country where every important resource in life—a job, a house, a social circle—is gained through family connections, it seemed foolhardy to cut oneself off from a supportive social network and depend solely on one person for happiness and success.

Six years later I returned to India to again do fieldwork, this time among the middle class in Bombay, a modern, sophisticated city. From the experience of my earlier visit, I decided to include a study of arranged marriages in my project. By this time I had met many Indian couples whose marriages had been arranged and who seemed very happy. Particularly in contrast to the fate of many of my married friends in the United States who were already in the process of divorce, the positive aspects of arranged marriages appeared to me to outweigh the negatives. In fact, I thought I might even participate in arranging a marriage myself. I had been fairly successful in the United States in "fixing up" many of my friends, and I was

confident that my matchmaking skills could be easily applied to this new situation, once I learned the basic rules. "After all," I thought, "how complicated can it be? People want pretty much the same things in a marriage whether it is in India or America."

An opportunity presented itself almost immediately. A friend from my previous Indian trip was in the process of arranging for the marriage of her eldest son. In India there is a perceived shortage of "good boys," and since my friend's family was eminently respectable and the boy himself personable, well educated, and nice looking, I was sure that by the end of my year's fieldwork, we would have found a match.

The basic rule seems to be that a family's reputation is most important. It is understood that matches would be arranged only within the same caste and general social class, although some crossing of subcastes is permissible if the class positions of the bride's and groom's families are similar. Although dowry is now prohibited by law in India, extensive gift exchanges took place with every marriage. Even when the boy's family do not "make demands," every girl's family nevertheless feels the obligation to give the traditional gifts, to the girl, to the boy, and to the boy's family. Particularly when the couple would be living in the joint family—that is, with the boy's parents and his married brothers and their families, as well as with unmarried siblings—which is still very common even among the urban, upper-middle class in India, the girls' parents are anxious to establish smooth relations between their family and that of the boy. Offering the proper gifts, even when not called "dowry," is often an important factor in influencing the relationship between the bride's and groom's families and perhaps, also, the treatment of the bride in her new home.

> **In a society where divorce is still a scandal and where, in fact, the divorce rate is exceedingly low, an arranged marriage is the beginning of a lifetime relationship not just between the bride and groom but between their families as well.**

In a society where divorce is still a scandal and where, in fact, the divorce rate is exceedingly low, an arranged marriage is the beginning of a lifetime relationship not just between the bride and groom but between their families as well. Thus, while a girl's looks are important, her character is even more so, for she is being judged as a prospective daughter-in-law as much as a prospective bride. Where she would be living in a joint family, as was the case with my friend, the girls's ability to get along harmoniously in a family is perhaps the single most important quality in assessing her suitability.

My friend is a highly esteemed wife, mother, and daughter-in-law. She is religious, soft-spoken, modest, and deferential. She rarely gossips and never quarrels, two qualities highly desirable in a woman. A family that has the reputation for gossip and conflict among its womenfolk will not find it easy to get

Even today, almost all marriages in India are arranged. It is believed that parents are much more effective at deciding whom their daughters should marry.

good wives for their sons. Parents will not want to send their daughter to a house in which there is conflict.

My friend's family were originally from North India. They had lived in Bombay, where her husband owned a business, for forty years. The family had delayed in seeking a match for their eldest son because he had been an Air Force pilot for several years, stationed in such remote places that it had seemed fruitless to try to find a girl who would be willing to accompany him. In their social class, a military career, despite its economic security, has little prestige and is considered a drawback in finding a suitable bride. Many families would not allow their daughters to marry a man in an occupation so potentially dangerous and which requires so much moving around.

The son had recently left the military and joined his father's business. Since he was a college graduate, modern, and well traveled, from such a good family, and, I thought, quite hand-some, it seemed to me that he, or rather his family, was in a position to pick and choose. I said as much to my friend.

While she agreed that there were many advantages on their side, she also said, "We must keep in mind that my son is both short and dark; these are drawbacks in finding the right match." While the boy's height had not escaped my notice, "dark" seemed to me inaccurate; I would have called him "wheat" col-ored perhaps, and in any case, I did not realize that color would be a consideration. I discovered, however, that while a boy's

skin color is a less important consideration than a girl's, it is still a factor.

An important source of contacts in trying to arrange her son's marriage was my friend's social club in Bombay. Many of the women had daughters of the right age, and some had already expressed an interest in my friend's son. I was most enthusiastic about the possibilities of one particular family who had five daughters, all of whom were pretty, demure, and well educated. Their mother had told my friend, "You can have your pick for your son, whichever one of my daughters appeals to you most."

I saw a match in sight. "Surely," I said to my friend, "we will find one there. Let's go visit and make our choice." But my friend held back; she did not seem to share my enthusiasm, for reasons I could not then fathom.

When I kept pressing for an explanation of her reluctance, she admitted, "See, Serena, here is the problem. The family has so many daughters, how will they be able to provide nicely for any of them? We are not making any demands, but still, with so many daughters to marry off, one wonders whether she will even be able to make a proper wedding. Since this is our eldest son, it's best if we marry him to a girl who is the only daughter, then the wedding will truly be a gala affair." I argued that surely the quality of the girls themselves made up for any deficiency in the elaborateness of the wedding. My friend admitted this point but still seemed reluctant to proceed.

"Is there something else," I asked her, "some factor I have missed?" "Well," she finally said, "there is one other thing. They have one daughter already married and living in Bombay. The mother is always complaining to me that the girl's in-laws don't let her visit her own family often enough. So it makes me wonder, will she be that kind of mother who always wants her daughter at her own home? This will prevent the girl from adjusting to our house. It is not a good thing." And so, this family of five daughters was dropped as a possibility.

Somewhat disappointed, I nevertheless respected my friend's reasoning and geared up for the next prospect. This was also the daughter of a woman in my friend's social club. There was clear interest in this family and I could see why. The family's reputation was excellent; in fact, they came from a subcaste slightly higher than my friend's own. The girl, who was an only daughter, was pretty and well educated and had a brother studying in the United States. Yet, after expressing an interest to me in this family, all talk of them suddenly died down and the search began elsewhere.

"What happened to that girl as a prospect?" I asked one day. "You never mention her any more. She is so pretty and so educated, what did you find wrong?"

"She is too educated. We've decided against it. My husband's father saw the girl on the bus the other day and thought her forward. A girl who 'roams about' the city by herself is not the girl for our family." My disappointment this time was even greater, as I thought the son would have liked the girl very much. But then I thought, my friend is right, a girl who is going to live in a joint family cannot be too independent or she will make life miserable for everyone. I also learned that if the family of the girl has even a slightly higher social status than the family of the boy, the bride may think herself too good for them, and this too will cause problems. Later my friend admitted to me that this had been an important factor in her decision not to pursue the match.

The next candidate was the daughter of a client of my friend's husband. When the client learned that the family was looking for a match for their son, he said, "Look no further, we have a daughter." This man then invited my friends to dinner to see the girl. He had already seen their son at the office and decided that "he liked the boy." We all went together for tea, rather than dinner—it was less of a commitment—and while we were there, the girl's mother showed us around the house. The girl was studying for her exams and was briefly introduced to us.

After we left, I was anxious to hear my friend's opinion. While her husband liked the family very much and was impressed with his client's business accomplishments and reputation, the wife didn't like the girl's looks. "She is short, no doubt, which is an important plus point, but she is also fat and wears glasses." My friend obviously thought she could do better for her son and asked her husband to make his excuses to his client by saying that they had decided to postpone the boy's marriage indefinitely.

By this time almost six months had passed and I was becoming impatient. What I had thought would be an easy matter

to arrange was turning out to be quite complicated. I began to believe that between my friend's desire for a girl who was modest enough to fit into her joint family, yet attractive and educated enough to be an acceptable partner for her son, she would not find anyone suitable. My friend laughed at my impatience: "Don't be so much in a hurry," she said. "You Americans want everything done so quickly. You get married quickly and then just as quickly get divorced. Here we take marriage more seriously. We must take all the factors into account. It is not enough for us to learn by our mistakes. This is too serious a business. If a mistake is made we have not only ruined the life of our son or daughter, but we have spoiled the reputation of our family as well. And that will make it much harder for their brothers and sisters to get married. So we must be very careful."

> **If a mistake is made we have not only ruined the life of our son or daughter, but we have spoiled the reputation of our family as well.**

What she said was true and I promised myself to be more patient, though it was not easy. I had really hoped and expected that the match would be made before my year in India was up. But it was not to be. When I left India my friend seemed no further along in finding a suitable match for her son than when I had arrived.

Two years later, I returned to India and still my friend had not found a girl for her son. By this time, he was close to thirty, and I think she was a little worried. Since she knew I had friends all over India, and I was going to be there for a year, she asked me to "help her in this work" and keep an eye out for someone suitable. I was flattered that my judgment was respected, but knowing now how complicated the process was, I had lost my earlier confidence as a matchmaker. Nevertheless, I promised that I would try.

It was almost at the end of my year's stay in India that I met a family with a marriageable daughter whom I felt might be a good possibility for my friend's son. The girl's father was related to a good friend of mine and by coincidence came from the same village as my friend's husband. This new family had a successful business in a medium-sized city in central India and were from the same subcaste as my friend. The daughter was pretty and chic; in fact, she had studied fashion design in college. Her parents would not allow her to go off by herself to any of the major cities in India where she could make a career, but they had compromised with her wish to work by allowing her to run a small dress-making boutique from their home. In spite of her desire to have a career, the daughter was both modest and home-loving and had had a traditional, sheltered upbringing. She had only one other sister, already married, and a brother who was in his father's business.

I mentioned the possibility of a match with my friend's son. The girl's parents were most interested. Although their daughter was not eager to marry just yet, the idea of living in

Appendix
Further Reflections on Arranged Marriage . . .

This essay was written from the point of view of a family seeking a daughter-in-law. Arranged marriage looks somewhat different from the point of view of the bride and her family. Arranged marriage continues to be preferred, even among the more educated, Westernized sections of the Indian population. Many young women from these families still go along, more or less willingly, with the practice, and also with the specific choices of their families. Young women do get excited about the prospects of their marriage, but there is also ambivalence and increasing uncertainty, as the bride contemplates leaving the comfort and familiarity of her own home, where as a "temporary guest" she had often been indulged, to live among strangers. Even in the best situation she will now come under the close scrutiny of her husband's family. How she dresses, how she behaves, how she gets along with others, where she goes, how she spends her time, her domestic abilities—all of this and much more—will be observed and commented on by a whole new set of relations. Her interaction with her family of birth will be monitored and curtailed considerably. Not only will she leave their home, but with increasing geographic mobility, she may also live very far from them, perhaps even on another continent. Too much expression of her fondness for her own family, or her desire to visit them, may be interpreted as an inability to adjust to her new family, and may become a source of conflict. In an arranged marriage the burden of adjustment is clearly heavier for a woman than for a man. And that is in the best of situations.

In less happy circumstances, the bride may be a target of resentment and hostility from her husband's family, particularly her mother-in-law or her husband's unmarried sisters, for whom she is now a source of competition for the affection, loyalty, and economic resources of their son or brother. If she is psychologically, or even physically abused, her options are limited, as returning to her parents' home, or divorce, are still very stigmatized. For most Indians, marriage and motherhood are still considered the only suitable roles for a woman, even for those who have careers, and few women can comfortably contemplate remaining unmarried. Most families still consider "marrying off" their daughters as a compelling religious duty and social necessity. This increases a bride's sense of obligation to make the marriage a success, at whatever cost to her own personal happiness.

The vulnerability of a new bride may also be intensified by the issue of dowry, which although illegal, has become a more pressing issue in the consumer conscious society of contemporary urban India. In many cases, where a groom's family is not satisfied with the amount of dowry a bride brings to her marriage, the young bride will be constantly harassed to get her parents to give more. In extreme cases, the bride may even be murdered, and the murder disguised as an accident or suicide. This also offers the husband's family an opportunity to arrange another match for him, thus bringing in another dowry. This phenomena, called dowry death, calls attention not just to the "evils of dowry" but also to larger issues of the powerlessness of women as well.

Serena Nanda
March 1998

Bombay—a sophisticated, extremely fashion-conscious city where she could continue her education in clothing design—was a great inducement. I gave the girl's father my friend's address and suggested that when they went to Bombay on some business or whatever, they look up the boy's family.

Returning to Bombay on my way to New York, I told my friend of this newly discovered possibility. She seemed to feel there was potential but, in spite of my urging, would not make any moves herself. She rather preferred to wait for the girl's family to call upon them. I hoped something would come of this introduction, though by now I had learned to rein in my optimism.

A year later I received a letter from my friend. The family had indeed come to visit Bombay, and their daughter and my friend's daughter, who were near in age, had become very good friends. During that year, the two girls had frequently visited each other. I thought things looked promising.

Last week I received an invitation to a wedding: My friend's son and the girl were getting married. Since I had found the match, my presence was particularly requested at the wedding. I was thrilled. Success at last! As I prepared to leave for India, I began thinking, "Now, my friend's younger son, who do I know who has a nice girl for him . . . ?"

Critical Thinking

1. To what extent are marriages arranged in India? How do middle class families in modern urban India feel about marriage? What is a "love match"?

2. How does the author describe the process of the parents' "getting them married" (with regard to young men and women)? Why did the author find this "oppressive"?

3. Describe the arguments and counter-arguments regarding arranged marriages as revealed in the verbal exchanges between the author and Sita.

4. In what sense did the author see arranged marriage as successful in contrast to marriage in the United States?

5. Why was the author so sure that a match could be made quickly for her friend's son?

6. What factors must be taken into account in arranging a marriage?

7. Why was the friend's son originally not considered a good match? What happened that would change his prospects? What drawbacks remained?

8. Describe the "problems" that arose with regard to the various "prospects" as well as the positive factors involved in the final match.

Create Central

www.mhhe.com/createcentral

Internet References

Kinship and Social Organization
www.umanitoba.ca/anthropology

Sex and Marriage
http://anthro.palomar.edu/marriage/default.htm
Wedding Traditions and Customs
http://worldweddingtraditions.com

Edited by Philip R. DeVita.

Article   Prepared by: Elvio Angeloni, *Pasadena City College*

Who Needs Love!
In Japan, Many Couples Don't

NICHOLAS D. KRISTOF

Learning Outcomes

After reading this article, you will be able to:

• Determine whether the stability of Japanese marriages implies compatibility and contentment.

• Discuss the ingredients that lead to a strong marriage in Japan.

Yuri Uemura sat on the straw tatami mat of her living room and chatted cheerfully about her 40-year marriage to a man whom, she mused, she never particularly liked.

"There was never any love between me and my husband," she said blithely, recalling how he used to beat her. "But, well, we survived."

A 72-year-old midwife, her face as weathered as an old baseball and etched with a thousand seams, Mrs. Uemura said that her husband had never told her that he liked her, never complimented her on a meal, never told her "thank you," never held her hand, never given her a present, never shown her affection in any way. He never calls her by her name, but summons her with the equivalent of a grunt or a "Hey, you."

"Even with animals, the males cooperate to bring the females some food," Mrs. Uemura said sadly, noting the contrast to her own marriage. "When I see that, it brings tears to my eyes."

In short, the Uemuras have a marriage that is as durable as it is unhappy, one couple's tribute to the Japanese sanctity of family.

The divorce rate in Japan is at a record high but still less than half that of the United States, and Japan arguably has one of the strongest family structures in the industrialized world. As the United States and Europe fret about the disintegration of the traditional family, most Japanese families remain as solid as the small red table on which Mrs. Uemura rested her tea.

It does not seem that Japanese families survive because husbands and wives love each other more than American couples, but rather because they perhaps love each other less.

A study published last year by the Population Council, an international nonprofit group based in New York, suggested that the traditional two-parent household is on the wane not only in America but throughout most of the world. There was one prominent exception: Japan.

In Japan, for example, only 1.1 percent of births are to unwed mothers—virtually unchanged from 25 years ago. In the United States, the figure is 30.1 percent and rising rapidly.

Yet if one comes to a little Japanese town like Omiya to learn the secrets of the Japanese family, the people are not as happy as the statistics.

"I haven't lived for myself," Mrs. Uemura said, with a touch of melancholy, "but for my kids, and for my family, and for society."

Mrs. Uemura's marriage does not seem exceptional in Japan, whether in the big cities or here in Omiya. The people of Omiya, a community of 5,700 nestled in the rain-drenched hills of the Kii Peninsula in Mie Prefecture, nearly 200 miles southwest of Tokyo, have spoken periodically to a reporter about various aspects of their daily lives. On this visit they talked about their families.

Survival Secrets, Often the Couples Expect Little

Osamums Torida furrowed his brow and looked perplexed when he was asked if he loved his wife of 33 years.

"Yeah, so-so, I guess," said Mr. Torida, a cattle farmer. "She's like air or water. You couldn't live without it, but most of the time, you're not conscious of its existence."

The secret to the survival of the marriage, Mr. Torida acknowledged, was not mutual passion.

"Sure, we had fights about our work," he explained as he stood beside his barn. "But we were preoccupied by work and our debts, so we had no time to fool around."

That is a common theme in Omiya. It does not seem that Japanese families survive because husbands and wives love each other more than American couples, but rather because they perhaps love each other less.

"I think love marriages are more fragile than arranged marriages," said Tomika Kusukawa, 49, who married her high-school sweetheart and now runs a car repair shop with him. "In love marriages, when something happens or if the couple falls out of love, they split up."

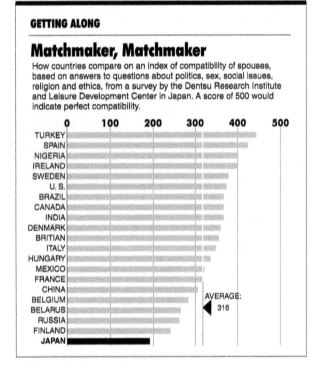

GETTING ALONG

Matchmaker, Matchmaker

How countries compare on an index of compatibility of spouses, based on answers to questions about politics, sex, social issues, religion and ethics, from a survey by the Dentsu Research Institute and Leisure Development Center in Japan. A score of 500 would indicate perfect compatibility.

TURKEY
SPAIN
NIGERIA
IRELAND
SWEDEN
U.S.
BRAZIL
CANADA
INDIA
DENMARK
BRITIAN
ITALY
HUNGARY
MEXICO
FRANCE
CHINA
BELGIUM
BELARUS
RUSSIA
FINLAND
JAPAN

AVERAGE: 316

If there is a secret to the strength of the Japanese family it consists of three ingredients: low expectations, patience, and shame.

The advantage of marriages based on low expectations is that they have built in shock absorbers. If the couple discover that they have nothing in common, that they do not even like each other, then that is not so much a reason for divorce as it is par for the course.

Even the discovery that one's spouse is having an affair is often not as traumatic in a Japanese marriage as it is in the West. A little sexual infidelity on the part of a man (though not on the part of his wife) was traditionally tolerated, so long as he did not become so besotted as to pay his mistress more than he could afford.

Tsuzuya Fukuyama, who runs a convenience store and will mark her 50th wedding anniversary this year, toasted her hands on an electric heater in the front of the store and declared that a woman would be wrong to get angry if her husband had an affair.

The durability of the Japanese family is particularly wondrous because couples are, by international standards, exceptionally incompatible.

"It's never just one side that's at fault," Mrs. Fukuyama said sternly. "Maybe the husband had an affair because his wife wasn't so hot herself. So she should look at her own faults."

Mrs. Fukuyama's daughter came to her a few years ago, suspecting that her husband was having an affair and asking what to do.

"I told her, 'Once you left this house, you can only come back if you divorce; if you're not prepared to get a divorce, then you'd better be patient,' " Mrs. Fukuyama recalled. "And so she was patient. And then she got pregnant and had a kid, and now they're close again."

The word that Mrs. Fukuyama used for patience is "gaman," a term that comes up whenever marriage is discussed in Japan. It means toughing it out, enduring hardship, and many Japanese regard gaman with pride as a national trait.

Many people complain that younger folks divorce because they do not have enough gaman, and the frequency with which the term is used suggests a rather bleak understanding of marriage.

"I didn't know my husband very well when we married, and afterward we used to get into bitter fights," said Yoshiko Hirowaki, 56, a store owner. "But then we had children, and I got very busy with the kids and with this shop. Time passed."

Now Mrs. Hirowaki has been married 34 years, and she complains about young people who do not stick to their vows.

"In the old days, wives had more gaman," she said. "Now kids just don't have enough gaman."

The durability of the Japanese family is particularly wondrous because couples are, by international standards, exceptionally incompatible.

One survey asked married men and their wives in 37 countries how they felt about politics, sex, religion, ethics, and social issues. Japanese couples ranked dead last in compatibility of views, by a huge margin. Indeed, another survey found that if they were doing it over again, only about one-third of Japanese would marry the same person.

A national survey found that 30 percent of fathers spend less than 15 minutes a day on weekends talking with or playing with their children.

Incompatibility might not matter so much, however, because Japanese husbands and wives spend very little time talking to each other.

"I kind of feel there's nothing new to say to her," said Masa-yuki Ogita, an egg farmer, explaining his reticence.

In a small town like Omiya, couples usually have dinner together, but in Japanese cities there are many "7-11 husbands," so called because they leave at 7 A.M. and return after 11 P.M.

Masahiko Kondo now lives in Omiya, working in the chamber of commerce, but he used to be a salesman in several big cities. He would leave for work each morning at 7, and about four nights a week would go out for after-work drinking or mah-jongg sessions with buddies.

"I only saw my baby on Saturdays or Sundays," said Mr. Kondo, a lanky good-natured man of 37. "But in fact, I really enjoyed that life. It didn't bother me that I never spent time with my kid on weekdays."

Mr. Kondo's wife, Keiko, had her own life, spent with her child and the wives of other workaholic husbands.

"We had birthday parties, but they were with the kids and the mothers," she remembers. "No fathers ever came."

A national survey found that 30 percent of fathers spend less than 15 minutes a day on weekdays talking with or playing with their children. Among eighth graders, 51 percent reported that they never spoke with their fathers on weekdays.

Traditionally, many companies were reluctant to promote employees who had divorced or who had major problems at home.

As a result, the figures in Japan for single-parent households can be deceptive. The father is often more a theoretical presence than a homework-helping reality.

Still, younger people sometimes want to see the spouses in daylight, and a result is a gradual change in focus of lives from work to family. Two decades ago, nearly half of young people said in surveys that they wanted their fathers to put priority on work rather than family. Now only one-quarter say that.

Social Pressures
Shame Is Keeping Bonds in Place
For those who find themselves desperately unhappy, one source of pressure to keep plugging is shame.

"If you divorce, you lose face in society," said Tatsumi Kinoshita, a tea farmer. "People say, 'His wife escaped.' So folks remain married because they hate to be gossiped about."

Shame is a powerful social sanction in Japan, and it is not just a matter of gossip. Traditionally, many companies were reluctant to promote employees who had divorced or who had major problems at home.

"If you divorce, it weakens your position at work," said Akihiko Kanda, 27, who works in a local government office. "Your bosses won't give you such good ratings, and it'll always be a negative factor."

The idea, Mr. Kanda noted, is that if an employee cannot manage his own life properly, he should not be entrusted with important corporate matters.

Financial sanctions are also a major disincentive for divorce. The mother gets the children in three-quarters of divorces, but most mothers in Japan do not have careers and have few financial resources. Fathers pay child support in only 15 percent of all divorces with children, partly because women often hesitate to go to court to demand payments and partly because men often fail to pay even when the court orders it.

"The main reason for lack of divorce is that women can't support themselves," said Mizuko Kanda, a 51-year-old housewife. "My friends complain about their husbands and say that they'd divorce if they could, but they can't afford to."

The result of these social and economic pressures is clear.

Even in Japan, there are about 24 divorces for every 100 marriages, but that compares with 32 in France, and 42 in England, and 55 in the United States.

The Outlook
Change Creeps in, Imperiling Family
But society is changing in Japan, and it is an open question whether these changes will undermine the traditional family as they have elsewhere around the globe.

The nuclear family has already largely replaced the extended family in Japan, and shame is eroding as a sanction. Haruko Okumura, for example, runs a kindergarten and speaks openly about her divorce.

"My Mom was uneasy about it, but I never had an inferiority complex about being divorced," said Mrs. Okumura, as dozens of children played in the next room. "And people accepted me easily."

Mrs. Okumura sees evidence of the changes in family patterns every day: fathers are playing more of a role in the kindergarten. At Christmas parties and sports contests, fathers have started to show up along with mothers. And Mrs. Okumura believes that divorce is on the upswing.

"If there's a weakening of the economic and social pressures to stay married," she said, "surely divorce rates will soar."

Already divorce rates are rising, approximately doubling over the last 25 years. But couples are very reluctant to divorce when they have children, and so single-parent households account for exactly the same proportion today as in 1965.

Shinsuke Kawaguchi, a young tea farmer, is one of the men for whom life is changing. Americans are not likely to be impressed by Mr. Kawaguchi's open-mindedness, but he is.

"I take good care of my wife," he said. "I may not say 'I love you,' but I do hold her hand. And I might say, after she makes dinner, 'This tastes good.'"

"Of course," Mr. Kawaguchi quickly added, "I wouldn't say that unless I'd just done something really bad."

Even Mrs. Uemura, the elderly woman whose husband used to beat her, said that her husband was treating her better.

"The other day, he tried to pour me a cup of tea," Mrs. Uemura recalled excitedly. "It was a big change. I told all my friends."

Critical Thinking

1. How does the author describe the marriage of Yuri Uemura?
2. How does the current Japanese divorce rate compare with the past and with that of the United States?
3. What are the statistics regarding unwed mothers?
4. In what sense are love marriages more fragile than arranged marriages?
5. What three ingredients add to the strength of Japanese marriages?
6. How do low expectations strengthen Japanese marriages?
7. Why is an affair "not as traumatic"?
8. What is "gaman" and how important is it to the Japanese?

9. To what extent are Japanese couples incompatible? What is the measure of this? Why does it not seem to matter much?

10. How much time do Japanese fathers spend with their children? What trend does the author see in this regard?

11. What are the social pressures working against divorce?

12. What changes does the author see with regard to the nuclear family versus the extended family and with regard to shame as a social sanction?

13. What changes are occurring with regard to the role of the father?

14. Are divorce rates rising? Under what specific circumstances?

Create Central

www.mhhe.com/createcentral

Internet References

Women Watch
www.un.org/womenwatch/about

Sex and Marriage
http://anthro.palomar.edu/marriage/default.htm

Unit 5

UNIT

Prepared by: Elvio Angeloni, *Pasadena City College*

Gender and Status

The feminist movement in the United States has had a significant impact upon the development of anthropology. Feminists have rightly charged that anthropologists have tended to gloss over the lives of women in studies of society and culture. In part this is because, until recent times, most anthropologists have been men. The result has been an undue emphasis on male activities as well as male perspectives in descriptions of particular societies.

These charges, however, have proven to be a firm corrective. In the last few decades, anthropologists have studied women and, more particularly, the division of labor based on gender and its relation to biology, as well as to social and political status. In addition, these changes in emphasis have been accompanied by an increase in the number of women in the field.

Feminist anthropologists have critically attacked many of the established anthropological beliefs. They have shown, for example, that field studies of nonhuman primates, which were often used to demonstrate the evolutionary basis of male dominance, distorted the actual evolutionary record by focusing primarily on baboons. While male baboons, for instance, have been shown to be especially dominant and aggressive, other, less-quoted primate studies show how dominance and aggression are highly situational phenomena, sensitive to ecological variation. Feminist anthropologists have also shown that the subsistence contribution of women was likewise ignored by anthropologists. A classic case is that of the !Kung, a hunting and gathering group in southern Africa, where women provide the bulk of the foodstuffs, including most of the available protein, and who, not coincidentally, enjoy a more egalitarian relationship than usual with men. Thus, since political control is a matter of cultural variation, male authority is not biologically predetermined. In fact, there are many cultures in which some men may play a more feminine or, at least, asexual role, showing that gender relationships are deeply embedded in social experience and that the gender categories employed in any given culture may be inadequate to the task of doing justice to the actual diversity that exists.

Lest we think that gender issues are primarily academic, we should keep in mind that gender equality in this world is still a distant dream.

Article   Prepared by: Elvio Angeloni, *Pasadena City College*

The Berdache Tradition

WALTER L. WILLIAMS

Learning Outcomes

After reading this article, you will be able to:

- Define berdache and explain how it highlights the ways in which different societies accommodate atypical individuals.
- Discuss Native American beliefs regarding the berdache.

Because it is such a powerful force in the world today, the Western Judeo-Christian tradition is often accepted as the arbiter of "natural" behavior of humans. If Europeans and their descendant nations of North America accept something as normal, then anything different is seen as abnormal. Such a view ignores the great diversity of human existence.

This is the case of the study of gender. How many genders are there? To a modern Anglo-American, nothing might seem more definite than the answer that there are two: men and women. But not all societies around the world agree with Western culture's view that all humans are either women or men. The commonly accepted notion of "the opposite sex," based on anatomy, is itself an artifact of our society's rigid sex roles.

Among many cultures, there have existed different alternatives to "man" or "woman." An alternative role in many American Indian societies is referred to by anthropologists as *berdache*. . . . The role varied from one Native American culture to another, which is a reflection of the vast diversity of aboriginal New World societies. Small bands of hunter-gatherers existed in some areas, with advanced civilizations of farming peoples in other areas. With hundreds of different languages, economies, religions, and social patterns existing in North America alone, every generalization about a cultural tradition must acknowledge many exceptions.

This diversity is true for the berdache tradition as well, and must be kept in mind. My statements should be read as being specific to a particular culture, with generalizations being treated as loose patterns that might not apply to peoples even in nearby areas.

Briefly, a berdache can be defined as a morphological male who does not fill a society's standard man's role, who has a non-masculine character. This type of person is often stereotyped as effeminate, but a more accurate characterization is androgyny. Such a person has a clearly recognized and accepted social status, often based on a secure place in the tribal mythology.

Berdaches have special ceremonial roles in many Native American religions, and important economic roles in their families. They will do at least some women's work, and mix together much of the behavior, dress, and social roles of women and men. Berdaches gain social prestige by their spiritual, intellectual, or craftwork/artistic contributions, and by their reputation for hard work and generosity. They serve a mediating function between women and men, precisely because their character is seen as distinct from either sex. They are not seen as men, yet they are not seen as women either. They occupy an alternative gender role that is a mixture of diverse elements.

In their erotic behavior berdaches also generally (but not always) take a nonmasculine role, either being asexual or becoming the passive partner in sex with men. In some cultures the berdache might become a wife to a man. This male-male sexual behavior became the focus of an attack on berdaches as "sodomites" by the Europeans who, early on, came into contact with them. From the first Spanish conquistadors to the Western frontiersmen and the Christian missionaries and government officials, Western culture has had a considerable impact on the berdache tradition. In the last two decades, the most recent impact on the tradition is the adaptation of a modern Western gay identity.

To Western eyes berdachism is a complex and puzzling phenomenon, mixing and redefining the very concepts of what is considered male and female. In a culture with only two recognized genders, such individuals are gender nonconformist, abnormal, deviant. But to American Indians, the institution of another gender role means that berdaches are not deviant—indeed, they do conform to the requirements of a custom in which their culture tells them they fit. Berdachism is a way for society to recognize and assimilate some atypical individuals without imposing a change on them or stigmatizing them as deviant. This cultural institution confirms their legitimacy for what they are.

Societies often bestow power upon that which does not neatly fit into the usual. Since no cultural system can explain everything, a common way that many cultures deal with these inconsistencies is to imbue them with negative power, as taboo, pollution, witchcraft, or sin. That which is not understood is seen as a threat. But an alternative method of dealing with such things, or people, is to take them out of the realm of threat and to sanctify them.[1] The berdaches' role as mediator is thus not just between women and men, but also between the physical and the spiritual. American Indian cultures have taken what Western culture calls negative, and made it a positive; they have successfully utilized the different skills and insights of a class of people that Western culture has stigmatized and whose spiritual powers have been wasted.

Many Native Americans also understood that gender roles have to do with more than just biological sex. The standard Western view that one's sex is always a certainty, and that one's gender identity and sex role always conform to one's morphological sex is a view that dies hard. Western thought is typified by such dichotomies of groups perceived to be mutually exclusive: male and female, black and white, right and wrong, good and evil. Clearly, the world is not so simple; such clear divisions are not always realistic. Most American Indian worldviews generally are much more accepting of the ambiguities of life. Acceptance of gender variation in the berdache tradition is typical of many native cultures' approach to life in general.

Overall, these are generalizations based on those Native American societies that had an accepted role for berdaches. Not all cultures recognized such a respected status. Berdachism in aboriginal North America was most established among tribes in four areas: first, the Prairie and western Great Lakes, the northern and central Great Plains, and the lower Mississippi Valley; second, Florida and the Caribbean; third, the Southwest, the Great Basin, and California; and fourth, scattered areas of the Northwest, western Canada, and Alaska. For some reason it is not noticeable in eastern North America, with the exception of its southern rim. . . .

American Indian Religions

Native American religions offered an explanation for human diversity by their creation stories. In some tribal religions, the Great Spiritual Being is conceived as neither male nor female but as a combination of both. Among the Kamia of the Southwest, for example, the bearer of plant seeds and the introducer of Kamia culture was a man-woman spirit named Warharmi.[2] A key episode of the Zuni creation story involves a battle between the kachina spirits of the agricultural Zunis and the enemy hunter spirits. Every four years an elaborate ceremony commemorates this myth. In the story a kachina spirit called *ko'lhamana* was captured by the enemy spirits and transformed in the process. This transformed spirit became a mediator between the two sides, using his peacemaking skills to merge the differing lifestyles of hunters and farmers. In the ceremony, a dramatic reenactment of the myth, the part of the transformed *ko'lhamana* spirit, is performed by a berdache.[3] The Zuni word for berdache is *lhamana*, denoting its closeness to the spiritual mediator who brought hunting and farming together.[4] The moral of this story is that the berdache was created by the deities for a special purpose, and that this creation led to the improvement of society. The continual reenactment of this story provides a justification for the Zuni berdache in each generation.

In contrast to this, the lack of spiritual justification in a creation myth could denote a lack of tolerance for gender variation. The Pimas, unlike most of their Southwestern neighbors, did not respect a berdache status. *Wi-kovat*, their derogatory word, means "like a girl," but it does not signify a recognized social role. Pima mythology reflects this lack of acceptance in a folk tale that explains male androgyny as due to Papago witchcraft. Knowing that the Papagos respected berdaches, the Pimas blamed such an occurrence on an alien influence.[5] While the Pimas' condemnatory attitude is unusual, it does point out the importance of spiritual explanations for the acceptance of gender variance in a culture.

Other Native American creation stories stand in sharp contrast to the Pima explanation. A good example is the account of the Navajos, which presents women and men as equals. The Navajo origin tale is told as a story of five worlds. The first people were First Man and First Woman, who were created equally and at the same time. The first two worlds that they lived in were bleak and unhappy, so they escaped to the third world. In the third world lived two twins, Turquoise Boy and White Shell Girl, who were the first berdaches. In the Navajo language the world for berdache is *nadle,* which means "changing one" or "one who is transformed." It is applied to hermaphrodites—those who are born with the genitals of both male and female—and also to "those who pretend to be *nadle,*" who take on a social role that is distinct from either men or women.[6]

In the third world, First Man and First Woman began farming, with the help of the changing twins. One of the twins noticed some clay and, holding it in the palm of his/her hand, shaped it into the first pottery bowl. Then he/she formed a plate, a water dipper, and a pipe. The second twin observed some reeds and began to weave them, making the first basket. Together they shaped axes and grinding stones from rocks, and hoes from bone. All these new inventions made the people very happy.[7]

The message of this story is that humans are dependent for many good things on the inventiveness of *nadle.* Such individuals were present from the earliest eras of human existence, and their presence was never questioned. They were part of the natural order of the universe, with a special contribution to make.

Later on in the Navajo creation story, White Shell Girl entered the moon and became the Moon Bearer. Turquoise Boy, however, remained with the people. When First Man realized that Turquoise Boy could do all manner of women's work as well as women, all the men left the women and crossed a big river. The men hunted and planted crops. Turquoise Boy ground the corn, cooked the food, and weaved cloth for the men. Four years passed with the women and men separated, and the men were happy with the *nadle.* Later, however the women wanted to learn how to grind corn from the *nadle,* and both the men and women had decided that it was not good to continue living separately. So the women crossed the river and the people were reunited.[8]

They continued living happily in the third world, until one day a great flood began. The people ran to the highest mountaintop, but the water kept rising and they all feared they would be drowned. But just in time, the ever-inventive Turquoise Boy found a large reed. They climbed upward inside the tall hollow reed, and came out at the top into the fourth world. From there, White Shell Girl brought another reed, and they climbed again to the fifth world, which is the present world of the Navajos.[9]

These stories suggest that the very survival of humanity is dependent on the inventiveness of berdaches. With such a mythological belief system, it is no wonder that the Navajos held *nadle* in high regard. The concept of the *nadle* is well formulated in the creation story. As children were educated by these stories, and all Navajos believed in them, the high status accorded to gender variation was passed down from generation to generation. Such stories also provided instruction for *nadle* themselves to live by. A spiritual explanation guaranteed a special place for a person who was considered different but not deviant.

For American Indians, the important explanations of the world are spiritual ones. In their view, there is a deeper reality than the here-and-now. The real essence or wisdom occurs when one finally gives up trying to explain events in terms of "logic" and "reality." Many confusing aspects of existence can better be explained by actions of a multiplicity of spirits. Instead of a concept of a single god, there is an awareness of "that which we do not understand." In Lakota religion, for example, the term *Wakan Tanka* is often translated as "god." But a more proper translation, according to the medicine people who taught me, is "The Great Mystery."[10]

While rationality can explain much, there are limits to human capabilities of understanding. The English language is structured to account for cause and effect. For example, English speakers say, "It is raining," with the implication that there is a cause "it" that leads to rain. Many Indian languages, on the other hand, merely note what is most accurately translated as "raining" as an observable fact. Such an approach brings a freedom to stop worrying about causes of things, and merely to relax and accept that our human insights can go only so far. By not taking ourselves too seriously, or overinflating human importance, we can get beyond the logical world.

The emphasis of American Indian religions, then, is on the spiritual nature of all things. To understand the physical world, one must appreciate the underlying spiritual essence. Then one can begin to see that the physical is only a faint shadow, a partial reflection, of a supernatural and extrarational world. By the Indian view, everything that exists is spiritual. Every object—plants, rocks, water, air, the moon, animals, humans, the earth itself—has a spirit. The spirit of one thing (including a human) is not superior to the spirit of any other. Such a view promotes a sophisticated ecological awareness of the place that humans have in the larger environment. The function of religion is not to try to condemn or to change what exists, but to accept the realities of the world and to appreciate their contributions to life. Everything that exists has a purpose.[11]

One of the basic tenets of American Indian religion is the notion that everything in the universe is related. Nevertheless, things that exist are often seen as having a counterpart: sky and earth, plant and animal, water and fire. In all of these polarities, there exist mediators. The role of the mediator is to hold the polarities together, to keep the world from disintegrating. Polarities exist within human society also. The most important category within Indian society is gender. The notions of Woman and Man underlie much of social interaction and are comparable to the other major polarities. Women, with their nurtural qualities, are associated with the earth, while men are associated with the sky. Women gatherers and farmers deal with plants (of the earth), while men hunters deal with animals.

The mediator between the polarities of woman and man, in the American Indian religious explanation, is a being that combines the elements of both genders. This might be a combination in a physical sense, as in the case of hermaphrodites. Many Native American religions accept this phenomenon in the same way that they accept other variations from the norm. But more important is their acceptance of the idea that gender can be combined in ways other than physical hermaphroditism. The physical aspects of a thing or a person, after all, are not nearly as important as its spirit. American Indians use the concept of a person's *spirit* in the way that other Americans use the concept of a person's *character*. Consequently, physical hermaphroditism is not necessary for the idea of gender mixing. A person's character, their spiritual essence, is the crucial thing.

The Berdache's Spirit

Individuals who are physically normal might have the spirit of the other sex, might range somewhere between the two sexes, or might have a spirit that is distinct from either women or men. Whatever category they fall into, they are seen as being different from men. They are accepted spiritually as "Not Man." Whichever option is chosen, Indian religions offer spiritual explanations. Among the Arapahos of the Plains, berdaches are called *haxu'xan* and are seen to be that way as a result of a supernatural gift from birds or animals. Arapaho mythology recounts the story of Nih'a'ca, the first *haxu'xan*. He pretended to be a woman and married the mountain lion, a symbol for masculinity. The myth, as recorded by ethnographer Alfred Kroeber about 1900, recounted that "These people had the natural desire to become women, and as they grew up gradually became women. They gave up the desires of men. They were married to men. They had miraculous power and could do supernatural things. For instance, it was one of them that first made an intoxicant from rainwater."[12] Besides the theme of inventiveness, similar to the Navajo creation story, the berdache role is seen as a product of a "natural desire." Berdaches "gradually became women," which underscores the notion of woman as a social category rather than as a fixed biological entity. Physical biological sex is less important in gender classification than a person's desire—one's spirit.

They myths contain no prescriptions for trying to change berdaches who are acting out their desires of the heart. Like many other cultures' myths, the Zuni origin myths simply sanction the idea that gender can be transformed independently of biological sex.[13] Indeed, myths warn of dire consequences when interference with such a transformation is attempted. Prince Alexander Maximilian of the German state of Wied, traveling in the northern Plains in the 1830s, heard a myth about a warrior who once tried to force a berdache to avoid women's clothing. The berdache resisted, and the warrior shot him with an arrow. Immediately the berdache disappeared, and the warrior saw only a pile of stones with his arrow in them. Since then, the story concluded, no intelligent person would try to coerce a berdache.[14] Making the point even more directly, a Mandan myth told of an Indian who tried to force *mihdake* (berdaches) to give up their distinctive dress and status, which led the spirits to punish many people with death. After that, no Mandans interfered with berdaches.[15]

With this kind of attitude, reinforced by myth and history, the aboriginal view accepts human diversity. The creation story of the Mohave of the Colorado River Valley speaks of a time when people were not sexually differentiated. From this perspective, it is easy to accept that certain individuals might combine elements of masculinity and femininity.[16] A respected Mohave elder, speaking in the 1930s, stated this viewpoint simply: "From the very beginning of the world it was meant that there should be [berdaches], just as it was instituted that there should be shamans. They were intended for that purpose."[17]

This elder also explained that a child's tendencies to become a berdache are apparent early, by about age nine to twelve, before the child reaches puberty: "That is the time when young persons become initiated into the functions of their sex. . . . None but young people will become berdaches as a rule."[18] Many tribes have a public ceremony that acknowledges the acceptance of berdache status. A Mohave shaman related the ceremony for his tribe: "When the child was about ten years old his relatives would begin discussing his strange ways. Some of them disliked it, but the more intelligent began envisaging an initiation ceremony." The relatives prepare for the ceremony without letting the boy know of it. It is meant to take him by surprise, to be both an initiation and a test of his true inclinations. People from various settlements are invited to attend. The family wants the community to see it and become accustomed to accepting the boy as an *alyha.*

On the day of the ceremony, the shaman explained, the boy is led into a circle: "If the boy showed a willingness to remain standing in the circle, exposed to the public eye, it was almost certain that he would go through with the ceremony. The singer, hidden behind the crowd, began singing the songs. As soon as the sound reached the boy he began to dance as women do." If the boy is unwilling to assume *alyha* status, he would refuse to dance. But if his character—his spirit—is *alyha*, "the song goes right to his heart and he will dance with much intensity. He cannot help it. After the fourth song he is proclaimed." After the ceremony, the boy is carefully bathed and receives a woman's skirt. He is then led back to the dance ground, dressed as an *alyha*, and announces his new feminine name to the crowd. After that he would resent being called by his old male name.[19]

Among the Yuman tribes of the Southwest, the transformation is marked by a social gathering, in which the berdache prepares a meal for the friends of the family.[20] Ethnographer Ruth Underhill, doing fieldwork among the Papago Indians in the early 1930s, wrote that berdaches were common among the Papago Indians, and were usually publicly acknowledged in childhood. She recounted that a boy's parents would test him if they noticed that he preferred female pursuits. The regular pattern, mentioned by many of Underhill's Papago informants, was to build a small brush enclosure. Inside the enclosure they placed a man's bow and arrows, and also a woman's basket. At the appointed time the boy was brought to the enclosure as the adults watched from outside. The boy was told to go inside the circle of brush. Once he was inside, the adults "set fire to the enclosure. They watched what he took with him as he ran

out and if it was the basketry materials, they reconciled themselves to his being a berdache."[21]

What is important to recognize in all of these practices is that the assumption of a berdache role was not forced on the boy by others. While adults might have their suspicions, it was only when the child made the proper move that he was considered a berdache. By doing woman's dancing, preparing a meal, or taking the woman's basket he was making an important symbolic gesture. Indian children were not stupid, and they knew the implications of these ceremonies beforehand. A boy in the enclosure could have left without taking anything, or could have taken both the man's and the woman's tools. With the community standing by watching, he was well aware that his choice would mark his assumption of berdache status. Rather than being seen as an involuntary test of his reflexes, this ceremony may be interpreted as a definite statement by the child to take on the berdache role.

Indians do not see the assumption of berdache status, however, as a free will choice on the part of the boy. People felt that the boy was acting out his basic character. The Lakota shaman Lame Deer explained:

> They were not like other men, but the Great Spirit made them *winktes* and we accepted them as such. . . . We think that if a woman has two little ones growing inside her, if she is going to have twins, sometimes instead of giving birth to two babies they have formed up in her womb into just one, into a half-man/half-woman kind of being. . . . To us a man is what nature, or his dreams, make him. We accept him for what he wants to be. That's up to him.[22]

While most of the sources indicate that once a person becomes a berdache it is a lifelong status, directions from the spirits determine everything. In at least one documented case, concerning a nineteenth-century Klamath berdache named Lele'ks, he later had a supernatural experience that led him to leave the berdache role. At that time Lele'ks began dressing and acting like a man, then married women, and eventually became one of the most famous Klamath chiefs.[23] What is important is that both in assuming berdache status and in leaving it, supernatural dictate is the determining factor.

Dreams and Visions

Many tribes see the berdache role as signifying an individual's proclivities as a dreamer and a visionary. . . .

Among the northern Plains and related Great Lakes tribes, the idea of supernatural dictate through dreaming—the vision quest—had its highest development. The goal of the vision quest is to try to get beyond the rational world by sensory deprivation and fasting. By depriving one's body of nourishment, the brain could escape from logical thought and connect with the higher reality of the supernatural. The person doing the quest simply sits and waits for a vision. But a vision might not come easily; the person might have to wait for days.

The best way that I can describe the process is to refer to my own vision quest, which I experienced when I was living on a Lakota reservation in 1982. After a long series of prayers and blessings, the shaman who had prepared me for the ceremony took me out to an isolated area where a sweat lodge had been set up for my quest. As I walked to the spot, I worried that I might not be able to stand it. Would I be overcome by hunger? Could I tolerate the thirst? What would I do if I had to go to the toilet? The shaman told me not to worry, that a whole group of holy people would be praying and singing for me while I was on my quest.

He had me remove my clothes, symbolizing my disconnection from the material would, and crawl into the sweat lodge. Before he left me I asked him, "What do I think about?" He said, "Do not think. Just pray for spiritual guidance." After a prayer he closed the flap tightly and I was left in total darkness. I still do not understand what happened to me during my vision quest, but during the day and a half that I was out there, I never once felt hungry or thirsty or the need to go to the toilet. What happened was an intensely personal experience that I cannot and do not wish to explain, a process of being that cannot be described in rational terms.

When the shaman came to get me at the end of my time, I actually resented having to end it. He did not need to ask if my vision quest was successful. He knew that it was even before seeing me, he explained, because he saw an eagle circling over me while I underwent the quest. He helped interpret the signs I had seen, then after more prayers and singing he led me back to the others. I felt relieved, cleansed, joyful, and serene. I had been through an experience that will be a part of my memories always.

If a vision quest could have such an effect on a person not even raised in Indian society, imagine its impact on a boy who from his earliest years had been waiting for the day when he could seek his vision. Gaining his spiritual power from his first vision, it would tell him what role to take in adult life. The vision might instruct him that he is going to be a great hunter, a craftsman, a warrior, or a shaman. Or it might tell him that he will be a berdache. Among the Lakotas, or Sioux, there are several symbols for various types of visions. A person becomes *wakan* (a sacred person) if she or he dreams of a bear, a wolf, thunder, a buffalo, a white buffalo calf, or Double Woman. Each dream results in a different gift, whether it is the power to cure illness or wounds, a promise of good hunting, or the exalted role of a *heyoka* (doing things backward).

A white buffalo calf is believed to be a berdache. If a person has a dream of the sacred Double Woman, this means that she or he will have the power to seduce men. Males who have a vision of Double Woman are presented with female tools. Taking such tools means that the male will become a berdache. The Lakota word *winkte* is composed of *win,* "woman," and *kte,* "would become."[24] A contemporary Lakota berdache explains, "To become a *winkte,* you have a medicine man put you up on the hill, to search for your vision. "You can become a *winkte* if you truly are by nature. You see a vision of the White Buffalo Calf Pipe. Sometimes it varies. A vision is like a scene in a movie."[25] Another way to become a *winkte* is to have a vision given by a *winkte* from the past.[26]...

By interpreting the result of the vision as being the work of a spirit, the vision quest frees the person from feeling responsible for his transformation. The person might even claim that the change was done against his will and without his control.

Such a claim does not suggest a negative attitude about berdache status, because it is common for people to claim reluctance to fulfill their spiritual duty no matter what vision appears to them. Becoming any kind of sacred person involves taking on various social responsibilities and burdens.[27]...

A story was told among the Lakotas in the 1880s of a boy who tried to resist following his vision from Double Woman. But according to Lakota informants "few men succeed in this effort after having taken the strap in the dream." Having rebelled against the instructions given him by the Moon Being, he committed suicide.[28] The moral of that story is that one should not resist spiritual guidance, because it will lead only to grief. In another case, an Omaha young man told of being addressed by a spirit as "daughter," whereupon he discovered that he was unconsciously using feminine styles of speech. He tried to use male speech patterns, but could not. As a result of this vision, when he returned to his people he resolved himself to dress as a woman.[29] Such stories function to justify personal peculiarities as due to a fate over which the individual has no control.

Despite the usual pattern in Indian societies of using ridicule to enforce conformity, receiving instructions from a vision inhibits others from trying to change the berdache. Ritual explanation provides a way out. It also excuses the community from worrying about the cause of that person's difference, or the feeling that it is society's duty to try to change him.[30] Native American religions, above all else, encourage a basic respect for nature. If nature makes a person different, many Indians conclude, a mere human should not undertake to counter this spiritual dictate. Someone who is "unusual" can be accommodated without being stigmatized as "abnormal." Berdachism is thus not alien or threatening; it is a reflection of spirituality.

Notes

1. Mary Douglas, *Purity and Danger* (Baltimore: Penguin, 1966), p. 52. I am grateful to Theda Perdue for convincing me that Douglas's ideas apply to berdachism. For an application of Douglas's thesis to berdaches, see James Thayer, "The Berdache of the Northern Plains: A Socioreligious Perspective," *Journal of Anthropological Research 36* (1980): 292–93.

2. E. W. Gifford, "The Kamia of Imperial Valley," *Bureau of American Ethnology Bulletin 97* (1931): 12.

3. By using present tense verbs in this text, I am not implying that such activities are necessarily continuing today. I sometimes use the present tense in the "ethnographic present," unless I use the past tense when I am referring to something that has not continued. Past tense implies that all such practices have disappeared. In the absence of fieldwork to prove such disappearance, I am not prepared to make that assumption, on the historic changes in the berdache tradition.

4. Elsie Clews Parsons, "The Zuni La' Mana," *American Anthropologist 18* (1916): 521; Matilda Coxe Stevenson, "Zuni Indians," *Bureau of American Ethnology Annual Report 23* (1903): 37; Franklin Cushing, "Zuni Creation Myths," *Bureau of American Ethnology Annual Report 13* (1894): 401–3. Will Roscoe clarified this origin story for me.

5. W. W. Hill, "Note on the Pima Berdache," *American Anthropologist 40* (1938): 339.

6. Aileen O'Bryan, "The Dine': Origin Myths of the Navaho Indians," *Bureau of American Ethnology Bulletin 163* (1956): 5; W. W. Hill, "The Status of the Hermaphrodite and Transvestite in Navaho Culture," *American Anthropologist 37* (1935): 273.

7. Martha S. Link, *The Pollen Path: A Collection of Navajo Myths* (Stanford: Stanford University Press, 1956).

8. O'Bryan, "Dine'," pp. 5, 7, 9–10.

9. Ibid.

10. Lakota informants, July 1982. See also William Powers, *Oglala Religion* (Lincoln: University of Nebraska Press, 1977).

11. For this admittedly generalized overview of American Indian religious values, I am indebted to traditionalist informants of many tribes, but especially those of the Lakotas. For a discussion of native religions see Dennis Tedlock, *Finding the Center* (New York: Dial Press, 1972); Ruth Underhill, *Red Man's Religion* (Chicago: University of Chicago Press, 1965); and Elsi Clews Parsons, *Pueblo Indian Religion* (Chicago: University of Chicago Press, 1939).

12. Alfred Kroeber, "The Arapaho," *Bulletin of the American Museum of Natural History 18* (1902–7): 19.

13. Parsons, "Zuni La' Mana," p. 525.

14. Alexander Maximilian, *Travels in the interior of North America, 1832–1834,* vol. 22 of *Early Western Travels,* ed. Reuben Gold Thwaites, 32 vols. (Cleveland: A. H. Clark, 1906), pp. 283–84, 354. Maximilian was quoted in German in the early homosexual rights book by Ferdinand Karsch-Haack, *Das Gleichgeschlechtliche Leben der Naturvölker* (The same-sex life of nature peoples) (Munich: Verlag von Ernst Reinhardt, 1911; reprinted New York: Arno Press, 1975), pp. 314, 564.

15. Oscar Koch, *Der Indianishe Eros* (Berlin: Verlag Continent, 1925), p. 61.

16. George Devereux, "Institutionalized Homosexuality of the Mohave Indians," *Human Biology 9* (1937): 509.

17. Ibid., p. 501

18. Ibid.

19. Ibid., pp. 508–9.

20. C. Daryll Forde, "Ethnography of the Yuma Indians," *University of California Publications in American Archaeology and Ethnology 28* (1931): 157.

21. Ruth Underhill, *Social Organization of the Papago Indians* (New York: Columbia University Press, 1938), p. 186. This story is also mentioned in Ruth Underhill, ed., *The Autobiography of a Papago Woman* (Menasha, Wisc.: American Anthropological Association, 1936), p. 39.

22. John Fire and Richard Erdoes, *Lame Deer, Seeker of Visions* (New York: Simon and Schuster, 1972), pp. 117, 149.

23. Theodore Stern, *The Klamath Tribe: A People and Their Reservation* (Seattle: University of Washington Press, 1965), pp. 20, 24; Theodore Stern, "Some Sources of Variability in Klamath Mythology," *Journal of American Folklore 69* (1956): 242ff; Leshe Spier, *Klamath Ethnography* (Berkeley: University of California Press, 1930), p. 52.

24. Clark Wissler, "Societies and Ceremonial Associations in the Oglala Division of the Teton Dakota," *Anthropological Papers of the American Museum of Natural History 11,* pt. 1 (1916): 92; Powers, *Oglala Religion,* pp. 57–59.

25. Ronnie Loud Hawk, Lakota informant 4, July 1982.

26. Terry Calling Eagle, Lakota informant 5, July 1982.

27. James S. Thayer, "The Berdache of the Northern Plains: A Socioreligious Perspective," *Journal of Anthropological Research 36* (1980): 289.

28. Fletcher, "Elk Mystery," p. 281.

29. Alice Fletcher and Francis La Flesche, "The Omaha Tribe," *Bureau of American Ethnology Annual Report 27* (1905–6): 132.

30. Harriet Whitehead offers a valuable discussion of this element of the vision quest in "The Bow and the Burden Strap: A New Look at Institutionalized Homosexuality in Native North America," in *Sexual Meanings,* ed. Sherry Ortner and Harriet Whitehead (Cambridge: Cambridge University Press, 1981), pp. 99–102. See also Erikson, "Childhood," p. 329.

Critical Thinking

1. What is a berdache? What special roles have berdaches played in Native American societies?

2. What kinds of erotic behavior have they exhibited?

3. How have Europeans and American Indians differed in their treatment of the berdaches? How does the author explain these two different approaches?

4. How does the author contrast Western thought with Native American views regarding gender?

5. Why do Native Americans explain things in spiritual terms rather than "logic" and "reality"?

6. What is the emphasis of American Indian religions? What is the function of such religion?

7. What is one of the most basic tenets of American Indian religion? What kinds of polarities exist? Why are mediators necessary?

8. What is the most important category within Indian society? How do men and women differ?

9. Describe some of the Native American beliefs regarding the berdache.

Create Central

www.mhhe.com/createcentral

Internet References

Sexualities
http://sexualities.sagepub.com
Sexuality Studies
https://sxs.sfsu.edu
Sexuality Studies.net
http://sexualitystudies.net/programs
The Kinsey Institute
www.kinseyinstitute.org/about
Gender & History
www.blackwellpublishing.com/journal.asp?ref=0953-5233&site=1

Article   Prepared by: Elvio Angeloni, *Pasadena City College*

The Hijras: An Alternative Gender in India

SERENA NANDA

Learning Outcomes

After reading this article, you will be able to:

- Describe the transgender hijra of India in terms of their traditional social and religious roles.
- Discuss the ways in which the hijra of India challenge the binary sex/gender notions of the West.

My first encounter with the hijras was in 1971. While walking on Churchgate in Bombay with an Indian friend one day, we were confronted by two persons in female clothing, who stood before us, blocking our passage. They clapped their hands in a peculiar manner and then put out their upturned palms in the traditional Indian gesture of a request for alms. My friend hurriedly dropped a few rupees into the outstretched palms in front of us, and pulled me along at a quick pace, almost shoving me in front of her. Startled at her abrupt reaction, I took another look at the two people who had intercepted us. It was only then that I realized that they were not females at all, but men, dressed in women's clothing. Now curious, I asked my friend who these people were and why she had reacted so strongly to their presence, but she just shook her head and would not answer me. Sensing her discomfort, I let the subject drop but raised it with other friends at a later time. In this way I found out a little about the hijras, and became determined to learn more.

For the next 10 years my professional interests as an anthropologist centered on culture and gender roles. As part of my interest in sexual variation I read what little I could find on the hijras, asking my Indian friends and relatives about them, and extending this interest through several field trips over the next twenty years. I learned that the hijras, described as neither men nor women, performed on auspicious occasions such as births and marriages, where they are believed to have the power to confer blessings of fertility; from some male acquaintances I discovered that hijras may also be prostitutes. Hijras were called eunuchs, but also said to be born intersexed, a contradiction I could not untangle. I realized that without talking with hijras themselves, I could not distinguish fact from fiction, myth from reality.

In 1981 I lived in India for a year with my family and decided to learn more about the hijras. During this time I met and interviewed many hijras in several of the major cities in North and South India. I spent days with them in their homes, attended their performances, met their husbands and customers, and also members of their families, and formed some good friendships among them. As a result of one of these friendships, I was made a ritual younger sister to a hijra guru. I also visited the temple of Bahuchara Mataji, the special deity of the hijras, located close to Ahmadabad. In addition, I spoke at length with doctors and social scientists in India who had personal knowledge of individual hijras or had written about them. All of these investigators were males, however, and I think being a woman gave me a great advantage in getting to know individual hijras in a more personal, and therefore, deeper way.

While hijras are regarded as deviant, and even bizarre, perhaps, in Indian society, in my hundreds of conversations with them, I was most forcibly struck by them as individuals who share in our common humanity. Like human beings everywhere, hijras are both shaped by their culture and the role they play in society, but are also individuals who vary in their emotions, behavior, and outlook on life. Some hijras were outgoing, flirtatious, and jolly, and loved to dress up, perform, and have their photos taken. They met the difficulties of their lives with a good sense of humor, which they often turned on themselves. Kamladevi was one of these: she was a favorite friend of mine because she was so amusing and she spoke fluent English, having graduated from a convent high school. She was a great gossip and imitated her hijra friends and elders in funny and very insightful ways. In telling a story of how she and several other hijra prostitutes were picked up by the police one evening, she captured to perfection the intimidating attitude of the police, the arrogance of the magistrate, and the combination of innocence and boldness she had used in telling them off. Like many hijra prostitutes, Kamladevi worked very hard under the watchful and demanding eye of the hijra "madam" who swallowed most of her earnings. Although she made a fair living as a prostitute, Kamladevi always spent more than she had as she could not resist buying saris and jewelry. But in spite of her poverty, and ill health as well, she always had an eye for the humorous side of things.

Other hijras I knew were very serious and even shy. They saw their life as a fate "written on their forehead," and accepted with resignation whatever insults or abuses were meted out to them. They worked all day, every day, at whatever they did to earn a living, whether begging alms from shops, or serving in bathhouses, or at various domestic chores within their households, which included cooking, cleaning, or small tasks such as grinding spices, which they did for outsiders to earn a few extra rupees. These hijras had few interests or social contacts, some even relatively isolated within the hijra community itself. Hijras who earned a living performing at marriages and childbirths were the elite of their community. Although they also worked very hard, they were better rewarded financially and gained status within the hijra community for earning a living in this traditional manner, rather than practicing prostitution or eking out a living begging for alms. Kavita, for example, one of the hijra performers I knew well, was determined to sing and dance whenever she got the opportunity. She not only performed at marriages and childbirths, but also in more contemporary settings, such as "stag parties" and college functions. Her energy in dancing for hours at a time, as well as her ability to "keep her cool" in the face of the teasing and rowdiness of large crowds of men was a well deserved source of pride to her.

While younger hijras are often playful and sometimes even outrageously bold in public, hijra elders, or gurus, as they are called, most often maintain a great degree of dignity. They, like other middle aged and elderly Indian women, tend to wear simple clothing and little jewelry, though what they wear is often real gold. They are modest in their manner, and also, like many middle class housewives, do not "roam about" but stay close to home, supervising the households of which they are in charge. Hijra gurus are also the ones who are most familiar with their place in India, which is rooted both in Hindu mythology, which incorporates many transgender figures, and in Islam, with its tradition of eunuchs who served at the courts of kings (Nanda 1999). Most gurus I met were happy to share this information with me, as it is the basis of their power and respect in Indian society.

But whatever their personality, their age, or social status within the hijra community, I almost always found a very courteous, and even hospitable reception among the hijras I visited. Occasionally hijras in the largest cities were hostile or even aggressive, an attitude undoubtedly fostered by the abuse or prurient curiosity they sometimes receive from the larger society, including foreigners. Given the many reasons hijras have to resent outsiders, I was overcome by the welcome I received, and the several close relationships that I formed. But even when courteous and hospitable, not all the hijras I met were interested in being interviewed. Some hijras would reveal nothing about their lives before they joined the community, while others were more forthcoming.

My interviews convince me, however, that the common belief in India that all hijras are born intersexed (hermaphrodites) and are taken away from their parents and brought into the hijra community as infants, is not correct. Most hijras are physically normal men, whose effeminacy, sometimes

accompanied by an interest in homosexual activity, led them to seek out the hijra community in their late childhood or adolescence. Their childhood effeminacy, expressed in a wish to wear girl's clothing and imitate girl's behavior was the source of ridicule or abuse by their peers and family and the only solution appeared to be that of leaving their families and joining up with the hijras. While many hijras subsequently lose all contact with their families, others maintain a connection; they may occasionally visit their parents or siblings or these family members may visit them.

Rukhmini was a hijra whose break with her family was permanent and complete. She came from a middle class family and her father was a high ranking police officer. In spite of the many attempts of her father and brothers to prevent her, she persisted in acting and dressing as a girl. When it became known to her father that Rukhmini had had sexual relations with the gardener's son, he almost killed her by holding her head down in a barrel of water and beating her with his cross belt. "My mother cried tears of blood," she said. After this incident, Rukhmini ran away from her home and never returned.

In Sushila's case, she lived at home until her late teens, in relative peace with her family, until one night an elder brother falsely accused her of stealing some money from him. In his anger he told her to "use your own money that you get from selling your anus." She was more outraged at the false accusation of theft than the insult about her homosexuality and then and there left her home to join a hijra commune in a nearby city. Sushila keeps in touch with her family, and sends them gifts on the occasion of her brothers' and sisters' marriage. Meera, a hijra guru, joined the hijra community from a different and less typical route. She had grown up with the desires to be like a female, but followed the conventions of society by having her family arrange her marriage. She was married for over twenty years, and the father of several children, before she "upped one day and joined the hijras." She, too, keeps track of her family and occasionally sends them money when they need it.

As physically normal men, Kavita, Kamladevi, Rukhmini, Sushila, Rekha, and Meera were required to undergo an "operation" which removed their male genitals and transformed them into hijras. This operation, called "nirvana" or rebirth, is a religious ritual for hijras which positions them as ascetics, whose creative powers derive from their rejecting and thus transcending normal sexuality. This role connects them to Shiva, the great Hindu deity, who through his asceticism was given powers to create by Lord Brahma. The operation also identifies hijras with their special goddess and gives them the power to confer blessings of fertility, and equally, curse those who resist their demand for alms. For the small percentage of hijras who are born intersexed, no such operation is necessary. Salima, for example, a hijra from Bombay, told me that from a very early age she had "an organ that was very small." Her mother thought it would grow as she grew older, but when this did not happen her mother took her to many doctors, all to no avail. When Salima was about ten years old, a doctor told her mother, "nothing can be done, your child is neither a man nor a woman," and so Salima's mother gave her to a household of hijras who lived nearby. Salima lived with this group very happily and reported that they treated her with great kindness when she was a child.

But whatever their former lives had been, whether they had joined the hijras voluntarily, or been given to the community in despair by their parents, once an individual joins the community, they become subject to its rules and must adapt to its restrictions. This is not easy. In return for the emotional and economic security provided by the hijra community, an individual must give up some freedom, although probably not more than a young woman gives up when she becomes a bride living in a joint family. Unlike similar persons in the United States, who primarily live and work on their own, the hijras, shaped as they are by Indian culture in spite of their deviance, seem to prefer, like most Indians, to live in groups.

The Hijra Community

The hijra community in India has the qualities of both a religious cult and a caste and takes its customs, social organization and history from both Hinduism and Islam (Nanda 1999; Reddy 2005). Hijras find great pride in citing their identification with many of the great male figures of Hindu mythology who take on female forms in various situations. Familiar to all Hindus is Arjun's disguise as a eunuch in the Mahabharata and Shiva's form as Ardhanarisvara, half man/half woman, just two examples of powerful males in Hindu culture who act or dress as women or who partake of feminine qualities.

Many Hindu festivals include male transgenderism, like the one in south India that attracts thousands of hijras from all over India. This festival is based on a story of a king, who, in order to avert defeat in a war, promised to sacrifice his eldest son to the Gods, asking only that he first be allowed to arrange his son's marriage. Because no woman could be found who would marry a man about to be sacrificed, Lord Krishna came to earth as a woman to marry the King's son and the king won the battle, as the gods had promised. For the festival, men dress as women and go through a marriage ceremony with the deity. The priest performs the marriage, tying on the traditional wedding necklace. The next day the deity is carried to a burial ground and all of those who have "married" him remove their wedding necklaces, cry and beat their breasts, break their bangles, and remove the flowers from their hair, as a widow does in mourning. Hijra participation in this ritual affirms their identification with Krishna, one of the most important Indian deities.

The identification of males with female deities, expressed by the hijras through their cross dressing and emasculation, is a traditional part of Hinduism. This identification reinforces the legitimacy of the hijras as devotees of the Mother Goddess and vehicles of her power, which they use to confer blessings of fertility and prosperity at the births and weddings where they perform. The importance of the mother goddess in India is thus critical to understanding the role of the hijras. Hijra devotion to the goddess, Bahucharaji, a version of the Mother Goddess, closely identified with Durga, is central to their community. Bahucharaji's temple, near Ahmedabad, always has several hijra attendants present who bless visitors and tell them

the stories of the powers of the goddess, which has specific references to transgenderism. It is in the name of the goddess that the hijras undergo their emasculation operation, which to them is a ritual of rebirth, transforming them from men to hijras.

Hindu, Muslim, and even Christian hijras revere the goddess, while at the same time embracing elements of Islamic culture. The Indian tradition among both Hindus and Muslims of seeking blessings from saint-like figures whose personal power and charisma supersedes their ascribed religion permits the hijras to find some respect in both these religious communities. In pre-independence India, for example, Muslim rulers gave land grants and special rights to hijras in their kingdoms. And while the hijra role is definitely rooted in early Hinduism, the use of eunuchs in the Mughal courts also strengthened its emergence as a distinct sub-culture. The incorporation of both Hinduism and Islam in the hijras' identity and community is characteristic of the power of Indian culture to incorporate seeming contradictions and paradoxes, into itself, including gender ambiguity, variation, and contradictions (O'Flaherty 1980).

As a caste (jati), or community (quam), hijras have a highly structured social organization whose dominant feature is a hierarchical relationship between the elders, or gurus, and the juniors, or chelas (the guru/chela relationship models itself on the teacher/disciple relationships which are an important feature of Hinduism). Each hijra joins the community under the sponsorship of a guru, and the guru/chela relationship ideally lasts a lifetime. Chelas of the same guru consider themselves "sisters" and adopt fictive kinship relations, such as "aunty" and "grandmother" with hijra elders. As chelas get older, they may become gurus by recruiting chelas for themselves. This process both offers scope for social mobility within the hijra community and also helps maintain the community over time. Hijra social organization, particularly in the guru/chela relationship, thus attempts to substitute for the family life which hijras have abandoned: the guru offers protection, care, and security to the chela and receives in return obedience, loyalty, and a portion of their earnings. Another important advantage of belonging to the hijra community is that it provides a haven when a hijra becomes aged or ill, and can no longer work. A hijra guru with many chelas will be well taken care of, but even a hijra with no chelas will be taken care of by the members of her community.

The typical effective working group of hijras is a communal household, consisting of 5–15 people, headed by a guru. The household members contribute part or all of their earnings to the household and share household chores. In return they get a roof over their heads, food, protection from the police for those who engage in prostitution, and a place from which to carry on their business. Most importantly, as all of the work hijras do, whether begging, entertaining, or prostitution, is strictly divided up among all the hijra households in a city, joining a hijra commune is practically the only way a hijra can get work. The hijra household is thus both an economic and a residential unit, as well as a family-like group which provides emotional satisfaction and a network of social relationships.

Living in a hijra household puts many restrictions on behavior. Just as an Indian bride must make adjustments to her in-laws when she moves into a joint family, so a new hijra must make many accommodations to her new "family" in a hijra commune. Kumari, an independent sort of person, who, with her guru's permission, eventually moved out to her own place, told me that "living with the hijras was very difficult. There were so many jobs to do . . . like cooking and housework. After coming home from a whole day of dancing, I then had to cook and do other chores. If I did the household chores during the day, I wouldn't have time to go out and the whole day would be lost. Gurus are very strict. If you don't keep your hair covered with your sari, if you don't cook properly, if the house is not spotlessly clean, for all these things they give you trouble. You can't just throw your dirty clothes down anywhere, you have to hang them up. If you don't serve food on the proper dishes, they will shout, 'What, are you a man that you cannot do these things properly!' I got tired of all that and so asked my guru permission to live on my own."

But even for hijras like Kumari, who prefer to live on their own, the idea of living as a hijra without the support of a guru is unthinkable. "You can never be without a guru," says Kumari, "anymore than you people (non-hijras) can be without a mother. Just as a daughter is known by her mother, so we are known by our guru. To belong to the hijra community, to live in a sari like this, you must have a guru; otherwise you will have no respect in society."

An individual can only join the hijra community under the sponsorship of a guru, and as a member of her guru's "house" (gharana). The "houses" into which the hijra community is divided are similar to symbolic descent groups, like clans or lineages. Although there are few meaningful distinctions between these "houses," each has its own founder and history. Hijras say the "houses" are like several brothers from the same mother, or two countries, like England and America, which have a common origin. A hijra remains in the "house" of her guru even if she moves her residence to some other household or even some other city. When a hijra dies, it is the elders of her "house," rather than her household, who arrange for her funeral; and a guru will pass her property to chelas belonging to her "house" when she dies.

Each "house" has a naik, or chief and it is the naiks who get together locally, and also nationally, to decide on major policy issues for the hijra community, or to celebrate some event within the community, such as the death anniversary of a famous guru. At the local level, it is the naiks who get together in a jamaat (meeting of the elders) to resolve conflict among hijra individuals or households within a city or region.

One of the most important tasks of the jamaat is to make sure that hijras do not violate the rules of their community. Honesty is one of the unshakable hijra norms. Hijras frequently change their residence, both within and between cities, and a hijra who has been found guilty of stealing someone's property will not be accepted in any hijra household. Without a household, a hijra will find herself without friends, and more important, without access to work. In respectable hijra households, individuals are expected to behave with some propriety, and hijras who drink heavily, or who are quarrelsome, or cannot control their aggression, will find themselves out on the street. The punishment for misbehavior varies with the crime: in some cases fines are levied; in more serious cases a hijra's hair will be cut as a way of stigmatizing her within the community, as

hijras are obliged to wear their hair long, like women. For the most serious offenses, such as abusing or assaulting one's guru, a hijra may be cast out of the community altogether and have to pay a very heavy fine to re-enter.

This had happened to Rehka. Rehka had been in the hijra community for the last 15 years, earning her keep by playing the dholak (drum) which always accompanies hijra performances. Several years ago, provoked in an argument over men and money, Rehka insulted her guru and struck her. A meeting of the naiks determined that she should be cast out of the hijra community. From living very comfortably and with her future secure, Rehka now found herself, literally, on the street. Her sister chelas would no longer talk to her, not even, she said, "give me a drink of water." There was no place within walking distance she could work that was not already part of another hijra group's territory. If she tried to perform or even beg, she would be chased away by other hijras. With no money, and no work, Rehka took up residence on the street, earning a few rupees caring for some neighbor's children, or sometimes walking miles to a suburb to beg for alms. When it rained she slept under a bus. Living in the open, her clothes became tattered, her appearance and her health deteriorated and she was constantly insulted by neighborhood rowdies. It was a vicious cycle: Rekha was cast out of the community until she could raise the substantial fine of over 1,000 rupees that the naiks determined as the price of her re-entry into the community and apart from the community it was hopeless to even think of earning that sum, never mind saving it. Rehka's transformation was not lost on the hijras in her city. For all who knew her, it acted as a powerful incentive to maintain their own obedience and loyalty to their gurus.

The most important conflicts that naiks resolve are those that occur when the rigid territorial allotment of work within a city is violated. Naiks reach agreement about which hijra groups may work—whether begging alms from shop owners or in traditional performances—in particular areas of a city. When a hijra group finds others encroaching on their assigned territory, there may be arguments or even fist fights, and the naiks must negotiate new allotments of territory or maintain traditional boundaries. Because hijras can hardly go to the police or courts to settle their disputes—nor would they wish to give up such power to outsiders—disputes are settled within the community.

The hijras today are an example of a highly successful cultural adaptation. Their structured social organization, which imitates both a family and a caste, the use of the guru/chela relationship as a recruitment strategy, their willingness to move into new economic niches, and the effective control over economic rights exercised within the community, provide hijras with both the flexibility and control needed to succeed in today's complex and highly competitive society. In the face of dwindling opportunities for their traditional performances, prostitution, always a lucrative profession, has expanded. Hijras now bless girl infants as well as boys; they have become tax collectors, and have successfully run for political office. In politics, hijras have largely succeeded by emphasizing that their ascetic role as neither man nor woman, with no families to support, which they contrast to the widespread nepotism and corruption engaged in by so many Indian politicians (Reddy 2003).

Hijras have also successfully weathered the attempts of the Indian government to outlaw their emasculation operation, which serves as the definitive symbol of their identity. Indeed, they have become politically organized and have petitioned various state governments to grant them, as members of the "sexually marginalized," rights to jobs, marriage, legal recognition as a third gender and to consider sending a hijra into space as part of India's space program (Reddy 2010:140).

Gender Variation in Other Cultures

The assumption by a man of a woman's character, sex/gender role and identity in a spiritual or religious context, and even as a means of salvation, which has long been part of the Hindu tradition, is found in many other cultural traditions as well (Herdt 1996), particularly in Southeast Asia (Peletz 2009). In many great agricultural civilizations of the ancient world, arising around 10,000 years ago, Mother Goddess cults were prominent. Some of these goddesses were attended by a priesthood that included men who acted and dressed as women, either specifically during religious rituals, or permanently, while other cults involved male priests who castrated themselves while in ecstasy, in a gesture of renunciation and identification with her, very similar to the hijra nirvana ritual. The numerous images of Hermaphroditus (from which the English term hermaphrodite derives) found in Greek mythology and statuary, make it clear that androgyny and sex-change also had special meaning for the ancient Greeks.

By the end of the 4th century, B.C.E., however, cultural diffusion, through the spread of Christianity and later, in the 8th century C.E. through the spread of Islam, led to the dominance of male deities. By the 8th century C.E., mother goddess worship had virtually disappeared (India is one of the few places where it remained culturally central), and with it, of course, the sexually ambiguous priesthoods. Still later, European colonialism began to have its effect in repressing sexual and gender diversity in the New World as well as the old. The British, for example, outlawed the land grants to hijras in India, which had been awarded in various princely states, and repressed the many transgender roles in Southeast Asia (Peletz 2009), while the 19th century American occupation of Hawai'i, led to the decline of the indigenous role of the mahu (Matzner 2001).

In the mid-20th century, the European medical model, which pathologized gender diversity and homosexuality, spread throughout Asia, and had a particularly negative impact in Thailand. The kathoey, a third gender, mentioned in ancient Buddhist scriptures and tolerated by society, as well as homosexuality, came to be viewed as "social problems," and were subject to both attempted "treatment" and repression (Jackson 1999; Costa and Matzner 2007). The contemporary global spread of fundamental Islam has also affected Islamic states such as Malaysia and Indonesia, whose previous casual toleration of indigenous transgender roles and male same-sex relationships, is now replaced by increasing public surveillance; in Indonesia a ban on the transsexual operation is being proposed.

At the same time, in recent decades, there has been a countercurrent to the decline of gender diversity, as the effects of ethnography, international human rights, the internet, and global media have sent information and images all over the world. Transgender beauty contests, long practiced in the Philippines—and based on American images of beauty rooted in the American occupation of the turn of the 20th century—have proliferated throughout Asia and the Pacific (Johnson 1997; Besnier 2011). In Indonesia, the waria, an indigenous transgender role, has become a symbol of nationalism and warias dominate beauty salons which prepare brides for traditional Indonesian weddings (Boellstorff 2005). The diffusion of a global gay identity, which is now associated with many different transgender roles throughout Asia, is spread by the media and by internet-based solidarity, even as it is transformed in local cultures in a variety of ways. Similarly, many international NGOs have set up HIV/AIDS clinics throughout Asia and Africa, which form a nexus of homosexual and transgender relationships, although in fact, AIDS in Asia and Africa is spread more by heterosexual than by same-sex relationships. Global migration, too, has been an important source of cultural diffusion, bringing for example, large numbers of transgendered Filipinos to Israel, where they dominate in the care of the aged (Heymann 2006). These globalizing dimensions of sex/gender diversity, have also affected the United States.

Sex/Gender Diversity and Change in the United States

One of the most important roles of anthropology is to increase our awareness of our own culture by reflecting on the cultures of others; as the famous anthropologist, Claude Levi-Strauss said, ethnography makes an important contribution to an ongoing critique of Western culture. The descriptions of sex/gender diversity in other cultures provokes us to re-examine the nature and assumptions of our own sex/gender system; the cultural basis of its categories; the relations between sex, sexuality, gender, and other aspects of culture; and the ways in which this impacts on individuals with alternative sex/gender identities who engage in diverse sexual practices (Nanda 2000).

Until the late 20th century, the binary Western concept of sex and gender—male and female—as well as condemnation of homosexuality, described in the book of Genesis, left no room for alternative sex/gender identities or varied sexual practices. The emergence of medical technology which enabled sex reassignment surgery both reflected and intensified this dichotomy. For an individual whose gender identity or sexual relationships were in conflict with his or her biological sex, the sex change operation provided one way out of the dilemma. Transsexuals in American culture were defined as "biologically normal persons of one sex convinced that they were members of the *opposite* sex" (Stoller, cited in Kessler and McKenna, 1978:115). The aim of sex reassignment surgery and the psychological and medical treatments (such as hormone therapy) that were required to accompany it, was the transformation of an individual from their natal sex into the sex with which they identified. An important aspect of the treatment required the individual to demonstrate to psychological and medical professionals that the individual was committed to, and was able to, make this transition.

This construction of the transsexual was consistent with the binary American sex/gender system and was supported in the larger culture by permitting various legal changes as part of a revised life story (Bolin 1988). Unlike alternative sex/gender figures in other cultures, however, transsexuals were viewed as a source of cultural anxiety, pathology, and a social problem; at best, as figures of scorn or pity. While the gay liberation movement in the United States helped our society become more humane and egalitarian in its response to sex and gender variations, our culture has not yet been able to incorporate the wide tolerance or spiritual roles for gender difference and ambiguity that traditionally existed in India and in other societies.

Even with emerging cultural and indeed legal supports of the construct of the transsexual as someone who crosses over completely to the "opposite" sex, this concept was not—and is not today—wholly accepted in our society. In a 2002 legal case in which a transsexual claimed the estate of her deceased spouse, the Kansas Supreme Court stated that both science and the courts are divided on whether transsexuals are more appropriately defined in terms of their birth sex status or their post-operative sex/gender status [*In re Marshall G. Gardiner, deceased.* (2002), in Norgren and Nanda 2006]. The Court held that, while "through surgery and hormones, a transsexual can be made to look like a woman . . . the sex assignment surgery does not create the sexual organs of a woman." The Court further held that while the plaintiff (a male to female transsexual) "wants and believes herself to be a woman [and] . . . has made every conceivable effort to make herself a female . . . her female anatomy, however, is still all man-made. The body [the plaintiff] inhabits is a male body in all aspects other than what the physicians have supplied . . . From that the Court has to conclude, that . . . as a matter of law [the plaintiff] is a male."

In spite of American resistance to changing concepts of sex and gender, illustrated by the legal decision cited above, the increasing awareness of the sex/gender systems of other cultures has led to a change in our own society. Within the last three decades America's rigid binary cultural boundaries—nature/culture, male/female, homosexual/heterosexual—have become blurred. Transgenderism is now a recognized cultural category, one that transcends the historical American "incorrigible proposition" that tells us that sex and gender are ascribed and permanent.

Transgenderism today incorporates a variety of subjective experiences, identities, and sexual practices that range widely over a sex/gender continuum, from androgynous to transsexual (Valentine 2007). Increasingly, persons defining themselves as transpeople see transgenderism as a way "out of the constraints imposed by a dichotomous sex/gender system [with the aim] . . . not to mandate anything, but to . . . be able to play with the categories, . . . to challenge the reductionism and essentialism that has accompanied these [binary] categories for so many millennia" (Ducat 2006: 48). In spite of the many differences among individuals experiencing transgender identities, one repeated theme of the transgender movement is that gender and sex categories are improperly imposed by society and its "sexual identity gatekeepers," referring here to the gender identity professionals who accepted and furthered the binary system of American sex/gender roles (Bolin 1996: 447). The transgendered are challenging and stretching the boundaries of the American system of sex/gender binary oppositions, and renouncing the American definition of gender as dependent on a consistency of genitals, body type, identity, role behaviors, sexual orientation, and sexual practice. Contemporary transgender communities include a continuum of people, from those who wish to undergo sex reassignment surgery, to those who wish to live their lives androgynously (Winter 2006). The previous split between transsexuals who viewed surgery as the only authentic expression of a feminine nature, as opposed to "part time" gender crossers who did not wish to have sex reassignment surgery, has to some extent been reconciled by the emergence of a transgender community which attempts to validate a whole range of gender roles and identities. As one transperson expressed it, " . . . you no longer have to fit into a box . . . it is okay to be transgendered. You can now lay anywhere on the spectrum from non-gendered to full transsexual" (Bolin 1996: 475). Transpeople are trying not so much to do away with maleness and femaleness as to denaturalize them, that is, take away their privileged status in relation to all other possible combinations of behaviors, roles, and identities. The point for some transpeople is that gender categories should be something that individuals can construct for themselves, through self-reflection and observation (Cromwell 1997).

The dynamism of the contemporary transgender movement, which includes both transgender activists and mental health professionals, was recently acknowledged in a proposal by the New York City Board of Health to allow people to alter the sex on their birth certificate even if they have not had sex-change surgery (Cave 2006: A1). While this proposal, which emphasized the importance of separating anatomy from gender identity, ultimately failed, New York City has adopted other measures aimed at blurring the lines of gender identification. It has, for example, allowed beds in homeless shelters to be distributed according to appearance, applying equally to post-operative transsexuals, cross-dressers, and persons perceived to be androgynous. A Metropolitan Transit Authority policy also allows people to define their own gender when deciding whether to use men's or women's bathrooms. These new, even radical, policies are just one of the many aspects of the current transgender movement. Other aims of this movement are the redefining of gender diversity as a naturally occurring phenomenon rather than a psychological disorder; dismantling gender stereotypes, and reducing harassment and discrimination against those who do not wish to conform to current sex/gender norms (Brown 2006: A1). As Sam Winter, director of the Transgender Asia website suggests, although treating gender disorders as a mental illness, as in the United States, is useful for Western transsexuals in obtaining medical services, it extracts too high a price in substantially contributing to transphobia. For contemporary transpeople he says, "transgender is one aspect of human diversity. . . . It is a difference, not a disorder. . . . If we can speak to any gender identity disorder at all, it is in the inability of many societies to accept the particular gender identity difference we call transgender" (Winter, accessed 2006).

A core American cultural pattern which places a high value on the "authentic self"—on integrating the inner person with external actions—is central to the current transgender movement, as well as to contemporary gay activism. This core American cultural value is not universal, which makes it easier for sex/gender diversity to exist in other societies. In Thailand, for example, little value is attached to acknowledging or displaying one's private sexual orientation in public. In Thailand, how one acts is more important than how one feels. Leading a "double life" is a generally accepted feature of Thai culture, not necessarily equated with duplicity or deception as in the United States. Thus, "coming out" as a homosexual in Thailand brings shame or "loss of face" both to the individual and to the family without the compensation of expressing one's "true self" so valued in the United States. Similar values also hold in Indonesia (Wieringa 2008). In Malaysia, too, the Islamic emphasis on marriage and family takes precedence over asserting one's individuality and agency, as required in the process of "coming out" (Peletz 2009). Martin Manalansan, in his ethnography of transgendered Philippine migrants in New York, makes a similar point, quoting a "bakla" informant: "The Americans are different, darling. Coming out is their drama. When I studied at [a New England college] the queens had nothing better to talk about than coming out . . . the whites, my God, shedding tears, leaving the families. The stories are always so sad" (2003).

This contrast between cultural values, as they affect homosexuals and transgender people in Thailand, Malaysia and the Philippines, and those in the United States, casts a revealing perspective on the demand for repeal of "Don't Ask, Don't Tell," the shortsighted, politically motivated policy that banned openly gay men and women from the American military. That policy, which burdened the individual with the necessity of hiding his or her "true self" is quite simply incompatible with American culture and is now in the process of being repealed.

Unlike transsexualism, which reinforces the binary American sex/gender system, transgenderism is culturally subversive: it calls into question the rightness of binary sex/gender categories. It also provides a wider range of individual possibilities for those who experience distress by trying to conform to exclusively binary sex/gender categories, including sexual practices. The American transgender movement has been empowered by knowledge about alternative sex/gender systems throughout the world. Some of these sex/gender systems have offered American transpeople a source of meaning, and especially spiritual meaning, that they do not find in the binary, transphobic culture that is still dominant within the United States. As the West becomes more aware of alternatives and variations in gender roles in other cultures, both past and present, it can also perhaps become more accommodating of those individuals who do not fit into their traditionally prescribed—and limited—sex/gender categories.

References

Besnier, N. 2011. *On the edge of the global: Modern anxieties in a Pacific Island nation.* Stanford, CA: Stanford University Press.

Boelstorff, T. 2005. *The gay archipelago: Sexuality and nation in Indonesia.* Princeton, NJ: Princeton University Press.

Bolin, A. 1988. *In search of Eve: Transsexual rites of passage.* South Hadley, MA: Bergin and Garvey.

Bolin A. 1996. "Transcending and transgendering: Male-to-female transsexuals, dichotomy and diversity." In G. Herdt (Ed.), *Third sex third gender: Beyond sexual dimorphism in culture and history* (pp. 447–485). New York: Zone Books.

Brown, P.L. 2006. "Supporting boys or girls when the line isn't clear." *The New York Times,* December 2, p. A1.

Cave, D. 2006. "New York plans to make gender personal choice." *The New York Times,* November 7, p. A1.

Costa, L. and Andrew Matzner, A. 2007. *Male bodies, women's souls: Personal narratives of Thailand's transgendered youth.* Binghamton, NY: Haworth Press.

Cromwell, J. 1977. "Traditions of gender diversity and sexualities: A female-to-male transgendered perspective." In S. Jacobs, W. Thomas, and S. Lang (Eds.). *Two spirit people: Native American gender identity, sexuality, and spirituality.* Urbana, IL: University of Illinois Press.

Ducat, S. 2006. "Slipping into something more comfortable: Towards a liberated continuum of gender." *LiP,* Summer, pp. 46–61.

Herdt, G. 1996. *Third sex third gender: Beyond sexual dimorphism in culture and history.* New York: Zone Books.

Heymann, T. 2006. *Paper Dolls.* (film). Strand Releasing.

Jackson, P. 1999. *Lady boys, tom boys, rentboys: Male and female homosexualities in contemporary Thailand.* Binghamton, NY: Haworth Press.

Johnson, M. 1997. *Beauty and power: Transgendering and cultural transformation in the Southern Philippines.* New York: Berg.

Kessler, S.J., and W. McKenna. 1978. *Gender: An ethnomethodological approach.* New York: Wiley.

Manalansan, M. 2003. *Global divas: Filipino gay men in the diaspora.* Durham, NC: Duke University Press.

Matzner, A. 2001. *'O au no keia: Voices from Hawai'i's Mahu and transgender community.'* Philadelphia: XLibris.

Nanda, S. 1999. *Neither man nor woman: the hijras of India.* 2nd Ed. Belmont, CA: Wadsworth.

Nanda, S. 2000. *Gender diversity: crosscultural variations.* Prospect Heights, IL: Waveland.

Norgren, J. and S. Nanda. 2006. *American cultural pluralism and law.* Westport, CN: Praeger.

O'Flaherty, W.D. 1980. *Women, androgynies, and other mythical beasts.* Chicago: University of Chicago Press.

Peletz, M. 2009. *Gender pluralism: southeast asia since early modern times.* NY: Routledge.

Reddy, G. 2003. "Men" who would be kings: celibacy, emasculation and reproduction of hijras in contemporary Indian politics. *Social Research,* 70, no. 1:163–198.

Reddy, G. 2005. *With respect to sex: negotiating hijra identity in South India.* Chicago: University of Chicago Press.

Reddy, G. 2010. "Crossing 'Lines' of difference: Transnational Movements and Sexual Subjectivities In Hyderabad, India." In Diane P. Mines and Sarah Lamb (Eds.), *Everyday life in south Asia,* 2nd Ed. Bloomington, IN: University of Indiana Press.

Valentine, D. 2007. *Imagining transgender: An ethnography of a category.* Durham, NC: Duke University Press.

Wieringa, S. 2008. "If there is no feeling . . . The Dilemma between Silence and Coming Out in a Working Class Butch/Femme Community in Jakarta." In Mark B. Padilla, Jennifer S. Hirsch, Miguel Munoz-Laboy, Robert E. Sember, and Richard G. Parker (Eds.), *Love and globalization: Transformations of intimacy in the contemporary world.* Nashville, TN: University of Vanderbilt Press, pp. 70–90.

Winter, S. 2006. "Transphobia: A price worth paying for gender identity disorder? Retrieved from http://web.hku.hk/~sjwinter/TransgenderASIA/index.htm.

Critical Thinking

1. Be aware of the various social roles played by the hijra and how individuals become part of a hijra community.

2. What is the significance of the operation known as "nirvana"?

3. Be familiar with the hijra community in terms of its religious and caste qualities.

4. Be familiar with the hijra household in terms of its structure and rules.

5. What kinds of tasks are carried out by the "naiks" and the "jamaat"?

6. In what respects are the hijras an example of a highly successful cultural adaptation?

7. What evidence is there of gender variation throughout history? How did cultural diffusion and colonialism suppress it? How and why have there been countercurrents to such suppression?

8. What is meant by the American notion of a "binary sex and gender"? How has this been reinforced by medical technology?

9. What kinds of changes did the "transgender movement" bring about?

10. How and why is "coming out" treated differently in the United States and Thailand?

11. Why is "transgenderism" more subversive than "transsexualism"?

Create Central

www.mhhe.com/createcentral

Internet References

Indian Journal of Gender Studies
http://ijg.sagepub.com

Intersections: Gender, History and Culture in the Asian Context
http://intersections.anu.edu.au

Gay, Lesbian, Bisexual, Transgender and Queer Studies, Canadian Online Journal for Queer Studies in Education
http://jqstudies.library.utoronto.ca/index.php/jqstudies

International Journal of Transgenderism
www.haworthpress.com/store/product.asp?sid=PX1MHCJ72GN18MGKKNXMG90SQVEV15K4&sku=J485&AuthType=4

SERENA NANDA is Professor Emeritus, Anthropology, at John Jay College, City University of New York. Many thanks to Joan Gregg, Mary Winslow, Cory Harris, and Barry Kass for their encouragement and suggestions.

Article   Prepared by: Elvio Angeloni

Afghan Boys Are Prized, So Girls Live the Part

JENNY NORDBERT

Learning Outcomes

After reading this article, you will be able to:

- Discuss the Afghan motivations for dressing some girls up as boys before puberty sets in.

- Explain why some Afghan girls find dressing as a boy can be both disorienting and liberating.

Six-year-old Mehran Rafaat is like many girls her age. She likes to be the center of attention. She is often frustrated when things do not go her way. Like her three older sisters, she is eager to discover the world outside the family's apartment in their middle-class neighborhood of Kabul.

But when their mother, Azita Rafaat, a member of Parliament, dresses the children for school in the morning, there is one important difference. Mehran's sisters put on black dresses and head scarves, tied tightly over their ponytails. For Mehran, it's green pants, a white shirt and a necktie, then a pat from her mother over her spiky, short black hair. After that, her daughter is out the door—as an Afghan boy.

There are no statistics about how many Afghan girls masquerade as boys. But when asked, Afghans of several generations can often tell a story of a female relative, friend, neighbor or co-worker who grew up disguised as a boy. To those who know, these children are often referred to as neither "daughter" nor "son" in conversation, but as "bacha posh," which literally means "dressed up as a boy" in Dari.

Through dozens of interviews conducted over several months, where many people wanted to remain anonymous or to use only first names for fear of exposing their families, it was possible to trace a practice that has remained mostly obscured to outsiders. Yet it cuts across class, education, ethnicity and geography, and has endured even through Afghanistan's many wars and governments.

Afghan families have many reasons for pretending their girls are boys, including economic need, social pressure to have sons, and in some cases, a superstition that doing so can lead to the birth of a real boy. Lacking a son, the parents decide to make one up, usually by cutting the hair of a daughter and dressing her in typical Afghan men's clothing. There are no specific legal or religious proscriptions against the practice. In most cases, a return to womanhood takes place when the child enters puberty. The parents almost always make that decision.

In a land where sons are more highly valued, since in the tribal culture usually only they can inherit the father's wealth and pass down a name, families without boys are the objects of pity and contempt. Even a made-up son increases the family's standing, at least for a few years. A bacha posh can also more easily receive an education, work outside the home, even escort her sisters in public, allowing freedoms that are unheard of for girls in a society that strictly segregates men and women.

But for some, the change can be disorienting as well as liberating, stranding the women in a limbo between the sexes. Shukria Siddiqui, raised as a boy but then abruptly plunged into an arranged marriage, struggled to adapt, tripping over the confining burqa and straining to talk to other women.

The practice may stretch back centuries. Nancy Dupree, an 83-year-old American who has spent most of her life as a historian working in Afghanistan, said she had not heard of the phenomenon, but recalled a photograph from the early 1900s belonging to the private collection of a member of the Afghan royal family.

It featured women dressed in men's clothing standing guard at King Habibullah's harem. The reason: the harem's women could not be protected by men, who might pose a threat to the women, but they could not be watched over by women either.

"Segregation calls for creativity," Mrs. Dupree said. "These people have the most amazing coping ability."

It is a commonly held belief among less educated Afghans that the mother can determine the sex of her unborn child, so she is blamed if she gives birth to a daughter. Several Afghan doctors and health care workers from around the country said that they had witnessed the despair of women when they gave birth to daughters, and that the pressure to produce a son fueled the practice.

"Yes, this is not normal for you," Mrs. Rafaat said in sometimes imperfect English, during one of many interviews over several weeks. "And I know it's very hard for you to believe why one mother is doing these things to their youngest daughter. But I want to say for you, that some things are happening in Afghanistan that are really not imaginable for you as a Western people."

Pressure to Have a Boy

From that fateful day she first became a mother—Feb. 7, 1999—Mrs. Rafaat knew she had failed, she said, but she was too exhausted to speak, shivering on the cold floor of the family's small house in Badghis Province.

She had just given birth—twice—to Mehran's older sisters, Benafsha and Beheshta. The first twin had been born after almost 72 hours of labor, one month prematurely. The girl weighed only 2.6 pounds and was not breathing at first. Her sister arrived 10 minutes later. She, too, was unconscious.

When her mother-in-law began to cry, Mrs. Rafaat knew it was not from fear whether her infant granddaughters would survive. The old woman was disappointed. "Why," she cried, according to Mrs. Rafaat, "are we getting more girls in the family?"

Mrs. Rafaat had grown up in Kabul, where she was a top student, speaking six languages and nurturing high-flying dreams of becoming a doctor. But once her father forced her to become the second wife of her first cousin, she had to submit to being an illiterate farmer's wife, in a rural house without running water and electricity, where the widowed mother-in-law ruled, and where she was expected to help care for the cows, sheep and chickens. She did not do well.

Conflicts with her mother-in-law began immediately, as the new Mrs. Rafaat insisted on better hygiene and more contact with the men in the house. She also asked her mother-in-law to stop beating her husband's first wife with her walking stick. When Mrs. Rafaat finally snapped the stick in protest, the older woman demanded that her son, Ezatullah, control his new wife.

He did so with a wooden stick or a metal wire. "On the body, on the face," she recalled. "I tried to stop him. I asked him to stop. Sometimes I didn't."

Soon, she was pregnant. The family treated her slightly better as she grew bigger. "They were hoping for a son this time," she explained. Ezatullah Rafaat's first wife had given birth to two daughters, one of whom had died as an infant, and she could no longer conceive. Azita Rafaat delivered two daughters, double the disappointment.

Mrs. Rafaat faced constant pressure to try again, and she did, through two more pregnancies, when she had two more daughters—Mehrangis, now 9, and finally Mehran, the 6-year-old.

Asked if she ever considered leaving her husband, she reacted with complete surprise.

"I thought of dying," she said. "But I never thought of divorce. If I had separated from my husband, I would have lost my children, and they would have had no rights. I am not one to quit."

Today, she is in a position of power, at least on paper. She is one of 68 women in Afghanistan's 249-member Parliament, representing Badghis Province. Her husband is unemployed and spends most of his time at home. "He is my house husband," she joked.

By persuading him to move away from her mother-in-law and by offering to contribute to the family income, she laid the groundwork for her political life. Three years into their marriage, after the fall of the Taliban in 2002, she began volunteering as a health worker for various nongovernmental organizations. Today she makes $2,000 a month as a member of Parliament.

As a politician, she works to improve women's rights and the rule of law. She ran for re-election on Sept. 18, and, based on a preliminary vote count, is optimistic about securing another term. But she could run only with her husband's explicit permission, and the second time around, he was not easily persuaded.

He wanted to try again for a son. It would be difficult to combine pregnancy and another child with her work, she said—and she knew she might have another girl in any case.

But the pressure to have a son extended beyond her husband. It was the only subject her constituents could talk about when they came to the house, she said.

"When you don't have a son in Afghanistan," she explained, "it's like a big missing in your life. Like you lost the most important point of your life. Everybody feels sad for you."

As a politician, she was also expected to be a good wife and a mother; instead she looked like a failed woman to her constituents. The gossip spread back to her province, and her husband was also questioned and embarrassed, she said.

In an effort to preserve her job and placate her husband, as well as fending off the threat of his getting a third wife, she proposed to her husband that they make their youngest daughter look like a son.

"People came into our home feeling pity for us that we don't have a son," she recalled reasoning. "And the girls—we can't send them outside. And if we changed Mehran to a boy we would get more space and freedom in society for her. And we can send her outside for shopping and to help the father."

No Hesitation

Together, they spoke to their youngest daughter, she said. They made it an alluring proposition: "Do you want to look like a boy and dress like a boy, and do more fun things like boys do, like bicycling, soccer and cricket? And would you like to be like your father?" Mehran did not hesitate to say yes.

That afternoon, her father took her to the barbershop, where her hair was cut short. They continued to the bazaar, where she got new clothing. Her first outfit was "something like a cowboy dress," Mrs. Rafaat said, meaning a pair of blue jeans and a red denim shirt with "superstar" printed on the back.

She even got a new name—originally called Manoush, her name was tweaked to the more boyish-sounding Mehran.

Mehran's return to school—in a pair of pants and without her pigtails—went by without much reaction by her fellow students. She still napped in the afternoons with the girls, and changed into her sleepwear in a separate room from the boys. Some of her classmates still called her Manoush, while others called her Mehran. But she would always introduce herself as a boy to newcomers.

Khatera Momand, the headmistress, with less than a year in her job, said she had always presumed Mehran was a boy, until she helped change her into sleeping clothes one afternoon. "It was quite a surprise for me," she said.

But once Mrs. Rafaat called the school and explained that the family had only daughters, Miss Momand understood perfectly. She used to have a girlfriend at the teacher's academy who dressed as a boy.

Today, the family's relatives and colleagues all know Mehran's real gender, but the appearance of a son before guests and acquaintances is just enough to keep the family functioning, Mrs. Rafaat said. At least for now.

Mr. Rafaat said he felt closer to Mehran than to his other children, and thought of her as a son. "I am very happy," he said. "When people now ask me, I say yes and they see that I have a son. So people are quiet, and I am quiet."

Economic Necessity

Mehran's case is not altogether rare.

Ten-year old Miina goes to school for two hours each morning, in a dress and a head scarf, but returns about 9 A.M. to her home in one of Kabul's poorest neighborhoods to change into boys' clothing. She then goes to work as Abdul Mateen, a shop assistant in a small grocery store nearby.

Every day, she brings home the equivalent of about $1.30 to help support her Pashtun family of eight sisters, as well as their 40-year-old mother, Nasima.

Miina's father, an unemployed mason, is often away. When he does get temporary work, Nasima said, he spends most of his pay on drugs.

Miina's change is a practical necessity, her mother said, a way for the entire family to survive. The idea came from the shopkeeper, a friend of the family, Nasima said: "He advised us to do it, and said she can bring bread for your home."

She could never work in the store as a girl, just as her mother could not. Neither her husband nor the neighbors would look kindly on it. "It would be impossible," Nasima said. "It's our tradition that girls don't work like this."

Miina is very shy, but she admitted to a yearning to look like a girl. She still likes to borrow her sister's clothing when she is home. She is also nervous that she will be found out if one of her classmates recognizes her at the store. "Every day she complains," said her mother. " 'I'm not comfortable around the boys in the store,' she says. 'I am a girl.' "

Her mother has tried to comfort her by explaining that it will be only for a few years. After all, there are others to take her place. "After Miina gets too old, the second younger sister will be a boy," her mother said, "and then the third."

Refusing to Go Back

For most such girls, boyhood has an inevitable end. After being raised as a boy, with whatever privileges or burdens it may entail, they switch back once they become teenagers. When their bodies begin to change and they approach marrying age, parents consider it too risky for them to be around boys anymore.

When Zahra, 15, opens the door to the family's second-floor apartment in an upscale neighborhood of Kabul, she is dressed in a black suit with boxy shoulders and wide-legged pants. Her face has soft features, but she does not smile, or look down, as most Afghan girls do.

She said she had been dressing and acting like a boy for as long as she could remember. If it were up to her, she would never go back. "Nothing in me feels like a girl," she said with a shrug.

Her mother, Laila, said she had tried to suggest a change toward a more feminine look several times, but Zahra has refused. "For always, I want to be a boy and a boy and a boy," she said with emphasis.

Zahra attends a girls' school in the mornings, wearing her suit and a head scarf. As soon as she is out on the steps after class, she tucks her scarf into her backpack, and continues her day as a young man. She plays football and cricket, and rides a bike. She used to practice tae kwon do, in a group of boys where only the teacher knew she was not one of them.

Most of the neighbors know of her change, but otherwise, she is taken for a young man wherever she goes, her mother said. Her father, a pilot in the Afghan military, was supportive. "It's a privilege for me, that she is in boys' clothing," he said. "It's a help for me, with the shopping. And she can go in and out of the house without a problem."

Both parents insisted it was Zahra's own choice to look like a boy. "I liked it, since we didn't have a boy," her mother said, but added, "Now, we don't really know."

Zahra, who plans on becoming a journalist, and possibly a politician after that, offered her own reasons for not wanting to be an Afghan woman. They are looked down upon and harassed, she said.

"People use bad words for girls," she said. "They scream at them on the streets. When I see that, I don't want to be a girl. When I am a boy, they don't speak to me like that."

Zahra said she had never run into any trouble when posing as a young man, although she was occasionally challenged about her gender. "I've been in fights with boys," she said. "If they tell me two bad words, I will tell them three. If they slap me once, I will slap them twice."

Time to "Change Back"

For Shukria Siddiqui, the masquerade went too far, for too long.

Today, she is 36, a married mother of three, and works as an anesthesiology nurse at a Kabul hospital. Short and heavily built, wearing medical scrubs, she took a break from attending to a patient who had just had surgery on a broken leg.

She remembered the day her aunt brought her a floor-length skirt and told her the time had come to "change back." The reason soon became clear: she was getting married. Her parents had picked out a husband whom she had never met.

At that time, Shukur, as she called herself, was a 20-year old man, to herself and most people around her. She walked around with a knife in her back pocket. She wore jeans and a leather jacket.

She was speechless—she had never thought of getting married.

Mrs. Siddiqui had grown up as a boy companion to her older brother, in a family of seven girls and one boy. "I wanted to be like him and to be his friend," she said. "I wanted to look like him. We slept in the same bed. We prayed together. We had the same habits."

Her parents did not object, since their other children were girls, and it seemed like a good idea for the oldest son to have a

brother. But Mrs. Siddiqui remained in her male disguise well beyond puberty, which came late.

She said she was already 16 when her body began to change. "But I really had nothing then either," she said, with a gesture toward her flat chest.

Like many other Afghan girls, she was surprised the first time she menstruated, and worried she might be ill. Her mother offered no explanation, since such topics were deemed inappropriate to discuss. Mrs. Siddiqui said she never had romantic fantasies about boys—or of girls, either.

Her appearance as a man approaching adulthood was not questioned, she said. But it frequently got others into trouble, like the time she escorted a girlfriend home who had fallen ill. Later, she learned that the friend had been beaten by her parents after word spread through the neighborhood that their daughter was seen holding hands with a boy.

"My Best Time"

Having grown up in Kabul in a middle-class family, her parents allowed her to be educated through college, where she attended nursing school. She took on her future and professional life with certainty and confidence, presuming she would never be constricted by any of the rules that applied to women in Afghanistan.

Her family, however, had made their decision: she was to marry the owner of a small construction company. She never considered going against them, or running away. "It was my family's desire, and we obey our families," she said. "It's our culture."

A forced marriage is difficult for anyone, but Mrs. Siddiqui was particularly ill equipped. She had never cooked a meal in her life, and she kept tripping over the burqa she was soon required to wear.

She had no idea how to act in the world of women. "I had to learn how to sit with women, how to talk, how to behave," she said. For years, she was unable to socialize with other women and uncomfortable even greeting them.

"When you change back, it's like you are born again, and you have to learn everything from the beginning," she explained. "You get a whole new life. Again."

Mrs. Siddiqui said she was lucky her husband turned out to be a good one. She had asked his permission to be interviewed and he agreed. He was understanding of her past, she said. He tolerated her cooking. Sometimes, he even encouraged her to wear trousers at home, she said. He knows it cheers her up.

In a brief period of marital trouble, he once attempted to beat her, but after she hit him back, it never happened again. She wants to look like a woman now, she said, and for her children to have a mother.

Still, not a day goes by when she does not think back to "my best time," as she called it. Asked if she wished she had been born a man, she silently nods.

But she also wishes her upbringing had been different. "For me, it would have been better to grow up as a girl," she said, "since I had to become a woman in the end."

Like Mother, Like a Son

It is a typically busy day in the Rafaat household. Azita Rafaat is in the bathroom, struggling to put her head scarf in place, preparing for a photographer who has arrived at the house to take her new campaign photos.

The children move restlessly between Tom and Jerry cartoons on the television and a computer game on their mother's laptop. Benafsha, 11, and Mehrangis, 9, wear identical pink tights and a ruffled skirt. They go first on the computer. Mehran, the 6-year-old, waits her turn, pointing and shooting a toy gun at each of the guests.

She wears a bandage over her right earlobe, where she tried to pierce herself with one of her mother's earrings a day earlier, wanting to look like her favorite Bollywood action hero: Salman Khan, a man who wears one gold earring.

Then Mehran decided she had waited long enough to play on the computer, stomping her feet and waving her arms, and finally slapping Benafsha in the face.

"He is very naughty," Mrs. Rafaat said in English with a sigh, of Mehran, mixing up the gender-specific pronoun, which does not exist in Dari. "My daughter adopted all the boys' traits very soon. You've seen her—the attitude, the talking—she has nothing of a girl in her."

The Rafaats have not yet made a decision when Mehran will be switched back to a girl, but Mrs. Rafaat said she hoped it need not happen for another five or six years.

"I will need to slowly, slowly start to tell her about what she is and that she needs to be careful as she grows up," she said. "I think about this every day—what's happening to Mehran."

Challenged about how it might affect her daughter, she abruptly revealed something from her own past: "Should I share something for you, honestly? For some years I also been a boy."

As the first child of her family, Mrs. Rafaat assisted her father in his small food shop, beginning when she was 10, for four years. She was tall and athletic and saw only potential when her parents presented the idea—she would be able to move around more freely.

She went to a girls' school in the mornings, but worked at the store on afternoons and evenings, running errands in pants and a baseball hat, she said.

Returning to wearing dresses and being confined was not so much difficult as irritating, and a little disappointing, she said. But over all, she is certain that the experience contributed to the resolve that brought her to Parliament.

"I think it made me more energetic," she said. "It made me more strong." She also believed her time as a boy made it easier for her to relate to and communicate with men.

Mrs. Rafaat said she hoped the effects on Mehran's psyche and personality would be an advantage, rather than a limitation.

She noted that speaking out may draw criticism from others, but argued that it was important to reveal a practice most women in her country wished did not have to exist. "This is the reality of Afghanistan," she said.

As a woman and as a politician, she said it worried her that despite great efforts and investments from the outside world to help Afghan women, she has seen very little change, and an unwillingness to focus on what matters.

"They think it's all about the burqa," she said. "I'm ready to wear two burqas if my government can provide security and a rule of law. That's O.K. with me. If that's the only freedom I have to give up, I'm ready."

Critical Thinking

1. Why do some Afghan parents decide to raise their girls as boys?
2. What are some of the social pressures in Afghanistan to have sons rather than daughters?
3. What kind of internal conflicts do Afghan girls raised as boys experience when they reach puberty?

Internet References

Gender and Society
http://gas.sagepub.com/
International Journal of Gender & Women's Studies
http://ijgws.com/
Journal of Gender Studies
http://www.psypress.com/journals/details/0958-9236/

Article Prepared by: Elvio Angeloni, *Pasadena City College*

Rising Number of Dowry Deaths in India

Amanda Hitchcock

Learning Outcomes

After reading this article, you will be able to:

- Explain why there is a rising number of dowry deaths in India.
- Discuss the traditional function of the dowry and how it has been recently transformed.

May 27: Young Housewife Burnt Alive for Dowry

Lucknow: For nineteen-year-old Rinki the dream of a happily married life was never to be. Barely a month after her marriage, she was allegedly tortured and then set ablaze by her in-laws for dowry in Indiranagar in the small hours of Saturday. Daughter of late Gyan Chand, a fish contractor who expired a year ago, Rinki was married to Anil on April 19. . . . However, soon after the marriage, Balakram [Anil's father] demanded a colour television instead of a black and white one and a motorcycle as well. When Rinki's mother failed to meet their demands, the teenage housewife was subjected to severe physical torture, allegedly by her husband and mother-in-law. . . . On Saturday morning she [her mother] was informed that Rinki was charred to death when a kerosene lamp accidentally fell on her and her clothes caught fire. However, prima-facie it appeared that the victim was first attacked as her teeth were found broken. Injuries were also apparent on her wrist and chest.

June 7: Woman Ends Life Due to Dowry Harassment

Haveri: Dowry harassment claimed yet another life here recently. Jyoti, daughter of Chandrashekhar Byadagi, married to Ajjappa Siddappa Kaginelle in Guttal village (Haveri taluk) had taken her life after being allegedly harassed by her husband Ajjappa, mother-in-law Kotravva, sister-in-law Nagavva and father-in-law Siddappa for more dowry, the police said. Police said that the harassment compelled her to consume poison. . . . The Guttal police have arrested her husband and father-in-law.

June 7: Body Found Floating

Haveri: The police said that a woman's body was found floating in a well at Tilawalli (Hanagal taluk) near here. . . . The deceased has been identified as Akhilabanu Yadawad (26). The police said that Akhilabanu was married to Abdul Razaksab Yadawad five years ago. In spite of dowry being given, her husband and his family tortured her to bring some more dowry. Her father, Abdulrope Pyati in his complaint, alleged that she was killed by them. Her husband and his two brothers have been arrested, the police added.

These three chilling reports from *The Times of India* are typical of the many accounts of dowry-related deaths that take place in the country every year. One cannot help but be struck by the offhand way in which a young woman's life and death is summed up, matter of factly, without any undue cause for alarm or probing of the causes. It is much as one would report a traffic accident or the death of a cancer patient—tragic certainly, but such things are to be expected.

The character of the articles points to the fact that the harassment, beating and in some cases murder of women over dowry is both common and commonly ignored or even tacitly condoned in official circles—by the police, the courts, politicians and media. These crimes are not isolated to particular groups, social strata, geographical regions or even religions. Moreover, they appear to be on the rise.

According to an article in *Time* magazine, deaths in India related to dowry demands have increase 15-fold since the mid-1980s from 400 a year to around 5,800 a year by the middle of the 1990s. Some commentators claim that the rising number simply indicates that more cases are being reported as a result of increased activity of women's organisations. Others, however, insist that the incidence of dowry-related deaths has increased.

An accurate picture is difficult to obtain, as statistics are varied and contradictory. In 1995, the National Crime Bureau of the Government of India reported about 6,000 dowry deaths every year. A more recent police report stated that dowry deaths had risen by 170 percent in the decade to 1997. All of these official figures are considered to be gross understatements of the real situation. Unofficial estimates cited in a 1999 article by Himendra Thakur "Are our sisters and daughters for sale?" put the number of deaths at 25,000 women a year, with many more left maimed and scarred as a result of attempts on their lives.

Some of the reasons for the under-reporting are obvious. As in other countries, women are reluctant to report threats and abuse to the police for fear of retaliation against themselves and their families. But in India there is an added disincentive. Any attempt to seek police involvement in disputes over dowry transactions may result in members of the woman's own family being subject to criminal proceedings and potentially imprisoned. Moreover, police action is unlikely to stop the demands for dowry payments.

The anti-dowry laws in India were enacted in 1961 but both parties to the dowry—the families of the husband and wife—are criminalised. The laws themselves have done nothing to halt dowry transactions and the violence that is often associated with them. Police and the courts are notorious for turning a blind eye to cases of violence against women and dowry associated deaths. It was not until 1983 that domestic violence became punishable by law.

Many of the victims are burnt to death—they are doused in kerosene and set light to. Routinely the in-laws claim that what happened was simply an accident. The kerosene stoves used in many poorer households are dangerous. When evidence of foul play is too obvious to ignore, the story changes to suicide—the wife, it is said, could not adjust to new family life and subsequently killed herself.

Research done in the late 1990s by Vimochana, a women's group in the southern city of Bangalore, revealed that many deaths are quickly written off by police. The police record of interview with the dying woman—often taken with her husband and relatives present—is often the sole consideration in determining whether an investigation should proceed or not. As Vimochana was able to demonstrate, what a victim will say in a state of shock and under threat from her husband's relatives will often change markedly in later interviews.

Of the 1,133 cases of "unnatural deaths" of women in Bangalore in 1997, only 157 were treated as murder while 546 were categorised as "suicides" and 430 as "accidents". But as Vimochana activist V. Gowramma explained: "We found that of 550 cases reported between January and September 1997, 71 percent were closed as 'kitchen/cooking accidents' and 'stove-bursts' after investigations under section 174 of the Code of Criminal Procedures." The fact that a large proportion of the victims were daughters-in-law was either ignored or treated as a coincidence by police.

Figures cited in *Frontline* indicate what can be expected in court, even in cases where murder charges are laid. In August 1998, there were 1,600 cases pending in the only special court in Bangalore dealing with allegations of violence against women. In the same year three new courts were set up to deal with the large backlog but cases were still expected to take six to seven years to complete. Prosecution rates are low. *Frontline* reported the results of one court: "Of the 730 cases pending in his court at the end of 1998, 58 resulted in acquittals and only 11 in convictions. At the end of June 1999, out of 381 cases pending, 51 resulted in acquittals and only eight in convictions."

Marriage as a Financial Transaction

Young married women are particularly vulnerable. By custom they go to live in the house of their husband's family following the wedding. The marriage is frequently arranged, often in response to advertisements in newspapers. Issues of status, caste and religion may come into the decision, but money is nevertheless central to the transactions between the families of the bride and groom.

The wife is often seen as a servant, or if she works, a source of income, but has no special relationship with the members of her new household and therefore no base of support. Some 40 percent of women are married before the legal age of 18. Illiteracy among women is high, in some rural areas up to 63 percent. As a result they are isolated and often in no position to assert themselves.

Demands for dowry can go on for years. Religious ceremonies and the birth of children often become the occasions for further requests for money or goods. The inability of the bride's family to comply with these demands often leads to the daughter-in-law being treated as a pariah and subject to abuse. In the worst cases, wives are simply killed to make way for a new financial transaction—that is, another marriage.

A recent survey of 10,000 Indian women conducted by India's Health Ministry found that more than half of those interviewed considered violence to be a normal part of married life—the most common cause being the failure to perform domestic duties up to the expectations of their husband's family.

The underlying causes for violence connected to dowry are undoubtedly complex. While the dowry has roots in traditional Indian society, the reasons for prevalence of dowry-associated deaths have comparatively recent origins.

Traditionally a dowry entitled a woman to be a full member of the husband's family and allowed her to enter the marital home with her own wealth. It was seen as a substitute for inheritance, offering some security to the wife. But under the pressures of cash economy introduced under British colonial rule, the dowry like many of the structures of pre-capitalist India was profoundly transformed.

Historian Veena Oldenburg in an essay entitled "Dowry Murders in India: A Preliminary Examination of the Historical Evidence" commented that the old customs of dowry had been perverted "from a strongly spun safety net twist into a deadly noose". Under the burden of heavy land taxes, peasant families were inevitably compelled to find cash where they could or lose their land. As a result the dowry increasingly came to be seen as a vital source of income for the husband's family.

Oldenburg explains: "The will to obtain large dowries from the family of daughters-in-law, to demand more in cash, gold and other liquid assets, becomes vivid after leafing through pages of official reports that dutifully record the effects of indebtedness, foreclosures, barren plots and cattle dying for lack of fodder. The voluntary aspects of dowry, its meaning as a mark of love for the daughter, gradually evaporates. Dowry becomes dreaded payments on demand that accompany and follow the marriage of a daughter."

What Oldenburg explains about the impact of money relations on dowry is underscored by the fact that dowry did not wither away in India in the 20th century but took on new forms. Dowry and dowry-related violence is not confined to rural areas or to the poor, or even just to adherents of the Hindu religion. Under the impact of capitalism, the old custom has been transformed into a vital source of income for families desperate to meet pressing social needs.

A number of studies have shown that the lower ranks of the middle class are particularly prone. According to the Institute of Development and Communication, "The quantum of dowry exchange may still be greater among the middle classes, but 85 percent of dowry death and 80 percent of dowry harassment occurs in the middle and lower stratas." Statistics produced by Vimochana in Bangalore show that 90 percent of the cases of dowry violence involve women from poorer families, who are unable to meet dowry demands.

There is a definite market in India for brides and grooms. Newspapers are filled with pages of women seeking husbands and men advertising their eligibility and social prowess, usually using their caste as a bargaining chip. A "good" marriage is often seen by the wife's family as a means to advance up the social ladder. But the catch is that there is a price to be paid in the form of a dowry. If for any reason that dowry arrangements cannot be met then it is the young woman who suffers.

One critic, Annuppa Caleekal, commented on the rising levels of dowry, particularly during the last decade. "The price of the Indian groom astronomically increased and was based on his qualifications, profession and income. Doctors, charted accountants and engineers even prior to graduation develop the divine right to expect a 'fat' dowry as they become the most sought after cream of the graduating and educated dowry league."

The other side of the dowry equation is that daughters are inevitably regarded as an unwelcome burden, compounding the already oppressed position of women in Indian society. There is a high incidence of gender-based abortions—almost two million female babies a year. One article noted the particularly crass billboard advertisements in Bombay encouraging pregnant women to spend 500 rupees on a gender test to "save" a potential 50,000 rupees on dowry in the future. According to the UN Population Fund report for the year 2000, female infanticide has also increased dramatically over the past decade and infant mortality rates are 40 percent higher for girl babies than boys.

Critics of the dowry system point to the fact that the situation has worsened in the 1990s. As the Indian economy has been opened up for international investment, the gulf between rich and poor widened and so did the economic uncertainty facing the majority of people including the relatively well-off. It was a recipe for sharp tensions that have led to the worsening of a number of social problems.

One commentator Zenia Wadhwani noted: "At a time when India is enjoying unprecedented economic advances and boasts the world's fastest growing middle class, the country is also experiencing a dramatic escalation in reported dowry deaths and bride burnings. Hindu tradition has been transformed as a means to escaping poverty, augmenting one's wealth or acquiring the modern conveniences that are now advertised daily on television."

Domestic violence against women is certainly not isolated to India. The official rate of domestic violence is significantly lower than in the US, for example, where, according to UN statistics, a woman is battered somewhere in the country on average once every 15 seconds. In all countries this violence is bound up with a mixture of cultural backwardness that relegates women to an inferior status combined with the tensions produced by the pressures of growing economic uncertainty and want.

In India, however, where capitalism has fashioned out of the traditions of dowry a particularly naked nexus between marriage and money, and where the stresses of everyday life are being heightened by widening social polarisation, the violence takes correspondingly brutal and grotesque forms.

Critical Thinking

1. What is implied by the character of the three articles cited, according to the author?
2. Why are the number of dowry deaths in India under-reported?
3. What are the typical explanations for why a woman might be burned to death?
4. Why are so many such deaths quickly written off by the police?
5. Why are young married women in such a vulnerable situation?
6. Why does the dowry system lead to their abuse?
7. How did the dowry function traditionally? How and why has it been transformed? In what segment of society are women most vulnerable?
8. What have been the consequences with respect to gender-based abortion and female infant mortality rates?

Create Central

www.mhhe.com/createcentral

Internet References

Women Watch
www.un.org/womenwatch/about
Population Council
www.popcouncil.org
Violence Against Women
http://vaw.sagepub.com

Article   Prepared by: Elvio Angeloni

Headscarves and Hymens: Why the Middle East Needs a Sexual Revolution

MONA ELTAHAWY, NAUREEN CHOWDHURY FINK, AND JOANNE J. MYERS

Learning Outcomes

After reading this article, you will be able to:

- Discuss the "trifecta" of women's oppression in the Middle East and the need for a "double revolution."

- Explain why the author is fighting both military rule and political Islam.

- Describe the way in which some Middle Eastern women have internalized misogyny.

- Discuss the "A'isha/Khadijah complex" and why there is not more emphasis upon Khadijah among Islamic clerics.

- Understand the actual history of feminism in the Middle East.

- Explain the importance of fighting misogyny in one's own country rather than invading other ones.

Introduction

JOANNE MYERS: Good afternoon. I'm Joanne Myers, and on behalf of the Carnegie Council I would like to welcome you all to this Public Affairs program.

Our guest is Mona Eltahawy, author of *Headscarves and Hymens: Why the Middle East Needs a Sexual Revolution*. This book expands upon her wildly popular and controversial 2012 *Foreign Policy* essay on Middle Eastern gender relations, in which she asked: "Why do they hate us?" Now, please note, if you think "they" and "us" refer to Muslims and Americans, you'd be wrong. "They" are the Arab men and the "us" she refers to are Arab women. From the response this article

received, there is no denying that misogyny in the Arab world is an explosive issue, and continues to be so.

In *Headscarves and Hymens,* Mona expands on this theme as she addresses some very difficult issues in highlighting the egregious record of women's rights in the Middle East. For Mona, the issue is a highly personal one—but you will hear more about that shortly.

But suffice it to say that in recent years we have increasingly been made aware of how women in the Arab world face unspeakable sexism, from the limitations on their movements, to child marriage, and genital mutilation. They are also used as political pawns. What rarely happens is an airing of their opinions, especially on any mainstream, widespread scale. Mona is succeeding in bringing their views to our attention.

Interviewing Mona will be Naureen Chowdhury Fink, head of research and analysis at the Global Center on Cooperative Security. She is an expert on violent extremism, including how it relates to women. . . .

Discussion

NAUREEN CHOWDHURY FINK: Thank you all of you for joining us here today, and of course thank you, Mona, for being here and for this fantastic book. It has been a difficult book, but a really, really fascinating read.

I'm going to jump right into one of the key questions that came to my mind as you were describing how women fought alongside men for the revolutions and how the Arab Spring was as much a citizen uprising that included both men and women.

But you ask the really potent question then: Whose revolution and what did it do for women? After all of that fighting together, women ended up scarred, beaten, sexually assaulted, and facing a number of issues on the street that you've talked about.

So I come back to that question: Whose revolution was it and what did women get out of the Arab Spring? Are they better off now?

MONA ELTAHAWY: Undoubtedly, the revolutions that began with Tunisia in 2010 were not revolutions about gender or women's equality or women's liberation. They were revolutions that were driven by the insistence that people wanted to be free and wanted to lead dignified lives. You could see that from the chants that you heard on the streets. People were chanting, "Bread, freedom, social justice, and human dignity." You could hear these chants across the various countries where the uprisings and revolutions took place.

But what drew people on the street was a recognition that the state oppressed everybody, men and women, and you saw men and women side by side.

But the points that I'm trying to raise in my book are: What happened when women went home, and what did they realize about the kind of oppression that they as women had to face? That's where I draw what I call the "trifecta." The trifecta is basically the recognition that the state, the street, and the home together oppress women specifically.

That's where what I call the "double revolution," the social and sexual revolution, comes in, because we began a political revolution that was directed toward the state. But, unless we have the social/sexual revolution that takes the fight to the street and to the home as well, in an attempt to destroy the patriarchy of that trifecta, then clearly it is only the men's revolution.

You see that playing out in so many of the countries, but specifically my own country, where I moved back in 2013, Egypt. All we have done is play basically political musical chairs, where we got rid of Mubarak, then we got a military junta of 19 Mubaraks, then we got Mohamed Morsi, then we got Sisi—and it's just one man replacing another. Unless we take that revolution to the streets and to the home, with gender at its heart, and have a social/sexual revolution, the political revolution as far as I'm concerned will fail because it will always be a men's revolution.

NAUREEN CHOWDHURY FINK: You are painting this picture of a quest for freedom, a quest for equality, a quest for rights, and you are sort of complicating this image we have of the Middle East, with the men and women fighting side by side, but then this continued revolution of women. Certainly in our line of work, working on countering violent extremism and counterterrorism, we are faced with another very puzzling image, which is of young women leaving homes, presumably in the West, where they do have some of these rights, where they are at least legally protected, and

then going to join perhaps the most extreme of some of these misogynist movements in ISIL [Islamic State of Iraq and the Levant], in Iraq and Syria.

How do you square that image between the desire for freedom and the sexual revolution you were talking about and young women choosing to leave places where they should have some of those rights and then going to join ISIL? Those pictures are very puzzling put together.

MONA ELTAHAWY: Another of the points that I want to raise in the book as well is too often when we look at the Middle East and North Africa, the only options that we see available for people are either military rule or Islamic rule, as if that is the only thing available, as if, in a country like Egypt of 85 to 90 million people, that's the only thing we could come up with.

I call them *Daesh*. I don't call them ISIS or ISIL because *Daesh* is the Arab acronym [for *Ad-Dawlah al-Islamiyah fi al-'Iraq wash-Sham*] and they don't like that acronym and I don't like them, so I will continue to call them by the name that they don't like.

I think that we have to place *Daesh* along the spectrum of that political Islam that I am also fighting. I am fighting military rule and political Islam because I think they are two sides of the same coin, authoritarianism, paternalistic rule, and this very misogynistic approach to life and religion. I think that *Daesh* belongs to the far right extreme.

In my book, I mention *Daesh* as one of the many groups that are killing and maiming people in Syria and Iraq, and they specifically target women. But most of my focus is on the Salafi groups and the Muslim Brotherhood in the region.

But if I were to take my arguments from the book and extend them to the UK and parts of Europe, and in some instances here in the United States, I think what those women represent are the more extreme version of the women of the Muslim Brotherhood and the Salafi groups, who in my opinion have internalized this misogyny, have basically understood that to survive in the kind of culture that we live in, there are certain things that you have to learn and regurgitate back, and in that case be protected and comforted by that group.

When it comes to the Muslim Brotherhood, for example, we have women who were advisors to Mohamed Morsi and who were the heads of the women's committee of the Muslim Brotherhood who made outrageous statements, such as "female genital mutilation [FGM] is a form of beautification," "women should not protest because it's undignified." In the middle of the revolution, we had the head of the women's committee of the Muslim Brotherhood's Freedom and Justice Party actually saying, "It's undignified for women to protest; they should let their brothers and fathers protest."

If I were to draw that line to those women who go and join *Daesh,* I would also complicate it by this idea of choice feminism that we often talk about now.

I'm often asked, when it comes to the veil and various veils, "Why are you so opposed to the veil? A woman has chosen to do this." This idea of choice has to be complicated beyond "a woman has chosen to do this."

Just because a woman has chosen to do something does not oblige me as a woman to support that choice. Unless that choice is a feminist choice, this is where we part ways.

So these young women who go and join *Daesh* in my opinion are not making feminist choices; they are committing what I believe is as egregious as the women who joined the Charles Manson gang.

I would make a difference also between men and women who joined things like the Baader Meinhof gang in West Germany, because at least the women who joined the Baader Meinhof gang actually fought. There were quotes from West German police in which they would say "shoot the women first." Why would they want to shoot the women of Baader Meinhof first? Because they were actually fighting with the men. These women had agency beyond going to be the bride of some jihadi, being covered from head to toe and basically dropping out of existence.

So it's very puzzling to me. I do not support that choice and I think it is an internalization of a very dangerous kind of misogyny.

NAUREEN CHOWDHURY FINK: Moving into this idea— and you mentioned this repeatedly in your book—that women have to some extent internalized this message so much that they have become the main protagonist. You talk about the mothers who take their daughters to be mutilated, or mothers who agree on this.

So let's complicate the notion of what it means to be a woman in Islam. We talk a lot about—and you've mentioned this certainly in the book, and you mentioned about the "A'isha/Khadijah complex." There is this enormous focus on the youngest wife of the Prophet and what she did in that relationship.

There is very little discussion about Khadijah, who was to all intents and purposes his boss. She was older, she was his only wife as long as she was alive, and she proposed to him. Why are we not talking more about Khadijah and why aren't women abroad in the diaspora communities and these girls that you are saying have this very simplified notion—why is Khadijah not more the role model? A'isha may have been a good role model—I don't want to say no—but why aren't we talking more about Khadijah?

MONA ELTAHAWY: This thing about Khadijah is really interesting to me. Khadijah, many of you might know, was

the first person who accepted Muhammad's message. She was the first person who believed in him. This is a woman who, as you said, was 15 years older than him, a divorcee, by some accounts also a widow. Apparently, she had more than three husbands. She proposed to Muhammad. She was his only wife. He was 25 and she was 40 when he married her. She was his only wife until she died when she was 60, I think it was.

I think the reason that our clerics do not bring Khadijah up is because, clearly, this was a woman who fully was empowered and was the best symbol of consent and agency. One of the ideas that I also want to talk about when we talk about revolution is consent and agency. So when our clerics look at a woman like Khadijah, who was the boss of the man who became the Prophet of Islam, and who was older than him, for them she represents the worst kind of thing that a woman is. This is a woman who is in control of her life. This is a woman who was the boss of the founder of Islam. She was clearly not a woman who was going to be molded in any way by Muhammad.

But they focus—they obsess—over A'isha. There is a huge fight over how old she was. Some people say she was six, some say she was nine, some say she was 19. I say in 2015 it doesn't matter how old she was, because in 2015 marrying a child anywhere in the world is pedophilia and should be against the law.

But this is a real issue of life and death in countries like Yemen, Saudi Arabia, my country Egypt, Sudan, where women's rights activists who very courageously try to put an age to marriage, a limit to how young a girl can be when she gets married, they are fought with charges of blasphemy by clerics who hold onto this idea of A'isha.

What they do is they say, "You are breaking the *sunnah,* the tradition of the Prophet, by questioning this." But they never say, "It's *sunnah* to marry an older woman." I joke about this, but it's really not a joke.

We have huge levels of male unemployment in the Middle East and North Africa, and in many parts of the so-called Muslim world I've never seen a cleric say, "Practice the *sunnah* of the Prophet. Marry a woman who's older because if you're unemployed she can take care of you." [Laughter] I never hear this.

What I do hear is these men being silent when these young girls are dying in childbirth at the age of eight or nine because they have essentially been raped on their wedding night by men five times their age. This is a crime under anybody's imagination.

Now, we can have arguments about how many cultures in the year 620 allowed child marriage. But again, it's beside the point. What happened in the seventh century should not be something that we have to abide by in the twenty-first century.

This image of Khadijah is not only the clerics' worst nightmare but she is the worst nightmare of *Daesh.* If the young women who are joining *Daesh* knew about Khadijah, knew about this woman who practiced consent and agency in the best way, I wonder would they be rushing to join *Daesh* at the age of 15 and being told to be happy with their lot, as the so-called jihadi bride of god knows who, who is ruining the lives of people in Iraq and Syria and is involved in systematic rape of the Yazidi women, as we all know.

NAUREEN CHOWDHURY FINK: Which brings me to the question, then, this complicated notion in this sort of more complex history that you are painting here: How much of that is accessible? I know that a lot of times when we talk about women's rights and we talk about gender issues, especially in countries dealing with extremism and conflict, we hear about this as a Western import—"these are Western values. These are not local values; these are not our values. You've brought them from abroad."

And yet, in your book you very powerfully highlight women in the Middle East who have been fighting for equal rights historically and in a contemporary setting. As a Medieval historian myself, I could say that a lot of these stories are really revolutionary when you do think of what was happening in Europe in the year 620 and then you have Muhammad fighting for a divorce and alimony and things like that. It is quite revolutionary.

But there does not seem to be that access to that history among women in the diaspora community. So you can have young girls who will go over to *Daesh* and say, "This is the historical image I follow."

How do we increase that access to information? How do we muddy the waters a little and bring this complexity into the history?

MONA ELTAHAWY: What I try to do in the book, as you say, is mention, name drop, as often as I can, a lot of feminists who belong to my heritage, whom I can turn to. As much as I admire and love Gloria Steinem and Germaine Greer, until she went culturally relativist on me and I had to part ways with her—but there are a lot of Western feminists that I do admire—they are not the only ones that have informed my own feminism.

I have women like Huda Sha'arawi, who in the 1920s removed her veil and said, "This is a thing of the past." I have women like Doria Shafik, who in the 1950s led a group of 1,500 Egyptian women into storming the Egyptian Parliament to demand political rights. Most people in Egypt do not know that Doria Shafik did this. I have women like Nawal El Saadawi, who is still alive today—she is 83 now—who was one of the first Egyptian feminists to my knowledge to write so openly and poignantly about her own genital cutting and to talk about how it has affected her life. And there is the Moroccan sociologist

feminist Fatema Mernissi, whose books on veiling informed my own decision to remove my *hijab,* because I wore a *hijab* for nine years. So we have all these women.

And we have contemporary women as well. In Saudi Arabia, where a lot of people would say, "Feminists in Saudi Arabia?" I say, "Yes, there are women like Manal al-Sharif, who, every year up until she had to leave and go to Dubai because she was hounded out of her job, took part in driving campaigns as part of civil disobedience to break the ban on women driving in Saudi Arabia. And several other women, all the way back to the 1990s, when you had at least 40 Saudi women who, after Saddam invaded Kuwait, had their own driving protest to break the ban on women's driving.

All these women exist in countries as conservative as Saudi Arabia and as liberal as Tunisia and Morocco. But you never hear their names. Now, internally you never hear their names because of that trifecta—the state, the street, and the home—that are not interested in promoting this kind of feminist message.

But one of the positive things that came about in the revolution in Egypt was many grassroots groups that came about after the revolution, like one group called Baheya Ya Misr. It was launched by a woman who is also a diplomat in the Arab League [Inas S. Mekkawy], who brought together lots of young men and women. What they would do when they went out on protest was they would put the pictures of these women that I mentioned, all these names, on these big banners, and they would march through downtown Cairo with the women's names as they waved these banners around, so that people could see these women from our own history that had basically just been entirely forgotten.

When the Muslim Brotherhood was in power and Mohamed Morsi was president for that brief year, one of the things that they wanted to do in the curriculum was to remove all pictures of Doria Shafik because she wasn't wearing a headscarf.

We were actively continuing to erase these women who should be our heroes. So these feminist groups who are coming about on the ground in Egypt were trying to bring her back. But I know that outside of the Middle East and North Africa very few young women know about these women.

And I'm talking about women just in my region. But I'm sure if you talk about Pakistan, I can talk about women like Hina Jilani and Asma Jahangir. These are two sisters who formed the first legal firm formed by women in Pakistan, and who to this day defend women who have been attacked by acid attacks; they defend women who have been hounded by their families because of so-called honor crimes.

There is a whole list of women who have been intentionally or indirectly erased who our young women today, both in various Muslim-majority countries and outside, must know about. The question is, why don't we know about them?

My book is just one of many that we need. But I think that those who work in counterterrorism and those who work in international organizations that want to counter the narrative of groups like *Daesh* would do well to start repeating these names, would do well to bring light.

In Oslo in January, I took part in a conference for Muslim women that was put together by a Norwegian-Pakistani woman called Deeyah Khan. Deeyah is a singer-songwriter who made a film about a young woman who was killed in a so-called honor killing in England because she had the nerve to escape her family and marry the man that she wanted. We have so many women like Deeyah. In that conference in Oslo she brought together women from dozens of countries.

Why don't more people know about them? Why aren't they in our mainstream media?

NAUREEN CHOWDHURY FINK: You touched on that earlier, and I think Joanne did in her question—who's "them," who's "us?" We have this notion that it always happens "over there." It's always "them," it's not "us." I think there are some very important campaigns. There's a documentary film called *Honor Diaries* that looks at the amount of honor killings, even here in the United States. It's really quite frightening.

You mentioned this phrase in the book that really stuck with me, "the misogyny of the state and the misogyny of the street." I don't know that any country has really gotten rid of both. When we debate "equal pay for equal work" here, I don't see that we've defeated misogyny.

But I think that is a very important point you make. There are two types. We think about violence against women in these big conflict settings and revolutions during conflicts and *Daesh* and these big settings. But there is this low-level misogyny—I don't want to say low-level because people are dying of it—but there is this constant misogyny too in the home that you have talked about. And in many cases, of course, the power is with the father in the household. It's negative when we think of this poor little girl in Saudi Arabia or these girls you talked about in the Yemeni wedding night.

But there are also some very powerful forces for good, which certainly we see in homes, if you think about Malala's father—or, presumably, in our homes, fathers—that can play a very positive role.

So how can we engage men? You have some great examples in the book—the Eritrean couple with the man wearing the sign on his wedding day saying, "I will only marry a liberated woman."

MONA ELTAHAWY: "An uncut woman."

NAUREEN CHOWDHURY FINK: That's right—and defying his family to marry her.

So how do we engage men more, because the reality is that right now in the home, in the state, and in the street a lot of men in these regions still have that defining role? How can men play more of a role in this revolution?

MONA ELTAHAWY: In order to answer that, I have to start with what you said about the misogyny not just being "over there." One of the points that I tried to make in my book and in all my appearances on book tours so far is that it is really important to see my book not as something that just indicts men from my part of the world and to somehow make it out to be that all Arab or all Muslim men have this structure and deity that makes them especially misogynist. I think it's this trifecta that I am trying to unpack here that encourages it because it institutionalizes it on many levels.

But I make comparisons to what happens here in the United States, especially in the Southern states. I often say that in the Middle East and North Africa I fight the Muslim Brotherhood; here in the United States I fight what I call the "Christian Brotherhood." These are the right-wing Christian groups who have been instrumental in fighting against women's reproductive rights. These are the kind of right-wing political groups that have led to something like the case of Purvi Patel, the Hindu woman in Indiana, who was recently sent to jail for 20 years on the charge on infanticide. This is unheard of. The entire world sat back and thought, "What is going on in the United States that this woman, who said that she had a miscarriage, was sent to jail on charges of infanticide?"

Basically a woman is considered an incubator in some of these states. There are some states also in the South where women have very little access to either contraception or reproductive rights generally, especially abortions.

So I draw the line between what I call "purity culture" here in the United States, this obsession with virginity, this obsession with women's bodies, this obsession with vaginas, and I connect it to the obsession with modesty; in modesty cultures where I come from, again an obsession with vagina. The saying now that I want to put on all T-shirts across the world is "Stay Out of My Vagina Unless I Want You in There." [Laughter] These very religious conservative men are obsessed with our vaginas.

So the purity culture here and the modesty culture over there have to be connected so that you don't think that I'm just talking about the men of my part of the world. Misogyny exists on a spectrum globally, but each country has made its own progress along that spectrum, thanks to the efforts of feminists and thanks to its ability to break that trifecta of the state, the street, and the home.

Going back to my region now and what's going on in the home, I think it is very important to realize that, because of that trifecta, what ends up happening is the misogynies are reflected back and forth.

For example, in March of 2011, when the military in Egypt subjected women revolutionaries to so-called virginity tests—essentially sexual assaults—the military knew it could get away with this because this concept of a virginity test exists in the Egyptian home.

I have been told many stories about this. But one story I was actually told was someone said, "My friend was engaged. The engagement broke up for whatever reason, and her fiancé actually contacted her parents and said, 'I think you should have your girl checked.'"

You can actually go to a forensics doctor and basically ask him to issue a virginity certificate. This exists in Turkey, this exists in parts of Iraq, this exists in Egypt. This is outrageous. This is a crime against the body of a girl or a woman.

I connect that crime—again, it is under this idea of consent and agency—to one of the earliest crimes that happens in the home again.

Now, this virginity test that was perpetrated by the state—the state knew that the people on the street and in the home would not be outraged. When I heard about these virginity tests, I thought, "For sure we are going to have another revolution now. How could they violate our revolutionaries like this?"

Nothing happened. The women who exposed these tests were called liars and they were told, "You are trying to malign our honorable military that is trying to protect us against Mubarak."

The state knew the home would be quiet, just as the home knows the state will be quiet when the home perpetrates one of the earliest crimes against the body of the girl, and that is in the form of genital mutilation or cutting.

So the misogynies are constantly reflected back. That is all underpinned by the legislation that allows this to happen and that allows street sexual harassment to go unpunished and unaccountable. That trifecta again allows all of this to happen.

Now, you mentioned the case of Lama. Lama is a young girl who at the age of four was—four or five, I can't remember now, but it is a horrific case.

NAUREEN CHOWDHURY FINK: Five. Too young.

MONA ELTAHAWY: She was raped by her father, who was a televangelist in Saudi Arabia. He claimed that he raped her because she wasn't a virgin. She's a girl who was five. Again this obsession with virginity. He managed to get away with it because her mother—he had divorced her mother—accepted blood money from him because she was a very poor single mother.

According to Saudi law, the crime of rape is punishable by death, but a man cannot be punished by death—and I am against the death sentence under any circumstances—but a man in Saudi Arabia cannot be sentenced to death if the crime that he supposedly committed was against his wife or his children.

So here again you have multiple levels of complicity between the state and the home, and in many instances the street as well.

This crime that happened against Lama—the people who stood up to it very bravely and courageously were Saudi activists. Now, I talked about Saudi feminists who many people do not know exist. There are also Saudi human rights defenders who many people outside of the kingdom do not know exist. They very bravely and courageously took up the case of Lama, and they also took up the case of domestic violence laws, so that they could take the crimes that happen in the home to the highest level.

But they are fighting against incredible odds. One of the worst odds that they are fighting against is something that the state allows to happen. It is called the guardianship system. In Saudi Arabia a woman is essentially a child her entire life because she must depend on a male guardian—be it her father, her husband, her brother, and in some instances her son—to give her permission to do the most basic of things.

According to this domestic violence law—this is a country where a woman cannot drive—you are basically supposed to depend on your male guardian to take you to the law enforcers to complain about domestic violence. How are you supposed to go and complain about the violence of the home if the person in the home who is going to take you to the police is the person abusing you?

So despite the fact that we have these incredibly courageous people fighting against the highest odds, that trifecta (the state, the street, and the home) must be taken apart in order for their courageous work to actually have an impact in helping the girls and women who are at the center of this trifecta.

NAUREEN CHOWDHURY FINK: I could go on forever, but I don't want to take up too much time from the floor. I will ask one more question because I think it is particularly key.

The book is in many ways inspiring because it catalogues so many difficult issues. It is a catalogue of things that need to be addressed—and I would add addressed quickly. But what can we do about it? There is a spectrum of actors you highlight—from the feminists, the ideologues, the civil society actors, to governments, to international organizations. What range of actions do you think is the best way to actually address it? Much as I think we need to raise awareness about the problems, I'd also love a chance to think about what the solution is and how we can move forward.

MONA ELTAHAWY: Right. I think the solutions belong on many levels. Kind of the ultimate solution—I'm not a policymaker, but my quickest answer to "What can we do?" is destroy the patriarchy. How can we destroy the patriarchy takes many levels.

I think, whenever I am asked at gatherings like this "What can I do to help you and women from your background?" I say, "Nothing. You as individuals can do nothing because only we can help ourselves." I didn't write this book because I want anyone to come and rescue us. I'm not waiting for someone to come and save us. Only we can save ourselves and only we can have this fight.

But what you as individuals can do at the local level—and that's why I always connect it to the misogyny that is available—

NAUREEN CHOWDHURY FINK: It's on sale at your local store.

MONA ELTAHAWY: Exactly, and at a 50 percent reduction.

In every country I've traveled there are obviously examples of misogyny. So I say fight the misogyny in your country. Believe me, when the Muslim Brotherhood or the state or anybody in my country finds out about a case like Purvi Patel or finds out that women in the United States don't get equal pay or you haven't had a woman president yet, the first thing they say to me is, "Don't you know they beat women up in America as well? Don't you know that a rape happens every four minutes in America as well?" Their excuse is always that "There's misogyny over there."

Of course there is. There is misogyny everywhere. So I say, fight the misogyny in your own community because that lifts up feminism on a global level. That way you won't have anyone over there saying, "Well, it's just as bad." The easiest way to shut down feminist discussions or a discussion about the importance of feminism is to say, "It happens everywhere—shrug—what can I do? It happens everywhere."

So fight it. Fight it wherever you are and don't accept it. I think in a lot of the Western contexts I speak in, people have gotten to this place of complacency, which is incredibly dangerous. A lot of my second-wave feminist friends, like Robin Morgan and Gloria Steinem—I'm going to be in a conversation with Robin Morgan at the PEN Festival on Saturday—a lot of them will tell you that the fights that they were having on the barricades in the 1960s and the 1970s have come back. How, in a country like the United States, have they come back? How, in a country like the United States, have civil rights and the crimes of the civil rights come back again, that we are still talking about police brutality against black men?

I went to Beijing in 1995. The Beijing platform was one of the most progressive platforms on reproductive rights. We have not been able to as a global community have another women's conference. You know why? Because all these religious fundamentalists in concert with the Vatican will destroy what we were able to produce in Beijing because of the religious fundamentalists and the regimes who support them.

So fight it in your own community and fight complacency.

On the political level, ask your politicians why they are silent when they buy billions of dollars' worth of oil from Saudi Arabia, sell Saudi Arabia billions of dollars' worth of weapons, and they know what Saudi Arabia does to women. The Swedish foreign minister tried to say something about this and she was banned from speaking at the Arab League. But worse, in Sweden, this paragon of feminism, she was attacked by the business community because they didn't want to lose money, she was attacked by politicians for being "too emotional"—too emotional! This is the Swedish foreign minister.

Again, misogyny has not been erased anywhere. So on a political level ask your politicians why they are shamefully silent. They basically throw women away like cheap currency and bargaining chips when they sit with our regimes. Again, I'm not saying, in the way that Laura Bush did when she took over the presidential address just before this country invaded Afghanistan, "We are invading Afghanistan to liberate the women from their *burkas*," which was just ludicrous. This is not why this country invaded Afghanistan.

I am not asking for anyone to invade, because most Western countries have terrible records when it comes to colonialism and imperialism in my part of the world, and hypocrisy when it comes to using women's issues. So don't come invading us for our sake.

But talk to your politicians about why they are hypocritical when it comes to women's issues and why they are so easily able to strike these deals.

And then, on a UN and international level, I want to know why the United Nations allows so many countries from my part of the world to place these asterisks that allow them to get away with violating exactly the kind of provisions in something like CEDAW, that basically destroy the meaning of the Convention on the Elimination of All Forms of Discrimination Against Women. Why, if this convention is aimed at protecting women from cultural and religious discrimination, do you allow countries to basically opt out, if according to their religion and culture, it somehow violates it?

I honestly want someone from the United Nations to sit and explain to me why these countries continuously violate the very conventions that—and basically, when you sign on to these conventions, you can then say, "You know what? The United States hasn't signed CEDAW, but we have." But then you look into the details of the various provisions they violate, and it's meaningless. All it does is it gives them cachet and the ability to say, "We signed this convention. . . ."

Critical Thinking

1. What is meant by the "trifecta" of women's oppression in the Middle East?

2. How is it that some women in the Middle East have internalized misogyny?

3. Who was Khadijah and why would a proper understanding of her represent a threat to the misogyny within the Islamic world of today?

4. Why would it be more effective for those who are opposed to misogyny in other cultures to actually fight it in their own culture?

Internet References

Evolutionary Demography Group
http://blogs.lshtm.ac.uk/evolutionarydemography/

Evolutionary Demography Society
http://www.sdu.dk/en/om_sdu/institutter_centre/maxo/evodemos

Eltahawy, Mona; Chowdhury Fink, Naureen; Myers, Joanne J., "Headscarves and Hymens", from *Carnegie Council for Ethics in International Affairs.* © 2015. Reprinted by permission.

Article

Prepared by: Elvio Angeloni

Poverty Is Sexist

Why Girls and Women Must Be at the Heart of the Fight to End Extreme Poverty

ONE

Learning Outcomes

After reading this article, you will be able to:

- Discuss the ways in which poverty is sexist.

- Discuss the solutions to the problem of poverty, given the fact that it goes hand-in-hand with sexism.

- Show how health issues are important to understanding and eliminating poverty.

- Discuss the evidence that shows that giving women access to employment, education, financial, and political opportunities reduces poverty.

- Describe the ways in which technology can help empower women in the developing world.

An Introduction

In Switzerland, for every 100,000 births, six women die in childbirth or just after. In Sierra Leone, 1,100 do.[1] That's right. A woman in Sierra Leone is 183 times more likely to die bringing a new life into the world than a woman in Switzerland.

It would be hard to find a statistic that more accurately reflects the injustice of a world in which whether you live or die depends on an accident of geography—on where you were born.

And think about the stories, and the lives, behind that statistic. In one part of the world, the bloodstained sheets, the clinics with flickering lights and intermittent electricity, few supplies and not enough trained nurses and doctors; the grieving husbands and parents, the children bewildered that Mum isn't coming home with a new brother or sister—in fact, that she's not coming home at all. And in the other part of the world,

none of that: just the quotidian expectation that when a woman goes into hospital to give birth she, and her baby, will come home safely in a few days, and rejoin her family with all the happiness and giddy promise for the future with which such moments are endowed.

The challenges and injustices that girls and women in the developing world face are many, across all aspects of life, and include structural, social, economic and political barriers—barriers that men, and women who live in richer countries, experience to far lesser degrees.

The numbers are sobering, even beyond maternal mortality. About 39,000 girls under the age of 18 become child brides every day, with a greater chance of suffering abuse from their husbands.[2] Only a little over 20% of poor rural girls in Africa complete primary education; fewer than 10% finish lower secondary school;[3] and in many countries women in paid work earn 10–30% less than men.[4] What is more, land, safe energy, technology, inheritance and financial services are often out of reach for women. Around the world, only about 22% of parliamentarians are female.[5] Women can be disproportionately affected by corruption because of reduced access to resources, lower participation in governance, and weaker protection of their rights.[6] Cultural and legal limitations create these disparities, despite the fact that women provide the backbone of many aspects of life: in the home, at work and in the community. Violence against women—physical and sexual—reflects the sexism, disrespect, and abuse of women's basic rights that occur in all countries across the world. Beyond gross abuses of human rights, imagine trying to productively farm, or fix a car, or stitch a tapestry, or code a new software program, with one hand tied behind your back; yet that is precisely the situation in which a society finds itself when it ignores women's potential.

What Needs to Happen

This situation needs to change—and not only because it is a source of endemic, global injustice.

Put simply, *poverty is sexist*, and we won't end it unless we face up to the fact that girls and women get a raw deal.

That means:

1. **Refocusing the development agenda so that girls and women are centre stage**—they are half of the current population of those living in poverty[7] and often the most vulnerable to falling into and staying in poverty. The global community must seize the opportunity to unleash the social, political, and economic potential of women everywhere.
2. **Better targeted investments** in health, education, and the economic empowerment of girls and women to dismantle the barriers that prevent so many living healthy and productive lives. In this brief, *ONE* sets out policy recommendations across key sectors to do just that.

If we take those two steps, all members of society could benefit. A mounting body of evidence shows that, if we invest in girls and women, it helps their families and communities too.

Why Now?
2015 is Just the Year To Do It

This year will see the world commit to a new set of Sustainable Development Goals[8] (SDGs) designed to replace the Millennium Development Goals[9] and eradicate extreme poverty by 2030—and so thinking about the place of women in the development story is more important than ever. Chancellor Angela Merkel of Germany and Chair of the African Union Commission (AUC) Nkosazana Dlamini-Zuma are leading the way on the issue: each will convene a women's summit this year, and Merkel is putting girls and women at the heart of her G7 agenda. In the following pages, we look at what the challenges—and opportunities—involved in such an agenda are.

- Secondary school enrolment for girls is **3x higher** in non-LDCs at 80.2% of girls, on average, compared with 26.8% of girls enrolled in LDCs.
- The percentage of working women who are in vulnerable employment[11] is three times higher in LDCs than in non-LDCs, with 86.2% of employed women on average working in vulnerable employment in LDCs.
- Almost half (45%) of the world's maternal deaths occur amongst the 13% of the world's poorest women living in LDCs: **131,000** in total. Across LDCs, the average ratio is 1 in 217 (i.e., 1 maternal death per 217 live births) compared with 1 in 1,250 on average across non-LDCs.

The Challenge for Girls and Women

Poverty and gender inequality go hand-in-hand; girls and women in the poorest countries suffer a double whammy, of being born both in a poor country and female. To see the extent of this disadvantage, *ONE* analysed the situation for girls and women in least developed countries (LDCs)[10] across key gender indicators. On every indicator, life is significantly harder for girls and women in LDCs compared with those living in other countries. While that may not be surprising—because men in poor countries are also disadvantaged—*ONE* also found that the gender gap between males and females is larger in the poorest countries.

ONE's calculations are based on data from:
World Bank, World Development Indicators
World Bank, Global Financial Inclusion Database (Findex)
UNESCO Institute for Statistics, Education Database
International Labour Organization, ILOSTAT

- In LDCs, on average, the rate of literacy among women is only **two-thirds** (68.5%) the rate of men. In non-LDCs, the gender gap remains, but to a lesser degree: women's rates are on average 94.8% those of men's.
- In LDCs, 20% more female workers than male workers are in vulnerable employment, a gender gap that is only 7% in other countries.

Country Comparisons

- **Madagascar** has 144 times more out-of school girls than **Germany**, which has 3.5 times the population of Madagascar.
- The number of girls enrolled in primary school in the **UK**, which has a population of 64.1 million, is equal to the number of out-of-school girls of primary age in **Ethiopia**, with a population of 94.1 million people.
- In **France**, 97% of women have a bank account—in **Chad**, less than 7% of women do, nearly 40% fewer than men.

The Opportunity

- Globally, providing female farmers with the same access to productive resources as male farmers could reduce the number of people living in chronic hunger by 100—150 million.[12]

- Reducing differences in the employment rate between men and women by 2017 could generate an additional $1.6 trillion in global output (measured in purchasing power parity).[13]
- Increasing the amount spent on key health interventions for women and children by $5 per person per year to 2035 across 74 developing countries could yield a nine times return on investment in economic and social benefits.[14]
- Ensuring that all students in low-income countries, including girls, leave school with basic readings skills could cut extreme poverty globally by as much as 12%.[15]

Women farmers could significantly raise economic output and decrease the number of people globally suffering from chronic hunger. Strong health systems could mean that maternal and child deaths drop dramatically. Safe, reliable energy could mean that businesses would be better able to thrive, the quality of education for girls and boys would improve and health clinics would provide better care. All of this could boost economic and social development. Improvement in access to quality education for girls could significantly boost their future income, drastically reduce rates of child malnutrition, save mothers' and children's lives and reduce overall poverty levels. Getting more women into the labour force and increasing women's access to information and communication technology (ICT) and the Internet could boost the overall economy. Affording women more control over finances could greatly improve quality of life at the household level. For all those reasons, the fundamental message is plain: if we are going to end extreme poverty, we need to start with girls and women.

A Deeper Look: Agriculture
What's Needed
Agricultural training and research and development should be tailored to women's needs; women's access to hired labour and other productive inputs should be increased; and women's land tenure rights should be strengthened (e.g., by such means as formalised registration of tenure, expansion of co-titling and enabling individual titling for women, and reforming inheritance and family laws).[16] All six World Health Assembly nutrition targets[17] should be integrated into the SDGs.

The Challenge

- Agricultural productivity for female farmers in a sample of sub-Saharan African countries is between 23% and 66% lower than that of male farmers.[18] Though data are limited, only 10–20% of all land-holders globally are female.[19] Female farmers' access to credit is lower than that of males.[20]

Women provide roughly half of all agricultural labour in Africa, yet female farmers continue to have less access to farm labour,

tools, extension services and financing for their farms compared with men, and get less return on the same investments.[21]

The Potential

- Globally, providing female farmers with the same access to productive resources as male farmers (i.e., closing the gender gap in agriculture) could increase agricultural yields by 20–30%, raise economic output by 2.5–4%, and reduce the number of people who go hungry by 12–17% (100–150 million people).[22]

Studies show that growth in the agriculture sector in sub-Saharan Africa is 11 times more effective at reducing poverty than growth in any other sector of the economy.[23] In developing countries, nearly half of the reduction in hunger that occurred between 1970 and 1995 can be correlated with increases in women's education,[24] and Bread for the World recently showed that countries with greater levels of gender equality tend to have lower rates of child malnutrition.[25]

A Deeper Look: Health
What's Needed
Investments in the health of girls and women must be scaled up and health programmes must more effectively target and engage them as their beneficiaries and partners. The health of girls and women must remain a foundational priority on the global development agenda, and leaders must chart a clear pathway towards the virtual elimination of preventable maternal and child deaths. As part of this effort, investments must be targeted in ways that aggressively fight specific diseases that adversely impact women; help make women's access to essential health commodities universal; and strengthen human resources for health, which can extend the reach of health systems to the most vulnerable.

The Challenge

- Of adults living with HIV in sub-Saharan Africa, 58% are women; and, globally women aged 15–24 face double the risk of HIV infection compared with their male peers.[26]
- Almost 800 women die every day from complications in pregnancy or childbirth. Of the 68 countries with the highest burden of maternal and child deaths, 53 do not have the 23 physicians, nurses and midwives per 10,000 people deemed necessary to deliver essential health services;[27] and an estimated 225 million women are not able to access the tools needed to plan and space the births of their children. Some 43 million women do not deliver their babies in a health facility.[28]

Far too many women and girls still lack access to the quality health services, programmes, and commodities they need to stay healthy. Compounding this problem, women experience physiological, economic and socio-cultural obstacles that make them more vulnerable to many diseases and conditions than their male counterparts. In addition, many African women spend a lot of their time playing the crucial role of health care providers and primary care-givers, looking after sick family members.[29]

The Potential

- In 2013, more than two-thirds of pregnant women living with HIV in low- and middle-income countries received treatment to prevent transmission of the virus to their babies.[30] Fast-tracking efforts on HIV/AIDS could see the world eliminate mother-to-child transmission of HIV, save millions of lives, and return $15 for every $1 invested.[31]
- If all women could access the care, commodities and services recommended by the World Health Organization (WHO), maternal deaths would drop by 67%, and newborn deaths would fall by 77%.[32]

In recent years, a significant increase in donor and domestic investments in women's and children's health has made a real impact: there are now fewer unintended pregnancies, fewer women dying in childbirth, and fewer children dying from preventable causes than ever before. Yet it is clear from the statistics that better and more investments in women's health, including training and retaining health care workers, are critical to saving lives of both women and children and to improving their overall health. As a side benefit, strengthened formal health systems could free up the time of women who traditionally play that (unpaid) role in the family, allowing them to pursue more economically productive activities.

A Deeper Look: Energy
What's Needed
Universal access to safe, sustainable, affordable, reliable, and modern energy services must be achieved, while access to finance and capacity-building resources in energy sector innovation, particularly for women, should be prioritised.

The Challenge

- In most countries, women tend to be in charge of cooking. When they cook over open fires or traditional stoves, they breathe in pollutants every day. This indoor smoke is responsible for over half a million deaths annually due to chronic obstructive pulmonary disease among women worldwide.[33]
- Around 60% of refrigerators used for vaccine storage in African health clinics have an unreliable electricity

supply, compromising the effectiveness of life-saving children's vaccines. Unreliable energy access for clinics also means the risk of unsafe delivery for women forced to give birth in the dark.[34]

Around 19% of the world's population, or 1.3 billion people, have no access to electricity at all.[35] Energy poverty (lack of access to safe, reliable, modern energy) is a crucial issue for women, as it results in premature deaths from cooking with unsafe and unhealthy fuel sources, wasted time in the collection of fuel (to say nothing of the dangers involved in collecting it), insufficient provision of health services, inability to properly store and process agricultural harvests, and lower quality of education. Further, many African businesses have cited the lack of reliable energy access as the biggest obstacle to growth.[36]

The Potential

- Women in sub-Saharan Africa currently spend up to eight hours per day collecting fuel for cooking and heating their homes; access to energy would mean that women could spend this time on income-generating pursuits.[37]
- In one study, women's employment in South Africa increased by 9.5% where electricity was provided, most probably because it released women from home production and enabled them to participate in micro-enterprises and other economic pursuits.[38]

Data on the direct positive effects of energy access for women on local and national economies are still too thin to draw direct global or even regional conclusions, but examples in a number of localities are proving promising. It is clear that providing reliable access to safe energy for all who lack it would improve educational opportunities, health service delivery, agricultural productivity, and women's safety.

A Deeper Look: Education
What's Needed
Focused attention must be paid to getting girls into school and helping them to stay there, through concrete policy measures such as improving infrastructure in order to create a gender-sensitive educational environment; providing female teachers trained in counselling; and recruiting professionally trained, motivated, and well-supported teachers of both sexes.

The Challenge

- If current trends continue, in sub-Saharan Africa, boys from the relatively richest families will achieve universal primary completion in 2021, but the poorest girls will not catch up until 2086.[39] Rural girls are more likely than rural boys and twice as likely as urban girls to be out of school.[40]

- Two-thirds of the 796 million people worldwide who are illiterate are women.[41]

While the gender gap in primary education is closing in much of the developing world,[42] it remains large in many sub-Saharan African countries and in some parts of Asia. It is estimated that almost two-thirds of the girls not in school in sub-Saharan Africa will never get there.[43] Globally, girls make up 54% (31 million) of the out-of-school population and it is likely that 17 million of them will never go to school.[44] The higher the grade level, the fewer the low-income countries (LICs) that achieve gender parity in education. Around 20% of LICs achieve parity at primary school, but only 10% achieve it at lower secondary level, and just 8% at upper secondary.[45] Sadly, since 1990, no progress has been made globally in improving women's rates of literacy, and in 12 of the 15 countries in West Africa that have some of the lowest adult literacy rates in the world, fewer than 50% of young women are literate.[46]

The Potential

- Every year that a girl spends in school can boost her future income by 10–20%.[47]
- If all women had primary education, there would be 15% fewer child deaths, saving 900,000 lives per year. If all women had secondary education, there would be 49% fewer child deaths, saving 2.8 million lives, 64% fewer early marriages, and 59% fewer young pregnancies.[48]

Studies show that investing in girls' and women's education goes beyond saving lives. Every year a girl spends in school can boost her future income by 10–20%.[49] Further, it is estimated that a 10% increase in educational equality can increase income per capita by 23% over 40 years. Put another way, if all students in LICs could leave school with basic reading skills, 171 million people could be lifted out of poverty, which would be equivalent to a 12% cut in world poverty.[50] In addition, globally, women are less likely to have access to vocational training; remedying this disadvantage would open up access to qualified, better-paying, more economically productive jobs.[51]

A Deeper Look: Financial, Legal, and Economic Empowerment
What's Needed

Employment, banking, and business policies must be better tailored to women, including the creation of decent, paid jobs; formalisation and growth of medium-sized, female-owned

enterprises; and access to financial services. The proportion of youth, particularly women, not in paid employment or vocational training should also be reduced. All legal differences on the basis of gender that limit women's economic empowerment must be dismantled.

The Challenge

- In sub-Saharan Africa, 86% of women are in vulnerable employment, compared with 70% of men, only a 1% decrease from 15 years ago.[52]
- More than 1.3 billion women do not have an account at a formal financial institution such as a bank, post office, or credit union.[53]

In the developing world, women are in vulnerable employment to a greater degree than men, meaning they are more vulnerable to economic risk, have less access to social protection, are paid on average less than men for work of equal value and access and use financial institutions at lower rates. Globally, almost half of women's productive potential is unutilised, compared with less than a quarter of men's.[54] In addition, in many countries legal barriers for women persist, with substantial gender-based differences in areas such as access to property, employment, credit, the justice system, and protection from violence.[55] All such barriers limit the extent to which women can be fully empowered economically.

The Potential

- Over the coming decade 1 billion women are poised to enter the global economy.[56]
- From programmes such as the social cash transfer in Niger, for instance, there is evidence that using mobile technology shifts intra-household decision-making in favour of women—the people who received the cash.[57]

A wealth of evidence suggests that giving women access to employment, educational, financial, and political opportunities reduces the likelihood of household poverty.[58] In South Africa, it was found that closing the gender gap in labour could result in a potential 10% increase in GDP.[59] In India, women who have been given more local decision-making power have provided more public goods such as water and sanitation.[60] Studies have demonstrated the development benefits when women have control over household income: for example, the PROGRESA cash transfer scheme in Mexico shifted family spending to areas including investments in the future and improved nutrition.[61] Another study found that child survival prospects are 20 times higher when a mother's earned income increases than when that of a father does.[62]

A Deeper Look: Access to Technology
What's Needed

To bring more women into the digital economy, policies that increase the affordability and use of technology, expand rural mobile access, digitise salary and government payments,[63] and boost digital literacy for women must be prioritised.

The Challenge

- In sub-Saharan Africa, women are 23% less likely than men to own a mobile phone,[64] and almost 45% fewer women than men have Internet access.[65]
- Globally, 300 million women do not own a mobile phone, amounting to $13 billion in missed revenues for mobile operators; women constitute an estimated two-thirds of the untapped mobile market.[66]

The Potential

- The World Bank estimates that every 10% increase in access to broadband is correlated with a 1.38% growth in GDP for developing countries;[67] closing the gender gap in broadband access could increase GDP growth, and surveys find that it increases women's income-earning potential.[68]

Technology is playing an ever more vital role in women's economic empowerment in the developing world. For example, among other aims, the Groupe Speciale Mobile Association's (GSMA) global "Connected Women" initiative[69] addresses two main challenges for women in developing countries concerning mobile technology—the access gap and the digital skills gap. Investments in information and communication technologies (ICTs) that are targeted towards women make economic sense in reaching an untapped or under-utilised market. Such investments also increase safety and access to mobile-based education and extension, financial services, and income-generating opportunities, all of which contribute to ending poverty. In Kenya, the arrival of mobile money transfers increased women's economic empowerment in rural areas by making it easier to request remittances from their husbands, who migrated to urban areas for work.[70] Some 46% of the clients for a Kenyan mobile-based micro-insurance programme for farmers are women; scaling up such programmmes elsewhere could prove enormously beneficial for female farmers.[71]

Why We Need a Data Revolution

More and better data are vital if women are to be placed at the centre of the development story. The data gaps for girls and women reflect an overall dearth of comprehensive data and statistics available for poverty analysis, and we need a data revolution to address the problem across the board.

The United Nations has defined a set of 52 indicators[72] that paint the full picture of women's economic empowerment, yet Bread for the World has found that, on average, in sub-Saharan Africa over 80% of these data points simply do not exist.[73] Without information on population, needs, or outcomes, there is no way of knowing how best to structure efforts to empower girls and women living in poverty, nor whether or not current efforts are succeeding. In response to this challenge, the No Ceilings initiative,[74] launching in March 2015 by the Clinton Foundation and partners, gives a data-driven evaluation of the progress that girls and women have made over the past 20 years and the challenges that remain to them achieving full participation in the 21st century. Data2X is another project seeking to close the gaps in our knowledge of women, so that support for them can be better targeted.[75] The Sustainable Development Solutions Network is prioritising a "Data Revolution" that will ensure that an adequate data system exists to monitor progress against the SDGs.[76]

2015 Could Change Everything

The case is clear across all sectors. Empowering women—giving them the power and tools they need to change their own status—allows them to take advantage of equal opportunities, break from cultural and social constraints that may be holding them back, and become drivers of poverty reduction. **Everyone could benefit**.

. . .

Endnotes

1. As of 2013; from the online UN Global Health Observatory data: http://www.who.int/gho/maternal_health/en/; also WHO. 2014. "Trends in Maternal Mortality 1990 to 2013". http://apps.who.int/iris/bitstream/10665/112682/2/9789241507226_eng.pdf?ua=1

2. United Nations Population Fund. 2014. "State of World Population: The Power of 1.8 Billion". http://www.unfpa.org/sites/default/files/pub-pdf/EN-SWOP14-Report_FINAL-web.pdf

3. UNESCO. 2014. "Education for All: Global Monitoring Report 2013/14". http://unesdoc.unesco.org/images/0022/002256/225660e.pdf

4. International Labour Organization (ILO). 2008. "Global Wage Report 2008–09: Minimum Wages and Collective Bargaining, Towards Policy Coherence". Geneva: ILO. http://www.ilo.org/wcmsp5/groups/public/-dgreports/—dcomm/documents/publication/wcms_100786.pdf

5. International Parliamentary Union. 2015. http://www.ipu.org/wmn-e/world.htm

6. United Nations Development Programme (UNDP). 2012. "Seeing Beyond the State: Grassroots Women's Perspectives on Corruption and Anti-Corruption". http://www.undp.org/content/dam/undp/library/Democratic%20Governance/Anti-corruption/Grassroots%20 women%20and%20anti-corruption.pdf

7. World Bank. 2013. "The State of the Poor". http://siteresources.worldbank.org/EXTPREMNET/Resources/EP125.pdf

8. https://sustainabledevelopment.un.org/focussdgs.html

9. http://www.un.org/millenniumgoals/

10. The UN determines LDC status based on three criteria: per capita income, human assets (indicators on nutrition, education, etc.) and economic vulnerability. http://unctad.org/en/Pages/ALDC/Least%20Developed%20Countries/UN-recognition-of-LDCs.aspx

11. The World Bank defines "vulnerable employment" in its World Development Indicators as "unpaid family workers and own-account workers as a percentage of total employment".

12. UN Food and Agriculture Organization (FAO). 2011. "The State of Food and Agriculture. Women in Agriculture: Closing the Gender Gap for Development". http://www.fao.org/docrep/013/i2050e/i2050e.pdf; using 2010 numbers for population, number of people suffering from chronic hunger and other variables.

13. ILO. 2012. "Global Employment Trends for Women." http://www.ilo.org/wcmsp5/groups/public/---dgreports/---dcomm/documents/publication/wcms_195447.pdf

14. Stenberg et al. 2013. "Advancing social and economic development by investing in women's and children's health: a new Global Investment Framework." *The Lancet 383: 1333-54*. http://www.thelancet.com/pdfs/journals/lancet/PIIS0140-6736(13)62231-X.pdf

15. UNESCO. 2014. "Education for All: Global Monitoring Report 2013/14", op. cit.

16. *ONE*. 2013. "Levelling the Field: Improving Opportunities for Women Farmers in Africa". http://one.org.s3.amazonaws.com/pdfs/ONE_Levelling_The_Field_Report_EN.pdf

17. FAO. 2011. "The State of Food and Agriculture. Women in Agriculture: Closing the Gender Gap for Development", op. cit.

18. Ibid.

19. *ONE*. 2013. "Levelling the Field: Improving Opportunities for Women Farmers in Africa", op. cit

20. FAO. 2011. "The State of Food and Agriculture", op. cit.; using 2010 numbers for population, number of people suffering from chronic hunger and other variables.

21. Other sectors include, for example, mining and utilities. Ligon, E. and Sadoulet, E. 2007. "Estimating the effects of aggregate agricultural growth on the distribution of expenditures". Background paper prepared for the "World Development Report 2008", World Bank, Washington, DC. http://siteresources.worldbank.org/INTWDRS/Resources/477365-1327599046334/8394679-1327614067045/

WDROver2008-ENG.pdf; L. Christiaensen, L. Demery and J. Kuhl. 2010. "The (evolving) role of agriculture in poverty reduction—an empirical perspective". Working Paper No. 2010/36. UNU-WIDER, Helsinki. http://www.oecd.org/agriculture/agricultural-policies/46412732.pdf

22. L.C. Smith and L. Haddad. 2000. "Explaining child malnutrition in developing countries: A cross-country analysis". Research Report 111, IFPRI: Washington DC.

23. Bread for The World. 2015. "Hunger Report". Online supplementary material: http://hungerreport.org/2015/empowerment-to-improve-nutrition/

24. *ONE* made these same recommendations in 2014 in a joint report with the World Bank, "Levelling the Field: Improving Opportunities for Women Farmers in Africa", op. cit.

25. In 2012, nations agreed at the UN World Health Assembly on six targets to cover all aspects of nutrition: stunting (too short for age), wasting (too light for height), anaemia, breastfeeding, low birth weight, and overweight. For more information on the far-reaching and life-long detrimental health effects of these aspects of malnutrition, especially when experienced in the first two years of life, see WHO. "Global Targets 2025". http://www.who.int/nutrition/global-target-2025/en/; and 1,000 Days. http://www.thousanddays.org

26. UNAIDS. 2014. "The Gap Report". http://www.unaids.org/sites/default/files/en/media/unaids/contentassets/documents/unaidspublication/2014/UNAIDS_Gap_report_en.pdf

27. UN World Health Organization (WHO). 2010. "Every Woman, Every Child: Access for All to Skilled, Motivated, and Supported Health Workers". http://www.who.int/pmnch/activities/jointactionplan/20101007_4_skilledworkers.pdf

28. Guttmacher Institute. 2014. "Adding It Up: The Costs and Benefits of Investing in Sexual and Reproductive Health in 2014". https://www.guttmacher.org/pubs/AddingItUp2014-summary.html

29. WHO. 2012. "Addressing the Challenge of Women's Health in Africa. Report of the Commission on Women's Health in the African Region". http://apps.who.int/iris/bitstream/10665/94309/1/AFR_RC63_8.pdf?ua=1

30. WHO. http://www.who.int/hiv/data/arvpmtct2014.png?ua=1

31. UNAIDS, press release, 18 November 2014. http://www.unaids.orgen/resources/presscentre/pressreleaseandstatementarchive/2014/november/20141118_PR_WAD2014report

32. Guttmacher Institute. 2014. "Adding It Up", op. cit.

33. See WHO's collection of studies in: WHO. 2006. "Fuel for Life: Household Energy and Health". http://www.who.int/indoorair/publications/fuelforlife.pdf

34. GAVI Alliance. 2012. "National Ownership of Innovative Supply Chain Technologies". Partners Forum 2012. http://www.gavi.org/library/pf2012-sessions/11-%E2%80%93-national-ownership-of-innovative-supply-chain-technologies/

35. International Energy Agency (IEA). 2014. "World Energy Outlook: Energy access database". http://www.worldenergyoutlook.org/resources/energydevelopment/energyaccessdatabase/

36. IEA. 2014. "African Energy Outlook." http://www.iea.org/publications/freepublications/publication/africa-energy-outlook.html

37. Practical Action. 2014. "Poor People's Energy Outlook (PPEO)". http://practicalaction.org/ppeo2014.

38. K. O'Dell, S. Peters, and K. Wharton. 2014. "Women, energy, and, economic empowerment: Applying a gender lens to amplify the impact of energy access". Deloitte University Press, p.8.

39. UNESCO. 2014. "Education for All Global Monitoring Report 2013/14", op. cit.

40. United Nations. 2010. "Millennium Development Goals Report". http://www.un.org/millenniumgoals/pdf/MDG%20Report%202010%20En%20r15%20-low%20res%2020100615%20-.pdf

41. United Nations Women Watch. 2012. "Facts & Figures: Rural Women and the Millennium Development Goals". www.un.org/womenwatch/feature/ruralwomen/facts-figures.html

42. World Bank. 2012. "World Development Report: Gender Equality and Development." http://siteresources.worldbank.org/INTWDR2012/Resources/7778105-1299699968583/7786210-1315936222006/Complete-Report.pdf

43. UNESCO. 2014. "Education for All Global Monitoring Report 2013-14". op. cit.

44. Ibid.

45. Ibid.

46. Ibid.

47. Ibid.

48. UNESCO. 2013. "Education Transforms Lives". http://unesdoc.unesco.org/images/0022/002231/223115E.pdf

49. UNESCO. 2014. "Education for All Global Monitoring Report 2013/14". http://unesdoc.unesco.org/images/0022/002256/225660e.pdf, op. cit.

50. Ibid.

51. World Bank. 2012. "World Development Report 2012: Gender Equality and Development", op. cit.

52. UN Statistics Division/UN Women. 2014. "MDGs Gender Chart". http://www.unwomen.org/~/media/headquarters/attachments/sections/library/publications/2014/gender%20gap%202014%20for%20web%20pdf.ashx

53. UN Women. 2014. "Women & Poverty". http://beijing20.unwomen.org/eninfographic/poverty

54. ILO. 2010. "Women in labour markets: measuring progress and identifying challenges", p.3. http://www.ilo.org/wcmsp5/groups/public/---ed_emp/---emp_elm/---trends/documents/publication/wcms_123835.pdf

55. World Bank. 2013. "Women, Business and the Law 2014". http://wbl.worldbank.org/~/media/FPDKM/WBL/Documents/Reports/2014/Women-Business-and-the-Law-2014-FullReport.pdf

56. Booz and Company. 2012. "Empowering the Third Billion: Women and the World of Work in 2012." http://www.strategyand.pwc.com/media/uploads/Strategyand_Empowering-the-Third-Billion_Full-Report.pdf

57. J. Aker, R. Boumnijel, A. McClelland, and N. Tierne. 2013. "How Do Electronic Transfers Compare? Evidence from a Mobile Money Cash Transfer Experiment in Niger." Tufts University Working Paper (Tufts University, Massachusetts). http://sites.tufts.edu/jennyaker/files/2010/02/Zap-it-to-Me_12sept2013_No-Appendices.pdf

58. N. Kabeer. 2012. "Women's economic empowerment and inclusive growth: labour markets and enterprise development". http://www.idrc.ca/EN/Documents/NK-WEE-Concept-Paper.pdf

59. Booz and Company. 2012. "Empowering the Third Billion: Women and the World of Work in 2012," op. cit.

60. Ibid.

61. L. Rubalcava et al. 2008. "Investments, time preferences and public transfers paid to women". Economic Development and Cultural Change, Vol. 57, No. 3, pp.507–538. https://scholars.duke.edu/display/pub802127

62. D. Thomas (1990) "Intra-Household Resource Allocation: An Inferential Approach," pp. 635–664, *The Journal of Human Resources,* Vol. 25, No. 4 University of Wisconsin Press http://www.jstor.org/

63. GSMA, Cherie Blair Foundation for Women, Women and Mobile and Vital Wave, Inc. 2010. "Women and Mobile: A Global Opportunity". http://www.gsma.com/mobilefordevelopment/wp-content/uploads/2013/01/GSMA_Women_and_Mobile-A_Global_Opportunity.pdf

64. Intel. 2013. "Women and the Web". http://www.intel.com/content/dam/www/public/us/en/documents/pdf/women-and-the-web.pdf

65. GSMA et. al. 2010. "Women and Mobile: A Global Opportunity." op. cit.

66. World Bank. 2009. "Economic Impacts of Broadband in Information and Communications for Development: Extending Reach and Increasing Impact".

67. Intel. 2013. "Women and the Web", op. cit.

68. GSMA. 2015. "The Connected Women Opportunity". http://www.gsma.com/connectedwomen/the-connected-women-opportunity/

69. World Bank. 2009. "Poor People Using Mobile Financial Services: Observations on Customer Usage and Impact from M-PESA." https://openknowledge.worldbank.org/bitstream/handle/10986/9492/503060BRI0Box31MPESA1Brief01PUBLIC1.pdf?sequence=1

70. C. Manfre and C. Nordehn. 2013. "Exploring the promise of information and communication technologies for women farmers in Kenya". http://agrilinks.org/sites/default/files/resource/files/MEAS%20CS%20Kenya%20-%20Women%20

and%20ICT%20-%20Manfre%20et%20al%20-%20
August%202013.pdf

71. Recommended by: G20. 2014. "The Opportunities of Digitizing
Payments". https://docs.gatesfoundation.org/documents/
G20%20Report_Final.pdf

72. The recommended indicators can be explored at: http://
genderstats.org/. Examples include youth literacy rate, by
sex; maternal mortality ratio; prevalence of female genital
mutilation/cutting; proportion of adult population owning land,
by sex; and share of female judges.

73. Bread for the World. 2015. "Hunger Report". Online
supplementary material: http://hungerreport.org/
missingdata/

74. Clinton Foundation. "No Ceilings: The Full Participation
Project". https://www.clintonfoundation.org/our-work/
no-ceilings-full-participation-project

75. Data2X. 2014. http://data2x.org/

76. Sustainable Development Solutions Network. "Towards a Data
Revolution". http://unsdsn.org/. See also: http://unsdsn.org/
resources/publications/indicators/

Critical Thinking

1. In what ways is poverty sexist?
2. What are the various ways in which poverty can be eliminated by addressing gender issues?
3. Why do we need a "data revolution"?

Internet References

Finca
   http://www.finca.org/
UN Women
   http://beijing20.unwomen.org/en/in-focus/poverty

Unit 6

UNIT

Prepared by: Elvio Angeloni, *Pasadena City College*

Religion, Belief, and Ritual

The anthropological interest in religion, belief, and ritual is not concerned with the scientific validity of such phenomena but rather with the way in which people relate various concepts of the supernatural to their everyday lives. From this practical perspective, some anthropologists have found that some traditional spiritual healing is just as helpful in the treatment of illness as is modern medicine; that religious beliefs and practices may be a form of social control; and that mystical beliefs and rituals are not absent from the modern world. In other words, this unit shows religion, belief, and ritual in relationship to practical human affairs. The placing of belief systems in social context thus helps to not only counter popular stereotypes, but also serves to promote a greater understanding of and appreciation for other viewpoints.

Every society is composed of feeling, thinking, and acting human beings who, at one time or another, are either conforming to or altering the social order into which they were born. Religion is an ideological framework that gives special legitimacy and validity to human experience within any given sociocultural system. In this way, monogamy as a marriage form, or monarchy as a political form, ceases to be simply one of many alternative ways in which a society can be organized, but becomes, for the believer, the only legitimate way. Religion considers certain human values and activities as sacred and inviolable. It is this mythic function that helps explain the strong ideological attachments that some people have, regardless of the scientific merits of their points of view.

While, under some conditions, religion may in fact be "the opiate of the masses," under other conditions such a belief system may be a rallying point for social and economic protest. A contemporary example of the former might be the "Moonies" (members of the Unification Church founded by Sun Myung Moon), while a good example of the latter is the role of the Black Church in the American Civil Rights movement, along with the prominence of religious figures such as Martin Luther King Jr. and Jesse Jackson. A word of caution must be set forth concerning attempts to understand belief systems of other cultures. At times, the prevailing attitude seems to be, "What I believe in is religion, and what you believe in is superstition." While anthropologists generally do not subscribe to this view, some tend to explain such behavior as incomprehensible and impractical without considering its full meaning and function within its cultural context. The articles in this unit should serve as a strong warning concerning the pitfalls of that approach.

Article   Prepared by: Elvio Angeloni, *Pasadena City College*

The Adaptive Value of Religious Ritual

Rituals promote group cohesion by requiring members to engage in behavior that is too costly to fake.

RICHARD SOSIS

Learning Outcomes

After reading this article, you will be able to:

- Explain how beliefs about the supernatural contribute to a sense of personal security, individual responsibility, and social harmony.

- Discuss the relationship between the demands upon members of a religious group and the levels of devotion and commitment achieved.

I was 15 years old the first time I went to Jerusalem's Old City and visited the 2,000-year-old remains of the Second Temple, known as the Western Wall. It may have foreshadowed my future life as an anthropologist, but on my first glimpse of the ancient stones I was more taken by the people standing at the foot of the structure than by the wall itself. Women stood in the open sun, facing the Wall in solemn worship, wearing long-sleeved shirts, head coverings and heavy skirts that scraped the ground. Men in their thick beards, long black coats and fur hats also seemed oblivious to the summer heat as they swayed fervently and sang praises to God. I turned to a friend, "Why would anyone in their right mind dress for a New England winter only to spend the afternoon praying in the desert heat?" At the time I thought there was no rational explanation and decided that my fellow religious brethren might well be mad.

Of course, "strange" behavior is not unique to ultraorthodox Jews. Many religious acts appear peculiar to the outsider. Pious adherents the world over physically differentiate themselves from others: Moonies shave their heads, Jain monks of India wear contraptions on their heads and feet to avoid killing insects, and clergy almost everywhere dress in outfits that distinguish them from the rest of society. Many peoples also engage in some form of surgical alteration. Australian aborigines perform a ritual operation on adolescent boys in which a bone or a stone is inserted into the penis through an incision in the urethra. Jews and Muslims submit their sons to circumcision, and in some Muslim societies daughters are also subject to circumcision or other forms of genital mutilation. Groups

as diverse as the Nuer of Sudan and the latmul of New Guinea force their adolescents to undergo ritual scarification. Initiation ceremonies, otherwise known as rites of passage, are often brutal. Among Native Americans, Apache boys were forced to bathe in icy water, Luiseno initiates were required to lie motionless while being bitten by hordes of ants, and Tukuna girls had their hair plucked out.

How can we begin to understand such behavior? If human beings are rational creatures, then why do we spend so much time, energy and resources on acts that can be so painful or, at the very least, uncomfortable? Archaeologists tell us that our species has engaged in ritual behavior for at least 100,000 years, and every known culture practices some form of religion. It even survives covertly in those cultures where governments have attempted to eliminate spiritual practices. And, despite the unparalleled triumph of scientific rationalism in the 20th century, religion continued to flourish. In the United States a steady 40 percent of the population attended church regularly throughout the century. A belief in God (about 96 percent), the afterlife (about 72 percent), heaven (about 72 percent) and hell (about 58 percent) remained substantial and remarkably constant. Why do religious beliefs, practices and institutions continue to be an essential component of human social life?

Such questions have intrigued me for years. Initially my training in anthropology did not provide an answer. Indeed, my studies only increased my bewilderment. I received my training in a subfield known as human behavioral ecology, which studies the adaptive design of behavior with attention to its ecological setting. Behavioral ecologists assume that natural selection has shaped the human nervous system to respond successfully to varying ecological circumstances. All organisms must balance trade-offs: Time spent doing one thing prevents them from pursuing other activities that can enhance their survival or reproductive success. Animals that maximize the rate at which they acquire resources, such as food and mates, can maximize the number of descendants, which is exactly what the game of natural selection is all about.

Behavioral ecologists assume that natural selection has designed our decision-making mechanisms to optimize the rate at which human beings accrue resources under diverse ecological conditions—a basic prediction of *optimal foraging theory*. Optimality models offer predictions of the "perfectly adapted" behavioral response, given a set of environmental constraints. Of course, a perfect fit with the environment is almost never achieved because organisms rarely have perfect information and because environments are always changing. Nevertheless, this assumption has provided a powerful framework to analyze a variety of decisions, and most research (largely conducted among foraging populations) has shown that our species broadly conforms to these expectations.

If our species is designed to optimize the rate at which we extract energy from the environment, why would we engage in religious behavior that seems so counterproductive? Indeed, some religious practices, such as ritual sacrifices, are a conspicuous display of wasted resources. Anthropologists can explain why foragers regularly share their food with others in the group, but why would anyone share their food with a dead ancestor by burning it to ashes on an altar? A common response to this question is that people believe in the efficacy of the rituals and the tenets of the faith that give meaning to the ceremonies. But this response merely begs the question. We must really ask why natural selection has favored a psychology that believes in the supernatural and engages in the costly manifestations of those beliefs.

Ritual Sacrifice

Behavioral ecologists have only recently begun to consider the curiosities of religious activities, so at first I had to search other disciplines to understand these practices. The scholarly literature suggested that I wasn't the only one who believed that intense religious behavior was a sign of madness. Some of the greatest minds of the past two centuries, such as Marx and Freud, supported my thesis. And the early anthropological theorists also held that spiritual beliefs were indicative of a primitive and simple mind. In the 19th century, Edward B. Tylor, often noted as one of the founding fathers of anthropology, maintained that religion arose out of a misunderstanding among "primitives" that dreams are real. He argued that dreams about deceased ancestors might have led the primitives to believe that spirits can survive death.

Eventually the discipline of anthropology matured, and its practitioners moved beyond the equation that "primitive equals irrational." Instead, they began to seek functional explanations of religion. Most prominent among these early 20th-century theorists was the Polish-born anthropologist Bronislaw Malinowski. He argued that religion arose out of "the real tragedies of human life, out of the conflict between human plans and realities." Although religion may serve to allay our fears of death, and provide comfort from our incessant search for answers, Malinowski's thesis did not seem to explain the origin of rituals. Standing in the midday desert sun in several layers of black clothing seems more like a recipe for increasing anxiety than treating it. The classical anthropologists didn't have the right answers to my questions. I needed to look elsewhere.

Fortunately, a new generation of anthropologists has begun to provide some explanations. It turns out that the strangeness of

religious practices and their inherent costs are actually the critical features that contribute to the success of religion as a universal cultural strategy and why natural selection has favored such behavior in the human lineage. To understand this unexpected benefit we need to recognize the adaptive problem that ritual behavior solves. William Irons, a behavioral ecologist at Northwestern University, has suggested that the universal dilemma is the promotion of cooperation within a community. Irons argues that the primary adaptive benefit of religion is its ability to facilitate cooperation within a group—while hunting, sharing food, defending against attacks and waging war—all critical activities in our evolutionary history. But, as Irons points out, although everyone is better off if everybody cooperates, this ideal is often very difficult to coordinate and achieve. The problem is that an individual is even better off if everyone else does the cooperating, while he or she remains at home enjoying an afternoon siesta. Cooperation requires social mechanisms that prevent individuals from free riding on the efforts of others. Irons argues that religion is such a mechanism.

The key is that religious rituals are a form of communication, which anthropologists have long maintained. They borrowed this insight from ethologists who observed that many species engage in patterned behavior, which they referred to as "ritual." Ethologists recognized that ritualistic behaviors served as a form of communication between members of the same species, and often between members of different species. For example, the males of many avian species engage in courtship rituals—such as bowing, head wagging, wing waving and hopping (among many other gestures)—to signal their amorous intents before a prospective mate. And, of course, the vibration of a rattlesnake's tail is a powerful threat display to other species that enter its personal space.

Irons's insight is that religious activities signal commitment to other members of the group. By engaging in the ritual, the member effectively says, "I identify with the group and I believe in what the group stands for." Through its ability to signal commitment, religious behavior can overcome the problem of free riders and promote cooperation within the group. It does so because trust lies at the heart of the problem: A member must assure everyone that he or she will participate in acquiring food or in defending the group. Of course, hunters and warriors may make promises—"you have my word, I'll show up tomorrow"—but unless the trust is already established such statements are not believable.

It turns out that there is a robust way to secure trust. Israeli biologist Amotz Zahavi observes that it is often in the best interest of an animal to send a dishonest signal—perhaps to fake its size, speed, strength, health or beauty. The only signal that can be believed is one that is too costly to fake, which he referred to as a "handicap." Zahavi argues that natural selection has favored the evolution of handicaps. For example, when a springbok antelope spots a predator it often *stots*—it jumps up and down. This extraordinary behavior puzzled biologists for years: Why would an antelope waste precious energy that could be used to escape the predator? And why would the animal make itself more visible to something that wants to eat it? The reason is that the springbok is displaying its quality to

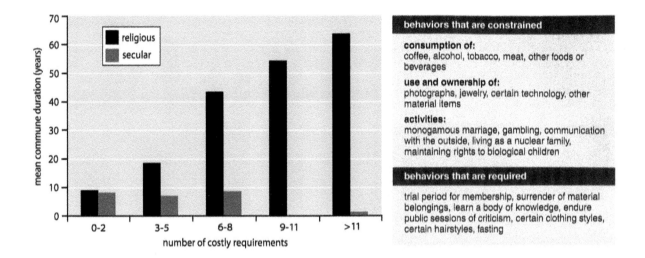

behaviors that are constrained

consumption of:
coffee, alcohol, tobacco, meat, other foods or beverages

use and ownership of:
photographs, jewelry, certain technology, other material items

activities:
monogamous marriage, gambling, communication with the outside, living as a nuclear family, maintaining rights to biological children

behaviors that are required

trial period for membership, surrender of material belongings, learn a body of knowledge, endure public sessions of criticism, certain clothing styles, certain hairstyles, fasting

the predator—its ability to escape, effectively saying, "Don't bother chasing me. Look how strong my legs are, you won't be able to catch me." The only reason a predator believes the springbok is because the signal is too costly to fake. An antelope that is not quick enough to escape cannot imitate the signal because it is not strong enough to repeatedly jump to a certain height. Thus, a display can provide honest information if the signals are so costly to perform that lower quality organisms cannot benefit by imitating the signal.

In much the same way, religious behavior is also a costly signal. By donning several layers of clothing and standing out in the midday sun, ultraorthodox Jewish men are signaling to others: "Hey! Look, I'm a *haredi* Jew. If you are also a member of this group you can trust me because why else would I be dressed like this? No one would do this *unless* they believed in the teachings of ultraorthodox Judaism and were fully committed to its ideals and goals." The quality that these men are signaling is their level of commitment to a specific religious group.

Adherence to a set of religious beliefs entails a host of ritual obligations and expected behaviors. Although there may be physical or psychological benefits associated with some ritual practices, the significant time, energy and financial costs involved serve as effective deterrents for anyone who does not believe in the teachings of a particular religion. There is no incentive for nonbelievers to join or remain in a religious group, because the costs of maintaining membership—such as praying three times a day, eating only kosher food, donating a certain part of your income to charity and so on—are simply too high.

Those who engage in the suite of ritual requirements imposed by a religious group can be trusted to believe sincerely in the doctrines of their respective religious communities. As a result of increased levels of trust and commitment among group members, religious groups minimize costly monitoring mechanisms that are otherwise necessary to overcome free-rider problems that typically plague communal pursuits. Hence, the adaptive benefit of ritual behavior is its ability to promote and maintain cooperation, a challenge that our ancestors presumably faced throughout our evolutionary history.

Benefits of Membership

One prediction of the "costly signaling theory of ritual" is that groups that impose the greatest demands on their members will elicit the highest levels of devotion and commitment. Only committed members will be willing to dress and behave in ways that differ from the rest of society. Groups that maintain more-committed members can also offer more because it's easier for them to attain their collective goals than groups whose members are less committed. This may explain a paradox in the religious marketplace: Churches that require the most of their adherents are experiencing rapid rates of growth. For example, the Church of Jesus Christ of Latter-day Saints (Mormons), Seventh-day Adventists and Jehovah's Witnesses, who respectively abstain from caffeine, meat and blood transfusions (among other things), have been growing at exceptional rates. In contrast, liberal Protestant denominations such as the Episcopalians, Methodists and Presbyterians have been steadily losing members.

Economist Lawrence Iannaccone, of George Mason University, has also noted that the most demanding groups also have the greatest number of committed members. He found that the more distinct a religious group was—how much the group's lifestyle differed from mainstream America—the higher its attendance rates at services. Sociologists Roger Finke and Rodney Stark, of Penn State and the University of Washington, respectively, have argued that when the Second Vatican Council in 1962 repealed many of the Catholic Church's prohibitions and reduced the level of strictness in the church, it initiated a decline in church attendance among American Catholics and reduced the enrollments in seminaries. Indeed, in the late 1950s almost 75 percent of American Catholics were attending Mass weekly, but since the Vatican's actions there has been a steady decline to the current rate of about 45 percent.

The costly signaling theory of ritual also predicts that greater commitment will translate into greater cooperation within groups. My colleague Eric Bressler, a graduate student at McMaster University, and I addressed this question by looking at data from the records of 19th-century communes. All

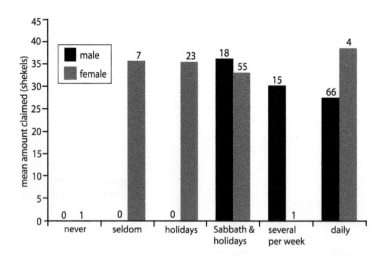

communes face an inherent problem of promoting and sustaining cooperation because individuals can free ride on the efforts of others. Because cooperation is key to a commune's survival, we employed commune longevity as a measure of cooperation. Compared to their secular counterparts, the religious communes did indeed demand more of their members, including such behavior as celibacy, the surrender of all material possessions and vegetarianism. Communes that demanded more of their members survived longer, overcoming the fundamental challenges of cooperation. By placing greater demands on their members, they were presumably able to elicit greater belief in and commitment toward the community's common ideology and goals.

I also wanted to evaluate the costly signaling theory of ritual within modern communal societies. The kibbutzim I had visited in Israel as a teenager provided an ideal opportunity to examine these hypotheses. For most of their 100-year history, these communal societies have lived by the dictum, "From each according to his abilities, to each according to his needs." The majority of the more than 270 kibbutzim are secular (and often ideologically antireligious); fewer than 20 are religiously oriented. Because of a massive economic failure—a collective debt of more than $4 billion—the kibbutzim are now moving in the direction of increased privatization and reduced communality. When news of the extraordinary debt surfaced in the late 1980s, it went largely unnoticed that the religious kibbutzim were financially stable. In the words of the Religious Kibbutz Movement Federation, "the economic position of the religious kibbutzim is sound, and they remain uninvolved in the economic crisis."

The success of the religious kibbutzim is especially remarkable given that many of their rituals inhibit economic productivity. For example, Jewish law does not permit Jews to milk cows on the Sabbath. Although rabbinic rulings now permit milking by kibbutz members to prevent the cows from suffering, in the early years none of this milk was used commercially. There are also significant constraints imposed by Jewish law on agricultural productivity. Fruits are not allowed to be eaten for the first few years of the tree's life, agricultural fields must lie fallow every seven years, and the corners of fields can never

be harvested—they must be left for society's poor. Although these constraints appear detrimental to productivity, the costly signaling theory of ritual suggests that they may actually be the key to the economic success of the religious kibbutzim.

I decided to study this issue with economist Bradley Ruffle of Israel's Ben Gurion University. We developed a game to determine whether there were differences in how the members of secular and religious kibbutzim cooperated with each other. The game involves two members from the same kibbutz who remain anonymous to each other. Each member is told there are 100 shekels in an envelope to which both members have access. Each participant decides how many shekels to withdraw and keep. If the sum of both requests exceeds 100 shekels, both members receive no money and the game is over. However, if the requests are less than or equal to 100 shekels, the money remaining in the envelope is increased by 50 percent and divided evenly among the participants. Each member also keeps the original amount he or she requested. The game is an example of a common-pool resource dilemma in which publicly accessible goods are no longer available once they are consumed. Since the goods are available to more than one person, the maintenance of the resources requires individual self-restraint; in other words, cooperation.

After we controlled for a number of variables, including the age and size of the kibbutz and the amount of privatization, we found not only that religious kibbutzniks were more cooperative with each other than secular kibbutzniks, but that male religious kibbutz members were also significantly more cooperative than female members. Among secular kibbutzniks we found no sex differences at all. This result is understandable if we appreciate the types of rituals and demands imposed on religious Jews. Although there are a variety of requirements that are imposed equally on males and females, such as keeping kosher and refraining from work on the Sabbath, male rituals are largely performed in public, whereas female rituals are generally pursued privately. Indeed, none of the three major requirements imposed exclusively on women—attending a ritual bath, separating a portion of dough when baking bread and lighting Shabbat and holiday candles—are publicly performed. They are not rituals that signal commitment to a wider group; instead they appear to signal commitment to the family. Men, however, engage in highly visible rituals, most notably public prayer, which they are expected to perform three times a day. Among male religious kibbutz members, synagogue attendance is positively correlated with cooperative behavior. There is no similar correlation among females. This is not surprising given that women are not required to attend services, and so their presence does not signal commitment to the group. Here the costly signaling theory of ritual provides a unique explanation of these findings. We expect that further work will provide even more insight into the ability of ritual to promote trust, commitment and cooperation.

We know that many other species engage in ritual behaviors that appear to enhance trust and cooperation. For example, anthropologists John Watanabe of Dartmouth University and Barbara Smuts at the University of Michigan have shown that greetings between male olive baboons serve to signal trust and commitment between former rivals. So why are human rituals often cloaked in mystery and the supernatural? Cognitive anthropologists Scott Atran of the University of Michigan and Pascal Boyer at Washington University in St. Louis have pointed out that the counterintuitive nature of supernatural concepts are more easily remembered than mundane ideas, which facilitates their cultural transmission. Belief in supernatural agents such as gods, spirits and ghosts also appears to be critical to religion's ability to promote long-term cooperation. In our study of 19th-century communes, Eric Bressler and I found that the strong positive relationship between the number of costly requirements imposed on members and commune longevity only held for religious communes, not secular ones. We were surprised by this result because secular groups such as militaries and fraternities appear to successfully employ costly rituals to maintain cooperation. Cultural ecologist Roy Rappaport explained, however, that although religious and secular rituals can both promote cooperation, religious rituals ironically generate greater belief and commitment because they sanctify unfalsifiable statements that are beyond the possibility of examination. Since statements containing supernatural elements, such as "Jesus is the son of God," cannot be proved or disproved, believers verify them "emotionally." In contrast to religious propositions, the kibbutz's guiding dictum, taken from Karl Marx, is not beyond question; it can be evaluated by living according to its directives by distributing labor and resources appropriately. Indeed, as the economic situation on the kibbutzim has worsened, this fundamental proposition of kibbutz life has been challenged and is now disregarded by many who are pushing their communities to accept differential pay scales. The ability of religious rituals to evoke emotional experiences that can be associated with enduring supernatural concepts and symbols differentiates them from both animal and secular rituals and lies at the heart of their efficiency in promoting and maintaining long-term group cooperation and commitment.

Evolutionary research on religious behavior is in its infancy, and many questions remain to be addressed. The costly signaling theory of ritual appears to provide some answers, and, of course, it has given me a better understanding of the questions I asked as a teenager. The real value of the costly signaling theory of ritual will be determined by its ability to explain religious

phenomena across societies. Most of us, including ultraorthodox Jews, are not living in communes. Nevertheless, contemporary religious congregations that demand much of their members are able to achieve a close-knit social community—an impressive accomplishment in today's individualistic world.

Religion has probably always served to enhance the union of its practitioners; unfortunately, there is also a dark side to this unity. If the intragroup solidarity that religion promotes is one of its significant adaptive benefits, then from its beginning religion has probably always played a role in intergroup conflicts. In other words, one of the benefits for individuals of intragroup solidarity is the ability of unified groups to defend and compete against other groups. This seems to be as true today as it ever was, and is nowhere more apparent than the region I visited as a 15-year-old boy—which is where I am as I write these words. As I conduct my fieldwork in the center of this war zone, I hope that by appreciating the depth of the religious need in the human psyche, and by understanding this powerful adaptation, we can learn how to promote cooperation rather than conflict.

References

Atran, S. 2002. *In Gods We Trust.* New York: Oxford University Press.

Iannaccone, L. 1992. Sacrifice and stigma: Reducing free-riding in cults, communes, and other collectives. *Journal of Political Economy* 100:271–291.

Iannaccone, L. 1994. Why strict churches are strong. *American Journal of Sociology* 99:1180–1211.

Irons, W. 2001. Religion as a hard-to-fake sign of commitment. In *Evolution and the Capacity for Commitment,* ed. R. Nesse, pp. 292–309. New York: Russell Sage Foundation.

Rappaport, R. 1999. *Ritual and Religion in the Making of Humanity.* Cambridge: Cambridge University Press.

Sosis, R. 2003. Why aren't we all Hutterites? Costly signaling theory and religious behavior. *Human Nature* 14:91–127.

Sosis, R., and C. Alcorta. 2003. Signaling, solidarity, and the sacred: The evolution of religious behavior. *Evolutionary Anthropology* 12:264–274.

Sosis, R., and E. Bressler. 2003. Cooperation and commune longevity: A test of the costly signaling theory of religion. *Cross-Cultural Research* 37:211–239.

Sosis, R., and B. Ruffle. 2003. Religious ritual and cooperation: Testing for a relationship on Israeli religious and secular kibbutzim. *Current Anthropology* 44:713–722.

Zahavi, A., and A. Zahavi. 1997. *The Handicap Principle.* New York: Oxford University Press.

Critical Thinking

1. What is the universal dilemma with regard to cooperation in a community, according to William Irons?

2. In what sense is religious ritual a form of communication?

3. What is the only kind of signal that can be believed? How does the example of the springbok antelope illustrate the point?

4. Why is there no incentive for nonbelievers to join or remain in a religious group? Are there costly monitoring mechanisms? Explain.

5. What is the relationship between demands upon members and levels of devotion and commitment? What paradox does this explain?

6. What groups have the most committed members?

7. What was observed among American Catholics once the Vatican Council reduced the level of strictness in the church?

8. Which 19th-century communes survived long and why?

9. Which kibbutzim survived better and why? What constraints existed among the religious kibbutzim and what effect did they have?

10. Describe the overall results of the game experiment with regard to religious versus secular kibbutzim and men versus women.

11. Why are religious rituals more successful at promoting belief than are secular rituals?

12. What is the "dark side" to the unity provided by religious intragroup solidarity?

Create Central

www.mhhe.com/createcentral

Internet References

Apologetics Index
www.apologeticsindex.org/site/index-c

Journal of Anthropology of Religion
www.mehtapress.com/social-science-a-humanities/
journal-of-anthropology-of-religion.html

RICHARD SOSIS is an assistant professor of anthropology at the University of Connecticut. His research interests include the evolution of cooperation, utopian societies and the behavioral ecology of religion. Address: Department of Anthropology, U-2176, University of Connecticut, Storrs, CT 06269–2176. Internet: richard.sosis@uconn.edu

Sosis, Richard. From *American Scientist*, March/April 2004, pp. 166–172. Copyright © 2004 by American Scientist, magazine of Sigma Xi, The Scientific Research Society. Reprinted by permission.

Article   Prepared by: Elvio Angeloni, *Pasadena City College*

Understanding Islam

KENNETH JOST

Learning Outcomes

After reading this article, you will be able to:

- Describe the basic tenets of Islam.
- Discuss whether Islam really clashes with Western values.

Is Islam Compatible with Western Values?

With more than 1 billion adherents, Islam is the world's second-largest religion after Christianity. Within its mainstream traditions, Islam teaches piety, virtue and tolerance. Ever since the Sept. 11, 2001, terrorist attacks in the United States, however, many Americans have associated Islam with the fundamentalist groups that preach violence against the West and regard "moderate" Muslims as heretics. Mainstream Muslims and religious scholars say Islam is wrongly blamed for the violence and intolerance of a few. But some critics say Muslims have not done enough to oppose terrorism and violence. They also contend that Islam's emphasis on a strong relationship between religion and the state is at odds with Western views of secularism and pluralism. Some Muslims are calling for a more progressive form of Islam. But radical Islamist views are attracting a growing number of young Muslims in the Islamic world and in Europe.

Overview

Aishah Azmi was dressed all in black, her face veiled by a *niqab* that revealed only her brown eyes through a narrow slit.

"Muslim women who wear the veil are not aliens," the 24-year-old suspended bilingual teaching assistant told reporters in Leeds, England, on Oct. 19. "Integration [of Muslims into British society] requires people like me to be in the workplace so that people can see that we are not to be feared or mistrusted."

But school officials defended their decision to suspend Azmi for refusing to remove her veil in class with a male teacher, saying it interfered with her ability to communicate with her students—most of them Muslims and, like Azmi, British Asians.

"The school and the local authority had to balance the rights of the children to receive the best quality education possible and Mrs. Azmi's desire to express her cultural beliefs," said local Education Minister Jim Dodds.

Although an employment tribunal rejected Azmi's discrimination and harassment claims, it said the school council had handled her complaint poorly and awarded her 1,100 British pounds—about $2,300.

Azmi's widely discussed case has become part of a wrenching debate in predominantly Christian England over relations with the country's growing Muslim population.

In September, a little more than a year after subway and bus bombings in London claimed 55 lives, a government minister called on Muslim parents to do more to steer their children away from violence and terrorism. Then, in October, a leaked report being prepared by the interfaith adviser of the Church of England complained that what he called the government's policy of "privileged attention" toward Muslims had backfired and was creating increased "disaffection and separation."

The simmering controversy grew even hotter after Jack Straw, leader of the House of Commons and former foreign secretary under Prime Minister Tony Blair, called full-face veils "a visible statement of separation and difference" that promotes separatism between Muslims and non-Muslims. Straw, whose constituency in northwestern England includes an estimated 25 percent Muslim population aired the comments in a local newspaper column.

Hamid Qureshi, chairman of the Lancashire Council of Mosques, called Straw's remarks "blatant Muslim-bashing."

"Muslims feel they are on center stage, and everybody is Muslim-bashing," says Anjum Anwar, the council's director of education. "They feel very sensitive."

Britain's estimated 1.5 million Muslims—comprising mostly Pakistani or Indian immigrants and their British-born children—are only a tiny fraction of Islam's estimated 1.2 billion adherents worldwide. But the tensions surfacing in the face-veil debate exemplify the increasingly strained relations between the predominantly Christian West and the Muslim world.

The world's two largest religions—Christianity has some 2 billion adherents—have had a difficult relationship at least since the time of the European Crusades against Muslim rulers, or caliphs, almost 1,000 years ago. Mutual suspicion and hostility have intensified since recent terrorist attacks around the world by militant Islamic groups and President George W. Bush proclaimed a worldwide "war on terror" in response to the Sept. 11, 2001, attacks in the United States.

Bush, who stumbled early on by referring to a "crusade" against terrorism, has tried many times since then to dispel perceptions of any official hostility toward Islam or Muslims generally. In Britain, Blair's government has carried on a 40-year-old policy of "multiculturalism" aimed at promoting cohesion among the country's various communities, Muslims in particular.

Despite those efforts, widespread distrust of Islam and Muslims prevails on both sides of the Atlantic. In a recent poll in the United States, 45 percent of those surveyed said they had an unfavorable view of Islam—a higher percentage than registered in a similar poll four years earlier.

British Muslim leaders also say they feel increasingly hostile anti-Muslim sentiments from the general public and government officials. "Muslims are very fearful, frustrated, upset, angry," says Asghar Bukhari, a spokesman for the Muslim Public Affairs Committee in London. "It's been almost like a mental assault on the Muslim psyche here."

As the face-veil debate illustrates, the distrust stems in part from an array of differences between today's Christianity and Islam as variously practiced in the so-called Muslim world, including the growing Muslim diaspora in Europe and North America.

In broad terms, Islam generally regards religion as a more pervasive presence in daily life and a more important source for civil law than contemporary Christianity, according to the British author Paul Grieve, who wrote a comprehensive guide to Islam after studying Islamic history and thought for more than three years. "Islam is a system of rules for all aspects of life," Grieve writes, while Western liberalism limits regulation of personal behavior. In contrast to the secular nation-states of the West, he explains, Islam views the ideal Muslim society as a universal community—such as the *ummah* established by the Prophet Muhammed in the seventh century.

Those theological and cultural differences are reflected, Grieve says, in Westerners' widespread view of Muslims as narrow-minded and extremist. Many Muslims correspondingly view Westerners as decadent and immoral.

The differences also can be seen in the debates over the role Islam plays in motivating terrorist violence by Islamic extremist groups such as al Qaeda and the objections raised by Muslims to what they consider unflattering and unfair descriptions of Islam in the West.

Muslim leaders generally deny responsibility for the violence committed by Islamic terrorists, including the 9/11 terrorist attacks in the United States and subsequent attacks in Indonesia, Spain and England. "Muslim organizations have done more than ever before in trying to advance community cohesion," Anwar says. They also deny any intention to deny freedom of expression, even though Muslims worldwide denounced a Danish cartoonist's satirical portrayal of Muhammad and Pope Benedict XVI's citation of a medieval Christian emperor's description of Islam as a violent religion.

For many Westerners, however, Islam is associated with radical Muslims—known as Islamists—who either advocate or appear to condone violence and who take to the streets to protest unfavorable depictions of Islam. "A lot of traditional or moderate Islam is inert," says Paul Marshall, a senior fellow at

Freedom House's Center for Religious Freedom in Washington. "Many of the people who disagree with radicals don't have a developed position. They keep their heads down."

Meanwhile, many Muslims and non-Muslims alike despair at Islam's sometimes fratricidal intrafaith disputes. Islam split within the first decades of its founding in the seventh century into the Sunni and Shiite (Shia) branches. The Sunni-Shiite conflict helps drive the escalating insurgency in Iraq three years after the U.S.-led invasion ousted Saddam Hussein, a Sunni who pursued generally secularist policies. "A real geopolitical fracturing has taken place in the Muslim world since the end of the colonial era," says Reza Aslan, an Iranian-born Shiite Muslim now a U.S. citizen and author of the book *No god but God*.

The tensions between Islam and the West are on the rise as Islam is surging around the world, growing at an annual rate of about 7 percent. John Voll associate director of the Prince Alwaleed bin Talal Centre for Christian-Muslim Understanding at Georgetown University, notes that the growth is due largely to conversions, not the high birth rates that are driving Hinduism's faster growth.

Moreover, Voll says, Muslims are growing more assertive. "There has been an increase in intensity and an increase in strength in the way Muslims view their place in the world and their place in society," he says.

Teaching assistant Azmi's insistence on wearing the *niqab* exemplifies the new face of Islam in parts of the West. But her choice is not shared by all, or even, most of her fellow Muslim women. "I don't see why she needs to wear it," says Anwar. "She's teaching young children under 11." (Azmi says she wears it because she works with a male classroom teacher.)

Muslim experts generally agree the Koran does not require veils, only modest dress. Observant Muslim women generally comply with the admonition with a head scarf and loose-fitting attire. In particularly conservative cultures, such as Afghanistan under Taliban rule, women cover their entire bodies, including their eyes.

Still, despite the varying practices, many Muslim groups see a disconnect between the West's self-proclaimed tolerance and its pressure on Muslims to conform. "It's a Muslim woman's right to dress as she feels appropriate, given her religious views," says Ibrahim Hooper, director of communications for the Council on American-Islamic Relations in Washington. "But then when somebody actually makes a choice, they're asked not to do that."

Indeed, in Hamtramck, Mich., a judge recently came under fire for throwing out a small-claims case because the Muslim plaintiff refused to remove her full-face veil.

As the debates continue, here are some of the questions being considered:

Is Islam a Religion That Promotes Violence?

Within hours of the London subway and bus bombings on July 7, 2005, the head of the Muslim World League condemned the attacks as un-Islamic. "The heavenly religions, notably Islam, advocate peace and security," said Abdallah al-Turki, secretary-general of the Saudi-funded organization based in Mecca.

The league's statement echoed any number of similar denunciations of Islamist-motivated terrorist attacks issued since 9/11 by Muslims in the United States and around the world. Yet many non-Muslim public officials, commentators, experts and others say Muslims have not done enough to speak out against terrorism committed in the name of their religion.

"Mainstream Muslims have not stepped up to the plate, by and large," says Angel Rabasa, a senior fellow at the Rand Corp., a California think tank, and lead author of a U.S. Air Force-sponsored study, *The Muslim World after 9/11*.

Muslim organizations voice indignant frustration in disputing the accusation. "We can always do more," says Hooper. "The problem is that it never seems to be enough. But that doesn't keep us from trying."

Many Americans, in fact, believe Islam actually encourages violence among its adherents. A CBS poll in April 2006 found that 46 percent of those surveyed believe Islam encourages violence more than other religions. A comparable poll four years earlier registered a lower figure: 32 percent.

Those perceptions are sometimes inflamed by U.S. evangelical leaders. Harsh comments about Islam have come from religious leaders like Franklin Graham, Jerry Falwell, Pat Robertson and Jerry Vines, the former president of the Southern Baptist Convention. Graham called Islam "a very evil and wicked religion," and Vines called Muhammad, Islam's founder and prophet, a "demon-possessed pedophile." Falwell, on the CBS news magazine "60 Minutes" in October 2002, declared, "I think Muhammad was a terrorist."

Mainstream Muslims insist Islam is a peaceful religion and that terrorist organizations distort its tenets and teachings in justifying attacks against the West or other Muslims. But Islamic doctrine and history sometimes seem to justify the use of violence in propagating or defending the faith. The dispute revolves around the meaning of *jihad,* an Arabic word used in the Koran and derived from a root meaning "to strive" or "to make an effort for." Muslim scholars can point to verses in the Koran that depict *jihad* merely as a personal, spiritual struggle and to others that describe *jihad* as encompassing either self-defense or conquest against non-believers.

Georgetown historian Voll notes that, in contrast to Christianity, Islam achieved military success during Muhammad's life and expanded into a major world empire within decades afterward. That history "reinforces the idea that militancy and violence can, in fact, be part of the theologically legitimate plan of the Muslim believer," says Voll.

"Islam, like all religions, has its historical share of violence," acknowledges Stephen Schwartz, an adult convert to Islam and executive director of the Center for Islamic Pluralism in Washington. "But there's no reason to single out Islam."

Modern-day jihadists pack their public manifestos with Koranic citations and writings of Islamic theologians to portray themselves as warriors for Allah and defenders of true Islam. But Voll and others stress that the vast majority of Muslims do not subscribe to their views. "You have a highly visible minority that represents a theologically extreme position in the Muslim world," Voll says.

In particular, writes Seyyed Hossein Nasr, a professor of Islamic studies at George Washington University, Islamic law prohibits the use of force against women, children or civilians— even during war. "Inflicting injuries outside of this context," he writes, "is completely forbidden by Islamic law."

Rabasa says, however, that Muslims who disapprove of terrorism have not said enough or done enough to mobilize opposition to terrorist attacks. "Muslims see themselves as part of a community and are reluctant to criticize radical Muslims," he says.

In addition, many Muslims are simply intimidated from speaking out, he explains. "Radicals are not reluctant to use violence and the threat of violence," he says. Liberal and moderate Muslims are known to receive death threats on their cell phones, even in relatively peaceful Muslim countries such as Indonesia.

Voll also notes that Islamic radicals have simply outorganized the moderates. "There is no moderate organization that even begins to resemble some of the radical organizations that have developed," he says.

In Britain, Bukhari of the Muslim Public Affairs Committee criticizes Muslim leaders themselves for failing to channel young people opposed to Britain's pro-U.S. foreign policy into non-violent political action. "Children who could have been peaceful react to that foreign policy in a way that they themselves become criminals," he says.

The Council on American-Islamic Relations' Hooper details several anti-terrorism pronouncements and drives issued following the London bombings by various Muslim groups and leaders in Britain and in the United States, including *fatwas,* or legal opinions, rejecting terrorism and extremism.

For his part, Omid Safi, an associate professor of Islamic studies at the University of North Carolina in Chapel Hill, points out that virtually every Muslim organization in the United States issued condemnations of violence almost immediately after the 9/11 terrorist attacks.

"How long must we keep answering this question?" Safi asks in exasperation. But he concedes a few moments later that the issue is more than perception. "Muslims must come to terms with our demons," he says, "and one of those demons is violence."

Is Islam Compatible with Secular, Pluralistic Societies?

In 2003, Germany's famed Deutsche Oper staged an avant-garde remake of Mozart's opera "Idomeneo," which dramatizes the composer's criticism of organized religion, with a scene depicting the severed heads of Muhammad, Jesus, Buddha and Poseidon. That production was mounted without incident, but the company dropped plans to restage it in November 2006 after police warned of a possible violent backlash from Muslim fundamentalists.

The cancellation prompted protests from German officials and artistic-freedom advocates in Europe and in the United States, who saw the move as appeasement toward terrorists. Wolfgang Bornsen, a spokesman for conservative Chancellor Angela Merkel, said the cancellation was "a signal" to other artistic companies to avoid any works critical of Islam.

The debate continued even after plans were discussed to mount the production after all—with enhanced security and the blessing of German Muslim leaders. "We live in Europe, where democracy was based on criticizing religion," remarked Philippe Val, editor of the French satirical magazine *Charlie Hebdo*. "If we lose the right to criticize or attack religions in our free countries . . . we are doomed."

As with the issue of violence, Islam's doctrines and history can be viewed as pointing both ways on questions of pluralism and tolerance. "There are a great many passages [in the Koran] that support a pluralistic interpretation of Islam," says the Rand Corp.'s Rabasa. "But you also find a great many that would support an intolerant interpretation."

"Intellectual pluralism is traditional Islam," says Schwartz at the Center for Islamic Pluralism. An oft-quoted verse from the Koran specifically prohibits compulsion in religion, he says. Voll and other historians agree that Muslim countries generally tolerated Christians and Jews, though they were often subject to special taxes or other restrictions.

"Islam is the only major religious system that has built-in protections for minorities," says Hooper at the Council on American-Islamic Relations. "You don't see the kind of persecutions of minorities that we often saw in Europe for hundreds of years. Many members of the Jewish community fled to find safety within the Muslim world."

Even so, Islam's view of religion and politics as inseparable creates difficult issues. Outside the Arab world, most Muslims live in practicing democracies with fair to good human-rights records. But some Muslim countries—Arab and non-Arab—have either adopted or been urged to adopt provisions of Islamic law—*sharia*—that are antithetical to modern ideas of human rights, such as limiting women's rights and prescribing stoning or amputations as criminal penalties.

Muslims participating in a society as a minority population face different issues, according to author Grieve. "Islam is difficult to accommodate in a determinedly secular Western society where almost all views are equally respected, and none is seen as either right or wrong," he writes.

The tensions played out in a number of controversies in recent years were provoked by unflattering depictions of Islam in Europe. A Danish cartoonist's satirical view of Muhammad provoked worldwide protests from Muslim leaders and groups after they were publicized in early 2006. Scattered violence resulted in property damage and more than 30 deaths.

Somewhat similarly, Pope Benedict XVI drew sharp criticism after a Sept. 12, 2006, lecture quoting a medieval Christian emperor's description of Islam as "evil and inhuman." Along with verbal denunciations, protesters in Basra, Iraq, burned an effigy of the pope. Within a week, he disclaimed the remarks and apologized.

Freedom House's Marshall says such controversies, as well as the cancellation of the opera in Berlin, strengthens radical Muslim elements. "Bending to more radical demands marginalizes the voices of moderate Muslims and hands over leadership to the radicals," he says.

Many Muslims in European countries, however, view the controversies—including the current debate over the veil in

Basic Tenets of Islam

Islam is the youngest of the world's three major monotheistic religions. Like the other two, Judaism and Christianity, Islam (the word means both "peace" and "submission") holds there is but one God (Allah). Muslims believe God sent a number of prophets to teach mankind how to live according to His law. Muslims consider Jesus, Moses and Abraham as prophets of God and hold the Prophet Muhammad as his final and most sacred messenger. Many accounts found in Islam's sacred book, the Koran (Qur'an), are also found in sacred writings of Jews and Christians.

There are five basic pillars of Islam:

- Creed—Belief in God and Muhammad as his Prophet.
- Almsgiving—Giving money to charity is considered a sacred duty.
- Fasting—From dawn to dusk during the month of Ramadan.
- Prayer—Five daily prayers must be given facing Mecca, Islam's holiest city.
- Pilgrimage—All Muslims must make a baff to Mecca at least once during their lifetime, if they are physically able.

England—as evidence of pervasive hostility from the non-Muslim majorities. "There is a growing hatred of Muslims in Britain, and anybody who bashes Muslims can only get brownie points," says Bukhari of the Muslim Public Affairs Committee.

"These are not friendly times for Western Muslims," says Safi, at the University of North Carolina. "Whenever people find themselves under assault, opening their arms and opening their hearts is difficult."

Does Islam Need a "Reformation"?

If Pakistan's Punjab University expected a chorus of approval when it decided to launch a master's program in musicology in fall 2006, it was in for a surprise. At the Lahore campus, the conservative Islamic Assembly of Students, known as I.J.T., rose up in protest.

Handbills accused school authorities of forsaking Islamic ideological teachings in favor of "the so-called enlightened moderation" dictated by "foreign masters." Undeterred, administrators opened the program for enrollment in September. When fewer students applied than expected, they blamed the poor response in part on the I.J.T. campaign.

The episode reflects how Islam today is evolving differently in the West and in some parts of the Muslim world. Many Muslim writers and scholars in the United States and Europe are calling for Islam to adapt to modern times by, for example, embracing pluralism and gender equality. Introducing a collection of essays by "progressive" Muslims, the University of North Carolina's Safi says the movement seeks to "start swimming through the rising waters of Islam and modernity, to strive for justice in the midst of society."

In much of the Muslim world, however, Islam is growing—in numbers and intensity—on the strength of literal interpretations of the Koran and exclusivist attitudes toward the non-Muslim world. "In the Muslim world in general, more extreme or reactionary forms of Islam are getting stronger—in Africa, Asia and the Middle East," says Freedom House's Marshall, who has previously worked on issues pertaining to persecution of Christians around the world.

Islamist groups such as I.J.T. talk about "reforming" or "purifying" Islam and adopting Islamic law as the primary or exclusive source of civil law. In fact, one version of reformed Islam—Wahhabism[1] or the currently preferred term Salafism—espouses a literalistic reading of the Koran and a puritanical stance toward such modern practices as listening to music or watching television. It has been instituted in Saudi Arabia and has advanced worldwide because of financial backing from the oil-rich kingdom and its appeal to new generations of Muslims.

"The Salafi movement is a fringe," says the Rand Corp.'s Rabasa. "But it's growing because it's dynamic and revolutionary, whereas traditional Islam tends to be conservative. It has this appeal to young people looking for identity."

But the Center for Islamic Pluralism's Schwartz, an outspoken critic of Salafism, says many Muslims are rejecting it because of its tendency to view other branches of Islam as apostasy. "People are getting sick of this," he says. "They're tired of the social conflict and upheaval."

Voll at the Center for Christian-Muslim Understanding also says some Muslim legal scholars are disputing literalistic readings of *sharia* by contending that the Islamic law cited as divinely ordained is actually "a human construct subject to revision."

Some Western commentators refer to a "reformation" in calling for a more liberal form of Islam. Nicholas D. Kristof, a *New York Times* columnist who focuses on global human-rights issues, sees "hopeful rumblings . . . of steps toward a Muslim Reformation," especially on issues of gender equality. He notes that feminist Muslim scholars are reinterpreting passages in the Koran that other Muslims cite in justifying restrictions on women, such as the Saudi ban on women driving.

Safi says he avoids the term reformation because it has been adopted by Salafists and also because it suggests a need to break from traditional Islam. He says "progressive" Muslims return to the Prophet's vision of the common humanity of all human beings and seek "to hold Muslim societies accountable for justice and pluralism."

Rabasa also says reformation is historically inappropriate as a goal for liberal or progressive Muslims. "What is needed is not an Islamic reformation but an Islamic enlightenment," says Rabasa. The West's liberal tradition, he notes, was produced not by the Reformation but by the Enlightenment—the 18th-century movement that used reason to search for objective truth.

Whatever terms are used, the clash between different visions of Islam will be less susceptible to resolution than analogous disputes within most branches of Christianity because Islam lacks any recognized hierarchical structure. Islam has no pope or governing council. Instead, each believer is regarded as having a direct relationship with God, or Allah, with no ecclesiastical intermediary.

"In the face of contemporary Islam, there is absolutely the sense of an authority vacuum," says Safi. Islam's future, he adds, "is a question that can only be answered by Muslims."

Note

1. Wahhabism originated in the Arabian peninsula in the late 1700s from the teachings of Arabian theologian Muhammand ibn Abd al Wahhab (1703–1792).

Critical Thinking

1. What are the main points of contention regarding the strained relationship between the Christian West and Muslim world?

2. Does Islam encourage violence? Explain.

3. Is Islam compatible with secular, pluralistic societies? Explain.

4. Does Islam need a "Reformation"? Explain.

Create Central

www.mhhe.com/createcentral

Internet References

Journal of Anthropology of Religion
    www.mehtapress.com/social-science-a-humanities/
    journal-of-anthropology-of-religion.html
Journal of Islamic Studies
    http://jis.oxfordjournals.org

Article   Prepared by: Elvio Angeloni, *Pasadena City College*

Five Myths of Terrorism

MICHAEL SHERMER

Learning Outcomes

After reading this article, you will be able to:

- Discuss the actual motives of terrorists in contrast to what is commonly believed.

- Discuss the actual effectiveness of terrorism in contrast to its goals.

Because terrorism educes such strong emotions, it has led to at least five myths. The first began in September 2001, when President George W. Bush announced that "we will rid the world of the evildoers" and that they hate us for "our freedoms." This sentiment embodies what Florida State University psychologist Roy F. Baumeister calls "the myth of pure evil," which holds that perpetrators commit pointless violence for no rational reason.

This idea is busted through the scientific study of aggression, of which psychologists have identified four types that are employed toward a purposeful end (from the perpetrators' perspective): instrumental violence, such as plunder, conquest, and the elimination of rivals; revenge, such as vendettas against adversaries or self-help justice; dominance and recognition, such as competition for status and women, particularly among young males; and ideology, such as religious beliefs or Utopian creeds. Terrorists are motivated by a mixture of all four.

In a study of 52 cases of Islamist extremists who have targeted the U.S. for terrorism, for example, Ohio State University political scientist John Mueller concluded that their motives are often instrumental and revenge-oriented, a "boiling outrage at U.S. foreign policy—the wars in Iraq and Afghanistan, in particular, and the country's support for Israel in the Palestinian conflict." Ideology in the form of religion "was a part of the

consideration for most," Mueller suggests, "but not because they wished to spread Sharia law or to establish caliphates (few of the culprits would be able to spell either word). Rather they wanted to protect their coreligionists against what was commonly seen to be a concentrated war on them in the Middle East by the U.S. government."

As for dominance and recognition, University of Michigan anthropologist Scott Atran has demonstrated that suicide bombers (and their families) are showered with status and honor in this life and the promise of women in the next and that most "belong to loose, homegrown networks of family and friends who die not just for a cause but for each other." Most terrorists are in their late teens or early 20s and "are especially prone to movements that promise a meaningful cause, camaraderie, adventure, and glory," he adds.

Busting a second fallacy—that terrorists are part of a vast global network of top-down centrally controlled conspiracies against the West—Atran shows that it is "a decentralized, self-organizing and constantly evolving complex of social networks." A third flawed notion is that terrorists are diabolical geniuses, as when the 9/11 Commission report described them as "sophisticated, patient, disciplined, and lethal." But according to Johns Hopkins University political scientist Max Abrahms, after the decapitation of the leadership of the top extremist organizations, "terrorists targeting the American homeland have been neither sophisticated nor masterminds, but incompetent fools."

Examples abound: the 2001 airplane shoe bomber Richard Reid was unable to ignite the fuse because it was wet from rain; the 2009 underwear bomber Umar Farouk Abdulmutallab succeeded only in torching his junk; the 2010 Times Square bomber Faisal Shahzad managed merely to burn the inside of his Nissan Pathfinder; and the 2012 model airplane bomber Rezwan Ferdaus purchased faux C-4 explosives from FBI agents. Most recently, the 2013 Boston Marathon bombers appear to have been equipped with only one gun and had no exit strategy beyond hijacking a car low on gas that Dzhokhar Tsarnaev used to run over his brother, Tamerlan, followed by a failed suicide attempt inside a land-based boat.

A fourth fiction is that terrorism is deadly. Compared with the annual average of 13,700 homicides, however, deaths from terrorism are statistically invisible, with a total of 33 in the U.S. since 9/11.

Finally, a fifth figment about terrorism is that it works. In an analysis of 457 terrorist campaigns since 1968, George Mason University political scientist Audrey Cronin found that not one extremist group conquered a state and that a full 94 percent failed to gain even one of their strategic goals. Her 2009 book is entitled *How Terrorism Ends* (Princeton University Press). It ends swiftly (groups survive eight years on average) and badly (the death of its leaders).

We must be vigilant always, of course, but these myths point to the inexorable conclusion that terrorism is nothing like what its perpetrators wish it were.

Critical Thinking

1. Contrast the "myth of pure evil" with the actual motives for terrorist acts.
2. Discuss the notion that terrorists are part of a vast global network.
3. Discuss the evidence for the notion that terrorists are diabolical geniuses.
4. How deadly has terrorism actually been?
5. To what extent does terrorism achieve its goals?

Create Central

www.mhhe.com/createcentral

Internet References

Center for Terrorism and Security Studies
http://www.uml.edu/Research/CTSS/default.aspx
Critical Studies on Terrorism
www.tandfonline.com

Article   Prepared by: Elvio Angeloni

Losing Our Religion

GRAHAM LAWTON

Learning Outcomes

After reading this article, you will be able to:

- Discuss the worldwide trend towards secularization in the modern world and the reasons for it.

- Describe the human mind's receptivity to religious ideas and what it means for a secular society.

- Describe the various kinds of atheism and the reasons for them.

O n an unseasonably warm Sunday morning in London, I do something I haven't done for more than 30 years: get up and go to church. For an hour and a half, I sing, listen to readings, enjoy moments of quiet contemplation and throw a few coins into a collection. At the end there is tea and cake, and a warm feeling in what I guess must be my soul.

This is like hundreds of congregations taking place across the city this morning, but with one notable exception: there is no god.

Welcome to the Sunday Assembly, a "godless congregation" held every other week in Conway Hall, home of the world's oldest free-thought organisation. On the day I went there were at least 200 people in the hall; sometimes as many as 600 turn up.

Founded by comedians Sanderson Jones and Pippa Evans in 2013, the Sunday Assembly aims to supply some of the uplifting features of a religious service without any of the supernatural stuff. Atheism is also off the agenda: the Assembly is simply about celebrating being alive. "Our mission is to help people live this one life as fully as possible," says Jones.

The Assembly's wider goal is "a godless congregation in every town, city and village that wants one". And many do: from a humble start in a deconsecrated church in London, there are now 28 active assemblies in the UK, Ireland, US and Australia. Jones now works full-time to fulfil the demand for more; he expects to have 100 by the end of this year.

The people I joined on that sunny Sunday are a small part of the world's fastest-growing religious identity—the "nones". Comprising non-believers of all stripes, from convinced atheists like me to people who simply don't care about religion, they now number more than some major world religions.

In London, admittedly, they are nothing special. The UK is one of the least religious countries in the world, with around half of the population saying they don't belong to any religion.

But elsewhere, their rise is both rapid and remarkable. A decade ago, more than three-quarters of the world's population identified themselves as religious. Today, less than 60 percent do, and in about a quarter of countries the nones are now a majority. Some of the biggest declines have been seen in countries where religion once seemed part of the furniture, such as Ireland. In 2005, 69 percent of people there said they were religious; now only 47 percent do.

"We have a powerful secularisation trend worldwide," says Ara Norenzayan, a psychologist at the University of British Columbia in Vancouver, Canada. "There are places where secularisation is making huge inroads: western and northern Europe, Canada, Australia, New Zealand, Japan and China."

Even in the US—a deeply Christian country—the number of people expressing "no religious affiliation" has risen from 5 percent in 1972 to 20 percent today; among people under 30, that number is closer to a third.

That's not to say that they have all explicitly rejected religion; only 13 percent of people around the world say they are "committed" atheists. Even so, it means there are almost a billion atheists globally. Only Christianity and Islam can claim more adherents. And alongside them are another billion and a half who, for whatever reason, don't see themselves as religious.

A century ago, these trends would have seemed inevitable. The founders of sociology, Émile Durkheim and Max Weber, expected scientific thinking to lead to the gradual erosion and eventual demise of religion. They saw the rise of humanist, rationalist and free thought organisations in western Europe as the start of a secular revolution.

Born to Believe

It didn't quite work out that way. Although parts of western Europe, Australia, Canada and New Zealand did secularise after the second world war, the rest of the world remained resolutely god-fearing. Even the official atheism of the communist bloc didn't really take hold at grass-roots level.

If anything, at the end of the twentieth century, religion seemed to be resurgent. Fundamentalist movements were gaining ground around the world; Islam was becoming a powerful political force; the US remained stubbornly religious. Increasingly, secular Europe looked like an outlier.

Now, though, secularisation is back in business. "The past 20 years has seen a precipitous decline in religiosity in all societies," says Phil Zuckerman, a sociologist at Pitzer College in Claremont, California. "We are seeing religion withering across the board. Yes, there are pockets of increased fundamentalism, but overall we are seeing rising rates of secularism in societies where we have never seen it before—places like Brazil, Ireland, even in Africa."

So is the nineteenth century prediction of a godless world finally coming true? Is it possible that one day the majority of people will see themselves as non-religious? And if that happens, will the world be a better place?

To answer these questions, we need to know why people believe in god in the first place.

For many, the answer is obvious: because god exists. Whether or not that is the case, it illustrates something very interesting about the nature of religious belief. To most people, probably the vast majority who have ever lived, belief in god is effortless. Like being able to breathe or learning one's native language, faith in god is one of those things that comes naturally.

Why is that? In recent years, cognitive scientists have produced a comprehensive account of the human mind's receptivity to religious ideas. Called cognitive by-product theory, it holds that certain features of human psychology that evolved for non-religious reasons also create fertile ground for god. As a result, when people encounter religious stories and claims, they find them intuitively appealing and plausible.

For example, our early ancestors were regularly on the dinner menu of predators, and so evolved a "hypersensitive agency detection device"—a fancy name for an assumption that events in the environment are caused by sentient beings, or agents. That makes evolutionary sense: when any rustle in the bushes might be a prowling predator it is better to err on the side of caution. But it also primes us to assume agency where there is none. That, of course, is a central claim of most religions: that an unseen agent is responsible for doing and creating things in the world.

Existential Comfort

Humans have evolved other quirks that encourage the spread of religious beliefs. Notions of a benevolent personal god, higher purpose and an afterlife, for example, help people to manage the existential dread and uncertainty that are part of being human.

We also have a tendency to imitate high status individuals—think of modern celebrity culture—and to conform to social norms, both of which promote the spread and maintenance of belief. We are especially impressed by what social scientists call CREDs or "credibility-enhancing displays"—costly and extravagant acts of faith such as fasting, self-flagellation or martyrdom.

Finally, people who think they are being watched tend to behave themselves and cooperate more. Societies that chanced on the idea of supernatural surveillance were likely to have been more successful than those that didn't, further spreading religious ideas.

Taken together, the way our minds work makes us naturally receptive to religious ideas and extremely likely to acquire them when we encounter them. Once humans stumbled on the idea of god, it spread like wildfire.

Cognitive by-product theory is a very successful account of why humans gravitate towards religious ideas. However, it has also been turned on the opposite problem: if belief in god comes so easily, why are there atheists?

Until quite recently, it was widely assumed that people had to reason their way to atheism: they analysed the claims of religion and rejected them on the grounds of implausibility. This explained why atheism was a minority pursuit largely practised by more educated people, and why religion was so prevalent and durable. Overcoming all of those evolved biases, and continuing to do so, requires hard cognitive work.

This "analytical atheism" is clearly an important route to irreligion and might explain some of the recent increase in secularity. It certainly flourishes in places where people are exposed to science and other analytical systems of thought. But it is by no means the only flavour of irreligion. In the US, for example, among the 20 percent of people who say they have no religious affiliation, only about 1 in 10 say they are atheists; the vast majority, 71 percent, are "nothing in particular".

"There are many pathways and motivations for becoming atheist," says Norenzayan. "Disbelief does not always require hard cognitive effort."

So if people aren't explicitly rejecting religious claims, what is causing them to abandon god? To Norenzayan, the answer lies in some of the other psychological biases that make religious ideas so easy to digest.

One of the main motivations for abandoning god is that people increasingly don't need the comfort that belief in god brings. Religion thrives on existential angst: where people feel insecure and uncertain, religion provides succour. But as societies become more prosperous and stable, this security blanket becomes less important.

By this reckoning it is no coincidence that the world's least religious countries also tend to be the most secure. Denmark, Sweden and Norway, for example, are consistently rated as among the most irreligious. They are also among the most prosperous, stable and safe, with universal healthcare and generous social security.

Conversely, the world's most religious countries are among its poorest. And within countries, poorer segments of society tend to be more religious, according to the Global Index of Religion and Atheism.

The link is supported by laboratory studies showing that making people aware of existential threats such as pain, randomness and death temporarily strengthens their belief in god. It seems to hold in the real world too: after the 2011 Christchurch earthquake in New Zealand—normally a stable and safe country with corresponding low levels of religiosity—religious commitment in the area increased.

Norenzayan refers to the kind of atheism that exists in these places as "apatheism". "This is not so much doubting or being sceptical, but more about not caring," he says. "They simply don't think about religion."

Counter-intuitively, he adds, apatheism could also explain the strength of religion in the US. In comparison to other rich nations, the US has high levels of existential angst. A lack of universal healthcare, widespread job insecurity and a feeble social safety net create fertile conditions for religion to flourish.

Another important source of irreligion is "inCREDulous atheism". That doesn't mean incredulous as in unbelieving, but as in not being exposed to CREDs, those dramatic displays of faith. "These have a powerful effect on how religion is transmitted," says Norenzayan. "Where people are willing to die for their beliefs, for example, those beliefs become more contagious. When people don't see extravagant displays, even if they are surrounded by people who claim to believe, then there is some evidence that this leads to decline of religion."

Norenzayan has yet to work out the relative importance of these different routes to atheism, partly because they are mutually reinforcing. But he says his hunch is that apatheism is the most important. "That is probably surprising to a lot of people who think you get atheism by analytical thinking. But I see striking evidence that as societies become more equal and there are social safety nets, secularisation follows," he says.

To some religious proponents, this is evidence that most of the "nones" aren't really atheists at all—a claim that is backed by a recent survey from UK-based Christian think tank Theos. It found that even as formal religion is waning in the UK,

spiritual beliefs are not. Almost 60 percent of adults questioned said they believed in some form of higher power or spiritual being; a mere 13 percent agreed with the line "humans are purely material beings with no spiritual element".

Some scientists—notably Pascal Boyer at Washington University in St Louis—have even claimed that atheism is psychologically impossible because of the way humans think. They point to studies showing, for example, that even people who claim to be committed atheists tacitly hold religious beliefs, such as the existence of an immortal soul.

To Norenzayan, this is all semantics. "Labels don't concern me as much as psychology and behaviour. Do people say they believe in god? Do they go to a church or synagogue or mosque? Do they pray? Do they find meaning in religion? These are the variables that should interest us." By these measures, most of the nones really are irreligious, meaning atheism is much more durable and widespread than would be the case if the only route to atheism was actively rejecting religious ideas.

Nones on the Run

Will the trend continue? On the face of it, it looks unlikely. If godlessness flourishes where there is stability and prosperity, then climate change and environmental degradation could seriously slow the spread of atheism. "If there was a massive natural disaster I would expect a resurgence of religion, even in societies that are secularised," says Norenzayan. The Christchurch earthquake is a case in point.

It is also not clear that European secularisation will be replicated elsewhere. "The path that countries take is historically contingent and there are exceptions," says Stephen Bullivant, a theologian at St Mary's University in the UK and co-editor of *The Oxford Handbook of Atheism*.

Nonetheless, he says, there is widespread agreement that if prosperity, security and democracy continue to advance, secularisation will probably follow. Ireland's shift towards irreligion coincided with its economic boom, says Michael Nugent, chairperson of Atheist Ireland. Interestingly, Ireland is showing no signs of a religious revival despite its recent economic woes, suggesting that once secularisation gets going it is hard to stop.

Ireland's experience also suggests that the most unlikely of places can begin to turn their back on long-held beliefs. "Ireland was always one of Europe's exceptions. If it can happen there it can happen elsewhere—Poland, or even the Philippines," says Bullivant.

And then there's the fact that the US seems to be moving away from god. The "nones" have been the fastest growing religious group there for the past 20 years, especially among young adults. One explanation for this is one of those historical contingencies: the cold war. For decades, Americans defined themselves in opposition to godless communists and atheism was seen as unpatriotic. The generation that grew up after the fall of the Berlin Wall in 1989 are the most irreligious since records began.

Interestingly, after the cold war Russia rebounded in the other direction. In 1991, 61 percent of Russians identified as nones; by 2008, that had dropped to just 18 percent. But even the Russians now seem to have joined the recent secularisation trend: according to the Global Index of Religion and Atheism, only 55 percent of people polled there in 2012 regard themselves as religious.

Bullivant thinks the secularisation trend will continue for another reason: the way religion is passed down the generations. "The strongest predictor of whether a person grows up to be religious is whether their parents are," he says. A child whose parents are actively religious has about a 50 percent chance of following them. A child whose parents are not has only about a 3 percent chance of becoming religious.

"In terms of keeping people, the nonreligious are doing very well indeed," says Bullivant. "It is extremely unusual for somebody brought up in a non-religious household to join a religion, but it is not at all unusual for somebody brought up with a religious affiliation to end up as nonreligious." In the UK, for every 10 people who leave the Catholic church, only one joins—usually from another Christian denomination.

Bullivant also points out that religiosity tends to be fixed by the time people reach their mid-20s. So the 30 percent or so of young people in the US who don't identify with any religion are unlikely to change their minds as they get older, and are likely to pass their irreligion on to their own children. "The very fact that there is such a group, that it is quite big and that there wasn't such a group before is an indicator of secularisation," says Bullivant.

So can the world really give up on god? "I think it is possible," says Norenzayan, "because we are seeing it happen already."

What would a world without god actually look like? One oft-voiced concern is that religion is the moral glue that holds society together, and that if you get rid of it, everything collapses. "That position is constantly articulated in the US—even secular people buy into it," says Zuckerman.

The evidence, however, suggests otherwise. In 2009, Zuckerman ran a global analysis comparing levels of religiosity in various countries with measures of societal health: wealth, equality, women's rights, educational attainment, life expectancy, infant mortality, teenage pregnancy, STI rates, crime rates, suicide rates and murder rates. "On just about every measure of societal health, the more secular a country or a state, the better it does." The same holds for the 50 US states.

That, of course, doesn't necessarily mean that secularism creates a healthy society: perhaps the rise of apatheists is a

consequence rather than a cause. "But it allows us to debunk the notion that religion is necessary for a healthy society," says Zuckerman.

He goes further, however, arguing that secularisation can lead to social improvements. "I now believe there are aspects of the secular world view that contribute to healthy societies," he says. "First, if you believe that this is the only world and there is no afterlife, that's going to motivate you to make it as good a place as possible. Number two is the emphasis on science, education and rational problem-solving that seems to come with the secular orientation—for example, are we going to pray to end crime in our city or are we going to look at the root causes?"

It is also hard to discuss mass atheism without invoking the spectre of the Soviet Union, the Khmer Rouge, North Korea and many other regimes that suppressed or banned religion. Is there a risk that a majority secular world will be more like Stalingrad than Stockholm?

To Zuckerman, there is a very good reason to think not. "I distinguish between coercive atheism that is imposed from above by a dictatorial regime, and organic atheism that emerges in free societies. It is in the latter that we see positive societal health outcomes."

Perhaps a more credible worry is what would happen to our physical and mental health. The past 20 years have seen a great deal of research into the benefits of being religious, and most studies claim to find a small association between religiosity, health and happiness. This is usually explained by religious people leading healthier lifestyles and having strong social support networks.

Some researchers have therefore jumped to the conclusion that if religion brings health and happiness, then atheism must come at a corresponding cost. Yet the link between religion and health is nowhere near as well established as is often claimed. A meta-analysis of 226 such studies, for example, found a litany of methodological problems and erroneous conclusions. What's more, the little research that has been done on atheists' physical and psychological health found no difference between them and religious people. And at a societal level, of course, a greater proportion of atheism is associated with better public health.

But if you think an atheist world would be a paradise of rationality and reason, think again. "When people no longer believe in god, it doesn't mean they don't have intuitions that are powerfully connected to the supernatural," says Norenzayan. "Even in societies that are majority atheist, you find a lot of paranormal belief—astrology, karma, extraterrestrial life, things that don't have any scientific evidence but are intuitively obvious to people."

That, however, isn't necessarily a bad thing. "It is important to appreciate that there are powerful psychological reasons why we have religion," says Norenzayan. "We can't just say 'it is a superstition, we need to get rid of it'. We need to find alternative solutions to the deep and perennial problems of life that religion tries to solve. If societies can do that I think atheism is a viable alternative."

Godless congregations like the Sunday Assembly can help, by serving the needs of nones who yearn for a sense of community and a common moral vision. They also articulate secular values and get the message across that godless societies can be healthy ones. If that means accepting a certain level of new-agey irrationality, then so be it.

All of which adds up to a vision of an atheist future rather different from the coldly rational one that Weber and Durkheim—and more recently Richard Dawkins and the other New Atheists—envisaged. A bit happy-clappy, a bit spiritual, driven more by indifference to religion rather than hostility to it—but a good society nonetheless. In fact, a society not unlike modern Britain. And as I walk back to my car on a sunny Sunday morning, I can't help feeling that wouldn't be so bad.

Critical Thinking

1. Why is atheism on the rise in today's world?
2. What kinds of atheism are there and why?
3. What seems to be the relationship between secularism and social and economic health?
4. What do you think is the future of religion and why?

Internet References

Anthropology of Religion-Indiana University
http://www.indiana.edu/~wanthro/religion.htm

Journal of Anthropology of Religion
http://www.publicationhosting.org/mehtapress/Journals/Journal-of-Anthropology-of-Religion/

Society for the Anthropology of Religion
http://www.aaanet.org/sections/sar/

The Journal for the Study of Religion, Nature & Culture
http://www.religionandnature.com/journal/editorial-board.htm

Article   Prepared by: Elvio Angeloni

The Age of Disbelief

JOEL ACHENBACH

Skepticism about science is on the rise, and polarization is the order of the day. What's causing reasonable people to doubt reason?

Learning Outcomes

After reading this article, you will be able to:

- Explain why there is so much public distrust of science today.
- Describe the scientific method.
- Explain why we cling to our intuitions even in the face of evidence for such ideas as a sun-centered solar system and organic evolution.
- Discuss "confirmation bias" and the scientific approach to overcome it.

There's a scene in Stanley Kubrick's comic masterpiece *Dr. Strangelove* in which Jack D. Ripper, an American general who's gone rogue and ordered a nuclear attack on the Soviet Union, unspools his paranoid worldview—and the explanation for why he drinks "only distilled water, or rainwater, and only pure grain alcohol" to Lionel Mandrake, a dizzy-with-anxiety group captain in the Royal Air Force.

RIPPER: Have you ever heard of a thing called fluoridation? Fluoridation of water?
MANDRAKE: Ah, yes, I have heard of that, Jack. Yes, yes.
RIPPER: Well, do you know what it is?
MANDRAKE: No. No, I don't know what it is. No.
RIPPER: Do you realize that fluoridation is the most monstrously conceived and dangerous communist plot we have ever had to face?

The movie came out in 1964, by which time the health benefits of fluoridation had been thoroughly established, and antifluoridation conspiracy theories could be the stuff of comedy. So you might be surprised to learn that, half a century later, fluoridation continues to incite fear and paranoia. In 2013 citizens in Portland, Oregon, one of only a few major American cities that don't fluoridate their water, blocked a plan by local officials to do so. Opponents didn't like the idea of the government adding "chemicals" to their water. They claimed that fluoride could be harmful to human health.

Actually fluoride is a natural mineral that, in the weak concentrations used in public drinking water systems, hardens tooth enamel and prevents tooth decay—a cheap and safe way to improve dental health for everyone, rich or poor, conscientious brusher or not. That's the scientific and medical consensus.

To which some people in Portland, echoing antifluoridation activists around the world, reply: We don't believe you.

We live in an age when all manner of scientific knowledge—from the safety of fluoride and vaccines to the reality of climate change—faces organized and often furious opposition. Empowered by their own sources of information and their own interpretations of research, doubters have declared war on the consensus of experts. There are so many of these controversies these days, you'd think a diabolical agency had put something in the water to make people argumentative. And there's so much talk about the trend these days—in books, articles, and academic conferences—that science doubt itself has become a pop-culture meme. In the recent movie *Interstellar,* set in a futuristic, downtrodden America where NASA has been forced into hiding, school textbooks say the *Apollo* moon landings were faked.

In a sense all this is not surprising. Our lives are permeated by science and technology as never before. For many of us this new world is wondrous, comfortable, and rich in rewards—but also more complicated and sometimes unnerving. We now face risks we can't easily analyze.

We're asked to accept, for example, that it's safe to eat food containing genetically modified organisms (GMOs) because, the experts point out, there's no evidence that it isn't and no reason to believe that altering genes precisely in a lab is more dangerous than altering them wholesale through traditional breeding. But to some people the very idea of transferring genes between species conjures up mad scientists running amok—and so, two centuries after Mary Shelley wrote *Frankenstein,* they talk about Frankenfood.

The world crackles with real and imaginary hazards, and distinguishing the former from the latter isn't easy. Should we be afraid that the Ebola virus, which is spread only by direct contact with bodily fluids, will mutate into an airborne super-plague? The scientific consensus says that's extremely unlikely: No virus has ever been observed to completely change its mode of transmission in humans, and there's zero evidence that the latest strain of Ebola is any different. But type "airborne Ebola" into an Internet search engine, and you'll enter a dystopia where this virus has almost supernatural powers, including the power to kill us all.

In this bewildering world we have to decide what to believe and how to act on that. In principle that's what science is for. "Science is not a body of facts," says geophysicist Marcia McNutt, who once headed the U.S. Geological Survey and is now editor of *Science,* the prestigious journal. "Science is a method for deciding whether what we choose to believe has a basis in the laws of nature or not." But that method doesn't come naturally to most of us. And so we run into trouble, again and again.

The trouble goes way back, of course. The scientific method leads us to truths that are less than self-evident, often mind-blowing, and sometimes hard to swallow. In the early 17th century, when Galileo claimed that the Earth spins on its axis and orbits the sun, he wasn't just rejecting church doctrine. He was asking people to believe something that defied common sense—because it sure looks like the sun's going around the Earth, and you can't feel the Earth spinning. Galileo was put on trial and forced to recant. Two centuries later Charles Darwin escaped that fate. But his idea that all life on Earth evolved from a primordial ancestor and that we humans are distant cousins of apes, whales, and even deep-sea mollusks is still a big ask for a lot of people. So is another 19th-century notion: that carbon dioxide, an invisible gas that we all exhale all the time and that makes up less than a tenth of one percent of the atmosphere, could be affecting Earth's climate.

Even when we intellectually accept these precepts of science, we subconsciously cling to our intuitions—what researchers call our naive beliefs. A recent study by Andrew Shtulman of Occidental College showed that even students with an advanced science education had a hitch in their mental gait when asked to affirm or deny that humans are descended from sea animals or that Earth goes around the sun. Both truths are counterintuitive.

The students, even those who correctly marked "true," were slower to answer those questions than questions about whether humans are descended from tree-dwelling creatures (also true but easier to grasp) or whether the moon goes around the Earth (also true but intuitive). Shtulman's research indicates that as we become scientifically literate, we repress our naive beliefs but never eliminate them entirely. They lurk in our brains, chirping at us as we try to make sense of the world.

Most of us do that by relying on personal experience and anecdotes, on stories rather than statistics. We might get a prostate-specific antigen test, even though it's no longer generally recommended, because it caught a close friend's cancer—and we pay less attention to statistical evidence, painstakingly compiled through multiple studies, showing that the test rarely saves lives but triggers many unnecessary surgeries. Or we hear about a cluster of cancer cases in a town with a hazardous waste dump, and we assume pollution caused the cancers. Yet just because two things happened together doesn't mean one caused the other, and just because events are clustered doesn't mean they're not still random.

We have trouble digesting randomness; our brains crave pattern and meaning. Science warns us, however, that we can deceive ourselves. To be confident there's a causal connection between the dump and the cancers, you need statistical analysis showing that there are many more cancers than would be expected randomly, evidence that the victims were exposed to chemicals from the dump, and evidence that the chemicals really can cause cancer.

Even for scientists, the scientific method is a hard discipline. Like the rest of us, they're vulnerable to what they call confirmation bias—the tendency to look for and see only evidence that confirms what they already believe. But unlike the rest of us, they submit their ideas to formal peer review before publishing them. Once their results are published, if they're important enough, other scientists will try to reproduce them—and, being congenitally skeptical and competitive, will be very happy to announce that they don't hold up. Scientific results are always provisional, susceptible to being overturned by some future experiment or observation. Scientists rarely proclaim an absolute truth or absolute certainty. Uncertainty is inevitable at the frontiers of knowledge.

Sometimes scientists fall short of the ideals of the scientific method. Especially in biomedical research, there's a disturbing trend toward results that can't be reproduced outside the lab that found them, a trend that has prompted a push for greater transparency about how experiments are conducted. Francis Collins, the director of the National Institutes of Health, worries about the "secret sauce"—specialized procedures, customized software, quirky ingredients—that researchers don't share with their colleagues. But he still has faith in the larger enterprise.

"Science will find the truth," Collins says. "It may get it wrong the first time and maybe the second time, but ultimately it will find the truth." That provisional quality of science is another thing a lot of people have trouble with. To some climate change skeptics, for example, the fact that a few scientists in the 1970s were worried (quite reasonably, it seemed at the time) about the possibility of a coming ice age is enough to discredit the concern about global warming now.

Last fall the Intergovernmental Panel on Climate Change, which consists of hundreds of scientists operating under the auspices of the United Nations, released its fifth report in the past 25 years. This one repeated louder and clearer than ever the consensus of the world's scientists: The planet's surface temperature has risen by about 1.5 degrees Fahrenheit in the past 130 years, and human actions, including the burning of fossil fuels, are extremely likely to have been the dominant cause of the warming since the mid-20th century. Many people in the United States—a far greater percentage than in other countries—retain doubts about that consensus or believe that climate activists are using the threat of global warming to attack the free market and industrial society generally. Senator James Inhofe of Oklahoma, one of the most powerful Republican voices on environmental matters, has long declared global warming a hoax.

The idea that hundreds of scientists from all over the world would collaborate on such a vast hoax is laughable—scientists love to debunk one another. It's very clear, however, that organizations funded in part by the fossil fuel industry have deliberately tried to undermine the public's understanding of the scientific consensus by promoting a few skeptics.

The news media give abundant attention to such mavericks, naysayers, professional controversialists, and table thumpers. The media would also have you believe that science is full of shocking discoveries made by lone geniuses. Not so. The (boring) truth is that it usually advances incrementally, through the steady accretion of data and insights gathered by many people over many years. So it has been with the consensus on climate change. That's not about to go poof with the next thermometer reading.

But industry PR, however misleading, isn't enough to explain why only 40 percent of Americans, according to the most recent poll from the Pew Research Center, accept that human activity is the dominant cause of global warming.

The "science communication problem," as it's blandly called by the scientists who study it, has yielded abundant new research into how people decide what to believe—and why they so often don't accept the scientific consensus. It's not that they can't grasp it, according to Dan Kahan of Yale University. In one study he asked 1,540 Americans, a representative sample, to rate the threat of climate change on a scale of zero to ten. Then he correlated that with the subjects' science literacy. He found that higher literacy was associated with stronger views—at both ends of the spectrum. Science literacy promoted polarization on climate, not consensus. According to Kahan, that's because people tend to use scientific knowledge to reinforce beliefs that have already been shaped by their worldview.

Americans fall into two basic camps, Kahan says. Those with a more "egalitarian" and "communitarian" mind-set are generally suspicious of industry and apt to think it's up to something dangerous that calls for government regulation; they're likely to see the risks of climate change. In contrast, people with a "hierarchical" and "individualistic" mind-set respect leaders of industry and don't like government interfering in their affairs; they're apt to reject warnings about climate change, because they know what accepting them could lead to—some kind of tax or regulation to limit emissions.

In the U.S., climate change somehow has become a litmus test that identifies you as belonging to one or the other of these two antagonistic tribes. When we argue about it, Kahan says, we're actually arguing about who we are, what our crowd is. We're thinking, People like us believe this. People like that do not believe this. For a hierarchical individualist, Kahan says, it's not irrational to reject established climate science: Accepting it wouldn't change the world, but it might get him thrown out of his tribe.

"Take a barber in a rural town in South Carolina," Kahan has written. "Is it a good idea for him to implore his customers to sign a petition urging Congress to take action on climate change? No. If he does, he will find himself out of a job, just as his former congressman, Bob Inglis, did when he himself proposed such action."

Science appeals to our rational brain, but our beliefs are motivated largely by emotion, and the biggest motivation is remaining tight with our peers. "We're all in high school. We've never left high school," says Marcia McNutt. "People still have a need to fit in, and that need to fit in is so strong that local values and local opinions are always trumping science. And they will continue to trump science, especially when there is no clear downside to ignoring science."

Meanwhile the Internet makes it easier than ever for climate skeptics and doubters of all kinds to find their own information and experts. Gone are the days when a small number of powerful institutions—elite universities, encyclopedias, major news organizations, even *National Geographic*—served as gatekeepers of scientific information. The Internet has democratized information, which is a good thing. But along with cable TV, it has made it possible to live in a "filter bubble" that lets in only the information with which you already agree.

How to penetrate the bubble? How to convert climate skeptics? Throwing more facts at them doesn't help. Liz Neeley, who helps train scientists to be better communicators at an organization called Compass, says that people need to hear from believers they can trust, who share their fundamental values. She has personal experience with this. Her father is a climate change skeptic and gets most of his information on the issue from conservative media. In exasperation she finally confronted him: "Do you believe them or me?" She told him she believes the scientists who research climate change and knows many of them personally. "If you think I'm wrong," she said, "then you're telling me that you don't trust me." Her father's stance on the issue softened. But it wasn't the facts that did it.

If you're a rationalist, there's something a little dispiriting about all this. In Kahan's descriptions of how we decide what to believe, what we decide sometimes sounds almost incidental. Those of us in the science-communication business are as tribal as anyone else, he told me. We believe in scientific ideas not because we have truly evaluated all the evidence but because we feel an affinity for the scientific community. When I mentioned to Kahan that I fully accept evolution, he said, "Believing in evolution is just a description about you. It's not an account of how you reason."

Maybe—except that evolution actually happened. Biology is incomprehensible without it. There aren't really two sides to all these issues. Climate change is happening. Vaccines really do save lives. Being right does matter—and the science tribe has a long track record of getting things right in the end. Modern society is built on things it got right.

Doubting science also has consequences. The people who believe vaccines cause autism—often well educated and affluent, by the way—are undermining "herd immunity" to such diseases as whooping cough and measles. The anti-vaccine movement has been going strong since the prestigious British medical journal the *Lancet* published a study in 1998 linking a common vaccine to autism. The journal later retracted the study, which was thoroughly discredited. But the notion of a vaccine-autism connection has been endorsed by celebrities and reinforced through the usual Internet filters. (Anti-vaccine activist and actress Jenny McCarthy famously said on the *Oprah Winfrey Show,* "The University of Google is where I got my degree from.")

In the climate debate the consequences of doubt are likely global and enduring. In the U.S., climate change skeptics have achieved their fundamental goal of halting legislative action to combat global warming. They haven't had to win the debate on the merits; they've merely had to fog the room enough to keep laws governing greenhouse gas emissions from being enacted.

Some environmental activists want scientists to emerge from their ivory towers and get more involved in the policy battles. Any scientist going that route needs to do so carefully, says Liz Neeley. "That line between science communication and advocacy is very hard to step back from," she says. In the debate over climate change the central allegation of the skeptics is that the science saying it's real and a serious threat is politically tinged, driven by environmental activism and not hard data. That's not true, and it slanders honest scientists. But it becomes more likely to be seen as plausible if scientists go beyond their professional expertise and begin advocating specific policies.

It's their very detachment, what you might call the cold-bloodedness of science, that makes science the killer app. It's the way science tells us the truth rather than what we'd like the truth to be. Scientists can be as dogmatic as anyone else—but their dogma is always wilting in the hot glare of new research. In science it's not a sin to change your mind when the evidence demands it. For some people, the tribe is more important than the truth; for the best scientists, the truth is more important than the tribe.

Scientific thinking has to be taught, and sometimes it's not taught well, McNutt says. Students come away thinking of science as a collection of facts, not a method. Shtulman's research has shown that even many college students don't really understand what evidence is. The scientific method doesn't come naturally—but if you think about it, neither does democracy. For most of human history neither existed. We went around killing each other to get on a throne, praying to a rain god, and for better and much worse, doing things pretty much as our ancestors did.

Now we have incredibly rapid change, and it's scary sometimes. It's not all progress. Our science has made us the dominant organisms, with all due respect to ants and blue-green algae, and we're changing the whole planet. Of course we're right to ask questions about some of the things science and technology allow us to do. "Everybody should be questioning," says McNutt. That's a hallmark of a scientist. But then they should use the scientific method, or trust people using the scientific method, to decide which way they fall on those questions." We need to get a lot better at finding answers, because it's certain the questions won't be getting any simpler.

Critical Thinking

1. Why is there so much public distrust of science today?
2. What is the scientific method?
3. Why do we cling to our intuitions in spite of scientific evidence to the contrary?
4. What is meant by the "confirmation bias" and how should we use the scientific approach to overcome it?
5. Why is science literacy not always enough to overcome science denial?

Internet References

Faraday Institute for Science and Religion
www.faraday-institute.org

National Center for Science Education
http://ncse.com

Washington Post science writer Joel Achenbach has contributed to *National Geographic* since 1998.

Article

Prepared by: Elvio Angeloni, *Pasadena City College*

Body Ritual among the Nacirema

HORACE MINER

Learning Outcomes

After reading this article, you will be able to:

- Discuss the role of rituals and taboos in our modern industrial society.

- Discuss the ways in which this article serves as a cautionary note in interpreting other people's customs.

The anthropologist has become so familiar with the diversity of ways in which different peoples behave in similar situations that he is not apt to be surprised by even the most exotic customs. In fact, if all of the logically possible combinations of behavior have not been found somewhere in the world, he is apt to suspect that they must be present in some yet undescribed tribe. This point has, in fact, been expressed with respect to clan organization by Murdock (1949: 71). In this light, the magical beliefs and practices of the Nacirema present such unusual aspects that it seems desirable to describe them as an example of the extremes to which human behavior can go.

Professor Linton first brought the ritual of the Nacirema to the attention of anthropologists twenty years ago (1936: 326), but the culture of this people is still very poorly understood. They are a North American group living in the territory between the Canadian Cree, the Yaqui and Tarahumare of Mexico, and the Carib and Arawak of the Antilles. Little is known of their origin, though tradition states that they came from the east. According to Nacirema mythology, their nation was originated by a culture hero, Notgnishaw, who is otherwise known for two great feats of strength—the throwing of a piece of wampum across the river Pa-To-Mac and the chopping down of a cherry tree in which the Spirit of Truth resided.

Nacirema culture is characterized by a highly developed market economy which has evolved in a rich natural habitat. While much of the people's time is devoted to economic pursuits, a large part of the fruits of these labors and a considerable portion of the day are spent in ritual activity. The focus of this activity is the human body, the appearance and health of which loom as a dominant concern in the ethos of the people. While such a concern is certainly not unusual, its ceremonial aspects and associated philosophy are unique.

The fundamental belief underlying the whole system appears to be that the human body is ugly and that its natural tendency is to debility and disease. Incarcerated in such a body, man's only hope is to avert these characteristics through the use of the powerful influences of ritual and ceremony. Every household has one or more shrines devoted to this purpose. The more powerful individuals in the society have several shrines in their houses and, in fact, the opulence of a house is often referred to in terms of the number of such ritual centers it possesses. Most houses are of wattle and daub construction, but the shrine rooms of the more wealthy are walled with stone. Poorer families imitate the rich by applying pottery plaques to their shrine walls.

While each family has at least one such shrine, the rituals associated with it are not family ceremonies but are private and secret. The rites are normally only discussed with children, and then only during the period when they are being initiated into these mysteries. I was able, however, to establish sufficient rapport with the natives to examine these shrines and to have the rituals described to me.

The focal point of the shrine is a box or chest which is built into the wall. In this chest are kept the many charms and magical potions without which no native believes he could live. These preparations are secured from a variety of specialized practitioners. The most powerful of these are the medicine men, whose assistance must be rewarded with substantial gifts. However, the medicine men do not provide the curative potions for their clients, but decide what the ingredients should be and then write them down in an ancient and secret language. This writing is understood only by the medicine men and by the herbalists who, for another gift, provide the required charm.

The charm is not disposed of after it has served its purpose, but is placed in the charm-box of the household shrine. As these magical materials are specific for certain ills, and the real or imagined maladies of the people are many, the charm-box is usually full to overflowing. The magical packets are so numerous that people forget what their purposes were and fear to use them again. While the natives are very vague on this point, we can only assume that the idea in retaining all the old magical materials is that their presence in the charm-box, before which the body rituals are conducted, will in some way protect the worshipper.

Beneath the charm-box is a small font. Each day every member of the family, in succession, enters the shrine room, bows his head before the charm-box, mingles different sorts of holy water in the font, and proceeds with a brief rite of ablution. The holy waters are secured from the Water Temple of the community, where the priests conduct elaborate ceremonies to make the liquid ritually pure.

In the hierarchy of magical practitioners, and below the medicine men in prestige, are specialists whose designation is best translated "holy-mouth-men." The Nacirema have an almost pathological horror and fascination with the mouth, the condition of which is believed to have a supernatural influence on all social relationships. Were it not for the rituals of the mouth, they believe that their teeth would fall out, their gums bleed, their jaws shrink, their friends desert them, and their lovers reject them. (They also believe that a strong relationship exists between oral and moral characteristics. For example, there is a ritual ablution of the mouth for children which is supposed to improve their moral fiber.)

The daily body ritual performed by everyone includes a mouth-rite. Despite the fact that these people are so punctilious about care of the mouth, this rite involves a practice which strikes the uninitiated stranger as revolting. It was reported to me that the ritual consists of inserting a small bundle of hog hairs into the mouth, along with certain magical powders, and then moving the bundle in a highly formalized series of gestures.

In addition to the private mouth-rite, the people seek out a holy-mouth-man once or twice a year. These practitioners have an impressive set of paraphernalia, consisting of a variety of augers, awls, probes, and prods. The use of these objects in the exorcism of the evils of the mouth involves almost unbelievable ritual torture of the client. The holy-mouth-man opens the client's mouth and, using the above mentioned tools, enlarges any holes which decay may have created in the teeth. Magical materials are put into these holes. If there are no naturally occurring holes in the teeth, large sections of one or more teeth are gouged out so that the supernatural substance can be applied. In the client's view, the purpose of these ministrations is to arrest decay and to draw friends. The extremely sacred and traditional character of the rite is evident in the fact that the natives return to the holy-mouth-men year after year, despite the fact that their teeth continue to decay.

It is to be hoped that, when a thorough study of the Nacirema is made, there will be a careful inquiry into the personality structure of these people. One has but to watch the gleam in the eye of a holy-mouth-man, as he jabs an awl into an exposed nerve, to suspect that a certain amount of sadism is involved. If this can be established, a very interesting pattern emerges, for most of the population shows definite masochistic tendencies. It was to these that Professor Linton referred in discussing a distinctive part of the daily body ritual which is performed only by men. This part of the rite involves scraping and lacerating the surface of the face with a sharp instrument. Special women's rites are performed only four times during each lunar month, but what they lack in frequency is made up in barbarity. As part of this ceremony, women bake their heads in small ovens for about an hour. The theoretically interesting point is that what seems to be a preponderantly masochistic people have developed sadistic specialists.

The medicine men have an imposing temple, or *latipso*, in every community of any size. The more elaborate ceremonies required to treat very sick patients can only be performed at this temple. These ceremonies involve not only the thaumaturge but a permanent group of vestal maidens who move sedately about the temple chambers in distinctive costume and headdress.

The *latipso* ceremonies are so harsh that it is phenomenal that a fair proportion of the really sick natives who enter the temple ever recover. Small children whose indoctrination is still incomplete have been known to resist attempts to take them to the temple because "that is where you go to die." Despite this fact, sick adults are not only willing but eager to undergo the protracted ritual purification, if they can afford to do so. No matter how ill the supplicant or how grave the emergency, the guardians of many temples will not admit a client if he cannot give a rich gift to the custodian. Even after one has gained admission and survived the ceremonies, the guardians will not permit the neophyte to leave until he makes still another gift.

The supplicant entering the temple is first stripped of all his or her clothes. In every-day life the Nacirema avoids exposure of his body and its natural functions. Bathing and excretory acts are performed only in the secrecy of the household shrine, where they are ritualized as part of the body-rites. Psychological shock results from the fact that body secrecy is suddenly lost upon entry into the *latipso*. A man, whose own wife has never seen him in an excretory act, suddenly finds himself naked and assisted by a vestal maiden while he performs his natural functions into a sacred vessel. This sort of ceremonial treatment is necessitated by the fact that the excreta are used by a diviner to ascertain the course and nature of the client's sickness. Female clients, on the other hand, find their naked bodies are subjected to the scrutiny, manipulation, and prodding of the medicine men.

Few supplicants in the temple are well enough to do anything but lie on their hard beds. The daily ceremonies, like the rites of the holy-mouth-men, involve discomfort and torture. With ritual precision, the vestals awaken their miserable charges each dawn and roll them about on their beds of pain while performing ablutions, in the formal movements of which the maidens are highly trained. At other times they insert magic wands in the supplicant's mouth or force him to eat substances which are supposed to be healing. From time to time the medicine men come to their clients and jab magically treated needles into their flesh. The fact that these temple ceremonies may not cure, and may even kill the neophyte, in no way decreases the people's faith in the medicine men.

There remains one other kind of practitioner, known as a "listener." This witch-doctor has the power to exorcise the devils that lodge in the heads of people who have been bewitched. The Nacirema believe that parents bewitch their own children. Mothers are particularly suspected of putting a curse on children while teaching them the secret body rituals. The counter-magic of the witch-doctor is unusual in its lack of ritual. The patient simply tells the "listener" all his troubles and fears, beginning with the earliest difficulties he can remember. The memory displayed by the Nacirema in these exorcism sessions is truly remarkable. It is not uncommon for the patient to bemoan the rejection he felt upon being weaned as a babe, and a few individuals even see their troubles going back to the traumatic effects of their own birth.

In conclusion, mention must be made of certain practices which have their base in native esthetics but which depend upon the pervasive aversion to the natural body and its functions. There are ritual fasts to make fat people thin and ceremonial feasts to make thin people fat. Still other rites are used to make women's breasts large if they are small, and smaller if they are large. General dissatisfaction with breast shape is symbolized in the fact that the ideal form is virtually outside the range of human variation. A few women afflicted with almost inhuman hypermammary development are so idolized that they make a handsome living by simply going from village to village and permitting the natives to stare at them for a fee.

Reference has already been made to the fact that excretory functions are ritualized, routinized, and relegated to secrecy. Natural reproductive functions are similarly distorted. Intercourse is taboo as a topic and scheduled as an act. Efforts are made to avoid pregnancy by the use of magical materials or by limiting intercourse to certain phases of the moon. Conception is actually very infrequent. When pregnant, women dress so as to hide their condition. Parturition takes place in secret, without friends or relatives to assist, and the majority of women do not nurse their infants.

Our review of the ritual life of the Nacirema has certainly shown them to be a magic-ridden people. It is hard to understand how they have managed to exist so long under the burdens which they have imposed upon themselves. But even such exotic customs as these take on real meaning when they are viewed with the insight provided by Malinowski when he wrote (1948:70):

> Looking from far and above, from our high places of safety in the developed civilization, it is easy to see all the crudity and irrelevance of magic. But without its power and guidance early man could not have mastered his practical difficulties as he has done, nor could man have advanced to the higher stages of civilization.

References

Linton, Ralph. 1936. *The Study of Man.* New York, D. Appleton-Century Co.

Malinowski, Bronislaw. 1948. *Magic, Science, and Religion.* Glencoe, The Free Press.

Murdock, George P. 1949. *Social Structure.* New York, The Macmillan Co.

Critical Thinking

1. What is "Nacirema" spelled backwards? Where are they actually located on a map? Who are they, really?

2. Why do the customs of the Nacirema seem so bizarre when they are written about in anthropological style?

3. Having read the article, do you view American culture any differently than you did before? If so, how?

4. Has this article helped you to view other cultures differently? If so, how?

5. If this article has distorted the picture of American culture, how difficult is it for all of us, anthropologists included, to render objective descriptions of other cultures?

Create Central

www.mhhe.com/createcentral

Internet References

Apologetics Index
www.apologeticsindex.org/site/index-c
Journal of Anthropology of Religion
www.mehtapress.com/social-science-a-humanities/journal-of-anthropology-of-religion.html
Magic and Religion
http://anthro.palomar.edu/religion/default.htm

Miner, Horace. From *American Anthropologist,* by Horace Miner, June 1956, pp. 503–507.

Unit 7

UNIT

Prepared by: Elvio Angeloni, *Pasadena City College*

Sociocultural Change

The origins of academic anthropology lie in the colonial and imperial ventures of the past five hundred years. During this period, many people of the world were brought into a relationship with Europe and the United States that was usually exploitative and often socially and culturally disruptive. For over a century, anthropologists have witnessed this process and the transformations that have taken place in those social and cultural systems brought under the umbrella of a world economic order. Early anthropological studies—even those widely regarded as pure research—directly or indirectly served colonial interests. Many anthropologists certainly believed that they were extending the benefits of Western technology and society, while preserving the cultural rights of those people whom they studied. But representatives of poor nations challenge this view and are far less generous in describing the past role of the anthropologist. Most contemporary anthropologists, however, have a deep moral commitment to defending the legal, political, and economic rights of the people with whom they work.

When anthropologists discuss social change, they usually mean the change brought about in pre-industrial societies through longstanding interaction with the nation-states of the industrialized world. In early anthropology, contact between the West and the remainder of the world was characterized by the terms *acculturation* and *culture contact*. These terms were used to describe the diffusion of cultural traits between the developed and the less-developed countries. Often this was analyzed as a one-way process, in which cultures of the less-developed world were seen, for better or worse, as receptacles for Western cultural traits. Nowadays, many anthropologists believe that the diffusion of cultural traits across social,

political, and economic boundaries was emphasized at the expense of the real issues of dominance, subordination, and dependence that characterized the colonial experience. Just as important, many anthropologists recognize that the present-day forms of cultural, economic, and political interaction between the developed and the so-called underdeveloped world are best characterized as neocolonial. They take the perspective that anthropology should be critical as well as descriptive and they raise questions about cultural contact and subsequent economic and social disruption.

None of this is to say that indigenous peoples can or even should be left entirely alone to live in isolation from the rest of the world. A much more sensible, as well as more practical, approach would involve some degree of self-determination and considerably more respect for their cultures.

Of course, traditional peoples are not the only losers in the process of technological "progress" and cultural destruction. The very same climate change that now seems to be flooding some of the low-lying Pacific islands may also be causing the most highly destructive hurricanes ever to hit the American coasts such as Katrina and Sandy and should be taken as a warning to the rest of us. The more we deprive the traditional stewards (the Indigenous peoples) of their land, the greater the loss in overall biodiversity.

Finally, all of humanity stands to suffer as resources dwindle and as a vast store of human knowledge—embodied in tribal subsistence practices, language, medicine, and folklore—is obliterated, in a manner not unlike the burning of the library of Alexandria 1,600 years ago. We can only hope that it is not too late to save what is left.

Article   Prepared by: Elvio Angeloni

Quiet Revolutions

BOB HOLMES

Learning Outcomes

After reading this article, you will be able to:

- Discuss the various circumstances in which farming first developed.

- In the light of new evidence discuss the various theories as to why crop domestication originally occurred.

- Explain how, in some cases, there was a long overlap between the use of wild foods and the domestication of crops.

In February 1910, British botanist Lilian Gibbs walked across North Borneo and climbed Mount Kinabalu, a lone white woman among 400 locals. She later wrote: "The 'untrodden jungle' of fiction seems to be nonexistent in this country. Everywhere the forest is well worked and has been so for generations."

What Gibbs saw was a seemingly curated tropical forest, regularly set alight by local tribes and with space carefully cleared around selected wild fruit trees, to give them room to flourish. The forest appeared to be partitioned and managed to get the most rattan canes, fibre for basketry, medicinal plants and other products. Generation after generation of people had cared for the trees, gradually shaping the forest they lived in. This wasn't agriculture in the way we know it today but a more ancient form of cultivation, stretching back more than 10,000 years. Half a world away from the Fertile Crescent, Gibbs was witnessing a living relic of the earliest days of human farming. In recent years, archaeologists have found signs of this "proto-farming" on nearly every continent, transforming our picture of the dawn of agriculture. Gone is the simple story of a sudden revolution in what is now the Middle East with benefits so great that it rapidly spread around the world. It turns out farming was invented many times, in many places and was rarely an instant success. In short, there was no agricultural revolution. "We're going to have to start thinking about things in a different way," says Tim Denham, an archaeologist at the Australian National University in Canberra.

Farming is seen as a pivotal invention in the history of humanity. Before, our ancestors roamed the landscape gathering edible fruits, seeds, and plants and hunting whatever game they could find. They lived in small mobile groups that usually set up temporary homes according to the movement of the prey they hunted. Then one fine day in the Fertile Crescent, around 8000 to 10,000 years ago—or so the story goes—someone noticed sprouts growing out of seeds they had accidentally left on the ground. Over time, people learned how to grow and care for plants in order to get the most out of them. Doing this for generations gradually transformed the wild plants into rich domestic varieties, most of which we still eat today.

This accidental revolution is credited with irreversibly shaping the course of humanity. As fields began to appear on the landscape, more people could be fed. Human populations—already on the rise and stretching the resources available to hunter-gatherers—exploded. At the same time, our ancestors traded their migratory habits for sedentary settlements: these were the first villages, with adjoining fields and pastures. A steadier food supply freed up time for new tasks. Craftspeople were born: the first specialised toolmakers, farmers, carers. Complex societies began to develop, as did trade networks between villages. The rest, as they say, is history.

The enormous impact of farming is widely accepted, but in recent decades the story of how it all began has been completely turned on its head. For starters, while the inhabitants of the Fertile Crescent were undoubtedly some of the earliest farmers, they weren't the only ones. Archaeologists now agree farming was independently "invented" in at least 11 regions, from Central America all the way to China. Decades of digging have kicked up numerous instances of ancient proto-farming, similar to what Gibbs saw in Borneo.

Another point archaeologists are rethinking is the notion that our ancestors were forced into farming when their populations outgrew what the land could provide naturally. If humans had turned to crops out of hunger and desperation, you would expect their efforts to have intensified when the climate took a turn for the worse. In fact, archaeological sites in Asia and the Americas show that most early cultivation happened during periods of relatively stable, warm climates when wild foods would have been plentiful, says Dorian Fuller of University College London.

Nor is there much evidence that early farming coincided with overpopulation. When crops first appeared in eastern North America, for example, people were living in small, scattered settlements. "The sites are less than 10 houses and they're not very numerous," says Bruce Smith, an archaeologist at the Smithsonian Institution in Washington DC. "There's no real evidence that population increase was the prime mover causing them to shift over to domesticated crops." The earliest South American farmers also lived in the very best habitats, where resource shortages would have been least likely. Similarly, in China and the Middle East, domesticated crops appear well before dense human populations would have made foraging impractical.

Instead, Smith suggests, the first farmers appear to have been pulled into experimenting with cultivation, presumably out of curiosity rather than necessity. "These are additional food supply sources, but otherwise the subsistence system based on wild species pretty much remains unchanged," he says. That lack of pressure would explain why so many societies kept crops as a low-intensity sideline—a hobby, almost—for so many generations. Only much later in the process would densely populated settlements have forced people to abandon wild foods in favour of near-exclusive reliance on farming.

Those first experiments most likely happened when bands of hunter-gatherers started tweaking the landscape to encourage the most productive habitats. On the islands of South-East Asia, people were burning patches of tropical forest way back during the last ice age. This created clearings where plants with edible tubers could flourish. In Borneo, evidence of this stretches back 53,000 years; in New Guinea, 20,000 years. We know the burns were deliberate because the charcoal they left behind peaks during wet periods, when natural fires would be less common and people would be fighting forest encroachment, says Christopher Hunt of Liverpool John Moores University, UK, who has worked in Borneo for many years.

Burnt Riches

Burning forest would have paid off for hunters too, as game is easier to spot at forest edges. At Niah Cave on the northern coast of Borneo, Hunt's colleagues have found hundreds of orangutan bones among the remains of early hunters, suggesting forest regrowth after a burn brought the apes low enough to catch, even before the invention of blowpipes. Burning probably intensified as the last ice age gave way to the warmer, wetter Holocene beginning about 13,000 years ago. Rainfall in Borneo doubled, producing a denser forest that would have been much harder to forage without fire.

This wasn't only happening in South-East Asia. Changing climates also pushed hunter-gatherers into landscape management in Central and South America. At the end of the last ice age, the perfect open hunting grounds of the savannahs began to give way to closed forest. By 13,000 years ago, people were burning forests during the dry season when fires would carry, says Dolores Piperno, also at the Smithsonian Institution. Researchers are now turning up evidence of similar management activities in Africa, Brazil and North America.

From burning, it is just a short step to actively nurturing favoured wild species, something that also happened soon after the end of the ice age in some places. Weeds that thrive in cultivated fields appear in the Fertile Crescent at least 13,000 years ago, for example, and New Guinea highlanders were building mounds on swampy ground to grow bananas, yams, and taro about 7000 years ago. In parts of South America, traces of cultivated crops such as gourds, squash, arrowroot, and avocado appear as early as 11,000 years ago, says Piperno. Evidence suggests that these people lived in small groups, often sheltering under rock overhangs or in shallow caves, and they tended small plots along the banks of seasonal streams in addition to foraging for wild plants.

Their early efforts wouldn't have looked much like farming is today. "It's better to see it as small gardens," says Fuller. "Small, intensively managed plots on riverbanks and alluvial fans—possibly not all that important in terms of the overall calories." Instead, Fuller thinks these gardens may have provided high-value foods, such as rice, for special occasions. "It's like growing something for Christmas dinner instead of year-round meals," he says.

As Gibbs discovered in Borneo, and others have seen elsewhere since, this kind of proto-farming is still practised by some hunter-gatherer tribes today. They often move every few years as local game populations are depleted, leaving behind fruit trees that their descendants may return to decades later. Hunt recalls meeting a man gathering fruit in the forest near Niah who told him he was harvesting the trees "that my grandfather planted for me". (Sadly, as younger people abandon their traditional lifestyles, this multi-generational knowledge is rapidly being lost, says Hunt.)

Archaeologists have long assumed that this proto-farming was a shortlived predecessor to fully domesticated crops. They believed that the first farmers quickly transformed the plants' genetic make-up by selecting traits like larger seeds and easier harvesting to produce modern domestic varieties. After all, similar selection has produced great changes in dogs within just the past few hundred years.

We'll Farm Maybe

But new archaeological sites and better techniques for recognising ancient plant remains have made it clear that crop domestication was often very slow. Through much of the Middle East, Asia, and New Guinea, at least a thousand—and often several thousand—years of proto-farming preceded the first genetic hints of domestication.

In China, for example, people began cultivating wild forms of rice on a small scale about 10,000 years ago. But physical traits associated with domesticated rice, such as larger grains that stay in the seed head instead of falling off to seed the next generation, didn't appear until about two-and-a-half millennia later. Fully domesticated rice didn't appear until 6000 years ago, says Fuller.

Even after crops were domesticated, there was often a lag, sometimes of thousands of years, before people began to rely on them for most of their calories. During this prolonged transition period, people often act as though they haven't made up their mind how much to trust the newfangled agricultural technology.

The inhabitants of China's Yangtze delta about 6900 years ago, for example, lived primarily on wild foods like acorns and water chestnuts. They also grew a small amount of partially domesticated rice, often in small depressions just a metre or two across. But Fuller has found that rice makes up only 8 per cent of plant remains in archaeological sites in the region. Three hundred years later, the use of rice had tripled, and yet wild foods still made up the bulk of the diet. "They're keeping their options open," says Fuller.

The record also shows a long period of overlap in other regions, with cultures using both wild foods and domesticated crops. We know from the type of starch grains found on their teeth that people living in southern Mexico 8700 years ago were eating domesticated maize, yet large-scale slash-and-burn agriculture did not begin until nearly a millennium later. In several cases—Scandinavia, for example—societies began to rely on domesticated crops, then switched back to wild foods when they couldn't make a go of farming. And in eastern North America, Native Americans had domesticated squash, sunflowers and several other plants by about 3800 years ago, but only truly committed to agriculture about AD 900, says Smith.

Indeed, some cultures didn't commit to domesticated crops until modern times. The highlanders of Borneo, for example, only began growing domestic rice after the second world war. Many of the indigenous crops grown by traditional New Guineans, like sago palm and some tubers, are even now only semi-domesticated at best, says Denham. One reason may be that traditional gardening hunter-gatherers use so many plants—often a different mix for each month of the year—that their crops experience very little evolutionary pressure toward domestication.

The story of agriculture, in short, is not the sudden agricultural revolution of textbooks, but rather an agricultural evolution. "The evidence is showing a much more patchwork-quilt mosaic, with different sorts of practices and different plants being used in different ways," says Denham. "In those conditions, when agriculture emerges over time, it's a long, drawn-out process. It's a much more diffuse event, both in time and in space."

That means people's motivations for making the switch were equally complex, as crops become gradually more dominant in their lives. "If people are cultivating plots, their life is going to be oriented to those areas," says Denham. "That would require a shift in their way of engaging with the landscape, and with each other as well. That's really why we're interested in it— because it's a story about us."

Where Did All the Potatoes Come From?

Our picture of the dawn of farming is being redrawn. Gone is the simple story of a sudden agricultural revolution in the Fertile Crescent at the end of the last ice age that spread around the world. Archaeologists now agree that farming was "invented" at least 11 times in 11 different places

The ingredients you cook with were once separated by oceans. We now know that most went through long periods of "proto-farming" before being grown in recognisable fields and turned into the crops we still eat today. Proto-farmers would tend to wild plants, perhaps planting some in small gardens

Cuscus to Slaughter

Domestic food animals, traditionally viewed as a later add-on in the development of agriculture, may have been part of the picture from the very beginning. In fact, the roots of animal husbandry probably stretch back into the last ice age.

There is some evidence that the common cuscus, a small marsupial native to New Guinea, appeared on remote islands such as New Ireland 20,000 and 10,000 years ago, at the same time as the first humans arrived. The cuscus is a favoured prey for modern hunter-gatherers, so the suspicious timing may mean early Pacific islanders brought the animals with them to seed their new home with prey.

In the Fertile Crescent of south-west Asia, skeletal remains of sheep and goats suggest that by 10,500 years ago, humans living in what is now Turkey were preferentially killing young male animals, says Melinda Zeder, an archaeologist at the Smithsonian Institution. This implies that they were not just hunting the animals, but deliberately managing herds to maintain fertile females. She is now looking at 11,700-year-old sites for evidence that the practice began even earlier. If she is successful, it would imply people began domesticating animals in the region at the same time as they began domesticating crops like wheat and barley.

So why have historians assumed that animal domestication came second? Further south in the Levant, the most common prey animal back then was a species of gazelle whose behaviour made it unsuitable for domestication.

Since most archaeologists working in the region have tended to study the Levant, which is more accessible, this may have led them to the erroneous conclusion that animal domestication lagged behind that of plants, says Zeder.

Critical Thinking

1. What were the apparent reasons for crop domestication—in contrast to previous theories?
2. Why was crop domestication a very slow process and not quite the revolution that was once thought?
3. Why was there often a long overlap between the use of wild foods and the domestication of crops?

Internet References

Ancient World History
http://earlyworldhistory.blogspot.com/2012/02/neolithic-age.html

Neolithic Revolution
http://www.regentsprep.org/regents/global/themes/change/neo.cfm

BOB HOLMES is a consultant for New Scientist based in Edmonton, Canada.

Article   Prepared by: Elvio Angeloni, *Pasadena City College*

Ruined

MICHAEL MARSHALL

Learning Outcomes

After reading this article, you will be able to:

- Discuss the relationship between climate change and the decline of civilizations in the past.

- Discuss the prospects of societal collapse as a result of climate change in the modern world.

The most beautiful woman in the world, Helen, is abducted by Paris of Troy. A Greek fleet of more than a thousand ships sets off in pursuit. After a long war, heroes like Achilles lead the Greeks to victory over Troy.

At least, this is the story told by the poet Homer around four centuries later. Yet Homer was not only writing about events long before his time, he was also describing a long-lost civilization. Achilles and his compatriots were part of the first great Greek civilization, a warlike culture centered on the city of Mycenae that thrived from around 1600 BC.

By 1100 BC, not long after the Trojan War, many of its cities and settlements had been destroyed or abandoned. The survivors reverted to a simpler rural lifestyle. Trade ground to a halt, and skills such as writing were lost. The script the Mycenaeans had used, Linear B, was not read again until 1952.

The region slowly recovered after around 800 BC. The Greeks adopted the Phoenician script, and the great city states of Athens and Sparta rose to power. "The collapse was one of the most important events in history, because it gave birth to two major cultures," says anthropologist Brandon Drake. "It's like the phoenix from the ashes." Classical Greece, as this second period of civilization is known, far outshone its predecessor. Its glory days lasted only a couple of centuries, but the ideas of its citizens were immensely influential. Their legacy is still all around us, from the math we learn in school to the idea of democracy.

But what caused the collapse of Mycenaean Greece, and thus had a huge impact on the course of world history? A change in the climate, according to the latest evidence. What's more, Mycenaean Greece is just one of a growing list of civilizations whose fate is being linked to the vagaries of climate. It seems big swings in the climate, handled badly, brought down whole societies, while smaller changes led to unrest and wars.

The notion that climate change toppled entire civilizations has been around for more than a century, but it was only in the 1990s that it gained a firm footing as researchers began to work out exactly how the climate had changed, using clues buried in lake beds or petrified in stalactites. Harvey Weiss of Yale University set the ball rolling with his studies of the collapse of one of the earliest empires: that of the Akkadians.

It began in the Fertile Crescent of the Middle East, a belt of rich farmland where an advanced regional culture had developed over many centuries. In 2334 BC, Sargon was born in the city state of Akkad. He started out as a gardener, was put in charge of clearing irrigation canals, and went on to seize power. Not content with that, he conquered many neighboring city states, too. The empire Sargon founded thrived for nearly a century after his death before it collapsed.

Excavating in what is now Syria, Weiss found dust deposits suggesting that the region's climate suddenly became drier around 2200 BC. The drought would have led to famine, he argued, explaining why major cities were abandoned at this time (*Science*, vol 261, p. 995). A piece of contemporary writing, called *The Curse of Akkad*, does describe a great famine (see end of article).

Weiss's work was influential, but there wasn't much evidence. In 2000, climatologist Peter deMenocal of Columbia University in New York found more. His team showed, based on modern records going back to 1700, that the flow of the region's two great rivers, the Tigris and the Euphrates, is linked to conditions in the north Atlantic: cooler waters reduce rainfall by altering the paths of weather systems. Next, they discovered that the north Atlantic cooled just before the Akkadian empire fell apart (*Science*, vol 288, p 2198). "To our surprise we got this big whopping signal at the time of the Akkadian collapse."

It soon became clear that major changes in the climate coincided with the untimely ends of several other civilizations. Of these, the Maya became the poster child for climate-induced decline. Mayan society arose in Mexico and Central America around 2000 BC. Its farmers grew maize, squashes and beans, and it was the only American civilization to produce a written language. The Maya endured for millennia, reaching a peak between AD 250 and 800, when they built cities and huge stepped pyramids.

Then the Maya civilization collapsed. Many of its incredible structures were swallowed up by the jungle after being abandoned. Not all was lost, though—Mayan people and elements of their culture survive to the present day.

Numerous studies have shown that there were several prolonged droughts around the time of the civilisation's decline. In 2003, Gerald Haug of the Swiss Federal Institute of Technology in Zurich found it was worse than that. His year-by-year reconstruction based on lake sediments shows that rainfall was abundant from 550 to 750, perhaps leading to a rise in population and thus to the peak of monument-building around 721. But over the next century there were not only periods of particularly severe drought, each lasting years, but also less rain than normal in the intervening years (*Science*, vol 299, p 1731). Monument construction ended during this prolonged dry period, around 830, although a few cities continued on for many centuries.

Even as the evidence grew, there was something of a backlash against the idea that changing climates shaped the fate of civilizations. "Many in the archaeological community are really reticent to accept a role of climate in human history," says deMenocal.

Much of this reluctance is for historical reasons. In the 18th and 19th centuries, anthropologists argued that a society's environment shaped its character, an idea known as environmental determinism. They claimed that the warm, predictable climates of the tropics bred indolence, while cold European climates produced intelligence and a strong work ethic. These ideas were often used to justify racism and exploitation.

Understandably, modern anthropologists resist anything resembling environmental determinism. "It's a very delicate issue," says Ulf Büntgen, also at the Swiss Federal Institute of Technology, whose work suggests the decline of the Western Roman Empire was linked to a period of highly variable weather. "The field is evolving really slowly, because people are afraid to make bold statements."

Yet this resistance is not really warranted, deMenocal says. No one today is claiming that climate determines people's characters, only that it sets limits on what is feasible. When the climate becomes less favorable, less food can be grown. Such changes can also cause plagues of locusts or other pests, and epidemics among people weakened by starvation. When it is no longer feasible to maintain a certain population level and way of life, the result can be collapse. "Climate isn't a determinant, but it is an important factor," says Drake, who is at the University of New Mexico in Albuquerque. "It enables or disables."

Some view even this notion as too simplistic. Karl Butzer of the University of Texas at Austin, who has studied the collapse of civilizations, thinks the role of climate has been exaggerated. It is the way societies handle crises that decides their fate, he says. "Things break through institutional failure." When it comes to the Akkadians, for instance, Butzer says not all records support the idea of a megadrought.

In the case of the Maya, though, the evidence is strong. Earlier this year, Eelco Rohling of the University of Southampton, UK, used lake sediments and isotope ratios in stalactites to work out how rainfall had changed. He concluded that annual rainfall fell 40 per cent over the prolonged dry period, drying up open water sources (*Science*, vol 335, p 956). This would

have seriously affected the Maya, he says, because the water table lay far underground and was effectively out of reach.

So after a century of plentiful rain, the Maya were suddenly confronted with a century of low rainfall. It is not clear how they could have avoided famine and population decline in these circumstances. Even today, our ability to defy hostile climes is limited. Saudi Arabia managed to become self-sufficient in wheat by tapping water reservoirs deep beneath its deserts and subsidising farmers, but is now discouraging farming to preserve what is left of the water. In dry regions where plenty of water is available for irrigation, the build-up of salts in the soil is a serious problem, just as it was for some ancient civilisations. And if modern farmers are still at the mercy of the climate despite all our knowledge and technology, what chance did ancient farmers have?

Greek Dark Ages

While many archaeologists remain unconvinced, the list of possible examples continues to grow. The Mycenaeans are the latest addition. The reason for their downfall has been the subject of much debate, with one of the most popular explanations being a series of invasions and attacks by the mysterious "Sea Peoples." In 2010, though, a study of river deposits in Syria suggested there was a prolonged dry period between 1200 and 850 BC—right at the time of the so-called Greek Dark Ages. Earlier this year, Drake analysed several climate records and concluded that there was a cooling of the Mediterranean at this time, reducing evaporation and rainfall over a huge area.

What's more, several other cultures around the Mediterranean, including the Hittite Empire and the "New Kingdom" of Egypt, collapsed around the same time as the Mycenaeans—a phenomenon known as the late Bronze Age collapse. Were all these civilisations unable to cope with the changing climate? Or were the invading Sea Peoples the real problem? The story could be complex: civilisations weakened by hunger may have become much more vulnerable to invaders, who may themselves have been driven to migrate by the changing climate. Or the collapse of one civilisation could have had knock-on effects on its trading partners.

Climate change on an even greater scale might be behind another striking coincidence. Around 900, as the Mayan civilisation was declining in South America, the Tang dynasty began losing its grip on China. At its height, the Tang ruled over 50 million subjects. Woodblock printing meant that written words, particularly poetry, were widely accessible. But the dynasty fell after local governors usurped its authority.

Since the two civilisations were not trading partners, there was clearly no knock-on effect. A study of lake sediments in China by Haug suggests that this region experienced a prolonged dry period at the same time as that in Central America. He thinks a shift in the tropical rain belt was to blame, causing civilisations to fall apart on either side of the Pacific (*Nature*, vol 445, p 74).

Critics, however, point to examples of climate change that did not lead to collapse. "There was a documented drought and even famines during the period of the Aztec Empire," says archaeologist Gary Feinman of the Field Museum in Chicago. "These episodes caused hardships and possibly even famines, but no overall collapse."

Realizing that case studies of collapses were not enough to settle the debate, in 2005 David Zhang of Hong Kong University began to look for larger patterns. He began with the history of the Chinese dynasties. From 2500 BC until the 20th century, a series of powerful empires like the Tang controlled China. All were eventually toppled by civil unrest or invasions.

When Zhang compared climate records for the last 1200 years to the timeline of China's dynastic wars, the match was striking. Most of the dynastic transitions and periods of social unrest took place when temperatures were a few tenths of a degree colder. Warmer periods were more stable and peaceful (*Chinese Science Bulletin,* vol 50, p 137).

The Thirty Years War

Zhang gradually built up a more detailed picture showing that harvests fell when the climate was cold, as did population levels, while wars were more common. Of 15 bouts of warfare he studied, 12 took place in cooler times. He then looked at records of war across Europe, Asia and North Africa between 1400 and 1900. Once again, there were more wars when the temperatures were lower. Cooler periods also saw more deaths and declines in the population.

These studies suggest that the effects of climate on societies can be profound. The problem is proving it. So what if wars and collapses often coincide with shifts in the climate? It doesn't prove one caused the other. "That's always been the beef," says deMenocal. "It's a completely valid point."

Trying to move beyond mere correlations, Zhang began studying the history of Europe from 1500 to 1800 AD. In the mid-1600s, Europe was plunged into the General Crisis, which coincided with a cooler period called the Little Ice Age. The Thirty Years War was fought then, and many other wars. Zhang analysed detailed records covering everything from population and migration to agricultural yields, wars, famines and epidemics in a bid to identify causal relationships. So, for instance, did climate change affect agricultural production and thus food prices? That in turn might lead to famine—revealed by a reduction in the average height of people—epidemics and a decline in population. High food prices might also lead to migration and social unrest, and even wars.

He then did a statistical analysis known as a Granger causality test, which showed that the proposed causes consistently occurred before the proposed effects, and that each cause was followed by the same effect. The Granger test isn't conclusive proof of causality, but short of rerunning history under different climes, it is about the best evidence there can be (*Proceedings of the National Academy of Sciences,* vol 108, p 17296).

The paper hasn't bowled over the critics. Butzer, for instance, claims it is based on unreliable demographic data. Yet others are impressed. "It's a really remarkable study," deMenocal says. "It does seem like they did their homework." He adds

that such a detailed breakdown is only possible for recent history, because older civilizations left fewer records.

So while further studies should reveal much more about how the climate changed in the past, the debate about how great an effect these changes had on societies is going to rumble on for many more decades. Let's assume, though, that changing climates did play a major role. What does that mean for us? On the face of it, things don't look so bad. It was often cooling that hurt past civilizations. What's more, studies of the past century have found little or no link between conflict and climate change. "Industrialized societies have been more robust against changing climatic conditions," says Jürgen Scheffran of the University of Hamburg, who studies the effects of climate change.

On the other hand, we are triggering the most extreme change for millions of years, and what seems to matter is food production rather than temperature. Production is expected to increase at first as the planet warms, but then begin to decline as warming exceeds 3°C. This point may not be that far away—it is possible that global average temperature will rise by 4°C as early as 2060. We've already seen regional food production hit by extreme heat waves like the one in Russia in 2010. Such extreme heat was not expected until much later this century.

And our society's interconnectedness is not always a strength. It can transmit shocks—the 2010 heat wave sent food prices soaring worldwide, and the drought in the US this year is having a similar effect. The growing complexity of modern society may make us more vulnerable to collapse rather than less.

We do have one enormous advantage, though—unlike the Mycenaeans and the Mayas, we know what's coming. We can prepare for what is to come and also slow the rate of change if we act soon. So far, though, we are doing neither.

The Curse of Akkad

'Look on my works, ye mighty, and despair!' All empires fall, but why?

A great drought did occur at the time this tablet was inscribed

For the first time since cities were built and founded,

The great agricultural tracts produced no grain,

The inundated tracts produced no fish,

The irrigated orchards produced neither syrup nor wine,

The gathered clouds did not rain, the masgurum did not grow.

At that time, one shekel's worth of oil was only one-half quart, One shekel's worth of grain was only one-half quart. . . .

These sold at such prices in the markets of all the cities!

He who slept on the roof, died on the roof,

He who slept in the house, had no burial,

People were flailing at themselves from hunger.

Critical Thinking

1. Discuss the causes of the decline of civilizations such as those of the Akkadian Empire and the Maya.

2. Why was there initially a backlash against the idea that changing climates shaped the fate of civilizations? Why is such resistance not warranted?

3. What are some of the specific consequences when the climate becomes less favorable?

4. Why does Karl Butzer view the notion of climate change's impact on civilizations as exaggerated?

5. What is the specific evidence for the impact of climate change on the Maya?

6. What evidence is there that our ability to defy hostile climes is limited even today?

7. Discuss the possible factors for Bronze Age collapse, i.e., the decline of the civilizations of the Mycenaeans (the Greek Dark Ages), the Hittite Empire, and the "New Kingdom" of Egypt.

8. What is the significance of the "striking coincidence" of the simultaneous collapse of the Tang dynasty in China and the Mayan civilization?

9. In what respect are the Aztecs an exception?

10. What do the climate records say about China's dynastic wars and transitions? About wars in Europe, Asia, and North Africa?

11. How was David Zhang able to "move beyond mere correlations" by using the "Granger causality test" with respect to the effects of climate change in Europe?

12. Why does there seem to have been little or no link between conflict and climate change over the past century?

13. Why might we become more vulnerable to collapse rather than less?

14. What is the one "enormous advantage" that we have today?

Create Central

www.mhhe.com/createcentral

Internet References

Murray Research Center
www.radcliffe.edu/murray_redirect/index.php

Small Planet Institute
www.smallplanet.org/food

MICHAEL MARSHALL is an environment reporter for *New Scientist*.

Marshall, Michael. From *New Scientist Magazine*, vol. 215, no. 2876, August 4, 2012, pp. 32–36. Copyright © 2012 by Reed Business Information, Ltd, UK. Reprinted by permission via Tribune Media Services.

Article   Prepared by: Elvio Angeloni, *Pasadena City College*

The Arrow of Disease

When Columbus and his successors invaded the Americas, the most potent weapon they carried was their germs. But why didn't deadly disease flow in the other direction, from the New World to the Old?

JARED DIAMOND

Learning Outcomes

After reading this article, you will be able to:

- Discuss the biological and social circumstances of disease transmission from animals to humans.

- Explain the "one-sidedness" to the disease transmission from Europeans to Native Americans.

The three people talking in the hospital room were already stressed out from having to cope with a mysterious illness, and it didn't help at all that they were having trouble communicating. One of them was the patient, a small, timid man, sick with pneumonia caused by an unidentified microbe and with only a limited command of the English language. The second, acting as translator, was his wife, worried about her husband's condition and frightened by the hospital environment. The third person in the trio was an inexperienced young doctor, trying to figure out what might have brought on the strange illness. Under the stress, the doctor was forgetting everything he had been taught about patient confidentiality. He committed the awful blunder of requesting the woman to ask her husband whether he'd had any sexual experiences that might have caused the infection.

As the young doctor watched, the husband turned red, pulled himself together so that he seemed even smaller, tried to disappear under his bed sheets, and stammered in a barely audible voice. His wife suddenly screamed in rage and drew herself up to tower over him. Before the doctor could stop her, she grabbed a heavy metal bottle, slammed it onto her husband's head, and stormed out of the room. It took a while for the doctor to elicit, through the man's broken English, what he had said to so enrage his wife. The answer slowly emerged: he had admitted to repeated intercourse with sheep on a recent visit to the family farm; perhaps that was how he had contracted the mysterious microbe.

This episode, related to me by a physician friend involved in the case, sounds so bizarrely one of a kind as to be of no possible broader significance. But in fact it illustrates a subject of great importance: human diseases of animal origins. Very few of us may love sheep in the carnal sense. But most of us platonically love our pet animals, like our dogs and cats; and as a society, we certainly appear to have an inordinate fondness for sheep and other livestock, to judge from the vast numbers of them that we keep.

Some of us—most often our children—pick up infectious diseases from our pets. Usually these illnesses remain no more than a nuisance, but a few have evolved into far more. The major killers of humanity throughout our recent history—smallpox, flu, tuberculosis, malaria, plague, measles, and cholera—are all infectious diseases that arose from diseases of animals. Until World War II more victims of war died of microbes than of gunshot or sword wounds. All those military histories glorifying Alexander the Great and Napoleon ignore the ego-deflating truth: the winners of past wars were not necessarily those armies with the best generals and weapons, but those bearing the worst germs with which to smite their enemies.

The grimmest example of the role of germs in history is much on our minds this month, as we recall the European conquest of the Americas that began with Columbus's voyage of 1492. Numerous as the Indian victims of the murderous Spanish conquistadores were, they were dwarfed in number by the victims of murderous Spanish microbes. These formidable conquerors killed an estimated 95 percent of the New World's pre-Columbian Indian population.

Why was the exchange of nasty germs between the Americas and Europe so unequal? Why didn't the reverse happen instead, with Indian diseases decimating the Spanish invaders, spreading back across the Atlantic, and causing a 95 percent decline in *Europe's* human population?

Similar questions arise regarding the decimation of many other native peoples by European germs, and regarding the decimation of would-be European conquistadores in the tropics of Africa and Asia.

Naturally, we're disposed to think about diseases from our own point of view: What can we do to save ourselves and to kill the microbes? Let's stamp out the scoundrels, and never mind what *their* motives are!

In life, though, one has to understand the enemy to beat him. So for a moment, let's consider disease from the microbes' point of view. Let's look beyond our anger at their making us sick in bizarre ways, like giving us genital sores or diarrhea, and ask why it is that they do such things. After all, microbes are as much a product of natural selection as we are, and so their actions must have come about because they confer some evolutionary benefit.

Basically, of course, evolution selects those individuals that are most effective at producing babies and at helping those babies find suitable places to live. Microbes are marvels at this latter requirement. They have evolved diverse ways of spreading from one person to another, and from animals to people. Many of our symptoms of disease actually represent ways in which some clever bug modifies our bodies or our behavior such that we become enlisted to spread bugs.

The most effortless way a bug can spread is by just waiting to be transmitted passively to the next victim. That's the strategy practiced by microbes that wait for one host to be eaten by the next—salmonella bacteria, for example, which we contract by eating already-infected eggs or meat; or the worm responsible for trichinosis, which waits for us to kill a pig and eat it without properly cooking it.

As a slight modification of this strategy; some microbes don't wait for the old host to die but instead hitchhike in the saliva of an insect that bites the old host and then flies to a new one. The free ride may be provided by mosquitoes, fleas, lice, or tsetse flies, which spread malaria, plague, typhus, and sleeping sickness, respectively. The dirtiest of all passive-carriage tricks is perpetrated by microbes that pass from a woman to her fetus—microbes such as the ones responsible for syphilis, rubella (German measles), and AIDS. By their cunning these microbes can already be infecting an infant before the moment of its birth.

Other bugs take matters into their own hands, figuratively speaking. They actively modify the anatomy or habits of their host to accelerate their transmission. From our perspective, the open genital sores caused by venereal diseases such as syphilis are a vile indignity. From the microbes' point of view, however, they're just a useful device to enlist a host's help in inoculating the body cavity of another host with microbes. The skin lesions caused by smallpox similarly spread microbes by direct or indirect body contact (occasionally very indirect, as when U.S. and Australian whites bent on wiping out "belligerent" native peoples sent them gifts of blankets previously used by smallpox patients).

More vigorous yet is the strategy practiced by the influenza, common cold, and pertussis (whooping cough) microbes, which induce the victim to cough or sneeze, thereby broadcasting the bugs toward prospective new hosts. Similarly the cholera bacterium induces a massive diarrhea that spreads bacteria into the water supplies of potential new victims. For modification of a host's behavior, though, nothing matches the rabies virus, which not only gets into the saliva of an infected dog but drives the dog into a frenzy of biting and thereby infects many new victims.

Thus, from our viewpoint, genital sores, diarrhea, and coughing are "symptoms" of disease. From a bug's viewpoint, they're clever evolutionary strategies to broadcast the bug. That's why it's in the bug's interests to make us "sick." But what does it gain by killing us? That seems self-defeating, since a microbe that kills its host kills itself.

Though you may well think it's of little consolation, our death is really just an unintended by-product of host symptoms that promote the efficient transmission of microbes. Yes, an untreated cholera patient may eventually die from producing diarrheal fluid at a rate of several gallons a day. While the patient lasts, though, the cholera bacterium profits from being massively disseminated into the water supplies of its next victims. As long as each victim thereby infects, on average, more than one new victim, the bacteria will spread, even though the first host happens to die.

So much for the dispassionate examination of the bug's interests. Now let's get back to considering our own selfish interests: to stay alive and healthy, best done by killing the damned bugs. One common response to infection is to develop a fever. Again, we consider fever a "symptom" of disease, as if it developed inevitably without serving any function. But regulation of body temperature is under our genetic control, and a fever doesn't just happen by accident. Because some microbes are more sensitive to heat than our own bodies are, by raising our body temperature we in effect try to bake the bugs to death before we get baked ourselves.

We and our pathogens are now locked in an escalating evolutionary contest, with the death of one contestant the price of defeat, and with natural selection playing the role of umpire.

Another common response is to mobilize our immune system. White blood cells and other cells actively seek out and kill foreign microbes. The specific antibodies we gradually build up against a particular microbe make us less likely to get reinfected once we are cured. As we all know there are some illnesses, such as flu and the common cold, to which our resistance is only temporary; we can eventually contract the illness again. Against other illnesses, though—including measles, mumps, rubella, pertussis, and the now-defeated menace of smallpox—antibodies stimulated by one infection confer lifelong immunity. That's the principle behind vaccination—to stimulate our antibody production without our having to go through the actual experience of the disease.

Alas, some clever bugs don't just cave in to our immune defenses. Some have learned to trick us by changing their antigens, those molecular pieces of the microbe that our antibodies recognize. The constant evolution or recycling of new strains of flu, with differing antigens, explains why the flu you got two years ago didn't protect you against the different strain that arrived this year. Sleeping sickness is an even more slippery customer in its ability to change its antigens rapidly.

Among the slipperiest of all is the virus that causes AIDS, which evolves new antigens even as it sits within an individual patient, until it eventually overwhelms the immune system.

Our slowest defensive response is through natural selection, which changes the relative frequency with which a gene appears from generation to generation. For almost any disease some people prove to be genetically more resistant than others. In an epidemic, those people with genes for resistance to that particular microbe are more likely to survive than are people lacking such genes. As a result, over the course of history human populations repeatedly exposed to a particular pathogen tend to be made up of individuals with genes that resist the appropriate microbe just because unfortunate individuals without those genes were less likely to survive to pass their genes on to their children.

Fat consolation, you may be thinking. This evolutionary response is not one that does the genetically susceptible dying individual any good. It does mean, though, that a human population as a whole becomes better protected.

In short, many bugs have had to evolve tricks to let them spread among potential victims. We've evolved counter-tricks, to which the bugs have responded by evolving counter-counter-tricks. We and our pathogens are now locked in an escalating evolutionary contest, with the death of one contestant the price of defeat, and with natural selection playing the role of umpire.

The form that this deadly contest takes varies with the pathogens: for some it is like a guerrilla war, while for others it is a blitzkrieg. With certain diseases, like malaria or hookworm, there's a more or less steady trickle of new cases in an affected area, and they will appear in any month of any year. Epidemic diseases, though, are different: they produce no cases for a long time, then a whole wave of cases, then no more cases again for a while.

Among such epidemic diseases, influenza is the most familiar to Americans, this year having been a particularly bad one for us (but a great year for the influenza virus). Cholera epidemics come at longer intervals, the 1991 Peruvian epidemic being the first one to reach the New World during the twentieth century. Frightening as today's influenza and cholera epidemics are, though, they pale beside the far more terrifying epidemics of the past, before the rise of modern medicine. The greatest single epidemic in human history was the influenza wave that killed 21 million people at the end of the First World War. The black death, or bubonic plague, killed one-quarter of Europe's population between 1346 and 1352, with death tolls up to 70 percent in some cities.

The infectious diseases that visit us as epidemics share several characteristics. First, they spread quickly and efficiently from an infected person to nearby healthy people, with the result that the whole population gets exposed within a short time. Second, they're "acute" illnesses: within a short time, you either die or recover completely. Third, the fortunate ones of us who do recover develop antibodies that leave us immune against a recurrence of the disease for a long time, possibly our entire lives. Finally, these diseases tend to be restricted to humans; the bugs causing them tend not to live in the soil or in other animals. All four of these characteristics apply to what Americans think of as the once more-familiar acute epidemic diseases of childhood, including measles, rubella, mumps, pertussis, and smallpox.

It is easy to understand why the combination of those four characteristics tends to make a disease run in epidemics. The rapid spread of microbes and the rapid course of symptoms mean that everybody in a local human population is soon infected, and thereafter either dead or else recovered and immune. No one is left alive who could still be infected. But since the microbe can't survive except in the bodies of living people, the disease dies out until a new crop of babies reaches the susceptible age—and until an infectious person arrives from the outside to start a new epidemic.

A classic illustration of the process is given by the history of measles on the isolated Faeroe Islands in the North Atlantic. A severe epidemic of the disease reached the Faeroes in 1781, then died out, leaving the islands measles-free until an infected carpenter arrived on a ship from Denmark in 1846. Within three months almost the whole Faeroes population—7,782 people—had gotten measles and then either died or recovered, leaving the measles virus to disappear once again until the next epidemic. Studies show that measles is likely to die out in any human population numbering less than half a million people. Only in larger populations can measles shift from one local area to another, thereby persisting until enough babies have been born in the originally infected area to permit the disease's return.

Rubella in Australia provides a similar example, on a much larger scale. As of 1917 Australia's population was still only 5 million, with most people living in scattered rural areas. The sea voyage to Britain took two months, and land transport within Australia itself was slow. In effect, Australia didn't even consist of a population of 5 million, but of hundreds of much smaller populations. As a result, rubella hit Australia only as occasional epidemics, when an infected person happened to arrive from overseas and stayed in a densely populated area. By 1938, though, the city of Sydney alone had a population of over one million, and people moved frequently and quickly by air between London, Sydney, and other Australian cities. Around then, rubella for the first time was able to establish itself permanently in Australia.

What's true for rubella in Australia is true for most familiar acute infectious diseases throughout the world. To sustain themselves, they need a human population that is sufficiently numerous and densely packed that a new crop of susceptible children is available for infection by the time the disease would otherwise be waning. Hence the measles and other such diseases are also known as "crowd diseases."

Crowd diseases could not sustain themselves in small bands of hunter-gatherers and slash-and-burn farmers. As tragic recent experience with Amazonian Indians and Pacific Islanders confirms, almost an entire tribelet may be wiped out by an epidemic brought by an outside visitor, because no one in the tribelet has any antibodies against the microbe. In addition, measles and some other "childhood" diseases are more likely to kill infected adults than children, and all adults in the tribelet are susceptible. Having killed most of the tribelet, the epidemic then disappears. The small population size explains why tribelets can't sustain epidemics introduced from the outside; at the same time it explains why they could never evolve epidemic diseases of their own to give back to the visitors.

That's not to say that small human populations are free from all infectious diseases. Some of their infections are caused by microbes capable of maintaining themselves in animals or in soil, so the disease remains constantly available to infect people. For example, the yellow fever virus is carried by African wild monkeys and is constantly available to infect rural human populations of Africa. It was also available to be carried to New World monkeys and people by the transAtlantic slave trade.

Other infections of small human populations are chronic diseases, such as leprosy and yaws, that may take a very long time to kill a victim. The victim thus remains alive as a reservoir of microbes to infect other members of the tribelet. Finally, small human populations are susceptible to nonfatal infections against which we don't develop immunity, with the result that the same person can become reinfected after recovering. That's the case with hookworm and many other parasites.

All these types of diseases, characteristic of small, isolated populations, must be the oldest diseases of humanity. They were the ones that we could evolve and sustain through the early millions of years of our evolutionary history, when the total human population was tiny and fragmented. They are also shared with, or are similar to the diseases of, our closest wild relatives, the African great apes. In contrast, the evolution of our crowd diseases could only have occurred with the buildup of large, dense human populations, first made possible by the rise of agriculture about 10,000 years ago, then by the rise of cities several thousand years ago. Indeed, the first attested dates for many familiar infectious diseases are surprisingly recent: around 1600 B.C. for smallpox (as deduced from pockmarks on an Egyptian mummy), 400 B.C. for mumps, 1840 for polio, and 1959 for AIDS.

Agriculture sustains much higher human population densities than do hunting and gathering—on average, 10 to 100 times higher. In addition, hunter-gatherers frequently shift camp, leaving behind their piles of feces with their accumulated microbes and worm larvae. But farmers are sedentary and live amid their own sewage, providing microbes with a quick path from one person's body into another person's drinking water. Farmers also become surrounded by disease-transmitting rodents attracted by stored food.

The explosive increase in world travel by Americans, and in immigration to the United States, is turning us into another melting pot—this time of microbes that we'd dismissed as causing disease in far-off countries.

Some human populations make it even easier for their own bacteria and worms to infect new victims, by intentionally gathering their feces and urine and spreading it as fertilizer on the fields where people work. Irrigation agriculture and fish farming provide ideal living conditions for the snails carrying schistosomes, and for other flukes that burrow through our skin as we wade through the feces-laden water.

If the rise of farming was a boon for our microbes, the rise of cities was a veritable bonanza, as still more densely packed human populations festered under even worse sanitation conditions. (Not until the beginning of the twentieth century did urban populations finally become self-sustaining; until then, constant immigration of healthy peasants from the countryside was necessary to make good the constant deaths of city dwellers from crowd diseases.) Another bonanza was the development of world trade routes, which by late Roman times effectively joined the populations of Europe, Asia, and North Africa into one giant breeding ground for microbes. That's when smallpox finally reached Rome as the "plague of Antonius," which killed millions of Roman citizens between A.D. 165 and 180.

Similarly, bubonic plague first appeared in Europe as the plague of Justinian (A.D. 542–543). But plague didn't begin to hit Europe with full force, as the black death epidemics, until 1346, when new overland trading with China provided rapid transit for flea-infested furs from plague-ridden areas of Central Asia. Today our jet planes have made even the longest intercontinental flights briefer than the duration of any human infectious disease. That's how an Aerolíneas Argentinas airplane, stopping in Lima, Peru, earlier this year, managed to deliver dozens of cholera-infected people the same day to my city of Los Angeles, over 3,000 miles away. The explosive increase in world travel by Americans, and in immigration to the United States, is turning us into another melting pot—this time of microbes that we previously dismissed as just causing exotic diseases in far-off countries.

When the human population became sufficiently large and concentrated, we reached the stage in our history when we could at last sustain crowd diseases confined to our species. But that presents a paradox: such diseases could never have existed before. Instead they had to evolve as new diseases. Where did those new diseases come from?

Evidence emerges from studies of the disease-causing microbes themselves. In many cases molecular biologists have identified the microbe's closest relative. Those relatives also prove to be agents of infectious crowd diseases—but ones confined to various species of domestic animals and pets! Among animals too, epidemic diseases require dense populations, and they're mainly confined to social animals that provide the necessary large populations. Hence when we domesticated social animals such as cows and pigs, they were already afflicted by epidemic diseases just waiting to be transferred to us.

For example, the measles virus is most closely related to the virus causing rinderpest, a nasty epidemic disease of cattle and many wild cud-chewing mammals. Rinderpest doesn't affect humans. Measles, in turn, doesn't affect cattle. The close similarity of the measles and rinderpest viruses suggests that the rinderpest virus transferred from cattle to humans, then became the measles virus by changing its properties to adapt to us. That transfer isn't surprising, considering how closely many peasant farmers live and sleep next to cows and their accompanying feces, urine, breath, sores, and blood. Our intimacy with cattle has been going on for 8,000 years since we domesticated them—ample time for the rinderpest virus to discover us nearby. Other familiar infectious diseases can similarly be traced back to diseases of our animal friends.

Given our proximity to the animals we love, we must constantly be getting bombarded by animal microbes. Those invaders get winnowed by natural selection, and only a few succeed in establishing themselves as human diseases. A quick survey of current diseases lets us trace four stages in the evolution of a specialized human disease from an animal precursor.

In the first stage, we pick up animal-borne microbes that are still at an early stage in their evolution into specialized human pathogens. They don't get transmitted directly from one person to another, and even their transfer from animals to us remains uncommon. There are dozens of diseases like this that we get directly from pets and domestic animals. They include cat scratch fever from cats, leptospirosis from dogs, psittacosis from chickens and parrots, and brucellosis from cattle. We're similarly susceptible to picking up diseases from wild animals, such as the tularemia that hunters occasionally get from skinning wild rabbits.

In the second stage, a former animal pathogen evolves to the point where it does get transmitted directly between people and causes epidemics. However, the epidemic dies out for several reasons—being cured by modern medicine, stopping when everybody has been infected and died, or stopping when everybody has been infected and become immune. For example, a previously unknown disease termed *o'nyong-nyong* fever appeared in East Africa in 1959 and infected several million Africans. It probably arose from a virus of monkeys and was transmitted to humans by mosquitoes. The fact that patients recovered quickly and became immune to further attack helped cause the new disease to die out quickly.

The annals of medicine are full of diseases that sound like no known disease today but that once caused terrifying epidemics before disappearing as mysteriously as they had come. Who alive today remembers the "English sweating sickness" that swept and terrified Europe between 1485 and 1578, or the "Picardy sweats" of eighteenth- and nineteenth-century France?

A third stage in the evolution of our major diseases is represented by former animal pathogens that establish themselves in humans and that do not die out; until they do, the question of whether they will become major killers of humanity remains up for grabs. The future is still very uncertain for Lassa fever, first observed in 1969 in Nigeria and caused by a virus probably derived from rodents. Better established is Lyme disease, caused by a spirochete that we get from the bite of a tick. Although the first known human cases in the United States appeared only as recently as 1962, Lyme disease is already reaching epidemic proportions in the Northeast, on the West Coast, and in the upper Midwest. The future of AIDS, derived from monkey viruses, is even more secure, from the virus's perspective.

The final stage of this evolution is represented by the major, long-established epidemic diseases confined to humans. These diseases must have been the evolutionary survivors of far more pathogens that tried to make the jump to us from animals—and mostly failed.

Diseases represent evolution in progress, as microbes adapt by natural selection to new hosts. Compared with cows' bodies, though, our bodies offer different immune defenses and different chemistry. In that new environment, a microbe must evolve new ways to live and propagate itself.

The best-studied example of microbes evolving these new ways involves myxomatosis, which hit Australian rabbits in 1950. The myxoma virus, native to a wild species of Brazilian rabbit, was known to cause a lethal epidemic in European domestic rabbits, which are a different species. The virus was intentionally introduced to Australia in the hopes of ridding the continent of its plague of European rabbits, foolishly introduced in the nineteenth century. In the first year, myxoma produced a gratifying (to Australian farmers) 99.8 percent mortality in infected rabbits. Fortunately for the rabbits and unfortunately for the farmers, the death rate then dropped in the second year to 90 percent and eventually to 25 percent, frustrating hopes of eradicating rabbits completely from Australia. The problem was that the myxoma virus evolved to serve its own interest, which differed from the farmers' interests and those of the rabbits. The virus changed to kill fewer rabbits and to permit lethally infected ones to live longer before dying. The result was bad for Australian farmers but good for the virus: a less lethal myxoma virus spreads baby viruses to more rabbits than did the original, highly virulent myxoma.

For a similar example in humans, consider the surprising evolution of syphilis. Today we associate syphilis with genital sores and a very slowly developing disease, leading to the death of untreated victims only after many years. However, when syphilis was first definitely recorded in Europe in 1495, its pustules often covered the body from the head to the knees, caused flesh to fall off people's faces, and led to death within a few months. By 1546 syphilis had evolved into the disease with the symptoms known to us today. Apparently, just as with myxomatosis, those syphilis spirochetes evolved to keep their victims alive longer in order to transmit their spirochete offspring into more victims.

How, then, does all this explain the outcome of 1492—that Europeans conquered and depopulated the New World, instead of Native Americans conquering and depopulating Europe?

In the century or two following Columbus's arrival in the New World, the Indian population declined by about 95 percent. The main killers were European germs, to which the Indians had never been exposed.

Part of the answer, of course, goes back to the invaders' technological advantages. European guns and steel swords were more effective weapons than Native American stone axes and wooden clubs. Only Europeans had ships capable of crossing the ocean and horses that could provide a decisive advantage in battle. But that's not the whole answer. Far more Native Americans died in bed than on the battlefield—the victims of germs, not of guns and swords. Those germs undermined Indian resistance by killing most Indians and their leaders and by demoralizing the survivors.

The role of disease in the Spanish conquests of the Aztec and Inca empires is especially well documented. In 1519 Cortés landed on the coast of Mexico with 600 Spaniards to conquer the fiercely militaristic Aztec Empire, which at the time had a population of many millions. That Cortés reached the Aztec capital of Tenochtitlán, escaped with the loss of "only" two-thirds of his force, and managed to fight his way back to the coast demonstrates both Spanish military advantages and the initial naïveté of the Aztecs. But when Cortés's next onslaught came, in 1521, the Aztecs were no longer naïve; they fought street by street with the utmost tenacity.

What gave the Spaniards a decisive advantage this time was smallpox, which reached Mexico in 1520 with the arrival of one infected slave from Spanish Cuba. The resulting epidemic proceeded to kill nearly half the Aztecs. The survivors were demoralized by the mysterious illness that killed Indians and spared Spaniards, as if advertising the Spaniards' invincibility. By 1618 Mexico's initial population of 20 million had plummeted to about 1.6 million.

Pizarro had similarly grim luck when he landed on the coast of Peru in 1531 with about 200 men to conquer the Inca Empire. Fortunately for Pizarro, and unfortunately for the Incas, smallpox had arrived overland around 1524, killing much of the Inca population, including both Emperor Huayna Capac and his son and designated successor, Ninan Cuyoche. Because of the vacant throne, two other sons of Huayna Capac, Atahuallpa and Huáscar, became embroiled in a civil war that Pizarro exploited to conquer the divided Incas.

When we in the United States think of the most populous New World societies existing in 1492, only the Aztecs and Incas come to mind. We forget that North America also supported populous Indian societies in the Mississippi Valley. Sadly,

these societies too would disappear. But in this case conquistadores contributed nothing directly to the societies' destruction; the conquistadores' germs, spreading in advance, did everything. When De Soto marched through the Southeast in 1540, he came across Indian towns abandoned two years previously because nearly all the inhabitants had died in epidemics. However, he was still able to see some of the densely populated towns lining the lower Mississippi. By a century and a half later, though, when French settlers returned to the lower Mississippi, almost all those towns had vanished. Their relics are the great mound sites of the Mississippi Valley. Only recently have we come to realize that the mound-building societies were still largely intact when Columbus arrived, and that they collapsed between 1492 and the systematic European exploration of the Mississippi.

When I was a child in school, we were taught that North America had originally been occupied by about one million Indians. That low number helped justify the white conquest of what could then be viewed as an almost empty continent. However, archeological excavations and descriptions left by the first European explorers on our coasts now suggest an initial number of around 20 million. In the century or two following Columbus's arrival in the New World, the Indian population is estimated to have declined by about 95 percent.

The main killers were European germs, to which the Indians had never been exposed and against which they therefore had neither immunologic nor genetic resistance. Smallpox, measles, influenza, and typhus competed for top rank among the killers. As if those were not enough, pertussis, plague, tuberculosis, diphtheria, mumps, malaria, and yellow fever came close behind. In countless cases Europeans were actually there to witness the decimation that occurred when the germs arrived. For example, in 1837 the Mandan Indian tribe, with one of the most elaborate cultures in the Great Plains, contracted smallpox thanks to a steamboat traveling up the Missouri River from St. Louis. The population of one Mandan village crashed from 2,000 to less than 40 within a few weeks.

The one-sided exchange of lethal germs between the Old and New Worlds is among the most striking and consequence-laden facts of recent history. Whereas over a dozen major infectious diseases of Old World origins became established in the New World, not a single major killer reached Europe from the Americas. The sole possible exception is syphilis, whose area of origin still remains controversial.

That one-sidedness is more striking with the knowledge that large, dense human populations are a prerequisite for the evolution of crowd diseases. If recent reappraisals of the pre-Columbian New World population are correct, that population was not far below the contemporaneous population of Eurasia. Some New World cities, like Tenochtitlán, were among the world's most populous cities at the time. Yet Tenochtitlán didn't have awful germs waiting in store for the Spaniards. Why not?

One possible factor is the rise of dense human populations began somewhat later in the New World than in the Old. Another is that the three most populous American centers—the Andes, Mexico, and the Mississippi Valley—were never connected by regular fast trade into one gigantic breeding ground for microbes, in the way that Europe, North Africa, India, and China became connected in late Roman times.

The main reason becomes clear, however, if we ask a simple question: From what microbes could any crowd diseases of the Americas have evolved? We've seen that Eurasian crowd diseases evolved from diseases of domesticated herd animals. Significantly, there were many such animals in Eurasia. But there were only five animals that became domesticated in the Americas: the turkey in Mexico and parts of North America, the guinea pig and llama/alpaca (probably derived from the same original wild species) in the Andes, and Muscovy duck in tropical South America, and the dog throughout the Americas.

That extreme paucity of New World domestic animals reflects the paucity of wild starting material. About 80 percent of the big wild mammals of the Americas became extinct at the end of the last ice age, around 11,000 years ago, at approximately the same time that the first well-attested wave of Indian hunters spread over the Americas. Among the species that disappeared were ones that would have yielded useful domesticates, such as American horses and camels. Debate still rages as to whether those extinctions were due to climate changes or to the impact of Indian hunters on prey that had never seen humans. Whatever the reason, the extinctions removed most of the basis for Native American animal domestication—and for crowd diseases.

The few domesticates that remained were not likely sources of such diseases. Muscovy ducks and turkeys don't live in enormous flocks, and they're not naturally endearing species (like young lambs) with which we have much physical contact. Guinea pigs may have contributed a trypanosome infection like Chagas' disease or leishmaniasis to our catalog of woes, but that's uncertain.

Initially the most surprising absence is of any human disease derived from llamas (or alpacas), which are tempting to consider as the Andean equivalent of Eurasian livestock. However, llamas had three strikes against them as a source of human pathogens: their wild relatives don't occur in big herds as do wild sheep, goats, and pigs; their total numbers were never remotely as large as the Eurasian populations of domestic livestock, since llamas never spread beyond the Andes; and llamas aren't as cuddly as piglets and lambs and aren't kept in such close association with people. (You may not think of piglets as cuddly, but human mothers in the New Guinea highlands often nurse them, and they frequently live right in the huts of peasant farmers.)

The importance of animal-derived diseases for human history extends far beyond the Americas. Eurasian germs played a key role in decimating native peoples in many other parts of the world as well, including the Pacific islands, Australia, and southern Africa. Racist Europeans used to attribute those conquests to their supposedly better brains. But no evidence for such better brains has been forthcoming. Instead, the conquests were made possible by Europeans' nastier germs, and by the technological advances and denser populations that Europeans ultimately acquired by means of their domesticated plants and animals.

So on this 500th anniversary of Columbus's discovery, let's try to regain our sense of perspective about his hotly debated achievements. There's no doubt that Columbus was a great visionary, seaman, and leader. There's also no doubt that he and his successors often behaved as bestial murderers. But those facts alone don't fully explain why it took so few European immigrants to initially conquer and ultimately supplant so much of the native population of the Americas. Without the germs Europeans brought with them—germs that were derived from their animals—such conquests might have been impossible.

Critical Thinking

1. What are the major killers of humanity and where do they come from? How did most victims of war die before World War II? What determined the winners of past wars? What percentage of the pre-Columbian Indian population was killed by Spanish microbes?

2. How might a bug such as salmonella be passively transmitted to its next victim? What examples does the author provide of microbes getting a "free ride" to its next victim? How might they modify the anatomy or habits of their host in order to accelerate their transmission?

3. How does the author, therefore, describe such "symptoms" of disease? Why is it in the bug's interest to make us "sick"? Is it in the bug's interest to kill us? How does the author explain death? How do bacteria survive even though the hosts die?

4. What "common responses" do we use to stay alive?

5. Explain the principle of vaccination. How do the bugs "trick us"? Why is the AIDS virus one of the "slipperiest of all"?

6. What is our slowest defense mechanism? How does the author describe the "escalating evolutionary context"?

7. Explain the difference between pathogens that fight a "guerrilla war," creating a steady trickle of new cases, versus those that conduct a "blitzkrieg" and cause epidemics.

8. What characteristics are shared by infectious diseases that visit us as epidemics?

9. Why does measles die out in populations of less than half a million people but persists in larger population?

10. Why can't such "crowd diseases" sustain themselves in small bands of hunter-gatherers and slash-and burn farmers?

11. Does this mean that small human populations are free from all infectious diseases? Explain. Why does the author believe these to be the oldest diseases of humanity?

12. When did crowd diseases first develop and what are the various reasons for their increased frequency?

13. What is the paradox regarding these diseases? Where did they come from? Why does the author say we must be constantly bombarded by them?

14. Describe the four stages in the evolution of a specialized human disease from an animal precursor.

15. In what sense do diseases represent evolution in progress? How do the mixoma virus and the Australian rabbits provide an example?

16. How were Europeans technologically superior to Native Americans? What gave Cortez the decisive advantage over the Aztecs? Why were the surviving Aztecs demoralized? What was Pizarro's similar "grim luck"? What happened to the Mound Builders of the Mississippi Valley?

17. What was the author taught in school that originally justified conquest? What do we know now?

18. Why was there "one-sidedness" to the disease transmission in spite of the large Native American populations? Explain the author's reasoning.

Create Central

www.mhhe.com/createcentral

Internet References

Evolution and Medicine Network
http://evmedreview.com

World Health Organization
www.who.int/mental_health/en

JARED DIAMOND is a contributing editor of *Discover,* a professor of physiology at the UCLA School of Medicine, a recipient of a MacArthur genius award, and a research associate in ornithology at the American Museum of Natural History. Expanded versions of many of his *Discover* articles appear in his book *The Third Chimpanzee: The Evolution and Future of the Human Animal,* which won Britain's 1992 COPUS prize for best science book. Not least among his many accomplishments was his rediscovery in 1981 of the long-lost bowerbird of New Guinea. Diamond wrote about pseudo-hermaphrodites for *Discover*'s special June issue on the science of sex.

Article   Prepared by: Elvio Angeloni, *Pasadena City College*

The Price of Progress

JOHN BODLEY

Learning Outcomes

After reading this article, you will be able to:

- Discuss "economic development" as an ethnocentric Western concept.
- Determine if wealth and power are distributed fairly across the world.

> *In aiming at progress . . . you must let no one suffer by too drastic a measure, nor pay too high a price in upheaval and devastation, for your innovation.*
>
> Maunier, 1949: 725

Until recently, government planners have always considered economic development and progress beneficial goals that all societies should want to strive toward. The social advantage of progress—as defined in terms of increased incomes, higher standards of living, greater security, and better health—are thought to be positive, *universal* goods, to be obtained at any price. Although one may argue that tribal peoples must sacrifice their traditional cultures to obtain these benefits, government planners generally feel that this is a small price to pay for such obvious advantages.

In earlier chapters [in *Victims of Progress,* 3rd ed.], evidence was presented to demonstrate that autonomous tribal peoples have not *chosen* progress to enjoy its advantages, but that governments have *pushed* progress upon them to obtain tribal resources, not primarily to share with the tribal peoples the benefits of progress. It has also been shown that the price of forcing progress on unwilling recipients has involved the deaths of millions of tribal people, as well as their loss of land, political sovereignty, and the right to follow their own life style. This chapter does not attempt to further summarize that aspect of the cost of progress, but instead analyzes the specific effects of the participation of tribal peoples in the world-market economy. In direct opposition to the usual interpretation, it is argued here that the benefits of progress are often both illusory and detrimental to tribal peoples when they have not been allowed to control their own resources and define their relationship to the market economy.

Progress and the Quality of Life

One of the primary difficulties in assessing the benefits of progress and economic development for any culture is that of establishing a meaningful measure of both benefit and detriment. It is widely recognized that *standard of living,* which is the most frequently used measure of progress, is an intrinsically ethnocentric concept relying heavily upon indicators that lack universal cultural relevance. Such factors as GNP, per capita income, capital formation, employment rates, literacy, formal education, consumption of manufactured goods, number of doctors and hospital beds per thousand persons, and the amount of money spent on government welfare and health programs may be irrelevant measures of actual *quality* of life for autonomous or even semiautonomous tribal cultures. In its 1954 report, the Trust Territory government indicated that since the Micronesian population was still largely satisfying its own needs within a cashless subsistence economy, "Money income is not a significant measure of living standards, production, or well-being in this area" (TTR, 1953: 44). Unfortunately, within a short time the government began to rely on an enumeration of certain imported consumer goods as indicators of a higher standard of living in the islands, even though many tradition-oriented islanders felt that these new goods symbolized a lowering of the quality of life.

A more useful measure of the benefits of progress might be based on a formula for evaluating cultures devised by Goldschmidt (1952: 135). According to these less ethnocentric criteria, the important question to ask is: Does progress or economic development increase or decrease a given culture's ability to satisfy the physical and psychological needs of its population, or its stability? This question is a far more direct measure of quality of life than are the standard economic correlates of development, and it is universally relevant. Specific indication of this *standard* of living could be found for any society in the nutritional status and general physical and mental health of its population, the incidence of crime and delinquency, the demographic structure, family stability, and the society's relationship to its natural resource base. A society with high rates of malnutrition and crime, and one degrading its natural environment to the extent of threatening its continued existence, might be described as at a lower standard of living than is another society where these problems did not exist.

Careful examination of the data, which compare, on these specific points, the former condition of self-sufficient tribal peoples with their condition following their incorporation into the world-market economy, leads to the conclusion that their standard of living is *lowered,* not raised, by economic progress—and often to a dramatic degree. This is perhaps the most outstanding and inescapable fact to emerge from the years of research that anthropologists have devoted to the study of culture change and modernization. Despite the best intentions of those who have promoted change and improvement, all too often the results have been poverty, longer working hours, and much greater physical exertion, poor health, social disorder, discontent, discrimination, overpopulation, and environmental deterioration—combined with the destruction of the traditional culture.

Diseases of Development

Perhaps it would be useful for public health specialists to start talking about a new category of diseases. . . . Such diseases could be called the "diseases of development" and would consist of those pathological conditions which are based on the usually unanticipated consequences of the implementation of developmental schemes.

Hughes & Hunter, 1972: 93

Economic development increases the disease rate of affected peoples in at least three ways. First, to the extent that development is successful, it makes developed populations suddenly become vulnerable to all of the diseases suffered almost exclusively by "advanced" peoples. Among these are diabetes, obesity, hypertension, and a variety of circulatory problems. Second, development disturbs traditional environmental balances and may dramatically increase certain bacterial and parasite diseases. Finally, when development goals prove unattainable, an assortment of poverty diseases may appear in association with the crowded conditions of urban slums and the general breakdown in traditional socioeconomic systems.

Outstanding examples of the first situation can be seen in the Pacific, where some of the most successfully developed native peoples are found. In Micronesia, where development has progressed more rapidly than perhaps anywhere else, between 1958 and 1972 the population doubled, but the number of patients treated for heart disease in the local hospitals nearly tripled, mental disorder increased eightfold, and by 1972 hypertension and nutritional deficiencies began to make significant appearances for the first time (TTR, 1959, 1973, statistical tables).

Although some critics argue that the Micronesian figures simply represent better health monitoring due to economic progress, rigorously controlled data from Polynesia show a similar trend. The progressive acquisition of modern degenerative diseases was documented by an eight-member team of New Zealand medical specialists, anthropologists, and nutritionists, whose research was funded by the Medical Research Council of New Zealand and the World Health Organization. These researchers investigated the health status of a genetically

related population at various points along a continuum of increasing cash income, modernizing diet, and urbanization. The extremes on this acculturation continuum were represented by the relatively traditional Pukapukans of the Cook Islands and the essentially Europeanized New Zealand Maori, while the busily developing Rarotongans, also of the Cook Islands, occupied the intermediate position. In 1971, after eight years of work, the team's preliminary findings were summarized by Dr. Ian Prior, cardiologist and leader of the research, as follows:

We are beginning to observe that the more an islander takes on the ways of the West, the more prone he is to succumb to our degenerative diseases. In fact, it does not seem too much to say our evidence now shows that the farther the Pacific natives move from the quiet, carefree life of their ancestors, the closer they come to gout, diabetes, atherosclerosis, obesity, and hypertension.

Prior, 1971: 2

In Pukapuka, where progress was limited by the island's small size and its isolated location some 480 kilometers from the nearest port, the annual per capita income was only about thirty-six dollars and the economy remained essentially at a subsistence level. Resources were limited and the area was visited by trading ships only three or four times a year; thus, there was little opportunity for intensive economic development. Predictably, the population of Pukapuka was characterized by relatively low levels of imported sugar and salt intake, and a presumably related low level of heart disease, high blood pressure, and diabetes. In Rarotonga, where economic success was introducing town life, imported food, and motorcycles, sugar and salt intakes nearly tripled, high blood pressure increased approximately ninefold, diabetes two- to threefold, and heart disease doubled for men and more than quadrupled for women, while the number of grossly obese women increased more than tenfold. Among the New Zealand Maori, sugar intake was nearly eight times that of the Pukapukans, gout in men was nearly double its rate on Pukapuka, and diabetes in men was more than fivefold higher, while heart disease in women had increased more than sixfold. The Maori were, in fact, dying of "European" diseases at a greater rate than was the average New Zealand European.

Government development policies designed to bring about changes in local hydrology, vegetation, and settlement patterns and to increase population mobility, and even programs aimed at reducing certain diseases, have frequently led to dramatic increases in disease rates because of the unforeseen effects of disturbing the preexisting order. Hughes and Hunter (1972) published an excellent survey of cases in which development led directly to increased disease rates in Africa. They concluded that hasty development intervention in relatively balanced local cultures and environments resulted in "a drastic deterioration in the social and economic conditions of life."

Traditional populations in general have presumably learned to live with the endemic pathogens of their environments, and in some cases they have evolved genetic adaptations to specific diseases, such as the sickle-cell trait, which provided an immunity to malaria. Unfortunately, however, outside intervention has entirely changed this picture. In the late 1960s, sleeping sickness suddenly increased in many areas of Africa and even spread to areas where it did not formerly occur, due to the building of new roads and migratory labor, both of which caused increased population movement. Large-scale relocation schemes, such as the Zande Scheme, had disastrous results when natives were moved from their traditional disease-free refuges into infected areas. Dams and irrigation developments inadvertently created ideal conditions for the rapid proliferation of snails carrying schistosomiasis (a liver fluke disease), and major epidemics suddenly occurred in areas where this disease had never before been a problem. DDT spraying programs have been temporarily successful in controlling malaria, but there is often a rebound effect that increases the problem when spraying is discontinued, and the malarial mosquitoes are continually evolving resistant strains.

Urbanization is one of the prime measures of development, but it is a mixed blessing for most former tribal peoples. Urban health standards are abysmally poor and generally worse than in rural areas for the detribalized individuals who have crowded into the towns and cities throughout Africa, Asia, and Latin America seeking wage employment out of new economic necessity. Infectious diseases related to crowding and poor sanitation are rampant in urban centers, while greatly increased stress and poor nutrition aggravate a variety of other health problems. Malnutrition and other diet-related conditions are, in fact, one of the characteristic hazards of progress faced by tribal peoples and are discussed in the following sections.

The Hazards of Dietary Change

The traditional diets of tribal peoples are admirably adapted to their nutritional needs and available food resources. Even though these diets may seem bizarre, absurd, and unpalatable to outsiders, they are unlikely to be improved by drastic modifications. Given the delicate balances and complexities involved in any subsistence system, change always involves risks, but for tribal people the effects of dietary change have been catastrophic.

Under normal conditions, food habits are remarkably resistant to change, and indeed people are unlikely to abandon their traditional diets voluntarily in favor of dependence on difficult-to-obtain exotic imports. In some cases it is true that imported foods may be identified with powerful outsiders and are therefore sought as symbols of greater prestige. This may lead to such absurdities as Amazonian Indians choosing to consume imported canned tunafish when abundant high-quality fish is available in their own rivers. Another example of this situation occurs in tribes where mothers prefer to feed their infants expensive nutritionally inadequate canned milk from unsanitary, but *high status,* baby bottles. The high status of these items is often promoted by clever traders and clever advertising campaigns.

Aside from these apparently voluntary changes, it appears that more often dietary changes are forced upon unwilling tribal peoples by circumstances beyond their control. In some areas, new food crops have been introduced by government decree, or as a consequence of forced relocation or other policies designed to end hunting, pastoralism, or shifting cultivation. Food habits have also been modified by massive disruption of the natural environment by outsiders—as when sheepherders transformed the Australian Aborigines' foraging territory or when European invaders destroyed the bison herds that were the primary element in the Plains Indians' subsistence patterns. Perhaps the most frequent cause of diet change occurs when formerly self-sufficient peoples find that wage labor, cash cropping, and other economic development activities that feed tribal resources into the world-market economy must inevitably divert time and energy away from the production of subsistence foods. Many developing peoples suddenly discover that, like it or not, they are unable to secure traditional foods and must spend their newly acquired cash on costly, and often nutritionally inferior, manufactured foods.

Overall, the available data seem to indicate that the dietary changes that are linked to involvement in the world-market economy have tended to *lower* rather than raise the nutritional levels of the affected tribal peoples. Specifically, the vitamin, mineral, and protein components of their diets are often drastically reduced and replaced by enormous increases in starch and carbohydrates, often in the form of white flour and refined sugar.

Any deterioration in the quality of a given population's diet is almost certain to be reflected in an increase in deficiency diseases and a general decline in health status. Indeed, as tribal peoples have shifted to a diet based on imported manufactured or processed foods, there has been a dramatic rise in malnutrition, a massive increase in dental problems, and a variety of other nutritional-related disorders. Nutritional physiology is so complex that even well-meaning dietary changes have had tragic consequences. In many areas of Southeast Asia, government-sponsored protein supplementation programs supplying milk to protein-deficient populations caused unexpected health problems and increased mortality. Officials failed to anticipate that in cultures where adults do not normally drink milk, the enzymes needed to digest it are no longer produced and milk *intolerance* results (Davis & Bolin, 1972). In Brazil, a similar milk distribution program caused an epidemic of permanent blindness by aggravating a preexisting vitamin A deficiency (Bunce, 1972).

Teeth and Progress

There is nothing new in the observation that savages, or peoples living under primitive conditions, have, in general, excellent teeth. . . . Nor is it news that most civilized populations possess wretched teeth which begin to decay almost before they have erupted completely, and that dental caries is likely to be accompanied by periodontal disease with further reaching complications.

Hooton, 1945: xviii

Anthropologists have long recognized that undisturbed tribal peoples are often in excellent physical condition. And it has often been noted specifically that dental caries and the other dental abnormalities that plague industrialized societies are absent or rare among tribal peoples who have retained their traditional diets. The fact that tribal food habits may contribute to the development of sound teeth, whereas modernized diets may do just the opposite, was illustrated as long ago as 1894 in an article in the *Journal of the Royal Anthropological Institute* that described the results of a comparison between the teeth of ten Sioux Indians who were examined when they came to London as members of Buffalo Bill's Wild West Show and were found to be completely free of caries and in possession of all their teeth, even though half of the group were over thirty-nine years of age. Londoners' teeth were conspicuous for both their caries and their steady reduction in number with advancing age. The difference was attributed primarily to the wear and polishing caused by the traditional Indian diet of coarse food and the fact that they chewed their food longer, encouraged by the absence of tableware.

One of the most remarkable studies of the dental conditions of tribal peoples and the impact of dietary change was conducted in the 1930s by Weston Price (1945), an American dentist who was interested in determining what caused normal, healthy teeth. Between 1931 and 1936, Price systematically explored tribal areas throughout the world to locate and examine the most isolated peoples who were still living on traditional foods. His fieldwork covered Alaska, the Canadian Yukon, Hudson Bay, Vancouver Island, Florida, the Andes, the Amazon, Samoa, Tahiti, New Zealand, Australia, New Caledonia, Fiji, the Torres Strait, East Africa, and the Nile. The study demonstrated both the superior quality of aboriginal dentition and the devastation that occurs as modern diets are adopted. In nearly every area where traditional foods were still being eaten, Price found perfect teeth with normal dental arches and virtually no decay, whereas caries and abnormalities increased steadily as new diets were adopted. In many cases the change was sudden and striking. Among Eskimo groups subsisting entirely on traditional food he found caries totally absent, whereas in groups eating a considerable quantity of store-bought food approximately 20 percent of their teeth were decayed. This figure rose to more than 30 percent with Eskimo groups subsisting almost exclusively on purchased or government-supplied food, and reached an incredible 48 percent among the Vancouver Island Indians. Unfortunately for many of these people, modern dental treatment did not accompany the new food, and their suffering was appalling. The loss of teeth was, of course, bad enough in itself, and it certainly undermined the population's resistance to many new diseases, including tuberculosis. But new foods were also accompanied by crowded, misplaced teeth, gum diseases, distortion of the face, and pinching of the nasal cavity. Abnormalities in the dental arch appeared in the new generation following the change in diet, while caries appeared almost immediately even in adults.

Price reported that in many areas the affected peoples were conscious of their own physical deterioration. At a mission school in Africa, the principal asked him to explain to the native schoolchildren why they were not physically as strong as children who had had no contact with schools. On an island in the Torres Strait the natives knew exactly what was causing their problems and resisted—almost to the point of

bloodshed—government efforts to establish a store that would make imported food available. The government prevailed, however, and Price was able to establish a relationship between the length of time the government store had been established and the increasing incidence of caries among a population that showed an almost 100 percent immunity to them before the store had been opened.

In New Zealand, the Maori, who in their aboriginal state are often considered to have been among the healthiest, most perfectly developed of people, were found to have "advanced" the furthest. According to Price:

> *Their modernization was demonstrated not only by the high incidence of dental caries but also by the fact that 90 percent of the adults and 100 percent of the children had abnormalities of the dental arches.*

> Price, 1945: 206

Malnutrition

Malnutrition, particularly in the form of protein deficiency, has become a critical problem for tribal peoples who must adopt new economic patterns. Population pressures, cash cropping, and government programs all have tended to encourage the replacement of traditional crops and other food sources that were rich in protein with substitutes, high in calories but low in protein. In Africa, for example, protein-rich staples such as millet and sorghum are being replaced systematically by high-yielding manioc and plantains, which have insignificant amounts of protein. The problem is increased for cash croppers and wage laborers whose earnings are too low and unpredictable to allow purchase of adequate amounts of protein. In some rural areas, agricultural laborers have been forced systematically to deprive nonproductive members (principally children) of their households of their minimal nutritional requirements to satisfy the need of the productive members. This process has been documented in northeastern Brazil following the introduction of large-scale sisal plantations (Gross & Underwood, 1971). In urban centers the difficulties of obtaining nutritionally adequate diets are even more serious for tribal immigrants, because costs are higher and poor quality foods are more tempting.

One of the most tragic, and largely overlooked, aspects of chronic malnutrition is that it can lead to abnormally undersized brain development and apparently irreversible brain damage; it has been associated with various forms of mental impairment or retardation. Malnutrition has been linked clinically with mental retardation in both Africa and Latin America (see, for example, Mönckeberg, 1968), and this appears to be a worldwide phenomenon with serious implications (Montagu, 1972).

Optimistic supporters of progress will surely say that all of these new health problems are being overstressed and that the introduction of hospitals, clinics, and the other modern health institutions will overcome or at least compensate for all of these difficulties. However, it appears that uncontrolled population growth and economic impoverishment probably will keep most of these benefits out of reach for many tribal peoples, and the intervention of modern medicine has at least partly contributed to the problem in the first place.

The generalization that civilization frequently has a broad negative impact on tribal health has found broad empirical support (see especially Kroeger & Barbira-Freedman [1982] on Amazonia; Reinhard [1976] on the Arctic; and Wirsing [1985] globally), but these conclusions have not gone unchallenged. Some critics argue that tribal health was often poor before modernization, and they point specifically to tribals' low life expectancy and high infant mortality rates. Demographic statistics on tribal populations are often problematic because precise data are scarce, but they do show a less favorable profile than that enjoyed by many industrial societies. However, it should be remembered that our present life expectancy is a recent phenomenon that has been very costly in terms of medical research and technological advances. Furthermore, the benefits of our health system are not enjoyed equally by all members of our society. High infant mortality could be viewed as a relatively inexpensive and egalitarian tribal public health program that offered the reasonable expectation of a healthy and productive life for those surviving to age fifteen.

Some critics also suggest that certain tribal populations, such as the New Guinea highlanders, were "stunted" by nutritional deficiencies created by tribal culture and are "improved" by "acculturation" and cash cropping (Dennett & Connell, 1988). Although this argument does suggest that the health question requires careful evaluation, it does not invalidate the empirical generalizations already established. Nutritional deficiencies undoubtedly occurred in densely populated zones in the central New Guinea highlands. However, the specific case cited above may not be widely representative of other tribal groups even in New Guinea, and it does not address the facts of outside intrusion or the inequities inherent in the contemporary development process.

Ecocide

"How is it," asked a herdsman . . . "how is it that these hills can no longer give pasture to my cattle? In my father's day they were green and cattle thrived there; today there is no grass and my cattle starve." As one looked one saw that what had once been a green hill had become a raw red rock.

Jones, 1934

Progress not only brings new threats to the health of tribal peoples, but it also imposes new strains on the ecosystems upon which they must depend for their ultimate survival. The introduction of new technology, increased consumption, lowered mortality, and the eradication of all traditional controls have combined to replace what for most tribal peoples was a relatively stable balance between population and natural resources, with a new system that is imbalanced. Economic development is forcing *ecocide* on peoples who were once careful stewards of their resources. There is already a trend toward widespread environmental deterioration in tribal areas, involving resource depletion, erosion, plant and animal extinction, and a disturbing series of other previously unforeseen changes.

After the initial depopulation suffered by most tribal peoples during their engulfment by frontiers of national expansion, most tribal populations began to experience rapid growth. Authorities generally attribute this growth to the introduction of modern medicine and new health measures and the termination of intertribal warfare, which lowered morality rates, as well as to new technology, which increased food production. Certainly all of these factors played a part, but merely lowering mortality rates would not have produced the rapid population growth that most tribal areas have experienced if traditional birth-spacing mechanisms had not been eliminated at the same time. Regardless of which factors were most important, it is clear that all of the natural and cultural checks on population growth have suddenly been pushed aside by culture change, while tribal lands have been steadily reduced and consumption levels have risen. In many tribal areas, environmental deterioration due to overuse of resources has set in, and in other areas such deterioration is imminent as resources continue to dwindle relative to the expanding population and increased use. Of course, population expansion by tribal peoples may have positive political consequences, because where tribals can retain or regain their status as local majorities they may be in a more favorable position to defend their resources against intruders.

Swidden systems and pastoralism, both highly successful economic systems under traditional conditions, have proved particularly vulnerable to increased population pressures and outside efforts to raise productivity beyond its natural limits. Research in Amazonia demonstrates that population pressures and related resource depletion can be created indirectly by official policies that restrict swidden peoples to smaller territories. Resource depletion itself can then become a powerful means of forcing tribal people into participating in the world-market economy—thus leading to further resource depletion. For example, Bodley and Benson (1979) showed how the Shipibo Indians in Peru were forced to further deplete their forest resources by cash cropping in the forest area to replace the resources that had been destroyed earlier by the intensive cash cropping necessitated by the narrow confines of their reserve. In this case, certain species of palm trees that had provided critical housing materials were destroyed by forest clearing and had to be replaced by costly purchased materials. Research by Gross (1979) and others showed similar processes at work among four tribal groups in central Brazil and demonstrated that the degree of market involvement increases directly with increases in resource depletion.

The settling of nomadic herders and the removal of prior controls on herd size have often led to serious overgrazing and erosion problems where these had not previously occurred. There are indications that the desertification problem in the Sahel region of Africa was aggravated by programs designed to settle nomads. The first sign of imbalance in a swidden system appears when the planting cycles are shortened to the point that garden plots are reused before sufficient forest regrowth can occur. If reclearing and planting continue in the same area, the natural patterns of forest succession may be disturbed irreversibly and the soil can be impaired permanently. An extensive tract of tropical rainforest in the lower Amazon of Brazil was reduced to a semiarid desert in just fifty years through such a process (Ackermann, 1964). The soils in the Azande area are also now seriously threatened with laterization and other problems as a result of the government-promoted cotton development scheme (McNeil, 1972).

The dangers of overdevelopment and the vulnerability of local resource systems have long been recognized by both anthropologists and tribal peoples themselves. But the pressures for change have been overwhelming. In 1948 the Maya villagers of Chan Kom complained to Redfield (1962) about the shortening of their swidden cycles, which they correctly attributed to increasing population pressures. Redfield told them, however, that they had no choice but to go "forward with technology" (Redfield, 1962: 178). In Assam, swidden cycles were shortened from an average of twelve years to only two or three within just twenty years, and anthropologists warned that the limits of swiddening would soon be reached (Burling, 1963: 311–312). In the Pacific, anthropologists warned of population pressures on limited resources as early as the 1930s (Keesing, 1941: 64–65). These warnings seemed fully justified, considering the fact that the crowded Tikopians were prompted by population pressures on their tiny island to suggest that infanticide be legalized. The warnings have been dramatically reinforced since then by the doubling of Micronesia's population in just the fourteen years between 1958 and 1972, from 70,600 to 114,645, while consumption levels have soared. By 1985 Micronesia's population had reached 162,321.

The environmental hazards of economic development and rapid population growth have become generally recognized only since worldwide concerns over environmental issues began in the early 1970s. Unfortunately, there is as yet little indication that the leaders of the new developing nations are sufficiently concerned with environmental limitations. On the contrary, governments are forcing tribal peoples into a self-reinforcing spiral of population growth and intensified resource exploitation, which may be stopped only by environmental disaster or the total impoverishment of the tribals.

The reality of ecocide certainly focuses attention on the fundamental contrasts between tribal and industrial systems in their use of natural resources, who controls them, and how they are managed. Tribal peoples are victimized because they control resources that outsiders demand. The resources exist because tribals managed them conservatively. However, as with the issue of the health consequences of detribalization, some anthropologists minimize the adaptive achievements of tribal groups and seem unwilling to concede that ecocide might be a consequence of cultural change. Critics attack an exaggerated "noble savage" image of tribals living in perfect harmony with nature and having no visible impact on their surroundings. They then show that tribals do in fact modify the environment, and they conclude that there is no significant difference between how tribals and industrial societies treat their environments. For example, Charles Wagley declared that Brazilian Indians such as the Tapirape

are not "natural men." They have human vices just as we do. . . . They do not live "in tune" with nature any more than I do; in fact, they can often be as destructive of their environment, within their limitations, as some civilized men. The Tapirape are not innocent or childlike in any way.

Wagley, 1977: 302

Anthropologist Terry Rambo demonstrated that the Semang of the Malaysian rain forests have a measurable impact on their environment. In his monograph *Primitive Polluters*, Rambo (1985) reported that the Semang live in smoke-filled houses. They sneeze and spread germs, breathe, and thus emit carbon dioxide. They clear small gardens, contributing "particulate matter" to the air and disturbing the local climate because cleared areas proved measurably warmer and drier than the shady forest. Rambo concluded that his research "demonstrates the essential functional similarity of the environmental interactions of primitive and civilized societies" (1985: 78) in contrast to a "noble savage" view (Bodley, 1983) which, according to Rambo (1985: 2), mistakenly "claims that traditional peoples almost always live in essential harmony with their environment."

This is surely a false issue. To stress, as I do, that tribals tend to manage their resources for sustained yield within relatively self-sufficient subsistence economies is not to make them either innocent children or natural men. Nor is it to deny that tribals "disrupt" their environment and may never be in absolute "balance" with nature.

The ecocide issue is perhaps most dramatically illustrated by two sets of satellite photos taken over the Brazilian rain forests of Rôndonia (Allard & McIntyre, 1988: 780–781). Photos taken in 1973, when Rôndonia was still a tribal domain, show virtually unbroken rain forest. The 1987 satellite photos, taken after just fifteen years of highway construction and "development" by outsiders, show more than 20 percent of the forest destroyed. The surviving Indians were being concentrated by FUNAI (Brazil's national Indian foundation) into what would soon become mere islands of forest in a ravaged landscape. It is irrelevant to quibble about whether tribals are noble, childlike, or innocent, or about the precise meaning of balance with nature, carrying capacity, or adaptation, to recognize that for the past 200 years rapid environmental deterioration on an unprecedented global scale has followed the wresting of control of vast areas of the world from tribal groups by resource-hungry industrial societies.

Deprivation and Discrimination

Contact with European culture has given them a knowledge of great wealth, opportunity and privilege, but only very limited avenues by which to acquire these things.

Crocombe, 1968

Unwittingly, tribal peoples have had the burden of perpetual relative deprivation thrust upon them by acceptance—either by themselves or by the governments administering them—of the standards of socioeconomic progress set for them by industrial civilizations. By comparison with the material wealth of industrial societies, tribal societies become, by definition, impoverished. They are then forced to transform their cultures and work to achieve what many economists now acknowledge to be unattainable goals. Even though in many cases the modest GNP goals set by development planners for the developing nations during the "development decade" of the 1960s were often met, the results were hardly noticeable for most of the tribal people involved. Population growth, environmental limitations, inequitable distribution of wealth, and the continued rapid growth of the industrialized nations have all meant that both the absolute and the relative gap between the rich and poor in the world is steadily widening. The prospect that tribal peoples will actually be able to attain the levels of resource consumption to which they are being encouraged to aspire is remote indeed except for those few groups who have retained effective control over strategic mineral resources.

Tribal peoples feel deprivation not only when the economic goals they have been encouraged to seek fail to materialize, but also when they discover that they are powerless, second-class citizens who are discriminated against and exploited by the dominant society. At the same time, they are denied the satisfactions of their traditional cultures, because these have been sacrificed in the process of modernization. Under the impact of major economic change family life is disrupted, traditional social controls are often lost, and many indicators of social anomie such as alcoholism, crime, delinquency, suicide, emotional disorders, and despair may increase. The inevitable frustration resulting from this continual deprivation finds expression in the cargo cults, revitalization movements, and a variety of other political and religious movements that have been widespread among tribal peoples following their disruption by industrial civilization.

References

Ackermann, F. L. 1964. *Geologia e Fisiografia da Região Bragantina, Estado do Pará*. Manaus, Brazil: Conselho Nacional de Pesquisas, Instituto Nacional de Pesquisas da Amazonia.

Allard, William Albert, and Loren McIntyre. 1988. Rondônia's settlers invade Brazil's imperiled rain forest. *National Geographic* 174(6):772–799.

Bodley, John H. 1970. *Campa Socio-Economic Adaptation*. Ann Arbor: University Microfilms.

———. 1983. *Der Weg der Zerstörung: Stammesvölker und die industrielle Zivilization*. Munich: Trickster-Verlag. (Translation of *Victims of Progress*.)

Bodley, John H., and Foley C. Benson. 1979. Cultural ecology of Amazonian palms. *Reports of Investigations*, no. 56. Pullman: Laboratory of Anthropology, Washington State University.

Bunce, George E. 1972. Aggravation of vitamin A deficiency following distribution of non-fortified skim milk: An example of nutrient interaction. In *The Careless Technology: Ecology and International Development*, ed. M. T. Farvar and John P. Milton, pp. 53–60. Garden City, N.Y.: Natural History Press.

Burling, Robbins. 1963. *Rengsanggri: Family and Kinship in a Garo Village*. Philadelphia: University of Pennsylvania Press.

Davis, A. E., and T. D. Bolin. 1972. Lactose intolerance in Southeast Asia. In *The Careless Technology: Ecology and International Development*, ed. M. T. Farvar and John P. Milton, pp. 61–68. Garden City, N.Y.: Natural History Press.

Dennett, Glenn, and John Connell. 1988. Acculturation and health in the highlands of Papua New Guinea. *Current Anthropology* 29(2):273–299.

Goldschmidt, Walter R. 1972. The interrelations between cultural factors and the acquisition of new technical skills. In *The Progress of Underdeveloped Areas*, ed. Bert F. Hoselitz, pp. 135–151. Chicago: University of Chicago Press.

Gross, Daniel R., et al. 1979. Ecology and acculturation among native peoples of Central Brazil. *Science* 206(4422):1043–1050.

Hughes, Charles C., and John M. Hunter. 1972. The role of technological development in promoting disease in Africa. In *The Careless Technology: Ecology and International Development*, ed. M. T. Farvar and John P. Milton, pp. 69–101. Garden City, N.Y.: Natural History Press.

Keesing, Felix M. 1941. *The South Seas in the Modern World*. Institute of Pacific Relations International Research Series. New York: John Day.

Kroeger, Axel, and François Barbira-Freedman. 1982. *Culture Change and Health: The Case of South American Rainforest Indians*. Frankfurt am Main: Verlag Peter Lang. (Reprinted in Bodley, 1988a:221–236.)

McNeil, Mary. 1972. Lateritic soils in distinct tropical environments: Southern Sudan and Brazil. In *The Careless Technology: Ecology and International Development*, ed. M. T. Farvar and John P. Milton, pp. 591–608. Garden City, N.Y.: Natural History Press.

Mönckeberg, F. 1968. Mental retardation from malnutrition. *Journal of the American Medical Association* 206:30–31.

Montagu, Ashley. 1972. Sociogenic brain damage. *American Anthropologist* 74(5):1045–1061.

Rambo, A. Terry. 1985. *Primitive Polluters: Semang Impact on the Malaysian Tropical Rain Forest Ecosystem*. Anthropological Papers no. 76, Museum of Anthropology, University of Michigan.

Redfield, Robert. 1953. *The Primitive World and Its Transformations*. Ithaca, N.Y.: Cornell University Press.

———. 1962. *A Village That Chose Progress: Chan Kom Revisited*. Chicago: University of Chicago Press, Phoenix Books.

Smith, Wilberforce. 1894. The teeth of ten Sioux Indians. *Journal of the Royal Anthropological Institute* 24:109–116.

TTR: *See under* United States.

United States, Department of the Interior, Office of Territories. 1953. *Report on the Administration of the Trust Territory of the Pacific Islands* (by the United States to the United Nations) for the Period July 1, 1951 to June 30, 1952.

———. 1954. *Annual Report, High Commissioner of the Trust Territory of the Pacific Islands to the Secretary of the Interior* (for 1953).

United States, Department of State. 1955. *Seventh Annual Report to the United Nations on the Administration of the Trust Territory of the Pacific Islands* (July 1, 1953 to June 30, 1954).

———. 1959. *Eleventh Annual Report to the United Nations on the Administration of the Trust Territory of the Pacific Islands* (July 1, 1957 to June 30, 1958).

———. 1964. *Sixteenth Annual Report to the United Nations on the Administration of the Trust Territory of the Pacific Islands* (July 1, 1962 to June 30, 1963).

———. 1973. *Twenty-Fifth Annual Report to the United Nations on the Administration of the Trust Territory of the Pacific Islands* (July 1, 1971 to June 30, 1972).

Critical Thinking

1. Why is "standard of living" an intrinsically ethnocentric concept as a measure of progress? What is a more useful measure and why? What does a careful examination based upon the specific points show?

2. In what ways does economic development increase the disease rate of affected peoples?

3. How does the author answer critics who argue that such figures simply represent better health monitoring? List the examples cited.

4. Explain the effects of government policy on peoples' adaptations to local environmental conditions.

5. Describe the circumstances under which peoples' dietary habits have been changed as a result of outside influences. What has happened to nutritional levels and why?

6. To what was attributed the differences in dental health between the Sioux Indians of Buffalo Bill's Wild West Show and Londoners?

7. What did Weston Price find in his studies?

8. Describe the chain of events that goes from the adoption of new economic patterns to changes in the kinds of crops grown to low wages to nutritional deprivation (principally of children).

9. What is one of the most tragic, and largely overlooked, aspects of chronic malnutrition?

10. What are the prospects that modern health institutions will overcome these problems?

11. How does the author respond to critics who charge that tribal peoples have always had low life expectancies, high infant mortality rates, and nutritional deficiencies?

12. What factors have contributed to population growth?

13. What are the consequences for each of the following:
    - Official policy restricting swidden people to smaller territories?
    - Resource depletion forcing people to participate in the world-market economy?
    - The settling of nomadic herders and the removal of prior controls on herd size?
    - Shortening the planting cycles?

14. How does the reality of ecocide focus attention on the fundamental contrasts between tribal and industrial systems in their use of natural resources? Who controls such resources and how are they managed?

15. What do the critics of the "noble savage" image claim? How does the author respond?

16. In what respects do tribal peoples feel deprivation as a result of "modernization"?

Create Central

www.mhhe.com/createcentral

Internet References

Association for Political and Legal Anthropology
www.aaanet.org/apla/index.htm

Human Rights and Humanitarian Assistance
www.etown.edu/vl/humrts.html

The Indigenous Rights Movement in the Pacific
www.inmotionmagazine.com/pacific.html

Murray Research Center
www.radcliffe.edu/murray_redirect/index.php

WWW Virtual Library: Indigenous Studies
www.cwis.org

Article   Prepared by: Elvio Angeloni

Sanctioned Theft: Tribal Land Loss in Massachusetts

CULTURAL SURVIVAL QUARTERLY

Learning Outcomes

After reading this article, you will be able to:

- Discuss the "legal" methods used by the English in claiming native lands in colonial New England.

- Discuss the contrast between Native Peoples' concepts of customary access to land versus the colonists' views on property ownership.

- Discuss the English guardianship as it was used by the colonists to acquire native lands.

- Describe the effect of the Enfranchisement Act of 1869 upon Indian communal land holdings.

- Describe the far-reaching consequences of the European appropriation of tribal land for Native Americans.

Native land loss, the policies that enabled it, and the subsequent consequences on Native American tribes in Massachusetts was the subject of a panel discussion at Suffolk University last April. "A Hidden History: How Massachusetts Law and Policy Facilitated the Loss of Tribal Lands" convened with an opening blessing by Jim Peters, executive director of the Massachusetts Commission on Indian Affairs. Panelists included Ann Marie Plane, an associate professor of history at the University of California-Santa Barbara; Cheryll Toney Holley, chief of the Nipmuc Nation and Hassanamisco Band of Nipmuc Indians; Raymond Trusty Williams, Jr. (Golden Hawk), vice president of the Tribal Council for the Chappaquiddick Wampanoag Tribe; Alma Gordon-Smith, sachem (chief) of the Chappaquiddick Wampanoag Tribe; and

Bill Hunt, vice chairman of the Herring Pond Wampanoag Tribe in Southern Plymouth, Massachusetts.

Plane provided the context for the discussion, explaining "how a land-holding Native majority population became a landless minority over the span of just a few centuries [and] was virtually erased from the awareness of local society." She pointed to the imposition of legal wardship, nineteenth-century ideas about so-called racial purity defining "real" Native Americans, and the misapplication of concepts of equal rights and blind justice as keys to colonial-era land procurement.

The advent of legal control over Native populations dates back to the seventeeth century as colonists established land claims under the auspices of both crown and religious law; such efforts included "praying towns," which were set up in an attempt to convert Native people to Christianity and organize their interactions with English colonists. Native subjugation was aided by widespread pandemics and the ensuing decimation of tribes, events interpreted by the non-Native settlers as divine retribution and further solidifying their notions of the righteousness of colonial settlements.

English doctrine about land ownership—namely, that unoccupied lands could be legally claimed—also contributed to Native land loss. Since Native people had different concepts of governance and land use, their migration patterns created vacant territories. Holley explained: "We weren't wanderers and vagrants; it's just how our traditional way of life was. We knew where to go and at what time to go there. We never had that concept of ownership before." Even after losing official title to their lands, however, Native people often retained customary rights of access to the areas and returned to places that were culturally significant.

"Despite the fact that they felt completely entitled, legally and religiously, to these lands, colonists did purchase land from Native landholders and sachems," Plane said, noting how multiple lines of descent and competition for resources complicated the deals. Because there was no Free, Prior and Informed Consent, Native people were forced to operate within an imposed foreign legal and tax system with little understanding of the consequences for the future. Toward the end of the eighteenth century, English settlers developed a guardianship system ostensibly to prevent the abuse of Native Americans during land negotiations, but in reality only furthering the fraud, abuse, and corruption. Guardians were paid by the tribes, but often the tribes' only sources of income were from sales of land or resources. Holley described how the majority of the Hassanamesit Nipmuc reservation, near today's town of Grafton, was sold to English families for £2,500. "They're supposed to distribute the funds from the purchase to the Native people when they need it, but instead what happens is that it disappears," she said.

Multiple state congressional reports from the mid-1800s investigating such guardianships acknowledged that many guardians had siphoned trust funds for personal use and that the state was indebted to several tribes. "Without the money from these trust funds, the Nipmuc people began to sell off the remaining land to pay off debts, back taxes, and care for the sick and elderly, to build English-style houses and fences, the things they could have used the trust funds for," Holley explained. "People accumulated little debts like the general store bill, and they would have 10 acres of land sold off to settle those. Loss of land destroyed communities. Families could not support themselves on dwindling acreage, could not farm, hunt, or gather because these were someone else's property and fences were put up. They had to move away to find jobs."

Today, only three acres remain of the original Hassanamesit reservation in Grafton. Although no Nipmuc people live on their traditional lands, they continue to congregate for cultural events that serve as an important connection to their ancestors.

Community Disrupted; Rebuilt

The Chappaquiddick Wampanoag once inhabited the entire island of Chappaquiddick, a small island off the eastern end of Martha's Vineyard. But by 1788, European expansion via unscrupulous land deals left the Chappaquiddick with just one-fifth of the island—mostly sandy soil that was difficult to cultivate. The Enfranchisement Act of 1869 granted full citizenship rights to Native people and also removed the special status possessed by the state's 10 reservations, effectively eliminating Indian communal land holding. Thousands of acres of reservation land were divided up or sold in the intervening years, and the previously held Chappaquiddick territory became part

of Edgartown. After the land reallotment most Chappaquiddick dispersed to the mainland in search of employment, mainly in domestic servitude. "It was a struggle for our people to maintain our sense of community and eke out a living," GordonSmith said. Today, two large Chappaquiddick families remain on the island; the tribe is working to reclaim lands by untangling the complex history of title transfers and land sales.

Although Native people lost control over their lands, they never lost their cultural connection, and in fact have maintained a continual presence in most areas. Hunt spoke about the Wampanoag tribal land of Herring Pond, which traditionally ranges from Plymouth, Massachusetts to parts of upper Cape Cod. The original reservation was laid out in the 1700s totaling 3,000 acres, but in 1742 the Commonwealth ordered all remnants of historical tribes to move to one of four communities with functioning governments: Mashpee, Aquinnah, Herring Pond, or Hassanamesit.

During Herring Pond's assimilation, the Wampanoag struggled with issues of debt, earning a living, and creating a stable community, difficulties encountered by many other tribes. In order to survive, many moved off of reservations and adopted English habits. When the balance of Herring Pond was finally auctioned off in 1873, the tribe largely disappeared from historical records—but its people persisted, remaining in traditional areas and continuing key aspects of their culture. In 1928 the tribe organized its first powwow in over 200 years, and since then has also turned the Pondville Baptist Church Meeting House into a central place of congregation. "Considering all of the things that have been done to remove Natives from their land, whether it was legal or illegal, the fact that we're still here says a lot," Hunt said, adding that the tribe is still discovering property to which it holds the title and is working to rebuild the community.

The European appropriation of tribal land has had far-reaching consequences for Native Americans, as traditional healing methods, arts, governance, original language, and spiritual beliefs related to the land were all disrupted. Speaking about the Chappaquiddick, Gordon-Smith said that "the allocation of their land has taken a toll on many levels: community ties are challenged, there is conflict within tribes, they could not comfortably visit the land, and it's difficult to build self-esteem as a people." But as Plane said, "Native peoples never gave up their identity. They never gave up their connection to the land. They never let the state decide who was or was not Native," and that "this long and proud tradition of activism in these communities is continued today in the efforts of many in the state of Massachusetts who are trying to obtain resources essential to continue cultural survival." Hunt concurred, enumerating ways that tribes keep their culture and history present today: "Through our youth and our elders. Our elders transfer a lot of the knowledge and wisdom that they have. We have classes making skins, dancing, singing. We have a language reclamation project where children can learn to speak Wampanoag," he said.

Holley summed up the significance of the intergenerational commitment to rebuilding Native communities: "I think the reason why my people still exist is there have always been people in every generation that kept reminding us who we were, and that we always had one piece of land to cling on to. So I am very grateful to the people who came before me that held on to that."

Critical Thinking

1. How did the tribal customary access to land differ from the colonists' view of property ownership?

2. What were the various tactics used by the colonists and their descendants to wrest the land "legally" from Native Americans?

3. What have been the far-reaching consequences of the European appropriation of tribal land for Native Americans?

Internet References

A Brief History of the Trail of Tears
http://www.cherokee.org/AboutTheNation/History/TrailofTears

National Museum of the American Indian
http://www.nmai.si.edu/

Article   Prepared by: Elvio Angeloni

The Lost World

The insatiable global-lunger for palm oil and timber are closing in on Borneo's last hunter-gatherers and their ancient way of life.

ALEX SHOUMATOFF

Learning Outcomes

After reading this article, you will be able to:

- Describe the link between Borneo's rainforest and world-wide consumer demand.

- Describe the political obstacles to preserving the hunting grounds of the Penan.

- Describe the three stages of rainforest destruction.

- Discuss the impact of rainforest destruction on the Penan way of life, the wildlife, and the environment in general.

There's a magic moment in the tropics, 15 minutes before sunset, when the horizontal shafts of the sinking sun filter through the surface vapor. The foliage turns iridescent blue and everything glows. I'm watching this transformation through the window of a silver Mitsubishi 4x4 pickup as we rise into Borneo's dramatic central highlands. We pass a looming jungle-smothered limestone spire, then a long waterfall spilling over a ledge. At the top of a knife-edged ridge, we look out on a 50-mile vista of nothing but rainforest and mist-filled valleys, with the 7,795-foot Mount Mulu rising in the distance. We can even see the curvature of the earth.

On closer inspection, we see that all the ridges in the foreground have logging roads on them, like the one we are on. There are eroded gashes on the hillsides where big trees, cut into 30- to 40-foot lengths, were slid down to the valley floors. We hear the rumble of logging trucks down below.

Borneo's epic rainforests are being cleared at a faster rate per acre than the Amazon's. This might seem like a minor concern, since the island accounts for only 1 percent of the earth's land. But according to the World Wildlife Fund, Borneo's forests

hold 6 percent of the planet's plant and animal species. Many are now being driven toward extinction, or being extinguished before they can even be identified—all because of consumer demands around the world. Timber companies fell the ancient trees and export their wood, mostly to other Asian nations. The palm oil industry follows closely, clearing the land for enormous plantations. Ninety percent of Borneo's primary forest cover is now gone, along with some of the tallest tropical trees in the world. In their place, much of the island is now covered with a tossing ocean of oil palm trees. The oil they produce goes out to markets in the United States, Europe, and just about everywhere else: It's an essential ingredient in processed foods, baked goods, ice cream, cosmetics, cleaning agents, biodiesel, toothpaste, shampoo, and countless other products.

I've come to Borneo to camp with a group of Penan hunter-gatherers who live the way their ancestors did, in raised huts that they throw up in no time at all, hunting with blowguns and moving every few months to a new encampment. Of the 10,000 or so Penan on Borneo, only several dozen are still semi-nomadic. The island's deforestation, along with a series of proposed massive dams, is impacting their way of life, just as it's threatening the orangutan, the pygmy hippo, and many other living things on the island. As these hunter-gatherers roam their 7,400-acre homeland, they know the big corporations are never far behind.

Our journey began early in the morning in Miri, in the Malaysian state of Sarawak. Miri is a teeming coastal city of about 300,000 people. Most of the state's milled lumber and processed palm oil are shipped abroad from here. These industries, along with oil and gas, have endowed Miri with nice restaurants, manicured parks, and a steady stream of tourists.

As we gathered provisions in the midday sun, Christmas carols blasted from overhead loudspeakers all over the city. Not surprisingly, many of the products we threw into the shopping cart contained palm oil: the canned evaporated milk, the crackers, the pasta, the peanut butter, the freeze-dried noodle soup. In the United States, Canada, Australia, and England, an estimated 40 to 50 percent of supermarket and drugstore items contain palm oil. Over the past 25 years, the global output has grown from 14.5 million to 61 million tons a year—making palm oil a $40 billion industry—and the land covered by oil palm plantations grew from 15 million to 40 million acres. And Malaysia and Indonesia produce 85 percent of the world's supply. Over Borneo's central ridge, in the Indonesian portion of the island, orangutans have lost 50 percent of their forest habitat in the last two decades.

Before we left the store, we added a 50-pound bag of rice, coffee, tins of sardines, plates and cutlery, a big cook pot, a frying pan and spatula, and a big case of plastic-bottled water. "If they ask why we need all this stuff, say we're going to Mulu National Park, not to the Penan," whispered my guide, a laid-back guy in his 40s. "Foreign activists, outside agitators, are not popular in Sarawak."

Now, some eight hours later, darkness is falling as we approach the Baram River at Long Lama. We drive the pickup onto a ferry, and when we reach the other side, we're in the land of the Orang Ulu—the 20 or so tribes who live in the mountainous jungle of Borneo's interior. My guide is a member of another one of these groups, but he grew up deep in the forest with the Penan and speaks their language. He's been mapping the Penans' traditional hunting grounds using GPS in the hope they will be recognized by the courts in Kuching, Sarawak's capital city: According to Malaysian law, ethnic lands can be deemed "customary" if the group farmed them before 1958. But there's currently no protection for hunting grounds, and my guide knows his efforts may be futile—especially because the longtime former chief minister of Sarawak state, Abdul Taib Mahmud, seems to have profited tremendously from the state's deforestation. He and his extended family have reportedly made more than $15 billion from timber and oil palm licensing and exports.

A torrential rain starts to pour down. The steep logging roads become treacherous and our progress slows. At one point, my guide's furious last-minute steering keeps us from plunging into a deep gorge. We pass trucks laden with huge logs: Some have pulled over because of the dangerous conditions and others are coming right at us.

At around 9, we approach a Penan settlement and decide to stay the night. This is not the group we've come to visit: The majority of Penan, and all the other Orang Ulu, now live in settlements. They supplement their diets by hunting in the forest, but they come home to modern longhouses with zinc roofs. In this village, a long concrete walkway leads to a small shop selling junk food, cigarettes, and soda. We're welcomed into a flat occupied by an extended family. There's a large room floored with linoleum, where several kids and women are watching TV. Beans boil on a gas stove. A woman washes vegetables in the sink. In back are an outhouse and several large barrels of water with a faucet for doing laundry.

The next morning, I go down to the river that curves sharply around a wall of shale and ease myself into the muddy brown water. A young woman arrives after a few minutes and, giggling, performs her ablutions facing the other way. Across the river is thick rainforest. A bird keeps letting out a four-note call that sounds like a bell chime, or a ringing cellphone.

Heading back to the longhouse, I pass a large clearing where a babui, or a Bornean bearded pig, is chasing a boy on a dirt bike. After the Penan kill an animal, they adopt its orphaned babies as pets until they are old enough to return to the forest. The orphan is known as molong, which has several other meanings. If you molong a sago palm, you lay claim to it for your family's exclusive use. The Penan also use molong to describe the conservationist principle of taking no more than you need. If the forest is going to provide for you, you can't clean it out.

Ian Mackenzie, an ethnographer and linguist who has lived with the Penan on and off for almost 25 years, warns that this ecological definition of molong is an entirely Western projection. Indeed, when the Penan use the word in this way, it can be hard to tell whether they're reflecting a foreign notion of the "ecologically noble savage." But based on everything I observed, Penans have absorbed this definition of molong into their own culture, the way they merged the Christian God with their own traditional pantheon of spirits. They may have adopted this concept initially for the benefit of foreign tourists, but acculturated Penans now insist it's the most important value they have to offer the world.

Back in the pickup, we travel a road that sinks down into valleys, passes over bridges, and forks off in several directions. Each ridge takes us higher, until we are close to 2,500 feet. Soon, we reach a place where clothes are drying on a line between two poles. Four dirt bikes are parked nearby. We've found the Ba Marong band.

The camp is 150 yards from the road. We hear chatter and laughter floating down the steep, muddy trail. Several young men appear and help us carry our bags and provisions up to a flat area, where we see four huts raised on poles lashed with strands of rotan, or rattan palm vines, from the forest. At the front of each hut's pole floor, a fire burns in an earthen hearth and pots hang over the flames, a stack of machete-split wood off to one side. The interior of the hut is for eating, sleeping, sitting and talking, and weaving baskets and bracelets.

There are 23 people here. All of them are under 35 except a stout, strong-faced woman in her 50s named Choeling who is weaving nine-yard strands of rotan that cascade down the side of her hut. Her husband, the group's headman, died last year. The current headman is married to her daughter, who is here with her own five daughters. These people are strikingly good-looking, glowing with fitness and well-being. The headman, Sagung, has a wispy mustache and elaborate dragon tattoos on his arms and torso, along with dozens of woven bracelets, some plastic rings, and a wristwatch. He looks like a martial arts master from central casting.

In the other two huts are a young couple with an infant, and three young women with their babies. Three teenage boys are migrating among the four huts. In fact, everybody is constantly visiting each other's huts. It's a cozy scene, the way humans have lived from time immemorial, though there are some modern amenities as well: a CD player, flashlights, flip-flops, store-bought clothes and disposable diapers from Long Bedian, the trading center we passed several hours back.

Half a dozen emaciated dogs are snoozing under the huts. They spring to life when it's time to go out with the hunters, or when they smell something cooking and know scraps and bones might be thrown their way. This camp is only three days old. Anticipating our arrival, the Penan built it nearer the road than they usually do so it would be easier for us to find.

The kids are full of beans and constantly playing in the huts, in the forest, down by the stream. Some of them have runny noses and mildly elevated temperatures, and their mothers ask if I have medicine. I give the women the small aspirins I take as a heart attack preventive, and it seems to do some good. But these balmy highlands are incredibly salubrious. In the course of this trip, I will lose 20 pounds.

There are few mosquitoes up here. I was worried about leeches, but there are not many. The ones we do find are small and easily pinched off, and their wound is antiseptic. You can feel the suction on both ends as they move across your palm. They have both male and female sexual organs—leeches are hermaphroditic.

I've heard a Penan myth about leeches—how demons create them out of the veins of dead people. Mackenzie, the source of this story, told me it took him a long time to gather traditional teachings like this. "The missionaries had anathematized the old beliefs, so most people had willfully forgotten them," he said. "After seven years, I came to a group I'd never visited. There I met Galang, who, though nominally Christian, knew all the myths, and after some years trusted me enough to disclose the secrets of their cosmos, which contains seven or eight different worlds. Today, I am almost certain he is the last good Penan informant."

One night in the Ba Marong camp, I ask a young man named Nelson to tell me about the old ways. "Because we are now Christian, we only believe in Lord Jesus," he says cautiously.

"I know there are other spirits, but I do not belong to them anymore." He goes on, though. Every living thing has a spirit, and humans can harness it. "The horn-bill spirit can make people walk very fast. Normally what takes two, three days to walk, they do it in one. The leopard spirit is even more powerful."

I've heard similar animal-human transformation myths from Amazon Indians, Pygmies in Africa, and bush-men. Hunter-gatherers have to be fully engaged in the unfathomably intricate ecosystems around them. The forest gives them everything, but learning to survive in it—without provoking the ghosts of the dead or the spirits of the animals and the trees—is a completely absorbing, lifelong process.

A three-inch-long green praying mantis lands on my plate. Hundreds of ephemerids swarm the light from our cooking fire. "The most important thing about being in the forest is to look after your own self so there will be no problem," Nelson continues. "The first thing in the forest is smell. It can tell you something. You smell what food is being cooked. The smell of a tree fallen, the smell of an animal that pissed three hours ago. I can smell the durian fruit in your plastic bag." He promises to show me the next day how the spirit talks to his people. "What I wish to show you tomorrow is this is not magic but the reality."

This way of thinking can be hard to put into words. As Gerardo Reichel-Dolmatoff, the anthropologist of the Colombian Amazon, reflected in 1987: "I did not find the 'noble savage.' What I did find was a world with a philosophy so coherent, with morals so high, with social and political organizations of great complexity, and with sound environmental management based on well-founded knowledge."

Or, as Nelson tells me, "The knowledge about the nature, you can ask every man anywhere, but there is no one who can teach you. Even Penan don't know how to teach you the experience we have. It's so deep."

There's a common romantic notion that the Penan have been hunter-gatherers since the dawn of time. In fact, Mackenzie told me, they were most likely farmers who migrated from Taiwan between 5,000 and 2,500 BC Once they got to Borneo, the Penan left farming behind and started living entirely off the abundant game, fruits, nuts, and sago palm. Unlike other Orang Ulu, they never made war on other groups or took heads as trophies; they had no need for land to farm and it wouldn't have made sense for them to lug a bunch of skulls around as they wandered from place to place. They kept living in this nomadic way until after World War II, when missionaries began to penetrate what was still one of the least-known quarters of the world.

One morning in the camp, after a night of pouring rain, the sun comes up over the ridge into clear blue sky and shines through the gap in the trees. The forest's day shift comes to life. We hear a chorus of gibbons down in the valley, then the crickets, then the six o'clock cicadas starting their grating B-flat drone. They do this every day of the year at dawn and dusk, followed by other kinds of cicadas with different songs. Asian paradise flycatchers and other birds come in. The morning bio-phony, tutti specie.

Choeling, stoking the fire in her hut, sings a traditional song to the men:

> *Wake up, don't you hear the gibbon? It's time to go hunting.*
>
> *I will stay and prepare to cook what you bring.*
>
> *You wake up in the morning before the clouds rise up in the sky.*
>
> *You are already moving like the leopard, through the hills and mountains.*
>
> *But I am still not prepared for your return.*

Sagung and one of the young men have already gone off with the dogs and their shotguns. Why not blowguns? "They are taking shotguns because they want to make it faster," Nelson says. "They don't want to waste time in the forest with you here. If they have bullets, they prefer the shotgun."

Breakfast is barking deer, also known as muntjac, and a thick, gelatinous porridge of sago palm. Everybody is sticking a wooden utensil with four prongs into the porridge and swirling it, dunking the blob that gloms onto it into venison juice. Yesterday it was sago porridge with small tree snails.

Several drongos, black songbirds with forked tails, land in the treetops to check us out. I ask about the clouded leopard, the biggest of Borneo's spotted cats, protected under Malaysian law. There are still some, but not many. Sagung killed one last year. He is wearing one of its teeth around his neck. Pythons are everywhere, in the forest and in the rivers, Nelson says. Sagung's father-in-law once had a python wrapped around his leg. It tried to kill him, but luckily he had his machete.

The hunters return with a big dead babui and four dead silvered leaf monkeys. They also bring back a live silvered leaf infant and lash it to a post of Sagung's hut. It looks on with what I can only imagine is horror and sorrow as its parents' bodies are thrown on the lashed-pole floor and butchered. Sagung's father guts the pig and scoops out the copious amount of blood and innards into a bowl. Then the five animals are roasted in their skin and smoked on a big fire that Sagung makes in the middle of the camp. Food for everybody for the next few days. (A vegetarian, I'll be sticking to the canned goods and produce I brought with me from the grocery store in Miri.)

After lunch and a nap, we set out into the forest. Sagung's 10-year-old daughter brings along the silvered leaf monkey and showers it with affection. Imprinting on its new, furless

caregivers, the animal seems decidedly less traumatized by the death of its parents, who are now in the Ba Marongs' stomachs.

Sagung's father and some of the children have gone ahead of us and left messages along the way, using bent and split branches. A branch bending slightly up to the right tells us the direction the advance party has taken. The next sign, a branch with crossed leaves in its fork, means the sign-sender is accompanied by two others, both family members. The next sign is in a split sapling, a larger cross and a series of cuts: Hurry, don't waste time. A branch cut into four prongs, like a sago porridge swirler, leads us to a sago palm, which another sign declares molong—it's been claimed by Sagung's family. Sagung tells me the Ba Marong have a hundred of these signs. His father left them for us; the children no longer know them. Even forest-dwelling Penan kids spend much of their time visiting friends who live in longhouses, watching TV, and using other modern amenities. Learning the old ways isn't high on their priority list.

Sagung hacks down the sago palm's multiple stems with their pinnate leaflets, cuts out a section of its yellowish white heart and chops it up. He passes around pieces. It's the best palmito I have ever had. Ambrosial.

Farther up the path, Sagung finds an agarwood tree and cuts out a yard-long section of its mold-blackened pith. The perfumed resin extracted from this tree has been esteemed for its fragrance and medical properties in China, India, and the Middle East for thousands of years. In the U.S., the best-grade agarwood can fetch $5,000 a pound. The pith will bring Sagung good money when he sells it locally. One of the main reasons for the high cost of agarwood is that there is relatively little left in the wild. It's listed by the Convention on International Trade in Endangered Species of Wild Fauna and Flora (CITES) as a potentially threatened species.

We wander through a forest of mixed second-growth dipterocarp—tropical lowland trees whose globular fruits have wings that slow them down as they fall from the canopy. They grow as high as 200 feet, their smooth gray bark spotted with luminous green bull's-eyes of lichen. Borneo is the dipterocarp center of the world. It has 267 of the 680 species. The tallest one ever measured, a 288-foot Shorea faguetiana, was in Sabah, Borneo's other Malaysian state. Some Penan believe these trees have particularly powerful spirits, and that angering them can bring all kinds of trouble.

The destruction of these trees is playing out in three stages. First, timber companies go in and cut the commercial hardwoods. They call this "selective logging," but the process of felling and removing these trees destroys most of the surrounding forest and cripples its ability to regenerate. In the lowlands, at least, this destructive logging doesn't really matter, because step two burns off what is left of the forest. If it is peat swamp forest, the fire can burn for months with no easy way to put it out.

These peat fires release more carbon than any other incinerated forest on earth. And at their worst, they shroud Southeast Asia in a pall of black smoke for months at a time, as they did last fall.

Step three is to plant oil palm wherever possible. The tree is native to the swamps and riverbanks of West Africa. The British discovered it could thrive in the steamy equatorial climate of Southeast Asia and put in the first plantations in Malaysia during World War I. The vast majority of the world's palm oil now comes from converted forests in Indonesia and Malaysia.

There are no tall native trees left around the Ba Marong camp. All we find are their rotting stumps. The only tree we see emerging through the canopy is a towering Alstonia pneumatophora, whose wood is presumably too soft to be of commercial interest. It's used to make the sape, the traditional sitar-like stringed instrument of the Orang Ulu.

According to my guide, the road below us was built and the big dipterocarps harvested during the early 1990s. At the time, various Penan groups were mounting protests to stop loggers from cutting the surrounding trees, but the Ba Marong were unable to save theirs. A Swiss activist named Bruno Manser brought international attention to the Penans' plight. He arrived in Sarawak in 1984, part of an expedition to explore the extensive cave systems of Gunung Mulu National Park. After his British caving companions left, he set off on a quest to "learn from a people who still live close to their source," trekking alone into the interior, over Mount Mulu to its eastern side, where he found some still-nomadic Penan. He lived with them for six years and recorded their oral histories in his journals. His notebooks are full of watercolor portraits and sketches of the Penan going about their lives.

The nomadic Penan weren't the only groups being threatened by Borneo's deforestation. The Penan who lived in longhouses were also vulnerable. So were the other Orang Ulu, and the Dyak people on the southern, Indonesian side of the central ridge. Most of them lived and hunted in territories that weren't officially recognized (and still aren't today), and they were struggling to keep the chain saws and bulldozers out of their lands. Still, it was the nomadic Penan who captured Manser's imagination. After seeing their game depleted, their rivers polluted, and their tana, or customary hunting grounds, destroyed, he started helping them organize peaceful blockades against logging trucks. Rumors spread that the Malaysian authorities had put a bounty on his head. Manser was captured by police officers but escaped by leaping out of their vehicle and diving into a thundering cataract. Returning to Europe in 1990, he devoted the next 10 years to rallying outside support for the Penan cause. For a while, the world took notice. In 1991, Al Gore, then a U.S. senator, condemned the logging activities in Sarawak, and in a speech at Kew Gardens, Prince Charles described the

treatment of the Penan as part of a global "collective genocide." Manser went on a 60-day hunger strike in front of the Federal Palace of Switzerland, in an attempt to inspire a ban on unsustainably harvested timber imports. Ultimately, though, none of those actions had much of an impact on Sarawak. In 2000, Manser slipped back over the Kalimantan border and headed for Bukit Batu Lawi, a 6,700-foot limestone pinnacle. He told the Penan who were helping carry his gear that he wanted to climb it alone and sent them back to their band. That was May 2000. Manser was never seen again. The machete slash marks he left behind were tracked to the swamp at the base of the pinnacle. In August 2014, on what would have been Manser's 60th birthday, a new species of goblin spider was named in his honor: *Aposphragisma brunomanseri*. Vladimir Nabokov wrote that no form of immortality compares to a Latin species name. But given the way things are going in Borneo, how much longer will this goblin spider survive?

I'm reflecting on this at the end of my visit when Sagung asks for money to build a longhouse. I'm taken aback to learn that this group of nomadic Penan wants to move into a stationary dwelling. Sagung explains that he wants to establish a permanent presence on this land. It makes me wonder to what extent this camp has been a Potemkin village. During our visit, I've seen a stylishly dressed Chinese man, a representative of a timber firm, driving back and forth along the ridge. According to my guide, the company has already felled many of the trees in the Ba Marong territory, and it wants to pay them the equivalent of $30 apiece to come in and do a second cut. Sagung claims he isn't going to give in, but more and more Penan groups are accepting offers like this.

I suspect that the Ba Marongs' wandering lifestyle is losing its appeal for other reasons, too. The members of this group move feluidly between the forest and their friends' longhouses down the road. After they've experienced what life is like with electricity, television, and running water, it's not hard to understand why they might be hankering after a longhouse of their own. That doesn't mean they won't be gone for days at a time hunting babui and gathering sago palm, fruit, and nuts in the forest. But there's a reason so few Penans still live like the Ba Marong in raised pole huts. According to Mackenzie, that number has dropped from 300 to fewer than 50 during the past 10 years. In another generation, that way of life will probably be gone.

After we leave the Ba Marong camp, we spend three glorious days in Gunung Mulu National Park, a Unesco World Heritage site. In 1978, the Royal Geographical Society embarked on a 15-month inventory of the park's flora and fauna, and researchers identified one of the largest collections of ants ever found in such a small area: 458 species. The lepidopterist J. D. Holloway was so blown away by what he found in the park that he undertook a monumental 18-volume series called *Moths of Borneo*. In Deer Cave, one of the largest subterranean chambers on earth, two million to three million free-tailed bats spend all day roosting from the ceiling. At dusk, they stream out of the cave in long floating ribbons, consuming as many as 30 tons of insects per night and pollinating numerous trees and flowering plants. Animals ranging from barking and sambar deer to the gargantuan Rajah Brooke's bird-wing papilio butterfly consume the salts in the bat excrement. Mulu, the British scientists discovered, was a naturalist's paradise.

Brian Clark, Mulu's park manager, has nothing but praise for Sarawak's former chief minister. "Without Taib, we'd still be a backwater," he tells me. "He's developed the state and maintained peace between all the different tribes and races. Every country on earth has exploited its resources. The West can't condemn any country for it. Canada, the U.S.A., Africa—where isn't there deforestation? It's part of the nature of the beast."

I hear something different when I visit Long Mera'an, a community of several hundred people on the Mago River. The Penan who live here belong to the group Manser lived with between 1984 and 1990. At the time, they were nomadic, like the Ba Marong. They moved into a settlement in the 1990s, but their longhouse burned down, and then a logging company cleared their land to build an oil pipeline. The Mera'an had blockaded the pipeline three times. The fourth time, the state ministry in charge of pipeline routes negotiated a settlement of about $53,500. At least some of that money went to build new dwellings and buy electric guitars and big speakers for the new church.

The new community consists of several dozen free-standing houses built in a variety of styles, from shacks to a few well-built two-story structures with gardens and fences. Many residents own dirt bikes, which they use to cross the narrow suspension bridge across the Mago River.

At Long Mera'an, I meet Radu, a master sape player. Through a translator, he tells me he learned his melodies from the birds in the forest, messengers of the spirit Balei Pu'un. "The world was not created by Balei Pu'un," says Radu. "It was already there. His job is to help people be good to each other. The way he communicates is through a bird or animal, because people cannot see him, so he needs a translator, a special person who is able to understand animals. My father was one of these people, and he taught me how to do it."

Is there a best time of day to hear Balei Pu'un speaking through the animals? "No time of day is better. If it happens, it happens." Where will Balei Pu'un go if the forest is destroyed? "He will try to find another place where there is still forest." What if there is no more forest anywhere? "We don't know, but it could be the end of the world." This is what the Penan believe. If their forest goes, it will be not only the end of them and the vast diversity of creatures who live there. The balei, the spirits who travel around the nine worlds of the Karawara, will also have nowhere to gather water and honey.

And what does this mean for the rest of us? Here in Borneo, I've been struck by the dramatic way people all over the world are shaping the fate of this island. The demand for tropical timber and palm oil is ending the Penans' way of life and extirpating hundreds of species found only on this island. It's also igniting peat fires that release more carbon dioxide than highways jammed with cars. If the deforestation continues at its current rate, there will be a cascade of negative impacts on everything from human health to the humid climate of Southeast Asia. The governments now promoting the logging and palm-oil industries will be crippled by the economic and ecological damage. And all of this will happen because of purchases made by consumers thousands of miles away. I, for one, am drastically cutting down on the number of palm-oil products I consume now that I've seen their hidden cost with my own eyes.

"We have to look after the whole thing," Radu tells me. "If people want to have more and more, they have to understand that without molong there is nothing left."

Critical Thinking

1. What is the connection between the destruction of Borneo's rainforest and world-wide consumer demand?
2. What obstacles in particular do the Penan face in preserving their land?
3. What impact will rainforest destruction have on the Penan, on wildlife, and on the environment in general?

Internet References

Association for Political and Legal Anthropology
   www.aaanet.org/apla/index.htm
Human Rights and Humanitarian Assistance
   www.etown.edu/vl/humrts.html

Article   Prepared by: Elvio Angeloni

We Walk on Our Ancestors: The Sacredness of the Black Hills

LEONARD LITTLE FINGER

Learning Outcomes

After reading this article, you will be able to:

• Discuss the importance of the Black Hills to the Lakota.

• Describe the treaties and how and why they were broken.

• Understand the legal struggles over the Black Hills and their outcomes.

• Describe the ways in which the Black Hills have been desecrated in the eyes of the Lakota.

I n 1883, my grandfather, Saste, was a child of seven years. With his parents, he traveled in a group into the Black Hills in South Dakota for a sacred prayer journey to Washun Niye, a site from which Mother Earth breathes. They were following a path that had been a journey for his people for thousands of years. In preparation for the ceremony, the women dried the hide of apte, or tatanka (buffalo), which was carried to this site for the sacred ceremony. The cannupa (sacred pipe) acknowledged apte by returning the hide to the world; upon completion of the prayers, the hide would be dropped into the hole. As my grandfather watched, Washun Niye carried the hide downward in a spiraling motion, soon to be enveloped into the darkness. The power of the sacred circle which has no ending was affirmed.

I heard this story in 1947, in Lakota, at the age of eight, seven years before he was to make his spirit journey—from which we all come as a spirit or soul. It took me many years to understand the importance of his story, because we must revisit anything of importance many times before we can fully understand its significance. When one finally understands, then begins the process of interpretation. The spiritual quest of truth, especially for Indigenous people, is in this process.

My grandfather and I are from a sub-band of the Teton, a member of the Nation of the Seven Council Fires. We are called the Mniconjou, or People Who Plant Near the Water. In the 1500s, one of our villages was the location of present day Rapid City along the streams of Mniluzahan Creek, or Rapid Creek, which is today's northern gateway to the Black Hills of South Dakota. Our family has had a spiritual relationship with this special land for over 500 years.

The Black Hills were recognized as the Black Hills because of the darkness from the distance. The term also referred to a container of meat; in those days people used a box made out of dried buffalo hide to carry spiritual tools, like the sacred pipe, or the various things that were used in prayers or to carry food. That's the term that was used for the Black Hills: they were a container for our spiritual need as well as our needs of food and water, whatever it is that allows survival.

A Legacy of Threats

The story of the Black Hills is an age-old conflict between imperialism and the understanding of their spiritual significance as a sacred site. The threats to our sacred lands began when the first two treaties were drawn up with the federal government. The first was in 1851 recognizing several tribes, including the People of the Seven Council Fires, and identified the territories of each tribe. In 1868 the Fort Laramie treaty designated an area that included the entire western half of South Dakota, with the eastern line marked by the Missouri River and a portion of North Dakota and Wyoming. We would not, as a nation, be recognized.

When gold was discovered in Montana, the trails leading to it came into the territory of the Sioux. In 1872, General Custer led a contingent of gold mining experts, theologists, and botanists into the Black Hills. Although just traces of gold were found in the streams, it was an indication that there was probably gold, veins of gold in the hills, so the US government sent two commissions to renegotiate the treaty. One of the articles stated that three-fourths of the male population had to agree to any amendments. Both commissions failed to achieve an agreement, so in 1874 Congress declared that treaties would no longer be used. Following this action (which nullified Article 6 of the US Constitution), more than 25,000 gold seekers came into the Black Hills over a very short period of time, essentially claiming that land. It's been estimated that during that time up until 2005, when the last gold mine was shut down, approximately 500 billion ounces, or $9 trillion worth, of gold were extracted.

Problems continued in 1888 when North and South Dakota were admitted into the union and the Sioux were forced onto reservations to become US citizens. In 1876 the Sioux had wiped out General Custer and the entire 7th Cavalry in Montana, becoming the only nation to ever defeat the United States in battle. That really marked us for violation, leading to the massacre at Wounded Knee in 1890. All of these things led to the people moving away from the Black Hills, away from the sacred sites for their spiritual journeys; we could no longer go back without the threat of being jailed or killed.

In the early 1920s the Sioux filed a complaint with the Indian Claims Commission alleging that the United States had illegally taken the land that had been designated to us by the treaties of 1851 and 1868. The claim entered the Supreme Court in 1962 and took nearly 20 years to settle, enduring as the longest court case in US history. On June 30,1980 the Supreme Court determined that the United States had indeed violated the treaty of the People of the Seven Council Fires: not just the Sioux, but the original title that we were known by. However, the federal government argued that it could not give back the land since it is occupied and includes the national monument of Mount Rushmore, a sculpture on a sacred site. The government offered compensation—for the value of the land in 1876, prior to its occupation and the gold that was extracted, including interest—of $350 million. Of course the People of the Seven Council Fires rejected that offer. The Black Hills is a sacred grandmother to us, filled with sacred power sites. How can one sell a sacred grandmother?

Now we have an opportunity to sit down in a unified way to discuss the Black Hills and the threat that is coming from ourselves as a people, as we have begun to travel the road of assimilation. Less and less people speak our native language, Lakota. Less and less adhere to the spiritual significance because of the introduction of Christianity to the reservations. One of my fears is that there is a day coming that the Bureau of Indian Affairs will sit down at a table with the offer and our people will accept the money. At that point, thousands and thousands of years of spiritual significance of the Black Hills will be left to the wayside because the new culture of the new people that have come onto the reservation will see the same meaning in the value of the money.

Our Place in History

Recently we were asked as elders to look at some aerial photos of the southern Black Hills. We looked at them as sacred circles, and in an aerial photo we saw the image of the big dipper. This is an image of what we are, the journey of the Black Hills, the sacred journey known as "seeking sacred goodness" and the pipe that is used, the cannupa. Today the UN Declaration on the Rights of Indigenous Peoples gives us the modern tools to stand up and declare our rights. We have come back to the table on the basis of what is recognized for Indigenous Peoples' rights and on the basis of what sacredness is. Our beliefs are substantiated by the image of the aerial rock formations in the sacred circle that were left by our ancestors thousands of years ago.

The desecration of the Black Hills is indicative of the violation of the sacredness of who we are as a people. The insides of Grandmother Earth are being taken; the atmosphere, the area that's there to protect us and all things is being destroyed. Earth is our grandmother, as animate as we all are, because she provides us with all of our needs to live. From the time of birth until now I look at that relationship as sacred. When our life ends here on Grandmother Earth, we become as one. This sacredness means that we walk on our ancestors. As Indigenous Peoples we are guided by the spiritualism of greater powers than we humans. We don't seek equality, we seek justice. This is who we are, and this is where we come from.

Critical Thinking

1. Why are the Black Hills sacred to the Lakota?
2. How have the Black Hills been desecrated, according to the Lakota?
3. What have been the legal claims set forth by the Lakota with respect to the Black Hills and what have been the results?

Internet References

Association for Political and Legal Anthropology
www.aaanet.org/apla/index.htm

Human Rights and Humanitarian Assistance
www.etown.edu/vl/humrts.html

Sioux Treaty of 1868—The U.S. National Archives and Records Administration
https://www.archives.gov/education/lessons/sioux-treaty/

LEONARD LITTLE FINGER is a respected Lakota elder and the founder-director of Sacred Hoop School, a Lakota language school in Ogalala, South Dakota.

Article

Prepared by: Elvio Angeloni

Dambusters

SUE BRANFORD AND MAURICIO TORRES

After a 40-year battle, Brazil's grandiose plan to tap the hydropower of the Amazon is coming apart at the seams.

Learning Outcomes

After reading this article, you will be able to:

- Discuss the Brazilian government's plan to build a hydro-electric dam on the Tapajos River and its potential consequences for the rainforest environment and the Munduruku.

- Discuss the legal process for building the dam and the efforts to bypass it.

- Discuss the evidence for the legal claims of the Munduruku.

- Explain why the building of the dam may not be practical after all.

About 20 men, their arms painted like tortoise shells, are silently hacking away at the forest, opening up a corridor about 4 metres wide. When they have finished, the corridor will stretch for 230 kilometres, encircling the land they call Sawré Muybu. Every so often the men, indigenous Munduruku, erect a sign asserting their ownership of the land in their own language and in Portuguese. The ancestors of these men used to decapitate their enemies and stick their heads on poles. Although the Munduruku gave up head-hunting long ago, some of the signs feature a painting of a head on a pike. This is their none-too-veiled way of telling the Brazilian government they are determined to defend this tract of Amazon forest that has been theirs for hundreds of years.

The government has other ideas. If it gets its way, work will soon begin on a huge hydroelectric dam close to Sawré Muybu on the Tapajos River, one of the major tributaries of the Amazon. Six other large dams are also on the drawing board for the

Tapajos basin. If the Sao Luiz do Tapajos dam goes ahead, parts of Sawré Muybu will be flooded.

Dreams of tapping into the immense power of the Amazon began in the 1970s, at a time when little attention was paid to climate and biodiversity. The military dictatorship in power at the time decided to start with a chain of dams on the Xingu River, another mighty tributary of the Amazon. However, after a lengthy battle with environmentalists and local people, it scaled back its plans to a single dam, albeit a huge one.

Belo Monte finally got the go-ahead in 2011. When it comes on stream in 2019 it will be the third-largest hydroelectric dam in the world. The building site is so big that it seems as if a new Panama Canal is being carved out of the forest. Even if one harbours reservations about the wisdom of this massive undertaking, one can't help but be impressed by the speed and efficiency with which huge layers of rock are blasted into the air and the rubble carted away by a phalanx of giant lorries. This scene could eventually be replicated across large swathes of the Amazon. According to ecologist Philip Fearnside, a senior researcher at the National Institute for Amazon Research in Manaus, the government has ambitions to turn much of the basin into chains of reservoirs for the production of hydropower. Most of the energy will be used to power big mineral extraction and refining projects in the Amazon itself, particularly aluminium smelting and gold mining.

The issues surrounding the construction of these dams are painfully familiar: habitat destruction, loss of biodiversity and heritage, and the trampling of the rights of vulnerable people. But the scale on which it could happen adds up to a huge transformation of one of the world's most important natural environments.

No Surrender

Before they resorted to direct action to defend their land, the Munduruku tried to go through the proper channels. Brazil is a signatory to the International Labour Organization's Convention 169, under which indigenous and tribal people shouldn't be removed from their land without their free and informed consent. It also states that before licensing a dam, a government must canvass the opinion of all affected groups and only then undertake viability studies. However, in early 2013 the Brazilian government authorised a research company to send in teams of scientists to carry out the viability studies, even though proper consultations with the Munduruku hadn't happened. Incensed, in June 2013 the Munduruku took three biologists hostage and paraded them, hands bound, in the square of Jacareacanga, a town beside the Tapajos. The government reacted quickly, promising to carry out the consultations and the biologists were released. However, three weeks later, the government sent the scientists back in under the protection of 250 policemen—still without any proper consultation. According to reports from the Munduruku and other local people, the police created an atmosphere of intimidation and terror by entering villages unannounced, sometimes arriving by helicopter. In a surreal episode which recalled the days of the dictatorship, a policeman bearing a machine gun tried to bar our way as we approached a group of biologists in a roadside cafe in a remote area of the Tapajos valley. Brazil's constitution also appears to be on the Munduruku's side, as it bans the permanent removal of indigenous people from their land. But the land claim has to be recognised by the authorities, which can only happen after a report giving the coordinates is officially published by FUNAI, the National Indian Foundation.

FUNAI began mapping Sawré Muybu eight years ago and completed the job in September 2013, but has yet to publish its report. Until that happens, the territory isn't formally recognised as belonging to the Munduruku. The Munduruku believe that the government is deliberately dragging its heels.

We obtained a leaked copy of the report, which shows that FUNAI accepts the Munduruku's claim to the land. The Munduruku are using its coordinates to mark out the boundary of their territory. But it is a long and laborious process.

The Munduruku's troubles have created a dilemma for the scientists carrying out the viability studies, for whom it has become embarrassingly clear that they are involved not in impartial research but in a fait accompli. Talking off the record, some are distraught at the prospect of the overwhelming losses that will be borne by people and ecosystems if the dam goes ahead. Yet they are reluctant to protest or resign, fearing that they will be blacklisted by the government and their career prospects harmed. So they dutifully produce their reports hoping to get the government to rethink its policies. But the government simply cherry-picks the evidence.

A more vigorous response has come from archaeologists. Evidence is being unearthed that the Tapajos basin was occupied by indigenous people for thousands of years before the Portuguese arrived, and archaeologists have been contracted to carry out environmental impact studies. This has caused widespread unease. At their meeting in August 2014, the northern branch of the Brazilian Archaeological Society passed a motion stating: "We are gravely concerned by the involvement of archaeologists in a process that relies on the presence of the National Security Force to guarantee the fulfilment of the research. For this reason we are calling on our professional colleagues not to take part in activities related to the environmental licensing of the dams along the Tapajos River." The concern at the biodiversity loss and the threat to indigenous people is exacerbated by a growing awareness that the drive to harness the power of the rivers may, in the long term, be futile. Sao Paulo, the industrial heartland of Brazil, is in the grip of the worst drought in living memory. The clouds from the Amazon that make the basin itself so wet and also deliver rain to the south of the country—dubbed "flying rivers" by one Brazilian scientist—have failed to materialise.

While this may be a result of natural climate variability, Antonio Nobre, a senior researcher at Brazil's National Institute for Space Research in Sao José dos Campos, says that the disruption is linked to deforestation. Recent research has shown that Amazon vegetation, particularly large trees, play a central role in maintaining the hydrological cycle. "In a single day a large tree in the rainforest can pump over 1000 litres of moisture from the soil into the atmosphere. If this is scaled up for the whole forest, it means the Amazon forest transpires 20 billion tonnes of water a day," he says. Cut down the forest and you destroy the flying rivers.

According to official satellite data, 22 percent of the forest has been felled. But this is an underestimate as it fails to account for selective logging, which the satellite images don't detect. After several years of marked declines in forest clearance, which won Brazil international plaudits, the level of deforestation has risen again.

It seems probable that continued forest destruction will sooner or later trigger a dramatic transformation of the Amazon. The tipping point was spelled out in 2013 by the Brazilian Panel on Climate Change: "Modelling studies have suggested that, if deforestation reaches 40 percent in the region, drastic changes will likely occur in the hydrological cycle, with a 40 percent reduction in rainfall during the months from July to November."

Even scientists with a less alarmist outlook than Nobre believe that, if deforestation continues, the viability of the large dams may be compromised. Until recently most scientists thought that cutting down trees near dams increased the amount of water flowing into them. But a recent study by the Amazon Environmental Research Institute in San Francisco, California, came to a very different conclusion. It found that by 2050, when on present trends at least 40 percent of Brazil's Amazon forest will be gone, there will be a significant decline in river flows and energy generation (PNAS, vol 110, p 9601). This would make the reliability of the dams as an energy source highly questionable.

Another difficulty is that big development projects always provoke an unruly influx of illegal loggers, land thieves, cattle ranchers, and slash-and-burn farmers, who exacerbate the deforestation. The government promises it will be different with Sao Luiz do Tapajos, through the use of river platforms similar to North Sea oil rigs to make it possible to bring people in using helicopters rather than roads.

But Juan Doblas of the non-profit Social-Environmental Institute in [. . .] out a flaw: "Yes, when a dam is up and running, you can bring workers in by helicopter. But the main environmental damage is done during the building of the dam, when thousands of labourers are needed. You can't bring in this volume by helicopter. Big projects always cause forest felling and there is no sign of that ending."

A radical solution would be to see if Brazil could do without dams on the Amazon. Nobre says that much could be done to save energy. "Brazil wastes 55 percent of public street lighting because the lenses spread the beam wider than is necessary. By refocusing the light we would save as much energy as Belo Monte will generate," he says. Another source of waste is electric showers. "If we were to install solar water heaters, which would not be difficult with the amount of sunshine we get, there would be no need for further hydroelectric dams in the Amazon."

Along with growing doubts from scientists, another factor is creating the perception that the authorities' love affair with Amazon hydropower may be waning. Historically, one of the biggest drivers of dam-building has been a cosy relationship between big engineering companies and their political allies. "Energy planning in Brazil is not treated as a strategic issue but as a source of money for engineering companies and politicians," says Felicio Pontes, prosecutor for the Federal Public Ministry in Para.

But many of the companies are now caught up in a massive corruption scandal involving bribery and money laundering by the state-owned oil company, Petrobras. Investigators are examining the contracts for the Belo Monte dam, and a leading executive of one of the companies, Camargo Correa, which has been funding viability studies for the Sao Luis do Tapajos dam, has been arrested.

As a result, there is no longer the same impetus to push ahead with the dams. Until recently, the government was planning to generate electricity from all the main tributaries of the Amazon east of the city of Manaus. But in a leaked copy of its latest 10-year energy plan, obtained by the *O Estado de S. Paulo* newspaper, all dams except Sao Luiz do Tapajos have been removed. Even this is no longer on the list of priority projects to be built over the next five years. If confirmed, this amounts to a major rethink of Brazil's energy plans, and a possible reprieve for the Amazon.

Meanwhile, the Munduruku fight on. Emboldened by a judicial decision that "full, free and prior consultations" must be carried out, a delegation of 30 made the five-day bus journey to Brasilia at the end of January to present their demands—the central one being the cancellation of the dam.

They are still a long way from achieving victory. But after decades of bitter struggle, the battle for the Amazon finally seems to be going their way.

Critical Thinking

1. What are the official and the unofficial motivations of the Brazilian government and the private companies involved with respect to building a dam on the Tapajos River in Brazil?
2. What are the potential consequences for the environment and the Munduruku?
3. Discuss the legal roadblocks to building such a dam and the legal claims of the Munduruku.
4. Why might the dam be impractical after all?

Internet References

Amazon Watch
 http://amazonwatch.org
International Waters
 https://www.internationalrivers.org

Article   Prepared by: Elvio Angeloni

On Thin Ice

Katya Wassillie

Learning Outcomes

After reading this article, you will be able to:

- Describe the reciprocal relationship between Alaskan Native communities and marine life that has existed for thousands of years.
- Discuss the ways in which this traditional relationship is being threatened by climate change.
- Discuss the real threat to Alaskan Native subsistence communities and what they think should be done about it.

Subsistence Walrus Hunting and the Adaptation to a Changing Climate in Alaska

Alaska Native communities along the coast of the Bering, Chukchi, and Beaufort Seas have lived in close connection with the ocean for thousands of years. The bounty of this rich environment, which includes marine mammals, fish, birds, and plant life, has sustained Alaska's St. Lawrence Island Yupik, Iñupiaq, Central Yup'ik, and Aleut communities since time immemorial. These Alaska Native communities are an integral part of the ocean ecosystem, maintaining their ties to the ocean through the continuation of the marine subsistence lifestyle. This lifestyle represents a reciprocal relationship with the environment and the animals in which traditions of respect are maintained through sustainable stewardship practices and spiritual expressions of song and dance. It has always been characterized by balance, which has allowed for successful coexistence with the ocean environment.

But this balance is now threatened by climate change, which is resulting in a rapidly and dramatically changing ocean environment. One of the species most impacted by these changes is the Pacific walrus, an important subsistence resource for many Alaska Native communities. In a 2004 interview for a

traditional knowledge project, Alexander Akeya, an elder from the community of Savoonga, said, "This walrus has been our food for centuries . . . our food has an overseer. Although I wanted to harvest more, our elders would say, 'Quit hunting, that is enough. Take care of your food, do not be wasteful. If you waste, you yourself will cause the Creator to cut you off . . . take home enough of what you need, with a limit. This animal, your food, is very important. We want it to live just as we strive to live'".

Pacific walrus depend on sea ice as a platform for resting, calving, and nursing, and this sea ice habitat is rapidly deteriorating due to climate change. This has opened the door for other impacts to the environment of the Pacific walrus, such as increased shipping and resource exploration activities in the area. Global carbon dioxide emissions are resulting in the rapid acidification of the Bering, Chukchi, and Beaufort Seas, whose waters are particularly vulnerable to ocean acidification due to their cold temperatures. This in turn has implications for the viability of walrus prey resources, mainly clams, whose shell formation is impacted by the acidity of the water.

These cumulative pressures, largely caused by excessive global carbon dioxide emissions, are of great concern to Alaska Native subsistence communities that depend on healthy and sustainable marine ecosystems. Climate change impacts are already being felt by the subsistence communities in many ways. Thinner sea ice makes for more dangerous hunting conditions and hunters must now travel farther to access marine mammals. Changing weather patterns, partially caused by decreased sea ice presence, are resulting in more severe storms that affect both hunting opportunity and the integrity of shorelines through increased erosion.

In an interview for another traditional knowledge project in April 2015, Vince Pikonganna, an elder from the King Island Native community, offered his perspective on the impacts of climate change: "Everything is changing. One thing affects another. Mother Nature can take care of herself, it's just that we the humans are the culprit of what she's suffering through.

She's reacting to what we've been doing to her for a couple hundred years now—all this pollution, destroying the land, and destroying the oceans. We have been told by our ancestors about the future. We've been told that [we] will need to watch out for the four winds. The four winds will be getting stronger in the future and unexpected weather patterns will start to be happening. And now it's happening, right before our eyes. I was practicing how to tell the weather in our Iñupiaq way 30 years ago. But some 20 years ago, everything got chaotic. This weather got chaotic."

One stark example of climate change impacts on marine subsistence is the walrus harvest disaster that occurred in the communities of Gambell and Savoonga on St. Lawrence Island in 2013. That year, unusual weather conditions and sea ice patterns prevented hunters from accessing the walrus as they migrated past the island, resulting in a record low harvest and food shortages for the communities. The state of Alaska declared a disaster, which leveraged support for food aid from many organizations, but the question remains as to how the communities will adapt if these conditions continue. Since 2013 harvest numbers for Gambell and Savoonga have not returned to normal levels, and the communities of Diomede and Wales, located in the Bering Straits region, have also declared harvest disasters due to similar ice and weather conditions.

Not only does the walrus provide large amounts of nutrition for the communities, but the continued consumption of this subsistence resource is culturally and spiritually important to the people of the communities. Furthermore, raw materials provided by walrus also help meet the material and financial needs of the communities. Alaska Native ivory carvers are renowned for their skill, and the sale of walrus ivory artwork and jewelry are an important source of income in the extremely limited cash economy of rural Alaska. Other material and cultural needs of the communities are also dependent on walrus subsistence, including the making of walrus skin boats for hunting and walrus stomach drums for Native dancing.

In a 2004 interview, Leonard Apangalook of Gambell explained how changing weather has impacted his community: "The ice recedes, goes so fast that our walrus season is very short. And of course we get a lot of wind, too. It's affecting us now. The animals that we hunt are affected by it and that is how it affects us. I have seen so much change with our climate over the years . . . the enormity of the problem is so big it involves many countries and the whole world."

The ability of Alaska Natives to continue to sustainably subsist on walrus and other marine mammal resources is an inherent Indigenous right, and climate change is threatening this right. The Pacific walrus is currently under review by the US Fish and Wildlife Service for listing under the Endangered Species Act, not because of current population decline, but because

of anticipated impacts to the population over the next 100 years caused by climate change and ocean acidification. As a mitigation measure the Service has suggested future restrictions to subsistence walrus hunting, an approach that the Eskimo Walrus Commission takes issue with. The Eskimo Walrus Commission is an Alaska Native co-management entity representing 19 walrus hunting communities from Barrow to the Bristol Bay region, which advocates on behalf of Alaska Native walrus hunters in the management process. Its mission is to protect the Pacific walrus population. The Commission has expressed the view that because subsistence walrus hunting is not the root cause of the issue with the walrus population, solely focusing on hunting restrictions cannot be a viable management solution.

The gravest threat to the Pacific walrus population, and thus to the Alaska Native subsistence communities that depend on them, is carbon emissions. In December 2014, the Commission passed a resolution urging the US Fish and Wildlife Service to make clear recommendations to the federal government to significantly reduce US carbon emissions and invest in clean energy. Through this resolution, the Commission identified the fact that the current management approach would not only be ineffective in the long term, but would threaten the continued survival of subsistence communities. As an Indigenous organization, the Eskimo Walrus Commission recognizes that threats to the Pacific walrus cannot be addressed on its own. A truly effective management approach must seek to protect not only the walrus, but the whole ecosystem in which it exists, recognizing that the rights of human subsistence communities that interact with and depend on this ecosystem must be protected also.

Critical Thinking

1. What has been the reciprocal relationship between Alaskan Native communities and marine life that has existed for thousands of years?
2. What are the ways in which this traditional relationship is being threatened by climate change?
3. What is the real threat to Alaskan Native subsistence communities and what do they think should be done about it?

Internet References

Association for Environmental Studies and Sciences
http://www.aess.info
International Journal of Environmental Studies
http://www.tandfonline.com/toc/genv20/current
Journal of Environmental Studies and Sciences
http://phys.org/journals/journal-of-environmental-studies-and-sciences
Journal of Environment and Ecology
http://www.macrothink.org/journal/index.php/jee

KATYA WASSILLIE (Yup'ik/Iñupiaq) is the Eskimo Walrus Commission specialist at Kawerak, Inc., the tribal consortium for the Bering Straits region of Alaska. She is from the communities of Pilot Station and White Mountain, Alaska, and is an active participant in the subsistence lifestyle.

Article   Prepared by: Elvio Angeloni, *Pasadena City College*

Being Indigenous in the 21st Century

With a shared sense of history and a growing set of tools, the world's Indigenous Peoples are moving into a future of their own making without losing sight of who they are and where they come from.

WILMA MANKILLER

Learning Outcomes

After reading this article, you will be able to:

- Discuss the values Indigenous People share about the natural world.
- Explain why we should care about the loss of human cultures.

There are more than 300 million Indigenous People, in virtually every region of the world, including the Sámi peoples of Scandinavia, the Maya of Guatemala, numerous tribal groups in the Amazonian rainforest, the Dalits in the mountains of Southern India, the San and Kwei of Southern Africa, Aboriginal people in Australia, and, of course the hundreds of Indigenous Peoples in Mexico, Central and South America, as well as here in what is now known as North America.

There is enormous diversity among communities of Indigenous Peoples, each of which has its own distinct culture, language, history, and unique way of life. Despite these differences, Indigenous Peoples across the globe share some common values derived in part from an understanding that their lives are part of and inseparable from the natural world.

Onondaga Faith Keeper Oren Lyons once said, "Our knowledge is profound and comes from living in one place for untold generations. It comes from watching the sun rise in the east and set in the west from the same place over great sections of time. We are as familiar with the lands, rivers, and great seas that surround us as we are with the faces of our mothers. Indeed, we call the earth Etenoha, our mother from whence all life springs."

Indigenous people are not the only people who understand the interconnectedness of all living things. There are many thousands of people from different ethnic groups who care deeply about the environment and fight every day to protect the earth. The difference is that Indigenous People have the benefit of being regularly reminded of their responsibilities to the land by stories and ceremonies. They remain close to the land, not only in the way they live, but in their hearts and in the way they view the world. Protecting the environment is not an intellectual exercise; it is a sacred duty. When women like Pauline Whitesinger, an elder at Big Mountain, and Carrie Dann, a Western Shoshone land rights activist, speak of preserving the land for future generations, they are not just talking about future generations of humans. They are talking about future generations of plants, animals, water, and all living things. Pauline and Carrie understand the relative insignificance of human beings in the totality of the planet.

Aside from a different view of their relationship to the natural world, many of the world's Indigenous Peoples also share a fragmented but still-present sense of responsibility for one another. Cooperation always has been necessary for the survival of tribal people, and even today cooperation takes precedence over competition in more traditional communities. It is really quite miraculous that a sense of sharing and reciprocity continues into the 21st century given the staggering amount of adversity Indigenous Peoples have faced. In many communities, the most respected people are not those who have amassed great material wealth or achieved great personal success. The greatest respect is reserved for those who help other people, those who understand that their lives play themselves out within a set of reciprocal relationships.

There is evidence of this sense of reciprocity in Cherokee communities. My husband, Charlie Soap, leads a widespread self-help movement among the Cherokee in which low-income volunteers work together to build walking trails, community centers, sports complexes, water lines, and houses. The self-help movement taps into the traditional Cherokee value of cooperation for the sake of the common good. The projects also build a sense of self-efficacy among the people.

Besides values, the world's Indigenous Peoples are also bound by the common experience of being "discovered" and subjected to colonial expansion into their territories that has led to the loss of an incalculable number of lives and millions and millions of acres of land and resources. The most basic rights of Indigenous Peoples were disregarded, and they were subjected to a series of policies that were designed to dispossess them of their land and resources and assimilate them into colonial society and culture. Too often the policies resulted in poverty, high infant mortality, rampant unemployment, and substance abuse, with all its attendant problems.

The stories are shockingly similar all over the world. When I read Chinua Achebe's *Things Fall Apart,* which chronicled the systematic destruction of an African tribe's social, cultural, and economic structure, it sounded all too familiar: take the land, discredit the leaders, ridicule the traditional healers, and send the children off to distant boarding schools.

And I was sickened by the Stolen Generation report about Aboriginal children in Australia who were forcibly removed from their families and placed in boarding schools far away from their families and communities. My own father and my Aunt Sally were taken from my grandfather by the U.S. government and placed in a government boarding school when they were very young. There is a connection between us. Indigenous Peoples everywhere are connected both by our values and by our oppression.

When contemplating the contemporary challenges and problems faced by Indigenous Peoples worldwide, it is important to remember that the roots of many social, economic, and political problems can be found in colonial policies. And these policies continue today across the globe.

Several years ago Charlie and I visited an indigenous community along the Rio Negro in the Brazilian rainforest. Some of the leaders expressed concern that some environmentalists, who should be natural allies, focus almost exclusively on the land and appear not to see or hear the people at all. One leader pointed out that a few years ago it was popular for famous musicians to wear T-shirts emblazoned with the slogan "Save the Rainforests," but no one ever wore a T-shirt with the slogan "Save the People of the Rainforest," though the people of the forest possess the best knowledge about how to live with and sustain the forests.

With so little accurate information about Indigenous Peoples available in educational institutions, in literature, films, or popular culture, it is not surprising that many people are not even conscious of Indigenous Peoples.

The battle to protect the human and land rights of Indigenous Peoples is made immeasurably more difficult by the fact that so few people know much about either the history or contemporary lives of our people. And without any kind of history or cultural context, it is almost impossible for outsiders to understand the issues and challenges faced by Indigenous Peoples.

This lack of accurate information leaves a void that is often filled with nonsensical stereotypes, which either vilify Indigenous Peoples as troubled descendants of savage peoples, or romanticize them as innocent children of nature, spiritual but incapable of higher thought.

Public perceptions will change in the future as indigenous leaders more fully understand that there is a direct link between public perception and public policies. Indigenous Peoples must frame their own issues, because if they don't frame the issues for themselves, their opponents most certainly will. In the future, as more indigenous people become filmmakers, writers, historians, museum curators, and journalists, they will be able to use a dazzling array of technological tools to tell their own stories, in their own voice, in their own way.

Once, a journalist asked me whether people in the United States had trouble accepting the government of the Cherokee Nation during my tenure as principal chief. I was a little surprised by the question. The government of the Cherokee Nation predated the government of the United States and had treaties with other countries before it executed a treaty with one of the first U.S. colonies.

Cherokee and other tribal leaders sent delegations to meet with the English, Spanish, and French in an effort to protect their lands and people. Traveling to foreign lands with a trusted interpreter, tribal ambassadors took maps that had been painstakingly drawn by hand to show their lands to heads of other governments. They also took along gifts, letters, and proclamations. Though tribal leaders thought they were being dealt with as heads of state and as equals, historical records indicate they were often objects of curiosity, and that there was a great deal of disdain and ridicule of these earnest delegates.

Tribal governments in the United States today exercise a range of sovereign rights. Many tribal governments have their own judicial systems, operate their own police force, run their own schools, administer their own clinics and hospitals, and operate a wide range of business enterprises. There are now more than two dozen tribally controlled community colleges. All these advancements benefit everyone in the community, not just tribal people. The history, contemporary lives, and future of tribal governments is intertwined with that of their neighbors.

One of the most common misperceptions about Indigenous Peoples is that they are all the same. There is not only great diversity among Indigenous Peoples, there is great diversity within each tribal community, just as there is in the larger society. Members of the Cherokee Nation are socially, economically, and culturally stratified. Several thousand Cherokee continue to speak the Cherokee language and live in Cherokee communities in rural northeastern Oklahoma. At the other end of the spectrum, there are enrolled tribal members who have never been to even visit the Cherokee Nation. Intermarriage has created an enrolled Cherokee membership that includes people with Hispanic, Asian, Caucasian, and African American heritage.

So what does the future hold for Indigenous Peoples across the globe? What challenges will they face moving further into the 21st century?

To see the future, one needs only to look at the past. If, as peoples, we have been able to survive a staggering loss of land, of rights, of resources, of lives, and we are still standing in the early 21st century, how can I not be optimistic that we will survive whatever challenges lie ahead, that 100 or 500 years from now we will still have viable indigenous communities? Without question, the combined efforts of government and various religious groups to eradicate traditional knowledge systems has had a profoundly negative impact on the culture as well as the social and economic systems of Indigenous Peoples. But if we have been able to hold onto our sense of community, our languages, culture, and ceremonies, despite everything, how can I not be optimistic about the future?

And though some of our original languages, medicines, and ceremonies have been irretrievably lost, the ceremonial fires of many Indigenous Peoples across the globe have survived all the upheaval. Sometimes indigenous communities have almost had to reinvent themselves as a people but they have never given up their sense of responsibility to one another and to the land. It is this sense of interdependence that has sustained tribal people thus far and I believe it will help sustain them well into the future.

Indigenous Peoples know about change and have proven time and time again they can adapt to change. No matter where they go in the world, they hold onto a strong sense of tribal identity while fully interacting with and participating in the larger society around them. In my state of Oklahoma alone, we have produced an indigenous astronaut, two United States congressmen, a Pulitzer Prize-winning novelist, and countless others who have made great contributions to their people, the state, and the world.

One of the great challenges for Indigenous Peoples in the 21st century will be to develop practical models to capture, maintain, and pass on traditional knowledge systems and values to future generations. Nothing can replace the sense of continuity that a genuine understanding of traditional tribal knowledge brings. Many communities are working on discrete aspects of culture, such as language or medicine, but it is the entire system of knowledge that needs to be maintained, not just for Indigenous Peoples but for the world at large.

Regrettably, in the future the battle for human and land rights will continue. But the future does look somewhat better for tribal people. Last year, after 30 years of advocacy by Indigenous Peoples, the United Nations finally passed a declaration supporting their distinct human rights. The challenge will be to make sure the provisions of the declaration are honored and that the rights of Indigenous Peoples all over the world are protected.

Indigenous Peoples simply do better when they have control of their own lives. In the case of my own people, after we were forcibly removed by the United States military from the southeastern part of the United States to Indian Territory, now Oklahoma, we picked ourselves up and rebuilt our nation, despite the fact that approximately 4,000 Cherokee lives were lost during the forced removal. We started some of the first schools west of the Mississippi, Indian or non-Indian, and built schools for the higher education of women. We printed our own newspapers in Cherokee and English and were more literate than our neighbors in adjoining states. Then, in the early 20th century, the federal government almost abolished the Cherokee Nation, and within two decades, our educational attainment levels dropped dramatically and many of our people were living without the most basic amenities. But our people never gave up the dream of rebuilding the Cherokee Nation. In my grandfather's time, Cherokee men rode horses from house to house to collect dimes in a mason jar so they could send representatives to Washington to remind the government to honor its treaties with the Cherokee people.

Over the past 35 years, we have revitalized the Cherokee Nation and once again run our own school, and we have an extensive array of successful education programs. The youth at our Sequoyah High School recently won the state trigonometry contest, and several are Gates Millennium Scholars. We simply do better when we have control over our own destiny.

Critical Thinking

1. What do the 300 million Indigenous People of the world have in common? Where does such knowledge come from?
2. In what ways do Indigenous People differ from others who care about the environment?
3. In what respects is there a "shared sense of responsibility for one another" among Indigenous People?
4. Describe the Indigenous People's common experience of "being discovered" and "being subjected to colonial expansion."
5. Why is it important to not just "save the rainforests," but also to "save the people"?
6. How is the battle to protect the human and land rights of Indigenous Peoples made immeasurably more difficult? How does the author suggest that such public perceptions be changed?
7. In what respects were tribal groups, such as the Cherokee, independent entities at one time?
8. In what respects do tribal governments in the United States still exercise a range of sovereign rights?
9. Why is the author optimistic about the future survival of indigenous communities?
10. What challenges lie ahead for Indigenous Peoples and how does the author suggest that they are meeting these challenges?
11. How have the Cherokee shown that "Indigenous Peoples simply do better when they have control over their own lives"?

Create Central

www.mhhe.com/createcentral

Internet References

Association for Political and Legal Anthropology
www.aaanet.org/apla/index.htm
Human Rights and Humanitarian Assistance
www.etown.edu/vl/humrts.html
The Indigenous Rights Movement in the Pacific
www.inmotionmagazine.com/pacific.html
Murray Research Center
www.radcliffe.edu/murray_redirect/index.php
Small Planet Institute
www.smallplanet.org/food
WWW Virtual Library: Indigenous Studies
www.cwis.org

Mankiller, Wilma. From *Cultural Survival Quarterly*, Spring 2009. Copyright © 2009 by Cultural Survival Inc. Reprinted by permission.

Article   Prepared by: Elvio Angeloni

The Organ Detective: A Career Spent Uncovering a Hidden Global Market in Human Flesh

ETHAN WATTERS

Learning Outcomes

After reading this article, you will be able to:

- Describe the general movement of organs and tissues in the world today.
- Describe and explain "transplant tourism."
- Discuss Nancy Scheper-Hughes 'call for "barefoot anthropologists" versus Roy Andrade's criticism that it is a "moral model."
- Describe the "organ mafia."

W hen she first heard about the organ thieves, the anthropologist Nancy Scheper-Hughes was doing fieldwork in northeastern Brazil. It was 1987, and a rumor circulating around the shantytown of Alto do Cruzeiro, overlooking the town of Timbaúba, in a sugarcane farming region of Pernambuco, told of foreigners who traveled the dirt roads in yellow vans, looking for unattended children to snatch up and kill for their transplantable organs. Later, it was said, the children's bodies would turn up in roadside ditches or in hospital dumpsters.

Scheper-Hughes, then an up-and-coming professor at the University of California-Berkeley, had good reason to be skeptical. As part of her study of poverty and motherhood in the shantytown, she had interviewed the area's coffin makers and the government clerks who kept the death records. The rate of child mortality there was appalling, but surgically eviscerated

bodies were nowhere to be found. "Bah, these are stories invented by the poor and illiterate," the manager of the municipal cemetery told her.

And yet, while Scheper-Hughes doubted the literal truth of the tales, she was unwilling to dismiss the rumors. She subscribed to an academic school of thought that swore off imposing Western notions of absolute or objective truth. As much as she wanted to show solidarity with the beliefs of her sources, she struggled with how to present the rumors in her 1992 book, *Death Without Weeping: The Violence of Everyday Life in Brazil*.

In the end, she argued that the organ stealing stories could only be understood in light of all the bodily threats faced by this impoverished population. In addition to pervasive hunger and thirst, the locals also faced mistreatment at the hands of employers, the military, and law enforcement. The medical care available, she suggested, often did more harm than good. Local health care workers and pharmacists gave the malnourished and chronically ill locals the catchall diagnosis of *nervos* and prescribed tranquilizers, sleeping pills, vitamins, and elixirs. The locals were well aware that wealthier people in their country and abroad had access to better medical care—including exotic procedures like tissue and organ transplants.

"The people of the Alto can all too easily imagine that their bodies may be eyed longingly as a reservoir of spare parts by those with money," Scheper-Hughes wrote in *Death Without Weeping*. The stories of transplant teams murdering local children and harvesting their organs persisted, she wrote, "because the 'misinformed' shantytown residents are onto something. They are on the right track and are refusing to give up on their intuitive sense that something is seriously amiss." The book, which was widely praised and nominated for the National Book Critics Circle Award, solidified her reputation as one of the leading anthropologists of her generation.

In 1995, Scheper-Hughes was the sole anthropologist invited to speak at a medical conference on the practice of organ trafficking held in Bellagio, Italy. Although there remained no solid evidence that people were being murdered for viable organs, rumors similar to the ones Scheper-Hughes had documented in Brazil had now spread from South America to Sweden, Italy, Romania, and Albania. In France, one popular story told of children being abducted from Euro Disney for their kidneys. The conference organizers asked Scheper-Hughes to explain the persistence of this gruesome meme.

The trade in kidneys particularly fascinated her. Unlike the trade in heart valves or corneas, kidneys were being shipped from country to country inside the living bodies of sentient individuals.

If the other participants at the conference, who were mainly transplant surgeons, were hoping to learn from Scheper-Hughes what was factual and what was false among these rumors, they were likely disappointed. She told them the stories were "true at that indeterminate level between fact and metaphor," as she'd later write. Looking back, she feels certain that the surgeons—whom she thinks of as bright and skilled, like fighter pilots, but not very intellectual—didn't really understand her more theoretical analyses. "We were speaking different languages," she told me.

Still, Scheper-Hughes made the best of her time among the doctors. In Bellagio, she decided to do some on-the-fly ethnographic research into the current practices of transplant surgeons. As she spoke with them during boat rides on Lake Como or while touring the olive groves of Villa Serbelloni, the doctors answered her questions candidly. One surgeon told her that he knew of patients who had traveled to India to purchase kidneys. She remembers an Israeli surgeon telling her that Palestinian laborers were "very generous" with their kidneys, and often donated to strangers in exchange for "a small honorarium." A heart surgeon from Eastern Europe admitted his concern that medical tourism would encourage doctors from his country to harvest organs from brain-dead donors who were "not quite as dead as we might like them to be." In these new practices, Scheper-Hughes began to understand, human organs and tissue generally moved from south to north, from the poor to the rich, and from brown-skinned to lighter-skinned people.

While none of the surgeons' accounts confirmed the kidnapping-for-organs rumors, Scheper-Hughes came to believe that the "really real" traffic in human body parts, as she has called it, was ripe for further study. "There were so many unanswered questions," she recalls. "How were patients finding out about available organs in other countries? Who were the poor people who were selling their body parts? Nobody had gone into the trenches to find out."

Scheper-Hughes' investigation of the organ trade would be a test case for a new kind of anthropology. This would be the study not of an isolated, exotic culture, but of a globalized, interconnected black market—one that crossed classes, cultures, and borders, linking impoverished paid donors to the highest-status individuals and institutions in the modern world. For Scheper-Hughes, the project presented an opportunity to show how an anthropologist could have a meaningful, real-time, and forceful impact on an ongoing injustice. "There is a joke in our discipline that goes, 'If you want to keep something a secret, publish it in an anthropology journal,'" she once told me. "We are perceived as benign, amusing characters." Scheper-Hughes had grander ambitions. She decided it was time, as she puts it, to stop following the rumors and start following bodies.

IN her writing, Scheper-hughes has described her years of research into the international black market for organs as a disorienting "descent into Hades." When she discusses the topic in person, she is animated and energetic. At 69, Scheper-Hughes presents a brassy mix of grandmother and urban hipster. On the winter day when I visited her home near the U.C. Berkeley campus, her hair was short, spiked, and highlighted with streaks of magenta, and she wore a short-sleeved shirt that revealed a stylized tattoo of a turtle—a gift, she said, from her son for her 60th birthday. As she talked about her dozens of international journeys to interview surgeons, donors, recipients, and various intermediaries, she showed me her office, which had formerly been the home's garage. Inside were thousands of files, stored in dozens of large plastic bins and black file cabinets, along with drawers full of cassette tapes and field notebooks.

Since the mid-1990s, Scheper-Hughes has published some 50 articles and book chapters about the organ trade, and she is currently in the process of synthesizing that material into a book, tentatively titled *A World Cut in Two*. Over the years, she has had an outsize impact on the intellectual trends in her field, and her study of the organ trade is likely to be her last major statement on the meaning and value of the discipline to which she has devoted her life. Whether this body of work represents a triumph of anthropological research or a cautionary tale about scholarly vigilantism is already a hotly disputed question among her colleagues.

When Scheper-Hughes began to focus on the organ trade in the 1990s, she was a leading voice in a contentious debate about the future of anthropology, which was then in the midst of a long-brewing identity crisis. In the 1940s and 1950s, anthropologists had carried the banner of science into the field. Back in those days, a graduate student heading out to complete an ethnography of some far-flung people could be expected to carry with him a copy of George Murdock's *Outline of Cultural Materials*, which lists more than 500 categories, cultural institutions, and behaviors under headings like "family," "religious practices," "agriculture," and so on. Anthropologists were expected to document kinship relations and answer straightforward questions like: How is food stored and preserved? Are farm crops grown for animal fodder? Does the groom move in with the bride's family after marriage, or vice versa? Because everyone was collecting the same types of information, the data could be replicated and updated, and cultures large and small could be classified and compared. Anthropologists of the era sought to create a taxonomy of human social behavior, and the doggedness and objectivity of the researcher were prized.

Scholars who came of age in the political tumult of the 1960s rejected this model. Scheper-Hughes was among a cohort of anthropologists who suggested that the scientific, taxonomic approach was just imperialism in another form, and that any claims of objectivity or literal truth were ultimately illusory or, worse, an excuse for exploitation and violence.

Of course, there remained a question: If not just collecting and cataloging facts about other cultures, what *should* anthropologists be doing? In a 1995 debate with the anthropologist Roy D'Andrade in the pages of *Current Anthropology*, Scheper-Hughes argued for what she called a "militant anthropology," in which practitioners would become traitors to their class and nation by joining political battles arm in arm with their subjects. The job of the anthropologist wasn't simply to document the quotidian but to strip away appearances and reveal the hidden forces and ideologies that leave people dominated and oppressed. To do this, she suggested throwing off the traditional guise of the academic—in "the spirit of the Brazilian 'carnavalesque'"—and joining the powerless in their fight against bourgeois institutions like hospitals and universities.

"The new cadre of 'barefoot anthropologists' that I envision," she wrote, "must become alarmists and shock troopers—the producers of politically complicated and morally demanding texts and images capable of sinking through the layers of acceptance, complicity, and bad faith that allow the suffering and the deaths to continue."

D'Andrade and others saw grave danger for the discipline in Scheper-Hughes' call to the barricades (or to the carnival). D'Andrade believed that Scheper-Hughes and her intellectual allies were leading the field away from an objective science and toward what he called a "moral model" based on the simplistic duality of the oppressed and the oppressor. Her militant style

of anthropology, he feared, would turn a once promising discipline into an exercise in "moralistic pamphleteering."

"With the moral model, the truth ain't exactly the thing that everyone strives for," D'Andrade, who is now retired and living in Northern California, told me. "What you strive for is a denunciation of a real evil." I asked him who prevailed in his public debate with Scheper-Hughes. "I believed that after the kerfuffle that people would get back to asking, 'How do you know something is true or not?' But in the end, the moral model swept the country and cultural anthropology stopped being anything that a self-respecting social scientist would call a science. The hegemony of the Scheper-Hughes position became total."

Another loose consensus that emerged out of the debates of the 1990s was a widely shared belief that cultural anthropology's focus on far-away, exotic societies had run its course: Why shouldn't anthropologists turn their gaze on institutions that have real power in the modern world—banks, multinational corporations, courts, and governmental agencies? Or, for that matter, transplant units in major hospitals?

At the time, there were only a handful of papers in the medical literature addressing the rise of the global organ market. Since the 1970s, live organ transplants had changed from experimental procedures to a common practice in the United States, most European and Asian countries, half a dozen South American nations, and four countries in Africa. In 1983, the introduction of the immunosuppressant drug cyclosporine dramatically increased the potential donor pool for any given patient. By the mid-1990s, there were hints in the medical literature of the rise of a new phenomenon: transplant tourism. In 1989, a small article had appeared in *The Lancet* reporting an inquiry into allegations that four Turks had been brought to Humana Hospital Wellington, in London, to sell their kidneys. Other research suggested that the selling of kidneys from living donors was rapidly growing in India, and that in China human organs were being harvested from the bodies of executed prisoners.

While most governments and international medical associations condemned the sale of human organs, laws and professional guidelines were inconsistent and often poorly enforced. What was clear was that the demand for organs outstripped the supply in nearly every country. In the United States, despite significant public outreach campaigns to encourage donations, there were already more than 37,000 people on organ waiting lists. Each year 10 percent of patients waiting for a heart transplant died before a donated organ could become available.

Scheper-Hughes' research into the organ trade began in earnest not long after the Bellagio conference, when she teamed up with the event's organizer, a medical historian at Columbia University named David Rothman; his wife, Sheila, a professor of sociomedical sciences at Columbia; and Lawrence Cohen, a fellow anthropologist from U.C. Berkeley. The four decided to spread out across the globe, dividing up the burgeoning global hot spots for transplant tourism. The Rothmans would focus their research on China; Cohen would investigate India; and Scheper-Hughes would travel mainly to Brazil and South Africa.

The research got off to a swift start. During breaks from teaching in the late 1990s, Scheper-Hughes visited African and South American dialysis units, organ banks, police morgues, and hospitals to interview surgeons, pathologists, nephrologists, nurses, patient's rights activists, and public officials. "It became like detective work," she told me. "I used a simple snowballing technique. I'd go to a morgue or a transplant ward and I'd get one person to tell me something—and then ask, 'Where do I go from here?' I found it enormously satisfying to begin to put the pieces together."

Her collaborators, too, quickly made headway. While reliable estimates of how many transplants were happening on the black market were difficult to come by, evidence that this market existed appeared nearly everywhere the collaborators looked. In India, Cohen found people selling their kidneys to private transplant clinics that catered to patients all over the world, despite a 1994 law that made such transactions illegal. Selling kidneys, he discovered, had become so common in India that some poor parents even talked of selling an organ to raise a dowry for a daughter. David Rothman, for his part, had become convinced that a Chinese anti-crime campaign was associated with a growing enterprise that sold organs from executed prisoners.

In both Brazil and South Africa, Scheper-Hughes discovered that the dead bodies of many poor people were harvested, without permission, for useful tissues—corneas, skin, heart valves—to be exported to wealthier countries. In São Paulo, she worked with a city council member who had been tracking illegal commerce in human tissue taken from the cadavers of indigents and nursing-home patients. He showed her documents suggesting that more than 30,000 pituitary glands had been shipped to the United States over a three-year period. In South Africa, the director of a research unit in a public medical school showed her documents approving the sale of heart valves to medical centers in Austria and Germany. She also discovered, at private medical centers in both Brazil and South Africa, that kidneys from live donors were being bought and sold.

In 1998, while Scheper-Hughes was still writing up her first major papers on her field research, she and her collaborators met at a Starbucks in Tokyo during a medical ethics conference to compare notes. The material they were turning up seemed so remarkable that they brainstormed starting an organization called Organs Watch, which would serve as a repository for information on global transplant activity and a center for future

research. By 1999, they had secured a $230,000 grant from the Open Society Institute, along with a commitment from the University of California, to help create the new organization.

As she gathered more information on Rosenbaum and his ties to multiple American hospitals, Scheper-Hughes made another unusual decision for an anthropologist: She began to share her findings with U.S. law enforcement.

But the collaboration between the Rothmans and Scheper-Hughes was short-lived. Scheper-Hughes' first major article on the organ trade, which she published in April 2000 in *Current Anthropology*, chronicled her findings in the morgues and hospitals in Brazil and South Africa; it was also so impassioned that it sounded, at times, like the setup for a horror movie. "Global capitalism and advanced biotechnology have together released new medically incited 'tastes' for human bodies, living and dead, for the skin and bones, flesh and blood, tissue, marrow, and genetic material of 'the other,'" she wrote. She called organ and tissue transplant a "post-modern form of human sacrifice" and accused transplant surgeons of conspiring to invent an "artificially created need . . . for an ever-expanding sick, aging, and dying population."

Some anthropologists saw the paper as groundbreaking. Elliott Leyton, of Memorial University of Newfoundland, wrote that the paper was nothing less than the "beginning of a long-awaited moral vindication of much of modern anthropology, lost for so long in the contemplation of its own navel." Other anthropologists, however, felt that Scheper-Hughes played fast and loose with source identification, and that her writing came off more like muckraking journalism than anthropology.

To her collaborator David Rothman, Scheper-Hughes' rhetoric didn't seem like scholarship at all. He was particularly taken aback by her contention that doctors were intentionally creating the demand for transplants. Rothman remembers traveling with his wife (and co-collaborator) to Berkeley in November of 1999 to attend the public launch of Organs Watch. "When Sheila and I saw the website that had been created, we were—let me see if I can get the right word—disturbed," Rothman said. "It was sensationalistic, emotive, and provocative, with pictures of bodies but no charts. We realized that we operated in very different ways from Nancy." After a heated argument, the Rothmans cut ties with Scheper-Hughes and ended their work with Organs Watch. But Scheper-Hughes was just getting started.

As soon as Organs Watch went public in 1999, Scheper-Hughes began to receive hundreds of leads through emails and phone calls from people who claimed behind-the-scenes knowledge of the tissue and organ trade. She began to personally track down many of the stories. "I was traveling in a blur, like a whirling dervish," she said.

She also began to push what she acknowledged were the accepted ethical boundaries of anthropological research. On her trips, as she wrote in a 2006 paper published in the *Annals of Transplantation,* she sometimes posed as a patient seeking a transplant or as someone looking to purchase a kidney for a sick family member. On a visit to Turkey, she pretended to be shopping for a kidney for a sick husband at a flea market near a minibus station in Askaray, a poor immigrant neighborhood of Istanbul. She found an unemployed baker who said he was willing to sell one of his kidneys, and she went so far as to sit with him at a local cafe to negotiate a price. At other times, she wrote, she'd simply walk into hospitals or clinics to confront a surgeon or an administrator or to learn what she could from patients. When stopped or questioned by staff or security, she would identify herself as "Dr. Scheper-Hughes," knowing that the questioner wouldn't likely suspect that she was referring to her doctorate in anthropology. Faced with what she called an international "organs Mafia," Scheper-Hughes argued in a 2009 article for *Anthropology News* that she had no choice but to abandon many accepted rules of her profession. "When one researches organized, structured and largely invisible violence," she wrote, "there are times one must ask if it is more important to strictly follow a professional code or to intervene."

Her research during this period yielded a wealth of information and insight into the illicit networks of organ brokers. The trade in kidneys particularly fascinated her. Unlike the trade in cadaveric heart valves or corneas, kidneys were being shipped from country to country inside the living bodies of sentient individuals. In the Philippines, kidney sellers she interviewed often pulled up their shirts, displaying their nephrectomy scars with evident pride. They spoke of the surgery as a sacrifice made for their families, and members of their community sometimes compared their abdominal incisions to the lance wounds Christ received on the cross. In Moldova, as she reported in a 2003 paper published in the *Journal of Human Rights,* people who had sold their kidneys were considered so morally and physically compromised that they were treated as social pariahs. "That son of a bitch left me an invalid," one Moldovan paid donor said of his surgeon. Young Brazilian men who had been flown to South Africa to sell their kidneys described to Scheper-Hughes how the experience had gained them a pass into the world of tourism and medical marvels. One told her that his main regret was not having spent more time in the

hospital. "There were clean sheets, hot showers, lots of food," he recalled. As he recovered, he went down to the hospital courtyard and bought himself his first cappuccino. "It was like ambrosia," he said. "I really felt like a big tourist." In the end, some attested that they would make the deal again, and some regretted the decision. "They treated me OK until they got what they wanted," another seller told her. "Then I was thrown away like garbage."

In her travels, Scheper-Hughes was also able to develop some relationships with kidney brokers, the middlemen who sought out donors in poor countries and neighborhoods. One convicted broker, Gadalya "Gaddy" Tauber, gave her lengthy interviews while serving out his sentence in Henrique Dias military prison in Recife, Brazil. Tauber, she learned, had facilitated a trafficking scheme that sent poor Brazilians to a private medical center in South Africa to supply kidneys for Israeli transplant tourists. He employed a number of "kidney hunters," some of whom were young men who had already donated their kidneys, to find new recruits. In the end, it wasn't difficult. Once the first young men came back from surgery centers in South Africa showing off their thick rolls of cash, Tauber and his associates had more willing donors than they needed. They began to drop the price they offered to donors from $10,000 to $6,000 and then to $3,000, Scheper-Hughes reported in a 2007 profile of Tauber.

Scheper-Hughes' portrayals of organ donors, recipients, and even brokers like Tauber show a great deal of nuance and empathy. At other times, however—particularly when she writes about transplant doctors, bioethicists, or members of the "transplant establishment"—her writing turns markedly more strident.

"Transplant surgeons vie only with the Vatican and its cardinals with respect to their assumption of privilege, irrefutability and of a kind of 'divine election' that seems to place them above (or outside) the mundane laws that govern ordinary mortals," she wrote in one article. "Like child-molesting priests among Catholic clergy, these outlaw surgeons are protected by the corporate transplant professionals hierarchy."

As Scheper-Hughes began to present her findings to doctors and transplant professionals, she experienced a series of harsh rebuffs and rejections. She remembers being called a liar by a senior pathologist at a 1999 medical ethics meeting in Cape Town. In 2002, at a special meeting on organ trafficking in Bucharest, she was shouted down by delegates in the audience: "Who invited this person? Why should we believe this slander?"

Scheper-Hughes recounts these confrontations as proof that she was telling truths that those in the "transplant establishment" were unwilling to face. Her conclusion at the time, as she wrote me in an email, was that "nobody, absolutely nobody cares about this topic." This suggestion, however, is somewhat hard to square with what was going on around her. A number of international meetings—events that Scheper-Hughes attended—had been called to address the growing illicit market in human organs and tissue, and they were producing unambiguous recommendations and declarations to curtail the trade. In October of 2000, the World Medical Association condemned the sale of human organs and tissue, and urged countries to adopt laws to prevent such abuses. The next month, the United Nations General Assembly adopted the Palermo protocols, which, among other things, defined coercive organ sales and coercive donation as a type of human trafficking.

Colleagues have suggested that, in large part, the medical establishment reacted negatively to Scheper-Hughes not because of her facts but because of her rhetorical style and penchant for confrontation. "I think it's fair to say that Nancy has a suspicion, bordering on hostility, of the medical enterprise," says David Rothman, her former collaborator. ("I have used strong language at times—a phrase like *neocannibalism* isn't going to make me any friends," Scheper-Hughes said after I related Rothman's criticism. "This is how the interpretive anthropologist works. We work with language and subtext.")

A few of Scheper-Hughes' colleagues have told me that she seems to become most energized when embattled. And indeed, discomfiting members of the medical establishment—rather than cultivating a collegial influence among them—may have been her plan all along. Although she rejects Rothman's contention that she is hostile to doctors, Scheper-Hughes has long argued that it is her job to investigate an insulated surgical profession prone to self-glorification. She felt obligated to challenge doctors who talked of "saving lives"—as if the benefits to organ recipients trumped all other concerns. She saw bioethicists who argued for a regulated market in kidneys as "handmaidens of free-market medicine." And she likewise criticized tame, "clinically applied" medical anthropologists who work closely with doctors to provide the spoonful of cultural knowledge that helps the Western medicine go down.

Back in 1990, she argued that the job of a medical anthropologist was to question, even ridicule, Western medicine. "Let us play the court jester, that small, sometimes mocking, sometimes ironic, but always mischievous voice from the sidelines," she wrote in a prominent journal. "To the young, up-and-coming medical anthropologist I would say: 'Take off that white jacket, immediately! Hang it up, and put on the white face of the harlequin.'" She warned even then that there would be a cost to those who assumed such a contentious stance. If your goal was to gain the respect of doctors, or to avoid "derision within conventional academic circles," she wrote, the work of the militant anthropologist was not for you.

> **"It became like detective work," she told me. "I used a simple snowballing technique. I'd go to a morgue or a transplant ward and I'd get one person to tell me something—and then ask, 'Where do I go from here?'"**

In the early 2000s, as she was trying to piece together a more complete picture of the brokers, kidney hunters, and networks that made up the international kidney trade, Scheper-Hughes made a breakthrough—one that appeared to connect the global organ market to major U.S. hospitals. Research informants in Israel had told her in the late 1990s that a man named Levy Izhak Rosenbaum was a big player in international "kidney matchmaking." Then, a few years later, in the summer of 2002, Scheper-Hughes began receiving emails from a man asking for her help in extricating himself from an organization—called United Lifeline, and headed by Rosenbaum—that he described as "the link between Israel and the United States in the illegal kidney trafficking business."

As she gathered more information on Rosenbaum and his ties to multiple American hospitals across the country, Scheper-Hughes took the information directly to the surgeons and the hospitals implicated. In 2002, she set up a meeting with the surgeons at Albert Einstein hospital in Philadelphia, so that she could confront them in person with what she was discovering about transplants there that had been arranged by Rosenbaum. "I was very nervous," she recalls. "I was thinking, What am I doing being madam prosecutor? But I felt that if I was going to publish this material I needed to inform them."

Around the same time, Scheper-Hughes also made another unusual decision for an anthropologist: She began to share her findings with U.S. law enforcement, including officials from the FBI, the Food and Drug Administration, and the State Department's visa fraud unit. Her information appeared to spark little interest and less action. She recalls one particularly frustrating meeting with an agent from the FBI in 2003. "I could see that the guy's mind was elsewhere," she recounted. "He didn't seem to understand that this was a major crime." Frustrated, she found herself thinking, "Look, I can do this. Give me a badge and I'll go make an arrest," she told me.

Scheper-Hughes acknowledges that other anthropologists consider turning over information to law enforcement to be crossing an ethical line, but counters that, given what she was documenting, she was more than justified. "I don't care if some anthropologists think that we have an absolute vow of secrecy to our subjects," she told me. "I think that kind of purity stinks to high heaven."

For Scheper-Hughes, the apparent disinterest of U.S. authorities stood in sharp contrast to her reception by law enforcement officials elsewhere. In 2004, she was invited to brief police investigators and state prosecutors in South Africa regarding their investigation into illegal transplants involving Brazilian donors at several prominent hospitals in Durban, Johannesburg, and Cape Town. She shared with a mustachioed police captain named Louis Helberg the names and contact information of brokers, surgeons, organ recipients, and donors in Brazil and Israel, as well as the names of hospitals she believed were involved in the trade. In return, Helberg gave Scheper-Hughes access to confiscated hospital files and billing records, which she helped sift through and decipher. With Scheper-Hughes' help and advice, Helberg eventually retraced the steps of her international investigation, traveling to Brazil and Israel and meeting with many of her sources. As a result of the investigation, South Africa's largest hospital group, Netcare, admitted to more than a hundred illegal transplants and agreed to pay substantial fines. The story, when it broke, was front-page news in South Africa. One nephrologist there pled guilty to 90 counts of contravening the country's Human Tissue Act. Four other Netcare surgeons and two hospital staffers were charged with various offenses (although the charges were later dropped).

In the U.S., however, it wasn't until the summer of 2009—some seven years after she began sharing her information with the FBI—that federal prosecutors called Scheper-Hughes to tell her they had arrested Rosenbaum. He had been swept up as a minor player in New Jersey's largest-ever political corruption and money laundering sting, which included the arrest of 44 people. Now that they were building a case against Rosenbaum, federal prosecutors were finally very interested in Scheper-Hughes' research, and they met with her on several occasions. She offered to testify at trial, but in October 2011 Rosenbaum pleaded guilty to brokering three illegal kidney transplants and conspiring to broker an illegal transplant.

So far, his is the only successful prosecution for organ trafficking under the 1984 National Organ Transplant Act. Scheper-Hughes had hoped that the Rosenbaum case would herald the beginning of many investigations and prosecutions, but it wasn't to be. "Why is he standing alone in the Trenton courtroom?" she wrote me in an email after Rosenbaum pleaded guilty to conspiracy. "Where are the ones he conspired with?" Frustrated with the U.S. investigators' seeming unwillingness to take these crimes seriously, open new prosecutions, or pursue the surgeons and hospitals without whom the organ trade could not function, Scheper-Hughes continued her own investigation.

One day in January of 2012, Scheper-Hughes called me to say that she might be on the verge of another breakthrough: A retired doctor, formerly a transplant surgeon at a major

East Coast hospital, had agreed to a face-to-face interview, and Scheper-Hughes invited me to come along to witness the encounter. She and I met at the Institute for Advanced Study in Princeton, New Jersey, where she was spending the year working furiously to finish her book on the organ trade. She handed me the keys to drive: She gets anxious on highways, she said. She also gets claustrophobic on airplanes and in elevators, and has difficulty reading maps, she told me. After just a bit of traveling with her, I found the serial globe-trotting that has defined her professional life all the more remarkable.

As night fell, we arrived at a Holiday Inn. The retired surgeon, a dapper man, met us in the hotel bar. Scheper-Hughes called the waitress over, asked her to lower the volume of the basketball game, and encouraged the doctor to order a drink. She then asked him open-ended questions about his personal and professional history. Her body language was friendly and intimate. She laughed at his jokes and shook her head empathetically at his stories of battling hospital bureaucracy.

The surgeon volunteered that he had conducted transplants later revealed to have been set up by Rosenbaum, but said that he had no direct knowledge that the donors had been paid. "In the back of my mind there is always the possibility that there is some incentive, but you can't control it. Personally, I don't see anything wrong with it." Then he added: "I know it is illegal. We have a protocol."

Scheper-Hughes then told him that others had fingered him as the ringleader. "You have been identified . . . as having been the person who set this whole thing up," she said, referring to the Rosenbaum-brokered transplants. "I have to tell you that. I didn't believe it, but that is what they said. You were accused of being the one who set it all up."

"I didn't set anything up," he said, shaking his head. Alternatively cajoling and asking pointed questions, Scheper-Hughes pressed on. The doctor said that some of the transplants set up by Rosenbaum seemed "fishy." "Some of the recipients were from New York, and it did feel a little strange that they found this donor from Israel." He went on to suggest that it was likely that everyone involved at the hospital had good reason to be suspicious. "There is no question that everyone in the program felt that it would be very possible that there was some kind of incentive there. I didn't feel that I had to be the police. As long as I don't know and as long as I don't have any evidence, I'm not going to deny the transplant just because I have the suspicion," he said.

Scheper-Hughes had heard that same argument from surgeons around the world, and I could see her tensing up. When the surgeon suggested that all of his patients did well, her tone turned stern. "I want to tell you something," she said. "Your patients didn't all do so well—the donors didn't all do well," she said, adding, "There is no dependable aftercare. They go thousands of miles away and you don't know what happened to them. So you don't know who dies." The doctor seemed momentarily chastened, but he maintained that he had improved the health of patients who needed transplants and that he had done nothing wrong.

The next week, Scheper-Hughes had a phone conversation with assistant U.S. attorney Mark McCarren, one of the lead investigators on the Rosenbaum case, and she shared some of the information she had gleaned from her meeting with the retired surgeon. McCarren told me that he was grateful for her help: "She had a lot more information than I needed. I don't think there is any question that she has a lot of guts and courage in the way that she has pursued this issue."

Scheper-Hughes was less generous in describing McCarren's efforts. She told me repeatedly that she was deeply concerned that McCarren and the prosecution team didn't understand the full gravity of the crimes being committed. Why, she wanted to know, hadn't prosecutors more aggressively investigated surgeons in the American hospitals connected to Rosenbaum? (Beyond what's in court records, McCarren wouldn't comment on who he included in his investigation.) After all, at the end of the day, Scheper-Hughes has told me on more than one occasion, it is the surgeons who hold the knives.

In the U.S., The waiting list for a kidney now stretches past 100,000 people, while the rate of donations has remained relatively flat for the past decade or so. Recent data from the World Health Organization suggests that, in 2010, the 107,000 organ transplants carried out in the organization's 95 member countries satisfied just 10 percent of the global need. The WHO estimates that one in 10 of all those transplanted organs was procured on the black market.

What impact Scheper-Hughes has had on transplant practices is an open question. Organs Watch still exists. Though she doesn't have an office staff, Scheper-Hughes still trains graduate students and postdocs to do international fieldwork. The organization's website contains only the following sentence: "The Organs Watch Web Site is currently under reconstruction and will be moved to a new address in August 2009." Scheper-Hughes says she had to hurriedly take down the site after an organ broker told her she had been using information there to locate populations of the cheapest and most willing donors.

In anthropology, the kind of radical political advocacy and "militancy" that Scheper-Hughes championed in the 1990s has become less fashionable. "She is notorious in the field; she both attracts and alienates our professional colleagues," says Arthur Kleinman, a prominent medical anthropologist at Harvard. "I admire her responsible, even blunt, honesty, but I'm troubled by her provocative and accusatory stances."

She still has her fans in the discipline, among them the well-known anthropologist Paul Farmer. "The challenge she has

taken up is: How can you be an advocate when everything is pulling you towards an ivory-tower model of disengagement?" he told me. "She is pushing the boundaries of social engagement, and she has gone beyond all parameters for an academic. She is doing what she and a lot of us think is right."

In the medical community, despite her record of antagonization, many transplant surgeons give Scheper-Hughes credit for bringing widespread abuses to light, and for revealing the voices of donors and middlemen in the transplant trade. "She's pointed out that underground illegal markets really do exist," says Arthur Matas, the director of the Renal Transplant Program at the University of Minnesota. While most transplant surgeons like to think that their community would never participate in such a black market, Matas says, Scheper-Hughes has made it clear that they do—"sometimes unknowingly and sometimes knowingly."

In the Philippines, kidney sellers she interviewed often pulled up their shirts, displaying their nephrectomy scars with evident pride.

By and large, however, Scheper-Hughes is still eyed warily by many in the transplant world, in part for glossing over what many see as critical degrees of culpability. Organ brokers like Rosenbaum can go to great lengths to make recruited donors seem legitimate to doctors, who may be fooled into proceeding with a transplant. "Participating knowingly and unknowingly are two different categories," Matas says. "You have to be very careful when you cast wide blame."

But in Scheper-Hughes' view, surgeons either participate in illegal transplants with full volition, or they cultivate a willful blindness to their participation. As her writing shows, she prefers to focus on a larger thesis, which has not varied much since her time in northeastern Brazil: that Western medicine is often a weapon of violence used on the bodies of the poor or otherwise disempowered.

Rumors about people being murdered for their body parts still circulate in parts of the world. In 2009 a journalist named Donald Boström wrote an article in the Swedish newspaper *Aftonbladet* headlined "Our Sons Are Plundered of Their Organs." The article suggested that Palestinian casualties in conflicts in the West Bank were being used as unwilling organ donors. Amid statistics about intense Israeli demand for kidneys and livers, Boström recounted that he had met "parents who told of how their sons had been deprived of organs before being killed." The article caused an international rift between

Sweden and Israel and was condemned as baseless "blood libel" by Israeli Prime Minister Benjamin Netanyahu.

Scheper-Hughes came to Boström's defense in *Counter-Punch,* presenting what she called a "smoking gun" to back up the claims in his article. Her evidence was an interview she had conducted with an Israeli pathologist named Yehuda Hiss, the director of the the the Abu Kabir Forensic Institute, Israel's central facility for conducting autopsies. In the interview, which Scheper-Hughes had recorded in 2000 but had not previously written about, Hiss made the remarkable admission that his institute had, without family permission, taken corneas, skin, bone, and other tissues from the dead bodies of Palestinians, as well as from the dead bodies of Israel Defense Forces soldiers and other cadavers that came through his morgue. The organs and tissues were used for medical training and research, and for skin and cornea transplants. (After the tape was released, Hiss denied any wrongdoing.)

Scheper-Hughes' interview with Hiss was a testament to her extraordinary knack for obtaining access to sensitive information and making an impact. Hiss has since been removed from his post at Abu Kabir. The repercussions of the controversy, legal and otherwise, will likely be felt for many years.

But given the extraordinary political tensions that persist between Israelis and Palestinians, this would seem to be a case where it's especially important to clearly delineate rumors from facts. As horrifying as Hiss' taped admissions were, they did not confirm the stories circulating among Palestinian families, and reported by Bostroöm, that their sons' organs were being harvested while the young men were still alive. In a 2013 essay about the controversy that she co-wrote with Boström, Scheper-Hughes criticized the international media for construing the *Aftonbladet* story as claiming that "Israeli soldiers were deliberately hunting young Palestinians in order to cut out their organs." She wrote that this was a "distortion" of Boström's reporting, one that distracted from the issue of transplant practices. While it's true that the original article stops short of making precisely this claim about "hunting," it does uncritically report the perception that Palestinian victims were still breathing when they disappeared from their villages. It's not surprising that international audiences would find this a morally salient detail.

When I suggested that there seemed to be an important difference between the charges repeated in the Boström article and the revelations from her interview with Hiss about cadaveric tissue-harvesting, Scheper-Hughes became frustrated that I wasn't seeing the big picture. "The distinctions you are making are just getting into obfuscation," she said. "It is true that the dead don't care what happens to their body—but the living do care. Those Palestinian families care. It isn't that I don't understand the difference."

"Does my interview with Hiss support the Boström article? Absolutely. It's not that different," she said. "If you miss that point, you are missing what I'm all about. I care about the body, alive or dead. That is what medical anthropologists are good at. We're guardians of the body."

Other medical anthropologists, however, argue that Scheper-Hughes does not paint the world of the illegal organ trade in enough shades of gray. "She is not a scholar at heart," Kleinman told me, "for good and bad. She always begins with a partisan position and a sensibility of outrage at injustices. She lumps rather than splits. The details of the argument are less important than the advocacy, the lobbying."

In the summer of 2012, I met up with Scheper-Hughes on the steps of the federal courthouse in Trenton, New Jersey, for the sentencing hearing for Rosenbaum. In the fourth-floor courtroom, Scheper-Hughes took a seat in the front row where she could see Rosenbaum's bearded and portly profile. Arguing for a stiff sentence, prosecutor McCarren called four witnesses. He questioned an administrator from Albert Einstein hospital and a surgeon who worked there while Rosenbaum was running his kidney trade business. He called to the stand a middle-aged woman named Beckie Cohen, who tearfully described how grateful she was that her family had been able to pay Rosenbaum $150,000 to arrange a kidney transplant in a Minneapolis hospital for her ailing father, Max Cohen. McCarren also questioned Elahn Quick, a young man born in Israel of American parents, who was paid about $25,000 to donate one of his kidneys to Mr. Cohen.

In describing his dealings with Rosenbaum, Quick told of no overt pressure or threats. In the end he said he felt used and somewhat victimized by the transaction, but he didn't regret the operation. "I wanted to do something meaningful," Quick said. "I'm still holding on to the fact that I saved a life." At this point Scheper-Hughes leaned to me and said that this refrain about "saving a life" was bunk: "These people that get transplants are mostly just old."

Scheper-Hughes spent most of the hearing rapidly writing in her notebook, but she made clear, in whispered asides, her disapproval of the proceedings. When the judge mentioned that she had been moved by the letters of support for Rosenbaum sent by recipients of organ transplants he had arranged, Scheper-Hughes sighed and said, "Oh, Jesus Christ." When Beckie Cohen teared up recounting her family's distress over her father's illness, which led them to pay Rosenbaum to arrange for a kidney seller, Scheper-Hughes leaned to me and said: "She could have given him her kidney." When a doctor from Albert Einstein hospital testified that he had no certain knowledge in the early 2000s that the donors were being paid by Rosenbaum, Scheper-Hughes whispered: "McCarren is not a very good questioner. I could do better." During the course of the long hearing, Scheper-Hughes had a sharp comment for every player in the courtroom: the doctor, the donor, the recipient's daughter, McCarren, the defense attorneys, and the judge. She had become, almost literally, the court jester she describes in her writing, a mocking, dissenting voice from the sidelines.

After the hearing, Scheper-Hughes and I had an early dinner at a nearby Cuban restaurant. She hadn't eaten all day and her energy was flagging. She told me she was satisfied with the sentence Rosenbaum received at the end of the hearing—two and a half years in federal prison—but said that she hadn't seen or heard anything that day that might change her perceptions of Rosenbaum or of the kidney trade that she had tracked to American shores.

I asked her about one scene described on the stand by Elahn Quick, the donor. Quick remembered that when he woke up after the operation, the family of Max Cohen had gathered around his hospital bed and applauded his sacrifice. I thought it was a poignant moment, one that suggested that Quick wasn't just an anonymous donor to the Cohen family, but something more. Scheper-Hughes waved away the scene. "What I can't stand is false emotion," she said, reminding me that Quick ultimately felt betrayed and kicked aside. "It makes my hair stand up. I can smell it like a rat."

Critical Thinking

1. What is "transplant tourism" and why is it occurring?
2. What is Nancy Scheper-Hughes' call for "barefoot anthropologists" and why does Roy D'Andrade criticize it?
3. Has cultural anthropology's focus on far-away, exotic societies run its course? Explain.
4. What is the "organ mafia?"
5. Why does Nancy Scheper Huges feel that she is justified in crossing the "ethical line" of anthropology?

Internet References

The Declaration of Istanbul on Organ Trafficking and Transplant Tourism
http://www.declarationofistanbul.org/

Human Organ Trafficking Resources
http://www.vachss.com/help_text/organ_trafficking.html

Stop Organ Trafficking Now!
http://www.stoporgantraffickingnow.org/

Watters, Ethan. "The Organ Detective: A Career Spent Uncovering a Hidden Global Market in Human Flesh", *Pacific Standard*, July 2014. Copyright © 2014 by Pacific Standard. Used with permission.

Article   Prepared by: Elvio Angeloni

The Evolution of Diet

Ann Gibbons

Learning Outcomes

After reading this article, you will be able to:

- Discuss the consequences for native peoples when they change from a traditional diet to one of the modern age.

- Discuss the pros and cons of "Paleolithic diet" as a nutritional strategy for all peoples of the world.

- Discuss the notion that humans stopped evolving at the end of the Paleolithic period.

It's suppertime in the Amazon of lowland Bolivia, and Ana Cuata Maito is stirring a porridge of plantains and sweet manioc over a fire smoldering on the dirt floor of her thatched hut, listening for the voice of her husband as he returns from the forest with his scrawny hunting dog.

With an infant girl nursing at her breast and a seven-year-old boy tugging at her sleeve, she looks spent when she tells me that she hopes her husband, Deonicio Nate, will bring home meat tonight. "The children are sad when there is no meat," Maito says through an interpreter, as she swats away mosquitoes.

Nate left before dawn on this day in January with his rifle and machete to get an early start on the two-hour trek to the old-growth forest. There he silently scanned the canopy for brown capuchin monkeys and raccoonlike coatis, while his dog sniffed the ground for the scent of pig-like peccaries or reddish brown capybaras. If he was lucky, Nate would spot one of the biggest packets of meat in the forest—tapirs, with long, prehensile snouts that rummage for buds and shoots among the damp ferns.

This evening, however, Nate emerges from the forest with no meat. At 39, he's an energetic guy who doesn't seem easily defeated—when he isn't hunting or fishing or weaving palm fronds into roof panels, he's in the woods carving a new canoe from a log. But when he finally sits down to eat his porridge from a metal bowl, he complains that it's hard to get enough meat for his family: two wives (not uncommon in the tribe) and 12

children. Loggers are scaring away the animals. He can't fish on the river because a storm washed away his canoe.

The story is similar for each of the families I visit in Anachere, a community of about 90 members of the ancient Tsimane Indian tribe. It's the rainy season, when it's hardest to hunt or fish. More than 15,000 Tsimane live in about a hundred villages along two rivers in the Amazon Basin near the main market town of San Borja, 225 miles from La Paz. But Anachere is a two-day trip from San Borja by motorized dugout canoe, so the Tsimane living there still get most of their food from the forest, the river, or their gardens.

I'm traveling with Asher Rosinger, a doctoral candidate who's part of a team, co-led by biological anthropologist William Leonard of Northwestern University, studying the Tsimane to document what a rain forest diet looks like. They're particularly interested in how the Indians' health changes as they move away from their traditional diet and active lifestyle and begin trading forest goods for sugar, salt, rice, oil, and increasingly, dried meat and canned sardines. This is not a purely academic inquiry. What anthropologists are learning about the diets of indigenous peoples like the Tsimane could inform what the rest of us should eat.

Rosinger introduces me to a villager named José Mayer Cunay, 78, who, with his son Felipe Mayer Lero, 39, has planted a lush garden by the river over the past 30 years. José leads us down a trail past trees laden with golden papayas and mangoes, clusters of green plantains, and orbs of grapefruit that dangle from branches like earrings. Vibrant red "lobster claw" heliconia flowers and wild ginger grow like weeds among stalks of corn and sugarcane. "José's family has more fruit than anyone," says Rosinger.

Yet in the family's open-air shelter Felipe's wife, Catalina, is preparing the same bland porridge as other households. When I ask if the food in the garden can tide them over when there's little meat, Felipe shakes his head. "It's not enough to live on," he says. "I need to hunt and fish. My body doesn't want to eat just these plants."

As we look to 2050, when we'll need to feed two billion more people, the question of which diet is best has taken on new urgency. The foods we choose to eat in the coming decades will have dramatic ramifications for the planet. Simply put, a diet that revolves around meat and dairy, a way of eating that's on the rise throughout the developing world, will take a greater toll on the world's resources than one that revolves around unrefined grains, nuts, fruits, and vegetables.

Until agriculture was developed around 10,000 years ago, all humans got their food by hunting, gathering, and fishing. As farming emerged, nomadic hunter-gatherers gradually were pushed off prime farmland, and eventually they became limited to the forests of the Amazon, the arid grasslands of Africa, the remote islands of Southeast Asia, and the tundra of the Arctic. Today only a few scattered tribes of hunter-gatherers remain on the planet.

That's why scientists are intensifying efforts to learn what they can about an ancient diet and way of life before they disappear. "Hunter-gatherers are not living fossils," says Alyssa Crittenden, a nutritional anthropologist at the University of Nevada, Las Vegas, who studies the diet of Tanzania's Hadza people, some of the last true hunter-gatherers. "That being said, we have a small handful of foraging populations that remain on the planet. We are running out of time. If we want to glean any information on what a nomadic, foraging lifestyle looks like, we need to capture their diet now."

So far studies of foragers like the Tsimane, Arctic Inuit, and Hadza have found that these peoples traditionally didn't develop high blood pressure, atherosclerosis, or cardiovascular disease. "A lot of people believe there is a discordance between what we eat today and what our ancestors evolved to eat," says paleo-anthropologist Peter Ungar of the University of Arkansas. The notion that we're trapped in Stone Age bodies in a fast-food world is driving the current craze for Paleolithic diets. The popularity of these so-called caveman or Stone Age diets is based on the idea that modern humans evolved to eat the way hunter-gatherers did during the Paleolithic—the period from about 2.6 million years ago to the start of the agricultural revolution—and that our genes haven't had enough time to adapt to farmed foods.

A Stone Age diet "is the one and only diet that ideally fits our genetic makeup," writes Loren Cordain, an evolutionary nutritionist at Colorado State University in his book *The Paleo Diet: Lose Weight and Get Healthy by Eating the Foods You Were Designed to Eat*. After studying the diets of living hunter-gatherers and concluding that 73 percent of these societies derived more than half their calories from meat, Cordain came up with his own Paleo prescription: Eat plenty of lean meat and fish but not dairy products, beans, or cereal grains—foods introduced into our diet after the invention of cooking and agriculture. Paleo-diet advocates like Cordain say that if we stick to the foods our hunter-gatherer ancestors once ate, we can avoid the diseases of civilization, such as heart disease, high blood pressure, diabetes, cancer, even acne.

That sounds appealing. But is it true that we all evolved to eat a meat-centric diet? Both paleontologists studying the fossils of our ancestors and anthropologists documenting the diets of indigenous people today say the picture is a bit more complicated. The popular embrace of a Paleo diet, Ungar and others point out, is based on a stew of misconceptions.

Meat has played a starring role in the evolution of the human diet. Raymond Dart, who in 1924 discovered the first fossil of a human ancestor in Africa, popularized the image of our early ancestors hunting meat to survive on the African savanna. Writing in the 1950s, he described those humans as "carnivorous creatures, that seized living quarries by violence, battered them to death. . . slaking their ravenous thirst with the hot blood of victims and greedily devouring livid writhing flesh."

Eating meat is thought by some scientists to have been crucial to the evolution of our ancestors' larger brains about two million years ago. By starting to eat calorie-dense meat and marrow instead of the low-quality plant diet of apes, our direct ancestor, *Homo erectus,* took in enough extra energy at each meal to help fuel a bigger brain. Digesting a higher quality diet and less bulky plant fiber would have allowed these humans to have much smaller guts. The energy freed up as a result of smaller guts could be used by the greedy brain, according to Leslie Aiello, who first proposed the idea with paleoanthropologist Peter Wheeler. The brain requires 20 percent of a human's energy when resting; by comparison, an ape's brain requires only 8 percent. This means that from the time of *H. erectus,* the human body has depended on a diet of energy-dense food—especially meat.

Fast-forward a couple of million years to when the human diet took another major turn with the invention of agriculture. The domestication of grains such as sorghum, barley, wheat, corn, and rice created a plentiful and predictable food supply, allowing farmers' wives to bear babies in rapid succession— one every 2.5 years instead of one every 3.5 years for hunter-gatherers. A population explosion followed; before long, farmers outnumbered foragers.

Over the past decade anthropologists have struggled to answer key questions about this transition. Was agriculture a clear step forward for human health? Or in leaving behind our hunter-gatherer ways to grow crops and raise livestock, did we give up a healthier diet and stronger bodies in exchange for food security?

When biological anthropologist Clark Spencer Larsen of Ohio State University describes the dawn of agriculture, it's a grim picture. As the earliest farmers became dependent on crops, their diets became far less nutritionally diverse than hunter-gatherers' diets. Eating the same domesticated grain every day gave early farmers cavities and periodontal disease rarely found in hunter-gatherers, says Larsen. When farmers began domesticating animals, those cattle, sheep, and goats became sources of milk and meat but also of parasites and new infectious diseases. Farmers suffered from iron deficiency and developmental delays, and they shrank in stature.

Despite boosting population numbers, the lifestyle and diet of farmers were clearly not as healthy as the lifestyle and diet of hunter-gatherers. That farmers produced more babies, Larsen says, is simply evidence that "you don't have to be disease free to have children."

The real paleolithic diet, though, wasn't all meat and marrow. It's true that hunter-gatherers around the world crave meat more than any other food and usually get around 30 percent of their annual calories from animals. But most also endure lean times when they eat less than a handful of meat each week. New studies suggest that more than a reliance on meat in ancient human diets fueled the brain's expansion.

Year-round observations confirm that hunter-gatherers often have dismal success as hunters. The Hadza and !Kung bushmen of Africa, for example, fail to get meat more than half the time when they venture forth with bows and arrows. This suggests it was even harder for our ancestors who didn't have these weapons. "Everybody thinks you wander out into the savanna and there are antelopes everywhere, just waiting for you to bonk them on the head," says paleoanthropologist Alison Brooks of George Washington University, an expert on the Dobe Kung of Botswana. No one eats meat all that often, except in the Arctic, where Inuit and other groups traditionally got as much as 99 percent of their calories from seals, narwhals, and fish.

So how do hunter-gatherers get energy when there's no meat? It turns out that "man the hunter" is backed up by "woman the forager," who, with some help from children, provides more calories during difficult times. When meat, fruit, or honey is scarce, foragers depend on "fallback foods," says Brooks. The Hadza get almost 70 percent of their calories from plants. The !Kung traditionally rely on tubers and mongongo nuts, the Aka and Baka Pygmies of the Congo River Basin on yams, the Tsimane and Yanomami Indians of the Amazon on plantains and manioc, the Australian Aboriginals on nut grass and water chestnuts.

"There's been a consistent story about hunting defining us and that meat made us human," says Amanda Henry, a paleobiologist at the Max Planck Institute for Evolutionary Anthropology in Leipzig. "Frankly, I think that misses half of the story. They want meat, sure. But what they actually live on is plant foods." What's more, she found starch granules from plants on fossil teeth and stone tools, which suggests humans may have been eating grains, as well as tubers, for at least 100,000 years—long enough to have evolved the ability to tolerate them.

The notion that we stopped evolving in the Paleolithic period simply isn't true. Our teeth, jaws, and faces have gotten smaller, and our DNA has changed since the invention of agriculture. "Are humans still evolving? Yes!" says geneticist Sarah Tishkoff of the University of Pennsylvania.

One striking piece of evidence is lactose tolerance. All humans digest mother's milk as infants, but until cattle began being domesticated 10,000 years ago, weaned children no longer needed to digest milk. As a result, they stopped making the enzyme lactase, which breaks down the lactose into simple sugars. After humans began herding cattle, it became tremendously advantageous to digest milk, and lactose tolerance evolved independently among cattle herders in Europe, the Middle East, and Africa. Groups not dependent on cattle, such as the Chinese and Thai, the Pima Indians of the American Southwest, and the Bantu of West Africa, remain lactose intolerant.

Humans also vary in their ability to extract sugars from starchy foods as they chew them, depending on how many copies of a certain gene they inherit. Populations that traditionally ate more starchy foods, such as the Hadza, have more copies of the gene than the Yakut meat-eaters of Siberia, and their saliva helps break down starches before the food reaches their stomachs.

These examples suggest a twist on "You are what you eat." More accurately, you are what your ancestors ate. There is tremendous variation in what foods humans can thrive on, depending on genetic inheritance. Traditional diets today include the vegetarian regimen of India's Jains, the meat-intensive fare of Inuit, and the fish-heavy diet of Malaysia's Bajau people. The Nochmani of the Nicobar Islands off the coast of India get by on protein from insects. "What makes us human is our ability to find a meal in virtually any environment," says the Tsimane study co-leader Leonard.

Studies suggest that indigenous groups get into trouble when they abandon their traditional diets and active lifestyles for Western living. Diabetes was virtually unknown, for instance, among the Maya of Central America until the 1950s. As they've switched to a Western diet high in sugars, the rate of diabetes has skyrocketed. Siberian nomads such as the Evenk reindeer herders and the Yakut ate diets heavy in meat, yet they had almost no heart disease until after the fall of the Soviet Union, when many settled in towns and began eating market foods. Today about half the Yakut living in villages are overweight, and almost a third have hypertension, says Leonard. And Tsimane people who eat market foods are more prone to diabetes than those who still rely on hunting and gathering.

For those of us whose ancestors were adapted to plant-based diets—and who have desk jobs—it might be best not to eat as much meat as the Yakut. Recent studies confirm older findings that although humans have eaten red meat for two million years, heavy consumption increases atherosclerosis and cancer in most populations—and the culprit isn't just saturated fat or cholesterol. Our gut bacteria digest a nutrient in meat called L-carnitine. In one mouse study, digestion of L-carnitine boosted artery-clogging plaque. Research also has shown that the human immune system attacks a sugar in red meat that's called Neu5Gc, causing inflammation that's low level in the young but that eventually could cause cancer. "Red meat is great, if you want to live to 45," says Ajit Varki of the University of California, San Diego, lead author of the Neu5Gc study.

Many paleoanthropologists say that although advocates of the modern Paleolithic diet urge us to stay away from unhealthy processed foods, the diet's heavy focus on meat doesn't replicate the diversity of foods that our ancestors ate—or take into account the active lifestyles that protected them from heart disease and diabetes. "What bothers a lot of paleoanthropologists is that we actually didn't have just one caveman diet," says Leslie Aiello, president of the Wenner-Gren Foundation for Anthropological Research in New York City. "The human diet goes back at least two million years. We had a lot of cavemen out there."

In other words, there is no one ideal human diet. Aiello and Leonard say the real hallmark of being human isn't our taste for meat but our ability to adapt to many habitats—and to be able to combine many different foods to create many healthy diets. Unfortunately the modern Western diet does not appear to be one of them.

The latest clue as to why our modern diet may be making us sick comes from Harvard primatologist Richard Wrangham, who argues that the biggest revolution in the human diet came not when we started to eat meat but when we learned to cook. Our human ancestors who began cooking sometime between 1.8 million and 400,000 years ago probably had more children who thrived, Wrangham says. Pounding and heating food "predigests" it, so our guts spend less energy breaking it down, absorb more than if the food were raw, and thus extract more fuel for our brains. "Cooking produces soft, energy-rich foods," says Wrangham. Today we can't survive on raw, unprocessed food alone, he says. We have evolved to depend upon cooked food.

To test his ideas, Wrangham and his students fed raw and cooked food to rats and mice. When I visited Wrangham's lab at Harvard, his then graduate student, Rachel Carmody, opened the door of a small refrigerator to show me plastic bags filled with meat and sweet potatoes, some raw and some cooked. Mice raised on cooked foods gained 15 to 40 percent more weight than mice raised only on raw food.

If Wrangham is right, cooking not only gave early humans the energy they needed to build bigger brains but also helped them get more calories from food so that they could gain weight. In the modern context the flip side of his hypothesis is that we may be victims of our own success. We have gotten so good at processing foods that for the first time in human evolution, many humans are getting more calories than they burn in a day. "Rough breads have given way to Twinkies, apples to apple juice," he writes. "We need to become more aware of the calorie-raising consequences of a highly processed diet."

It's this shift to processed foods, taking place all over the world, that's contributing to a rising epidemic of obesity and related diseases. If most of the world ate more local fruits and vegetables, a little meat, fish, and some whole grains (as in the highly touted Mediterranean diet), and exercised an hour a day, that would be good news for our health—and for the planet.

On my last afternoon visiting the Tsimane in Anachere, one of Deonicio Nate's daughters, Albania, 13, tells us that her father and half-brother Alberto, 16, are back from hunting and that they've got something. We follow her to the cooking hut and smell the animals before we see them—three raccoonlike coatis have been laid across the fire, fur and all. As the fire singes the coatis' striped pelts, Albania and her sister, Emiliana, 12, scrape off fur until the animals' flesh is bare. Then they take the carcasses to a stream to clean and prepare them for roasting.

Nate's wives are cleaning two armadillos as well, preparing to cook them in a stew with shredded plantains. Nate sits by the fire, describing a good day's hunt. First he shot the armadillos as they napped by a stream. Then his dog spotted a pack of coatis and chased them, killing two as the rest darted up a tree. Alberto fired his shotgun but missed. He fired again and hit a coati. Three coatis and two armadillos were enough, so father and son packed up and headed home.

As family members enjoy the feast, I watch their little boy, Alfonso, who had been sick all week. He is dancing around the fire, happily chewing on a cooked piece of coati tail. Nate looks pleased. Tonight in Anachere, far from the diet debates, there is meat, and that is good.

Science prevented the last food crisis. Can it save us again?

Critical Thinking

1. What is the "Paleolithic diet"? What are some of the misconceptions surrounding it?
2. What kinds of negative consequences for humans as well as the planet developed as a result of agriculture?

Internet References

Journal of Human Evolution
   http://www.journals.elsevier.com/journal-of-human-evolution/
The Future of Food
   http://food.nationalgeographic.com/

ANN GIBBONS is the author of *The First Human: The Race to Discover Our Earliest Ancestors.*

Gibbons, Ann. "The Evolution of Diet", from *National Geographic*, September, 2014, pp. 30–61, Washington, D.C., © 2014.

Article   Prepared by: Elvio Angeloni, *Pasadena City College*

Population Seven Billion

By 2045 global population is projected to reach nine billion. Can the planet take the strain? As we reach the milestone of seven billion people this year, it's time to take stock. In the coming decades, despite falling birthrates, the population will continue to grow—mostly in poor countries. If the billions of people who want to boost themselves out of poverty follow the path blazed by those in wealthy countries, they too will step hard on the planet's resources. How big will the population actually grow? What will the planet look like in 2045? Throughout the year we'll offer an in-depth series exploring those questions. The answers will depend on the decisions each of us makes.

ROBERT KUNZIG

Learning Outcomes

After reading this article, you will be able to:

- Define what is meant by the *demographic transition* and discuss the role it has played in world population growth.

- Discuss whether we should be alarmed by population growth, the environment, or both.

One day in Delft in the fall of 1677, Antoni van Leeuwenhoek, a cloth merchant who is said to have been the long-haired model for two paintings by Johannes Vermeer—"The Astronomer" and "The Geographer"—abruptly stopped what he was doing with his wife and rushed to his worktable. Cloth was Leeuwenhoek's business but microscopy his passion. He'd had five children already by his first wife (though four had died in infancy), and fatherhood was not on his mind. "Before six beats of the pulse had intervened," as he later wrote to the Royal Society of London, Leeuwenhoek was examining his perishable sample through a tiny magnifying glass. Its lens, no bigger than a small raindrop, magnified objects hundreds of times. Leeuwenhoek had made it himself; nobody else had one so powerful. The learned men in London were still trying to verify Leeuwenhoek's earlier claims that unseen "animalcules" lived by the millions in a single drop of lake water and even in French wine. Now he had something more delicate to report: Human semen contained animalcules too. "Sometimes more than a thousand," he wrote, "in an amount of material the size of a grain of sand." Pressing the glass to his eye like a jeweler, Leeuwenhoek watched his own animalcules swim about, lashing their long tails. One imagines sunlight falling through leaded windows on a face lost in contemplation, as in the Vermeers. One feels for his wife.

Leeuwenhoek became a bit obsessed after that. Though his tiny peephole gave him privileged access to a never-before-seen microscopic universe, he spent an enormous amount of time looking at spermatozoa, as they're now called. Oddly enough, it was the milt he squeezed from a cod one day that inspired him to estimate, almost casually, just how many people might live on Earth.

Nobody then really had any idea; there were few censuses. Leeuwenhoek started with an estimate that around a million people lived in Holland. Using maps and a little spherical geometry, he calculated that the inhabited land area of the planet was 13,385 times as large as Holland. It was hard to imagine the whole planet being as densely peopled as Holland, which seemed crowded even then. Thus, Leeuwenhoek concluded triumphantly, there couldn't be more than 13.385 billion people on Earth—a small number indeed compared with the 150 billion sperm cells of a single codfish! This cheerful little calculation, writes population biologist Joel Cohen in his book *How Many People Can the Earth Support?*, may have been the first attempt to give a quantitative answer to a question that has become far more pressing now than it was in the 17th century. Most answers these days are far from cheerful.

Historians now estimate that in Leeuwenhoek's day there were only half a billion or so humans on Earth. After rising very slowly for millennia, the number was just starting to take off. A century and a half later, when another scientist reported the discovery of human egg cells, the world's population had doubled to more than a billion. A century after that, around 1930, it had doubled again to two billion. The acceleration since then has been astounding. Before the 20th century, no human had lived through a doubling of the human population, but there are people alive today who have seen it triple. Sometime in late 2011, according to the UN Population Division, there will be seven billion of us.

And the explosion, though it is slowing, is far from over. Not only are people living longer, but so many women across the world are now in their childbearing years—1.8 billion—that the global population will keep growing for another few decades at least, even though each woman is having fewer children than she would have had a generation ago. By 2050 the total number could reach 10.5 billion, or it could stop at eight billion—the difference is about one child per woman. UN demographers consider the middle road their best estimate: They now project that the population may reach nine billion before 2050—in 2045. The eventual tally will depend on the choices individual couples make when they engage in that most intimate of human acts, the one Leeuwenhoek interrupted so carelessly for the sake of science.

With the population still growing by about 80 million each year, it's hard not to be alarmed. Right now on Earth, water tables are falling, soil is eroding, glaciers are melting, and fish stocks are vanishing. Close to a billion people go hungry each day. Decades from now, there will likely be two billion more mouths to feed, mostly in poor countries. There will be billions more people wanting and deserving to boost themselves out of poverty. If they follow the path blazed by wealthy countries—clearing forests, burning coal and oil, freely scattering fertilizers and pesticides—they too will be stepping hard on the planet's natural resources. How exactly is this going to work?

There may be some comfort in knowing that people have long been alarmed about population. From the beginning, says French demographer Hervé Le Bras, demography has been steeped in talk of the apocalypse. Some of the field's founding papers were written just a few years after Leeuwenhoek's discovery by Sir William Petty, a founder of the Royal Society. He estimated that world population would double six times by the Last Judgment, which was expected in about 2,000 years. At that point it would exceed 20 billion people—more, Petty thought, than the planet could feed. "And then, according to the prediction of the Scriptures, there must be wars, and great slaughter, &c.," he wrote.

As religious forecasts of the world's end receded, Le Bras argues, population growth itself provided an ersatz mechanism of apocalypse. "It crystallized the ancient fear, and perhaps the ancient hope, of the end of days," he writes. In 1798 Thomas Malthus, an English priest and economist, enunciated his general law of population: that it necessarily grows faster than the food supply, until war, disease, and famine arrive to reduce the number of people. As it turned out, the last plagues great enough to put a dent in global population had already happened when Malthus wrote. World population hasn't fallen, historians think, since the Black Death of the 14th century.

In the two centuries after Malthus declared that population couldn't continue to soar, that's exactly what it did. The process started in what we now call the developed countries, which were then still developing. The spread of New World crops like corn and the potato, along with the discovery of chemical fertilizers, helped banish starvation in Europe. Growing cities remained cesspools of disease at first, but from the mid-19th century on, sewers began to channel human waste away from drinking water, which was then filtered and chlorinated; that dramatically reduced the spread of cholera and typhus.

Moreover in 1798, the same year that Malthus published his dyspeptic tract, his compatriot Edward Jenner described a vaccine for smallpox—the first and most important in a series of vaccines and antibiotics that, along with better nutrition and

sanitation, would double life expectancy in the industrializing countries, from 35 years to 77 today. It would take a cranky person to see that trend as gloomy: "The development of medical science was the straw that broke the camel's back," wrote Stanford population biologist Paul Ehrlich in 1968.

Ehrlich's book, *The Population Bomb,* made him the most famous of modern Malthusians. In the 1970s, Ehrlich predicted, "hundreds of millions of people are going to starve to death," and it was too late to do anything about it. "The cancer of population growth . . . must be cut out," Ehrlich wrote, "by compulsion if voluntary methods fail." The very future of the United States was at risk. In spite or perhaps because of such language, the book was a best seller, as Malthus's had been. And this time too the bomb proved a dud. The green revolution—a combination of high-yield seeds, irrigation, pesticides, and fertilizers that enabled grain production to double—was already under way. Today many people are undernourished, but mass starvation is rare.

Ehrlich was right, though, that population would surge as medical science spared many lives. After World War II the developing countries got a sudden transfusion of preventive care, with the help of institutions like the World Health Organization and UNICEF. Penicillin, the smallpox vaccine, DDT (which, though later controversial, saved millions from dying of malaria)—all arrived at once. In India life expectancy went from 38 years in 1952 to 64 today; in China, from 41 to 73. Millions of people in developing countries who would have died in childhood survived to have children themselves. That's why the population explosion spread around the planet: because a great many people were saved from dying.

And because, for a time, women kept giving birth at a high rate. In 18th-century Europe or early 20th-century Asia, when the average woman had six children, she was doing what it took to replace herself and her mate, because most of those children never reached adulthood. When child mortality declines, couples eventually have fewer children—but that transition usually takes a generation at the very least. Today in developed countries, an average of 2.1 births per woman would maintain a steady population; in the developing world, "replacement fertility" is somewhat higher. In the time it takes for the birthrate to settle into that new balance with the death rate, population explodes.

When child mortality declines, couples eventually have fewer children—but that transition takes a generation.

Demographers call this evolution the demographic transition. All countries go through it in their own time. It's a hallmark of human progress: In a country that has completed the transition, people have wrested from nature at least some control over death and birth. The global population explosion is an inevitable side effect, a huge one that some people are not sure our civilization can survive. But the growth rate was actually at its peak just as Ehrlich was sounding his alarm. By the early 1970s, fertility rates around the world had begun dropping faster than anyone had anticipated. Since then, the population growth rate has fallen by more than 40 percent.

The fertility decline that is now sweeping the planet started at different times in different countries. France was one of the first. By the early 18th century, noblewomen at the French court were knowing carnal pleasures without bearing more than two children. They often relied on the same method Leeuwenhoek used for his studies: withdrawal, or coitus interruptus. Village parish records show the trend had spread to the peasantry by the late 18th century; by the end of the 19th, fertility in France had fallen to three children per woman—without the help of modern contraceptives. The key innovation was conceptual, not contraceptive, says Gilles Pison of the National Institute for Demographic Studies in Paris. Until the Enlightenment, "the number of children you had, it was God who decided. People couldn't fathom that it might be up to them."

Other countries in the West eventually followed France's lead. By the onset of World War II, fertility had fallen close to the replacement level in parts of Europe and the U.S. Then, after the surprising blip known as the baby boom, came the bust, again catching demographers off guard. They assumed some instinct would lead women to keep having enough children to ensure the survival of the species. Instead, in country after developed country, the fertility rate fell below replacement level. In the late 1990s in Europe it fell to 1.4. "The evidence I'm familiar with, which is anecdotal, is that women couldn't care less about replacing the species," Joel Cohen says.

The end of a baby boom can have two big economic effects on a country. The first is the "demographic dividend"—a blissful few decades when the boomers swell the labor force and the number of young and old dependents is relatively small, and there is thus a lot of money for other things. Then the second effect kicks in: The boomers start to retire. What had been considered the enduring demographic order is revealed to be a party that has to end. The sharpening American debate over Social Security and last year's strikes in France over increasing the retirement age are responses to a problem that exists throughout the developed world: how to support an aging population. "In 2050 will there be enough people working to pay for pensions?" asks Frans Willekens, director of the Netherlands Interdisciplinary Demographic Institute in The Hague. "The answer is no."

In industrialized countries it took generations for fertility to fall to the replacement level or below. As that same transition takes place in the rest of the world, what has astonished demographers is how much faster it is happening there. Though its population continues to grow, China, home to a fifth of the world's people, is already below replacement fertility and has been for nearly 20 years, thanks in part to the coercive one-child policy implemented in 1979; Chinese women, who were bearing an average of six children each as recently as 1965, are now having around 1.5. In Iran, with the support of the Islamic regime, fertility has fallen more than 70 percent since the early '80s. In Catholic and democratic Brazil, women have reduced their fertility rate by half over the same quarter century. "We still don't understand why fertility has gone down so fast in so many societies, so many cultures and religions. It's just

mind-boggling," says Hania Zlotnik, director of the UN Population Division.

"At this moment, much as I want to say there's still a problem of high fertility rates, it's only about 16 percent of the world population, mostly in Africa," says Zlotnik. South of the Sahara, fertility is still five children per woman; in Niger it is seven. But then, 17 of the countries in the region still have life expectancies of 50 or less; they have just begun the demographic transition. In most of the world, however, family size has shrunk dramatically. The UN projects that the world will reach replacement fertility by 2030. "The population as a whole is on a path toward nonexplosion—which is good news," Zlotnik says.

The bad news is that 2030 is two decades away and that the largest generation of adolescents in history will then be entering their childbearing years. Even if each of those women has only two children, population will coast upward under its own momentum for another quarter century. Is a train wreck in the offing, or will people then be able to live humanely and in a way that doesn't destroy their environment? One thing is certain: Close to one in six of them will live in India.

I have understood the population explosion intellectually for a long time. I came to understand it emotionally one stinking hot night in Delhi a couple of years ago. . . . The temperature was well over 100, and the air was a haze of dust and smoke. The streets seemed alive with people. People eating, people washing, people sleeping. People visiting, arguing, and screaming. People thrusting their hands through the taxi window, begging. People defecating and urinating. People clinging to buses. People herding animals. People, people, people, people.

—Paul Ehrlich

In 1966, when Ehrlich took that taxi ride, there were around half a billion Indians. There are 1.2 billion now. Delhi's population has increased even faster, to around 22 million, as people have flooded in from small towns and villages and crowded into sprawling shantytowns. Early last June in the stinking hot city, the summer monsoon had not yet arrived to wash the dust from the innumerable construction sites, which only added to the dust that blows in from the deserts of Rajasthan. On the new divided highways that funnel people into the unplanned city, oxcarts were heading the wrong way in the fast lane. Families of four cruised on motorbikes, the women's scarves flapping like vivid pennants, toddlers dangling from their arms. Families of a dozen or more sardined themselves into buzzing, bumblebee-colored auto rickshaws designed for two passengers. In the stalled traffic, amputees and wasted little children cried for alms. Delhi today is boomingly different from the city Ehrlich visited, and it is also very much the same.

At Lok Nayak Hospital, on the edge of the chaotic and densely peopled nest of lanes that is Old Delhi, a human tide flows through the entrance gate every morning and crowds inside on the lobby floor. "Who could see this and not be worried about the population of India?" a surgeon named Chandan Bortamuly asked one afternoon as he made his way toward his vasectomy clinic. "Population is our biggest problem." Removing the padlock from the clinic door, Bortamuly stepped into a small operating room. Inside, two men lay stretched out on examination tables, their testicles poking up through holes in the green sheets. A ceiling fan pushed cool air from two window units around the room.

Bortamuly is on the front lines of a battle that has been going on in India for nearly 60 years. In 1952, just five years after it gained independence from Britain, India became the first country to establish a policy for population control. Since then the government has repeatedly set ambitious goals—and repeatedly missed them by a mile. A national policy adopted in 2000 called for the country to reach the replacement fertility of 2.1 by 2010. That won't happen for at least another decade. In the UN's medium projection, India's population will rise to just over 1.6 billion people by 2050. "What's inevitable is that India is going to exceed the population of China by 2030," says A. R. Nanda, former head of the Population Foundation of India, an advocacy group. "Nothing less than a huge catastrophe, nuclear or otherwise, can change that."

China is already below replacement fertility, thanks in part to its coercive one-child policy.

Sterilization is the dominant form of birth control in India today, and the vast majority of the procedures are performed on women. The government is trying to change that; a no-scalpel vasectomy costs far less and is easier on a man than a tubal ligation is on a woman. In the operating theater Bortamuly worked quickly. "They say the needle pricks like an ant bite," he explained, when the first patient flinched at the local anesthetic. "After that it's basically painless, bloodless surgery." Using the pointed tip of a forceps, Bortamuly made a tiny hole in the skin of the scrotum and pulled out an oxbow of white, stringy vas deferens—the sperm conduit from the patient's right testicle. He tied off both ends of the oxbow with fine black thread, snipped them, and pushed them back under the skin. In less than seven minutes—a nurse timed him—the patient was walking out without so much as a Band-Aid. The government will pay him an incentive fee of 1,100 rupees (around $25), a week's wages for a laborer.

The Indian government tried once before to push vasectomies, in the 1970s, when anxiety about the population bomb was at its height. Prime Minister Indira Gandhi and her son Sanjay used state-of-emergency powers to force a dramatic increase in sterilizations. From 1976 to 1977 the number of operations tripled, to more than eight million. Over six million of those were vasectomies. Family planning workers were pressured to meet quotas; in a few states, sterilization became a condition for receiving new housing or other government benefits. In some cases the police simply rounded up poor people and hauled them to sterilization camps.

The excesses gave the whole concept of family planning a bad name. "Successive governments refused to touch the subject," says Shailaja Chandra, former head of the National Population Stabilisation Fund (NPSF). Yet fertility in India has dropped anyway, though not as fast as in China, where it was nose-diving even before the draconian one-child policy took effect. The national average in India is now 2.6 children per woman, less than half what it was when Ehrlich visited. The southern half of the country and a few states in the northern half are already at replacement fertility or below.

In Kerala, on the southwest coast, investments in health and education helped fertility fall to 1.7. The key, demographers there say, is the female literacy rate: At around 90 percent, it's easily the highest in India. Girls who go to school start having children later than ones who don't. They are more open to contraception and more likely to understand their options.

So far this approach, held up as a model internationally, has not caught on in the poor states of northern India—in the "Hindi belt" that stretches across the country just south of Delhi. Nearly half of India's population growth is occurring in Rajasthan, Madhya Pradesh, Bihar, and Uttar Pradesh, where fertility rates still hover between three and four children per woman. More than half the women in the Hindi belt are illiterate, and many marry well before reaching the legal age of 18. They gain social status by bearing children—and usually don't stop until they have at least one son.

As an alternative to the Kerala model, some point to the southern state of Andhra Pradesh, where sterilization "camps"—temporary operating rooms often set up in schools—were introduced during the '70s and where sterilization rates have remained high as improved hospitals have replaced the camps. In a single decade beginning in the early 1990s, the fertility rate fell from around three to less than two. Unlike in Kerala, half of all women in Andhra Pradesh remain illiterate.

Amarjit Singh, the current executive director of the NPSF, calculates that if the four biggest states of the Hindi belt had followed the Andhra Pradesh model, they would have avoided 40 million births—and considerable suffering. "Because 40 million were born, 2.5 million children died," Singh says. He thinks if all India were to adopt high-quality programs to encourage sterilizations, in hospitals rather than camps, it could have 1.4 billion people in 2050 instead of 1.6 billion.

Critics of the Andhra Pradesh model, such as the Population Foundation's Nanda, say Indians need better health care, particularly in rural areas. They are against numerical targets that pressure government workers to sterilize people or cash incentives that distort a couple's choice of family size. "It's a private decision," Nanda says.

In Indian cities today, many couples are making the same choice as their counterparts in Europe or America. Sonalde Desai, a senior fellow at New Delhi's National Council of Applied Economic Research, introduced me to five working women in Delhi who were spending most of their salaries on private-school fees and after-school tutors; each had one or two children and was not planning to have more. In a nationwide survey of 41,554 households, Desai's team identified a small but growing vanguard of urban one-child families. "We were totally blown away at the emphasis parents were placing on their children," she says. "It suddenly makes you understand—that is why fertility is going down." Indian children on average are much better educated than their parents.

That's less true in the countryside. With Desai's team I went to Palanpur, a village in Uttar Pradesh—a Hindi-belt state with as many people as Brazil. Walking into the village we passed a cell phone tower but also rivulets of raw sewage running along the lanes of small brick houses. Under a mango tree, the keeper of the grove said he saw no reason to educate his three daughters. Under a neem tree in the center of the village, I asked a dozen farmers what would improve their lives most. "If we could get a little money, that would be wonderful," one joked.

The goal in India should not be reducing fertility or population, Almas Ali of the Population Foundation told me when I spoke to him a few days later. "The goal should be to make the villages livable," he said. "Whenever we talk of population in India, even today, what comes to our mind is the increasing numbers. And the numbers are looked at with fright. This phobia has penetrated the mind-set so much that all the focus is on reducing the number. The focus on people has been pushed to the background."

It was a four-hour drive back to Delhi from Palanpur, through the gathering night of a Sunday. We sat in traffic in one market town after another, each one hopping with activity that sometimes engulfed the car. As we came down a viaduct into Moradabad, I saw a man pushing a cart up the steep hill, piled with a load so large it blocked his view. I thought of Ehrlich's epiphany on his cab ride all those decades ago. People, people, people, people—yes. But also an overwhelming sense of energy, of striving, of aspiration.

The annual meeting of the Population Association of America (PAA) is one of the premier gatherings of the world's demographers. Last April the global population explosion was not on the agenda. "The problem has become a bit passé," Hervé Le Bras says. Demographers are generally confident that by the second half of this century we will be ending one unique era in history—the population explosion—and entering another, in which population will level out or even fall.

But will there be too many of us? At the PAA meeting, in the Dallas Hyatt Regency, I learned that the current population of the planet could fit into the state of Texas, if Texas were settled as densely as New York City. The comparison made me start thinking like Leeuwenhoek. If in 2045 there are nine billion people living on the six habitable continents, the world population density will be a little more than half that of France today. France is not usually considered a hellish place. Will the world be hellish then?

Some parts of it may well be; some parts of it are hellish today. There are now 21 cities with populations larger than ten million, and by 2050 there will be many more. Delhi adds hundreds of thousands of migrants each year, and those people arrive to find that "no plans have been made for water, sewage, or habitation," says Shailaja Chandra. Dhaka in Bangladesh and Kinshasa in the Democratic Republic of the Congo are 40 times larger today than they were in 1950. Their slums are filled with desperately poor people who have fled worse poverty in the countryside.

Whole countries today face population pressures that seem as insurmountable to us as India's did to Ehrlich in 1966. Bangladesh is among the most densely populated countries in the world and one of the most immediately threatened by climate change; rising seas could displace tens of millions of Bangladeshis. Rwanda is an equally alarming case. In his book *Collapse,* Jared Diamond argued that the genocidal massacre of some 800,000 Rwandans in 1994 was the result of several factors, not only ethnic hatred but also overpopulation—too many farmers dividing the same amount of land into increasingly small pieces that became inadequate to support a farmer's family. "Malthus's worst-case scenario may sometimes be realized," Diamond concluded.

Many people are justifiably worried that Malthus will finally be proved right on a global scale—that the planet won't be able to feed nine billion people. Lester Brown, founder of Worldwatch Institute and now head of the Earth Policy Institute in Washington, believes food shortages could cause a collapse of global civilization. Human beings are living off natural capital, Brown argues, eroding soil and depleting groundwater faster than they can be replenished. All of that will soon be cramping food production. Brown's Plan B to save civilization would put the whole world on a wartime footing, like the U.S. after Pearl Harbor, to stabilize climate and repair the ecological damage. "Filling the family planning gap may be the most urgent item on the global agenda," he writes, so if we don't hold the world's population to eight billion by reducing fertility, the death rate may increase instead.

Eight billion corresponds to the UN's lowest projection for 2050. In that optimistic scenario, Bangladesh has a fertility rate of 1.35 in 2050, but it still has 25 million more people than it does today. Rwanda's fertility rate also falls below the replacement level, but its population still rises to well over twice what it was before the genocide. If that's the optimistic scenario, one might argue, the future is indeed bleak.

But one can also draw a different conclusion—that fixating on population numbers is not the best way to confront the future. People packed into slums need help, but the problem that needs solving is poverty and lack of infrastructure, not overpopulation. Giving every woman access to family planning services is a good idea—"the one strategy that can make the biggest difference to women's lives," Chandra calls it. But the most aggressive population control program imaginable will not save Bangladesh from sea level rise, Rwanda from another genocide, or all of us from our enormous environmental problems.

People packed into slums need help, but the problem that needs solving is poverty, not overpopulation.

Global warming is a good example. Carbon emissions from fossil fuels are growing fastest in China, thanks to its prolonged economic boom, but fertility there is already below replacement; not much more can be done to control population. Where population is growing fastest, in sub-Saharan Africa, emissions per person are only a few percent of what they are in the U.S.—so population control would have little effect on climate. Brian O'Neill of the National Center for Atmospheric Research has calculated that if the population were to reach 7.4 billion in 2050 instead of 8.9 billion, it would reduce emissions by 15 percent. "Those who say the whole problem is population are wrong," Joel Cohen says. "It's not even the dominant factor." To stop global warming we'll have to switch from fossil fuels to alternative energy—regardless of how big the population gets.

The number of people does matter, of course. But how people consume resources matters a lot more. Some of us leave much bigger footprints than others. The central challenge for the future of people and the planet is how to raise more of us out of poverty—the slum dwellers in Delhi, the subsistence farmers in Rwanda—while reducing the impact each of us has on the planet.

The World Bank has predicted that by 2030 more than a billion people in the developing world will belong to the "global middle class," up from just 400 million in 2005. That's a good thing. But it will be a hard thing for the planet if those people are eating meat and driving gasoline-powered cars at the same rate as Americans now do. It's too late to keep the new middle class of 2030 from being born; it's not too late to change how they and the rest of us will produce and consume food and energy. "Eating less meat seems more reasonable to me than saying, 'Have fewer children!'" Le Bras says.

It's too late to keep the new middle class of 2030 from being born. But it's not too late to change the ways we all consume.

How many people can the Earth support? Cohen spent years reviewing all the research, from Leeuwenhoek on. "I wrote the book thinking I would answer the question," he says. "I found out it's unanswerable in the present state of knowledge." What he found instead was an enormous range of "political numbers, intended to persuade people" one way or the other.

For centuries population pessimists have hurled apocalyptic warnings at the congenital optimists, who believe in their bones that humanity will find ways to cope and even improve its lot. History, on the whole, has so far favored the optimists, but history is no certain guide to the future. Neither is science. It cannot predict the outcome of *People* v. *Planet,* because all the facts of the case—how many of us there will be and how we will live—depend on choices we have yet to make and ideas we have yet to have. We may, for example, says Cohen, "see to it that all children are nourished well enough to learn in school and are educated well enough to solve the problems they will face as adults." That would change the future significantly.

The debate was present at the creation of population alarmism, in the person of Rev. Thomas Malthus himself. Toward the end of the book in which he formulated the iron law by which unchecked population growth leads to famine, he declared that law a good thing: It gets us off our duffs. It leads us to conquer the world. Man, Malthus wrote, and he must have meant woman too, is "inert, sluggish, and averse from labour, unless compelled by necessity." But necessity, he added, gives hope:

"The exertions that men find it necessary to make, in order to support themselves or families, frequently awaken faculties that might otherwise have lain for ever dormant, and it has been commonly remarked that new and extraordinary situations generally create minds adequate to grapple with the difficulties in which they are involved."

Seven billion of us soon, nine billion in 2045. Let's hope that Malthus was right about our ingenuity.

Critical Thinking

1. Why should we be alarmed about continued world population growth?

2. How did Thomas Malthus explain world growth?

3. Discuss the "demographic transition" as an explanation for population growth.

4. How has medical science aided population growth?

5. What is meant by "replacement fertility"? Why do populations continue to expand for a period after reaching replacement fertility?

6. In what parts of the world has fertility fallen significantly? What was the "demographic dividend" and what did it mean for the United States? Where do we still find high fertility rates?

7. What have been some of the key factors in reducing fertility in such places as China and India?

8. Why do critics say is it more important to focus on health, education, and the personal decisions people make regarding fertility rather than on "numerical targets"?

9. Why are many people justifiably worried that Malthus will finally be proved right on a global scale?

10. In what respects do some say the focus on population rather than the environment is wrong? What matters more than simply the number of people, according to the author?

11. In what sense did Malthus express hope?

Create Central

www.mhhe.com/createcentral

Internet References

Murray Research Center
www.radcliffe.edu/murray_redirect/index.php

Small Planet Institute
www.smallplanet.org/food

ROBERT KUNZIG is *National Geographic*'s senior editor for the environment.

Kunzig, Robert. From *National Geographic*, January 2011, pp. 40, 42–43, 45, 48–49, 60–63. Copyright © 2011 by National Geographic Society. Reprinted by permission.